Avicenna and the Aristotelian Tradition

Avicenna and the Aristotelian Tradition

Introduction to Reading Avicenna's Philosophical Works

Second, Revised and Enlarged Edition,
Including an
Inventory of Avicenna's Authentic Works

By

Dimitri Gutas

BRILL

LEIDEN · BOSTON
2014

Cover illustration: Leiden University Library Or. 4, f. 1ᵃ. Title page of Avicenna's *Kitāb aš-Šifāʾ* (*The Cure*)

This paperback is also published in hardback under ISBN 978-90-04-25580-7 as volume 89 in the series IPTS.

The Library of Congress has cataloged the hardcover edition as follows

Gutas, Dimitri.
Avicenna and the Aristotelian tradition : introduction to reading Avicenna's philosophical works / by Dimitri Gutas. – Second, revised, and enlarged edition, including an inventory of Avicenna's authentic works.
pages cm. – (Islamic philosophy, theology, and science, ISSN 0169-8729 ; VOLUME 89)
Includes bibliographical references and index.
ISBN 978-90-04-25580-7 (hardback : alk. paper) – ISBN 978-90-04-26207-2 (e-book : alk. paper)
1. Avicenna, 980-1037. 2. Aristotle–Influence. I. Title.

B751.Z7G87 2014
181'.5–dc23

2013040355

This publication has been typeset in the multilingual "Brill" typeface. With over 5,100 characters covering Latin, IPA, Greek, and Cyrillic, this typeface is especially suitable for use in the humanities. For more information, please see www.brill.com/brill-typeface.

ISBN 978-90-04-20172-9 (paperback)
ISBN 978-90-04-26207-2 (e-book)

This book is printed on acid-free paper.

Printed by Printforce, the Netherlands

To the Memory of
DAVID C. REISMAN

رأيتُ المنايا خَبْطَ عَشْواءَ مَن تُصِبْ * تُمِتْه ومن تُخطِئ يُعَمَّرْ فيهرمِ

I have seen the Fates trample like a purblind camel; those they strike they slay, those they miss are left to live on into dotage.

Zuhayr ibn-Abī-Sulmā, *Muʿallaqa*

Translation by A.J. Arberry, *The Seven Odes*, London: George Allen & Unwin, 1957, 118.

Τί 'ναι, μωρέ, στὸν κόσμο τὰ παιδιὰ παρὰ μπουκιὲς τοῦ Χάρου;
Ἀνάθεμα τὸ ἀντρόυνο ποὺ γεννάει καὶ τὸ φονιὰ ταγίζει!

What in this world are children but morsels for grim Death?
Cursed be that couple that gives birth and feeds the Slayer!

Νίκος Καζαντζάκης, 'Οδύσσεια X,1126–1127
Nikos Kazantzakis, *The Odyssey. A Modern Sequel.* XXII, 1126–1127.

Translation into English Verse ... by Kimon Friar, New York: Simon and Schuster, 1958, 705.

Nell'impostazione dei problemi storico-critici, non bisogna concepire la discussione scientifica come un processo giudiziario, in cui c'è un imputato e c'è un procuratore che, per obbligo d'ufficio, deve dimostrare che l'imputato è colpevole e degno di essere tolto dalla circolazione. Nella discussione scientifica, poiché si suppone che l'interesse sia la ricerca della verità e il progresso della scienza, si dimostra piú "avanzato" chi si pone dal punto di vista che l'avversario può esprimere un'esigenza che deve essere incorporata, sia pure come un momento subordinato, nella propria costruzione. Comprendere e valutare realisticamente la posizione e le ragioni dell'avversario (e talvolta è avversario tutto il pensiero passato) significa appunto essersi liberato dalla prigione delle ideologie (nel senso deteriore, di cieco fanatismo ideologico), cioè porsi da un punto di vista "critico", l'unico fecondo nella ricerca scientifica.

Antonio Gramsci, *Il materialismo storico e la filosofia di Benedetto Croce*, Torino: Einaudi, 1949, 21.

In the formulation of historico-critical problems it is wrong to conceive of scientific discussion as a process at law in which there is an accused and a public prosecutor whose professional duty it is to demonstrate that the accused is guilty and has to be put out of circulation. In scientific discussion, since it is assumed that the purpose of discussion is the pursuit of truth and the progress of science, the person who shows himself most "advanced" is the one who takes up the point of view that his adversary may well be expressing a need which should be incorporated, if only as a subordinate aspect, in his own construction. To understand and to evaluate realistically one's adversary's position and his reasons (and sometimes one's adversary is the whole of past thought) means precisely to be liberated from the prison of ideologies in the bad sense of the word—that of blind ideological fanaticism. It means taking up a point of view that is "critical", which for the purpose of scientific research is the only fertile one.

Selections from the Prison Notebooks of Antonio Gramsci, edited and translated by Quintin Hoare and Geoffrey Nowell Smith, New York: International Publishers, 1971, 343–344.

CONTENTS

PART TWO

AVICENNA'S RECEPTION OF THE ARISTOTELIAN TRADITION

PART THREE

AVICENNA'S INTEGRATION OF THE ARISTOTELIAN TRADITION

APPENDIX

INVENTORY OF AVICENNA'S AUTHENTIC WORKS

PREFACE TO THE SECOND EDITION (2014)

The central and dominant position which Avicenna occupies in the history of philosophy in the Islamic world was acknowledged already in his lifetime and became increasingly evident after his death, as the philosophical tradition reacted almost exclusively to his teaching by following it, revising it, or attempting in parts to reject or refute it.[1] Among these various responses to his thought, there also began to develop in subsequent centuries a tradition which presented his teachings as having a mystical aspect which was claimed to represent his true philosophy, despite the fact that Avicenna never ceased to be regarded as the unchallenged representative of Arabic Peripateticism (he was ubiquitously hailed as the leader of the *maššāʾūn*, Peripatetics). In support of this view a number of pseudepigraphs began to be attributed to him, and with the passage of time the "mystical" persona of Avicenna became dominant in popular perception and in certain philosophical circles. Especially in Iran, where in later centuries (and also because of his presumed Persian origins) he was elevated to a most revered status, he was considered—and is considered to this day—the master of mystical illumination and esoteric "gnosis" (*ʿirfān*) whose origins allegedly go back to a pre-Islamic Persian spirituality. Western scholarship in the twentieth century followed by and large this spurious latter tradition,[2] with the result that the philosophical content of this eminent Peripatetic thinker was left, with a few notable exceptions, unexamined.

Such was the state of affairs, as I describe it in my original Introduction, when I began my Avicennan studies about four decades ago. Having myself succumbed to this approach to Avicenna that dominated scholarship in my student days, my interest in him was concentrated only on his commentaries on Aristotle—the few sections that survive from his *Fair Judgment* (*al-Inṣāf*)—and in particular on his *Marginal Glosses on Aristotle's De anima*: it would be difficult, I had thought, to make a mystical text out of *that* Aristotelian masterpiece, and I was curious to see what Avicenna could have done with it. During my post-doctoral stay in Cairo, I consulted the

---

[1] See the outline of the developments in philosophical directions after Avicenna in Gutas "Heritage."

[2] For a historical discussion of the various approaches to Arabic philosophy in the past century see Gutas "Historiography."

unique manuscript containing this work (Dār al-Kutub, Ḥikma 6 Muṣṭafā Fāḍil), collating Badawī's previous edition against it, and on this basis I prepared a revised edition and translation of it. I began to write an introduction, addressing some of the problems raised by the text, but it soon became clear to me that my approach to—and hence my understanding of—Avicenna were all wrong: more and more of what I was reading by Avicenna himself indicated that he was much more integrally related—and beholden—to the Aristotelian tradition than it was previously thought, and I had to dig deeper and more comprehensively into his entire thought in order to teach myself how to read his philosophical works. To this end I began to collect and translate the relevant documentary evidence and to discuss numerous problems at greater length, and the introduction soon grew out of all bounds until it became the book you hold in your hands; in the process, I had also found my subtitle, but the edition and translation of Avicenna's *Marginal Glosses on Aristotle's De anima* itself, my original project, has necessarily been postponed to future (and I hope not Greek) calends.[3]

The book has been received favorably since its first appearance exactly a quarter of a century ago—its approach having been found useful in providing what its subtitle promises—and the continuing demand for it has made a second edition necessary. The revision has been thorough. Apart from corrections of inaccuracies, recent research, both others' and mine, has been incorporated in the notes and, whenever necessary, accounted for in the narrative of my presentation. I should emphasize, though, that this is not a different book but a revised edition of the original: the scope, argument, tone, and direction are the same. In the body of the work, the major changes are two. In response to a suggestion by numerous readers, I have added a final chapter on Avicenna's philosophical project, reviewing the results not only of the preceding pages but also of my other work on Avicenna in the last twenty-five years,[4] and offering a comprehensive view of the philosopher's work.

Second, in the first edition of this book and in subsequent studies, I used the word "intuition" to render in English Avicenna's key epistemological concept, *ḥads*. In retrospect, this was rather unfortunate. This convenient one-word rendering of the Arabic term is serviceable if one understands it—and as I meant it to be understood—exclusively in the narrow sense given

---

[3] A preliminary report on the nature and context of these glosses, however, has appeared in the meantime in Gutas "Glosses."

[4] Now collected in a Variorum volume with the title *Orientations of Avicenna's Philosophy* (Ashgate 2014).

to it by Avicenna to mean the ability to hit upon, guess correctly, or "divine" the middle term of a syllogism. However, the more common meaning of the word, "sensing without the use of rational processes" (*The American Heritage College Dictionary*, [4]2004) tends to mislead—and it has misled even some serious scholars of Avicenna—and create a misunderstanding of this crucial concept as something mystical or extra rational, which is exactly the opposite of what was intended by Avicenna. I have accordingly avoided it in this edition and translated *ḥads* literally as "guessing correctly," which necessarily evokes the middle term as the object of the transitive verb in the reader's mind—precisely what Avicenna meant to express.

Outside the scope of the original publication, the major change is the addition of the Appendix including an inventory of Avicenna's authentic works, certainly something desirable in a book that purports to introduce a reading of them. The Appendix will increase the serviceability of this book both by providing easy access to essential information about Avivenna's works and by reformulating the objectives of future research, as described in the introductions to the various parts of the Appendix.

I have kept, finally, the text of the original introduction both to retain the record of what drove the original research and to give an indication of how much or how little has been done since then. I have only updated its notes to reflect current scholarship.

I hope that this new edition of the book will prove equally protreptic to sustained study of Avicenna as did the first, and that it will continue to be a useful general introduction to reading Avicenna's philosophical works, both as an orientation to the beginner and as a guide to the historical approach to their study. Avicenna is a particularly complex and multifaceted philosopher (as a worthy successor to Aristotle can only be expected to be), and a partial or superficial reading of some of his works can easily mislead the unwary.

ACKNOWLEDGMENTS

It would be a Sisyphean task to acknowledge all those who contributed to the second edition of this book. In the quarter century since its first appearance, I have had literally hundreds of conversations with friends, colleagues, and students about it, none of whom was sparing either in his appreciation of it or with suggestions for its improvement. Some of the suggestions were repeated by many; I frequently heard, for example, that the book comes to a sudden stop after a rather frenetic pace, without a final chapter for deceleration and retrospection, or that the absence of a bibliography and especially a subject index at the end made consulting it cumbersome. I am fortunate and happy to have been afforded this opportunity to oblige on these and all other counts, with an expression of sincere gratitude to all. Anonymous though they must necessarily remain, with my apologies, there is some consolation in that should they do me the honor of reading the second edition as well they will know who they are.

I am also indebted to all the reviewers of the first edition, and especially to the review by the late Michael Marmura ("Avicenna's Thought"), a lifelong and inspiring student of the philosophy of Avicenna, who alerted me to the inadequate treatment of a number of issues. It led me to their sustained study in subsequent publications, the results of which have been incorporated in this edition.

As in the first edition, I wish to thank the following libraries for kindly providing me with microfilms and CDs of manuscripts in their possession: Istanbul, Istanbul Üniversitesi Kütüphanesi, Süleymaniye Kütüphanesi, Topkapı Sarayı; Leiden, Bibliotheek der Rijksuniversiteit te Leiden, Department of Oriental Manuscripts; Milano, Biblioteca Ambrosiana; Oxford, Bodleian Library, Department of Oriental Books; Uppsala, Uppsala Universitetsbibliotek, Manuscript Department. My thanks also go to the Yale University library system which, as always, has provided invaluable assistance. And a special word of thanks to my Brill editors, Kathy van Vliet-Leigh and Maaike Langerak, and their team of assistant editors and typesetters for their care, expertise, and professionalism which have made our work together over the years a distinct pleasure.

I am delighted to be able to thank again my friend and lifelong colleague Hans Daiber for accepting the book once more in the Brill series he has been succesfully editing, and to extend my thanks also to Anna Akasoy and Emilie Savage-Smith, his recent co-editors, who will ensure and increase its success. The book was number four in the series when it first appeared; in its second reincarnation it is eighty-nine, a measure of the series' immense contribution to the study of Islamic philosophy and theology, and now science, in the past twenty-five years. And in this connection I might repeat my thanks to Professors Ehsan Yarshater and Gregory Sifakis for supporting the original publication: without the fourth there would have been no eigthy-ninth.

More specifically, as the revision was approaching its final stages, I had the good sense to solicit, and the good fortune to receive, help from numerous friends and colleagues who exceeded all bounds of generosity in answering specific questions or providing information. A big thank you to Maroun Aouad, Rüdiger Arnzen, Ahmed Q. Asad, Allan Bäck, Amos Bertolacci, Hans Daiber, Heidrun Eichner, Mohammad Javad Esmaeili, Silvia Fazzo, Frank Griffel, Jules Janssens, Cüneyt Kaya, Yahya Michot, Shady Nasser, Jamil Ragep, Tony Street, Fehrullah Terkan, Alexander Treiger, and Rob Wisnovsky.

Special and profound thanks are due to three individuals, without whose contributions in particular to the compilation of the Inventory it may not have seen the light of day as soon as it did, or inded in the form that it did, if at all. My former student Matthew Melvin-Koushki, while still in graduate school, found the time to enter in a Word file Mahdavī's *Fehrest* in English, including the lists of manuscripts, with astonishing expertise and accuracy, which saved me weeks of labor. My *Avicennisant* accomplice and friend Jules Janssens was never stinting with his prompt responses to a seemingly endless stream of questions, with precise information about books and articles, and with general advice and suggestions on questions of method. With David Reisman, finally, my friend, colleague, and former student, we had had long discussions as well as lengthy e-mail exchanges over the years about aspects of the book and especially about Avicenna's works. In particular he was planning a revision of Mahdavī's and Anawati's bibliographies, with additional information on manuscripts, mostly from Iran, and discussion of individual titles. At one point he stopped working on this subject, and in 2007 he sent me all the notes he had collected in a manuscript he had entitled *Avicenniana*. These notes, from which I benefited in the Inventory, together with his publications on the manuscripts of Avicenna (especially his *Avicennan Tradition*), constitute the most advanced analysis of the manuscript transmission of Avicenna's works and a model to be followed.

David is no longer with us for me to thank him, or indeed to see and enjoy the second edition of the book towards which he contributed so much. My indignation at his loss is somewhat, but futilely, tempered by the words of the Arab and Greek poets I cite above. I had dedicated to Ioanna the first edition of the book; Ioanna and I dedicate this second edition to his memory.

New Haven, June 2013

INTRODUCTION TO THE FIRST EDITION (1988)

The year 1370 after the *Hijra* (1950 AD) corresponded to the lunar millenary anniversary of Avicenna's traditional date of birth. The international scholarly community celebrated this felicitous event with due pomp and circumstance: almost countless congresses, conferences, and meetings were held, memorial volumes, articles, and editorials published, new editions of the Master's works launched, and radio and television programs broadcast. The enthusiasm and vigor that went into the production of these activities were hardly misplaced: few individuals ever influenced and graced intellectual history to the same breadth and extent.

These activities also brought to a head the scholarly production on Avicenna, which had been gathering momentum for approximately a century. By the mid-Fifties, the cascade of scholarship on Avicenna, as if in protest against the excesses of what had immediately preceded, was reduced to the routine trickle. Today, close to four decades later, the waters have been considerably stilled, reflecting more clearly the deficiencies and omissions of previous research. The picture makes sadly manifest the fact that Avicennan studies are at present in a rather confused state.

The confusion is due to many factors, both endemic to Avicenna's manner of philosophical approach and production and the tradition the latter generated, and extrinsic to it, stemming from errors of scholarly omission as well as commission. Although we are well informed, due to certain fundamental works on Avicenna, about the general outline of his thought and its influence, we are nevertheless in a relative haze about a number of subjects which for other philosophers of his caliber are considered indispensable for further research. To start with one of the more basic—elementary, one would say—subjects, his life: we are in the fortunate position of possessing both an autobiography and a biography by a close disciple; yet rarely has an autobiographical document been so extensively quoted, paraphrased, and retold, but so frequently misunderstood and so little analyzed. Furthermore, its very existence seems to have inhibited investigation into additional sources already from the very beginning: in his *Essential Information on the Generations of Physicians*, Ibn-Abī-Uṣaybiʿa, the thirteenth century bio-bibliographer, opens his section on Avicenna with a statement to that effect (L 26). The result of this for contemporary scholarship has been a lack of a comprehensive biography. We also have nothing serious about his "life and

2 times," and still less about his disciples who were, after all, responsible to a large extent for the edition and propagation of his works.[1]

We are also quite unclear about the most crucial subject, his works: their number, nature, transmission, present state, and most important, their relationship to each other, both in time and subject matter, and to Avicenna's work in general. Responsibility for this lies partly with Avicenna himself—he rarely kept second copies of his commissioned pieces—and partly with history: a number of his works was lost in pillages and fires. There exist three recent bibliographies of his works, with listings of the available manuscripts: one in Turkish (Ergin), another in Arabic (Anawati), and the third in Persian (Mahdavī), all superseding the previous bibliography in German by Brockelmann.[2] Extremely useful and fundamental for any future research as these are, because of the very nature of the work involved in their making—it is impossible for a single individual to examine personally the hundreds of existing manuscripts—they give widely conflicting and necessarily incomplete information. The determined Arabist may laboriously—and with gratitude—make his way through them and attempt to sort out the information provided, but Avicenna is a philosopher of the Latin West no less than he is of the Arabic East, and the interested Latin scholar who wishes to find out which works of Avicenna were *not* translated into Latin—for those that were he is forever indebted to the untiring efforts of d'Alverny[3]—and to gain an idea of what he is missing, has indeed very little to go on: the tentative (and necessarily redundant) inventory in a European language by Anawati[4] found no successors.

To the uncertainty about the exact number and nature of his works, buttressed as it is by the general knowledge that some of them have been lost, there has been added another misleading factor throughout the history of
3 Avicennan scholarship, and the combination of the two has created a scholarly hoax, or non-issue, of immense proportions that has consistently hampered research, especially in Western Arabic studies. Jaeger says of Aristotle

---

[1] For the state of research on Avicenna's biography see Chapter 2, Introduction, note 3. Regarding his disciples, the pioneering study by El-Khodeiri "Silsila" has now been supplemented by substantive research by Reisman, Michot, and al-Rahim.

[2] These bibliographies appeared in the following chronological order: Brockelmann *GALS* I,812–828 (1937); Ergin "İbni Sina Bibliyografyası" (^{1}1937); Anawati *Mu'allafāt Ibn Sīnā* (1950); Mahdavī *Fehrest* (1954); Ergin *İbni Sina Bibliografyası* (^{2}1956). See the comparative review by Sellheim (1958).

[3] See the series of articles on "Avicenna Latinus" by d'Alverny, reprinted in d'Alverny *Codices*, with addenda by S. Van Riet and P. Jordogne.

[4] Anawati "Tradition manuscrite."

that he "was the first thinker to set up along with his philosophy *a conception of his own position in history.*"[5] If Aristotle was the first, I propose that Avicenna was the second in importance, for the words of Jaeger which I emphasize here are particularly true in his case. There is a cluster of texts by Avicenna, all composed during a specific period in his literary career, which reflect an awareness on his part of the new stage in the history of philosophy which his works had achieved, and which are explicitly intended to represent a revision and development of philosophy as transmitted in the Aristotelian tradition. Avicenna saw fit to call these texts Eastern (*mašriqiyya*), but as chance would have it, the greater part of two of the works which date from that period is not extant. The historical fact of the loss of these works has given rise to two opposed interpretations which, however, are united in assuming that they are the very last which he composed, and in following an emotional approach of *bemoaning* the fact of their loss rather than the scholarly procedure of *studying* the extant sections and their relation to Avicenna's other works. The first interpretation sees the Eastern texts as the most mature expression of Avicenna's thought, concludes that "the secret of his evolution ... will remain concealed from us as long as we do not possess" them, and bemoans that "the irreparable lacuna in the transmission of his works does not allow us to understand in what respects he wished to complete, and even to correct, Aristotle."[6]

The other interpretation assumes the Eastern texts to represent not only the most mature, but also the *true* expression of Avicenna's thought, pitting it against and in contradiction to his other work. It creates a two-sided Avicenna: an exoteric side, rational and Aristotelian, and an esoteric, mystical and "Oriental."[7] Representative of this interpretation is the following fanciful passage:

> A close study of the "esoteric" writings of Ibn Sīnā will reveal that the "Oriental Philosophy" is not at all a philosophy in the rationalistic sense, nor a system of dialectic to fulfill certain mental needs; rather, it is a form of wisdom

---

[5] Werner Jaeger, *Aristotle. Fundamentals of the History of His Development*, trans. Richard Robinson, Oxford: Clarendon Press, [2]1948, 3.

[6] A.-M. Goichon, in *EI*[2], III.941b, 944a. Such statements can be multiplied at will. Cf. only the conclusion of Afnan's *Avicenna* 290: "And yet he [Avicenna] never lived to complete his work. Of that *Oriental Philosophy* which was to contain the results of his mature thought, nothing remains but a few leaves; admittedly full of promise but serving no useful purpose." Cf. the discussion below in Chapter 2, W9 and W10.

[7] Edward Said's definition of the "Oriental" as the "other" in Western literature is particularly applicable in this case. See his *Orientalism*, New York: Vintage, 1978.

> 4 or a "theosophy" which has for its purpose the deliverance of man from this world of imperfection to the "world of light." It is non-Greek in the sense that the specific "genius" of the Greeks of the historical period was dialectical. They even hid the Egyptian, Orphic, and Babylonian mysteries, upon which Pythagoreanism was based, under a veil of dialectics. The "Oriental Philosophy" removes this veil and seeks to present the *philosophia perennis* not as something to satisfy the need for thinking but as a guide, or at least doctrinal aid, for the illumination of man which arises from the inner experience of its author. Its language is therefore primarily symbolic rather than dialectical even if it begins with Aristotelian logic and employs some of the cosmological ideas of the Peripatetic philosophers.[8]

One recent variant of this interpretation is that the loss of the Eastern texts does not matter, but that both the "esoteric" and "exoteric" aspects of Avicenna's thought can be gleaned from his extant works. In this variant, although what gave originally rise to the esoteric/exoteric dichotomy is discarded, the nefarious conclusion that *there is* such a dichotomy is preserved.[9]

The combination of all of the above factors thus makes the confusion reign supreme, with a distorting effect on further scholarship.[10] Not only has there been provided no basis for situating Avicenna in his intellectual milieu—there are no comprehensive biographies, since Avicenna's stylized autobiography is taken at its face value—, not only is there a general lack of studies on his predecessors and immediate successors, not only, finally, has there been no critical investigation of the precise number and nature

---

8 Nasr *Cosmological Doctrines* (^{2}1978), 191. For the level of Nasr's scholarship in the history of Islamic science, his field of specialization, see David A. King "Islamic Mathematics and Astronomy," *Bibliotheca Orientalis* 35 (1978) 339–342; and for a critical assessment of his method and approach in general, see Joseph Needham, *Science and Civilization in China*, Vol. V, Part 4, Cambridge: Cambridge University Press, 1980, xxxv–xliv.

9 In a Harvard Ph.D. dissertation by S.A. Nuseibeh, *The Foundations of Avicenna's Philosophy*, 1978, xx. In a subsequent publication, Nuseibeh modified this view but persisted in the mystical expression of Avicenna: "it is not the case that there are two Avicennas, one rational and the second mystical, but that there is one Avicenna who once uses rational, and then mystical/poetic means to express the same views;" in "Al-ʿAql al-Qudsī: Avicenna's Subjective Theory of Knowledge," *SI* 69 (1989) 39n11.

10 Another subject of debate was the question whether Avicenna is a materialist (in the Marxist sense) or not. A work which summarized the state of the debate was Elisabeth Buschmann's dissertation, *Untersuchungen zum Problem der Materie bei Avicenna*, Frankfurt: Peter Lang, 1979. This question has but added to the confusion described above, if only because it has not been asked in the proper context, since most of the participants in the debate, including Buschmann herself, worked not from the Arabic texts but only the medieval Latin translations of Avicenna.

of his works—since the assumption that some of his most mature writings have perished is universal—but there is also the additional problem of his "esoteric" and "exoteric" teachings, which every researcher into Avicenna has had to face. A student of Avicenna is thus confronted at the very outset with a set of encumbering presuppositions and the straightjacket of biased attitudes, to which he must somehow make the facts which he discovers and analyzes fit. The result is that the conclusions he reaches inevitably reflect the initial distortions.

The present work is an attempt to set the record straight and provide a starting point for the future study of Avicenna. Since it is clear that Avicenna had a precise conception of his own position in the history of philosophy, the aim has been specifically to describe Avicenna's intellectual base and background, and the theoretical positions and orientations (*pace* Corbin, no pun on "orientations" intended) which provide the framework and field of activity of his philosophical work. Part One presents the documentation and the textual evidence upon which the detailed analyses and elaboration which follow in the remaining parts are based. It is divided into two chapters, the first of which presents translations of a series of texts in which Avicenna and his major disciples discuss his attitude toward his own philosophy and the Aristotelian tradition. The second chapter offers a critical inventory and relative chronology of Avicenna's major philosophical works.

Avicenna's philosophical work, as presented in Part One on the basis of his own statements and the inventory of his major philosophical writings, defines itself by constant reference, whether explicit or implicit, to the Aristotelian corpus and tradition, and stands in a manifest dialectical relationship to both of them. It is, in effect, a record of the way in which Avicenna received, disagreed with, modified, integrated, and communicated philosophical knowledge as conceived and transmitted in that tradition. Therefore the conscious and unconscious position of Avicenna vis-à-vis Aristotle and the Aristotelian tradition is of crucial importance for reading his works, and forms the subject proper of the remainder of the book. By "reading" I mean having an orientation toward his work commensurate with his overall point of view and consistent with his intention, and understanding his thought in its historical and semantic context and *thereby* first evaluating its relation to what preceded in philosophy and its relevance for what succeeded, and ultimately assessing its significance for the history of ideas. There is nothing novel in such an approach to a philosopher; the study of most major thinkers has benefited from numerous investigations that have taken it. The study of Arabic-writing philosophers, however, for reasons that properly belong to the history of scholarship rather than here, has been consistently hampered by a general lack of *historical investigations preceding and establishing the boundaries* of normative evaluations.[11]

6 This lack is making itself obtrusively manifest in the unwelcome consequences it entails: on a general level it creates the multiple and often discordant approaches to Avicenna which result in the confusion described above, and more specifically it compels almost every author dealing with Avicenna at a certain level of comprehensiveness to waste both his own and the reader's time by taking a position on the issue of the Eastern philosophy after citing only inadequate and recurrent arguments, often unassimilated.[12] This issue, however, as well as the more general one of determining the most appropriate approach to Avicenna, cannot be solved independently and in abstraction; they are integrally related to the central question of the position of Avicenna with regard to Aristotle and the Peripatetic tradition.

In order to determine this position, we need to consider his own *testimony* about his conscious stand vis-à-vis Peripatetic philosophy, *internal evidence* from his philosophical works about the same subject, and the *material* of the Aristotelian corpus and tradition which were available to him and shaped his ideas—we have to retrace, so to speak, his intellectual upbringing. In discussing the latter question, due account has to be taken of the fact, frequently overlooked and sometimes deliberately slighted, that the Aristotle and the Aristotelian tradition known to Avicenna are not those known to us. Avicenna had, in a way, both more and less of Aristotle: he had often incomplete and defective Arabic translations, we have the Greek original; he had access, unlike us, to numerous commentaries from the Peripatetic tradition, most of which have not survived; and most important, he was heir to a traditional understanding and analysis of Aristotle which are alien to both our

---

11 In his normative study of Avicenna's (?) *Throne Philosophy*, Meyer "Thronschrift" 227–228 is fully aware of the problems of an ahistorical approach. His apologies are perfectly justified on the basis of his succinct formulation of the problem.

12 So Finianos (1976) 27–28, reproducing the previous arguments by Anawati "Études" and Nasr *Cosmological Doctrines* (^{2}1978) 185–186, who insists on the impossible reading *mušriqiyya* more than fifty years after, and despite his references to the conclusive article by Nallino "Filosofia "Orientale"" (1923–1925). Nasr has persisted in his unfounded views about the "esoteric" "Oriental philosophy," and although in a 1994 publication he accepted the reading *mashriqiyyah* ("Oriental Philosophy" 247), in 1999 he innovated with the incomprehensible reading "*m(a)shriqiyyah*", which he explained as follows in a note: "Unable to convey this double meaning [?] in the Latin transliteration, I have chosen to write the word as *m(a)shriqiyyah*, keeping the (a) in parentheses" (Nasr and Aminrazavi 268).

philological and philosophical proclivities. In this light the central question thus becomes determining the position of Avicenna with regard to Aristotle and the Aristotelian tradition *as known* to Avicenna. All this, finally, has to be assessed within Avicenna's historical and Islamic context.

Part Two will discuss Avicenna's reception of the Aristotelian tradition. Reception is here to be understood in both its objective and subjective sense, or historical and epistemological; what there was, in other words, for Avicenna to receive, and how he says he received it. Among Avicenna's pronouncements on his own work and his position in the history of philosophy
none is more significant than his Autobiography, and most of the discussion 7
will accordingly focus on it. The Aristotelian tradition included not only a curriculum of higher studies to be followed in order to acquire a body of knowledge of supreme value—*the* knowledge according to its adherents—but also carried along with it procedural guidelines, expressed in both historical and normative terms, for its acquisition in specific social contexts. In its self-perception throughout the long history of its evolution, the tradition had developed concrete ideas about what it meant to do philosophy and how to do it in a society where it had to be (or alternately, where it should be) the occupation of a small minority. The need to reconcile these apparently contradictory facts—the blatant disproportion of the number of the individuals engaged in philosophy to the absolute worth of its goal—gave rise to concepts about the praxis of philosophy which, transmitted through generations of philosophers, were also part of the tradition received by Avicenna.

Part Three will treat Avicenna's reaction to the Aristotelian tradition so received, that is, the different aspects of its integration, modification, and communication in his works. There were major contradictions both within the received tradition and between it and the Islamic context in which Avicenna encountered it. For Avicenna, these represented areas of conflict which he could not, given his understanding of the philosophical praxis and his specific epistemology discussed in Part Two, either disregard or gloss over; they called for resolution and shaped to a large degree the direction his philosophical work was to take. At the same time, the very resolution of these problems, in ways that integrated the different strands of the tradition rather than reproduced it, implied the concomitant evolution of an independent attitude on his part toward the tradition. This attitude found concrete expression in the various methods he elaborated for the communication of his new systematization of the received knowledge. The identification of these methods and their description, treated in the final chapter, pave the way for a comprehensive reading of his books.

There is little need to remind the general reader, much less the specialist
of Arabic philosophy, that Avicenna did not work in a vacuum. The two
centuries that preceded Avicenna's emergence saw an intensive cultivation
of the philosophical sciences both in the central Islamic lands and further
afield to the East, in the countries where Avicenna grew up and worked. But
the formative period of philosophy in Islam, and especially the history of
Arabic Aristotelianism, have been very little studied and far too few texts
are available in translation for a proper appreciation of the significance of
these movements in general intellectual history. It was therefore necessary
8 to include in my discussions many translations of substantial passages from
related literature in order to give the reader a sense of the intellectual
context of Arabic and Avicennan philosophy. Although Avicenna already
has an unassailable position in the history of philosophy, his achievement
comes alive and its enormity is better realized when it is seen against this
background. Encomia of Avicenna abound; but they are for the most part
perfunctory and seem to follow, as he would have said, customary practice.
His works need to become available to world culture, and this book aspires
to foster a sober interest in them by facilitating their reading.

Bibliographical Note

There is an immense bibliography on Avicenna in many languages. I cannot claim to have consulted all of it, or even all of the material that falls within my linguistic range, but I believe to have seen, within the limits of human fallibility, the constraints of time, and reasonably ready availability of recondite sources, everything that is even remotely relevant to the subject of this book. Much of what I have seen is either outdated or of very little scholarly value—if not downright misleading—and references to secondary literature have accordingly been selective. The purpose of this book is neither antiquarian, to write the history of scholarship on Avicenna on this subject, nor bibliographic, to refer to every single publication regardless of its worth. If a reference that may be considered germane by some is found missing, then the omission was deliberate. As Avicenna put it, "I refrained from prolix arguments in contradiction of doctrines patently invalid or sufficiently dealt with through the fundamental principles which we establish and the rules we present" (T9, §1). For a descriptive and critical bibliography of works by and on Avicenna see the *Bibliography* by Janssens and its supplements.

The Bibliography at the end of the volume lists all the works actually referred to in the body of the book, where references are given by author and short title in cases when more than one work by the same author has been consulted, and mostly by author alone otherwise. The short titles used for this purpose are added in brackets after the citation in the Bibliography. Incidental single references in this book to works not directly relevant to the study of Avicenna have been provided with full bibliographical details in the appropriate notes and have not been repeated in the Bibliography.

Translation and Annotation

All translations from Arabic, Persian, and Greek are mine unless otherwise noted. However, the rather lamentable state of the editions of most Arabic works drawn upon here made it necessary to comment extensively, for the sake of the Arabists, on the text of the passages selected for translation, and to include information about variant manuscript readings and lexicographic details. This study, however, is also intended for the non-Arabist who would have no use for such information. Accordingly it appeared advisable to adopt a twofold system of annotation. Matters relating strictly to the choice or meaning of Arabic words are provided with notes indicated by superscript letters. The non-Arabist can skip these and concentrate on the numbered notes which contain the bibliographic references and other explanatory information.

Technical Terms

Avicenna uses a highly technical language. Many terms which he employs are common to Arabic philosophical and scholarly vocabulary, but others are peculiar to him and refer to specific concepts in his system. It has been necessary to alert the reader to the use of these terms in the texts of Avicenna as well as in my own discussion of them. In order to avoid giving in parentheses the Arabic word in every instance, these terms have been identified by capitalization. The Index of Technical Terms at the end of the volume lists them and refers to the chapters and sections where their specific definition is discussed.

Transliteration

The transliteration follows the rules established by the German Oriental Society (*Deutsche Morgenländische Gesellschaft*), with the following exceptions: *j* instead of *ǧ*, and *-aw* and *-ay* for the diphthongs instead of *-au* and *-ai*. The inflection (*iʿrāb*) is indicated only when necessary for the comprehension of the transliterated passage.

For the benefit of non-Arabists, a hyphen (-) connects in the transliteration of proper names all the words that form a unit of nomenclature. Thus, Abū-l-Faraj Ibn-aṭ-Ṭayyib, ʿAlāʾ-ad-Dawla.

The Arabic article before single word proper names has been omitted in my text (e.g., Fārābī, Jūzjānī), but retained when it occurs in a translated passage.

Serial Numbers of Avicenna's Works

In the classification of Avicenna's works in the Appendix, and throughout this book, each work is identified by a serial number preceded by initials which indicate the category to which it belongs, all headed by an initial G for Gutas. See the Conspectus of Avicenna's Works in Part Three of the Appendix. The initials for the categories are:

L	Logic and Language
M	Metaphysics
Math	Mathematics
Med	Medicine
P	Physics
PP	Practical philosophy
Ps	Pseudepigraph
PW	Private Writings
S	Summae

References to Avicenna's Works and Other Primary Sources

All references to primary sources, including the works of Avicenna, are given by page (and on occasion, line) number of the editions listed in the Bibliography under the name of the editor, not the author. Other than the works of Avicenna himself, which are listed comprehensively in the Inventory, the primary sources consulted for this study are too disparate to be listed meaningfully in a separate section. In the case of Avicenna, in view of both the inadequacy and the proliferation of various printings of his works—and in anticipation of the glorious day when we will have properly critical editions as standard references—the following conventions of reference have been adopted:

Šifāʾ: Referred to by the name of the book, followed by the page number in the Cairo edition and the name of the editor(s). Full bibliographical details are listed in the Bibliography under the name of the editor(s).

Najāt: References are to the page numbers of the editions of al-Kurdī and Dānešpaǰūh, in that order, separated by a slash (/).

Išārāt: The references consist of Roman numerals I and II for the first (*anhāj*) and second (*anmāṭ*) parts respectively, followed by the number of the *nahj* or *namaṭ*, followed by the number of the *faṣl* as given in the edition by Zāreʿī. Then follow the page references to the editions of Forget and Zāreʿī, in that order, separated by a slash (/).

Bayhaqī's *Tatimma*, heavily used in this study, is referred to by the page numbers of the editions of Shafīʿ and Kurd ʿAlī, in that order, separated by a slash (/).

Signs and Marginal Numbers

The paragraph sign (§) after a Text or a Lemma refers to the paragraph numbers in the translated passage.

In the *translated texts* throughout the book, the following signs have been used:

(…) Parenthetical remarks by the author of the passage.
[…] My own explanatory additions in English to the author's text.
⟨…⟩ My conjectural additions to the Arabic text of the passage.

The numbers in the margins of the text refer to the pages of the first edition (1988).

Abbreviations and Reference Works

ASP	*Arabic Sciences and Philosophy. A Historical Journal*
Blachère *Dictionnaire*	R. Blachère, M. Chouémi, C. Denizeau, *Dictionnaire Arabe-Français-Anglais*, Paris: G.-P. Maisonneuve et Larose, 1967 ff.
BSOAS	*Bulletin of the School of Oriental and African Studies, University of London*
CAG	*Commentaria in Aristotelem Graeca*, Berlin 1882 ff. Cf. K. Praechter in *Byzantinische Zeitschrift* 18 (1909) 516–538, translated in R. Sorabji, ed., *Aristotle Transformed*, London: Duckworth, 1990, 31–54, and Sorabji's article in the volume, 1–30.
Dozy	Reinhart Pieter Anne Dozy, *Supplément aux dictionnaires arabes*, 2 vols., Leiden: E.J. Brill, 1881.
DPhA and *Supplément*	*Dictionnaire des Philosophes Antiques*, Richard Goulet, ed., Paris: CNRS, 1989 ff.
EI[1], *EI*[2], *EI*[3]	*The Encyclopaedia of Islam*, 1st ed., Leiden: E.J. Brill, 1913–1938; 2nd ed., Leiden: E.J. Brill, 1960–2009; 3rd ed., Leiden: Brill, 2007 ff.
EIr	*Encyclopædia Iranica*, Ehsan Yarshater, ed., vols. 1–4 published by Routledge & Kegan Paul, London, 1985–1990; vols.

5–8 published by Mazda Publications, Costa Mesa, California, 1992–1998; vols. 9–10 published by Bibliotheca Persica Press, New York, 1999–2001, vols. 11–15 published by Encyclopædia Iranica Foundation, New York.

GAL, GALS Carl Brockelmann, *Geschichte der arabischen Litteratur*, 2nd ed., Leiden: E.J. Brill, 1943–1949; *Supplement*, 3 vols., Leiden: E.J. Brill, 1936–1942.

GALex *A Greek and Arabic Lexicon. Materials for a Dictionary of the Medieval Arabic Translations from Greek into Arabic*, Gerhard Endress and Dimitri Gutas, eds. [Handbuch der Orientalistik. Erste Abteilung. Band 11], Leiden: Brill, 1992 ff.

GAS Fuat Sezgin, *Geschichte des arabischen Schrifttums*, Leiden: 11
E.J. Brill, 1967 ff.

JAOS *Journal of the American Oriental Society*

JIS *Journal of Islamic Studies*

JNES *Journal of Near Eastern Studies*

Kazimirski Albert de Biberstein Kazimirski, *Dictionnaire Arabe-Français*, Paris: Théophile Barrois, 1846–1860.

Lane Edward William Lane, *An Arabic-English Lexicon*, London, Edinburgh: Williams and Norgate, 1863–1893.

MIDEO *Mélanges de l'Institut Dominicaine d'Études Orientales*, Cairo / Turnhout

Reckendorf Hermann Reckendorf, *Die syntaktischen Verhältnisse des Arabischen*, Leiden: E.J. Brill, 1895–1898.

SI *Studia Islamica*

Steingass Francis Joseph Steingass, *A Comprehensive Persian-English Dictionary*, London: K. Paul, Trench, Trubner & Co., 1930.

TLG *Thesaurus Linguae Gaecae*. http://www.tlg.uci.edu/

WKAS Manfred Ullmann, *Wörterbuch der klassischen arabischen Sprache*, Wiesbaden: Harrassowitz, 1957–2009.

Wright William Wright, *A Grammar of the Arabic Language*, 3rd ed., Cambridge: Cambridge University Press, 1896–1898.

WZKM *Wiener Zeitschrift für die Kunde des Morgenlandes*

ZDMG *Zeitschrift der Deutschen Morgenländischen Gesellschaft*

ZGAIW *Zeitschrift für Geschichte der Arabisch-Islamischen Wissenschaften*

The following initials have been used to refer to the various sections and passages in the book:

L Lemmata, or passages cited, as numbered at the end of the indented lemma.
T Texts translated and numbered in Chapter 1.
W Works discussed and numbered in Chapter 2.

PART ONE

DOCUMENTS ON AVICENNA AND THE ARISTOTELIAN TRADITION

PERSONAL TEXTS BY AVICENNA AND HIS DISCIPLES ON HIS RELATION TO THE ARISTOTELIAN TRADITION

Introduction

Avicenna had few reservations about expressing his thoughts on the nature and practice of philosophy, both in history and in his immediate environment. Acutely aware of the historical progression of the acquisition of knowledge through philosophy, he was never content to follow tacitly or leave unchallenged the presuppositions that governed the philosophical praxis. In numerous introductions, epilogues, and private letters, texts that can be described as personal and some as private, he raised these very issues and stated his position on them. His views were also reflected in the writings of his disciples, who responded to the earnestness and intensity with which he approached the work of philosophy. The fourteen texts translated in this chapter present a selection of these texts. The selection contains, I believe, the most relevant and the most significant pronouncements by Avicenna on these issues, but it does not aim to be comprehensive. Many were excluded for considerations of space, and others doubtless escaped my attention for lack of ready availability. The task of collecting all these texts, and especially Avicenna's considerable correspondence with his disciples, is a major desideratum for the future.[1]

The first three texts provide the setting, or the normative background, for the rest. They inform about *what,* in Avicenna's view, is to be learned

[1] Recent publications are well on their way to remedying this deficiency. In particular the writings of Avicenna referring to his controversies with Abū-l-Qāsim al-Kirmānī have been used to good effect by Reisman *Avicennan Tradition* 166–185 to map the stages of composition of Avicenna's *Discussions,* and some of these texts themselves were soundly edited, translated, and studied by Michot *Abû Saʿd* and "Riz". The review of the former of Michot's publications by Reisman "New Standard" is by itself a major contribution to this subject, and cf. also my review in *JIS* 14 (2003) 379–381. The contribution of such documentation to a profounder understanding of Avicenna's social and intellectual context can be seen in Reisman "Patronage."

in philosophy (T1) and *how* it is to be learned (T2), and give an example of a person *who* learned it (T3). The remaining texts, except for the last, follow in chronological order the evolution of Avicenna's thoughts about Aristotle and the Aristotelian tradition, about the historical progression of philosophy, and about the place of his own work in this continuum. The last section (T14), finally, also Avicenna's very last work, presents his own summary of his philosophical system. These texts are intended to be read in the order presented. Since they constitute the focus and provide the documentation for much of the discussion in this book, a serial reading will bring out the major themes and points which, to borrow Avicenna's phrase, "had they been perceived, there would have been no need" for the rest of the book (T9, § 4).

Some of these texts are available in translations of varying accuracy; very
16 few are available in editions even marginally critical. It was therefore necessary to provide relatively full, and separate, textual annotation, indicated by superscript letters. As these notes show, critical editions of all of Avicenna's works still remain to be done. My notes, which are based on a necessarily narrow base of printed and manuscript evidence, merely aim to contribute toward an eventual critical edition of these texts; they are not intended to substitute for a critical apparatus. Their main purpose is to enable the Arabist to read my versions while comparing them with the available Arabic texts in the cited publications.

My translations aim to render Avicenna's meaning as precisely as possible and are based for the most part on the detailed analyses of the texts in the body of the book. For this reason recurring technical terms which have a special significance in Avicenna's thought are always written with a capital letter; the reader's attention is directed to the Index of Technical Terms. References to earlier translations have accordingly been kept to a minimum and have been made primarily when their renditions of key passages, representing accepted wisdom, differ substantially from my own. References to editions and manuscripts, and other bibliographical information, are given at the beginning of each selection.

Text 1. From *Compendium on the Soul* (GP 10)

The eighth chapter of Avicenna's first philosophical treatise lists the intelligible forms, i.e., theoretical knowledge, to be acquired by the rational soul. It is extraordinary because it presents these forms in the order and in terms of the philosophical sciences as classified in the Aristotelian tradition. (See the discussion below, Chapter 2, W1, and Chapter 3.1.)

The text was first edited and translated into German by Landauer (1875). The translation below is based on his edition (361.4–362.16 and 364.19–365.4, text; 404–408 and 410–411, translation, with useful annotation), but the paragraphing and numbering are mine. The text established by Landauer was reproduced by van Dyck *Hadiyya*, down to the very notes, except that on occasion van Dyck inexplicably offered a variant word or phrase, left unrecorded here. The text published by Ahwānī *Aḥwāl* 168–171, differs from that of Landauer only in minor and insignificant details, also left unrecorded here. In my notes, an occasional reference has been made to variant renderings of significant passages and terms in the Latin translation by Andrea Alpago ff. 1–39^{b} and in the English translation by van Dyck *Offering*. Van Dyck 9 refers to an earlier "studiedly literal" English translation by James Middleton MacDonald (Beirut 1884) which I have not seen.

Chapter 8

On the Stages of the Human Soul from Inception to Perfection

1. There is no doubt that the species of rational living beings is distinguished
from the irrational through a faculty by means of which it is able to con- 17
ceptualize the intelligibles. This faculty is the one called "rational soul," although it is also Customary to call it "material intellect," that is, potential intellect, by analogy to [prime] matter.

2. This faculty, which exists in the entire human species, does not in itself possess any intelligible forms, but these rather come about within it in one of two ways. The first is through divine inspiration [*ilhām*], without any process of learning or utilization of the senses, as is the case with self-evident intelligibles[1] like our conviction that the whole is greater than the part and that "two contraries cannot be present in a single thing simultaneously."[2] All adults with a sound intellect may attain these forms.

3. The second way is to acquire [them] through syllogisms and Discover [them] through demonstration, as is the case with:[3]

---

[1] "Self-evident intelligibles:" *al-maʿqūlāt al-badīhiyya*; "Axiome," Landauer; "mentally-grasped self-evident axioms," van Dyck. These are the primary intelligible concepts, the *awwaliyyāt*, upon which depend the secondary intelligibles that form the subject matter of logic. See Sabra 753ff., and Gutas "Empiricism" Section V for the *awwaliyyāt*.

[2] Landauer 406n2 marks the quotation from Aristotle's *Metaphysics* 1011b17–18.

[3] The remainder of this section (§3) consists of a single sentence. I have divided it and labeled each item in order to bring out Avicenna's extremely methodical and traditional enumeration of the subject matter of the sciences. Cf. the list below with the contents of Avicenna's *The Cure* in Chapter 2, W6a. For Avicenna's observance of the classification of the sciences in the Aristotelian tradition, and for the standard textbooks that corresponded to these sciences, see Chapter 3.1.

[I. Logic] The conceptualization of logical truths. Examples: genera, species, differentiae, properties, and accidents[4] [Porphyry's *Eisagoge*]; simple terms and the different kinds of compound terms [*De Interpretatione*];[5] the composition of syllogisms, both true and false [*Prior Analytics*]; propositions which, when organized[a] to form syllogisms, yield conclusions which are necessary and demonstrative [*Posterior Analytics*], or more [true than false] and dialectical [*Topics*], or equally [true and false] and rhetorical
18 [*Rhetoric*], or less[b] [true than false] and sophistical [*Sophistici Elenchi*], or impossible [i.e. totally false] and poetic [*Poetics*].[6]

[II. Physics] Verification of physical matters. Examples: matter, form, privation, nature, place, time, rest, and motion [*Physics*]; celestial bodies and bodies composed of the elements [*De Caelo*]; the principles of generation and corruption[7] [*De Generatione et Corruptione*]; generation of phenomena in the atmosphere, in the mines [*Meteorologica*][8] and on the surface of the earth: plants [ps.-Aristotelian *De Plantis*] and animals [*Historia, De Partibus,* and *De Generatione Animalium*]; the real nature of man and the real nature of the self-conceptualization of the soul [*De Anima*].

[III. Mathematics] Conceptualization of mathematical matters, namely, arithmetic [*Introduction to Arithmetic* by Nicomachus of Gerasa], pure geometry [Euclid's *Elements*], astronomical geometry [Ptolemy's *Almagest*], geometry of musical melodies [Ptolemy's *Harmonics*], and geometry of optics [Ptolemy's *Optics*].

---

[a] Perhaps *tašakkalat* is to be read for *šukkilat* in the printed texts.

[b] Reading *aqalliyya* for *awwaliyya* in the printed texts. See below, note 6, for the justification of this reading.

---

[4] The fifth of Porphyry's five predicables (the *quinque voces*), accident, is missing in the manuscripts used by Landauer and in the Hebrew translation, while it is found in Alpago's Latin. Despite Landauer's doubts, it is perhaps to be added to the text since it may have been omitted by the scribe of an archetype manuscript on account of a presumed dittography between *ḫawāṣṣ* and *aʿrāḍ* which look alike in Arabic.

[5] For the omission of the Categories see Chapter 6.4.

[6] This fivefold classification of propositions on the basis of their truth value and their correspondence to the last five books of Aristotle's *Organon* is standard late Alexandrian doctrine; it was transmitted into Syriac by Paul the Persian (fl. mid-sixth century) and naturalized in Arabic philosophy by Fārābī. See Gutas "Paul the Persian" 242–243 and Diagrams IVa, IVb, and V. Avicenna was later to abandon and criticize this doctrine: *Šifāʾ*, *Qiyās* 4 Zāyid; *Išārāt* I.9, 81/166 = Goichon *Directives* 224 = Inati *Logic* 148–149.

[7] Literally, "absolute generation and corruption" (*al-kawn wa-l-fasād al-muṭlaqayn*), that is, a discussion of the principles of generation and corruption in general, not related to specific things.

[8] For Aristotle's *Meteorology* in Arabic see the article by Pieter L. Schoonheim in *DPhA Supplément* 324–328. For the notorious Book IV in particular see Baffioni and, for Avicenna, Hasnaoui.

[IV. METAPHYSICS][9]

[A. Universal science: (i) Being-as-such] Conceptualization of divine matters. For example: getting to know [*maʿrifa*] the first principles of absolute being-as-such and its consequent properties [*lawāḥiq*], like potentiality, actuality, first principle, cause, substance, accident, genus, species, contradiction, congener-ness, congruence, incongruence, unity, and multiplicity.

[A. Universal Science: (ii) First Philosophy] Establishing the first principles of the theoretical sciences—namely Mathematics, Physics, and Logic—access to which can be gained only through this science [of Metaphysics].

[B. Theology: (iii) Natural Theology] Establishing the first creator, the 19
first created, and the universal soul; the way in which creation occurs; the rank of the intellect with respect to the creator,[c] of the soul to the intellect, of sublunar matter[10] and the forms to the soul, and of the spheres, stars, and generated beings to matter and form; and why there is such a stark divergence in priority and posteriority among them.[11]

[B. Theology: (iv) Metaphysics of the Rational Soul] Getting to know [*maʿrifa*] divine governance, the nature of the universe, the providence of the First One, prophetic revelation, the sanctified and Lordly spirit,[12] and the supernal angels; attaining the real meaning [*ḥaqīqa*] of the doctrines denying polytheism and the anthropomorphism of the creator;[13] attaining knowledge [*maʿrifa*] of the reward in store for the virtuous and the punishment for evildoers, and of the pleasure and pain befalling souls after their separation from the body.[14]

...

---

[c] Reading *al-mubdiʿ* for *al-ibdāʿ* in the printed texts.

---

[9] Much of the account of Metaphysics presented here is directly indebted to Fārābī's *On the Purposes of the Metaphysics*, translated below, L45. For the classification of the contents of Metaphysics by Avicenna, and for his sources other than Aristotle's *Metaphysics*, see Chapter 6.1 and 6.2.

[10] "Sublunar matter;" literally, "the matter of nature" (*al-hayūlā min aṭ-ṭabīʿa*). For the correct reading of the series enumerated here see Landauer 408n9.

[11] Avicenna later called this part "the fruit of Metaphysics." See T4, § 1, and Chapter 6.1 and 6.2.

[12] That is, the rational faculty of the prophets, or the so-called "prophetic intellect." See the next paragraph (§ 4).

[13] These two doctrines (*širk, tašbīh*) are subjects regularly treated in Islamic theology (*kalām*).

[14] Avicenna later called this part "the fruit of Physics." See T4, § 1, and Chapter 6.2.

4. [Another aspect of the second way in which intelligibles come about in the rational soul:] In some people, keenness of mind[15] and contact with the universal intellect may so predispose the rational faculty as to free it from having recourse to syllogisms and deliberation in order to become cognizant [*taʿarruf*]; inspiration and revelation, rather, are sufficient sustenance for it. This specific property of the rational faculty is called sanctification, in accordance with which it is then called sanctified spirit. None shall gain the enjoyment of this rank except prophets and messengers of God, peace and prayers be upon them.

Text 2. From *Philosophy for ʿAlāʾ-ad-Dawla* (GS 7)

Philosophy for ʿAlāʾ-ad-Dawla is the only philosophical summa by Avicenna written in Persian (see Chapter 2, W8). Like all his summae, the section on the human soul, which was a part of Physics, contained a discussion of the theory of learning. The chapter translated below, the penultimate in the Physics, deals with this subject. The importance of this chapter lies in the fact that it alone, among all similar sections in Avicenna's summae, adds an autobiographical perspective to his theory of learning. In this passage Avicenna situates himself on his own scale of learning, and states his own conception of how he acquired knowledge and how it relates to the transmitted body of knowledge, the Aristotelian philosophy.

The translation is based on the text edited by Meškāt *Ṭabīʿiyyāt*, pp. 141.10–145.3. There is a French translation by Achena and Massé II,87–89, and an English translation by Th. Gaskil in Nasr and Aminrazavi I,217–218.

Part III: Physics

Chapter: Exposition of the State of Powerful Souls

1. It is a fact that unknown [intelligible] things are acquired by means of the middle term [of a syllogism]. The middle term can be obtained either through quickness of comprehension, in that Guessing Correctly pours [it] into the soul[1] (and that is due to the soul's disposition to be affected by the active intellect), or from a teacher.

2. Guessing Correctly [the middle term] is likewise of two sorts: one comes about slowly and after delay, the other at once. There is no require-

[15] "Keenness of mind:" *yaqẓa*, cf. Dozy s.v.; Alpago and, following him, Landauer and van Dyck have "vigil:" *vigiliis*, "Nachtwachen," and "vigils," respectively. The reference here is to what Avicenna was later to call Guessing Correctly the middle term, *ḥads*. See Chapter 3.2.

[1] *Ke ḥads andar nafs afkand*; cf. Achena and Massé, "en ce sens que l'intuition intellectuelle jette dans l'âme ce moyen terme." See Avicenna's definitions of these terms cited below in L7–9, Chapter 3.2. The garbled translation of this paragraph by Gaskil does not correspond to the Persian text (e.g., he translates *afkand* by "thinks").

ment that Correct Guessing should occur with respect to some problems [only] and not others; as a matter of fact, if you want the truth, [the solution to] every problem has been found by means of Correct Guesses, since everybody has learned from somebody else but he who was the very first never learned from anybody; there was, therefore, someone who found [solutions and knowledge] all by himself.

3. If someone knows the things of the world by applying himself to the
utmost, his knowledge of most of the things will be either accurate or highly
doubtful, since what he has been doing was Discovering [middle terms].[2]
Accordingly among people [a] there is the person who needs a teacher for 21
most things, being completely incapable of any Correct Guesses—or even worse, he might be incapable of understanding even with a teacher; [b] there may be a person who knows most things by Guessing Correctly [the middle terms] and has slight need for a teacher; and [c] there may also be a person,[3] though rarely, who can attain whenever he wishes the sciences from beginning to end in the order in which Guessing Correctly [the middle terms] occurs,[4] without a teacher and in very little time. This is because he has made excellent contact with the active intellect so that he has absolutely no need of reflection, and therefore believes that [this knowledge] is being poured into his heart from one place[5]—and perhaps this is what the truth is. It is from this person that the basis of instruction for humans must come.

4. One must not be amazed at this. We ourselves have witnessed a person[6] who was not at this rank [of the prophet] and would learn things after reflection and hard work, but who nevertheless dispensed with excessive

---

[2] Literally, "since he has been a Discoverer" (*ke vey estenbāṭgar būde ast*; Achena and Massé: "parce qu'il aurait pratiqué des constatations [?]"). A more paraphrastic translation would be, "depending on how good he is at Discovering the middle terms". Avicenna is referring here, in an abbreviated fashion, to his theory that the ability to Guess Correctly the middle term (*ḥads*) varies from person to person according to how many middle terms and how fast each person can discover them. See the parallel passage cited in Chapter 3.2, L7, §3.

[3] I.e. a prophet.

[4] "In the order in which Guessing Correctly [the middle terms] occurs" (*be-tartīb-e ḥadsī*; Achena and Massé: "par voie [?] d'intuition"), i.e. the prophet does not learn wholesale and by heart, as it were, a body of doctrines in digest form without knowing how the different parts are interconnected, but rather Guesses Correctly and step by step, although with "computer" speed, and in a logical order which starts from axiomatic truths and proceeds by consecutive discoveries of middle terms, until he encompasses all things that can be known with rational certainty. See the parallel passages cited in Chapter 3.2, L7, §3, and L12, §3.

[5] I.e., from the active intellect.

[6] Avicenna is referring here to himself. See his Autobiography in T3 and compare the parallel formulations.

hard work through his strong [aptitude for] Guessing Correctly [the middle terms]. His Correct Guessing in most things corresponded with what is found in books,[7] and consequently he did not have to endure the hard work of excessive book reading. At the age of eighteen or nineteen this person understood the philosophical sciences—from logic and physics and metaphysics [to] geometry, arithmetic, astronomy, music, medicine, and many abstruse sciences—in such a way that he saw no one else like himself. After that, many years went by without his adding anything more to that initial state [of knowledge]—and it is known that each one of these sciences requires years of instruction.[8]

22 Text 3. The Autobiography

The Autobiography is readily available in numerous translations in many languages. I am including it here first because it is the focus of much discussion below (Chapter 3), and second because certain crucial passages have not received the care they deserve by translators if only through the inadvertence bred by familiarity. I therefore beg the reader to read once more with me this amazing text.

The only critical edition of the Arabic text, with facing English translation, is that by Gohlman 16–42, which has to be used in conjunction with the review by Ullmann. My translation below is based on this edition, and my textual comments and suggestions have been indicated in the notes.[a] Among scholarly translations,

[a] Crisp and efficient as this edition appears to be (cf. the reviews by Ullmann 149, and by M. van Damme, *Bibliotheca Orientalis* 33 [1976] 364), it will have to be done anew. Specifically, the following tasks would seem to be still on the agenda: (a) A more thorough understanding has to be gained of the relationship among the various manuscripts of the main recension. Gohlman 4 assumes his four primary manuscripts ABJN to derive independently from a common archetype. His documentation for this assumption, however, is exceedingly slim (he is content, in the examples he cites on p. 5, with only one separative error among them), and, in one case, unfounded: the separative error he cites (p. 5) between A and the other witnesses is that on p. 64, line 5 of his edition, A has *baynahum* and the other manuscripts have

[7] I.e., philosophical books in the Aristotelian tradition, mainly those referred to in Avicenna's list of the intelligible forms given in T1, § 3. See the comments in T5, note 3.

[8] This is not a rhetorical statement. In Paul the Persian's introduction to the works of Aristotle, based on Alexandrian sources in late antiquity, the time required for studying the philosophical sciences is specified as being between ten and twenty years: Miskawayh, *Kitāb as-Saʿāda*, Cairo 1335/1917, 71.10–11; see Gutas "Paul the Persian" 235. In another passage of similar provenance (Chapter 3.4, L27), the time required is said to be ten years. Avicenna, whose conception of the philosophical curriculum was shaped by such works, is therefore comparing this time period to the approximately six years it took him to master these subjects. See also below, Chapter 3.1, note 13.

the earliest, and one of the most accurate, is that by Kraus "Biographie" (1932). The very readable English translation by A.J. Arberry was first published in his *Theology* (1951) 9–14 and later reprinted in a number of other publications (listed by Gohlman 117n28), most notably in the volume edited by G.M. Wickens, *Avicenna* (1952) 9–20, where it was also provided with a running commentary. There is also, among others, a French translation by Achena and Massé 6–11, and a Spanish translation with commentary by Cruz Hernández 19–39.

The bibliography on the Autobiography is extensive, but its worth is inversely proportional to its extent. There is a list of publications in Gohlman, supplemented by Ullmann in his review. References to earlier Eastern European publications can be found in Brentjes and Brentjes (1979) and A.V. Sagadeev (1980). Among this mass of material, two studies stand out for their particularly perceptive analyses of the Autobiography: Sellheim's comments in his review of Ergin's bibliography, and the 23
idiosyncratic article by Lüling (1977).

The Autobiography

1. My father was a man of Balḫ. He moved from there to Buḫārā in the days of the Prince Nūḥ ibn-Manṣūr,[1] during whose reign he was employed in the administration as the governor of a village in one of the royal estates of Buḫārā called Ḫarmayṯan, which is one of the regional capitals[2] there.

---

bi-tatmīm. This, however, is not a separative error, but a variant reading of the same skeleton (*rasm*) of the word. For a case study of a faulty reading adopted in the text by Gohlman due to his inadequate analysis of the stemmatic relationship of the manuscripts see Lameer "Concupiscence." (b) A better understanding has to be gained of the relationship which the recension represented by the texts of Ibn-al-Qifṭī, 413–417 (Lippert) and Ibn-Abī-Uṣaybiʿa II.2–4 (Müller) bears to the main recension. If the variants in the former recension (which, incidentally, Gohlman calls "tradition," p. 6) are due to Ibn-al-Qifṭī's revision, as Gohlman assumes (pp. 5, 6), then they should either be discarded or, if they agree with the reading of some of the manuscripts of the main recension, explained and recorded in the apparatus, not taken in the text, as Gohlman says he has done (p. 6). (c) The paraphrase by Ẓahīr-ad-Dīn al-Bayhaqī must be studied in detail and the manuscript tradition which he used as a source identified. (Bayhaqī is cited below according to the two editions by Šafīʿ (1935) 38–62 and Kurd ʿAlī (1365/1946) 52–72). (d) Proper consideration ought to be given to the medieval Persian and Latin translations of the Autobiography.

---

1 Sāmānid ruler who reigned from 366/976 to 14 Rajab 387/23 July 997 (see further below, Chapter 2, W1, note 1). Internal evidence from the Autobiography—Avicenna redundantly refers to him further down (§ 10) as "the Sultan at that time in Buḫārā, Nūḥ ibn-Manṣūr"—and external evidence from the historical record indicate that Avicenna's father must have moved to Buḫārā before this ruler's reign. It has been suggested that Nūḥ ibn-Manṣūr in the text is a mistake for Manṣūr ibn-Nūḥ, his father, who ruled 350/961–366/976 (Sellheim 237), or even for Nūḥ ibn-Naṣr, his grandfather, who ruled 331/943–343/954 (Gutas "*Maḏhab*" 335–336); cf. also the remarks by Lüling 506n7.

2 "Capitals:" the Arabic term used (*ummahāt al-qurā*, "mother of cities" = metropolis) is Qurʾānic, where it refers to Mecca (Q 6:92 and 42:7; cf. Lüling 500 and note 25). The

Nearby is a village named Afšana, and there my father married my mother and took up his permanent residence.

2. I was born there,[3] as was my younger brother, and later we moved to Buḫārā. I was provided with a teacher of the Qur'ān and a teacher of literature, and when I reached the age of ten I had mastered the Qur'ān and a great deal of literature to such an extent that I evoked great amazement.[4]

3. My father was among those who responded to the proselytizer of the Egyptians and was considered one of the Ismāʿīlīs.[5] He had heard from them the account about the soul and the intellect in the way in which *they* tell it
24 and present it,[b] and so had my brother. They[6] would sometimes discuss this matter [i.e., the account about the soul and the intellect] among themselves,

---

[b] Reading *yuʿarrifūnahu* in the text (Gohlman 18.5), not *yaʿrifūnahu*: "auffassen," Kraus; "understand," Arberry; "know," Gohlman. The emphasis is in the Arabic.

---

expression was regularly employed in Arabic to indicate village or town centers; in Ibn-ʿAbd-Rabbihi's *Al-ʿIqd al-farīd*, for instance, it is used to refer to Medina, Ṭāʾif, and Ḫaybar in Arabia (Aḥmad Amīn et al., eds., Cairo 1948–1949, VI.27.5–7). See *EI*[2] s.v. "ḳarya" (al-Wohaibi). Lüling interprets it as follows: "Ḫarmayṯan was a metropolis *of former times*" ("Kharmīṯan war eine Metropole der *Vorzeit*," *ibid*., emphasis added). He understands the alleged reference to be to the importance of the town as a Buddhist center in pre-Islamic times, and he tries to associate Avicenna's family and the Sāmānids with this Buddhist tradition.

[3] Avicenna does not provide the date of his birth. At the end of his Biography of Avicenna, Jūzjānī calculates it to be 370/980, manifestly on the basis of his date of death, 428/1037, and his presumed age at the time, 58 lunar years (Gohlman 88–89). However, the available historical evidence, some of it not unrelated to that of the time of his father's arrival in Buḫārā mentioned in the second preceding note, clearly indicates that his birth has to be antedated by about a decade; see Sellheim 233–239, and Gutas "*Maḏhab*" 334–335.

[4] Avicenna is indirectly referring here and in what follows to the strength of his ability to Guess Correctly middle terms; cf. T2, § 4: "one must not be amazed at this," i.e. the ability of some people to learn uncommonly fast. See Chapter 3.2.

[5] In the tenth and eleventh centuries the Ismāʿīlī Šīʿīs from Fāṭimid Egypt were waging an intense conversion campaign in Central Asia. See the article on "Ismāʿīliyya" by W. Madelung in *EI*[2], IV,198a, and Gohlman 120n11.

[6] The antecedent of the pronoun here is problematical. The text established by Gohlman, apparently on the basis of the manuscripts containing the Autobiography and not its recensions in later biographers who incorporated it, uses the plural pronoun throughout in the rest of the paragraph. This implies at least three people, viz., Avicenna's father, brother, and one (or more?) Ismāʿīlī proselytizer. The plural pronoun would further imply that, since the young Avicenna and the still younger brother were present, the discussions took place in their home where the Ismāʿīlī proselytizer could apparently visit freely. The text of the Autobiography as it appears in Ibn-al-Qifṭī, however, uses the dual pronoun throughout, referring to Avicenna's father and brother (this variant in the textual tradition is not recorded by Gohlman). This is the natural pronoun to expect in the structure of the Arabic paragraph, and may be the original reading. In the next paragraph (4), Avicenna shifts to the singular, referring to his father.

while I would listen to them and comprehend what they were saying, but my soul would not accept it;[c] and they began to summon me to it[7] with[d] constant talk on their tongues about philosophy, geometry, and Indian arithmetic.[8]

4. Then he [my father] sent me for a while[e] to a greengrocer[9] who used Indian arithmetic and I would thus learn from him.

5. Then Abū-ʿAbdallāh an-Nātilī,[10] who claimed to be a philosopher, came to Buḫārā. My father had him stay in our house, and he occupied himself with my education. Before his arrival, I used to occupy myself with jurisprudence, attending frequently Ismāʿīl az-Zāhid[11] about it. I was one of the most skillful questioners, having become familiar with the methods of posing

---

[c] Gohlman punctuates incorrectly and mistranslates line 18.7: the period (or rather, comma) should be after *nafsī*, not *ilayhi*.

[d] A variant reading in a number of sources, not recorded by Gohlman, gives a different meaning to the whole sentence. For *yujrūna* in Gohlman 18.7, the Istanbul MS Üniversite 4755, f. 308ª (= B in Gohlman), Ibn-Abī-Uṣaybiʿa (II,2.13 Müller), and the otherwise unknown al-Kāšī (wrote in 754/1353: Ahwānī *Nukat* 10.6), read *wa-yujrūna*, while Ibn-al-Qifṭī reads *wa-yujriyāni* (413.16 Lippert), retaining the conjunction. If the conjunction *wa-* is retained, the sentence then means, "they began to summon me to it and they began to talk constantly about philosophy, geometry, and Indian arithmetic."

[e] Arabic: *kāna yuwajjihunī*. Ibn-al-Qifṭī and Ibn-Abī-Uṣaybiʿa have *wa-aḫaḏa yuwajjihunī*.

---

[7] I.e., specifically to the Ismāʿīlī doctrine about the soul and the intellect. The Arabic text does not support the more general interpretations of both Gohlman and Arberry: "They began to invite me to join the movement [!]" (Arberry); "And so [!] they began appealing to me to do it [to accept the Ismāʿīlī doctrines (!)]" (Gohlman).

[8] For Indian arithmetic see the article on "ʿIlm al-ḥisāb" by A.I. Sabra in *EI*^{2} III,1138a. Bayhaqī *Tatimma* 40.1–2/52–53, and, apparently following him (cf. Gohlman 6), the Istanbul MS of the Autobiography, Ahmet III 3447 (= J in Gohlman), add that he also studied parts of the *Rasāʾil Iḫwān aṣ-Ṣafāʾ*. This fateful—and misleading—addition is nothing else, however, but Bayhaqī's mistaken inference based on Avicenna's statements in this passage (Gutas "*Maḏhab*" 323–324); cf. Minorsky 6n1, and see below, Chapter 3.4, note 108.

[9] Bayhaqī *Tatimma* 40.3/53, calls him Maḥmūd al-Massāḥ; Massāḥī (or Misāḥī?) in Gohlman 20.

[10] This is Abū-ʿAbdallāh al-Ḥusayn ibn-Ibrāhīm ibn-al-Ḥusayn ibn-Ḫuršīd aṭ-Ṭabarī an-Nātilī, editor and adaptor of the Arabic translation of Dioscurides' *Materia medica*, which he completed in 380/990. It is preserved in the Leiden MS 289 Warner (1301) and was studied by Ullmann *Dioskurides* 318 ff.; cf. further Sellheim 238, question no. 1. He is listed as a physician also by Ibn-Abī-Uṣaybiʿa I,240.-9 Müller. Bayhaqī lists him primarily as a philosopher, with great accomplishments in metaphysics, but it appears that Bayhaqī is merely extrapolating from (and re-phrasing) Avicenna's Autobiography and that he did not have access to independent information; see Meyerhof 142–143 (= Bayhaqī *Tatimma* 22–23/37–38).

[11] Abū Muḥammad Ismāʿīl ibn-al-Ḥusayn ibn-ʿAlī az-Zāhid al-Buḫārī, a noted Ḥanafī jurist of Buḫārā, died in 8 Šaʿbān 402/5 March 1012: al-Ḫaṭīb al-Baġdādī, *Taʾrīḫ Baġdād*, Beirut 1968, VI,310, no. 3355. See further on him Gutas "*Maḏhab*" 327–330.

questions and ways[f] of raising objections to a respondent in the manner
Customary with these people.[12] Then I began to study the *Eisagoge* with an-
Nātilī, and when he mentioned to me the definition of "genus," viz., "what is
predicated of many things differing in species, in answer to [the question]
'What is it?',"[13] I surprised him[g] in Verifying this definition with something
26 whose like had never been heard.[14] He was extremely amazed at me and
cautioned my father that I should occupy myself with nothing else but Philosophy. Whatever problem he posed I conceptualized[15] it better then he,[h]

---

[f] Read *wujūh* for *wujūduhu* in Gohlman 20.6.

[g] The reading of the apodosis here must be, *fa-aḫaḏtuhu bi-mā lam yusmaʿ bi-miṯlihi*, the *lectio difficilior* (the *fa-* introducing the apodosis after *lammā* following the parenthetical *annahu* clause: see *WKAS* II.3, 1278b7 ff.). Gohlman reads *fa-aḫḫaḏtuhu*, allegedly following the manuscripts of the Autobiography, but the meaning "I captivated him" is not appropriate here (Gohlman translates, "I evoked his admiration"), while the recension of Ibn-al-Qifṭī and Ibn-Abī-Uṣaybiʿa reads *fa-aḫaḏtu*, "I set about," clearly a banalization.

[h] I follow here the reading of the recension in Ibn-al-Qifṭī (414.6–7 Lippert) and Ibn-Abī-ʿUṣaybiʿa (II,3.3–4 Müller). In the manuscripts of the Autobiography this sentence is placed after "amazed at me" (*kulla l-ʿajab*, Gohlman 22.3).

---

[12] "Posing questions ... raising objections:" *muṭālaba ... iʿtirāḍ*. These are specific terms in Aristotelian dialectics, not general concepts, as implied by the existing translations: "Argumentation ... widerleg[en]," Kraus; "postulation ... rebuttal," Arberry; "prosecution ... rebuttal," Gohlman. Only Achena and Massé are more precise: "interrogation ... objection." The context here is dialectical discussion as analyzed by Aristotle in the *Topics*. For *muṭālaba* cf. Avicenna's *Šifāʾ, Jadal* 315.12 Ahwānī, reflecting the Greek *zētein* (*Topics* 158a23 = *yuṭālab* in the Arabic translation, Badawī *Manṭiq* III,703); for *iʿtirāḍ* cf. ibid. 307.11 Ahwānī, reflecting the Greek *enstasis* (*Topics* 156a39 = *muʿāraḍa* and *munāqaḍa* [for 156b3] in the Arabic translation, Badawī *Manṭiq* III,694). See the discussion in Chapter 3.1.

[13] This is the definition of "genus" given by Porphyry in the *Eisagoge* (p. 2.15–16 Busse, *CAG* IV.1), in the wording of Avicenna, *Šifāʾ, Madḫal* 47.18–19 Anawati et al. Abū-ʿUṯmān ad-Dimašqī's translation of the Greek text reads, "*al-maḥmūl ʿalā kaṯīrīn muḫtalifīn bi-n-nawʿ min ṭarīq mā huwa*" (Badawī *Manṭiq* III,1024).

[14] Avicenna was conscious of his novel analysis of the question "What is it?" which he incorporated in most of his works on logic. In *Pointers and Reminders* he refers to this problem, and almost certainly to Nātilī, in similar words: "Literal minded logicians, when alerted, almost make no distinction between essential [universal] terms and the predicate in answer to [the question] 'What is it?' ... Then they become confused when one Verifies for them the status of essential terms which are more general [than the thing defined] but not themselves genera, like the things which they call generic differentiae" (*Išārāt* I.1.16, 10–11/51; cf. Goichon *Directives* 92–93, Inati *Logic* 58–59). For *ẓāhiriyyūn* see the second following note below.

[15] This is a reference to Avicenna's theory that "all knowledge is either forming concepts

until I finished [in this fashion] a literal[16] reading of Logic with him; as for its minute implications, though, he had no notion of them. Then I began to study the books [of the *Organon*] by myself and consult the commentaries until I had mastered Logic.

6. As for the book [the *Elements*] of Euclid, I studied the first five or six
figures[17] with him, and thereafter undertook on my own to solve the entire
remainder of the book. Next I moved on to the *Almagest* [of Ptolemy] and
when I had finished its introductory sections and reached the geometrical
figures,[18] an-Nātilī said to me, "Take over reading and solving them [i.e. the
geometrical figures] by yourself,[i] and then submit them to me so that I
can show you what is right and what is wrong." But the man could not 27
deal with the book, so I made the analysis myself; and many were the

---

[i] Or, following the vocalization suggested by Lippert, "Take over reading them and solve them (*ḥullahā*) by yourself" (Ibn-al-Qifṭī 414.12).

(*taṣawwur*) or acknowledging the truth (*taṣdīq*)" of a categorical statement (*Najāt* I,1, 3/20). For a detailed discussion of these two terms see Lameer *Conception*, Part One; cf. the earlier discussion by van Ess 95–113.

16 Avicenna is fond of explanatory descriptions which, though immediately apparent to his contemporaries, may seem colorful to us. Among the Islamic schools of law there was one known as the Ẓāhiriyya, i.e., "the literalists," "which would derive the law only from the literal text (*ẓāhir*) of the Qur'ān" and the Prophetic Traditions (R. Strothmann on "al-Ẓāhirīya" in *EI*^{1}, and similarly A.-M. Turki in *EI*^{2}); they were also called "Dā'ūdiyya" after the founder, Dā'ūd ibn-Ḫalaf (d. 270/884). On this analogy Avicenna divides logicians into "literalists" (*aẓ-ẓāhiriyyūn*, see the text quoted in the second preceding note above), i.e., those who would adhere uncritically to the literal text, or the apparent meaning, of Aristotle's *Organon*, and into those (like himself) who would delve into its deeper implications. In a statement reported in the memoirs of a disciple (Ibn-Zayla?) writing from Rayy, Avicenna describes the literalists as never having "suffered the pains of analyzing the details of problems so that they may gain a syllogistic habit" (T13, § 4), and as paying too much attention to the *form* of the syllogism rather than its contents (T13, §§ 5–6). Shehaby 8 suggests, without any argument, that "literalists" might refer to the Stoics, but this is highly unlikely, especially in view of the discussion here. On this basis, then, Avicenna classes Nātilī with the literalists and says that consequently he could only have finished a literal reading of the *Organon* (*ẓawāhir al-manṭiq*) with him. The implication is also that he read the entire *Organon* with Nātilī, not only some parts, as the translations of the Autobiography imply: "die einfachen Teile," Kraus; "les parties évidentes," Achena and Massé; "the straightforward parts," Arberry; "the simple parts," Gohlman.

17 I.e., Avicenna read with Nātilī the introductory definitions and postulates up to the sixth proposition of Book I of the *Elements*.

18 I.e., Avicenna read with Nātilī as far as Book I, Chapter 8 of the *Almagest*. Spherical astronomy proper, which contains the "geometrical figures" mentioned by Avicenna, starts with Chapter 9. Bayhaqī, who paraphrases this information from Avicenna's Autobiography and adds it to Nātilī's biography, misunderstands the reference here (*Tatimma* 22.4/37 end).

figures with which he was unfamiliar until I presented them to him and made him understand them! Then an-Nātilī took leave of me, heading for Gurgānj, and I occupied myself on my own with Determining the Validity of books on Physics and Theology [*ilāhiyyāt*], both their essential parts[19] and commentaries,[j] and the gates of the Philosophical Sciences began opening for me.

7. Next I desired [to learn] medicine and I read the books that have been written on this subject. Medicine is not one of the difficult sciences, and therefore I excelled in it in a very short time, to the point that distinguished physicians began to study medicine with me.[20] I cared for the sick, and there opened up to me indescribable possibilities of therapy which can only be acquired through experience.[21] At the same time I was also occupied with jurisprudence and would engage in legal disputations, being now sixteen years of age.

8. The next year and a half I devoted myself entirely to reading Philosophy: I read Logic and all the parts of philosophy once again. During this time I did not sleep completely through a single night, or occupy myself with anything else by day. I put together in front of me [sheaves of] scratch paper,[22] and for each argument that I examined, I recorded the syllogistic premisses it contained, the way in which they were composed,[k] and the conclusions[l]

---

[j] Read *šurūḥ* for *šurūʿ* in Gohlman 24.6.

[k] "Composed:" reading *wa-tarkībaha* for the transmitted *tartībaha*. See the analysis below, Chapter 3.3A and note 71.

[l] The correct text for this sentence is given by the oldest manuscript of the Autobiography, Üniversite 4755 (B in Gohlman's apparatus): *aṯbattu mā fīhā min al-muqqaddimāt al-qiyāsiyya wa-tartībahā wa-mā ʿasāhā tuntiju* (cf. Gohlman's apparatus to 28.1–2). Gohlman's reconstruction, *kuntu anẓuru fīhā aṯbattu* (*fīhā*) *mā fīhā min muqaddimāt qiyāsiyya* etc., confuses the evidence of the manuscripts and has one *fīhā* too many (if I am right in assuming that the *fīhā* in parentheses on 28.1 is intended as an editorial addition). For *tartībahā* I read *tarkībahā*; see the preceding note.

---

[19] "Essential parts," *fuṣūṣ*, as demonstrated at length by Bertolacci "Autobiography." This partial reading of texts in metaphysics would include, at the very least, *Alpha elatton* 1–2 and *Lambda* 6–10 from Aristotle's *Metaphysics*, parts of the *Theology of Aristotle*, and Themistius's paraphrase of *Lambda*, all texts contained in the Cairo MS Ḥikma 6M, which preserves copies of texts found in Avicenna's private library (cf. Gutas "Ṣiġnāḫī").

[20] It appears that Avicenna was not completely self-taught in medicine (as Lüling 504 would infer from his silence). There are reports mentioning two physicians who were his teachers: Abū-Manṣūr al-Ḥasan ibn-Nūḥ al-Qumrī and Abū-Sahl ʿĪsā ibn-Yaḥyā al-Masīḥī. See Ullmann *Medizin* 147 and 151, respectively, and his *Dioskurides* 322–324 for Avicenna's use of Nātilī's revision of Dioscurides in the *Canon*.

[21] The translation of this sentence is by Ullmann in his review of Gohlman.

[22] *Ẓuhūran*, or blank reverse of paper that has been used on one side. For this meaning of

which they might yield, and I would also take into account the conditions of its premisses [i.e. their modalities] until I had Ascertained that particular problem. Every time I was at a loss about a problem, concerning which I was unable to find the middle term in a syllogism, I would repair on its account to the mosque and worship, praying humbly to the All-Creator to disclose to me its obscurity and make its difficulty easy.[m] At 28
night I would return home, set the lamp before me, and occupy myself with reading and writing. Whenever I felt drowsy or weakening, I would turn aside to drink a cup of wine to regain my strength, and then I would go back to my reading. Whenever I fell asleep, I would see those very problems in my dream; and many problems became clear to me while asleep. So I continued until all the Philosophical Sciences became deeply rooted in me and I understood them as much as is humanly possible.[23] Everything that I knew at that time is just as I know it now; I have added nothing more to it to this day, such that I mastered Logic, Physics and Mathematics.

9. Ultimately I reached Theology [*al-ʿilm al-ilāhī*]. I read the *Metaphysics* [of Aristotle] but did not understand what it contained and was confused about the author's purpose to the point that I reread it forty times and consequently memorized it. In spite of this I still did not understand it or what was intended by it, and I said, despairing of myself, "There is no way to understand this book!" One afternoon I was at the booksellers' quarter when a crier came up holding a volume which he was hawking for sale. He offered it to me but I refused it in vexation, believing that there was no use in this particular science. But he said to me, "Buy it; its owner needs the money and it's cheap; I'll sell it to you for three dirhams." So I bought it and it turned out to be Abū-Naṣr al-Fārābī's book *On the Purposes of the Metaphysics*. I returned home and hastened to read it, and at once the

[m] The text in the recension of Ibn-al-Qifṭī and Ibn-Abī-Uṣaybiʿa reads, "praying humbly to the All-Creator until He disclosed to me its obscurity and made its difficulty easy."

ẓahr see Gacek *Manuscript Tradition* 96. Bayhaqī *Tatimma* 40/54 also feels the need to explain the term and adds, *ẓuhūran min al-qarāṭīs*, "[blank] reverse of sheets of paper."

[23] This formulation reflects and conflates two of the six canonical definitions of philosophy in Alexandrian Aristotelianism. Philosophy is the knowledge of the real nature of things and the imitation of God to the extent of human ability. See Gutas *Wisdom Literature* 225–227 and 333–335. For an analysis of Avicenna's methods of study described here see below, Chapter 3.3.

purposes of that book were disclosed to me because I had learned it by heart. I rejoiced at this and the next day I gave much in alms to the poor in gratitude to God Exalted.[24]

10. It happened that the Sultan at that time in Buḫārā, Nūḥ ibn-Manṣūr, had an illness which perplexed the physicians. Since my name had become well known among them for my complete devotion to the Philosophical Sciences and to reading, they mentioned me in his presence and asked him to summon me. So I presented myself and collaborated with them in treating him, and was enrolled in his service. One day I asked his permission to
29 enter their library, look through it, and read its contents. He gave me permission and I was admitted to a building with many rooms; in each room there were chests of books piled one on top of the other. In one of the rooms were books on the Arabic language and poetry, in another jurisprudence, and so on in each room a separate science. I looked through the catalogue of books by the ancients and requested those which I needed. I saw books whose very names are unknown to many and which I had never seen before nor have I seen since.[25] I read those books, mastered their teachings, and realized how far each man had advanced in his science.

11. So by the time I reached my eighteenth year I had completed my study in all these Philosophical Sciences. At that time my retention of Knowledge was better, but today my grasp of it is more mature; otherwise the Knowledge is the same, nothing new having come to me since.

12. In my neighborhood there lived a man called Abū-l-Ḥasan al-ʿArūḍī [the Prosodist], who asked me to compose for him a comprehensive work on this Knowledge [i.e., Philosophy]. I composed for him *The Compilation*, which I named after him [i.e., *Philosophy for ʿArūḍī*], and I treated in it all the sciences except mathematics.[26] At that time I was twenty-one years old.

13. Also in my neighborhood there lived a man called Abū-Bakr al-Baraqī, a Ḫwārizmian by birth. A prudent man, he favored jurisprudence, Qurʾānic exegesis, and asceticism, but also had an inclination for these Philosophical

---

[24] The significance of this incident for Avicenna's philosophy is discussed below, Chapter 6.1.

[25] An example of the rare books mentioned here is provided by Avicenna in the Prior Analytics of *The Cure*, Shehaby 159; see also below, Chapter 2, W6b. For this and the other libraries visited by Avicenna in his lifetime see Weisweiler.

[26] See Chapter 2, W2.

Sciences. He asked me to comment on the books [on Philosophy] and so I composed *The Available and the Valid* for him in about twenty volumes, and I also composed a book for him on Ethics which I called *Piety and Sin*. These two books exist only in his possession because he never lent them to anybody to copy from them.[27]

14. Then my father died. My situation changed drastically, and I assumed some post in the financial administration of the Sultan.[n] However, necessity led me to abandon Buḫārā and move to Gurgānj, where Abū-l-Ḥusayn as-Sahlī, a lover of the Philosophical Sciences, was minister.[28] I was introduced to the Prince there, ʿAlī ibn-Maʾmūn;[29] at that time I was in lawyer's garb, wearing the *ṭaylasān* scarf turned under the chin. They fixed for me a monthly salary which provided enough for someone like me.

15. Then necessity led me to move to Nasā, and from there to Bāward, and then to Ṭūs, then to Samanqān, then to Jājarm (the frontier of Ḫurāsān), and then to Jurjān. I was planning to go to Prince Qābūs, but it happened meanwhile that he was taken and imprisoned in some fortress, where he died. Then I departed for Dihistān, where I fell very ill. I returned to Jurjān, and there I became associated with Abū-ʿUbayd al-Jūzjānī.[30] He recited to me an ode on my state of affairs which contained the following verse by a poet:

When I became great, no city[31] was big enough for me;
When my price went up, no one would buy me.

---

[n] For the meaning of the terms *taṣarrafat al-aḥwāl* and *ʿamal/aʿmāl* see Dozy.

---

[27] See Chapter 2, W3. On Baraqī see Gutas "*Maḏhab*."

[28] Abū-l-Ḥusayn Aḥmad ibn-Muḥammad as-Sahlī was a well-known patron of the Greek sciences. Gohlman 124n41 notes that his name is given as as-Suhaylī by both Ṯaʿālibī and Yāqūt, but in all the manuscripts of the Autobiography and of the relevant works by Avicenna it is written as as-Sahlī, which, short of a comprehensive investigation, ought to be followed. He also commissioned works from Avicenna's teacher of medicine, Abū-Sahl al-Masīḥī. See Ullmann *Medizin* 151.

[29] The Ḫwārizm-Šāh ʿAlī ibn-Maʾmūn ruled from 387/997 to 399/1009.

[30] Kraus "Biographie" 1882a, note †††, hinted, and Lüling boldly proposed, that political reasons lay behind Avicenna's travels. For the geographical and chronological details see Lüling's maps, Gohlman's notes, and Chapter 2, W6, below.

[31] There is a pun here. *Miṣr* also means "Egypt," and the hemistich then means, "When I became great, even Egypt was not big enough for me."

Text 4. Introduction to *The Provenance and Destination* (GM 1)

The Provenance and Destination is the first extant work by Avicenna which sets forth his metaphysical theory in a format that is largely independent of Aristotelian models. It was copied extensively in both *The Cure* and *The Salvation* (see W4). The title refers to the place of origin of all being (Provenance, *al-mabda'*) and to the place of return of the rational soul (Destination, *al-ma'ād*).[1] These two concepts play a large role in Avicenna's metaphysics, and especially in what I have called the Metaphysics of the Rational Soul (see Chapter 6.2). The Introduction is significant for explicitly locating the center, in Avicenna's view, of Aristotelian Physics and Metaphysics, and for presenting his understanding and analysis of traditional methods of philosophical expression (see Chapter 8.1).

The printed text made available by Nūrānī, *Al-Mabda' wa-l-ma'ād* (1984), is unsatisfactory. A truly critical edition in preparation by Y. Michot has not been completed, but he has kindly made available on-line his draft translation in French, annotated with many variant readings from a number of manuscripts (*Livre de la genèse*). My translation below is based on the Istanbul MS Ahmet III, 3268, f. 61^{a} (I), as copied by Mahdavī 213 and Nūrānī 1,[a] and the Milan MS Ambrosiana 320 (Hammer), ff. 118^{b}–119^{a} (A). I have indicated the relevant variants in the notes.

31 ### *Introduction*

1. In this treatise I wish to indicate the real doctrine of the Validating[b] Peripatetic philosophers concerning Provenance and Destination in an effort to find favor with Master Abū-Aḥmad ibn-Muḥammad ibn-Ibrāhīm al-Fārisī.[c] This treatise of mine contains the fruits of two great sciences, one of which is characterized by being about metaphysical, and the other physical,

[a] In his introduction, Nūrānī says that he based his "edition" on the Istanbul MS Ahmet III, 3227, dated 580H, with due consideration of other manuscripts. His text, however, has no apparatus criticus, and furthermore, according to Mahdavī, it is MS Ahmet III, 3268 (and not 3227) that is dated 580H. The text of the introduction, finally, as given by both Mahdavī and Nūrānī, except for a single variant (below, note h), is verbatim identical. Although it is impossible to be certain without an examination of the manuscripts themselves, it would seem that they both copy from the same source and that the manuscript numbers have been confused. For the sake of brevity I treat their texts as representing a single witness.

[b] *Al-muḥaṣṣilūn* I; *al-muḫliṣūn* A, i.e., "the devotees" of the doctrine.

[c] *Taqarruban bihi ilā š-šayḫi Abī Aḥmad b. Muḥammad b. Ibrāhīm al-Fārisī* A, is omitted in I, in Nūrānī, and in Michot's translation.

[1] The subject of *ma'ād* was treated extensively by Michot *Destinée*. See in general the entry "Ma'ād" in EI^2, V,893b (R. Arnaldez).

matters. The fruit of the science dealing with metaphysical matters is that part of it known as *theologia*,[2] which treats [the subjects of] Lordship, the first principle,[3] and the relationship which beings bear to it according to their rank.[4] The fruit of the science dealing with physical matters is the knowledge that the human soul survives and that it has a Destination.[5]

2. I have divided this book into three parts: (a) Establishing the first principle of the universe and its oneness; enumeration of the attributes befitting it. (b) Indicating the order of the emanation of being from the being [of the first principle], beginning with the first being [emanating] from it and ending with the last beings after it. (c) Indicating the survival of the human soul; the real bliss in the Hereafter, and what is a certain kind of bliss that is not real;[d] the real misery in the Hereafter, and what is a certain kind of misery that is not real.[e]

3. In these parts I strive[f] to clarify what they [the Peripatetic philosophers] obscured,[g] proclaim what they concealed and suppressed, collect what they dispersed, and expand what they summarized,[6] to the best of the inadequate abilities of a person like me beset with these afflictions: 32
the age of scholarship is becoming extinct, interests are turning away from the philosophical sciences toward various pursuits, and hatred is heaped

[d] Reading *ġayr al-ḥaqīqiyya* for *wa-ġayr al-ḥaqīqiyya* A, and *wa-ġayr ḥaqīqiyya* I. See the next note. Retaining the conjunction would imply a tripartition of bliss (real bliss, a certain kind of bliss, unreal bliss), but Avicenna speaks only of two kinds in the work itself. See the headings of Chapters 14 and 15 in Mahdavī 216, Nūrānī 109 and 114.

[e] Reading *ġayr al-ḥaqīqiyya* A for *wa-ġayr al-ḥaqīqiyya* I.

[f] Reading *ataḥarrā* I for *ataḥaddā* A.

[g] Reading *aġlaqū* I for *aġfalū* A, though the *lectio difficilior* in A ("they neglected") may deserve consideration.

[2] Avicenna uses the transliteration of the Greek word here, *Uṯūlūjiyā*, a clear reference to the title of the Arabic *Enneads*, the *Theologia Aristotelis*. For Avicenna this is part of Peripatetic doctrine, despite the fact that he expressed some doubts about the validity of the ascription of the work to Aristotle. See T12, § 3.

[3] The word *mabda'* means both first principle and place of origin; Avicenna is referring here both to the subject matter of his treatise and to its title.

[4] Cf. T1, § 3, IV B iii, and note 11.

[5] Cf. T1, § 3, IV B iv, and note 14.

[6] These are the ways in which, according to later Aristotelian tradition, philosophical knowledge in published books could be Withheld from those unworthy to receive it. Hence the need for explanation, or decoding, a task which Avicenna sets for himself in this work, as he says in the first sentence of this Introduction, i.e., to expound the real doctrine of the Peripatetics hiding behind these subterfuges. See the discussion in Chapter 5.3.

upon those who concern themselves with[h] some part of truth; furthermore, earnestness is exhausted and energy dissipates[i] from the minds of those who have been tried as sorely, and subjected to as many vicissitudes of time, as I have been.[7] But God is our resort, with Him is the Power and the Might!

Text 5. Epilogue of the "Lesser" *Destination* (*State of the Human Soul*) (GM 3)

This treatise is the counterpart of *The Provenance and Destination* with regard to Avicenna's theory of the soul. It was also copied extensively in both *The Cure* and *The Salvation*. See Chapter 2, W5, and GM 3 in the Appendix, for the questions of its title and authenticity.

The text is translated from the edition by Ahwānī *Aḥwāl* 141–142. The transcription of the text by Ülken II,153–154 from MS Istanbul, Ahmet III 3447, riddled with errors, has not been taken into account. Ahwānī also used the Ahmet III MS for his edition, but the variants he cites frequently do not coincide with the readings in Ülken. No attempt has been made here to edit the brief passage translated below; any textual comments have been relegated to the notes. There is a French translation of this chapter in Michot *Destinée* 3n14 and Sebti "Authenticité" 352.

Chapter 16

[Epilogue:] The Occasion[a] of this Treatise

1. In this essay I have left out a discussion of the superficial aspects of the theory of the soul,[1] except for what was absolutely necessary, and have

---

[h] Both A and Nūrānī read *taʿāṭā*; Mahdavī reads *yuʿāṭā*, "those who are given."

[i] Reading *infilāl* I for *inqilāb* A.

[a] "Occasion:" *maḥall*. In the table of contents of this treatise given by Mahdavī 246, the reading is given as *mujmal*, "summary" (without indication of the manuscript from which it was taken), which is the reading also in the Istanbul MS Üniversite 4755, f. 127[a], though it is corrected there on the basis of another MS (*nusḫa*) to *maḥall*. The table of contents in Ahwānī *Aḥwāl* 47 also has *maḥall*.

---

[7] Avicenna's complaint about the times is not merely rhetorical, although such complaints were commonplace in much scholarly writing (see Chapter 5.3). At the time when Avicenna was writing this treatise, his social and political world had indeed collapsed. The Sāmānid state was destroyed, its lands and his home overrun by the Turkish Qarāḫānids; Avicenna was a man without a country. This work was written shortly after he had come to Jurjān after long travels, described in the Autobiography (T3, §15), during a period of great political instability in the area (cf. Lüling).

[1] By "superficial aspects [*al-umūr aẓ-ẓāhira*] of the theory of the soul [*ʿilm an-nafs*]," that is, of the Aristotelian *De anima* and its elaboration in the tradition, Avicenna is referring to

instead "removed the cover" [Qur'ān 50:22] lifted the veil, and indicated the 33
innermost ideas[2] stored in the depths of books[3] and Withheld from explicit mention.[4]

2. [I did this] in an effort to find favor with my friends and also because, first, I am confident that in our times there is no one who would either inherit these innermost ideas through instruction or be able to gain a comprehensive knowledge of them through Discovery,[5] and second, I have relinquished the hope that the person who desires to perpetuate the Philosophical Sciences and bequeath them to posterity has any means or device at his disposal other than to record them and put them down in writing in black and white. One cannot rely either on the student's desire to Ascertain them in the proper manner, uphold them, and bequeath them to posterity, or on the solicitude of our contemporaries and their like-minded successors to examine the symbolically expressed passages [in these books] and interpret

---

the discussion of the vegetative and animal souls (Books I and II of *De anima*), matters with which he dealt in detail both in his earlier *Compendium on the Soul* (W1) and later in *The Cure* (W6). In this treatise he concentrates primarily on the rational soul (see Chapter 2, W5).

[2] "Innermost ideas:" *asrār*. I have not used the word "secrets" to render *asrār* in order to avoid the association, in the mind of the English reader, first with the extended meaning of the word as "mystery," and second with any notion of a presumed "esoteric" doctrine of Avicenna. *Asrār* means here "secrets" only in the sense of something hidden from view because stored deep inside something else. This is evident in the above passage, where it is contrasted with "superficial," or external, matters, *al-umūr aẓ-ẓāhira*, and with things that are not expressed outwardly, or explicitly, *at-taṣrīḥ bihā*.

[3] "Books," that is, on the subject written by Aristotle and the philosophers in the tradition. Cf. a similar use of the absolute *kutub*, "books," in T2, §4, and in the Autobiography (T3, end of paragraph 6), where the reference to the Aristotelian tradition is evident: "I occupied myself on my own with Determining the Validity of *books* on Physics and Theology [*ilāhiyyāt*], both their essential parts and commentaries." See the discussion on *ʿilm*, below, end of Chapter 3.1. The expression "the depths of books" (*buṭūn al-kutub*) seems to be taken directly from the passage of Fārābī's treatise *The Agreement between Plato and Aristotle*, translated in Chapter 5.3, L43, §1. The attribution of this treatise to Fārābī is disputed, but Avicenna knew it as the work of Fārābī (*al-Ajwiba ʿan masāʾil Abī Rayḥān al-Bīrūnī* 40.12–13 Nasr and Mohaghegh) and thus for the purposes of this book it will be so treated. For the dispute see Marwan Rashed, "On the Authorship of the Treatise *On the Harmonization of the Opinions of the Two Sages* Attributed to al-Fārābī," *ASP* 19 (2009) 43–82, and the references there to earlier studies.

[4] "Withheld from explicit mention:" *al-maḍnūn bi-t-taṣrīḥ bihā*. See the discussion of the concept of "Withholding," *ḍanna*, below, Chapter 5.3.

[5] The reference here is to the twin sources of knowledge mentioned in Texts 1 and 2, instruction and Discovery, the latter either through syllogisms or Guessing Correctly the middle term. See Chapter 3.2.

them (should symbolic expression have in fact been used), and to elaborate their succinct passages (should the author have in fact restricted himself only to a succinct exposition).[6]

3. I have then forbidden all my friends who would read [this treatise][b] to squander[7] it on an evil or obdurate person, or to show it to him, or to deposit it where it does not belong, and bound them [by an oath] to God as their adversary in my behalf [should they violate the oath].[8]

34 Text 6. From *The Cure* (GS 5): Prologue and Epilogue of Sophistics

Aristotle's epilogue to the *Sophistici Elenchi* played a significant role in the Aristotelianism of late antique Alexandria, in the formation of a stylized conception of the history of philosophy (see Chapter 4). This conception was transmitted to Arabic philosophy, and Avicenna took the opportunity while paraphrasing the Aristotelian text in *The Cure* to express his views on the subject in general and on individual philosophers and philosophical traditions in particular (see Chapter 7).

The selection below is translated from *Safsaṭa* 4.11–5.10, 110–115 Ahwānī.

A. Prologue

[In the Prologue to the Sophistics, Avicenna follows Aristotle's argument (164a20–165a20) in an expanded paraphrase. After 165a20, he inserts the following parenthetical remarks based on his personal experience, and then resumes his paraphrase.]

1. [165a20–21] It seems that it is more preferable for some people—no, most of them—to be thought of as philosophers without being such than to be philosophers in themselves without being taken as such.

2. As a matter of fact, in our time we have seen and witnessed people who fit this description: for they would feign philosophy, advocate it, and summon people to it, despite the fact that their degree of its attainment

---

[b] The text here has the masculine pronoun, *yaqra'u-hu*, to refer to the feminine "essay," *maqāla*, at the beginning of this passage.

---

[6] For the "evil times" motif see T4. On the concepts of the philosophical praxis and methods of philosophical communication adumbrated here see Chapters 5 and 8.

[7] *Baḏala*, "to spend freely," is the antonym of *ḍanna*, "be stingy, withholding." See Chapter 5.3.

[8] Cf. the similar oath of reservation at the end of *Pointers and Reminders*, T10, § 8.

was miserable. When we advised them of their deficiency, and their situation became apparent to people, they denied that philosophy has any validity or usefulness. But as it was impossible for many of them to have sheer ignorance be imputed to them, to claim that philosophy is fundamentally worthless, and to abandon completely knowledge and reason, they attempted to slander the Peripatetics and to find fault with books on logic as well as those who built on their basis: they propagated the delusion that philosophy is [only] Platonic, wisdom [only] Socratic, and that among the ancients only the earliest, and among philosophers only the Pythagoreans[a] possessed knowledge.

3. Many of them said: "Although philosophy may have some validity, learning it is nevertheless futile. The human soul, like that of the beasts, perishes, and philosophy is [therefore] useless in this world; and as for the next [world], there is none." Whoever would like to be thought of as a philosopher but his powers fall short of attaining philosophy, or indolence and ample means prevent him from it, will find no other alternative but to espouse the discipline of the sophists. From this results deliberate sophistry, although sometimes it also arises out of fallacious reasoning.

[Avicenna then resumes his paraphrase of the Aristotelian text.]

B. Epilogue

Absolving Aristotle of Deficiency (*if indeed there was any*)

1. [183a27–36] We have explained the [different] aspects of sophistical arguments and their solution, how to ask questions using them, and how to argue against them. We must now restate our purpose in a few words.

2. [183a37–b9] Aristotle said: 'Since we have attempted to obtain rules which would enable us to adduce syllogisms based on generally accepted [endoxic] opinions for the purposes of dialectical [argumentation] or the art of examination, and since the art of sophistry resembles both of them, that is, dialectic and examination (dialectic because they have common subjects and because sophistry sometimes imitates dialectic and is accordingly called the art of pretense, and examination because of the attempt to deceive and because it is also associated with dialectic), we had [the *Topics*] followed by an investigation into this discipline [of sophistry]. But we

[a] Reading *illā ʿinda l-qudamāʾ min al-awāʾil wa-l-Fīṯāġūriyyīn min al-falāsifa*, without paragraph break.

did not restrict ourselves[b] in this subject to matters that pertain to the questioner [only], but also to the respondent, in his defense of his position[1] by means of homonyms,[2] to matters he should take into account concerning generally accepted opinions, and to matters that pertain to a person imitating a respondent in his defense of sophistical positions.[1] Defense, in short, is more difficult than interrogation, since interrogation is like destroying and defense like constructing, and the defender has to proceed by means of generally accepted opinions only and nothing else, while the questioner has at his disposal whatever comes his way. This is why[c] Socrates would not be a respondent, since he would acknowledge that he was not good at it,[3] but he would rather assume the position of a questioner.'

36 3. [183b9–34] It must not be understood from what follows next in Aristotle's text that he is talking about syllogism in general, but about sophistical syllogisms; and although he expressed himself as follows,[d] 'In the demonstrative and dialectical disciplines that we mentioned we took fundamental principles from our predecessors,' he does not mean that [he found] these principles [expressed in a theoretical manner,] abstracted from concrete things, but [that he perceived them] as they were used in concrete things. In demonstrative arguments—in geometry, for example—and in dialectical and rhetorical questions and answers there were used particulars from which universal rules could be extracted. When men first became aware of dialectic and rhetoric, these particulars were very few; only later did they branch out and multiply as talented people began to appear, build upon these particulars, alter them, and correct them. They acquired an aptitude [for dialectic and rhetoric], albeit not from rules, and they performed interrogations, offered solutions, and conducted disputes satisfactorily on the basis of particulars. Occasionally, they also suggested certain universals,

---

[b] The text has, "we did not branch out and we did not restrict ourselves," which makes little sense. The construction *wa-lam ... wa-lam* is also suspect; and *wa-lam nataša‘‘ab* does not belong to the preceding sentence.

[c] Reading *li-ḏālika* for *ka-ḏālika* in the text, along with four manuscripts (see the apparatus criticus) and Ibn-Zur‘a (Badawī *Manṭiq* 1010.1).

[d] *Wa-in kāna ka-ḏālika qāla*: the text seems doubtful here.

---

[1] *Waḍ‘*, i.e. *topos*.

[2] *Bi-l-muštarakāt*. This misunderstanding on Avicenna's part is due to the faulty translation of Ibn-Zur‘a, who renders *homotropōs* (183b6) by *bi-štirāki l-ism* (Badawī *Manṭiq* 1009.-2), as if it meant *homōnymōs*.

[3] *Lā yuḥsinu ḏālika* for *ouk eidenai* (183b8) is Ibn-Zur‘a's translation (Badawī *Manṭiq* 1010.2).

though few. Aristotle mentioned a succession of people in rhetorical education who followed after the ancients—like Tisias,[4] and after him Thrasymachus, the person who debated Socrates on the subject of justice, and then Theodorus.

4. [Then Aristotle says (183b34–36):] 'With regard to argumentation against the sophists, however, earlier scholars did not treat adequately any part of it that is of account because there was little need for it; as a matter of fact, they had nothing of this subject—be it with regard to principles or particulars—which we could inherit from them at all. Accordingly, as the need for the discipline of sophistry was little, they did not even finish posing its problems, let alone solving them; instead they talked about a few particular examples and some things related to rhetoric. For our part, however, we elaborated slightly on the subject, investigated and collected [different] aspects of captious questions, and abstracted[e] from concrete things a universal discipline.'

5. [183b36–184a9] 'A need *was* felt, on the other hand, for something like rhetoric, precisely in order to [be able to] choose certain things and avoid others. Early men first came upon this kind of rhetoric only, and then they made some discoveries. But they were in a hurry, and they would teach and
learn before abstracting the discipline [of rhetoric], for what was learned 37
from their teachers was by way of learning from an experienced teacher, not from one who can construct a syllogism; they would thus acquire neither a discipline nor something universal, except for things of no account but which would bring about an [immediate] benefit.' [There follows a long elaboration (pp. 112.11–113.5) of Aristotle's example from the cobbler's craft (184a5–9): giving people shoes does not teach them how to make them.][5] Aristotle said: 'We therefore did not acquire from our predecessors their discipline, but merely inherited from them ready-made examples[6] in rhetoric, dialectic, and demonstration.'

6. Aristotle said [184a9–end]: 'As for the form of syllogism, and the form of each individual syllogism, this is something in whose quest we toiled for

---

[e] Reading *jarradnā* for *jarradnāhā* in the text.

---

[4] Avicenna has *Ṭīṭīās*, a mistranscription of the name found only in Ibn-Zurʿa (Badawī *Manṭiq* 1011.6 app.).

[5] Avicenna's prolixity here is partly based on his attempt to elucidate the rather garbled translation by Ibn-Zurʿa which he was following.

[6] The analogy here is to the ready-made shoes instead of the cobbler's craft given to people.

a long time until we discovered it. If any deficiency appears in this single art, then let the person[f] who becomes conscious of this upon close scrutiny grant pardon, let him accept[g] the boon of whatever truth we have imparted to him, and let him know[h] that imparting principles and deriving the foundation of a discipline occupy a loftier position and higher rank than building upon it, especially when the discovery, despite its recent origin, comprehends the totality of the discipline and its rules, out of which only matters of consequence can sprout.' This is then what Aristotle says.

7. As for me [i.e. Avicenna], I say to my fellow students and scholars: Reflect upon what this great man said, and then consider: after almost one thousand three hundred and thirty years, was this goal reached by anyone who blamed Aristotle for being deficient, and who was right in identifying a defect in him because Aristotle was in fact deficient in such and such a matter? And did there appear after him anybody who added anything at all to this art beyond what Aristotle said? Certainly not; for what Aristotle did is complete and perfect. The distinction falls on him and cannot be transferred to anyone else. For our part, despite the fact that our investigation was profound (in the days when we applied ourselves to Philosophy in total absorption and did independent thinking we had a better mind and more time for worthier matters), we considered [this discipline], studied it thoroughly, scrutinized it closely, and found no method for [the study of] sophistical matters other than the one Aristotle gave.[7] If there is anything, it is some
38 details in certain chapters which we have taken from him—something for which we hope to provide more evidence in the *Appendices* when we hope to have more time for worthier matters.[8]

8. Aristotle's teacher [Plato] digressed from the due course and did not treat the subject adequately in what he wrote in the book which he called *The Sophist*.[9] His digression was due to his confusion of Logic with Physics and Theology, [subjects] feebly distinguished by philosophers before the appearance of this great man [Aristotle]. Plato's inadequate treatment was due to the fact that the only way for the occurrence of sophistry which he

---

[f] Reading *fa-l-yaʿḏir*.
[g] Reading *wa-l-yaqbal*.
[h] Reading *wa-l-yaʿlam*.

---

[7] Cf. the Autobiography (T3) and the Introduction to *The Easterners* (T8, §2).
[8] Cf. what Avicenna himself has to say about the Sophistics of *The Cure* in a later text, T13, §7.
[9] Literally, Sophistics (*sūfisṭīqā*).

understood was homonymy. It is proper, then, that the truth be told: if the extent of Plato's achievements in Philosophy is what came down to us of him, then his wares were paltry indeed and philosophy in his time had not matured to the point of reaping.[10] Whoever affects allegiance to him, having at his disposal only the amount of knowledge about Plato that has been transmitted to us, does it either out of envy for Aristotle or out of a foolish notion that the prior in time is also in a discipline prior in rank. The truth, however, is the opposite.

Text 7. Introduction to *The Cure* (GS 5), by Jūzjānī

Abū-ʿUbayd ʿAbd-al-Wāḥid ibn-Muḥammad al-Jūzjānī, one of Avicenna's closest disciples and his amanuensis (*mudawwin*) and biographer, wrote two accounts of the genesis of *The Cure*. The first was in the following Introduction, written shortly after the work was completed, and the second was incorporated in his Biography of Avicenna, written after the latter's death. These accounts provide significant information about Avicenna's attitude toward his work and Jūzjānī's perception of them (see W6).

The text is translated from *Madḫal* 1–4 Anawati et al. It has been compared with MS Leiden Golius 4 (No. 1444 in P. de Jong and M.J. de Goeje, *Catalogus Codicum Orientalium Bibliothecae Academiae Lugduno Batavae*, Leiden 1865, 316–319), which was not used in the Cairo edition. The text given in Mahdavī 127–129, apparently from MS Bodleian Pococke 119 and also not used in the Cairo edition, agrees almost verbatim with it. The Latin translation by Avendauth, edited by Birkenmajer 314–317, has been compared throughout. (In this connection it is to be noted
that Birkenmajer's identification, following Amable Jourdain, of Avendauth with 39
Johannes Hispalensis has been disproved by d'Alverny "Avendauth?".) The new edition of the Latin translation in the *Avicenna Latinus* project announced by Van Riet has not materialized.

Introduction to The Cure

1. My love for the philosophical sciences and my desire to acquire true knowledge prompted me to abandon my country and emigrate to the country where Avicenna—may God perpetuate his days[1]—resided, because the

[10] Cf. a similar formulation by Ḥunayn ibn-Isḥāq quoted below, Chapter 4, L30. This and the preceding two paragraphs are paraphrased by Šahrazūrī and Quṭb-ad-Dīn Šīrāzī in their commentaries on Suhrawardī's *Philosophy of Illumination* (*Ḥikmat al-išrāq*). They indicate that Suhrawardī had these passages by Avicenna in mind when he mentioned in the introduction to the work that Aristotle's importance should not be exaggerated. See Corbin *Opera II* 303–304.

[1] The implication is, naturally, that Avicenna is still alive. Some manuscripts have instead,

reports about him that came to my attention and his writings[a] to which I was exposed required that I favor him above everybody else known for this discipline and associated with this subject.[b] The reports that had reached me about him indicated that he was proficient in these sciences already as a young man—an adolescent still in his teens[c]—and that he had written many works, except that he would little Withhold them [from others] and showed little interest in keeping copies[d] [for himself]. My desire was thus confirmed that I should go to him and join his company, and insistently request from him to concern himself [only] with writing while I concerned myself with keeping[e] [what he wrote].[2]

2. So I went to Jurjān where he resided at the time; he was then approximately thirty-two years old. He was afflicted with serving the Sultan[3] in the financial administration,[f] something which occupied all his time,[4] and

[a] "Writings:" *kalām*, literally, "words;" Latin: *sermo* (17). [The numbers in parentheses after the Latin words refer to the lines of Birkenmajer's text.]

[b] "Subject:" *jumla*; literally, "set, or group [of sciences]." The Latin also translates according to the sense: *sciencia* (19).

[c] Literally, "not having exceeded two decades (reading *ʿaqdayn*) of life." The Latin has *XL* (22), which is difficult to account for (barring scribal errors) unless the translator mistook *ʿaqd* for "score" rather than "half-score."

[d] The Latin has *codice radices* (24), which might imply an original Arabic reading of *uṣūlihā* for the transmitted *nusaḫihā*, although such a reading is not attested in the Arabic apparatus. It seems that *codice radices* is the interpretation of the translator. See the following note.

[e] Again the Latin translator interprets "keeping" (*ḍabṭ*) as *mihi copiam faciendo* (27).

[f] "Financial administration:" *at-taṣarruf fī ʿamalihi*; cf. the Latin, *occupatus in ipsius negociis disponendis* (30), where *negotia* also would refer to finances. See above in the Autobiography, T3, §14.

"may God have mercy on his soul;" the Latin omits the phrase entirely. See the discussion in Chapter 2, W6.

[2] See a similar statement by Jūzjānī in *GAS* VI,281n3. When Jūzjānī's works are all collected and examined, it is likely that more such statements will emerge.—It appears that it was common practice for scholars to have secretaries who would record their books (*mudawwin*, amanuensis). See Bayhaqī *Tatimma* 102.3/109 for Ibrāhīm b. ʿAdī, Fārābī's amanuensis; Ibn-Abī-Uṣaybiʿa II,139.19 Müller.

[3] The Sultan at the time in Jurjān was the son of the Ziyārid Qābūs, Falak-al-Maʿālī Manūchihr (d. 420/1029; see Bosworth "Ziyārids"). Avicenna did not fare very well in this position, as is evident from Jūzjānī's choice of words, "afflicted with" (*buliya bi-*), an expression also used by Avicenna himself in the Introduction to *The Easterners* (T8, §4) and perhaps referring to his associates in Jurjān. In the Biography (Gohlman 45) Jūzjānī does not mention that Avicenna was employed in Manūchihr's court.

[4] The Latin adds, "to be able to accede on every occasion to my requests," *usquequaque meis postulacionibus annuendi* (31). The Arabic manuscripts show no indication of such an addition.

I could therefore avail myself of only a few opportunities during which I took down some dictation on Logic and Physics.[5] When I appealed to him to compose long works and commentaries, he referred to the commentaries he had written and books he had composed in his native country. I had heard, however, that these were widely dispersed and that people who owned a copy of them Withheld them [from others]; as for him, it was not his habit to save a copy for himself, just as it was not his habit to make a clean copy from his holograph or transcribe [a holograph] from his rough draft: he would only either dictate[g] or himself write the copy and give it to the person who had commissioned it from him. Moreover, he suffered from successive misfortunes, and disasters destroyed his books.[6]

3. For a number of years I kept moving with him from Jurjān to Rayy and from Rayy to Hamaḏān, where he was employed as the minister of King Šams-ad-Dawla,[h] an occupation that proved distressful to us and a waste of our time.[i,7] In the meantime, the hope of ever obtaining his lost works[j] 41
having dimmed, we[8] asked[k] him to rewrite them and he said, "I have neither

---

[g] It might be useful to give here the Arabic and Latin (38–42) technical terms for manuscript writing used in this passage: *nusḫa* = *codex*; *ḫazana* (or *ḫazzana*) = *in thesauriolo repono*; *ḥarrara* = *in textualem litteram redigo*; *dustūr* = *prima notula*; *amlā* = *ad notandum do*. The phrase *yuḫrija min as-sawād* is either omitted in the Latin or incorporated into the preceding *yuḥarrira min ad-dustūr* and together translated as *post primam notulam in textualem litteram redigeret*. For *dustūr* meaning archetype in the sense of holograph there is the authority of a marginal gloss in MS Vienna 105, f. 69^{a}, of Ibn-al-Qifṭī's *Taʾrīḫ al-ḥukamāʾ*, explaining the word (*dasātīr*, 120.13) as *an-nusḫa al-maʿmūla awwalan ṯumma yunqalu ʿanhā*, "the first [complete] copy from which other copies are made." This gloss is cited by D. Chwolsohn, *Die Ssabier und der Ssabismus*, St. Petersburg 1856, Vol. 2, pp. iii–iv. See also the various meanings of these terms given in Gacek.

[h] Some MSS add, "may God sanctify his soul." The Latin omits this.

[i] The Latin reads this sentence differently: *que utique occupacio mihi dampnosa extitit et ei non minime tediosa* (48–49).

[j] The Latin adds, *ad quas me transsumpserat* (50).

[k] The Latin elaborates: *a iugi precum instancia ... non desisterem* (51–52).

---

[5] Cf. Jūzjānī's Biography, Gohlman 45.

[6] See what follows next and the Biography.

[7] For details about their travels from Jurjān to Hamaḏān and the causes of their distress see the Biography, Gohlman 49–57.

[8] Jūzjānī is apparently referring here to himself and other disciples, if one is to judge by Avicenna's reply to them in the plural and Jūzjānī's use of the first person singular in other parts of the text where he is speaking only about himself. The Latin translation (lines 52, 53) has the singular, and Jūzjānī himself uses the singular in the parallel passage in the Biography; see the discussion below, Chapter 2, W6.

the time nor the inclination to occupy myself with close textual analysis[9] and commentary. But if you [pl.] would be content with whatever I have readily in mind [which I have thought] on my own, then I could write for you [pl.] a comprehensive[l] work arranged in the order which will occur to me."[10] We readily offered our consent to this and urged[m] that he start with Physics. He began with that and wrote approximately twenty folia, but was then interrupted by administrative disruptions.

4. But time dealt its blows destroying that King.[11] Avicenna saw fit not to remain in the same state nor to resume the same duties, and trusted that the prudent thing for him to do, in furthering his purposes in this regard, would be to hide in anticipation of an opportunity to leave that region. Availing myself of his unexpected seclusion and leisure, I pressed him to complete *The Cure*. He voluntarily applied himself with great earnestness to its composition, and in a period of twenty days he finished Metaphysics and Physics (except the two books on Zoology and Botany) without having available any book to consult, but by relying solely upon his natural talents. He also started on Logic and wrote the opening address and associated material.[12]

5. Then the notables of that state resented his being in hiding, and they were particularly displeased with his intentions to leave, thinking that it was in order to plot a conspiracy or join forces with the enemy. A close
42 servant, who coveted his downfall[n] in order to obtain whatever worldly possessions Avicenna had with him, informed on him to his persecutors. These people were among those to whom Avicenna had formerly done such

---

l "Comprehensive:" *jāmiʿ*; Latin *summata* (56).

m "Urged:" *ḥarraḍnā*, as in the MS Golius 4, p. 317.17, and the Latin *insistendo* (59); the Cairo edition has *ḥariṣnā*, "we desired."

n "His downfall:" *tawrīṭihi fī mahlaka*, literally, "to involve him in peril." The Latin interprets this as "death:" *mortem* (77).

---

9 "Close textual analysis:" *alfāẓ*; literally, "terms," "words;" the Latin has *sermones* (line 53). By *alfāẓ* Avicenna is not referring here to the simple and compound terms discussed in the *Categories* and *De Interpretatione* (cf. T1, § 3 I), but to the *ipsissima verba* of the Aristotelian text, i.e., to textual analysis.

10 For Jūzjānī's parallel report in the Biography see Chapter 2, W6. Cf. Avicenna's Prologue to *The Cure* (T9, § 1).

11 Šams-ad-Dawla died in 412/1021. The circumstances are described in the Biography, Gohlman 57.

12 Cf. the parallel passage in the Biography, Gohlman 57.6–59.8. Jūzjānī says there that Avicenna wrote "a part" (*juzʾan*) of Logic. This part, here identified as "opening address," is almost certainly chapters 2–4 in the Cairo edition, containing the introduction to philosophy and Logic, not the Prologue to *The Cure* (T9).

favors that should have prevented them from attempting to deprive him of his possessions, had they of good deeds been mindful. [The servant] told them his [hiding] place[o] and he was detained[p] by being imprisoned in the castle of Fardajān. He remained there for a period of four months during which time the affairs of that region were brought to a certain resolution and the contesting party withdrew from it.[q] Avicenna was released and was offered to be reinstated as minister, but he excused himself and asked for a leave of absence, which he received.[13]

6. There [in Hamaḏān] he worked on the Logic [of *The Cure*]. He had access to the books [of Aristotle], and it consequently happened that he followed a course parallel to them, proceeding according to the order followed by people [in the Aristotelian tradition][r] and discussing their statements of which he disapproved. As a result, the Logic grew longer and was completed in Iṣfahān. The Mathematics, on the other hand, he had written in a summary fashion much earlier, and thought that he would add it to *The Cure*. He composed also the Zoology and Botany [later],[14] finishing with these books.[s] In most of the Zoology he followed a course parallel to Aristotle, and expanded it[t] quite beyond the latter's book. At that time he had reached the age of forty.[15]

---

[o] Because of the long parenthetical phrase immediately preceding, the Latin elaborates: *Induxit itaque eos ad locum, ubi ipse latitabat, proditor memoratus* (82–83).

[p] "Detained:" *ustūṯiqa minhu*; the Latin also has, *captiuantes eum* (83); cf. Dozy s.v. The meaning of arrest comes from the literal sense of the verb: "to be secure against someone," and it is not unlikely that this may be the intended meaning here, i.e. the persecutors secured themselves against the presumed threat coming from Avicenna's actions by imprisoning him.

[q] I.e., from that region, Hamaḏān. The Latin misunderstands *wa-tārakahā l-munāziʿūn*, *eius detentores ad cor redeuntes* (86–87), i.e. "his detainers coming to their senses."

[r] The Latin also paraphrases: *antecessorum uestigia secutus est et ordinem* (90–91).

[s] "These books," *hāḏihi l-kutub*, must refer in the context to the two sections on Botany and Zoology, although normally one would have expected the dual number. In the Biography also (Gohlman 66.2–3) Jūzjānī neglects to use the dual when referring to these two books: *kitābay ... ṣannafahā* instead of *kitābay ... ṣannafahumā*. The Latin, on the other hand, omits *wa-fariġa min hāḏihi l-kutub*, which might raise the possibility that these words are a later addition.

[t] The pronoun is feminine, which is of dubious antecedent, if the transmitted text is correct: *wa-zāda fīhā min ḏālika ziyādātin*. The Latin understands the sentence to mean, *multas in libro suo addiciones et intenciones interserens ex eodem* (98–99), which makes little sense in the context.

---

[13] For the details see the Biography, Gohlman 59–61.

[14] That is, after his move to Iṣfahān. See the more detailed account in the Biography, Gohlman 61–67.

[15] This number is inaccurate. See the discussion in W6.

43 7. My purpose in recounting these stories is to tell the reason why Avicenna declined to comment on the texts [of Aristotle][16] and why there is a disparity between his organization of the Logic and that of the Physics and Metaphysics, and also to provoke wonder for his ability to compose the Physics and Metaphysics in a period of twenty days without having access to books but by taking dictation only from his heart which was preoccupied with the afflictions [then] besetting it.[u] The person who studies this book [*The Cure*] with attention and consideration will find such fine and rare statements, Derivations of Corollary Principles,[v] and explanations as he will never find in all the books of past authors.

Text 8. Introduction to *The Easterners* (GS 8)

Avicenna's famous Introduction to *The Easterners* (Chapter 2, W9) is a concrete exposition of his understanding of the philosophical work and of his own position in its historical development. It is, in essence, his manifesto of the philosophical praxis as he came to formulate it later in his life (see Chapter 5).

The Introduction has been the subject of considerable discussion and a number of translations; the text, however, still lacks a proper edition. It was first published in 1910 in Cairo, in a volume arbitrarily entitled by the publisher (al-Maktaba as-Salafiyya) *Manṭiq al-mašriqiyyīn*, 2–4. The text was printed on the basis of the Cairo MS Dār al-Kutub Ḥikma 6 M[uṣṭafā Fāḍil], ff. 116^{b}–117^{a},[1] but the person who copied it made many and serious errors. It was later reprinted by photo-offset in Tehran by Maktabat al-Jaʿfarī at-Tabrīzī (no date given, but probably in the Seventies), and, recast in a new type-font, in Beirut in 1982, with Šukrī Najjār appearing as the "editor." In his Arabic translation of Nallino's article, Badawī *Turāṯ* 279–282 copied the text from the Cairo edition, although it seems that he added his own corrections without recourse to the Cairo manuscript.

My translation below is based on the actual readings of the Cairo manuscript (C), the most significant of which have been indicated in the textual notes; the numerous mistranscriptions of the defective Cairo edition have not been recorded. The text of the Cairo edition was also collated by Mahdavī 89–91 with the Istanbul MS Ayasofya 4852, ff. 34^{b} ff. (I). I have adopted some of the readings of the Ayasofya manuscript, as recorded by Mahdavī, and indicated them in the notes.

---

[u] "By taking dictation … besetting it:" the Latin misreads, *sed solo sui cordis suffultus repositorio* (105–106), apparently reading *bi-mā yumlaʾu* (*repositorio*) for *wa-innamā yumlī*, but the rest is unclear.

[v] "Corollary Principles:" *tafrīʿāt*; The Latin has *extraneis inuencionibus* (107).

---

[16] "Comment on the texts:" *šarḥ al-alfāẓ*; see above, note 9.

[1] For a description of this manuscript see Gutas "Ṣiġnāḫī."

Among the numerous translations that have been made, most noteworthy are
those by Nallino 455–458, and especially Anawati "Études" 112–115. Badawī's own
translation appeared in his *Histoire* II,607–609. They were all based on the defective 44
Cairo edition, however, and their renderings accordingly suffer. The fact that none of them is, strictly speaking, complete, is attributable to the relative unintelligibility of the printed text (Nallino omits the last part of § 6, below, Anawati omits the phrase before "This is the utmost …" in § 1, and Badawī omits the entire §§ 5 and 6).[2]

A number of articles by A.-M. Goichon, all overlapping and occasionally copying each other, contain extended paraphrases of the Introduction interspersed with literal translations of key passages. These are significant for the discussion of the Introduction within the context of Avicenna's philosophical orientation in general and of the Autobiography and his life in particular. In chronological order, they are the following: "Évolution" (1948), reprinted as the first part of the "Introduction" of her *Directives* 1–19; "Personnalité" (1952), reappeared, with minor modifications, as "Unité" (1952); "Nouveauté" (1952); "Philosophie" (1955). Certain passages of the Introduction, finally, were translated and discussed by Pines, "Philosophie Orientale."

Introduction

1. We have resolved to compile a treatise on matters about which researchers[3] have disagreed. In it we shall neither proceed by following Partisan considerations, our own fancy,[4] Customary Practice, or personal habit,[5] nor be

---

[2] Regrettably, the translation of this very Introduction by S.H. Nasr, in Nasr and Aminrazavi I,268–270, which appeared (1999) after the publication of the first edition of this book (1988), and despite its reference to it in the Bibliography (p. 272), is also incomplete—it skips most of §§ 4 and 6, below, and all of § 5, though Nasr calls it "a complete translation" (p. 268)—and repeats some of the mistakes of the earlier ones.

[3] *Ahl al-baḥṯ*, i.e., those who do philosophy through study and syllogistic means, and not through *ḏawq*, as he is going to say later (below, T 14, § 11 and notes 16 and 18). *The Easterners*, in other words, is about research oriented philosophy, and not, as mistakenly (and stubbornly) taken, about an "oriental" mystical philosophy.

[4] "Our own fancy:" *hawan*. The term refers to one's subjective fanciful notions that are contrary to acceptable standards set by reason, custom, or law; it does not mean "passione" (Nallino) or "passion" (Anawati "Études"). Avicenna uses the term in the same sense and context in the Prologue to *The Cure*, T9, § 1. Heretics in Islam are called *ahl al-bidʿa wa-l-ahwāʾ*, "innovators and those who follow their own fancy," as in the title of Malaṭī's book, ed. S. Dedering (Bibliotheca Islamica 9), Wiesbaden 1936. As a matter of fact, *hawan* was used by Ḥunayn's nephew, Ḥubayš, to translate the Greek *hairesis*; see Biesterfeldt 213 s.v. Cf. also Dozy, s.v., and F. Pollak, "Beiträge zum arabischen Lexikon," *WZKM* 32 (1925) 253–254.

[5] Note the two pairs of opposites: Avicenna says that he will follow neither sectarian nor private opinion, and neither public custom nor individual habit. These two pairs are significant in indicating what Avicenna understood to be the objective philosophical method that leads to Knowledge, *al-ʿilm*; they should not be glossed over by such generalized renderings as, e.g., "impartially, disinterestedly, and without regard to accepted custom" (F.W.

concerned about any departure[6] that manifests itself on our part both from what those who study the books of the Greeks are accustomed to[a] out of unmindfulness and obtuseness, and from what our position has been understood to be in books which we composed for the common philosophasters,[7] who are infatuated with the Peripatetics and who think that no one else other than they was ever guided by God or attained to His mercy. At the same time we acknowledge the merit of the most excellent of their predecessors [Aristotle] in being awake to that concerning which his masters and teachers were in deep sleep, in distinguishing the parts of the sciences one from the other and in classifying them better than they,[8] in perceiving the truth in many things, in discerning sound and eminent[b] Fundamental Principles in most sciences, and in disclosing to people what his compatriots who preceded him had overlooked.[c] This is the utmost that can be accomplished by a person who is the first to try his hand at separating what lay confused and restoring what had been impaired; and it behooves his successors to gather the loose ends he left, repair any breach[d] they find in what he constructed, and Supply Corollaries to Fundamental Principles he presented. But his successors were unable to free themselves of the imperfections[9] of what they

---

[a] Reading *alifahu*, along with Badawī *Turāṯ* 279n1, for *allafahu*, as translated by Nallino: "[scritti] composti."

[b] Reading *sariyya* instead of *sirriyya*, as understood by Nallino: "segreti." Badawī *Histoire* 608 apparently also read *sariyya*: "riches."

[c] C, I: *ʿalā mā sahā fīhi s-salafu min ahli bilādihi.*

[d] Or, "breaches," reading *ṯulaman yajidūnahā* (I) for *ṯalman yajidūnahu* (C).

Zimmermann in Booth 107); see Chapter 5.1. In the Prologue to *The Cure* (T9, § 4) Avicenna describes the method he followed in *The Easterners* in positive terms as follows: "I presented philosophy as it is naturally [perceived]."

[6] As Avicenna clarifies in his Prologue to *The Cure* (T9, § 4), this "apparent departure" is due to his use of an indirect and conciliatory approach in that book as opposed to the direct method to be employed in the present one.

[7] Note the implication that even in his indirect and conciliatory works Avicenna maintained the same theories he is about to expound; the books for the "common philosophasters" are therefore not to be esteemed any less than the present one. The only difference between them is that they have been understood differently. Cf. Nallino's note (p. 455, note 3): "Cioè da ciò che gli altri avranno potuto trovare nei nostri libri."

[8] In the schematized history of philosophy which was developed in late antiquity in Alexandria and taken over in the Syriac and Arabic traditions, Aristotle figures as the classifier of the sciences (i.e., of the parts of philosophy) *par excellence*. See the discussion and the texts presented below, Chapter 4.

[9] As Nallino rightly saw, *ʿuhda* is here to be translated as "imperfection" ("difetti"). The metaphor is taken from the concept of liability for defects in the transferal of goods from one

inherited from him, and they spent their lives in efforts to understand what he accomplished best and in Partisan Adherence to some defective theories
he originated.[e] These people occupy themselves all their lives with what has 46
already been done, neither finding time in which to consult their own minds nor, had they found it, thinking it permissible[f] to consider the statements of the ancients in need of addition, correction, or revision.[10]

2. As for ourselves, getting to understand what they[11] said has been easy for us from the very moment when we first occupied ourselves with it since it is not unlikely that Philosophical Sciences may have come to us from a direction other than that of the Greeks.[12] We were occupied with it in the prime of our youth, and were granted such success by God that we were able thereby to come to comprehend in a short time what they bequeathed.[13]

---

[e] "Some defective theories he originated." The reading is somewhat uncertain here. C seems to have *mā fṭr min taqṣīrihi*, although the word *fṭr* is slightly smudged, while I, according to Mahdavī, has *fṭn*. The Cairo edition, followed by both Badawī *Turāṯ* and Mahdavī, has *far(r)aṭa*, which is certainly not the original reading and in any case unsatisfactory. I prefer to follow C, however lamely, reading perhaps *fuṭira*. More manuscript evidence will be required before the question is settled, though there is little doubt about the intended meaning.

[f] C, I: *wa-lā law wajadahā staḥalla.*

---

owner to the next. See Lane, s.v. Anawati and Badawī understood the term as "obligation": "l'obligation qu'ils avaient à l'égard de ce qu'ils ont hérité de lui," Anawati "Études"; "aucun … n'a pu s'acquitter de cette obligation," Badawī *Histoire*.

10 Cf. a similar statement in his introduction to the Physics of *The Cure*, cited below, Chapter 5.2, L38.

11 I.e., Aristotle and all the successors of Aristotle, both Greek and Arabic, and not only the Muslims as Nallino 456n2 remarks.

12 I.e., by learning not from teachers and books but by independent acquisition of knowledge through syllogistic thinking and the ability to Guess Correctly the middle terms (*ḥads*), which "in most things corresponded with what is found in [Greek philosophical] books." See the parallel passage in T2, § 4, and the discussion below, Chapter 3.2 and note 65. Some of the renditions of the word *jiha* (direction) in this passage given by earlier translators completely prejudge the interpretation. Thus Badawī translates it as "nation": "… quelques sciences nous sont parvenues d'autres nations [!] que de la nation grecque" (*Histoire* 608), whereas Pines and Anawati interpret the word to refer to different, *non*-Greek sciences: "des sciences qui ne dérivent pas [!] des Grecs," Pines "Philosophie Orientale" 24; "certains sciences … en dehors [!] de celles (transmises) par les Grecs," Anawati "Études" 113; "from non-Greek sources," Nasr in Nasr and Aminrazavi 269. The Arabic text is talking, of course, about acquiring (the same) sciences from a different *direction* and by different means, not about sciences from different nations or about sciences different from those of the Greeks.

13 In the articles listed above, Goichon translates as follows this crucial sentence ("Évolution" 326 = *Directives* 14 = "Personnalité" 280 = "Unité" 305 = "Nouveauté" 46 = "Philosophie" 31): "Depuis, par la grâce de Dieu, nous trouvâmes ce qui nous avait manqué à cause de cette

We then measured all that, word for word, against the sort[14] of science which the Greeks call logic—it is not unlikely that the Easterners may have another name for it[15]—and we thus came to know what could bear such a confrontation and what resisted it. For each thing, we sought its manner[g] [in which it was argued for], with the result that whatever is true was [actually shown to be] true, and whatever is false [was actually shown to be] false.[16]

47 3. Now since those who are occupied with Philosophy are forcefully asserting their descent from the Peripatetics among the Greeks, we were loath to create schisms and disagree with the majority of the people. We thus joined their ranks and Adhered in a Partisan spirit to the Peripatetics, since they were the sect among them most worthy of such an Adherence.[17] We perfected what they meant to say but[h] fell short of doing, never reaching their aim in it;[i] and we pretended not to see what they were mistaken about, devising reasons for it and pretexts, while we were conscious of its real nature and aware of its defect.[j,18] If ever we spoke out openly our disagreement with them, then it concerned matters which it was impossible to tolerate; the greater part [of these matters], however, we concealed with the veils of feigned neglect:

---

[g] C, I: *wajhahu*, correctly guessed by Nallino 457n1.
[h] C, I: *fa-qaṣarū* (C corrects from *wa-qaṣarū* above the line).
[i] C, I: *fīhi* for *minhu* in the printed text.
[j] Reading *ḫalalihi* with I; C sems to have *ẓlh*.

---

jeunesse, en réfléchissant assez longuement sur l'héritage transmis." Her grammatical analysis in "Philosophie" 31n36 of the Arabic text in defense of this reading is quite implausible.

[14] "Sort:" *namaṭ*; this is the name Avicenna gives to the chapters of the second part of the *Pointers and Reminders*. See W11.

[15] I.e., "the instrumental science," *al-ʿilm al-ālī*. See the discussion below, Chapter 6.5.

[16] Avicenna is referring here to his syllogistic analysis of all philosophy by means of his index cards, or "sheaves of scratch paper" as he says in the Autobiography: arguments that "could bear such a confrontation," i.e., that could be put in demonstrative syllogistic form, were proven to be true, and those that "resisted it," i.e., that defied syllogistic analysis, were shown to be baseless. This is what Avicenna means by seeking for every thing "its manner" (*wajh*) of argumentation. See T3, § 8, and the discussion below, Chapter 3.3A.

[17] This particular point, as well as the argument of this whole Introduction, are found at the conclusion of *The Principles of the Universe* (*Fī mabādiʾ al-kull*) attributed to Alexander of Aphrodisias. See the translation of this passage below, Chapter 4, L34.

[18] Cf. the similar expression in his introduction to the Physics of *The Cure*, Chapter 5.2, L38.

4. [a] Among these were matters ⟨about⟩ which[k] we were loath to have ignorant people become aware of [our] disagreement with something which was so widely accepted among them that they might have doubts about clear daylight but not about it, although parts of it were so subtle as to dim the mind's eyes of our contemporaries.[19] As a matter of fact, we were afflicted with a company of them—as devoid of understanding "as if they were propped-up blocks of wood" [Qur'ān 63:4]—who consider profound theoretical analysis a heresy, and disagreement with what is widely accepted a deviation from the right path, as if they were the Ḥanbalites among the authors[l] of Prophetic Traditions.[20] Had we found among them someone following the right course,[21] we would have convinced him about what we had Verified, thus benefiting them with it; and perhaps it would have been easy for them to penetrate into its meaning, thus benefiting us in turn with 48
something which they alone would have been able to fathom.[m]

5. [b] Also among ⟨these⟩ were matters which we Withheld from making public out of a desire to protect overlooked truths[n] lest they be Pointed to and not accepted except in a Partisan spirit.[22] For this reason, in many matters with whose difficulty[o] we were fully acquainted, we followed a course of accommodation [with the Peripatetics] rather than one of disputation, although[p] with regard to what was disclosed to us from the moment when

[k] Perhaps *fa-min jumlati ḏālika mā karihna ⟨fīhi⟩ an yaqifa …* is to be read; cf. note n below.

[l] C, I: *al-Ḥanābilatu min katabati l-ḥadīṯi.*

[m] C: *bi-t-tanaqquri*; I: *bi-t-tanqīri.*

[n] C, I: *wa-min jumlati ⟨ḏālika⟩ ma ḍanannā bi-iʿlānihi ġāʾirīna* (*ʿābirīna* C) *ʿalā ḥaqqin maġfūlin ʿanhu.* For my addition of *ḏālika* see above, note k, and cf. Anawati "Études" 114.20, "Au nombre des [questions] que …".

[o] C: *bi-najdatihi*; I: *yataḥaddaṯuhu* [!].

[p] C, I: *wa-in* instead of *wa-law* in the printed text.

[19] The reasons for Avicenna's unwillingness to have common people understand that he is disagreeing with what they believe are discussed in Chapter 8.2; cf. L75[b].

[20] The Ḥanbalī legal rite has been traditionally the most conservative in Islam. They set great store by the Traditions of the Prophet (*ḥadīṯ*), which they used in legal argumentation almost to the exclusion of all other accepted methods, such as analogy and individual opinion. Note the religious terminology throughout, with the implication that philosophers had become as dogmatic as the most conservative religious people.

[21] Literally, "someone rightly guided [by God]," continuing the religious metaphor. Cf. the similar description of the ideal student in T10, § 7 below.

[22] For the concept of Withholding knowledge and what is to be Withheld see Chapter 5.3.

we first applied ourselves to this field, we would expressly reconsider[q] our position and examine anew whatever we thought repeatedly demanded closer scrutiny because an opinion was confusing to us[r] and doubt crept in our beliefs, and we said "perhaps" and "maybe." But you, our friends, know what our position was at the beginning, at the end, and during the time[s] between our first statement [on these matters] and the second.[23]

6. If we find this [to be] our case,[t] then we should all the more trust in most of what we determined, judged, and emended, especially with regard to matters which are the greatest purposes and the ultimate goals which we have considered and reconsidered hundreds of times. And since such is the case,[t] and matters[t] stand as briefly described here, we wished to compile a book that will include the fundamental elements of true Philosophy
49 which was Discovered by someone who examined a lot, reflected[u] long, and Guessed nearly perfectly [middle terms],[24] and who, striving for Partisan Adherence to many things[v] discordant with truth, was in great demand[w] on account of his Partisanship and statements in everybody's eyes except his own. There is no one more worthy of being listened to than the Partisan[x]

---

[q] C, I: *nubdī* for *lam nbd* in the printed text.

[r] C, I: *li-mā bannatanā* (*blyn'* I) *fīhi ra'yunā* (*r'y'* C) *li-ḫtilāṭin* (*l'ḫtlṭ* C) *'alaynā r-ra'yu.* "Repeatedly demanded closer scrutiny:" *bannatanā fīhi ra'yunā. Bannata* is to question someone minutely and repeatedly. See Ṣaġānī, *At-Takmila ... li-Kitāb Tāj al-luġa*, Cairo 1970, I.302; cf. Kazimirski, s.v.

[s] Both Nallino and Anawati take the word *ṭūla* in *ṭūla l-mudda* not as a preposition but as a noun and the object of the preceding verb, *ta'lamūna*: "la lunghezza del tempo [trascorso]," Nallino; "la longue période qui sépare," Anawati "Études".

[t] "Case" and "matters": *ṣūra* and *qiṣṣa* (C, I, instead of *qaḍiyya* in the printed text), respectively, are used in their colloquial senses here, as taken over later by both Persian and Ottoman Turkish. Anawati "Études", however, translates the first *ṣūra* as "forme" and only the second as "la chose".

[u] C: *wa-afkara*; I: *wa-ftakara.*

[v] I: *li-kaṯīrin mimmā*; C: *li-kaṯīrin fī-mā.*

[w] C, I: *nafāqan* (C corrects from *wifāqan* above the line). Cf. Dozy s.v. *nafaqa 'alā.*

[x] *Al-muta'aṣṣib* Mahdavī; C, I: *at-ta'aṣṣub.*

---

[23] I.e., his position never changed; despite his repeated examination of difficult questions, his views remained essentially constant, as he says twice in the Autobiography (T3, §§ 8, 11). See the discussion below, Chapter 3.3Ei.

[24] "Guessed perfectly," *jūdat al-ḥads*, an expression that reflects the Arabic translation of Aristotle's *eustochia* in the *Posterior Analytics*, *ḥusnu ḥadsin.* See the discussion below, Chapter 3.2. As in the passage from the *Philosophy for 'Alā'-ad-Dawla* cited above (T2, § 4), Avicenna manifestly is referring here to himself (cf. Marmura "Avicenna's Thought" 338b and Michot *Abū Sa'd* 93*n1).

of a group when he requires them to follow truth,[y] for nothing but truth will save them from [their] faults.[25]

7. We have compiled this book to show it only to ourselves—I mean to those who are to us like ourselves; as for the common people among those who struggle to master this subject, we gave them in *The Cure* what is [already] too much for them and even more than what they need, and we shall give them again in the *Appendices* what is suitable for them in excess of what they have already received.[26]

In every case, God is our only recourse.

Text 9. From *The Cure* (GS 5): The Prologue

Avicenna wrote the Prologue to *The Cure* some time after the work had been completed, apparently in order to counter some of the implications of Jūzjānī's earlier Introduction (T7; see Chapter 2, W6). In the meantime Avicenna had also written *The Easterners*, and he took the opportunity afforded by the Prologue to state the relationship of the two works to each other and to his work and the Peripatetic tradition as a whole.

The Prologue created a stir in the West, both medieval and modern, and attracted attention quite beyond Avicenna's original intentions, primarily because of his mention of Eastern philosophy. *The Easterners*, however, was more than half lost quite early in the East (see W9), and was never available in the Muslim West in Arabic, let alone in a Latin translation. All medieval Western authors who referred to it, therefore, derived their information from Avicenna's few words about it in the Prologue. This is true of Roger Bacon, who read the Prologue in Avendauth's Latin
translation (edited by Birkenmajer, see T7), of Averroes, and especially of Ibn-Ṭufayl, 50
who interpreted Avicenna's reference to that work to suit his own purposes and used Avicenna's phrase as the subtitle of his "philosophical romance," *Ḥayy ibn-Yaqẓān, On the Secrets of the Eastern Philosophy* (*Fī asrār al-ḥikma al-mašriqiyya*; see the testimonia in W9). In modern times Ibn-Ṭufayl's subtitle was appropriated at the end of last century by M.A.F. Mehren who used it arbitrarily as the Arabic title of his own edition of a number of Avicenna's opuscula and selections from the *Pointers and Reminders*: *Rasāʾil ... Ibn Sīnā fī asrār al-ḥikma al-mašriqiyya* (Leiden 1889–1899). The French title, which presumably (but incorrectly) translated the Arabic, was *Traités mystiques ... d'Avicenne*, and these works have ever since been branded as mystical (see the extended discussion of this subject in Gutas "Ibn Ṭufayl" 231–234 and "Eastern Philosophy" 160–166).

---

[y] I read *aḫaḏa bi-ṣidqin ʿalayhim*; C does not dot the *bi-* of *bi-ṣidqin*. I has *mṣdq*.

---

[25] See the discussion in Chapter 2, W9e and Chapter 5.2.

[26] See Chapter 5.3.

The debate about the same issue has been continued in more recent times in the partial translations and paraphrases of the Prologue; there has never been a complete translation. The first of these was by Madkour 22–23, followed by Goichon "Nouveauté" 43–45, Anawati "Études" 111–112, and Badawī *Histoire* II,609–611. Goichon also discussed the issue in most of her articles listed above in T8, notably in "Philosophie" 29–31. In all these studies the remainder of the Prologue has received slight attention.

The translation is based on the edition of the Prologue in *Madḫal* 9.7–11.16 Anawati et al., collated for the most significant variants with the Latin translation; my comments are given in the notes. The text given by Mahdavī 129–131 reproduces that of the Cairo edition.

Prologue

1. Our purpose in this book, which we hope that time will allow us to complete, and that success granted by God will attend us in its composition, is to set down in it the gist of the Fundamental Principles which we have Ascertained—both the Fundamental Principles contained in the philosophical sciences[a] attributed to the ancients and based on methodical and Verified theoretical analysis, and the Fundamental Principles Discovered by [a series of] acts of comprehension[1] cooperating in the attain-
51 ment of truth which was diligently pursued for a long time until it culminated in a correct body [of such Principles] which gained the agreement of most views and helped dispel the veils of fanciful notions.[2] I sought to set down in it most of the discipline, indicate in every passage where ambiguity may occur, and solve it by setting forth clearly the correct answer to the extent of my ability. [I also sought] to Supply the Corollary Principles along with the Fundamental ones, excluding only what I trust will

---

[a] For *fī l-ʿulūm al-falsafiyya* the Latin has *in sentenciis* (11), which seems to be a mistranscription for *in scientiis*. The omission of *al-falsafiyya* in the Latin reflects the reading in some Arabic manuscripts. [The numbers in parentheses after the Latin words refer to the lines in Birkenmajer's edition.]

---

[1] "Acts of comprehension," literally *afhām*, as in the Latin translation, *intelligendi actiones* (13). As Marmura "Avicenna's Thought" 339 notes, Avicenna is referring here to the cumulative progress of knowledge by successive philosophers, each contributing his act of comprehension; cf. Madkour 22, "études ... collectives," and Anawati "Études" 111, "les intelligences qui collaborent." This is the mainstay of Avicenna's conception of the praxis of philosophy, for which see below Chapter 5.

[2] "Fanciful notions:" *ahwāʾ*. See note 4 in T8. The Latin renders, "*caligines uoluntatum* (17)."

be revealed to the person who is able to see what we are displaying and ascertain what we are depicting,[b] or what escaped my memory and did not occur to my thought. I strove in earnest to be concise and always to avoid repetition—barring mistakes and oversights—and I refrained from prolix arguments in conradicting doctrines patently[c] invalid or sufficiently dealt with[d] through the Fundamental Principles which we establish and the rules we present.

2. There is nothing of account to be found in the books of the ancients which we did not include in this book of ours; if it is not found in the place where it is Customary to record it, then it will be found in another place which I thought more appropriate for it. To this I added some of the things which I perceived through my own reflection and whose Validity I Determined through my own theoretical analysis, especially in Physics and Metaphysics—and even in Logic, if you will:[e] for although it is Customary to prolong [the discussion on] the first principles of logic with material that does not belong to Logic but only to the philosophical discipline—I mean the First Philosophy[3]—I avoided mentioning any of that [in Logic] and wasting thereby time, and deferred it to its [proper] place.

3. Then I thought it appropriate that I should write another book to follow this one. I have called it *Appendices*, and it will end with my life, finding its termination[f] in whatever will have been completed every year. It 52

[b] "Excluding ... depicting:" the Latin summarizes, *preterquam in hiis, de quorum presumebam manifestacione sufficienter ea intuenti* (21–22).

[c] The abbreviation in the Latin (26) should perhaps be read, *patente*.

[d] "Sufficiently dealt with:" *makfiyyat aš-šuġl*. See *WKAS* I,286a–b.

[e] "If you will," literally, "for whomever it please" (*li-man aḥabba*), is attested in three of the ten manuscripts used in the Cairo edition of the Arabic text, and in the Latin translation: *cui licet* (*libet*? Birkenmajer) *cordi fuerit* (app. crit. to line 34). One of the three manuscripts containing this phrase (Istanbul Yeni Cami 772) is dated 628/1230, and the Latin translation must be based on a manuscript copied a century after Avicenna's death at the latest. This *lectio difficilior* is in all probability original. Madkour 22, who was using the other two manuscripts containing the phrase (British Library Or. 7500 = M, and India Office 475 = H), translates, "et même en logique si l'on veut."

[f] "Finding its termination:" *yu'arraḫu*. For this meaning of *arraḫa* as "to appoint a terminus" see the definition of Ṣūlī (*Adab al-kuttāb* 178, Cairo 1341): "The *ta'rīḫ* of each thing is its goal (*ġāyatuhu*) and its final time;" translated in F. Rosenthal, *A History of Muslim Historiography*, 2nd ed., Leiden: E.J. Brill, 1968, 272; cf. also 14n3. The Latin, which transposes this

[3] The reference is to the Universal Science Part of Metaphysics. For the inclusion of the Categories in this science see Chapter 6.1 and 6.4.

is like a commentary to this book, Providing Corollaries to its Fundamental Principles and elaborating upon its briefly expressed concepts.

4. I also wrote a book other than these two, in which I presented philosophy as it is naturally [perceived][4] and as required by an unbiased view[g] which neither takes into account in [this book] the views of colleagues in the discipline, nor takes precautions[h] here against creating schisms among them as is done elsewhere;[5] this is my book on Eastern philosophy.[6] But as for the present book, it is more elaborate and more accommodating to my Peripatetic colleagues. Whoever wants the truth [stated] without

---

phrase to the end of this paragraph (after "concepts"), understands the word in its conventional sense of "to date:" *temporali illius anno numero annotabo* (43–44). The same applies to Anawati's version ("Études" 112): "chaque partie [!] portera la date de l'année de son achèvement."

g "Unbiased view," literally, "unadulterated view," *ar-ra'y aṣ-ṣarīḥ*; *opinio pura* (47).

h Reading *wa-lā yattaqī* for *wa-lā yuttaqā* in the passive as in the edition. See note 5.

---

4 "As it is naturally [perceived]:" *ʿalā mā hiya fī ṭ-ṭabʿ*, i.e., "as it is in the nature" of the perceiver to perceive it. For this interpretation see Marmura "Avicenna's Thought" 339–340 and Gutas "Eastern Philosophy" 160n7. Cf. the same use of *ṭabʿ* in the *Pointers and Reminders*, I,8.1, 76, 77/157, 158, *qarīb min/ilā ṭ-ṭabʿ*, "nous sont naturelles, est naturel," Goichon *Directives* 215, 217, "grasp naturally," Inati *Logic* 144.

5 "Which neither takes … elsewhere." This crucial phrase has been largely misinterpreted, with serious effects on the understanding of Avicenna's meaning. The Latin version contains a serious mistranslation: *non obseruando semitam aut partem, ad quam declinant participes in arte, neque formidando a suarum ictibus lancearum* [! *min šaqqi ʿaṣāhum*], *hoc quod fuit in aliis formidatum* (47–49). This led Roger Bacon to describe the book by saying that Avicenna was not afraid in it of the "*ictus lancearum contradicentium,*" the blows of the barbs of his opponents (Birkenmajer 308, 309). Among modern versions, the most accurate is that by Anawati "Études" 112: "l'opinion franche qui ne ménage pas le point de vue des compagnons dans la philosophie et où on ne craint pas [reading *yuttaqā*, as in the edition; cf. note h] de faire sécession comme on le ferait dans d'autres livres." Madkour 22 paraphrases: "sans tenir compte des autres philosophes, ni des doctrines qui s'opposent à nous et dont nous nous sommes occupé dans d'autres écrits." Goichon "Nouveauté" 44 translates: "à laquelle [à l'opinion pure] n'a point égard la majeure partie de ceux qui partagent cette discipline. Celui qui *shaqqa* [!] *'asâhum* (qui fit schisme, qui partit en dissidence) ne craint pas dans ce livre ce qu'il craint dans les autres." Badawī *Histoire* translates: "… l'opinion qui ne se soucie pas de la ligne adoptée par les confrères, et où celui qui se met [!] en désaccord avec eux ne craint pas de les contredire." Both Goichon and Badawī wrongly assume the subject of the first *yattaqī* to be *man* (*šaqqa*) and not *ar-ra'y aṣ-ṣarīḥ*. If this were the reading, and given the fact that the two clauses *lā yurāʿī* and *lā yattaqī* are relative in need of an *ʿā'id*, the pronouns in *fīhi* and *ġayrihi* would have to refer to *ar-ra'y aṣ-ṣarīḥ*, which makes little sense.—The taking of precautions mentioned here is the circumlocution referred to as "indirection" (*majmaja*) below in the same paragraph.

6 I.e., *The Easterners*; see W9.

indirection,[i] he should seek the former book; whoever wants the truth 53
[stated] in a way which is somewhat conciliatory to colleagues,[j] elaborates a lot, and alludes to things which, had they been perceived, there would have been no need for the other book, then he should read the present book.[7]

5. [A. Logic] In the first part of this book I began with Logic. I strove to have it run parallel to the order of Aristotle's books [on Logic],[k] supplying in addition [discussions on] hidden[l] and subtle issues which are lacking in available books.

[B. Physics] Logic is then followed by Physics, but [here] I was mostly unsuccessful[m] in pursuing a course parallel to the systematic treatise and the memoranda of Aristotle,[8] the paradigmatic master in this discipline.

---

i "Indirection:" *majmaja*. The word indicates lack of explicitness or forthrightness (cf. Lane, s.v.), and may be closer to "equivocation" or "prevarication" than to "circumlocution," although here it does not seem to have the negative implications of "prevaricate" or "equivocate." I have accordingly preferred the more neutral rendering "indirection." In any case, the context here provides the definition: *majmaja* is indirection qualified by whatever is described in the following sentence (viz. a way which seeks to be accommodating, etc.). An example of *majmaja* in the sense of "prevaricate" is found in the *Fihrist* of Ibn-an-Nadīm, 320.16 Flügel: when the Caliph al-Maʾmūn asked the Ṣābians if they had a book or a prophet, they prevaricated (*majmajū fī l-qawl*), thus provoking his ire (Dodge 751 mistranslates, "they stammered in replying"). The Latin translation has *titubacio* (52; "faltering," "hesitating"), apparently translating an Arabic original *jamjama* instead of *majmaja*. Although the apparatus of the Cairo edition does not list *jamjama* as a variant here, it must have existed because *jamjama* appears in some manuscripts of Ibn-Ṭufayl's *Ḥayy ibn-Yaqẓān*, who quotes this passage (p. 4.2 and 14.13 Gauthier; see Testimonium [12] in W9).

j The two Latin variants for *aš-šurakāʾ*, *principia* and *principes* (54), should read *participes*.

k The Latin has only, *ut logicorum libros imitarer* (60).

l The Latin apparently read a word other than *asrār*: *in intencionis* T, *imitaciones* C (60).

m The Latin should read, along with the manuscript C, *neque* (= *wa-lam*), instead of *ubi* (62).

---

7 For Avicenna's understanding of the method of "indirection" used to write philosophical books see Chapter 5.3. Cf. also note i above.

8 The division of Aristotle's works into systematic treatises and memoranda was part of the instruction in the Aristotelian school tradition. Cf. Paul the Persian, in Miskawayh's *Saʿāda*, Cairo 1335/1917, 69.3–5, 70.10–11: "Aristotle composed on the subject of Physics a book in which he mentioned the properties [*umūr*] common to all natural things, be they subject to generation or not, and he called it *Physikē akroasis*;" "Aristotle also wrote other treatises and books which he called memoranda [*taḏākīr* = *hypomnēmata*]; these are numerous, according to the catalogue of his books." Cf. Gutas "Paul the Persian" 235 and note 9, and Ullmann's review of Gohlman, p. 150.

[C. Mathematics] Physics is then followed by Geometry: I made a terse[n]
54 summary of Euclid's *Elements* in which I restricted[o] myself to the solution of its ambiguities. I then complemented Geometry with a similar summary of [Ptolemy's] *Almagest* on Astronomy, which contains, despite the abridgment, explanations and instructions. After I finished this, I appended to it such additions as are necessary for the student to know in order to complete[p] thereby [his study of] this discipline and bring into conformity astronomical observations with the laws of Physics. Astronomy is then followed by a terse summary of the *Introduction to Arithmetic* [by Nicomachus of Gerasa]. I then concluded the discipline of the mathematicians with an abridgment of the science of Music in a manner which was disclosed to me after long research and detailed theoretical analysis.

[D. Metaphysics] Finally, I concluded the book with the science that belongs to Metaphysics[9] in accordance with its parts and aspects, while referring in it [only] to the essential elements[q] of Ethics and Politics,[10] in anticipation of a comprehensive and separate book which I will write on these subjects.[11]

6. This book, though small in volume, contains much of Philosophy. The person who studies it attentively and reflects on it will hardly fail to acquire most of the [philosophical] discipline, including[r] the additions which were Customarily omitted from other books.[12]

---

[n] "Terse:" *laṭīf*. See Dozy s.v. "Explicatif" [?] Madkour 23.

[o] The Latin should perhaps read *contractus* for *cum temperatus* (67).

[p] Perhaps *yutimma* is preferable to *tatimma* in the edition. Cf. the following verb, *yuṭābiqa*.

[q] "Essential elements:" *jumal*. Cf. Blachère *Dictionnaire* 1724a–b. "Données" Madkour 23.

[r] The Arabic has *ilā*, "up to," but perhaps *min* is to be read, following the Latin *ex* (86), yielding the following sense: "most of the [philosophical] discipline from the additions which …".

---

[9] "The Science that belongs to Metaphysics:" see Chapter 6.1.

[10] For the contents of the tenth book of the *Ilāhiyyāt* see Chapter 6.2.

[11] Avicenna never wrote this book. For his works on practical philosophy see W3 in Chapter 2 below and section F in the Appendix. For the classification of the subjects mentioned in this Prologue see T1 and Chapter 3.1.

[12] These "additions" constitute the points about which Avicenna came in conflict with the Aristotelian tradition, and his own views which he integrated into the system. See Chapter 6.

Text 10. From *Pointers and Reminders* (GS 9): Prologues and Epilogue

In his last major work (W11), Avicenna touches briefly, in the form of advice to the reader, upon the essential elements that govern the philosophical praxis and gives particularly valuable information on the indicative method of composition (Chapter 8.3).

The translation is based on *Išārāt* I, Prologue, 2/33; II, Prologue, 90/185; II, Epilogue, 222/395. There is a French translation by Goichon *Directives* 77, 246, 525–526, and an English translation of the first part by Inati *Logic* 46 and of the third part by Inati *Mysticism* 107–108.

Prologue to Logic 55

1. I praise God, who graciously bestows success;
I ask God for guidance in His path,
for inspiration with the truth through its Verification,[1]
and to bless His servants chosen for His mission
and especially Muḥammad and his family.[2]

2. O you who are zealous to Ascertain the truth: I am bestowing upon you in these Pointers and reminders Fundamental Principles and essential elements[a] of philosophy; if sagacity takes hold of your hand [to guide you],[3] it will become easy for you to Derive Corollary Principles from the former and work out the details of the latter.

3. I will start with Logic and then proceed to Physics and on to the science that precedes it.[4]

---

[a] *Jumal.* See T9, note q.

---

[1] I.e., Avicenna is not asking for inspiration with the truth *tout court*—in which case the truth will have to be accepted through Partisan Adherence to an authoritative source, *taʿaṣṣuban*—but for inspiration with the truth at the end of a process of investigation and Verification by the researcher. See Chapter 3.3E.

[2] The five lines of this introduction are written in rhyming prose, *sajʿ*.

[3] "If sagacity takes hold of your hand," *in aḫaḏat al-faṭānatu bi-yadika*; Goichon *Directives* 77 reads the verb in the second person, "si tu en prends la compréhension avec la main," which she interprets as, "si tu en possèdes avec maîtrise la compréhension." Inati has, "if you are directed by intelligence." The reference with *faṭāna*, however, is again to Guessing Correctly the middle terms (*ḥads*).

[4] I.e., Metaphysics as First Philosophy, which precedes Physics because it provides its principles. See Chapter 6.1.

Prologue to Physics and Metaphysics

4. What follows are Pointers to Fundamental Principles and reminders of essential elements.[a] Whoever finds them easy will be able to gain insights through them, while he who finds them difficult will not benefit even from the most obvious of them.[5] We rely on God for success.

5. Here I repeat my admonition and restate my request that the contents of these parts be Withheld as much as possible from those who do not meet the conditions I stipulated at the end of these Pointers.

Epilogue

Admonition

6. Dear Friend:
I have churned for you in these Pointers the cream of truth and have fed you choice morsels of philosophy
in pithy[b] sayings.
56 Protect them from those who would hackney them,
the ignoramuses,
those not endowed with blazing[6] sagacity,
training, and practice,
those whose tendencies lie with the rabble,
or are among the deviants[7] and parasites[8]
of these philosophers.

7. If you find somebody whose heart you trust to be pure,
his way of life straight,
who abstains from the sudden insinuations of the Whisperer,[9]

---

[b] *Laṭāʾif*. See T9, note n.

---

[5] What Avicenna is doing here is publishing philosophy without publicizing it, like Aristotle. Those without the ability to Guess Correctly middle terms will find these pointers impenetrable, while those who have it will be able to Work Out the Corollaries. See T2, § 3 and Chapter 5.3.

[6] Cf. the passage on *ḥads* from *The Salvation* below, Chapter 3.2, L7, § 3: "he blazes with Correct Guessing."

[7] "Deviants:" *mulḥida*, a collective noun (cf. *WKAS* II,1, 289a). Apparently meaning in this context not so much "atheists" or "heretics" in a religious sense as those who deviate from true philosophy.

[8] "Parasites:" *hamaj*, literally, "gnats," "infecting the faces and eyes of sheep and donkeys," says Ṭūsī. Another meaning given is "riff-raff."

[9] The reference is to Satan, Qurʾān 113.

and who directs his attention to the truth
readily and sincerely,
then answer his questions in degrees,
in fragments,
in installments,
so that you can detect from what you just said
what to say next.
Bind him with inviolable oaths to God to follow your path in what you gave him,
finding solace in you.

8. If you publicize or squander this knowledge, then God [will judge] between us. "God suffices for a guardian."[10]

Text 11. From a Letter to an Anonymous Disciple (Bahmanyār) = *Mubāḥaṯa* II

Avicenna wrote this letter to a disciple, who remains anonymous in the manuscripts but who has been identified as Bahmanyār (Reisman *Avicennan Tradition* 207–213; Michot "Riz" 92), after the pillage of his books in 425/1034 (see W9), a few years before his death. It is a very personal letter, written in a dejected mood, tired and mellow in its tone. The burning zeal for philosophical discussion, however, and the intellectual self-assurance are still evident. Of particular significance are Avicenna's statements about method (see the last note to this Text below).

The letter is preserved among the *Discussions* (*Mubāḥaṯāt*; see W12). The translation below is based on the Later recension of the work, as preserved in the Bodleian MS Hunt. 534, ff. $5^{a}12$–6^{a} ult. (B).[1] This has been compared throughout with the Ṣiġnāḫī recension in the Cairo MS Dār-al-Kutub, Ḥikma 6 M[uṣṭafā Fāḍil], ff. $110^{b}21$–$111^{b}11$ (C) and the divergences are recorded in the notes. The Leiden MS Or. 864 Warn., ff. $16^{b}1$–$18^{a}3$ (L) follows the recension represented by the Bodleian MS in the
body of the text, but it was collated in the margins with a manuscript deriving from 57
the Ṣiġnāḫī recension (see note h below). Its readings have been compared but as a rule not recorded since they do not contribute in any significant way to the purposes of the present translation.

Badawī published the letter from the Cairo manuscript in his *Arisṭū* 245–246. He omitted the middle part of the text because it had already been excerpted and inserted among the rest of the *Mubāḥaṯāt* by the recensor (pp. 228.12–229.11

---

[10] The book ends with a quotation from the Qur'ān, 4:81, etc. (Arberry translation). The Epilogue is written entirely in *saj*ʿ.

[1] The various recensions of the *Mubāḥaṯāt* have been studied in great detail by Reisman *Avicennan Tradition*, whose conclusions I follow here; see below, W12. Although in the first edition of this book I used the siglum H to refer to the Bodleian MS, I switch here to B to avoid confusion and to accord with that used by both Reisman and Bīdārfar in his edition.

Badawī). In its Later recension of the Bodleian MS, the letter was also published by Bīdārfar in his edition of the *Mubāḥaṯāt*. All significant divergences between the readings of Badawī and Bīdārfar and those in MSS B and C are recorded in the notes. The part of the letter translated below corresponds to pp. 245, 228.12–14, 229.8–11, 246 in Badawī and pp. 49–54 in Bīdārfar. The beginning and end of the letter were also transcribed from the Bodleian MS by Mahdavī 203–204. This has not been taken into account.

The first paragraph of this letter was briefly discussed by Badawī *Arisṭū* 25–27 (introduction), whose conclusions were disputed by Pines "Philosophie Orientale" 22n1. Pines's own version and remarks were in turn marred by his dependence on the defective text in Badawī. The contents of the letter were discussed, in connection with the rest of the *Discussions*, by Reisman *Avicennan Tradition* 212–213 and Michot "Riz" 90–94; and cf. also the translation of § 1 on pp. 207–208 in the former, and of § 7 on pp. 91–92 in the latter.

The letter is written in the polite form of address, where the addressee is referred to in the third person—i.e., the opening line of the first paragraph translated below reads, "As for his expression of sorrow at the loss of *Pointers and Reminders* …". I have translated throughout using the second person, which is more natural in English and less likely to create confusion about the referents.

The Letter

1. You expressed sorrow at the loss of *Pointers and Reminders*, but I think that a copy of this book has been preserved. As for the Eastern questions,[2] I had packed them up[a]—no, most of them—[as they were] in their quires[3] so as[b] no one would look at them,[4] and I had also[c] written down on slips of

[a] "I had packed them up:" *fa-qad kuntu ʿabaʾtuhā* (*ʿabbaʾtuhā* Bīdārfar) B; *fa-qad ktb ʿabaʾtuhā* C; *fa-qad katabtu aʿyānahā* [!] Badawī.

[b] *Fī ajzāʾihā bi-ḥayṯu* B; *bi-ḥayṯu* om. C.

[c] *Ayḍan* B; *minhā* C.

[2] By Eastern questions and Eastern Fundamental Principles (§ 4 below) are meant the texts on Eastern philosophy, which were lost. See Chapter 2, W9.

[3] I.e., he packed the quires (*ajzāʾ*) away without having them transcribed clearly and bound as books for distribution. Suhrawardī must be referring to this very passage when he says that "[t]he quires (*karārīs*) which Avicenna attributed to the Easterners are extant separately in unbound form" (Chapter 2, W9a, Testimonium 14).

[4] For "so as no one would look at them" the Arabic has, *bi-ḥayṯu lā yaṭṭaliʿu ʿalayhā aḥadun*; Reisman *Avicennan Tradition* 208 translates, "in such a way that no one's attention would be drawn to them," which may be a valid interpretation, if stretched, of *iṭṭalaʿa ʿalā*; but Reisman further interprets this (p. 223n64) as meaning that Avicenna "put them away *so that no one would discover them* during the siege of Iṣfahān" (emphasis in the original). If that is so, it would mean that Avicenna knew beforehand that his books would be plundered and took precautions accordingly. But he could hardly have known that, and even if he did, why

paper some passages from the *Throne Philosophy*;[5] it is these which got lost. They were not voluminous, however, (although they did treat many subjects and were quite comprehensive,) and it would be easy to rewrite them. But yes, the *Fair Judgment*, on the other hand, could not but be extensive, and rewriting it would require work.[6]

2. But then, who is going to rewrite it, and who is he who is so free from 58
the worthless as to devote himself exclusively to truth, from this world to the next, and from superfluities to superiority? Indeed, fate has plunged in me the talons of vicissitudes and I don't know how to extricate and save myself. I have been driven to perform tasks I am not the man for, and I got so detached from Knowledge that it is as if I can catch a glimpse of it from behind a thick veil only. And yet I tender thanks to God Almighty, for He, despite the contending situations, the compounding tribulations, the obtruding peregrinations, and the conflicting alternations, will not leave me without a spark, will revive my heart, and steady my step. Him I praise for whatever helps or harms, hurts or cheers.

3. As for the questions which you asked me, they are significant questions about the Philosophical Sciences, and especially these particular ones.[d] But treating such questions briefly leads to error, while too many of them overtax a mind preoccupied with cares and it can hardly concentrate on the areas[e] requiring explanation, especially for somebody who is like me and in my situation. I have studied these questions carefully and I have found them

---

[d] *Lā siyyamā hāḏihi l-masāʾil* om. B, Bīdārfar.

[e] The reading is uncertain here. L has, and Badawī reads C as, *biqāʿ*, which seems suspect though better than the alternatives; B omits the phrase, and a second hand has added in the margin, *nqʾyḥ* [?] or *nqʾṯḥ* [?], which Bīdārfar suggests reading as the implausible *baqāʾiḥ* or *naqāʾiḥ*, while he prints *natāʾij* in his text.

---

protect only those books and not others—especially the *Fair Judgment*, this book in twenty volumes, which, according to Reisman, was also lost during this siege and would have been very difficult to rewrite? In any case, the precaution, if that is what it was, manifestly did not work.

[5] For this work see the Inventory in the Appendix, GM-Ps 1.

[6] It is to be noted that this passage implies that the *Fair Judgment* was *not* among the quires of the Eastern questions and the fragments of the *Throne Philosophy* which were lost on this occasion (i.e., in 425/1034). What was lost, as Avicenna says, was not "voluminous" (*kabīrat al-ḥajm*), while the *Fair Judgment* was "extensive" (*mabsūṭ*) and, "had it been transcribed clearly, would have comprised twenty volumes" (T12, § 3); it must therefore have been lost on another occasion (i.e., earlier, in 421/1030). See the discussion about the dating of these books and the events surrounding them in Chapter 2, W9 and W10.

to be the proper ones; some I have answered at sufficient length,[f] others by means of Pointers, and still other perhaps I have been unable to answer at all.

4. The invariable element in animals may be [a subject] more amenable to a clear exposition; as a matter of fact, I dealt with it thoroughly in the Eastern Fundamental Principles by first raising doubts and then solving them. In the case of plants, however, a clear exposition [of the same subject] is more difficult.

5. If there is no constant element [in plants] which would be infinite[g] and come about through the species, then it will come about through number ....

> [Avicenna next lists a series of questions and problems associated with establishing the constant principle in plants, corresponding to the soul in humans and animals, which lends them perpetuity and continuity.]

6. Let the members of our group strive to help each other to reach truth in this matter and not despair of God's comfort. That there is inevitably something constant under change is known to anybody who might wish to think a little; as for its problematic aspects, they are those which we
59 mentioned. I will be delighted with anybody who takes up these problems because the truth about them will appear,[h] as I estimate, at a short distance.

7. Indeed, I am delighted with you for having taken up this sort[i] of investigation which you resumed after [suggesting] a sort I disapproved of,[j] because this sort of investigation, i.e., an investigation with demonstrative methods,[k] is appropriate for the loftiest Philosophical Science [i.e., Metaphysics], while much of what you called for when I was in Rayy was inappropriate. You should engage in more such discussions [with me] on anything

---

[f] Reading *maqnaʿ* for *muqniʿ* (Badawī).

[g] Reading *ġayra mutanāhin* with B; C omits *mutanāhin* (as does Bīdārfar).

[h] Reading *wa-ana afraḥu mim-man ḫāḍa fī hāḏihi š-šubahi fa-innahu yalūḥu* with B and as printed by Bīdārfar; *wa-ammā l-faraju* (*frḥ* L) *fa-min ḫaṣāṣin li-hāḏihi š-šubahi yalūḥu* C. L has the reading of B in the text and of C in the margin. The latter reading, which seems to be the *lectio difficilior*, would mean, "As for the successful solutions [*al-faraj*?], the truth about these problems will glimmer through their cracks."

[i] Reading *la-afraḥu mim-man ḫāḍa min* [*sic*; *fī*?] *hāḏā n-namaṭ* with B and Bīdārfar; *mim-man ḫāḍa* om. C.

[j] "Resumed": *jaddadahu* Bīdārfar, *ḥaddadahu* Badawī; "disapproved": *kuntu astakrihuhu* Badawī; *ktb astakrihuhu* B and Bīdārfar (!).

[k] *Burhānī* B; *burhānī munāsib jiddan* C. The reading in C appears to be a marginal correction inserted into the text as a doublet. Perhaps *jiddan* should be read before the first *munāsib*: it "is eminently appropriate."

you wish, because in them lies pleasure and benefit. Whatever I am able to bring to light I will do so either openly, or from behind a veil which will act as a useful kind of stimulus and drill for it [i.e., the question at hand]; whatever I am unable to do so, I will excuse myself and admit it, since what is known to mankind is limited.

8. For my part, with regard to matters upon which I have spent great effort, I have come to know things which[l] I have Verified and cannot be improved, except that they are few. What I neither know nor have a way of knowing, on the other hand, is much indeed, but sometimes I have no hopes that about what I do not know I will ever come into possession of new knowledge which I have not[m] already achieved by the assiduous research I have been engaged in, despite the fact that my dedication to the search for truth is unmatched. Currently I am in such unpleasant circumstances and so overwhelmingly busy that I would be content[n] if I were able to track down [successfully] an idea at first try[7]—and yet, despite all this I praise God. He has granted me an incessant certainty[o] about Fundamental Principles which the seeker of salvation must without fail know,[p] and a wide-ranging competence[q] in subsequent areas.[r,8]

Text 12. Letter to Kiyā (GP 13)

This letter is addressed to a certain al-Kiyā Abū-Jaʿfar Muḥammad ibn-al-Ḥasan (or Ḥusayn) al-Marzubānī (or ibn-al-Marzubān), otherwise unknown. He is not to be identified with Bahmanyār—if only because Bahmanyār would have known the

---

[l] *ʿAlimtu ašyāʾa qad ḥaqqaqtuhā* B and Bīdārfar; *ʿalimtu kaṯīra* [!] *ašyāʾa maʿrifatan qad ḥaqqaqtuhā* Badawī.

[m] *Lam* C; *am* B and Bīdārfar (!).

[n] Reading *iqtanaʿtu bihi* with B; *aqnaʿtu* [?] Badawī.

[o] For "certainty," *yaqīnan*, the reading of both B and C, Bīdārfar prints *nafsan*, "soul," without specifying his source; presumably it is his conjecture.

[p] Reading *lā budda li-ṭālibi n-najāti minhā ʿārifan* with B; C omits *ʿārifan.*

[q] For the use of *majāl* as the *maṣdar* of the Ist form of the verb see Dozy, s.v. For the expression *ḍīq majāl* cf. T13, note g.

[r] C, along with some other MSS, but not B, adds at the end, *wa-maʿrifatan bi-mā lā aʿrifuhu bāliġatan*, "and a far-reaching [sufficient?] knowledge about what I do not know" [?].

---

[7] Avicenna frequently uses a hunting metaphor to refer to the acquisition of intelligible ideas; see, e.g., Text [17], § 2 in Gutas "Intuition and Thinking" 27.

[8] I.e., competence in the areas of Working Out Corollary Principles from the Fundamental Principles "and whatever is further derived from them," as the anonymous disciple from Rayy (Ibn-Zayla?) says in his Memoirs (T13, § 5). For the importance of this letter for Avicenna's method see Chapters 3.3A, 5.1, 8.

details about Avicenna's works narrated in the letter and would not need to be told about them—though he must have nevertheless possessed some significant philosophical erudition in order to ask and be told the specifics Avicenna details; and if Avicenna's patron and protector ʿAlāʾ-ad-Dawla is representative of the Kākūyid clan's open-mindedness and intellectual interests, he may well have been the ruler's cousin and governor of Šābūr-Ḫwāst, as Reisman suggests, *Avicennan Tradition* 186n72, who also stresses that the identification is "purely speculative." The letter, which is similar in tone to the preceding, was written about a year before Avicenna's death (W10) and sounds the basic themes of philosophical method (Chapters 5 and 8).

The text was first discovered by P. Kraus in the Cairo Avicenna *majmūʿa* Dār al-Kutub Ḥikma 6M[uṣṭafā Fāḍil], where it also forms uncharacteristically the opening selection of the *Discussions* (*Mubāḥaṯāt*, W12) because it is not, properly speaking, a part of it (Reisman *Avicennan Tradition* 63–64). In an extended footnote in his "Plotin" 272n3, Kraus presented an extract from it (§ 3 below). It was later edited by Badawī, on the basis of the Cairo manuscript, in his *Arisṭū* 120.9–122.8.

This letter is extant in a number of manuscripts (cf. M 12, A 259, and Reisman *Avicennan Tradition* 64–66), and it will require a critical edition. In his edition of the *Mubāḥaṯāt* pp. 371–375, Bīdārfar simply copied the text from Badawī's edition (and not the Cairo MS) and just added in the notes some variant readings from the Leiden MS Or. 864 Warn. My translation below is based on the actual readings of the Cairo manuscript (C), indicated in the textual notes. Here also, as in the case of the previous letter, I changed the third person of the addressee to the second.

Pines based his "Philosophie Orientale" on a translation (6–9) and study of this letter; Goichon discussed it briefly in "Philosophie" 21–22.

Letter to Kiyā

1. What you mentioned about the disagreement, obtuseness, and wavering of people on the subject of the soul and the intellect, and especially of the simple-minded Christians of Baġdād,[1] is just as you said. Already Alexander, Themistius, and others were perplexed on this issue, each being right in some respects and wrong in others. The reason for this is the obscurity of Aristotle's method [of composition],[2] which led them to think that he
61 took up the exposition of the survival of the soul or its annihilation upon death *only* when he was composing the last book of *De anima*.[3] This, how-

---

[1] The reference here is to the Christian philosophers in Baġdād, and particularly to Abū-l-Faraj Ibn-aṭ-Ṭayyib, Abū-l-Ḫayr Ibn-al-Ḫammār, and Ibn-as-Samḥ, the targets of Avicenna's philosophical ire in the dispute described in a disciple's (Ibn-Zayla's?) memoirs in T13, §§ 3–4, below.

[2] *Maḏhab* here means "method of composition" and not "doctrine," as translated by Pines "Philosophie Orientale". For the influence on Avicenna of the late antique doctrine of Aristotle's obscurity of method see Chapters 5.3 and 8.2.

[3] According to the division of the *De anima* in the translation used by Avicenna, the last

ever, is not so; on the contrary, already in the first book, in the course of his argument with Democritus on the subject of the soul, he Worked Out Corollary Principles[a] in a concealed fashion, and offered to those who have an understanding of this matter the Fundamental Principle, namely, that the thing in which the universal intelligibles are conceived is indivisible.[4] He thus precluded the possibility that it is corporeal substance which receives the [universal] intelligible concepts. What receives them, therefore, is a substance subsisting by itself, neither divisible [itself] nor [existing] in something divisible on account of which it could become divisible. It is free of any resemblance to a body or anything corporeal. Then, in the last book [of *De anima*], Aristotle devoted himself exclusively to an exposition of the faculties which accompany the soul in its survival only, since he had already indicated previously that the [faculties of] sense-perception, imagination, memory, and their likes, and the motive faculty, cannot subsist without a body, and it had become clear from the tenor of his argument that perceiving by both the external and internal senses can only come about by means of something divisible. He thus wished to investigate the intellectual faculties [in the last book of *De anima*]. He began with the faculty called material intellect [in Book III.4] and showed that it does not perish, and then he moved on to another faculty [in Book III.5] and stated plainly that it also does not perish. Now his word[b] "also" indicates that a second[c]

---

[a] Reading *qad farraʿa* with C, for *faraʿa* in Badawī.

[b] Reading *lafẓuhu* (C) for *lafẓat* in Badawī. Even though C never indicates the *tāʾ marbūṭa*, it is clear from what follows (see note 5) that the word *ayḍan* refers to Aristotle's text.

[c] Reading *ṯāniyan*, indicated clearly in C and correctly surmised by Finnegan "Alexandre" 135n4, for *ṯābitan* in Badawī.

"book" began with III.4, what Avicenna describes below as the discussion of the material intellect. The same translation was also used by Averroes for his lemmata in the Large Commentary; see Crawford 379. The various translations of the *De anima* used by these philosophers are discussed by Frank "*De anima*" and by Gätje *Psychologie*. For a complete account of the Arabic tradition of *De anima* see the articles by A. Elamrani-Jamal and R. Arnzen in *DPhA Supplément* 346–365.

[4] The passage of the *De anima* referred to here is I,2, 405a8–13 (not I,3, as suggested by Pines "Philosophie Orientale" 6n2). The statement of Aristotle which Avicenna considered as providing the Fundamental Principle read as follows in the Arabic translation (as reflected in the Latin version, Crawford 39.3–4): "Democritus said that the soul and the intellect are the same and that it is one of [*ex* = **min*?] the primary indivisible bodies." In the *Marginal Glosses on De anima* (GS 11c; see W10), Avicenna devotes a lengthy discussion to this very passage where he presents all the arguments alluded to here (Badawī *Arisṭū* 79–83).

62 pronouncement is analogous to the first;[5] but because a certain person imagined something else (on the basis of his belief that the material intellect is the rational soul itself, or that the material intellect[d] is a certain disposition of the heart, and that accordingly the intelligibles are received[e] by the body of the heart by means of this disposition),[6] he got confused,[f] came up with the wrong opinion, and strayed from the ideal path.[7] The truth is that this [material] intellect is a disposition of the *substance* of the soul, not of any *body*, and that it accompanies the substance of the soul in every state. Upon the subject that the divisible cannot receive the intelligible I have expatiated in a treatise [elsewhere] in precise[g] and unequivocal terms; perhaps I will present it to you, should God decree that I meet you.[8]

2. As for John Philoponus's book on the refutation of Aristotle,[9] it is a book which is apparently cogent but essentially weak, while applying oneself to

---

[d] I include here the phrase omitted in C by *homoioteleuton*, and found in the British Library MS Or. 8069, given by Pines "Philosophie Orientale" 7n2.

[e] Reading *fa-kāna* with C for *fa-ka-anna* in Badawī.

[f] There is no need to supply ⟨*wa-*⟩ here, as Badawī does.

[g] Bīdārfar registers the reading in the Leiden MS here as *mutqanan* for the unpointed skeleton in C which Badawī reads as *muġniyan*, and it seems preferable.

---

[5] The reference here is to *De anima* III,5, 430a17, which read as follows in the translation used by Avicenna (Crawford 440.1–2): "This intellect also [*etiam* = **ayḍan*] is separable, unmixed and impassive." This corresponds, as noted by Finnegan "Alexandre" 134n4, to the Greek *kai houtos ho nous chōristos kai apathēs kai amigēs*, where the first *kai* was translated by *ayḍan*. What Avicenna means is that since the active intellect is said to be "also" separable (the second pronouncement), then this must imply that the passive, or material, intellect is separable (the first pronouncement); he then proceeds, on this basis, to criticize those who denied the separability of the material intellect. It is interesting to note that Averroes understood the Aristotelian text in precisely the same manner: "I.e., this intellect also is separable, like the material intellect, and it is also impassive and unmixed like it" (Crawford 440.8–10).

[6] Avicenna refers to the same doctrine in much the same words in his *Marginal Glosses on De anima* (Badawī *Arisṭū* 92.15–16), as noted by Finnegan "Porphyrius" 195 and note 3.

[7] The reference here seems to be to Alexander of Aphrodisias, about whom Avicenna makes a similar comment in his *Marginal Glosses on De anima*, Badawī *Arisṭū* 101.17–19 (mentioned by Finnegan "Porphyrius" 192n1). That this doctrine should also be that of the Porphyrians, as Finnegan claims ("Porphyrius" 196) with some misgivings, seems open to doubt.

[8] Avicenna repeats the same wish below, in paragraph 4.

[9] The reference seems to be to Philoponus's book *De aeternitate mundi contra Aristotelem*; see the note by Pines "Philosophie Orientale" 7n4. For the Arabic translation and reception of this work, including Avicenna's view of Philoponus mentioned here, see the article on him by Emma Gannagé in *DPhA* Va,537 ff.

these problems[10] and succeeding in solving them [require] a powerful soul[11] and ample philosophical Knowledge. I did what should be done in this 63
regard, by means of commentary, detailed exposition, and Working Out of Corollary Principles on the basis of Fundamental Principles, in what I wrote in my comprehensive book, *The Cure*, which contains all the sciences of the ancients, even music. The complexities of these problems are such that they cannot be comprehended by the superficial[h] scholars you know, for their solution is built upon the Corollaries of Fundamental Principles [found] in the *Physics*: both[i] the *Physics* and the *De Caelo* [contain] Fundamental Principles which themselves are Corollaries of the Fundamental Principles set forth in the *Physics*, though these Corollary Principles are not stated explicitly in the *Physics* but only implicitly.[12] So whoever does not *first* churn the concepts of the *Physics* to produce the cream of these Corollary Principles, he will have wasted his efforts to gain an understanding and suffer the same fate as those [Christians of Baġdād] we are talking about and John Philoponus. Indeed, some people tried to refute his refutation, but they approached the house from the rear instead of the [front] door, and they misled themselves into contentment with what they wrote. As for ourselves, we have clarified these [Fundamental Principles] common to both books;[13] whoever comes to understand them will find all the problems vapid and undaunting.

3. You asked to find out how I go about in such matters. I will tell you: I had composed a book which I called *Fair Judgment*. I divided scholars into two groups, the Westerners and the Easterners, and I had the Easterners argue against the Westerners until I intervened to Judge Fairly when there was

---

[h] *Rasmiyyūn*. For the meaning see Jabre *Lexique* 108–109, and cf. Pines "Philosophie Orientale" 8n2, objected to by Goichon "Philosophie" 21n8. The reference is to the Christians of Baġdād.

[i] The use of *bayna … bayna* in this context is distributive (cf. Wright II,180D–181A), not limitative as understood by Pines "Philosophie Orientale" 8: "(pour passer) de la *Physique* au *De Caelo* (il est besoin) de principes …". Literally, the above passage reads, "for both the *Physics* and the *De Caelo* there are principles which …".

---

[10] "Problems:" *šukūk*, literally, "doubts, aporiai;" "critiques," Pines "Philosophie Orientale" 8. This is the technical term for the genre of scholarly literature in the form of *aporiai kai lyseis*, *dubitationes et solutiones*. Cf. the title of Ibn-al-Hayṯam's work, *aš-Šukūk ʿalā Baṭlamyūs*.

[11] By "powerful soul" Avicenna is referring to his theory of *ḥads*. See T2.

[12] For the understanding of Aristotle's method of composition indicated here see Chapters 5.3 and 8.

[13] I.e., *De Caelo* and *Physics*.

a real point of dispute between them.[j] This book had contained approximately twenty-eight thousand questions. I commented clearly on the difficult passages in the essential texts[14] up to the end of the *Theologia Aristotelis*,
64 despite the fact that the *Theologia* is somewhat suspect, and I talked about the oversights of the commentators. I wrote it in a short period of time—[a work] which, had it been transcribed clearly, would have comprised twenty volumes.[15] Then it was lost in the course of some rout, since there was only the first draft. Investigating it and these controversies was a pastime; after completing something I am working on [at present], I will occupy myself with rewriting it, although even thinking about rewriting is oppressive.[k] But it had contained a precise exposition[l] of the weakness of the Baġdādīs, and of their deficiency and ignorance. At the present moment it is impossible for me [to rewrite it]: I do not have the free time for it, but am occupied with men like Alexander [of Aphrodisias], Themistius, John Philoponus, and their likes. As for Abū-Naṣr al-Fārābī, he ought to be very highly thought of, and not to be weighed in the same scale with the rest:[m] he is all but the most excellent of our predecessors.[16]

4. Perhaps God will make it easy [for me] to meet with you; it will be mutually beneficial. Please excuse my disorderly writing and crooked letters, but I have not undertaken to correspond in my own hand for a year or two now. Debilitating and long diseases which sapped my strength have kept me immobilized and prevented my hand from writing. This is the first thing I write in my own hand.

---

[j] Reading *al-lidād* (C), the verbal noun of the 3rd stem (*WKAS* II 1, 436a), as correctly printed by Bīdārfar 375, against the *al-ladad* in Badawī's text. Pines "Philosophie Orientale" 9 reads, "Jusqu'à ce que la dispute eût été éclaircie [!] et que je procédasse à un arbitrage équitable." Cf. the better rendering of Anawati "Tradition manuscrite" 416, "quand l'opposition devient réelle, je m'avance pour les départager équitablement." For *ḥaqqa* used in this sense see Jūzjānī's Introduction to *The Cure* (T7, § 1).

[k] Literally, "even the shadow of rewriting is heavy," i.e. let alone the actual rewriting itself. See Lane s.v. *ẓill*.

[l] *Talḫīṣ*. See *WKAS* II 1, 428b.

[m] Literally, "not to be made to run in the same course with the others."

---

[14] I.e., the difficult core passages of books in the Aristotelian tradition, as listed in T1, § 3, that were the source of misunderstanding and dispute. For the term *fuṣūṣ* used here by Avicenna see above, T3, § 6, and note 19.

[15] Cf. the similar account of the disciple writing from Rayy (Ibn-Zayla?), T13, § 2.

[16] This is the beginning of the tradition that Fārābī is the "second teacher" after Aristotle. Bayhaqī, who cites this passage in his chapter on Abū-l-Ḫayr Ibn-al-Ḫammār (*Tatimma* 13.5–7/27), seems to have had a different text here.

Text 13. Memoirs of a Disciple (Ibn-Zayla?) Writing from Rayy[1]

These memoirs in the form of a letter present a lively picture of Avicenna as a philosopher and a teacher, and offer valuable information about his books and philosophical method. They were written in Rayy (§ 2, end) by a disciple of Avicenna who remains anonymous in the manuscripts, and addressed to an equally anonymous gentleman (*šayḫ*) in ʿIrāq, presumably in Baġdād (§ 4, middle). The author is in all probability Ibn-Zayla, as suggested by Reisman, but the identification is tentative; the recipient remains unidentified. The memoirs are preserved in some recensions of the *Discussions* (see W12), though by their very nature they do not properly belong to that collection of materials.[2]

The purpose of the letter is in the main apologetic. An emissary of Avicenna arrived in Baġdād and sought to buy the books by the eminent philosopher Abū-l-Faraj Ibn-aṭ-Ṭayyib, one of the last representatives of the illustrious line of Baġdād Aristotelians. Ibn-aṭ-Ṭayyib, however, was displeased at the idea of having Avicenna acquire his books, and in order to discourage the sale, and perhaps also insult Avicenna, asked for an exorbitant price. The reason for Ibn-aṭ-Ṭayyib's displeasure— 65
apparently scholarly rivalry—is not stated in the letter; the author merely says discreetly, "the fact that somebody like Avicenna had sent for Ibn-aṭ-Ṭayyib's books did not meet with the latter's pleasure" (§ 3, middle). The emissary, however, was instructed to purchase the books irrespective of the price, and thus the sale was made. The story must have circulated in Baġdād quickly. In the philosophical circles in which the rivalry between the two men was known, Avicenna's eagerness to acquire the books despite the insultingly inflated price was interpreted—perhaps even at the suggestion of Ibn-aṭ-Ṭayyib himself—as indicating a commensurate scholarly need for them on his part. The letter was written in order to dispel this notion. The author asks specifically the recipient to circulate the letter so that people could realize that "the need for [Ibn-aṭ-Ṭayyib's] books was not as great as implied by [the willingness to pay] such an exorbitant price and ... that there was no satisfaction with them" (§ 4, middle). It was written either at the request of the recipient, who must have heard the rumours in Baġdād and wished to find out the true facts from his acquaintance in Rayy, or else it was sent on the disciple's own initiative in order to restore Avicenna's reputation in Baġdād. In any case, we owe this letter and the useful information it contains to an all too human situation: philosophical rivalry, scholarly gossip, and the hurt pride of a disciple.

---

[1] Cf. Reisman *Avicennan Tradition* 195n99.

[2] For Ibn-Zayla see Reisman *Avicennan Tradition* 195–203; for the "Memoirs," which Reisman rightly places among the "accretional texts" of the *Discussions*, see p. 253. Reisman's identification of Ibn-Zayla as the author rests on two arguments, both good, but not conclusive. First, in some manuscripts of the *Discussions*, some entries, like the "Memoirs," are preceded by the abbreviation of the Arabic letter *ṭ*, which indicates that they were "in the handwriting (*bi-ḫaṭṭihi*) of" Avicenna, Bahmanyār, or Ibn-Zayla. Since the "Memoirs" are by neither of the first two, they are by elimination by Ibn-Zayla. Second, the "Memoirs" indicate a strong interest in Avicenna's *Fair Judgment*, which Ibn-Zayla certainly had.

The background of the letter is equally revealing. After the loss of the *Fair Judgment* during the sack of Iṣfahān, Avicenna would be neither enticed to rewrite it upon the request of his disciples in Rayy, nor provoked into polemics by sending for the new books of the philosophers in Baġdād. It was only when a rich young man—the Alcibiades of the group, who in all likelihood is to be identified as Bahmanyār[3]—offered to buy the books himself, thus suggesting that the real reason for Avicenna's refusal to consider rewriting the book was niggardliness, that Avicenna was moved to action and sent his emissary to Baġdād with the inevitable instructions that the books be bought at any price. We thus owe the events that prompted the letter also to a human situation: the young disciple's insolence and the master's *amour propre* and umbrageousness.

The events described in the letter took place in 421/1030, after the attack on Iṣfahān by the Ghaznavid Masʿūd and the loss of the *Fair Judgment* earlier that year. The letter itself was probably written shortly afterwards: after the death of the Ghaznavid Maḥmūd in May of 1030, who is referred to as "the late Sultan" (§ 2, beginning), but before the death of Avicenna in 428/1037, because he is referred to in the letter as "the man we are talking about" (*fulān*), without the customary (and in the case of a disciple, obligatory) benedictory formulae for the dead. In any case, the extreme upper limit is Ibn-aṭ-Ṭayyib's death in 435/1043, since he was alive at the time the letter was written. For further details on the chronology and the political events see Chapter 2, W10b.

The translation below is based on the text of the *Discussions* (*Mubāḥaṯāt*) in the Oxford MS Bodleian Hunt. 534, ff. 13^{b} ult.–15^{b}-2 (B) and compared throughout with the text in the Leiden MS Warn. Or. 864, ff. $64^{a}1$–$66^{a}11$ (L). The text of the letter was transcribed, apparently from the Bodleian manuscript but with numerous errors, in Mahdavī 206–210, and, with greater accuracy, by Bīdārfar §§ 127–141. The readings of both manuscripts and all instances where Mahdavī and Bīdārfar deviate from them are recorded in the textual notes. In the translation, the polite third person form of address was again changed to the second person.

The letter was first noted in the Bodleian manuscript by S.M. Stern, who brought
66 it to the attention of S. Pines just as the latter's "Philosophie Orientale" was about to be published. Pines could only include in an Appendix (pp. 35–36) a brief summary and a translation of the passage on the *Metaphysics* (§ 8, end; see also p. 21, n. 2). Stern himself apparently intended to edit the letter, as Pines reports, but the project never materialized. He only used the information on Ibn-as-Samḥ, and translated the relevant sentence (§ 3, middle), in his "Ibn al-Samḥ" 32–33.

Memoirs of a Disciple (Ibn-Zayla?) Writing from Rayy

1. God prolong your days! You are aware of the relationship between a group of us and Avicenna, just as you know the degree of attainment in all the sciences, and especially the true ones, with which God has distinguished him.

---

3 As suggested by Reisman *Avicennan Tradition* 191–192.

2. In the year when the horsemen of the late Sultan overran these lands,
Avicenna was prompted for some reason to occupy himself with a book
which he called *Fair Judgment*. It contained commentaries on all the books
by Aristotle, among which he even included the *Theologia* [*Aristotelis*],
about whose contents he brought out matters that had never been taken
into account.[4] He examined all divergences of exegesis and Judged every
question and every philosopher by bestowing Fairly praise or blame, and
appreciation or deprecation. God only knows the number of problems and
solutions, and Corollaries based on Fundamental Principles, which resulted,
although the period [in which the book was composed] was from the middle
of the month of Dey to the end of the month of Ḫordād in [less than] a
year![5] It came to more than six thousand folios written in a crowded hand
and ten thousand folios written in a straight hand;[6] it relieved him, however,
of what he needed to communicate and left him manifestly cheered. The
number of issues he discussed as lemmata[a] about which he traced where
previous statements were wrong, mistaken, deficient, or corrupt, was over
twenty-seven thousand. But before all this was transcribed into a clean copy,
he was hindered by a military rout in which all his belongings and books
were carried off at the gate of Iṣfahān. When he returned to Rayy, he was 67
urged to rewrite all that, but he found this repugnant,[b] since doing all over
again something that has just been completed is onerous.[7]

3. The instigations and incitements, however, continued: he was told, "If you would send for what our contemporaries in Baġdād have just produced,

---

[a] Reading *wa-ja'alahu mawḍi'an* for *mawḍi'* (nom. or gen.) in B, Mahdavī, and Bīdārfar. L has *mawḍū'* (nom. or gen.).

[b] Reading *fa-staqazza*, clearly indicated in B; L has *wa-staqarra*, where presumably the dot of the *zāy* was omitted, though the Xth form of *qzz* is not attested in the dictionaries. Both Mahdavī and Bīdārfar print *fa-stafazza*, which makes little sense in context.

---

[4] This is correct. The extant portions of Avicenna's commentary (see W10) are thorough and original. This is largely due, of course, to the fact that the *Theologia*, not being an Aristotelian text, had not been subjected to repeated commentaries in the Greek tradition.

[5] That is, from about mid-December to early June in 1029, or approximately five and a half months. For a discussion of these dates see W10b.

[6] Cf. a similar statement by Rāzī in his autobiography: "So great in fact have been my endeavours and endurance, that in a single year I have written as many as 20,000 pages in a script as minute as that used in amulets (*ḫaṭṭ at-ta'āwīḏ*)," Arberry *Physick* 16; Arabic text and French translation by Kraus "Raziana I" 320.12, 334.

[7] Cf. the similar account given by Avicenna himself in the letter to Kiyā, T12, § 3.

perhaps the new[c] ideas might move you into action to pass judgment on them[8] by declaring them valid or erroneous." Then an aristocratic young man, one of the sons of the commanders, came forth and said that he would send from his own money the initial payment[d] needed to procure whatever [books] could be found there by the two masters, both of whom were alive at the time (God prolong the life of the survivor!).[9] Avicenna resented this and, loath to behave like a miser, instructed one of his friends to purchase the recent[e] books by the two masters. However, only the books by the venerable master [Ibn-aṭ-Ṭayyib] who is still alive could be located (God be pleased with him!). Avicenna was dealt unfairly in the transaction and was asked an exorbitant price: the fact that somebody like him had sent for that master's books did not meet with the latter's pleasure. But Avicenna had directed his friend not to be deterred from the purchase by a high price, and thus a number of that master's books was procured. When we
68 studied them carefully, we found such befuddlement and mental confusion the likes of which accomplished people[10] had never seen. Avicenna then

[c] Reading the unpointed skeleton in B as *al-jadīda*, along with L. Mahdavī and Bīdārfar read *al-ḥadīda*; but cf. note e below. Pines "Philosophie Orientale" 35 also paraphrases, "idées nouvelles."

[d] *Yastaftiḥu*. For this meaning of the verb see Dozy s.v.

[e] Reading *mā tajaddada*, clearly indicated in B, Bīdārfar; *mimmā tajaddada* L; *mā yajidu* Mahdavī.

[8] Presumably the new ideas, although it would be more appropriate to understand by the feminine pronoun the books of the Baġdādīs.

[9] Three Baġdādī scholars are mentioned by name in this letter: Abū-l-Ḫayr Ibn-al-Ḫammār (born 331/942), Abū-ʿAlī Ibn-as-Samḥ (died 418/1027), and Abū-l-Faraj Ibn-aṭ-Ṭayyib (died 435/1043). Since the events described in this letter took place in 421/1030 (see W10b), the scholar still alive at the time the letter was written is thus definitely Ibn-aṭ-Ṭayyib, as is also obvious from what follows. Ibn-as-Samḥ is listed by Ibn-al-Qifṭī 412 Lippert as having died in 418/1027, and thus he cannot be one of "the two masters" mentioned in this sentence. This leaves Ibn-al-Ḫammār, whose date of death is not known but who must have died, according to the information provided by this letter, sometime during 421/1030, at the age of 88 solar years. However, this calculation of the date of his death is valid only if Ibn-al-Qifṭī's date for the death of Ibn-as-Samḥ is reliable; if not, one of "the two masters" could just as well be Ibn-as-Samḥ whose date of death will have to be revised accordingly. The information provided by Ibn-Buṭlān (in Ibn-Abī-Uṣaybiʿa I,242–243 Müller; cf. the English translation of the passage in Schacht and Meyerhof 62–63), that Ibn-as-Samḥ and Ibn-aṭ-Ṭayyib died within "a period of ten and some odd years" (*fī muddati biḍʿa ʿašrata sanatan*) of each other, is too vague to be of specific use here; nevertheless, it assures that the general range of these dates is correct.

[10] *Ahl at-taḥṣīl*. I translate this term as "accomplished people" rather than in Avicenna's

spoke upraidingly to his instigators: "Didn't I tell you that this is the level [of Ibn-aṭ-Ṭayyib] and this the procedure? And that Abū-l-Ḫayr Ibn-al-Ḫammār and Ibn-as-Samḥ,[f] because their scope is so narrow,[g] adhered[h] more closely than others to the [traditional] transmission[i] of certain books? To hear people magnify the substance and overrate the price [of Ibn-aṭ-Ṭayyib's books] you would think that they are brandishing[j] [for sale] something that no eye has ever seen or ear has ever heard." Then he said, "What one should do with these books is to send them back to their vendor and let him keep the money![11] On the other hand, I have heard that the master," meaning Abū-l-Faraj Ibn-aṭ-Ṭayyib, "had suffered[k] for a period from mental derangement due to illnesses that continuously befall thinkers;[12] perhaps this is one of his works from that period. Maybe time will cure him."[13]

4. Nevertheless, we are certainly astonished at those who are content with such a paltry[l] amount of research and then with such a deficient sort of exposition. Upon my life, these people relax and are satisfied with whatever they imagine to be the case which is easily treated, dismissing logic absolutely. With regard to the matters of syllogisms, their dismissal is complete and 69

---

[f] Reading *Ibn-as-Samḥ* with B L and Bīdārfar; *Ibn-al-Masḥ* Mahdavī.

[g] *ʿAlā ḍīqi majālihimā* seems to mean here "because their scope is so narrow," rather than "in spite of their limited capacity," as in Stern 33. The same expression is used again later on in this text, § 4, in this sense: *ḍīq majāl li-l-bayān*, "the narrow scope of exposition." Cf. Pines's paraphrase ("Philosophie Orientale" 36n1), "ces savants sans envergure." Cf. also T11, note q.

[h] Reading *kāna taʿalluquhumā* with L, Bīdārfar, and Mahdavī; *kāna wa-taʿalluquhumā* B.

[i] *Bi-riwāya* B; *bi-zāwiya* [!] L, followed by Stern 33 in his translation: "this or that little corner."

[j] Reading *yahuzzūna* with B; *yhḏwn* L; *yhdwn* Mahdavī and Bīdārfar.

[k] Reading *qad* for *fd* in Mahdavī.

[l] *Nazr* B L and Bīdārfar; *nḏr* Mahdavī.

---

special sense of "those who Determine the Validity [of philosophical texts]" (see the Index of Technical Terms) because the words are used by the disciple in what appears to be a broader meaning. Nevertheless, since Avicenna criticized Ibn-aṭ-Ṭayyib, among other things, for not Determining the Validity of philosophical statements, echoes of this narrower signification are certainly to be perceived in this term as it is used here.

[11] Bayhaqī repeats this statement of Avicenna in his chapter on Ibn-aṭ-Ṭayyib (*Tatimma* 28.1/43), as noted by Pines "Philosophie Orientale" 16n5, and Mahdavī 208n1.

[12] According to Galenic humoral pathology, continuous thinking, or brooding, causes an excess of black bile in the body, which in turn brings about "black bile diseases," i.e., mental disorders, collectively known as *melancholia, sawdāʾ*.

[13] That Ibn-aṭ-Ṭayyib suffered from some mental disorder on account of his excessive study of metaphysics is reported by his student, Ibn-Buṭlān. See Schacht and Meyerhof 87–88 (54 of the Arabic text).

they pay no attention whatever to them—and not only today, but they have been doing this for quite some time. As for the forms of syllogisms, specifically these people have disregarded them. Whenever they treated them, they strayed from the right path because they never acquired the habit of dealing with them and they never suffered the pains of analyzing the details of problems so that they may gain a syllogistic habit; their sole reliance, instead, is upon ideas not subject to rules.[14] I ask you to submit this account of the affair[m] to the accomplished[15] students of these sciences so that they will know, first, that the need for these books [by Ibn-aṭ-Ṭayyib] was not as great as implied by [the willingness to pay] such an exorbitant price, and second, that there was no satisfaction with them.[n] By God, among the books of confused people that we have studied carefully, never have our eyes fallen on anything more astray and tortuous[o] than the contents of these books: the[p] scant attention to the meaning [*al-maʿānī*, i.e., of the text commented upon], the narrow scope of exposition, the dubious argumentation that fails to convince,[q] the use of rhetorical and sophistical methods in the demonstrative sciences,[16] and the inconsistent procedures. These books [by Ibn-aṭ-Ṭayyib] that became available to us are those which he composed on the *Eisagoge* [of Porphyry], *Categories, De Interpretatione, Sophistici Elenchi, De Caelo, De Sensu et Sensato*, and *Metaphysics*. If anybody[r] in ʿIrāq to whom this letter is shown is doubtful that our group is right, let him turn to[s] any passage

---

[m] "Account of the affair:" *ṣūra*; cf. T8, note t.

[n] *Iqtirāru ʿaynin*: note the unusual VIIIth form of the verb for this familiar expression.

[o] Reading *aḫraj wa-aʿwaj* with B; *aḥraj wa-aḥwaj* Mahdavī and Bīdārfar. For the elative use of *afʿal* for deformities cf. W1 below in Chapter 2, note m.

[p] I read *min qillat* ... for *maʿa qillat* ... in the MSS and Mahdavī and Bīdārfar. If *maʿa* were to be retained the meaning could possibly be, "Despite the fact that the books of confused people normally pay scant attention to substance, have a narrow scope of exposition, etc., Ibn-aṭ-Ṭayyib's books are even *more* astray and tortuous than they."

[q] *Tabkīt* L, Mahdavī and Bīdārfar; unpointed skeleton in B.

[r] Reading *fa-man* with B L and Bīdārfar; *mimman* Mahdavī.

[s] Reading *fa-l-yaʿtanni* with B and Bīdārfar; *fa-l-yataʿayyan* [!] Mahdavī. L has *fa-l-yuʿayyin*, which corroborates the skeleton, if not the points of B. *Iʿtanna ʿalā*, in the VIIIth form, is not attested in the dictionaries; but cf. the base form, used with *ʿalā*, in Dozy, s.v.

---

[14] This "syllogistic habit" is of course what Avicenna says he acquired in his youth; cf. his Autobiography (T3, § 8) and the discussion in Chapter 3.3A.

[15] See above, note 10.

[16] What is meant here is that they use rhetorical or sophistical premisses or propositions when they deal with subjects that need to be analyzed by means of demonstrative propositions.

he wishes among the subjects [*al-maʿānī*] included in[t] these books—and especially in Physics and Theology—so that we may write some[u] of the corruptions, inconsistencies, and nonsense that it contains in such a manner that no one will have any more doubts and no two people will disagree about pronouncing us right on the subject. As for Avicenna, [he will not write such refutations] because he keeps himself above[v] engaging in arguments about everything and everybody and upsetting friends, and because he never mentions anybody except with good words and excessive regard[w].[17]

5. What is astonishing, though, is that one should dare to have such confounded writings be taken to someone like Avicenna, seeing that he is the person who taught us to analyze into simple terms [of syllogisms] all the Philosophical Sciences, all their Corollary Principles, and whatever is further derived from them, not according to the forms of the [syllogistic] figures but according to their matters. He also taught us how to take into account the relations existing among simple terms, as well as, among other things, his minute investigation of these relations and especially of the sciences of the demonstrative syllogism, seeing that he has enumerated every passage in the Philosophical Sciences in which middle terms are appropriate[x] and there is need to draw them from outside, and where they can be found and where they cannot. For he has a superbly detailed knowledge, unparalleled in others, of what does not constitute terms of premisses in demonstrative, dialectical, and sophistical syllogisms.

6. We constantly used to hear him say: "In analysis, do not spend too much time taking into account the forms of syllogisms for that's one of the easy

---

[t] *ʿAlayhi* sic B L and the editions for *ʿalayhā*.

[u] *Baʿḍan mā* [!] B and Bīdārfar; *baʿḍa mā* L, Mahdavī.

[v] B (and Bīdārfar) has the unusual VIIIth form, *yantazihu*, which is to be preferred. L "corrects" it to the Vth: *yatanazzahu*; *ytzh* Mahdavī.

[w] "Excessive regard:" *šahāda mufriṭa*; cf. the Persian-Turkish expression, *ḥosn-e* (*ḥüsn-ü*) *šehādet*.

[x] The skeletal text of this sentence appears to be clear, as is the sense, though the pointing is problematic. I read, *wa-huwa yaʿuddu kulla mawḍiʿin fī l-ʿulūmi yafiqu fīhi l-awsāṭu*. Mahdavī prints *baʿda* for *yaʿuddu*, which is preferred by Bīdārfar; *baʿda* is the reading in B, and L has the same skeleton text, but a second hand added points later to read *yaʿuddu*. For what I read as *yafiqu* B has *yaqifu* (adopted by both Mahdavī and Bīdārfar) and L has, again with dots added in a later hand, *ṯaqa/ifa*.

---

[17] This is a reference, stated in flattering terms, to what Avicenna repeatedly says about his unwillingness to write commentaries and detailed refutations. See T8, § 3; T9, § 1 end; L38 from the introduction to the Physics part of *The Cure*, and the discussion in Chapter 5.2.

parts and a sound instinct[y] rarely makes a mistake about it; you should rather practice examining in detail the matters [of syllogisms]."

7. We also heard from him that it is beneficial to Determine the Validity of these books because, [he said,] "the limited sophistical *topoi* are both verbal and semantic [in nature]. Those that Aristotle set down are few, but the Corollary Principles which we Worked Out are many and almost
71 equivalent to the dialectical *topoi*. The Sophistics [part of *The Cure*] is not short on account of their small number: the very same *topoi* are examined repeatedly in order that the book reach an appropriate length. All these *topoi* are provided in these compilations [of mine] with examples drawn from the Philosophical Sciences and supersede those examples [of Aristotle], some of which were derived[z] from common definitions and others from conversations current at that time [of Aristotle] but since forgotten."[18]

8. We also heard him say, "It distresses me that the belief in the permanence of the first principle and in the permanence of its unity should be arrived at by means of motion and the oneness of the moved world, as if[aa] [Aristotle's] *Metaphysics* could not yield its riches concerning God Almighty except in this way! This is to be regarded as distressing not on the part of our contemporaries only, but also on the part of all their masters like them." He further said, "Had they comprehended the innermost ideas of the *Metaphysics* they would have been ashamed of this sort of thing and not felt compelled[bb] to maintain that the course to be adopted includes[cc] both the Physical approach and the Theological approach—something totally unfounded because this book [Aristotle's *Metaphysics*] is distinguished by the Theological approach alone."[19]

9. As a matter of fact, Avicenna himself had composed a separate commentary on this book, whose part on the *Alpha Elatton* alone contained approximately everything in the commentary imported from Baġdād. Fur-

[y] *Al-ġarāʾiz* in B and L, and Mahdavī; Bīdārfar prints *al-qarāʾin*.
[z] Reading *al-mūrada* with B L and Bīdārfar; *mūrada* Mahdavī.
[aa] Reading *ka-anna* with B L and Bīdārfar; *li-anna* Mahdavī.
[bb] Reading *yuḥwi/ajū*, clearly indicated in B, Bīdārfar; *yaḫrujū* L and Mahdavī.
[cc] *Hāḏihi l-maʾāḫiḏ fīhi* sic B, and followed by Mahdavī and Bīdārfar; L has *ḥāḏā l-maʾḫaḏ fīhi*.

[18] See Chapters 3.3Ei and 5.2 for the implications of this passage for Avicenna's understanding of the philosophical method and of the historical contextuality of the philosophical praxis.
[19] See Chapter 6.3.

thermore, he did not include in it any problems whose Corollary Principles he had already Worked Out in Logic, Physics, or Mathematics. Nothing was repeated, and no exposition was lengthy but rather expressed as concisely as possible despite the inclusion of [all] the subjects [*al-maʿānī*].[20]

10. Frequently[dd] Avicenna used to say: "A commentator should provide all the premisses that are needed, and omit nothing but the obvious and the superfluous,[21] for the most incompetent commentator is he who uses in his 72
commentary premisses more cryptic than, or as cryptic as, the premisses of whatever he is commenting upon. These commentaries which [purport to] bring us the truth conceal in fact the theses better than the essential texts,[ee] while what they conceal[ff] most is errors."

Text 14. *On the Rational Soul* (GP 11)

On the Rational Soul is in all probability Avicenna's very last work. He refers in it to the *Compendium on the Soul*, which he wrote, he says, forty years previously, at the beginning of his career (§ 11 below; see W1). Fate appropriately decreed that Avicenna should start and end his career with a work on the human soul, the subject that focuses and animates his philosophy.

This essay presents *in nuce* Avicenna's philosophical system, structured around the central concept of the rational soul. All the philosophical sciences with which Avicenna was most intimately concerned and which engaged his sustained scholarly attention are brought into mutual relationship: logic, the fruits of metaphysics and physics, ethics, and even medicine (see Chapter 6.2). It is an integrated theoretical construct reflecting an integrated view of the universe and man's position in it.

The essay survives in a single manuscript, Leiden 958 Warner (catalogue number 1468), ff. 247ª–250ª, dated at the end of the treatise on 19 Ḏū l-Qaʿda 954 / 31 December 1547. It was edited from this manuscript, with rudimentary apparatus, by A.F. al-Ahwānī in the journal *Al-Kitāb* 5 (1952) 419–423, and reprinted, but without the apparatus, in his *Aḥwāl* 195–199. The text is translated here on the basis of the manuscript itself with the different readings in Ahwānī and my suggestions for improving the text indicated in the notes.

---

dd *Wa-kaṯīran* L, Mahdavī, Bīdārfar; *wa-kaṯīr* B.

ee "The essential texts:" *al-fuṣūṣ* L, and Bīdārfar; *al-quṣūṣ* [!] B; *an-nuṣūṣ* Mahdavī. For the word *fuṣūṣ* see above, T3, § 6 and note 19; T12, § 3.

ff Reading *ḫafāʾihā* with B L, Bīdārfar; *ḫafāʾan* Mahdavī.

---

20 In all likelihood this commentary formed part of Avicenna's early work, *The Available and the Valid*. See W3.

21 Literally, "that whose omission cannot be concealed and whose mention is not obligatory/appropriate (*yabrudu*)."

On the Rational Soul

In the Name of God, the Merciful, the Compassionate.

God bless our Master, Muḥammad, and his family, and grant them peace.

Make [my task] easy, O my gracious Lord!

Praise be to God alone.

1. Know that human beings alone, to the exclusion of all other living beings, posses a faculty highly capable of grasping the intelligibles. This faculty is sometimes called rational soul, sometimes "soul at peace,"[1] sometimes sacred soul, sometimes spiritual spirit, sometimes commanding[a] spirit, sometimes good word, sometimes word that unites and separates, sometimes divine secret,[2] sometimes governing light, sometimes chief command-
73 ing light,[b] sometimes true heart, sometimes core of the self [*lubb*], sometimes understanding [*nuhan*], and sometimes brains [*ḥijan*].[3] It exists in every single human being, young or old, adolescent or adult, insane or sane, sick or sound.

---

[a] The MS has *ʾmry*, which in all likelihood is to be read *āmirī*, i.e., commanding, rather than *amrī*, or, if one were slightly to emend it, *amīrī*. This would be the Arabic word corresponding to the Persian one Avicenna cites in the next line; see next note.

[b] The MS has, *wa-tāratan nūran isfahbadiyyan*, omitted by Ahwānī. *Ispahbad̠* is Persian for army chief, an ancient title also used in Islamic times until the Mongol invasions; see the article by Bosworth in *EI*², IV,207–208. The spelling of the word is interesting, if it reflects the usage by Avicenna and his environment; cf. Bosworth's article 207b for other Arabic variants.

---

[1] This is a reference to the Qur'ānic description of the soul that enters heaven (89:27–30): "O soul at peace,/ return unto thy Lord, well-pleased, well-pleasing!/ Enter thou among my servants!/ Enter thou My Paradise!" (Arberry's translation).

[2] Or perhaps "self" in the sense of core of the self, *sirr*. Cf. Goichon "Sirr."

[3] The practice of forming ecumenical lists to identify the same object in different intellectual and religious traditions comes from the multi-cultural early Islamic environment which generated the historiography of religions and heresiography. In Avicenna's context, it can be seen in the work by a member of the Jayhānī family of viziers to the Sāmānid rulers (see the article by Pellat in *EI*², Supplement, 265–266), who wrote on Zoroaster and who is quoted by Šahrastānī in his *al-Milal wa-n-niḥal* at the end of the section on Zoroaster: the passage in Šahrastānī, missing in the earlier editions, was first brought to light by M. b. Tavit et-Tanci, "Şehristanî'nin kitab'ul-milel ve'n-nihal'i," *İlâhiyat Fakültesi Dergisi* (Ankara Üniversitesi) 5 (1956) 1–16. Jayhānī there identifies the Zoroastrian divine power governing the universe with, among others, the active intellect of the philosophers, the Christian Holy Ghost, and the Qur'ānic "spirit," *rūḥ*, mentioned in the *Sūrat al-Qadr* (97:4), "the angels and the Spirit descend" (Arberry). The similarity in practice and contents of the lists in Jayhānī and Avicenna, even if one is talking about a divine faculty and the other human, cannot be accidental, given the latter's Sāmānid upbringing.

2. At the beginning of its existence this faculty is devoid of the forms of the intelligibles, and from this point of view it is then called material intellect.

3. Next there come about in it the forms of the primary intelligibles, which are concepts whose truth is Ascertained without [the use of] syllogisms or [a process of] learning and acquisition. They are called the starting point of intellections,[4] general notions, and natural primary knowledges, like, for example, the knowledge that the whole is greater than the part, and that a single body cannot occupy two places at the same time, or be simultaneously wholly black and white, existent and non-existent.[5] Through these forms, the faculty is prepared[c] to acquire the secondary intelligibles either by means of Thinking, which is an act of finding what ⟨results from⟩[d] these primary intelligibles by [their] composition and combination [to form definitions and syllogisms], or by means of Correct Guessing, which is the representation of the middle term in the faculty all at once[e] and without

---

[c] Reading *wa-tatahayya'u bi-hāḏihi ṣ-ṣuwar* for *wa-yatahayya'u* (*yutahayya'u*?) *bi-hāḏihi l-quwwa* in the MS and the edition.

[d] Reading *mā* ⟨*yaḥṣulu*⟩ *min* for *mā fī* in the text. As it stands, the text means, "finding out what these primary intelligibles contain by composition and combination," which makes no sense; the contents of the primary intelligibles are self-evident. For the emendation cf. *Naǧāt* 102/170–171: *fa-yartasimu ḥīna'iḏin fī l-ʿaqli l-maʿānī l-ūlā bi-t-taṣawwur, ṯumma yurakkabu minhā l-ḥudūdu* (text according to Dānešpažūh): "Thereupon the primary notions are impressed on the intellect by means of concept formation, and then definitions are composed out of them;" cf. Gutas "Empiricism" section V, L6.

[e] Reading *dufʿatan* only, without *wāḥidatan* as in Ahwānī, which is not in the MS.

---

[4] "Starting point of intellections," *bidāyat al-ʿuqūl*. Marmura "Avicenna's Thought" 340a made the excellent suggestion that the phrase should read, *badā'ih al-ʿuqūl*, presumably meaning (Marmura did not himself translate the phrase), "self-evident truths of intellects" which come naturally to the human mind, since Marmura translated the word *badīha* in the *Ilāhiyyāt* of *The Cure* as "innate/natural intelligence" (Marmura *Metaphysics* 40.32, 113.16 and 24; *badīha*, however, here as well as in *Naǧāt* 287/357, is used in a general way and not as a technical epistemological term). The MS has the skeletal form of the word without pointing for the *yā'* and *tā' marbūṭa*, so either reading would have the authority of our single witness. However, in the various discussions of the primary notions (*awwaliyyāt*) which Avicenna is mentioning here, he never once throughout his works does he use the word *badīha—badā'ih* to refer to these notions; the terms for natural intelligence and its operations that he uses are always *fiṭra*, *ġarīza* (as here in the next phrase), and *jibilla* (see Gutas "Empiricism" sections V–VI). I thus prefer to keep *bidāya* and understand *ʿuqūl* as the plural of the *maṣdar*, "intellections;" cf. the plural of the *maṣdar*, *afhām*, in T9, §1 and note 1.

[5] Cf. the same examples used by Avicenna in his very first work, T1, §2.

Thinking or considering. By "middle term" I mean the cause which makes acknowledging the existence or non-existence of a thing necessary—i.e., the evidence which justifies the judgment—and this sometimes comes about following search and a desire to attain the intelligibles, and sometimes initially, without desire or search; and whenever the evidence is attained, so is invariably that for which the evidence is provided.[f]

4. Through these acquired intelligibles this faculty next assumes an aspect and a state by means of which it is ready to call to presence the intelligibles whenever it wishes without needing to acquire them. This aspect is called *habitus* [disposition], and the faculty, in this state and from this point
74 of view, is called actual intellect. When the intelligibles are actually present in the faculty as being observed and represented[g] in it, then from this point of view it is called acquired intellect.[6]

5. This rational soul is a substance subsisting by itself, and is imprinted neither in a human body nor in any other corporeal entity. On the contrary, it is separable and abstracted from material and corporeal entities. It has a certain association with the human body as long as the person is alive, but this association is not like the relation [*taʿalluq*] of a thing to its receptacle; it is, rather, like the relation of a wielder of an instrument to the instrument. [This substance] comes into existence together with the body, not before, but it does not perish when the body perishes and dies; it survives, rather, as it was, except that ⟨it attains, after⟩[h] its association with the body is severed,[7] either bliss and pleasure or misery and pain.

---

[f] Reading *wa-mahmā ḥaṣala d-dalīlu, ḥaṣala l-madlūlu lā maḥālata* with the MS and the *Al-Kitāb* version of the edition.

[g] Reading *mušāhadatan mutamaṯṯilatan*, as in the parallel passage from the *Išārāt* II.3,10, 126.13/242.13.

[h] The text seems to be defective. For the words included in the angular brackets here Ahwānī provides the following: *illā annahu* ⟨*taḥṣulu lahu ḥālatun tusammā ʿindamā* [!]⟩ *tanqaṭiʿu ʿalāqatuhu … saʿādatan*. I suggest *illā annahu* ⟨*yanālu baʿda an*⟩ *tanqaṭiʿa ʿalāqatuhu … saʿādatan*. See also note 6.

---

[6] Cf. the very similar exposition of the subject in the passage from *Pointers and Reminders* translated below, Chapter 3.2, L11.

[7] I.e., after death. The text in the MS, as a matter of fact, adds, "that is, after the severance of the association through death" (*ay baʿda nqiṭāʿi l-ʿalāqati bi-l-mawt*). This could hardly have been what Avicenna wrote, however, and it looks like a marginal scribal gloss incorporated at some point into the main text.

6. The bliss [of the rational soul][i] comes about when its substance is rendered perfect,[8] and this is accomplished when it is purified through knowledge of God and works for God. Its purification through works for God consists of (a) its being purged of vile and wicked qualities of character, (b) its being far removed[j] from blameworthy attributes and evil and offensive habits by following reason and religious law, and (c) its being adorned with good habits, praiseworthy qualities of character, and excellent and pleasing traits by following reason and religious law.

7. Its purification through knowledge of God consists of its attainment a disposition of its own, by means of which it is ready to call all the intelligibles to presence whenever it wishes without needing to acquire them, and thus to have all the intelligibles present in it in actuality, or in a potentiality that is as close to actuality as possible.[9] The soul then becomes like a polished mirror upon which are reflected the forms of things as they are in themselves[10] 75
without any distortion, and whenever it stands face to face with them having been purified through knowledge, there ensues [an automatic] practicing of the theoretical philosophical sciences.

8. Purification through works is accomplished by methods mentioned in books on Ethics and by assiduous performance of religious duties, both legal and traditional, such as observances relating to [the functions of] the body, one's property, and to a combination of the two. For being restrained at the places where religious law and its statutes place such restraints,[k] and undertaking to submit to its commands, have a beneficial effect on subjugating the soul that "incites to evil" [and thus transforming it] into the rational soul which is "at peace,"[11] i.e., making the bodily faculties of the soul, the appetitive and the irascible, subservient to the rational soul which is "at peace."

---

[i] The text has the masculine pronoun (*saʿādatuhu*), presumably referring to the substance (*jawhar*) of the soul, but in the context only the soul can be meant.

[j] Reading *wa-taqdīsuhu* with the MS for *wa-taqwīmuhu* conjectured by Ahwānī.

[k] Reading with the MS, *fa-inna li-l-wuqūf ʿinda tawqīfāt* for *fa-inna* ⟨*fī*⟩ *l-wuqūf ʿinda marḍiyāt* printed by Ahwānī.

---

[8] "To render perfect," *takmīl*, is naturally to be understood in the Aristotelian sense of *entelecheia*, "to bring out into full actuality."

[9] That is, to attain the stages of acquired intellect and actual intellect, respectively.

[10] Cf. the similar turn of phrase used by Avicenna to describe the contents of *The Easterners* in the Prologue to *The Cure*, T9, § 4.

[11] The reference is again to a Qurʾānic verse, 12:53: "Surely the soul of man incites to evil" (Arberry). For the "soul at peace" that follows see above, note 1.

9. Now it has become clear in the physical sciences that personal qualities and habits follow the temperament of the body,[12] in the sense that the dominant characteristics of a phlegmatic (a person whose temperament is dominated by phlegm) are sedateness, dignity, and forbearance, a choleric (he whose temperament is dominated by yellow bile) anger, and a melancholic (he whose temperament is dominated by black bile) ill disposition. Each one of these [humors], furthermore, is followed by other qualities of character which we shall not mention here. There is thus no doubt that temperament is subject to change, in which case qualities of character are also subject to change thereby; and it is for this reason that the performance of the exercises mentioned in books on Ethics is specified. Whenever a person's temperament is balanced, his qualities of character are easily refined; his balanced temperament is thus influential in this process. The unbalanced temperament, on the other hand, is that which is overpowered by one or two of its four elements (when, for example, it is either hotter or drier than it ought to be, or both hotter and drier than it ought to be[l]). Since these four elements are [two pairs of elements that are] opposite to each other, the unbalanced temperament will be constituted of either one [excessive] opposite [element] or two opposite [elements in combination], whereas
76 the balanced temperament is the one which lacks these opposites[m] (that is, it will have [an excess of] neither heat [alone] nor cold [alone] but a quality intermediate between the two, nor humidity and dryness [alone] but a quality intermediate between the two[n]).[13] The closer a temperament

---

[l] The last phrase, *aw aḥarr wa-aybas maʿan mimmā yanbaġī* is omitted by Ahwānī.

[m] "Whereas … these opposites," adding from the MS, *wa-ammā l-mizāj al-muʿtadil fa-huwa llaḏī ʿadima hāḏihi l-aḍdād*, omitted by Ahwānī.

[n] "Nor humidity … the two," adding from the MS, *wa-laysa fīhi ruṭūbatun wa-yubūsatun bal kayfiyyatun mutawassiṭatun baynahumā*, omitted by Ahwānī.

---

[12] Galen wrote a book by this title, *That the Faculties of the Soul Are Consequent upon the Temperaments of the Body* (IV.767–822 Kühn, new edition by Athena Bazou, Athens: Academy of Athens, 2011), which was translated into Arabic and widely discussed in medical, physiological, and psychological writings. For the Arabic translation see Biesterfeldt. "Temperament" here is to be understood in its traditional sense, i.e., the particular blending (*krasis*, *mizāj*) of the four humors (blood, phlegm, black bile, yellow bile) which were thought to determine a person's mental and emotional constitution. This theory lies behind the etymology of the word idiosyncrasy, i.e., one's own particular blend of humors. Cf. the words "phlegmatic," "choleric," and "melancholic" next explained by Avicenna in the text.

[13] The excess of a single element produces the simple unbalanced temperament, while

is to a balanced state, the more is a person predisposed to develop excellent traits in both his knowledge and his works.

10. It has also become clear in the ⟨Physical⟩ sciences that the celestial bodies are not constituted from a mixture of these four elements but are totally lacking in these opposites. Furthermore, it is only the involvement with these opposites that hinders the reception of the divine effluence, by which I mean the inspiration coming from the Lord, occurring all at once and revealing some intellective truth. The closer, therefore, a temperament is to a balanced state, the more is a person predisposed to receive this effluence. Since the celestial bodies are totally devoid of the opposites, they are receptive to the divine effluence; human beings, on the other hand, no matter how balanced their temperaments may be, are not free from defects [due to the involvement with] the opposites. As long as the rational soul is associated with the human body, no corporeal entity [*jirm*] can be completely ready to receive[o] the divine effluence or have perfectly revealed to it all the intelligibles. But when a person expends all his efforts to purify [his rational soul] through knowledge, acquires the propensity for contact with the divine effluence (i.e., with the intellective substance which is the medium of the divine effluence and which is called "angel" in the language of Revelation and "active intellect" in philosophical terminology), has a balanced temperament, and lacks these opposites which hinder his reception of the divine effluence, then there comes about in him a certain similarity[p] to the celestial bodies and he resembles through this purification the seven mighty ones, i.e., the seven celestial spheres. When the association of the soul with the body is severed through death, something which is designated with the expression "separation of the form from the receivers"—for the appellation "form" may be applied to the soul and the appellation "the receiver of the soul" may be applied to the body, even if the meaning of this "receiving" is unlike that of a receptacle "receiving" what occupies it, but is rather like that of a place where an activity occurs "receiving" the activity: the body "receives" the activity of the soul, and from this point of view it is

[o] Reading *lā yaṣfū ⟨li-⟩qabūl.*

[p] Reading *fa-šākala* with the MS for *fa-šābaha* printed by Ahwānī, though the meaning is the same.

the excess of one element formed from the combination of two opposite elements produces the composite unbalanced temperament. For a concise account of humoral physiology see Ullmann *Medicine* 55–64.

77 possible (a) to call the body "receiver of the soul," (b) to call the soul "form," and (c) to designate the severance of the association between the two with the expression "separation of the form from the receivers"—when, then, this separation occurs after the soul has acquired excellent traits in its knowledge and works, and the obstacle that hindered it from receiving the divine effluence in its totality ceases to exist (the obstacle being the association of [the soul with the body, which consists of] its activity in the body), then the soul[q] will receive the divine effluence, will have revealed to it whatever was hidden from it before the separation, and there will come about it a similarity with the abstract intellects which are the principles of the causes of beings, since all the truths are revealed to these intellects. (You know that God Almighty first created an intellect, then by its means another intellect and a celestial sphere, then by means of the other intellect a third intellect and a second celestial sphere, and so on in the order we mentioned; the intellects, then, are the principles of the causes.)[r]

11. This, then, is what we wished to mention on this occasion in explanation of this divine word.[14] As for the demonstrative proof establishing that the rational soul is a substance, subsists by itself, is free of any corporeality, is not imprinted on any corporeal entity, survives after the death of the human body, and whether its condition after death is one of blessing or punishment, it involves a long and elaborate investigation and can be brought to light only after numerous premisses have been mentioned. As a matter of fact, I happened to write at the beginning of my career forty years ago a summary treatise[15] setting forth the knowledge about the soul and related matters by following the method of those who engage in philosophy through research;[16] whoever wishes to find out about the soul should study this trea-

---

[q] The pronoun is again masculine, which could refer, strictly speaking, to *jins* or *jawhar*; the meaning, however, is clear.

[r] Ahwānī adds here instead of in his apparatus three paraphrased quotations from the preceding text, which, as he notes, must be some marginal material copied into the text by an inadvertent scribe. They do not belong in Avicenna's text.

---

[14] I.e., the rational soul; cf. the list of names for it given above, paragraph 1. Landauer 338.4 assumes the reference to be to metaphysics ("metaphy."?).

[15] The reference is to the *Compendium on the Soul* (W1), from which the passage in T1 is extracted. Cf. Landauer 336–339.

[16] "Those who engage in philosophy through research:" *ahl al-ḥikma al-baḥṯiyya*, literally, "those of research philosophy;" i.e., those who use the method of logical demonstration and syllogisms, as implied in the preceding sentence. They are contrasted to the experiential philosophers following next. See the discussion in Chapter 3.2 at the end.

tise because it is suitable for students who do research. But God Almighty
"guides whomsoever He will"[17] to the way of those who engage in philosophy
through direct experience[18]—may He put us and you in the latter group! He 78
is in charge of such a thing, capable of it!

Praise be to God, Lord of the worlds.

God bless the best among the best of mankind, our Master Muḥammad, the members of his family, the good and pure, and all his companions.

---

17 A frequent Qurʾānic phrase which normally reads, "God guides whomsoever He will to a straight path:" Q2:142, Q2:213, etc. (Arberry translation).

18 "Those who engage in philosophy through direct experience:" *ahl al-ḥikma aḏ-ḏawqiyya*, literally, "those of philosophy by tasting," i.e., experiential philosophy. Toward the end of his life Avicenna developed the concept of "tasting", *ḏawq*, to express the intellectual pleasure (*al-laḏḏa al-ʿaqliyya*) enjoyed by those who have become adept at engaging in philosophy through syllogistic means (and Guessing Correctly the middle term) to such an extent that they gain a familiarity or intimacy (*alf*) with the intelligibles and a disposition or habit for them (*malaka*). At this point their experience of the intelligibles is such that "even though it is accompanied by the middle term it is as if it doesn't need it." See briefly below, Chapter 8.2.2, and the fuller discussion and related texts on this subject in Gutas "Absence of Mysticism" 365–369. For experiential knowledge in Avicenna and the later development of terminology with *ḏawq* in Ġazālī see Treiger *Inspired Knowledge* 60–63.

CHAPTER TWO

AN INVENTORY AND RELATIVE CHRONOLOGY OF AVICENNA'S MAJOR PHILOSOPHICAL WORKS. THEIR ORGANIZATION AND CONTENTS IN RELATION TO THE ARISTOTELIAN TRADITION

Introduction

After a youth spent in tranquillity in Buḫārā, Avicenna led an itinerant and turbulent life. His literary output, which spanned a period of more than forty years, was nevertheless immense. His works seem to approach one hundred, although their precise number has yet to be determined; they are extant in hundreds of manuscripts, while an equally large number of writings attributed to him and extant in as many manuscripts is apparently spurious or misattributed.

The transmission of Avicenna's works is extremely complicated. This is as much due to the peculiar way in which they were composed and distributed as it is to external factors affecting their preservation. His disciple and biographer, Jūzjānī, writes that Avicenna was very liberal with his works "and showed little interest in keeping copies [for himself]. ... [T]hese were widely dispersed and ... people who owned a copy of them Withheld them [from others]; as for him, it was not his habit to save a copy for himself, just as it was not his habit to make a clean copy from his holograph or transcribe [a holograph] from his rough draft: he would only either dictate or himself write the copy and give it to the person who had commissioned it from him" (T7, §§1–2). Another aspect of Avicenna's method of composition which Jūzjānī does not mention but which is crucial for establishing the relative chronology of the works is that Avicenna frequently copied entire passages from earlier works in later ones. This fact is also significant in enabling us to estimate the works of which Avicenna had kept copies. "Moreover," to quote Jūzjānī again, "he suffered from successive misfortunes, and disasters destroyed his books" (T7, §2). At the time of his death, the spread of Avicenna's books was thus in a rather chaotic state. Valiant efforts were made by successive generations of disciples and bibliographers, writing in the grand tradition of Arabic bibliography, to draw up accurate and complete lists of his works. In these lists, constantly new titles appear; some of these are obviously

spurious, but others are just as obviously authentic: some are variant titles of
80 works already known, others may be the lost commissioned pieces Jūzjānī talked about which resurfaced in the libraries of the descendants of the original sponsors. All this information has to be assessed and harmonized with the additional information about the transmission of a work contained in the preserved manuscripts (scribal and owners' notes) as well as with the internal evidence of the works themselves.[1]

The bibliographies of Avicenna's works by Anawati *Mu'allafāt* (1950), Mahdavī (1954), and Ergin (second edition, 1956), superseding the earlier one by Brockelmann *GAL* (1937), and the early lists of Avicenna's works collected and rationalized by Gohlman (1974) and presented in tabular form in the Tetrapla in the Appendix, manage, despite their inevitable imperfections, to bring this vast amount of source material under some kind of control and make it readily accessible. Mahdavī's bibliography is by far the most useful. In addition to listing the extant manuscripts, the incipits and explicits, and contents of the works—information also provided by Anawati—Mahdavī discusses, at times extensively, their origin and date. In a brief appendix, Gohlman describes the difficulties inherent in dating Avicenna's works and presents some of them in a rough chronological order, grouping them under the headings of works written in Buḫārā (before 392/1002), in Gurgānj (392/1002–402/1012), in Jurjān (402/1012–405/1014), in Rayy (405/1014–1015), in Hamaḏān (405/1015–415/1024), and in Iṣfahān (415/1024–428/1037).

Doubtless more manuscripts will be discovered in the future, some of those already known will be reevaluated and reassigned to a different work or rejected, the extant lists of works will be edited and studied with greater detail and accuracy, a complete collection of testimonia for each work will be compiled, and the chronological order of all the works will be established with greater certainty. At this stage, however, the task at hand is to prepare, with the material already available, a critical and descriptive catalogue raisonné of Avicenna's works by taking into consideration all of the factors decribed above, and to gain a clearer picture of the range and extent of Avicenna's authentic works by distinguishing them more sharply and

[1] See the synoptic tables of the titles listed in the four early bibliographies of Avicenna's works (Tetrapla) and their Inventory in the Appendix. Additional remarks about the "disastrous affair" of the preservation and transmission of Avicenna's works can be read in Reisman *Avicennan Tradition* 21–23, an exemplary study for the conduct of research I adumbrate in my last sentences above.

accurately from the pseudepigraphic and spurious. This task is accomplished in the Appendix. The purpose of this chapter is to present a critical inventory of the major philosophical works which are essential for the subject of the study that follows.

For each work treated, I will discuss the occasion, date, and details of its composition, and wherever relevant, trace the history of its transmission. This will be followed by a description of its contents, which intends to give a clear picture of the relation of the work to its predecessors and successors, including information about passages copied, and, consonant with the aim of this study, to assess its position relative to the canon of Aristotle's writings.

My selection of what I consider "major philosophical works" certainly 81
includes works universally acknowledged as "major," but it is also based on a criterion dictated by the subject of this book, namely, the extent to which a given work by Avicenna contributes to our understanding of the way in which he received, modified, and transmitted the Aristotelian tradition, thereby transforming the history of philosophy. I have thus included titles which although they may not be considered as major absolutely, nevertheless constitute important landmarks in the transformation of the Aristotelian tradition at the hands of Avicenna. In presenting the particulars of the composition of most of these works and dating them, my main purpose has been to establish their relative chronology only because absolute dating could not be offered consistently. Apart from the works for which it has been possible to give absolute dates on the basis of external evidence, the remaining can be dated only on the basis of Avicenna's age when he wrote them; converting his age into absolute dates, however, would necessarily have to depend on his birthdate, and this is uncertain.[2] An investigation of Avicenna's birthdate and a detailed description of the events in his life and their dates on the basis of all available evidence, and especially the private correspondence and private documents of Avicenna, are the subject of a much needed critical biography,[3] clearly beyond the scope of this study.

---

[2] The best exposition of the problems associated with dating the year of Avicenna's birth in 370/980 is again Sellheim's review of Ergin, pp. 232–239, overlooked by Gohlman, as Ullmann notes in his review of the latter. Further documentation along the lines suggested by Sellheim I provide in the Appendix of Gutas "*Maḏhab*." Although it is difficult to establish the exact date of his birth, it has become clear that it is much earlier than the traditionally cited year 370/980, which is no longer tenable.

[3] Biographies of Avicenna in many languages naturally abound, but none is completely satisfactory. Useful collections of all the traditional material, but with little critical analysis,

Each section below is introduced by the title of the work to be discussed,
followed by the serial number of the work assigned to it in the Inventory in
the Appendix; references to the numbers in the bibliographies of A[nawati]
and M[ahdavī] will be found there. Readers without Arabic may refer to
Anawati's "Tradition manuscrite" in French, where the same numbers of the
82 works have been used as those in his Arabic bibliography. The numbers after
the full names (and not only the initials) of Anawati and Mahdavī refer to
the pages in their works.

Work 1. *Compendium on the Soul* (*Kitāb fī n-Nafs ʿalā sunnat al-iḫtiṣār*) [GP 10]

Avicenna began his career as an author, at the age of seventeen, with a short treatise on the soul in ten chapters, dedicated to the Sāmānid ruler in Buḫārā, Nūḥ b. Manṣūr.[1] Avicenna refers to it in his introduction simply as "a book on the soul after the fashion of compendia," as entered above, but it has been given various titles in the bibliographical and manuscript traditions in order to distinguish it from the other works which he wrote on the subject. I have labeled it his "Dissertation" because it was written when he had completed what can be called his "graduate" education.[2]

The date of its composition was established quite convincingly by Landauer, who was the first to edit and translate it in German.[3] The most

---

are offered by the biographies written by three Iranian scholars, among others: Z. Safa, *Le Livre du Millénaire d'Avicenne* [Collection du Millénaire d'Avicenne, no. 27], Tehran 1953, 1–53 (French translation of the first part of the author's *Sargoḏašt va ta'līfāt va aš'ār va ārā'-ye Ebn-e Sīnā*, Tehran Š1331); Nafīsī *Pūr-e Sīnā*; A. Riḍvānī, *Abū 'Alī Sīnā*, Tehran Š1344. Anawati once mentioned ("Tradition manuscrite" 413n1) that Mahmoud El-Khodeiri had undertaken to compile a detailed biography of Avicenna, a project apparently unfinished because of El-Khodeiri's death (see the obituaries in *MIDEO* 6[1959–1961]533–560).—The available categories of sources, with a discussion of their relationship and the tasks of the future biographer, are analyzed in Gutas "Biography" 67–68. For an appreciation of the benefits that will accrue to the biography of Avicenna from a study of his private documents see the references in Chapter 1, note 1.

[1] A readily available survey of the Sāmānid dynasty in Ḫurāsān and Transoxania (204/819–395/1005) is the article "The Sāmānids" by Richard N. Frye in *The Cambridge History of Iran*, Cambridge: Cambridge University Press, 1975, IV,136–161. A chronology of the house with brief historical account is also offered by Clifford E. Bosworth, *The New Islamic Dynasties*, New York: Columbia University Press, 1996, 170–171.

[2] See Chapter 3.1.

[3] Landauer 336–339. Landauer's arguments are reproduced in English by van Dyck *Offering* 18–19.

compelling argument Landauer adduced is based on the internal evidence provided by Avicenna's last treatise, *On the Rational Soul*:

> … [T]he demonstrative proof establishing that the rational soul is a substance, subsists by itself, is free of any corporeality, is not imprinted on any corporeal entity, survives after the death of the human body, and whether its condition after death is one of blessing or punishment … involves a long and elaborate investigation and can be brought to light only after numerous premisses have been mentioned. As a matter of fact, I happened to write at the beginning of my career forty years ago a summary treatise setting forth the knowledge about the soul and related matters by following the method of those who engage in philosophy through research; whoever wishes to find out about the soul should study this treatise because it is appropriate for students who do research. [T14, § 11]

The list of the subjects given in this passage as treated by Avicenna in the earlier treatise corresponds quite accurately with chapters 9 and 10 (in the table of contents given below); particularly significant is Avicenna's mention of the "demonstrative proofs" (*barāhīn*) used to establish that the soul is a substance, because in chapter 9 of the *Compendium* Avicenna makes a point to
present demonstrative syllogisms, as opposed to mere "arguments" (*ḥujaj*) 83
presented elsewhere.[4] By Avicenna's own admission, therefore, his first work was on the soul and its contents fit those of the *Compendium*. Next, having correctly noted that the dedication to the Prince in the *Compendium* is written with an obsequiousness unparalleled in the other writings of Avicenna, Landauer inferred that it must have been dedicated to the first ruler with whom Avicenna had ever had dealings, namely Nūḥ b. Manṣūr. His inference is corroborated by Alpago's Latin translation of the *Compendium* which states at the very beginning that the work was dedicated "to Nūḥ, the King of Ḫurāsān."[5] Avicenna states in his Autobiography that he became proficient in medicine when he was sixteen (T3, § 7) and that he was subsequently summoned to Nūḥ's court to treat him. Landauer, assuming the traditional date of Avicenna's birth (370/980) to be correct, calculated that this could have taken place at the earliest in 386/996. Since forty lunar years after Nūḥ's

[4] For the difference between argument and proof in Avicenna see below, Chapter 3.3A and L18.

[5] *Ad Nuch regem Corrasan*, Alpago 1. Avicenna refers to the ruler as *amīr* in the dedication of this treatise (Landauer 340–341) and as *sulṭān* in the Autobiography (T3, § 10); the Latin *rex* of Alpago may correspond to either one term, though the latter is more likely, assuming that the author who is responsible for the title in the Arabic manuscript from which Alpago translated picked this term from the Autobiography.

death (387/997) brings us to the year 427, well within Avicenna's lifetime (he died in 428/1037), Laundauer concluded that the *Compendium* must have been written between 996 and 997.[6]

Two minor objections can be raised to Landauer's calculations. First, the "forty years" mentioned by Avicenna in his *On the Rational Soul* need not be taken literally, and second, the year of his birth has still to be established with certainty. However, these objections affect only the absolute dating of the *Compendium* between the years 996–997; the relative chronology still stands, for there can be very little doubt, for the reasons already stated, that the *Compendium* was indeed Avicenna's first work. In addition to Avicenna's testimony in his *On the Rational Soul* and Landauer's arguments, it can also be mentioned that Avicenna's unique theory of *ḥads* (Guessing Correctly the middle term), present in all his writings on the soul, had not yet developed in the *Compendium*.[7]

It may be possible to ascertain with greater precision the age in which Avicenna wrote this work. Two considerations are of relevance: (a) The description of metaphysics in the *Compendium* is heavily indebted, even in its very wording, to that in Fārābī's *On the Purposes of the Metaphysics*.[8] In the
84 Autobiography Avicenna mentions that after he was sixteen, he spent a year and a half studying all the parts of philosophy again, and that metaphysics was the last subject he mastered, with the help of Fārābī's book (T3, §§ 8–9). He was thus about seventeen and a half when he discovered Fārābī's book and he could accordingly have written the *Compendium* only after that time. (b) In the introduction of the *Compendium* Avicenna says that after "industrious scrutiny of the books of learned men (*kutub al-ʿulamāʾ*)," he found out that the subject of the faculties of the soul was among the hardest; a paragraph later he repeats that he "had read in the books of the ancients (*kutub al-awāʾil*)" how they undertook to study the soul upon being inspired from the saying "know yourself so that you may know your Lord" inscribed on the Temple of Asclepius.[9] This implies wide reading which, given that the *Compendium* was written over forty years before Avicenna's death, most likely took place in the royal library, as described in the Autobiography.

---

[6] Mahdavī 242 made the same calculation and came to the same conclusion, except that the Hijra year of the composition of the work is(mis-?) written as 378 (988) instead of 387 (997). In 378, according to this reckoning from the alleged date of Avicenna's birth, 370, he was eight years old.

[7] See the texts on this subject and the discussion in Chapter 3.2.

[8] See T1, § 3.IV, and Chapter 6.1 for discussion.

[9] Landauer 340.11–13, 341.1–4.

At about the same time that he discovered Fārābī's book, Avicenna was summoned to the royal court to help the physicians cure the ailing Nūḥ b. Manṣūr. He was successful and was enrolled in Nūḥ's service. Then, he continues,

> One day I asked his permission to enter [the physicians'] library, look through it, and read its contents. He gave me permission .... I looked through the catalogue of books by the ancients (*kutub al-awāʾil*) and requested those which I needed. I saw books whose very names are unknown to many and which I had never seen before nor have I seen since. I read those books, mastered their teachings, and realized how far each man had advanced in his science. So by the time I reached my eighteenth year I had completed my study in all these Philosophical Sciences. [T3, §§ 10–11]

The *Compendium* presupposes—and reflects—the learning acquired during the approximately six months spent in the royal library, a period of study which I have labeled Avicenna's "graduate education" (Chapter 3.1). The result was the treatise on the soul, dedicated to Nūḥ apparently in gratitude for the favor of allowing him to visit the library, and written between the ages of seventeen and a half and eighteen.

The contents of the work are listed by Avicenna in a table which he provides at the end of his introduction. The chapter headings presented there are fuller and more descriptive than they are in their respective places within the text; I translate them therefore from the table of contents and mark significant variations in the notes.[10]

Introduction and dedication; table of contents.

1. Establishing [the existence of] the faculties of the soul, with whose detailed presentation and explanation I begin.
2. Primary division[a] of the faculties of the soul; absolute [generic][b] definition of the soul. 85
3. None of the faculties of the soul originates from the mixture of the four elements; instead they come upon it from without.

---

[a] "Primary division" (*bi-l-qisma al-ūlā*) is the correct reading in the body of the text (Landauer 344; cf. *al-aqsām al-uwal*, Landauer 345.6–7); the table of contents has, "division of the primary faculties of the soul," *taqsīm al-quwā n-nafsāniyya al-ūlā*.

[b] For "absolute" Avicenna has *ʿalā l-iṭlāq*, which he interprets in the chapter itself as follows: "Definition of the universal [*kulliyya*] soul, i.e., the absolute [*muṭlaqa*] and generic [*jinsiyya*] soul" (Landauer 345.7–8).

---

[10] The table of contents (Landauer 341–342) is also given by Anawati *Muʾallafāt* 160–161 and Mahdavī 243.

4. Detailed statement of the vegetative faculties; mention of the need for each one of them.
5. Detailed statement of the animal faculties; mention of the need for each one of them.
6. Detailed statement of the external senses[c]; how they perceive; differences of opinion concerning vision.[d]
7. Detailed statement of the internal senses and of the faculty that moves the body.
8. The stages of the human soul from inception to perfection [partial translation in T1, above].
9. That the rational[e] soul is a substance:[f] setting up the necessary[g] demonstrative proofs following the method of logic.
10. Setting up the argument for the existence of an intellective substance separable from corporeal entities, which functions like a source for the rational faculties[h] or like light for vision; declaration that the rational souls remain united with it after the death of the body,[i] secure from corruption and change: it[j] is what is called 'universal intellect.'[k]

Avicenna's choice of a subject for his very first work is indicative of the direction which his philosophical thought was to take throughout his life. The study of the human soul, and particularly its rational part according to the Aristotelian division, to which he repeatedly reverted in numerous works throughout his career, constitutes the cornerstone of his philosophy. The
86 reason for this is that the study of the rational soul provides access to all the philosophical sciences as classified in the Aristotelian tradition: the focus of this study is epistemology (i.e., the acquisition by the rational soul of the intelligible forms), which leads to a study of ontology (i.e., the totality of the intelligible forms constitutes ontology), and the different aspects of ontol-

[c] The chapter heading in the treatise has instead "the five senses" (Landauer 353).

[d] The chapter heading omits the last phrase (Landauer 353).

[e] The chapter heading omits "rational" (Landauer 365).

[f] The chapter heading in the treatise adds, "and does not need the body to subsist" (Landauer 365).

[g] The chapter heading omits "necessary" (Landauer 365).

[h] The chapter heading has instead, "the human souls" (Landauer 370).

[i] "Declaration ... body:" the chapter heading reads, "establishing that when souls separate from corporeal entities they are united with it" (Landauer 370).

[j] I.e., the intellective substance, reading *wa-huwa l-musammā bi-l-ʿaql al-kullī*, with the Istanbul MS Üniversite 4755, fol. 104[b], and the body of the text itself in that chapter (Landauer 371.18–19). The table of contents in Landauer 342 and in both Anawati *Muʾallafāt* and Mahdavī read *wa-hiya*, the feminine pronoun, which in the context would have to be understood as referring to the "rational souls," which is wrong; it should be emended to read *wa-huwa*, as just cited.

[k] The chapter heading omits everything after "body."

ogy are studied in the various sciences of the Aristotelian canon. Thus epistemology reproduces ontology, and ontology reflects epistemology, i.e., by studying how one knows and what one knows, one studies the Aristotelian sciences, i.e., all philosophy, or as we shall discuss later, all knowledge: Logic, the instrument for further study; the theoretical sciences, Physics, Mathematics, and Metaphysics; and the practical sciences, and particularly Ethics, which render the rational soul pure enough to receive the intelligible forms.[11]

This direction which Avicenna's philosophy was to take is dramatically illustrated already in the *Compendium*, Chapter 8, translated above as Text 1. While discussing "the stages of the rational soul from inception to perfection," Avicenna describes the path which the intellect has to traverse in order to progress from the stage of pure potentiality to that of total actuality. This path is nothing else but the philosophical sciences as classified in the Aristotelian tradition, and it constitutes a blueprint, or an outline, of the comprehensive works he was to write in the future.

How did Avicenna come to treat of this subject, and why did he treat it in this way? In the introduction of the *Compendium* he merely says that he decided to write on this aspect of the philosophical sciences because he found "the researches on the faculties of the soul [were] among the most recalcitrant to having their Validity Determined[l] by thought, and the most blind[m] in their methods (Landauer 340.12–13)." This is not very illuminating; Avicenna took issue with the Aristotelian tradition on a number of crucial subjects (as we shall discuss below, Chapter 6), and for any one of them he could have said that they could not be easily ascertained. One 87
inference that might conceivably be drawn from his statement is that he found the methods of previous researches defective because he himself had

[l] To Determine Validity: *taḥṣīl*. In a long footnote Landauer (373n3) showed that the form *ḥaṣṣala* was used in the Graeco-Arabic translations to render *horizō*, and hence *muḥaṣṣal* = *hōrismenos*. Additional evidence, with full consideration of all the lexicographical data, was presented by Kutsch, though he had overlooked Landauer's note. From this it becomes clear that the meaning for *taḥṣīl* = "études, connaissances, savoir, sagesse" given by Dozy derives from the original concept of "determining, discriminating." The expression frequently used by Avicenna (and others), *al-muḥaṣṣil min al-ḥukamāʾ*, thus means "a philosopher who has ascertained, Verified, and Determined the Validity of the facts for himself." See Chapter 3.3E.

[m] For "most blind of the researches" Avicenna uses *aʿmā-hā*, an example of the elative use of a defect adjective. Cf. Reckendorf 116 and see the references in Manfred Ullmann, *Arabische Komparativsätze*, Nachr. d. Akad. d. Wiss. in Göttingen, 1985, Nr. 7, p. [3], note 2.

[11] This subject is discussed fully below, Chapter 3.2.

a good idea about how to proceed, and the organization of the *Compendium* informs us about it. In general, Avicenna follows the order of the discussion in Aristotle's *De anima*, but for the most part the organization and specific treatment of individual questions are relatively unprecedented in the extant Aristotelian tradition. The history of the discussions on the soul in the late Greek tradition is poorly documented,[12] while in the Arabic tradition up to the time of Avicenna there is nothing that is extant which might be considered as its predecessor, especially with regard to structure. This is an area where fruitful research can be conducted in the future to assess the extent of Avicenna's digression from tradition (or, affirmatively put, originality) in his maiden literary effort.

Work 2. *The Compilation*, or *Philosophy for ʿArūḍī* (*al-Majmūʿ*; *al-Ḥikma al-ʿArūḍiyya*) [GS 2]

In his Autobiography Avicenna says that a neighbor of his in Buḫārā, a certain Abū-l-Ḥasan Aḥmad ibn-ʿAbdallāh al-ʿArūḍī (full name given at the end of the work, f. 84[a] = 164 Ṣāliḥ), i.e., "the Prosodist," commissioned him to write a comprehensive work on philosophy ("this Knowledge," *hāḏā l-ʿilm*, T3, § 12). The youthful Avicenna complied, and thus was born the first medieval philosophical summa which can be said to have signaled the beginning of scholastic philosophy. The work was his first attempt to treat in a systematic fashion and within the confines of a single book all the branches of theoretical philosophy according to the Aristotelian classification, as already outlined in the *Compendium on the Soul*.[1] This "habilitation," as I have labeled it (Chapter 3.1), which lends credence to Avicenna's stylized account of his philosophical studies, actualized the entire philosophical curriculum latent in the classification of sciences since late antique times in Alexandria, and established a precedent for all subsequent philosophical summae,

---

12 Our knowledge of both the Greek and Arabic discussions on the theory of the soul is well summarized in the various essays and texts in Gätje's *Psychologie*. The Arabic translations and adaptations of the *De anima* and its tradition are summarized by A. Elamrani-Jamal and Rüdiger Arnzen in *DPhA Supplément* (2003) 346–365, while its reception among Avicenna's predecessors is studied by Ramón Guerrero.

1 Viz. Logic, Physics, and Metaphysics, with the exception of the four mathematical sciences, as Avicenna himself notes in the Autobiography (T3, § 12). Cf. Peters 105 (though *The Compilation* does not, of course, cover "only the first part of the Aristotelian *corpus*," as Peters states). For the probable absence of practical philosophy from this work see the introductions to sections E and F in the Inventory in the Appendix.

both by Avicenna himself and his successors, and both in the East and in the West.

The work fortunately survives. It is extant in a unique, though incomplete, independent manuscript, Uppsala 364; in various excerpts in later works by Avicenna;[2] in an extended paraphrase of apparently the entire text by Ġulām ʿAlī (1704–1786), recently discovered by Maroun Aouad;[3] and, in mostly verbatim quotations of the parts on dialectic, sophistics, rhetoric, and poetics, in the *Kitāb al-Muʿtabar* by Abū-l-Barakāt al-Baġdādī (d. after 1164).[4] One may hazard the guess that more such extracts by later authors may yet be identified. Although in this particular case there remains to be investigated whether the citations by these authors are from the *ʿArūḍiyya* itself or from one of Avicenna's own later works quoting himself, it is nevertheless somewhat astonishing that a work of such apparent popularity should have survived in only one known independent manuscript.

The Uppsala manuscript is undated, but the prevalent opinion is that it 88
was written in the seventh/thirteenth century (Mahdavī). From two marginal annotations referring to readings "in the author's holograph," it becomes apparent that there was at least one intermediary between this

---

[2] Anawati *"Ḥikma ʿarūḍiyya"* first reported on the manuscript in 1951 and stated his intention to publish it but the edition never materialized. The text of the manuscript itself was printed, though not accurately and without any annotation or consultation of previous partial editions (see GS 2 in the Appendix), by Ṣāliḥ (2007). The *ʿArūḍiyya* was copied extensively from all its parts, Logic, Physics, and Metaphysics, in the *Salvation* (see the details in Mahdavī); Ṣāliḥ 165–166 offers a comparative table of the common passages. The parts of the Logic on Topics, Sophistics, and Rhetoric (ff. 10^a–41^a = 47.19–98.4 Ṣāliḥ) were also copied, with some variations, in Avicenna's *Epitome of the Principles of Logic* (*ar-Risāla al-Mūjaza fī uṣūl al-manṭiq*, GL 2), as suggested by Mahdavī 223 and actually stated by Anawati "Nour Osmaniyye" 382. In the Istanbul MS Nuruosmaniye 4894, these passages correspond to ff. 39^b–57^b (and not as indicated by Anawati) of the text of the *Epitome*.

[3] The paraphrase is embedded in Ġulām ʿAlī's work entitled *Miḥakk an-naẓar* (*The Touchstone of Theoretical Inquiry*, like Ġazālī's title, cited below, Chapter 6.5), preserved in MS Arabe 4 in the Bibliothèque Nationale et Universitaire de Strasbourg, no. 4151 in the catalogue of E. Wickersheimer (Paris: Plon 1923). Maroun Aouad, who in addition to discovering this manuscript also identified its contents, was kind enough to provide me with this information for which I am thankful.

[4] Würsch 11 and elsewhere noted Abū-l-Barakāt's use of the *ʿArūḍiyya* for the Rhetoric, and was referred to by Maroun Aouad, "Les fondements de la *Rhétorique* d'Aristote ...," in *Peripatetic Rhetoric after Aristotle*, W.W. Fortenbaugh and D.C. Mirhady, eds., New Brunswick: Transaction, 1994, 265 and note 20. Van Gelder and Hammond 70 identified the Poetics part of the *Muʿtabar* as being dependent on the *ʿArūḍiyya*, and Jules Janssens noted the rest.

manuscript and the copy Avicenna gave to ʿArūḍī.[a] This is also indicated by the frequent lack of rubrics in the text; especially noteworthy is the absence of a heading to introduce the chapter on the soul.[5] If the scribe of the Uppsala manuscript were copying directly from Avicenna's holograph, which must have included the heading, he would certainly have reproduced it, as he did with the rest. The text thus seems to have been subjected to some deformation in the process of transmission, and the future editor of *The Compilation* will have to take into consideration and define more precisely the role of the intermediary copy (or copies).

At the very end of the work there is a note (f. 84^a = 164 Ṣāliḥ): "Avicenna wrote this book in the year 391"/1001.[6] This note may be taken to be either by Avicenna himself, put in the third person by a scribe, or by a subsequent scribe, calculated on the basis of Avicenna's statement in the Autobiography (T3, §12) that he was twenty-one years old when he completed *The Compilation*, and of Bayhaqī's report (*Tatimma* 39.3/52.6) that Avicenna was born in 370/980. The second alternative is much more likely, because although Avicenna does give *relative* dates for his achievements and works (see the Autobiography in general and T14, §11), he never gives *absolute* Hijrī dates; and in any case, the reason for his preoccupation with precise dating is his theory of Guessing Corrrectly the middle term of a syllogism, which developed after his twenty-first year.[7] Furthermore, the marginal annotations indicating which passages Avicenna crossed out imply that the scribe
89 was interested in presenting as detailed information about Avicenna's work as possible; it is thus more likely that it was this scribe (an editor?) who wrote the note at the end of the work.

---

[a] The two annotations referring to passages marked in the text read as follows: "The passage between the marks was crossed out in the author's holograph" (f. 73^b = 18 Ṣāliḥ: *mā bayna l-ʿalāmatayni kāna maḍrūban ʿalayhi fī aṣli l-muṣannif*); and "The passage between the marks is a gloss. It was thus found in the author's hand" (f. 74^a = 18 Ṣāliḥ: *mā bayna l-ʿalāmatayni ḥāšiya; kaḏā wujida bi-ḫaṭṭi l-muṣannif*). From the way these notes are written it is clear that the scribe was copying similar annotations in his exemplar. Cf. Mahdavī 77.

---

[5] The end of the fifth chapter of the Physics ("On Compounds," *fī l-murakkabāt*) runs directly into the beginning of the sixth ("On the Soul," *fī n-nafs*) without any indication of a break: f. 78^a15, corresponding verbatim to *Najāt* (*The Salvation*) 256.12–15/317.12–318.2: *li-t-taḥlīl wa-qad yatakawwanu* .... On p. 155, Ṣāliḥ adds the title of the section 〈*fī n-nafs*〉 in brackets but then prints the word *ṭābiʿ*, which does not exist in the MS, and also adds the same folio number, 78^w (= 78^a) a second time and in the wrong place.

[6] Cf. Mahdavī 76 and 80.

[7] See below, Chapter 3.2 and 3.4.

The manuscript has preserved only a partial text. Numerous folios are missing, and in one instance, four folios (ff. 2–5) have been bound out of place. The contents of the work, in the proper order and with indications of the missing parts, are the following:[8]

A. Logic

Ff. 1^{b}: Introduction. The need for logic. [Eisagoge, Categories (?) and part of De Interpretatione are missing.]
6^{a-b}: from De Interpretatione. [The last part of De Interpretatione, Prior Analytics, and the beginning of Posterior Analytics are missing.]
7^{a}–10^{a}: Posterior Analytics.
10^{a}–31^{a}: Topics (copied in the *Epitome*).
31^{b}–34^{a}: Sophistici Elenchi (copied in *The Salvation* and the *Epitome*).
34^{a}–45^{a}: Rhetoric (Aristotle, *Rhetoric* Bk. I); (copied in the *Epitome*)
$48^{b}14$–50^{a} ult.: Natural dispositions and affections of the soul (Aristotle, *Rhetoric* II.1–10).
45^{b}–48^{b}: Poetics.

B. Physics

Ff. 50^{b}–78^{a}: Physics; Meteorology (copied in *The Salvation*).
78^{a}–81^{b}: De Anima (the first page copied in *The Salvation*; the two texts then diverge. *The Salvation* reproduces the text on the soul from the "Lesser" *Destination*; see below, W5).

C. Metaphysics 90

(a) Universal Science: Being-as-such

Ff. [1. On being. Missing.]
2^{a}–$3^{a}4$: [2.] The order of being. Unity (copied in *The Salvation*).
$3^{a}5$-ult.: 3. Potentiality (copied in *The Salvation*).
$3^{b}1$–14: 4. Acting.
$3^{b}15$–$4^{a}12$: 5. Necessity and Possibility.
$4^{a}13$–$4^{b}4$: 6. Pre-existent and created.
$4^{b}5$–12: 7. The universal.
$4^{b}13$–16: 8. Perfection and imperfection (copied in *The Salvation*).
$4^{b}16$–$5^{a}5$: [8.i] The four causes as principles.
$5^{a}6$–$5^{b}15$: 9. Priority and posteriority (copied in *The Salvation*).
$5^{b}15$-ult.: [9.i: Essential creation] (copied in *The Salvation*).
[10. Kinds of unity and plurality. The end is missing.]

[8] Here only the major divisions of the work are given. Further details as well as the Arabic titles of the sections can be found in Mahdavī 77–78, and the latter also in Ṣāliḥ's printing of the text.

(b) Theology: Natural Theology

	[The necessary existent and its aspects; missing.]
82^a–84^a:	The necessary existent is immutable, intellect in actuality, one. The world emanates from it.

The above reconstruction needs a word of explanation. Placing the four folios (ff. 2–5) containing the universals, i.e. the categories and consequents of being, under Metaphysics may beg the question. As we shall see later (Chapter 6.4), the subject of the classification of the Categories under Logic or Metaphysics was of great importance to Avicenna, and deciding the matter for him on the basis of his later works may not correspond to his earlier position and thus prejudice our interpretation of the development of his thought. This possibility, however, is precluded by a reference in the text contained in these four folios to the logical part of the same work: "You [i.e. the reader] have understood the difference between the concomitant and the essential in the Logic" (f. 2^b12 = *Najāt* 340–341/515.3); these folios, therefore, do not belong to Logic. Moreover, Avicenna followed the example of Fārābī's essay *On the Purposes of the Metaphysics* already in the *Compendium on the Soul* (W1) and classified the discussion of the Categories under Uni-
91 versal Science (T1, § 3 IV A.i.); in *The Compilation* for ʿArūḍī, he also adhered very closely to Fārābī's description of the contents of the Universal Science.[9] The enumeration of the sections in C.a, finally, are those of the manuscript itself, where we read, "section three, four, etc., of *one*."[b] This "one" apparently refers to the first part of the chapter on Metaphysics, much like the division of the chapter in *The Salvation*. The misplaced folios thus do belong to the Metaphysics and, by a reasoning the reverse of that which led Avicenna to discuss the Categories under Metaphysics, they were placed, by a knowledgable owner or binder, at the beginning of the work, where the Categories would normally be discussed. In all probability this person was helped in this regard also by the explicit mention of the Categories in the first sentence of the section on acting: "'Acting' applies to what is meant by one of the ten categories …."[10]

[b] *Faṣl jīm*, *dāl*, etc., *min alif*, with circumflexes above the letters (pp. 34–37 Ṣāliḥ). Mahdavī 78 suggests that the *alif* here is an abbreviation for *Ilāhiyyāt* (Theology), but this is improbable.

[9] Cf. the entries in C.a, above, with Fārābī's explanation in his essay, L45, § 4.

[10] F. 3^b2, at the top of the page, p. 34 Ṣāliḥ.

There is, however, a further problem. In view of the many textual correspondences between this work and *The Salvation*, the question is raised—and it *was* raised by Anawati—whether the Uppsala manuscript consists in effect of "fragments of *The Compilation* itself and *The Salvation* arbitrarily joined together by a scribe."[11] If this is indeed the case, then most of the argument presented in the preceding paragraph is vitiated. But closer scrutiny and a comparison of the two texts invalidate this hypothesis. Two examples should suffice. a) In Chapter C.a of *The Compilation* (ff. 2^{a}–5^{b} = 31–39 Ṣāliḥ), sections 2 and 3 and then 8 and 9 are copied verbatim, and in that order, in *The Salvation*; the intermediary sections, however, are instead elaborated and improved upon in the later work. If the scribe of the Uppsala manuscript was copying for some purpose from the two books (one has to ascribe to him some discriminating purpose; otherwise he would have copied only one of them), it would be difficult to explain his procedure of first copying from *The Salvation* (sections 2–3), then switching to the manifestly more primitive text of *The Compilation* (sections 4–7), and then reverting to *The Salvation* (sections 8–9). b) More telling are the numerous instances where Avicenna changes the wording of a passage or, more particularly, substitutes one argument for another. For example, in the section of the Physics of *The Salvation* entitled, "Proof that the originating (*mubdiʿa*) motion is one in number and circular," Avicenna copies verbatim the introductory paragraph from *The Compilation* (ff. 71^{a}12–71^{b}1 *ʿArūḍiyya* [= 144 Ṣāliḥ] = 226.14–227.3/279.2–9 *Najāt*), then substitutes a different and longer argument for
the one in *The Compilation* designed to prove that motion in a straight line 92
cannot be continuous (f. 71^{b}1–6 *ʿArūḍiyya* ≠ 227.3–17/279.9–281.3 *Najāt*), and then continues with the rest of the section, copying again verbatim from *The Compilation* (f. 71^{b}6 ff. *ʿArūḍiyya* = *Najāt* 227.17 ff. / 281.3 ff.). A scribe copying arbitrarily would have no reason to alter the text in precisely this fashion. The Uppsala manuscript thus contains what is extant of *The Compilation*, and Avicenna copied himself quite extensively, years later, in *The Salvation*. This fact provides striking confirmation of his statement in the Autobiography that, "at that time [i.e., in his youth] my retention of Knowledge was better, but today my grasp of it is more mature; otherwise the Knowledge is the same, nothing new having come to me since" (T3, § 11), and affords a valuable opportunity to study, by comparing the variations between the two texts, precisely where his more mature grasp lies.

11 Anawati "*Ḥikma ʿarūḍiyya*" 176.

A final question with regard to the order in which *The Compilation* was written (i.e. in which it was intended to be read) concerns the section on "Natural dispositions and affections of the soul" (ff. 48^{b}–50^{a} = 110–112 Ṣāliḥ) which, though naturally belonging to the Rhetoric (it is a summary of Aristotle's *Rhetoric* II.1–10), follows in the manuscript immediately upon the end of the entire part on Logic where Avicenna explicitly says, "Let this be enough about our purpose to abridge the *Organon* (*manṭiq*)."[12] Because it begins in the middle of the page, there can be no question of misplaced folios in the manuscript; it has therefore to be assumed either that Avicenna intended it to be placed there,[13] or that the misplacement occurred in the intermediary copy (or copies, as discussed above). The former alternative, however, cannot be maintained for at least three reasons: a) The Arabic title of the section is, *fī l-aḫlāq wa-l-infiʿālāt an-nafsāniyya*. Now the word *aḫlāq* ("natural traits") in Arabic is also used to render "ethics" (it is a calque from the plural Greek term *ēthē*, whence *ēthika*) and it might be thought that Avicenna intended by this brief section to treat, after logic, first practical philosophy (ethics) and then theoretical philosophy (physics and metaphysics, omitting, as noted, mathematics). But Avicenna's opening sentence in this section makes it clear that he is still discussing a subject that belongs to logic, and indeed, to Rhetoric: "The most powerful means of eliciting assent and the one most appropriate to rhetoric is first a demonstrative statement and then provoking the following affections" [of the soul, i.e., emotions].[14] This statement, which is a summary of that in Aristotle's *Rhetoric* II,1 (1377b16 ff.), and is followed by a discussion of the emotions listed by Aristotle, is directly related to Avicenna's paraphrase, in his earlier section on the Rhetoric itself
93 (ff. $35^{a}6$–$35^{b}4$ = 88–89 Ṣāliḥ), of Aristotle's argument about the means of persuading an audience (*Rhetoric* 1356a1 ff.). Anyone reading Avicenna's paraphrase in the Rhetoric section could hardly fail to associate the section on "Natural dispositions and affections of the soul" with it, given the latter's opening sentence. Furthermore, in the extant works of Avicenna on ethics, there is no corresponding discussion of the subjects treated in this section, something which would have been expected on the basis of the relatively invariable structure of his philosophical works. b) By the same token, it is also highly unlikely that, had Avicenna intended this section as a brief

[12] F. $48^{b}11$ = 110 Ṣāliḥ. See the reproduction of the lower half of this folio in Remondon 26.

[13] Through "a weakness in his composition," suggests Remondon 19–20.

[14] F. 48^{b} = 110 Ṣāliḥ (who wrongly transcribes *iḫtilāf at-taṣdīq* for *ijtilāb at-taṣdīq* in the manuscript); cf. Remondon 23 and 27.

treatment of ethics or practical philosophy, he would have placed it between logic and physics in a book which dealt with theoretical philosophy.[15] c) In *The Cure*, finally, where rhetoric is treated extensively, the discussion of emotions corresponding to the second book of Aristotle's *Rhetoric* occurs in its proper place, not at the end of the entire logic. It thus appears that the section on "Natural dispositions and affections of the soul" of *The Compilation*, originally composed as a part of Avicenna's treatment of rhetoric, was misplaced in the process of transmission at the end of the entire section on logic.

Avicenna wrote *The Compilation* apparently according to the specifications required by ʿArūḍī. At the end of both the part on Logic and the part on Metaphysics (the end of the part on Physics is lost) he says: "I composed this book for Abū-l-Ḥasan Aḥmad ibn-ʿAbd-Allāh al-ʿArūḍī upon his request and *in the way in which* he requested it."[c] If, judging by the name alone—al-ʿArūḍī, the Prosodist—his patron was a man of letters, this might explain the disproportionately extensive coverage of the Topics, Sophistics, Rhetoric, and Poetics, all subjects of interest to such a person.[16] By the same token, it becomes relatively difficult to estimate what percentage of the work is missing. In view of Avicenna's habit of copying from his previous works, however, more lost parts may be recovered in some of his later essays as they have in the *Epitome* and *The Salvation*. This will have to be determined by future research on this, the first scholastic philosophical compendium.

---

[c] Ff. 48[b], 84[a] = 110, 164 Ṣāliḥ; Mahdavī 78, 80: *ʿamilnāhu li-mā arādahu* (*iltamasa*) *wa-ʿalā l-wajhi llaḏi arādahu* (*iltamasa*). On f. 48[b] the scribe wrote by mistake *ʿallamnāha* for *ʿamilnāhu*, and the wrong form was duly copied by Ṣāliḥ 110. Mahdavī 78 corrects to *ʿamilnāhā* but leaves the feminine pronoun, and I correct to *ʿamilnāhu*, as in the second phrase at the end of the work, f. 84[a] = 164 Ṣāliḥ.

---

[15] For a discussion of Avicenna's writings on practical philosophy see Chapter 6.2 and the introduction to Section F in the Appendix.

[16] These subjects cover 39ff. (ff. 10–48) in the manuscript, as compared to 32ff. for the entire Physics, including the section on the soul. Although the latter section is not complete, judging from the advanced stage of the discussion where it breaks off, hardly more than a folio or two from it can be missing. Even more indicative is a comparison between the section on poetics (4ff.) and that on the soul (5 or 6ff.), with the corresponding ones in *The Cure*, where both subjects are given their fullest treatment. In the Cairo edition of *The Cure*, Poetics covers 53 pages (Badawī *Šiʿr*), while the De anima section is over four times its size, covering 233 pages (Anawati and Zāyid). *The Salvation*, for its part, has only five small pages on the Topics, copies the Sophistics from *The Compilation*, and omits Rhetoric and Poetics altogether.

94 Work 3. Precursors of *The Cure* and *Fair Judgment: The Available and the Valid* [*of Theoretical Philosophy*] (*al-Ḥāṣil wa-l-maḥṣūl*) and *Piety and Sin* [*in Practical Philosophy*] (*al-Birr wa-l-iṯm*) [GS 10, GPP 1]

After having mentioned in the Autobiography that he completed *The Compilation* for ʿArūḍī when he was twenty-one, Avicenna says that another neighbor of his, Abū-Bakr al-Baraqī,

> asked me to comment on the books [on Philosophy] and so I composed *The Available and the Valid* for him in about twenty volumes [*mujallad*], and I also composed a book [*kitāb*] for him on Ethics which I called *Piety and Sin*. These two books [*kitābān*] exist only in his possession because he never lent them to anybody to copy from them. [T3, §13]

Avicenna thus wrote these books in his twenty-second or twenty-third year when he was still in Buḫārā. This report is echoed in the entry on these two works in the Longer Bibliography (LB below in the Appendix), which says that he wrote them "in his home city ... in the early part of his life" (*bi-baladihi ... fī awwali ʿumrihi*), adding that the two works existed only in one copy, the original, in the possession of Baraqī.[1] This explains their very poor survival record.

Of the two, we are relatively better informed from the literary record about the fate and contents of the work on Ethics, *Piety and Sin*. The Shorter Bibliography embedded in Jūzjānī's Biography and ascribed to him (see SB in the Appendix) mentions that it was in two volumes (*mujalladatān*);[2] this would indicate, especially in view of Avicenna's silence on the matter, that, if not Jūzjānī himself, then someone close to Avicenna's time and circle who compiled the Shorter Bibliography had seen it, or at least had heard of it. Furthermore, a copy was also said to be extant well over a century after Avicenna's death, and reportedly seen by Bayhaqī himself: "In the year 544[/1149–1150] I saw [a copy of] it, in an ugly and crowded hand, in the possession of the Imām Muḥammad al-Ḥāriṯān as-Saraḫsī."[3] It is possible that Bayhaqī had correctly identified the work—in his bibliographic information, at least, he appears to be reliable[4]—but in any case, there seems to

---

1 Gohlman 92–93.

2 Biography, Gohlman 46–47; this is also echoed in the Longer Bibliography, Gohlman 92–93.

3 Bayhaqī *Tatimma* 44/57; cf. Gohlman 123–124, notes 37 and 38.

4 See on this matter the discussion by Reisman *Avicennan Tradition* 129–130.

be little doubt that the book was in circulation also outside Baraqī's library and most likely also among Avicenna's disciples, because he refers to it as if it were widely available in a passage from *The Cure* where he also informs us about its contents. At the end of the Metaphysics of *The Cure*, after discussing the celestial influences on the world and the concept of 95
providence, Avicenna continues:

> Know that most of the matters which the masses [*al-jumhūr*] affirm, resort to, and profess are true; it is only those who act as if they were philosophers that reject them out of ignorance of their causes and reasons. As a matter of fact, we wrote on this subject the book *Piety and Sin*. You should study carefully the exposition of these matters there, count as true the stories about divine punishments descending upon corrupt cities and tyrants, and consider how truth emerges victorious. You should also know that the reason for [the efficacy of] our praying, almsgiving, etc., as well as for the occurrence of wrongdoing and sin, is only from There, for the first principles of all these matters are ultimately reducible to nature, will, and chance. ... When matters are resolved [into their constituent components], they are [found to be] dependent on the first principles that necessitate them,[a] which descend from God.[5] (L1)

It would thus seem that Avicenna treated the Metaphysics of the Rational Soul also in the context of Ethics and the practical sciences (see the discussion in Chapter 6.2, below, and the introductions to sections E and F in the Inventory in the Appendix). The extent to which he treated each one of those subjects and the way in which he treated them, however, cannot be decided at present.

The reason is that the picture that emerges from the manuscripts which purport to, or may, contain *Piety and Sin* is one of great confusion, while the information elicited from them is largely irreconcilable with the bibliographic reports just summarized. In brief, manuscripts do contain a work ascribed to Avicenna which they entitle *Piety and Sin* (*al-Birr wa-l-iṯm*), but it is a mere sixteen pages in the edition of Šamsaddīn (353–369), has quite disparate and disjointed contents, and no introduction. In addition, there are at least two other essays entitled *On Ethics* (*Risāla fī l-aḫlāq*) and a certain *Pledge* (*ʿAhd*) in the manuscripts, the texts of which are fluid among the

---

[a] *Najāt* reads *ilā mabādiʾ wujūdihā* for *ilā mabādiʾ īǧābihā* in the *Šifāʾ*.

---

[5] *Ilāhiyyāt* 439.6–17 Mūsā et al. = *Najāt* 496.1–15/705.8–706.9; cf. the English translation by Marmura *Metaphysics* 362–363.

various versions and interpenetrating one another, both in the manuscripts and in the various publications of these texts. Karlığa, who describes this confusion,[6] opines (p. 27) that one of the treatises titled *al-Aḫlāq* and what goes under the name of *al-Birr wa-l-iṯm* are actually two parts of the same book, *al-Birr wa-l-iṯm* (referred to as "two volumes" in the Shorter Bibliography), and claims to have discovered a "new treatise" in the second essay that goes by that name in the manuscripts. But the Shorter Bibliography lists this title under the rubric "*Kutub*," not "*Rasāʾil*," which comes later (see the Tetrapla in the Appendix), and two volumes (*mujalladatān*) thus means two volumes, not two parts; and some twenty-five odd pages of text of the two treatises combined can hardly count as two volumes. Besides, from the context in which Avicenna describes the book both in the Autobiography and in the passage from *The Cure* just cited (L1), it is clear that the exposition of the material in *Piety and Sin* was comprehensive and extensive, and twenty-five pages of notes cannot comprise it.

In addition, the problem is complicated by questions of the authenticity of these surviving texts, compounded by the fact that they contain quotations and material from Fārābī as well as from the Arabic translations of two paraphrases of the *Nicomachean Ethics*, one attributed to a certain Nicolaus and the other known as the *Summa Alexandrinorum* (*Iḫtiṣār al-Iskandarāniyyīn*).[7] A reasonable hypothesis would be, if all these extant texts are indeed by Avicenna, that they are various excerpts from the original *Piety and Sin*, extracted at various times and on various occassions by scribes, and copied, titled, and recombined to create the confused state in which we find them in the manuscripts. However, a final judgment cannot be made before the entire tradition of the *Nicomachean Ethics* in Arabic is studied and the various surviving texts are properly identified and classified. The starting point for this research has just been accomplished in the two masterful volumes of the language and vocabulary of the Arabic translation of the *Nicomachean Ethics* by Manfred Ullmann.[8]

---

[6] Karlığa "Traité d'éthique." Helpful as his spadework and elucidation of the complex situation are (cf. his very useful note 10 on p. 32), his own exposition is not without some opacity. Šamsaddīn's comments, strewn throughout the book and devoid of precise reference to manuscripts, are much less helpful. For the text of *al-Birr wa-l-iṯm* in particular, which he publishes as just stated, he refers to "*al-maḫṭūṭ al-maḏkūr min maktabat Isṭanbūl*" (p. 218), having mentioned quite a few Istanbul manuscripts previously.

[7] See Karlığa "Traité d'éthique" 29–32, and Janssens "Lawkari" 22 also for the Farabian background. For the complex history of the transmission of the *Nicomachean Ethics* in the Syriac and Arabic traditions see the entry by Mauro Zonta in *DPhA*, *Supplément* 191–198.

[8] Manfred Ullmann, *Die Nikomachische Ethik des Aristoteles in arabischer Überlie-*

The information about the fate and contents of the theoretical part of the book, *The Available and the Valid*, is even more sparse. Other than Avicenna's statement, repeated in the anonymous Longer Bibliography (LB 1), that Baraqī possessed the original and unique copy, the only report about its fate is provided by Bayhaqī: "There was a copy of it, now lost, in the library in Būzajān."[9] It would appear that no other copies were ever available; no manuscript identified as containing any part of the work has so far been located.

In this connection one further report is of interest. In the Biography, Jūzjānī reports the following about the evening sessions of Avicenna and his disciples while in Hamaḏān, before Šams-ad-Dawla's death in 412/1021: "Every night pupils would gather at [Avicenna's] house, while by turns I would read from *The Cure* and someone else would read from *The Canon* [*of Medicine*]."[10] In some later manuscripts of Bayhaqī's *Tatimma*, which reproduces this report from Jūzjānī, the text appears augmented as follows: "… while by turns Abū-ʿUbayd [al-Jūzjānī] would read from *The Cure*, al- 96
Maʿṣūmī from *The Canon*, Ibn-Zayla from *Pointers and Reminders*, and Bahmanyār from *The Available and the Valid*."[11] This is clearly a fabrication, if only because *Pointers and Reminders* had not yet been written at the time when the evening sessions were held. What it does indicate, however, is that somebody after the twelfth century wanted to associate the names of the closest pupils of Avicenna with reading and, implicitly, having a special interest in particular works of the master. *The Cure*, *The Canon*, and *Pointers and Reminders* were all by then famous works, widely circulated and studied. What is curious is why *The Available and the Valid* should have been mentioned as being read by Bahmanyār, if by then it was lost and virtually unknown. The association of the first three works with the specific names seems to be based on the following rationale: Jūzjānī was clearly connected in posterity with *The Cure* because by his own account he had urged Avicenna to write it and then provided a special introduction to it (T7); Maʿṣūmī was known as the scientist among Avicenna's pupils: it was he who was entrusted with answering Bīrūnī's objections to Avicenna's physical and astronomical theories; Ibn-Zayla, finally, was known as the exegete of

ferung. Teil I: Wortschatz; Teil II: Überlieferung, Textkritik, Grammatik, Wiesbaden: Harrassowitz, 2011–2012.

[9] Bayhaqī *Tatimma* 44/57.

[10] Gohlman 54–55.

[11] Bayhaqī *Tatimma* 49/62; cf. Gohlman 128n71.

the more allusive works of Avicenna, largely because of his commentary on *Ḥayy ibn-Yaqẓān*. Bahmanyār was known as the author of a large summa of Avicennan philosophy, entitled *Validated Knowledge* (*Kitāb at-Taḥṣīl*),[12] and it would seem that the association with Avicenna's *The Available and the Valid* (*Al-Ḥāṣil wa-l-maḥṣūl*) was made on the basis of the similarity of the titles. Now this similarity is most likely purely accidental and what struck the fancy of the person who interpolated the names of Avicenna's pupils in Bayhaqī's manuscripts; on the other hand, it cannot be completely discounted that it may indeed reflect a bibliographical fact that Bahmanyār may have had access in some form to *The Available and the Valid* and made some use of it in his work. The question cannot be resolved without further investigation into the transmission of *The Available and the Valid* and the works of Bahmanyār along the lines suggested by some recent research;[13] it would seem, however, premature to dismiss this work by Avicenna as completely lost.

As for the contents of the work, only some reasoned conjectures can be offered in the absence of any concrete evidence. The title, which itself presents some problems of interpretation, may be indicative of the contents. Achena and Massé seem to be the only scholars who expressed some doubts about its precise translation, placing a question mark after their suggested
97 version, *"La Somme et le produit?"* The other translations that have been offered include *Buch des Resultats und des Ergebnisses* (Kraus), *The Import and the Substance* (Arberry and Afnan), *The Sum and Substance* (Gohlman and, following him, a number of later scholars), and *La somme et ce qu'il en demeure* (Goichon).[14] Only Goichon's suggestion seems to point to the

---

12 Edited by Moṭahharī. The title may also mean, according to Bahmanyār's introduction, *The Digest*. This title is to be distinguished from *Taḥṣīlāt Bahmanyār* which is the title given to the earliest collection of *Mubāḥaṯāt* materials by Bahmanyār himself; see Reisman *Avicennan Tradition* 111–113.

13 Janssens "Bahmanyār" 196 made the important determination that Bahmanyār's *Taḥṣīl* in some respects "re-Aristotelizes" Avicenna. Now in all likelihood this early work by Avicenna showed closer adherence to Aristotelian tenets than did the more emancipated later writings of his, as I discuss below, Chapter 7. It would thus stand to reason that, if Bahmanyār was more beholden to Aristotle than was Avicenna in his later period, he would prefer a work such as *The Available and the Valid* if he had access to it. See also Janssens "Revision" where it is shown that in the metaphysics part of the *Taḥṣīl* Bahmanyār studiously avoids discussing subjects of the *kalām*—subjects, that is, which had been introduced by Avicenna to the Aristotelian roster.

14 Goichon explains, *"La Somme et ce qu'il en demeure*[,] comme l' or dégagé du minera[l];" review of Gohlman 98.

right direction. If one were to judge from *maḥṣūl*, which can be taken to be synonymous with *muḥaṣṣal* and hence mean "determined, verified, or Validated [philosophy, knowledge, theories or ideas]," it might be possible to interpret *al-ḥāṣil* to mean "the sum total of actually existing or proffered [philosophy, knowledge, theories, or ideas]." If this interpretation is correct, it would mean that by the title Avicenna wanted to present a description of the book's contents: it presented theoretical philosophy as it was actually transmitted in the Aristotelian tradition and available in his time (*al-ḥāṣil*), and then proceeded to comment upon this tradition (note his words in the Autobiography: Baraqī "asked me to *comment* [*šarḥ*] on the philosophical books") and to discuss and Determine its Validity, and offer an Ascertained version, its reformulated substance and extract (*al-maḥṣūl*).[15]

Since we do not possess the introduction of the work, in which the meaning of the title may have been explained or could be understood from the context, there cannot be certainty about this interpretation; it is consonant, however, with the tendency of Avicenna displayed in his later works: in *The Cure* he did not wish to discuss all the philosophical theories but merely to present those which seemed right to him, i.e., he wanted to pesent only the *maḥṣūl* part of the earlier work; in the *Fair Judgment* (W10) he reverted to the structure of *The Available and the Valid* and presented the transmitted theories (*ḥāṣil*) and judged between them and his own verified reformulations (*al-maḥṣūl*); in other words, in the *Fair Judgment* he judged fairly between the *ḥāṣil* and the *maḥṣūl*. Perhaps it is not entirely accidental that the *Fair Judgment* is also said to have been in twenty volumes, just like *The Available and the Valid.*

There are a few references in Avicenna's works suggesting that *The Available and the Valid* may indeed have been in commentary format. One is provided by the Avicenna—Bīrūnī debate. In his response to Bīrūnī's fifth question, Avicenna refers the reader to his own exegesis of the first book of the *Metaphysics*.[16] This correspondence took place around the year 390/1000, 98
and whatever the precise age of Avicenna at that time, he had written nothing more substantial than *The Available and the Valid* and certainly nothing that could be referred to with greater probability as a commentary on the *Metaphysics*.[17] Another is a reference to "a separate commentary [by

15 For the meaning of the root *ḥ/ṣ/l* and its derivatives see the references in note 1 to Work 1, above.

16 *Al-Ajwiba ʿan masāʾil al-Bīrūnī* 23.13–14 Nasr and Mohaghegh: [... *fī*] *tafsīrinā li-l-maqālati l-ūlā min Kitāb Māṭāfūsīqā fī Mā baʿd aṭ-ṭabīʿiyyāt.*

17 The correspondence is mentioned by Bīrūnī himself, who refers to Avicenna as "the

Avicenna] on this book [Aristotle's *Metaphysics*], whose part on the *Alpha Elatton* alone contained approximately everything in the commentary [by Abū-l-Faraj Ibn-aṭ-Ṭayyib] imported from Baġdād" (T13, § 9). Since the letter of Avicenna's disciple writing from Rayy (Ibn-Zayla?) in which this report occurs deals with the *Fair Judgment*, the phrase "separate commentary" cannot refer to the Metaphysics part of that book; and since none of the extant works of Avicenna deals with the *Metaphysics*, and especially Book *Alpha Elatton*, as extensively as described above, it is very likely that the disciple is referring to that part of *The Available and the Valid*. In addition, there are separate references to a commentary on the *Physics*, *De anima*, and the *Metaphysics*, all of which appear to be to those parts of *The Available and the Valid* dealing with those books (see the references in the Inventory in the Appendix, GS 10a, 10b, and 10c under Physics, and GS 10d under Metaphysics).

In general, then, it appears that the entire work was intended to be a summa in the form of a running commentary on the philosophical sciences, as classified in the Aristotelian tradition and conceived of in two units: the first, *The Available and the Valid*, dealt with Logic and theoretical philosophy (Physics, Mathematics, and Metaphysics) in about twenty volumes; the second, *Piety and Sin*, dealt with practical philosophy—both the traditional parts, Ethics and presumably also Oeconomics and Politics, and the new fourth part that Avicenna introduced, the relevant subjects that fall under the Metaphysics of the Rational Soul (especially its posthumous punishment and reward)—in two volumes. It thus represented the culmination of the process initiated by the *Compendium on the Soul* in which the plan of such a summa was first conceived and outlined, and continued by *The Compilation* in which the summa was executed in a summary fashion, almost as a first draft, and almost certainly without the part on practical philosophy. *The Available and the Valid* together with *Piety and Sin* were in this sense real precursors of *The Cure*—and perhaps also thereby explain Avicenna's diffidence in undertaking to write the latter work—as well as of the *Fair Judgment*, and close his first period of literary activity.

excellent youth" (*al-fatā al-fāḍil*). See E. Sachau, *Chronologie orientalischer Völker von Albērūnī*, Leipzig 1878, repr. 1923, p. 257.3–5 (text), and his Introduction, p. xxxv (= *The Chronology of Ancient Nations*, London 1879, p. 247, trans.); cf. Mahdavī 11–12.

Work 4. *The Provenance and Destination* (*al-Mabdaʾ wa-l-maʿād*) [GM 1]

Jūzjānī says in the Biography (44.6–7) that Avicenna wrote this treatise in Jurjān for his benefactor, a certain Abū-Muḥammad aš-Šīrāzī, who is described as an "amateur of these [philosophical] sciences."[1] The date of composition is therefore approximately 403/1013, shortly after Avicenna's 99
arrival in Jurjān and initial meeting with Jūzjānī.[2]

Thematically the subjects of the Provenance and the Destination belong to the De anima and Metaphysics parts in the classification of the philosophical sciences and constitute their essential doctrines, what Avicenna calls in his introduction to the work the "fruit" (*ṯamara*) of Physics and Metaphysics. Avicenna himself classified them in the Metaphysics and treated them in that section of it which I have called the Metaphysics of the Rational Soul (Chapter 6.2). This monograph marks a transition period in Avicenna's literary activity. With it he began to formulate his theories on these subjects in his own words and to strike a largely independent course from the transmitted Aristotelian models.

The work is divided into three parts, described by Avicenna in his Introduction (T4). The first two, dealing with the first principle and the emanation of being from it (pp. 2–90 Nūrānī, ff. 119^{a}–177^{a} in the Milan MS Ambrosiana 320 Hammer), were copied verbatim, with only some omissions, rearrangement, and additions, in the Metaphysics parts of both *The Cure* and *The Salvation*. They constitute most of the second chapter (*maqāla*) of the Metaphysics of *The Salvation* (*Najāt* 366–464/546–666), as well as most of books 8 and 9 of *The Cure* (*Ilāhiyyāt* 355–413 Mūsā et al.). The subject of the third part of *The Provenance and Destination*, the survival of the human soul, was treated more extensively by Avicenna in the "Lesser" *Destination*, and it was this work that was later incorporated in *The Cure* and *The Salvation* (see next Work, W5).

---

[1] In his dedication, Avicenna refers to this person as Abū-Aḥmad ibn-Muḥammad (or simply Abū-Muḥammad in the Istanbul MS Ahmet III 3268, Nūrānī 1 and Mahdavī 212) ibn-Ibrāhīm al-Fārisī. Neither person, if they are two, has been identified so far (cf. Nafīsī *Pūr-e Sīnā* 127, no. 3; Mahdavī 212, no. 106; Gohlman 139n3; Michot *Destinée* 6n27).

[2] The chronology of Avicenna's life after his arrival in Jurjān is discussed below, W6.

Work 5. The "Lesser" *Destination* (*al-Maʿād al-aṣġar*) [GM 3]

This treatise, written for one or a number of unspecified friends "of pure heart" (*ḫullaṣ*), is known in the manuscript tradition under a wide variety of titles, though it can now be safely identified as the *Destination, al-Maʿād*, which Jūzjānī says (Biography 50.1) Avicenna wrote in Rayy while in the service of the Būyid Majd-ad-Dawla, that is, approximately in 404/1014. Its relatively early date of composition is also clear from its style and occasional use of Greek rather than Arabic terminology.[1]

Avicenna himself describes it in his introduction as follows (Ahwānī *Aḥwāl* 45.4–7): "[This treatise] contains the marrow [of the theory] about the state of the human soul arrived at through demonstrative proofs, the heart of the matter about its survival—after the disintegration of the [physical] temperament and the decay of the body—provided by unequivocal research, and an examination of [the question of] resurrection and the circumstances that lead to it in the afterlife." As Mahdavī 244 rightly points out, given the contents of the work as just described by Avicenna, the title *Des-*
100 *tination* (*al-Maʿād*) for it is entirely appropriate. This treatise thus belongs to the same transition period of Avicenna's literary output as the preceding work and acts as its complement. Just as *The Provenance and Destination* established the version of Avicenna's doctrine of the "fruit" of Metaphysics with which he was most content, so also this *Destination* established the version of his doctrine of the "marrow" of Physics, i.e., his theory of the soul and its afterlife; and just as the former treatise was copied extensively in the Metaphysics part of *The Cure* and *The Salvation*, so also this one was copied in the De Anima parts of both works.

The treatise contains sixteen chapters, which correspond as follows to the text in *The Salvation*:[2]

---

[1] Michot "*La Définition de l'âme*" 240n6 argues for a very late date of composition for this treatise, while Sebti "Authenticité" questions the authenticity of three of its chapters. Briefly to review the evidence, Avicenna uses in his early works transliterated terms and some expressions which he does not do later on; for example, *ṭūbīqā* for Topics instead of *jadal* (55.8 Ahwānī), *fanṭāsiyā/banṭāsiyā* for the internal common sense instead of *ḥiss muštarak* (61.11, 120.1 and 8 Ahwānī, etc.), and he still calls Plato "divine," *al-ilāhī Aflāṭūn* (108.4 Ahwānī, not excised when copied in the *Najāt* 313.6/391.10; see also below, W7 note 2). For a full discussion of the identification, dating, and authenticity of this treatise see the Appendix, GM 2 and 3.

[2] The chapter headings are given in paraphrase only; cf. the contents of the *Compendium on the Soul* listed above, W1. For the correspondences between *The Destination, The Salvation*, and *The Cure* see also the tables in Goichon *Distinction* 499–500, the *Appendice* in Michot "Prophétie et divination" 532–534, and Sebti "Authenticité" 353–354.

The Destination	*The Salvation* (*Najāt*, ed. Kurdī)
Introduction: contents of the treatise.	
1. Definition of the soul.	
2. Brief description of the faculties of the soul.	258–272; 274–275
3. Various functions of the perceptive faculties of the soul.	275–279
4. The faculties can perceive particular forms only by means of an organ.	279–285
5. The faculties cannot perceive universal forms by means of an organ; the faculties do not subsist through a body.	285–292
6. How and when the soul uses the body; how it dispenses with the body, or rather, how the body harms it.	297–299
7. The soul does not need the body in order to subsist.	292–297
8. The soul comes into existence along with the body.	300–302
9. The survival of the soul.	302–309
10. Metempsychosis does not exist.	309–310
11. All the faculties belong to a single soul.	313–315
12. The actualization of the theoretical intellect.	315–316
13. On prophecy.	
14. The purification of the soul.	272–274
15. Eschatology (happiness and misery of the soul after death).	477–490
16. The occasion of this treatise (T5).	

Work 6. *The Cure* (*Aš-Šifā'*) [GS 5] 101

a. *Occasion of Composition and Contents*

Jūzjānī offers two slightly divergent accounts of the genesis of *The Cure*. The earlier one occurs in the Introduction which he wrote for the work right after its completion (as I will argue below in Section c); the later one is found in the Biography which he wrote after Avicenna's death. A juxtaposition of the two texts will best bring out their differences.

Introduction (*T7, §3*)	*Biography* (*54.1–5 Gohlman*)
The hope of ever obtaining his lost works having dimmed, we asked him to rewrite them and he said, "I have neither the time nor the inclination to occupy myself with close textual analysis and commentary.	Then I asked him myself to comment on the books of Aristotle, but he brought up that he had no leisure for this at that time.
But if you [pl.] would be content with whatever I have readily in mind [which I have thought] on my own,	"But if you [sing.] would like me to compose a book in which I will set forth what, in my opinion, is sound

Introduction (*T7*, *§3*)

then I could write for you [pl.] a comprehensive work arranged in the order which will occur to me."

We readily offered our consent to this and urged that he start with Physics.

Biography (*54.1–5 Gohlman*)

of these [philosophical] sciences, without debating with those who disagree or occupying myself with their refutation, then I will do that." I was pleased with this and he began with the Physics of a book which he called *The Cure*. (L2)

The two accounts emphasize different aspects of what is, essentially the same story, and are therefore complementary despite their apparent divergences. The only real difference is the shift in the Biography to the first person: in view of the discussion in Section c, below, it would seem that Jūzjānī wanted to take all the credit for urging Avicenna to write *The Cure* after he had seen that the other disciples who may have initially participated with him in their request preferred the later works of Avicenna.

The initial request was for Avicenna to rewrite the works which were inaccessible to his disciples in Hamaḏān because they were either lost or extant in single copies in the possession of individuals in Buḫārā and other cities visited by Avicenna in the course of his lengthy travels. This is clear from Jūzjānī's Introduction. The words in which Avicenna's reply is couched, as cited in the same document, suggest that what he was being asked to do in order to rewrite these books was to engage in "close textual analysis and
102 commentary," the implication being that this was also the format of the earlier works. What is implied in the Introduction is stated explicitly in the Biography, where the same request is presented this time as Jūzjānī asking Avicenna "to comment on the books of Aristotle." Avicenna's reply in the Biography again makes explicit what engaging in "close textual analysis and commentary" entailed: "debating with those who disagree or occupying [oneself] with their refutation." The one work written before *The Cure* that was comprehensive enough to fit the description of a commentary on "the books of Aristotle" and detailed enough to contain debates and refutations of opponents was, as suggested above in W3, *The Available and the Valid*. Clearly, then, Avicenna was unwilling to rewrite a similar work, partly for the reasons stated in T7, and partly because he wished to abandon the commentary format as it was employed, for the works of Aristotle at least, from the time of Alexander of Aphrodisias (active in 200 AD) to his own times. Instead he proposed to write a running exposition of the Philosophical Sciences as reconstructed according to his own opinion. This decision inaugurates the mature period of his literary activity, which saw the composition of his

classic summae of philosophy: *The Cure, The Salvation, Philosophy for ʿAlāʾ-ad-Dawla*, and *Pointers and Reminders*.

The overall plan of *The Cure* follows exactly the order of the philosophical sciences as classified in the Aristotelian tradition and as already presented by Avicenna himself in the *Compendium on the Soul, The Compilation*, and doubtless in *The Available and the Valid*. The variation in the order mentioned by Avicenna occurs, if at all, in the internal arrangement of each one of these sciences, and will have to be studied in detail in the future. The following are the contents of the work:

I. Logic

1. Eisagoge (Porphyry); 2. Categories; 3. De Interpretatione; 4. Syllogism (Prior Analytics); 5. Demonstration (Posterior Analytics); 6. Dialectic (Topica); 7. Sophistics; 8. Rhetoric; 9. Poetics.

II. Physics

1. Physica; 2. De Caelo; 3. De Generatione et Corruptione; 4. Qualities and Transformations of the Four Elements ("Chemistry") [Meteorology IV];[1] 5. Meteorology [Meteorology I–III]; 6. De Anima; 7. Botany; 8. Zoology.

III. Mathematics

1. Geometry [Euclid's *Elements*]; 2. Astronomy [Ptolemy's *Almagest*]; 3. Arithmetic [Nicomachus's *Introduction*]; 4. Music [Ptolemy's *Harmonics*].

IV. Metaphysics [cf. Chapter 6.1].

It has become a commonplace to refer to *The Cure* as an "encyclopaedia;" it is obvious from the above tabulation, however, that this is at best misleading. 103
In contemporary terminology, an encyclopaedia is a collection of unrelated and disparate articles on some or all branches of knowledge; it does not have the organic unity and coherent approach of a summa like *The Cure*. Avicenna himself calls it a "compendium" (*jumla*; T9, § 1), while in modern Arabic the word for encyclopaedia is "round, or course, of knowledges" (*dāʾirat al-maʿārif*), a calque from the Greek, *enkyklios paideia*.[2]

---

[1] Avicenna treats *Meteorology* IV before the first threee books, as pointed out by J.-M. Mandosio and C. Di Martino, "La 'Météorologie' d'Avicenne (Kitāb al-Šifāʾ V) et sa diffusion dans le monde latin," in Andreas Speer and Lydia Wegeners, eds., *Wissen über Grenzen. Arabisches Wissen und lateinishes Mittelalter* [Miscellanea Mediaevalia 33], Berlin / New York: Walter de Gruyter, 2006, 407n8. See also above T1, note 8.

[2] For the issue and meaningful application of the concept of encyclopaedia to medieval Arabic writings see the useful collection of articles in Gerhard Endress, ed., *Organizing*

b. *Dates of Composition*

The dates of composition of *The Cure* can be established with relative certainty. The sources available in this regard are primarily the two reports by Jūzjānī in his Introduction to *The Cure* (T7) and in the Biography, and secondarily the incidental chronological references provided by Avicenna himself in the work. Jūzjānī mentions no specific dates but only refers to political events corresponding to the various stages of the composition of *The Cure*. For the most part it is possible to date these events with precision.

The absolute chronology of Avicenna's life can be followed beginning with the first specific date that can be established, the death of Qābūs ibn-Vušmagīr, the Ziyārid ruler of Jurjān. This took place in the winter months of 403, i.e., approximately between January and March of 1013.[3] After the death of Qābūs, Avicenna says in the Autobiography, "I departed for Dihistān, where I fell very ill. I returned to Jurjān, and there I became associated with Abu-ʿUbayd al-Jūzjānī (T3, § 15)." Avicenna then went to Rayy where he remained until the Būyid "Šams-ad-Dawla arrived after the killing of Hilāl ibn-Badr ibn-Ḥasanwayh and the rout of the troops of Baġdād" (Biography 50.1–3). The battle between Šams-ad-Dawla and Hilāl, and the latter's death occurred in Ḏū-l-Qaʿda 405/April 1015.[4] From Rayy Avicenna departed for Qazwīn and from there to Hamaḏān, where he met Šams-ad-Dawla and accompanied him in his expedition against the ʿAnnāzids at Qarmīsīn (Biography 50.3–52.2). Given the number and the duration of the events that transpired between Hilāl's death and the expedition against the ʿAnnāzids, the latter could hardly have taken place before mid-406/Winter 1015–1016.[5]
104 Avicenna then returned to Hamaḏān and served as the vizier of Šams-ad-Dawla. Jūzjānī mentions both in the Biography (54–56) and in his Introduction (T7, §§ 3–4) that Avicenna started writing *The Cure* before Šams-ad-Dawla's death, which is known to have taken place in 412/1021–1022.[6] Avicenna thus began on his magnum opus some time between 406/1016 and

Knowledge. Encyclopaedic Activities in the Pre-Eighteenth Century Islamic World, Leiden: Brill, 2006, and especially the article by Josef van Ess, 3–19.

[3] See the article "Ḳābūs" by C.E. Bosworth in *EI*², IV,358, where all the literature is referred to. Cf. Gohlman 125n51.

[4] H. Busse, *Chalif und Grosskönig*, Beirut: F. Steiner, 1969, 89. Cf. Gohlman 127n62 and 63.

[5] See the article "ʿAnnāzids" by V. Minorsky in *EI*² I,512b, where the reference to the "autobiography" of Avicenna should be to the Biography. Cf. Gohlman 128n69.

[6] See Bosworth "Kākūyids" 74; cf. Gohlman 128n73.

412/1021. With the information available it is impossible to establish the date with greater precision; it may not be idle to suggest, however, that given the order in which the events are narrated in both of Jūzjānī's accounts, Avicenna started to work on *The Cure* not too long before Šams-ad-Dawla's death, about 411/1020.

Avicenna continued working on *The Cure* in Hamadān until the capture of the city by the Kākūyid ʿAlāʾ-ad-Dawla in 414/1023–1024[7] and shortly after it. "Some time" later (*zamān*, Biography 62.2), he decided to move to Iṣfahān, where he was received with honors by ʿAlāʾ-ad-Dawla. He completed the remaining parts of *The Cure* there, and wrote the last two books "in the year in which ʿAlāʾ-ad-Dawla headed for Šābūr-Ḫwāst, en route" (Biography 66.3–4). The events surrounding Šābūr-Ḫwāst that engrossed ʿAlāʾ-ad-Dawla's attention are in all likelihood those associated with the Kurdish rebellions in 417–418/1026–1027; ʿAlāʾ-ad-Dawla may have headed for Šābūr-Ḫwāst in connection with the battle at Nihāwand where he routed the rebels in 418/1027.[8] An earlier recorded expedition to Šābūr-Ḫwāst by ʿAlāʾ-ad-Dawla took place right after he had captured Hamadān in 414/1024, when Avicenna was still in Hamadān; whereas a later one took place in 421/1030, when Avicenna was already engaged in writing other works of a similar nature as that of *The Cure*, specifically the *Fair Judgment* (W10).[9] *The Cure* was thus completed at the latest by 418/1027.

On the basis of these dates in Avicenna's career and the details about the composition of the work provided by Jūzjānī, it is possible to offer the following chronological table:

406–412/1016–1021, possibly about 411/1020: Avicenna begins writing
The Cure in Hamadān at the request of Jūzjānī. Begins with
Physics 1; writes approximately twenty folia.

412–414/1022–1024: in Hamadān, writes:
Logic 1 (Eisagoge); Physics 1 (completed); Physics 2; Physics 3; 105
Physics 4; Physics 5; Physics 6; Metaphysics, entire, in twenty days.

414/1024: in Hamadān, writes,
Logic 2; Logic 3; Logic 4; Logic 5; Logic 6 (?);

---

7 Bosworth "Kākūyids" 74–75; cf. Gohlman 131n80. The year 414 AH fell between 26 March 1023 and 15 March 1024. Since Ibn-al-Aṯīr (IX,232 Tornberg) mentions that in the course of the operations some three hundred soldiers of ʿAlāʾ-ad-Dawla died because of the extreme cold, I would guess the conquest of the city to have taken place in late 414, or early 1024.

8 Bosworth "Kākūyids" 75.

9 Cf. Gohlman 132n89.

414–418/1024–1027: in Iṣfahān, writes,
Logic 7; Logic 8; Logic 9; Mathematics 2;
adds to the completed work,
Mathematics 1; Mathematics 3; Mathematics 4;

418/1027: en route to Šābūr-Ḫwāst, writes,
Physics 7; Physics 8.

The Cure was thus composed intermittently during a period of approximately eight years, from 1020 to 1027. The age of Avicenna at this time is again elusive. Jūzjānī offers two numbers, but they are mutually contradictory. In the Introduction to *The Cure* he says that Avicenna was "approximately thirty-two years old" when they met in Jurjān (T7, § 2); since this took place relatively shortly after the death of Qābūs, the year must have been 404/July 1013-July 1014. However, in the same Introduction Jūzjānī also specifies that Avicenna was forty years old when he completed *The Cure* (T7, § 6), i.e., in 418/1027. This is clearly impossible since between the year of their meeting (404) and the year of the completion of *The Cure* (418) there elapsed about fifteen years, not eight, as suggested by Jūzjānī's account.[10] His numbers are therefore wrong.

Assuming that Jūzjānī did not intentionally provide false information, the inaccuracies can perhaps be explained as errors of calculation starting with the figures Jūzjānī knew best. The year of Avicenna's death is firmly established as 428/1037.[11] Jūzjānī can also be trusted to have known the number of years he had been with Avicenna, which he says in the Biography (68.3) to have been twenty-five. Since he calculated that Avicenna lived to be fifty-eight (Biography 88.4–6), his conclusion that Avicenna was thirty-two when they met is thereby explained and is consistent with the other figures he provides. His statement that Avicenna was forty when he completed *The Cure*, on the other hand, is clearly either an error of calculation on Jūzjānī's part or possibly due to the erroneous transmission of the number (forty-eight?) in the transmission of the manuscripts.[12]

---

[10] Gohlman 133n89 fails to see the discrepancy when he cites these numbers. If Avicenna was forty in 421/1030, as he suggests, then he must have been born in 380/990, something which is clearly contradictory to the date of birth which is given by Jūzjānī (i.e., 370/980; Biography 89) and not disputed by Gohlman.

[11] See the references to the sources in Gohlman 137n113.

[12] The editor of *The Guidance* (*al-Hidāya*, 1974), Muḥammad ʿAbduh, comes to grips with the problem and tries to save Jūzjānī's figures by suggesting (pp. 14–15) that what perhaps Jūzjānī meant by the number "forty" was to indicate the age at which Avicenna started on *The Cure*, not when he completed it. Jūzjānī's text, however, is very explicit.

The incidental information which Avicenna himself provides in *The Cure* enables us to come tantalizingly close to establishing a precise chronology for the composition of the different parts of the work, but in fact it merely corroborates the general framework described above. In the Prior Analytics part of the Logic of *The Cure* he says that he came across a book on conditional propositions and syllogisms "about eighteen years after we had figured out this part of the Philosophical Sciences."[13] The period of his youth referred to here must be that when he was between sixteen and seventeen and a half: the word he uses here, "figured out" (*istaḫrajnā*), fits very well with his description in the Autobiography, "So I continued until all the Philosophical Sciences became deeply rooted in me and I understood them as much as is humanly possible. Everything that I knew at that time is just as I know it now; I have added nothing more to it to this day" (T3, §8). Avicenna thus came across this book when he was at least thirty-four or thirty-five, and when he was writing the Prior Analytics of *The Cure,* i.e. in 414/1024, he was older than that, something which is consistent with the chronology described above. More relevant is another dated reference Avicenna makes in the Meteorology section of the Physics of *The Cure* where he says that he saw a halo around the sun in 390–391 [/1000–1001] and then again approximately twenty years later.[14] Even if the conventional date of his birth is accepted (370/980), this would make him over forty years old when he was composing the Meteorology part of *The Cure* in 412–414/1022–1024. Jūzjānī's statement that Avicenna was forty when he completed the work is thus false and can be discounted; that he was thirty-two when they met has still to be verified, although it is consistent with the other figures that Jūzjānī provides. 106

c. *The Date and Purpose of Composition of Jūzjānī's Introduction and Avicenna's Prologue to* The Cure

The questions of the time and purpose of composition of Jūzjānī's Introduction to *The Cure* and its relation to his Biography need special consideration. 107
Jūzjānī himself says that he wrote the Introduction for the following purposes (T7): 1) To explain that Avicenna chose to write *The Cure per modum*

[13] *Al-Qiyās* 356.9–10 Zāyid: *wa-baʿda an kunnā staḫrajnā hāḏā l-juzʾa mina l-ʿilmi bi-qarībin min ṯamāniya ʿašra* ⟨*ta*⟩ *sanatan* .... The translation by Shehaby 159 is inaccurate ("nearly 18 years ago"), for it implies that Avicenna was thirty-four or thirty-five when he was writing the *Qiyās*, which is clearly impossible.

[14] *Al-Maʿādin* 49.13–16 Muntaṣir et al. Similar but less precise chronological references are found also in other parts of the same book. See the quoations assembled by Mahdavī 125n1.

expositionis rather than as a textual commentary on Aristotle because he had no time; 2) to explain that the reason that the Logic of *The Cure* follows the order and arrangement of Aristotle's *Organon* while the Physics and Metaphysics do not follow the order of Aristotle's corresponding books is that Avicenna wrote the former in leisure and with full access to books while the latter he wrote from memory; 3) to glorify Avicenna for his extraordinary abilities to write from memory something which in the Cairo edition of *The Cure* takes hundreds of pages.

These three points address the following problems and imply the following chronological context: No. (1) is an answer to those who were requesting from Avicenna commentaries on the text of Aristotle and who were not content with his works *per modum expositionis* which were then available, including *The Cure*. This situation could have existed only before the compilation of the *Fair Judgment* which addressed itself precisely to these requests. Jūzjānī's explanation, therefore, is temporally relevant only to the period before the compilation of the *Fair Judgment*, for if it were written afterwards one would have expected a reference to it, perhaps together with the account of its loss, as in the Biography (80.5–7; see below the discussion on W10).

Jūzjānī's attempt in No. (2) to claim that Avicenna wrote the entire Metaphysics and Physics 1 (?) through 6 "without having available any book to consult" is at the very least disingenuous. A comparison of the two accounts in the Introduction and the Biography is again edifying:

Introduction (T7, §4)	*Biography 58.2–8 Gohlman*
He voluntarily applied himself with great earnestness to [the] composition [of *The Cure*],	The Master wrote down the main topics [of *The Cure*] in approximately twenty octavo quires. He worked at this for two days until he had written down the main topics without the presence of a book or source to consult, but from his memory and by heart. Then he left these quires before him, took paper, and he would examine each topic and write the commentary on it.
and in a period of twenty days he finished Metaphysics and Physics (except the two books on Zoology and Botany), without having available any	He would write fifty folia every day, until he had completed the entire Physics and Metaphysics (except the two books on Zoology and Botany[a]).

[a] "And Botany" is found only in the Ibn-al-Qifṭī/Ibn-Abī-Uṣaybiʿa recension of the Biog-

Introduction (*T7*, *§4*)	*Biography* 58.2–8 *Gohlman*
book to consult, but by relying solely upon his natural talents.	
He also started on Logic and wrote the opening address and associated material.	He began on Logic and wrote one part of it. (L3)

108

Jūzjānī's remark in the Introduction that Avicenna wrote by heart the entire Physics and Metaphysics appears to be willfully inaccurate for two reasons: first, in the Biography he himself transfers that remark, more credibly, to the drafting of the outline only which Avicenna wrote prior to the actual composition of these books, and second, he fails to mention the fact, doubtless well known to him, that entire chapters in at least the De Anima and Metaphysics parts of *The Cure* were copied verbatim from earlier works, in particular *The Provenance and Destination* and the "Lesser" *Destination*. Even if one were to grant Avicenna prodigious mnemonic powers, it is hard to believe that he could have reproduced from memory every single word of scores of pages originally written over a decade before.

It thus seems quite certain that Jūzjānī in this instance is deliberately exaggerating a point—if not falsifying the facts—in an attempt to answer Avicenna's Peripatetic critics (actual or potential) who would have expected him to follow, albeit *per modum expositionis*, the order and the contents of the Aristotelian canon of writings. The justification offered here by Jūzjānī is again temporally tenable only for the period before the composition of Avicenna's later works, *The Easterners* and particularly *Pointers and Reminders*, which were written in Iṣfahān when Avicenna had both the time and the freedom to consult all the books that could have been physically available to him. If Jūzjānī were to offer the same explanation after their composition, it would have been immediately rejected on the grounds that in these later works Avicenna still followed the order and the arrangement of *The Cure* (and deviated even more from Aristotelian patterns).

The glorification of Avicenna in No. (3) and in paragraph 1 of Jūzjānī's Introduction in general ill accords with both the relatively more subdued tone in the Biography, which was written after Avicenna's death, and the openly critical attitude toward his master evident in later works. A good example is provided by his comments in the abridgment of an astronomical

---

raphy, but also in the margin of one of the MSS in the independent tradition preferred by Gohlman. Clearly it belongs to the text and it should not be left out.

work of his entitled, *On the Nature of the Construction of the Spheres*. In his introduction Jūzjānī says that he had been baffled for a long time by the concept of the equant sphere and did not know if the reason that there was no explanation available anywhere was because

> they (i.e. the astronomers) niggardly held it back from others, or it escaped them altogether, as in the case of [Avicenna], may God have mercy on his soul. When I asked him about this problem, he said: "I came to understand this problem after great effort and much toil, and I will not teach it to anybody.
> 109 Apply yourself to it and it may be revealed to you as it was revealed to me." I suspect that I was the first to achieve these results.[15] (L4)

The above considerations thus indicate that the tenor of Jūzjānī's Introduction is apologetic with a laudatory dimension, and that its main thrust is to defend Avicenna's Peripatetic orthodoxy. Such a depiction of Avicenna's relationship to the Aristotelian tradition could not have been maintained after, nor was it indeed maintained by Avicenna himself in the Prologue to *The Cure* (T9) and the Introduction to *The Easterners* (T8). It is therefore fair to assume that Jūzjānī's Introduction antedated both of them.

Three further considerations support this assumption. First, a comparison between Jūzjānī's Introduction and Biography indicates that in the latter he gives essentially the same account of the history of the composition of *The Cure*, but with some major differences: the Biography is for the most part more detailed in the narration of events, making the corresponding parts of the Introduction superfluous;[16] the Biography is relatively more specific in referring to the particular names of the personalities involved in the events, suggesting that the reticence or vagueness of the Introduction in this regard may be due to the concern lest these personalities be offended;[17] and the Biography, finally, is manifestly free of any attempt to claim Peripatetic

---

15 Saliba 380. (I am grateful to George Saliba for drawing my attention to his article and to this passage.) See *GAS* VI,281n2, for a differently worded account of the same conversation between the two men by Quṭb-ad-Dīn aš-Šīrāzī, presumably extracted from Jūzjānī's longer work. It is very likely that similar statements will come to light when Jūzjānī's extant works are studied.

16 See my references to the Biography in the notes to the translation of Jūzjānī's Introduction, T7.

17 Cf. for example, "the notables of that state" (T7, § 5), as opposed to the specific mention of Tāj-al-Mulk in the Biography (58.8); particularly striking is the absence of any mention of 'Alā'-ad-Dawla in the Introduction, presumably in order not to involve him explicitly in the events surrounding Avicenna's imprisonment in Fardajān and his subsequent move to Iṣfahān. If this argument is valid, then by the same reasoning the Biography, in which 'Alā'-ad-Dawla is mentioned, must have been written after the latter's death in 433/1041.

orthodoxy for Avicenna,[18] reflecting the philosopher's later position, as discussed in the next preceding paragraph under No. (2). All these differences indicate that the Biography was written after the Introduction.

Second, there is the matter of the benedictory formula after the name of
Avicenna in Jūzjānī's Introduction (T7, §1). Certain manuscripts of the work 110
have, "may God perpetuate his days," an indication that Avicenna was alive at the time of writing, while others have instead, "May God have mercy on his soul;" the Latin translation omits the phrase entirely. Scribes of Arabic manuscripts were notoriously free with the use of such formulae and can hardly be relied upon to reproduce the exact words originally used by the author, but the former formula wishing Avicenna a long life is by the nature of things the *lectio difficilior* and to be preferred in this case.

Third, there is the matter of Jūzjānī's misinformation at best, or patent lie at worst, concerning Avicenna's writing from memory: large parts of the Metaphysics are copied verbatim from *The Provenance and Destination*, and it is rather inconceivable that Avicenna should have had the text by heart. The only reason for this that I can suggest is that Jūzjānī wanted to gloss over Avicenna's blatant "innovations" in the hope that in a future work he could perhaps write an exposition of Aristotle's system. It is not unlikely that the *Fair Judgment* owes its genesis to such an insistence by Jūzjānī.

Jūzjānī therefore wrote the Introduction to *The Cure* before the Biography, when his master was still alive, and apparently even before Avicenna wrote any of the later comprehensive philosophical works, or summae. I would even argue that Jūzjānī wrote the Introduction immediately upon the completion of *The Cure*. In it he represents himself as the instigator and constant goad of the project, and if this was indeed the case, he must have considered it his right to introduce the finished product and could hardly have tarried to do so. What he originally envisaged the work to be (an exposition of Aristotle's philosophy) and the actual work he received at the end (Avicenna's version of Aristotle's philosophy) were apparently two different things, and this would explain the apologetic tenor of the Introduction. However the case may be, the fact remains that Jūzjānī prized *The Cure* above all of Avicenna's works: in the body of the Biography he does not

18 It is indicative that the Biography not only does not say that Avicenna wrote the Physics and Metaphysics from memory, but also omits the claim made by the Introduction (T7, §6), that the Logic follows the order of the *Organon* because Avicenna had access to books. Such a claim could not have been made in the Biography in view of Avicenna's later works.

even mention at all *The Easterners* and especially *Pointers and Reminders*, let alone describe the circumstances surrounding their composition, despite the fact that they were works about which such bibliographical information was sorely needed. This casts an interesting light on Jūzjānī, and will have to be taken seriously into consideration in an appraisal of his own work and his relation to Avicenna.

For his part, it appears that Avicenna at a later stage, after he had written *The Easterners*, thought Jūzjānī's Introduction to *The Cure* inadequate, if not misleading. To eliminate its apologetic impression and to answer to its implication that Avicenna was an anti-Aristotelian despite himself, i.e.,
111 because he could not help it due to objective conditions, he removed all references to the "extenuating" circumstances adduced by Jūzjānī: the lack of free time, the unavailability of books, the imprisonment, etc. Instead, he presented both the organization and contents of the book as being solely due to his deliberate plan. He says explicitly in the Prologue (T9, § 2; emphasis added), "There is *nothing of account* to be found in the books of the ancients *which we did not include in this book* of ours;" i.e., there are no omissions of significant theories due to the unavailability of sources, as Jūzjānī implied (the statement at the end of §1 of the Prologue, "excluding only ... what escaped my memory and did not occur to my thought," is a general disclaimer dictated by scholarly prudence and does not appear to have any specific reference); "if it is not found in the place where it is Customary to record it, then it will be found in another place which *I thought more appropriate for it*;" i.e., the displacement, or rather, the deviation from the axiomatic arrangement of subjects in the Aristotelian canon is deliberate and not due to the lack of sources to consult; "to this I added some of the things which I perceived through *my own* reflection and whose Validity I Determined through *my own* theoretical analysis, *especially in Physics and Metaphysics*," i.e., the two subjects which Jūzjānī specifically singles out repeatedly (T7, §§ 4, 7) as being organized differently from the works of Aristotle because of the lack of books. Avicenna here expressly rejects Jūzjānī's interpretation and states that the different organization (and contents) are due to his own research. "And even in logic, if you will," is again directed specifically against Jūzjānī's account in the Introduction (T7, §§ 6, 7) that the part on Logic followed the *Organon* because of the availability of books. Avicenna of course does follow a course "parallel to the order of Aristotle's books [on logic]" as he himself says in the Prologue (T9, § 5), but this has nothing to do with the availability of books, and the outward conformity to the Aristotelian canon does not, as Jūzjānī implies, bespeak a corresponding internal congruence: should one look more closely—and that is the thrust of the parenthetical,

"if you will"—there is a disparity between the Aristotelian tradition on logic and his own in substance as well (see Chapter 6.4 and 6.5).

Avicenna thus presents himself in the Prologue to *The Cure* not as an anti-Aristotelian despite himself, as Jūzjānī would have it, but as a conscious reformer of the Aristotelian tradition, an attitude which is also apparent in the Introduction to *The Easterners* and shared by other disciples of his like Bahmanyār.[19] The Prologue itself was added to the completed *The Cure* in
response to Jūzjānī's previous Introduction, and it was written in all prob- 112
ability shortly after *The Easterners*, to which it refers as a work of equal importance as *The Cure* and hence presumably very much in circulation—or at least available at the time, as opposed to Avicenna's later references to it as having been withdrawn from circulation (T11, § 1).[20]

Work 7. *The Salvation* (*an-Najāt*) [GS 6]

Jūzjānī says in the Biography (66.4) that Avicenna wrote *The Salvation* en route to Šābūr-Ḫwāst right after completing the last books of *The Cure*. This information is also repeated in the anonymous Longer Bibliography (LB 15 = 96.1–2 Gohlman). According to the chronology established for *The Cure* in the preceding section, *The Salvation* was thus written in 417/1026 or 418/1027.

This work also was a commissioned piece. In his brief introduction Avicenna mentions that a group of unspecified friends asked him to compile a book that would include the indispensable minimum of philosophical knowledge necessary for a person to acquire in order to be counted among the educated elite. In particular, they asked him to include only the Fundamental Principles of Logic and Physics, as much information from Geometry and Arithmetic as is necessary for one to deal with mathematical proofs, practical information from Astronomy related to calendars and *zīj*es, Music, and Metaphysics. This last section, which was to be written in as clear and concise a manner as possible, was also to contain information about the

19 Bahmanyār describes the contents of his *Taḥṣīl* (p. 1 Moṭahharī) as "the gist of the philosophy which Avicenna revised" (*lubāb* [thus to be read for *kitāb* in the text] *al-ḥikma allatī haḏḏabahā š-Šayḫ*).

20 Goichon "Nouvauté" 44.13–17 was the only scholar to have sensed that the Prologue to *The Cure* must have been written after the work itself, "vers la fin de sa vie." Although she proffered no arguments ("bien que nous n'ayons trouvé nulle part cette hypothèse") she deserves credit for being aware of the problem. S. Van Riet makes no mention of the matter.

Destination, or place of return, of the human soul, and about personal ethics in order for one "to attain salvation from drowning in the sea of errors."[1]

Avicenna granted their request and compiled *The Salvation* practically without composing a single line anew. As Jūzjānī informs us (Biography 74.9–76.1), for the Logic he used the *Shorter Summary on Logic* which he had written in Jurjān, i.e., approximately around 404/1013–1014. A comparison of the remaining parts of *The Salvation* with other works of Avicenna indicates that for the Physics he copied the corresponding chapters from *The*
113 *Compilation* or the *Philosophy for ʿArūḍī*, which he had written as a young man in Buḫārā, except for the De Anima, for which he used the chapter from the "Lesser" *Destination*. Most of the Metaphysics, finally, is copied verbatim from *The Provenance and Destination*. After putting together these various earlier compositions of his, obviously in a very short time, Avicenna did not complete his editorial patchwork.[2] Jūzjānī remarks that the reason for this was that "he was hindered by some obstacles," and therefore he, Jūzjānī, assumed the responsibility of completing the work. He says that he added the chapters on Geometry, Astronomy, and Music from earlier works by Avicenna found in his own possession, but that since he could find nothing appropriate for Arithmetic, he took it upon himself to abridge from Avicenna's larger work on Arithmetic in *The Cure* those passages that are especially pertinent to Music and include them in *The Salvation*. He also wrote a very brief preface to the part on Mathematics, from which the above information is derived.[3]

Jūzjānī's explanation of Avicenna's omission of the mathematical part again seems to be apologetic. After completing *The Cure*, Avicenna never wrote another mathematical part for any of his summae: neither *Philos-*

---

[1] *Najāt* 2–3/3–4; Mahdavī 226–227.

[2] Apparently he did not even edit the patchwork for inconsistencies. An understanding of his compositional technique in works that copy each other can be gained only after close scrutiny of and comparison among the repeated passages, a work that has yet to be done. For *The Salvation*, Fazlur Rahman had already noted in 1958 (*Prophecy* 72n30) that certain phrases of internal reference, taken over from *The Cure*, were not excised in *The Salvation* although the passages to which they referred in *The Cure* were not also copied in *The Salvation*. This lack of editing and revision is also responsible for the appearance of Plato in *The Salvation* as "divine," which is taken over unedited from the "Lesser" *Destination* and indicates the posteriority of *The Salvation* to that work, because "divine" is not something that Avicenna would have called Plato in 1027–1028 when he was compiling *The Salvation*; see above W5 and note 1, and the discussion of this subject below, Chapter 7 and in the Appendix, GM 3.

[3] Jūzjānī's preface is given in Mahdavī 234–235, and translated, from the Damascus MS (formerly) Ẓāhiriyya 9152, in Ragep and Ragep 3–4.

ophy for ʿAlāʾ-ad-Dawla (W8), nor *The Easterners* (W9), nor *Pointers and Reminders* (W11) has one. As a matter of fact, even before *The Cure* Avicenna frequently omitted this part in similar works such as *Elements of Philosophy* (*ʿUyūn al-ḥikma*, GS 3) and *The Guidance* (*al-Hidāya*, GS 4).[4] Avicenna states the reason in *The Easterners*: Mathematics, he says, and most of the practical sciences (Ethics, Oeconomics, Politics), are not areas in which philosophers have disagreed (Testimonium 19 in W9 below). This means that Avicenna did not find any major conflicts between his views on these subjects and those transmitted in the Aristotelian tradition. The standard books on these subjects were for the most part sufficient, and after treating them himself in several monographs and extensively in *The Cure*, he found no need for repeated expositions and successive elaborations, as he had for the other subjects. Jūzjānī's excuse that Avicenna was diverted by other engagements from incorporating these subjects in *The Salvation* thus appears another attempt to excuse Avicenna's deviation from traditional practice and to justify his Aristotelian orthodoxy.

The Salvation, both the parts compiled by Avicenna and those added by Jūzjānī, is a composite piece of work bringing together earlier compositions by Avicenna, written at various stages of his career. It is *not* a summary or abridgment of *The Cure*, as frequently stated,[5] but rather both it and *The* 114
Cure copy passages from earlier works by Avicenna, notably *The Philosophy for ʿArūḍī, The Provenance and Destination*, and *The Destination*. It is these passages from the last two, incorporated in the De anima and Metaphysics parts of *The Cure* and *The Salvation*, that Goichon and Michot identify in their tables of concordance, *Distinction* 499–503 and "Prophétie et divination" 532–534, respectively. The bibliographical usefulness of *The Salvation* lies in enabling us to trace the evolution of Avicenna's thought on all these subjects by comparing its text with that of chapters from earlier works, some of which were written almost thirty years previously.[6]

---

4 Though the editor of the *Hidāya*, M. ʿAbduh, suggests (pp. 25–27) that originally the work might have included such a section.

5 Especially in older literature, as, for example, in Afnan (1958) 71, S. Pines ("Philosophy," *The Cambridge History of Islam*, Cambridge: Cambridge University Press, 1970, II,806), and Fakhry ([1]1970) 135 (repeated in the [3]2004 edition), but not in some more recent works such as Goodman ([2]2006) 32 and McGinnis *Avicenna* (2010) 24, to name only accessible treatments in English.

6 See, for example, the remarks made above (W1) about some of the specific differences in wording and arrangement between *Philosophy for ʿArūḍī* and *The Salvation*.

Work 8. *Philosophy for ʿAlāʾ-ad-Dawla* (*Dānešnāme-ye ʿAlāʾī*) [GS 7]

This work was written in Persian (cf. Lazard 62–66) at the express request of the Kākūyid ʿAlāʾ-ad-Dawla during Avicenna's stay in Iṣfahān. Since Avicenna lived in Iṣfahān from 414/1023 until his death in 428/1037, it could have been written any time during this long period. Mahdavī 101 may be right in suggesting the earlier rather than the later years of this period as the date of composition; since it so closely resembles *The Salvation* in both scope and execution, I would also place it around 418/1027. It may be possible to arrive at a more precise relative date after its doctrinal points have been compared with those in other works in order to detect shifts in emphasis.

Avicenna says in the introduction that ʿAlāʾ-ad-Dawla specifically asked him to set down in as abridged a manner as possible the Fundamental Principles and major points of five sciences, Logic, Physics, Astronomy, Music, and Metaphysics. Avicenna, in fact, actually wrote only three, omitting the two parts of Mathematics (Astronomy and Music), and changed the order of presentation of the rest into Logic, Metaphysics, and Physics.[1] This change of order foreshadows the new arrangement Avicenna was later to follow in *The Easterners* (W9).

The book bears the title *Dānešnāme-ye ʿAlāʾī*, but it is not clear whether it is Avicenna's title or what was given to it by Jūzjānī (or others?). In any case, the word *dāneš* in the title, knowledge, is used in the special sense in which Avicenna used the Arabic *ʿilm*, Knowledge, meaning Philosophy (Chapter 3.1 below). The Persian usage is thus parallel to the Arabic title of Avicenna's other work, *al-Ḥikma al-ʿArūḍiyya, Philosophy for ʿArūḍī* (W2 above), and would correspond in Arabic to *al-Ḥikma al-ʿAlāʾiyya*. This is indicated by the fact that in his preface Avicenna does not refer to Philosophy as *dāneš* but uses the Arabic word, *ḥekmat*: he says the book will comprise "five sciences among the sciences of Philosophy" (*panj ʿelm az ʿelmhā-ye ḥekmat*). And Bahmanyār himself translated the Persian title precisely as *al-Ḥikma al-ʿAlāʾiyya* (*at-Taḥṣīl* 1 Moṭahharī). The Persian title thus properly means, "book comprising philosophy, or the philosophical sciences, dedicated to ʿAlāʾ-ad-Dawla," or *Philosophy for ʿAlāʾ-ad-Dawla* for short.

Jūzjānī completed the work by adding the part on Mathematics and including not only Astronomy and Music, as Avicenna was asked and had

[1] Mahdavī 102 = Achena and Massé I,63–64.

intended to do, but also Arithmetic and Geometry. This entire mathematical part, as a matter of fact, is largely a Persian translation of the corresponding parts Jūzjānī had added to *The Salvation*: Geometry, Astronomy, and Music from earlier works by Avicenna, and Arithmetic from his own selection of issues pertinent to Music from the Arithmetic of *The Cure*. In his brief preface to this part, which is almost verbatim identical with the one he had written for *The Salvation* (W7), he explains that he decided to complete the work because the part Avicenna himself had written was lost.[2] This explanation also can be discounted because, as in the case with *The Salvation*, it appears to be apologetic in nature.

Avicenna wrote the work apparently by translating into Persian sections that he had written earlier in Arabic. Such underlying texts have been identified by Janssens ("Dānesh-Nāmeh") in the compilation of Avicenna's jottings later collected into the *Notes* (W13), as well as in an independently circulating section on the uses of logic extant in the early Leiden MS Golius 184 (Janssens *Bibliography* 17).[3] It is not yet clear whether the entire text was translated from previously written Arabic sections or just those that have survived (or were selected to survive) in the *Notes* and elsewhere. In its turn, the Persian *Dānešnāme* was used as the base for the interpretive translation back into Arabic by Ġazālī in his *Intentions of the Philosophers* (*Maqāṣid al-falāsifa*).[4] Future research along these lines will shed more light on the composition and state of the text of the *Dānešnāme*.

Work 9. *The Easterners* (*al-Mašriqiyyūn*) [GS 8] 115

The questions of the nature and date of composition, transmission and survival of this book are complex and have been complicated even further by hasty scholarship. For a sober assessment, it is necessary to collect and sort out all the pertinent facts; these include statements by Avicenna and later philosophers, as well as the evidence provided by the extant parts of the work itself.[1]

---

[2] Mahdavī 110 = Achena and Massé II,91–92.

[3] The section on logic, which is the Arabic original of the very first chapter of the *Dānešnāme*, was published by Mohaghegh in Mohaghegh and Izutsu, pp. *do-seh*; cf. also Janssens "Structuration" 110n6. In this article Janssens offers (p. 110n5) some corrections to his previous article on "Dānesh-Nāmeh."

[4] See Janssens "*Maʿārij al-quds*" 31n13, and Afifi al-Akiti 197n23.

[1] Most of the available evidence has been collected in the useful discussion by Mahdavī 80–88.

a. *Testimonia*

I. Statements by Avicenna.

Avicenna mentions "Eastern" matters and the "Easterners" in all his currently known writings as follows:

A) "Eastern philosophy" (*al-ḥikma al-mašriqiyya*), 7 times:

[1] Prologue to *The Cure*, 1 time (T9, §4):

> I also wrote a book other than these two [*The Cure* and the *Appendices*], in which I presented philosophy as it is naturally [perceived] and as required by an unbiased view which neither takes into account in [this book] the views of colleagues in the discipline, nor takes precautions here against creating schisms among them as is done elsewhere; this is my book on Eastern philosophy [*wa-huwa kitābī fī l-falsafa al-mašriqiyya*]. ... Whoever wants the truth [stated] without indirection, he should seek [this] book.

[2] Commentary on the *Theologia*, 6 times (Badawī *Arisṭū* 43.10, 43.19, 53.19, 58.9, 61 ult., 72.12):[2]

> [In all these passages Avicenna says that the answer to the problem discussed should be sought "in the Eastern philosophy" (*ʿalā/min/fī l-ḥikma al-mašriqiyya*), without prefixing the word *kitāb* (book) to "Eastern philosophy." In one instance only (53.18–19) he says that the subject is discussed "in the books and in the Eastern philosophy" (*fī l-kutub wa-fī l-ḥikma al-mašriqiyya*).]

B) "Eastern questions" (*al-masāʾil al-mašriqiyya*), 1 time:

[3] Letter to an Anonymous Disciple (Bahmanyār) (T11, §1):

> You expressed sorrow at the loss of *Pointers and Reminders*, but I think that a copy of this book has been preserved. As for the Eastern questions, I had
> 116 packed them up—no, most of them—[as they were] in their quires so as no one would look at them, and I had also written down on slips of paper some passages from the *Throne Philosophy*; it is these which got lost. They were not voluminous, however (although they did treat many subjects and were quite comprehensive), and it would be easy to rewrite them. But yes, the *Fair Judgment*, on the other hand, could not but be extensive, and rewriting it would require work.

C) "Eastern Fundamental Principles" (*al-uṣūl al-mašriqiyya*), 1 time:

---

[2] These passages are identified by Vajda "Théologie" 348, and the subjects they deal with are listed in notes 2–7.

[4] Letter to an Anonymous Disciple (Bahmanyār) (T11, § 4):

> The invariable element in animals may be [a subject] more amenable to a clear exposition; as a matter of fact, I dealt with it thoroughly in the Eastern Fundamental Principles by first raising doubts and then solving them. In the case of plants, however, a clear exposition [of the same subject] is more difficult.

D) "Eastern demonstrative proof" (*al-burhān aš-šarqī/al-mašriqī*), 1 time:

[5] *Discussions* § 298 Bīdārfar (= § 107 Badawī *Arisṭū* 145.11):

> Bahmanyār (?) requests from Avicenna a demonstrative proof (*burhān*) that is "according to the Throne or Eastern" (*ʿaršī aw šarqī*), about the faculty of the intellect, that it is not imprinted in matter; Avicenna responds that it will be found in the *Throne Philosophy*. The Ṣiġnāḫī codex recension (ed. Badawī) summarizes the question only and interprets *ʿaršī aw šarqī* as referring to *two* proofs of the same kind, *al-burhānayn al-mašriqiyyayn*: "The two Eastern demonstrative proofs that it is impossible for the faculty of the intellect to be corporeal." This provides a good example of the kind of editorial changes wrought in the Šiġnāḫī codex.[3]

E) "The Easterners" (*al-mašriqiyyūn*), 46 times:

[6] Letter to Kiyā, 1 time (T12, § 3):

> I had composed a book which I called *Fair Judgment*. I divided scholars into two groups, the Westerners and the Easterners, and I had the Easterners argue against the Westerners until I intervened to Judge Fairly when there was a real point of dispute between them.

[7] Introduction to *The Easterners*, 1 time (T8, § 2):

> It is not unlikely that the Easterners may have another name for [logic].

[8] *Fair Judgment*: *Commentary on Book Lambda*, 1 time (Badawī *Arisṭū* 33.18); *Discussions* § 876 Bīdārfar (= § 333[bis] Badawī *Arisṭū* 193.8),[4] 1 time; *Marginal Glosses on De anima*, 42 times (Badawī *Arisṭū* 75–116, *passim*):

> [In all these passages either from the *Fair Judgment* or related to it (see W10), there are three kinds of references to the Easterners: (a) they are either quoted directly or in paraphrase; (b) they are referred to in general for the completion

[3] See Reisman *Avicennan Tradition* 77–82. A full translation of this passage with a discussion of its significance can be found *ibid.* 228–230.

[4] This passage in the *Discussions* is actually a quotation from the *Commentary on Book Lambda*: "Avicenna mentioned in a passage that … (= Badawī *Arisṭū* 25.2–7) and found that the discussion on this subject is best listened to from the Easterners."

117 of an argument or for the solution of a problem (e.g., Badawī *Arisṭū* 33.18, 86.16, 100.12, 193.8); (c) references are made to the books of the Easterners (Badawī *Arisṭū* 83.11, 96.16, 110.18, 116.13).]

II. Statements By Others

[9] Shorter Bibliography (SB 16), 46.10 Gohlman:

> Some of the *Eastern Philosophy*, one volume.[5]

[10a] Longer Bibliography (LB 47), 102.3–4 Gohlman:

> The book *Eastern Philosophy*, which is not extant in its entirety.

[10b] Extended Bibliography (EB 13), Bayhaqī *Tatimma* 187.14 Shafīʿ:

> The book *Eastern Philosophy*.

[11a] Bayhaqī (d. 1174), *Tatimma* 56.1–7/67–68:

> (i) Then Governor Abū-Sahl al-Ḥamdūnī along with a group of Kurds [troops] plundered the personal effects of the Master, among which were also his books. Of the *Fair Judgment* only some quires were [later] found, but then ʿAzīz-ad-Dīn al-Fuqqāʿī az-Zanjānī[6] claimed [the following] in some month of the year 545[/1150–1151]: "I bought a copy of it in Iṣfahān and took it to Marw." God knows best.
>
> (ii) As for the *Eastern Philosophy* in its entirety and the *Throne Philosophy*, the Imām Ismāʿīl al-Bāḫarzī said that they were in the libraries of Sultan Masʿūd ibn-Maḥmūd at Ghazna until [the libraries] were put to fire by the Ġūrid and Oġuz troops of the king of Jibāl, al-Ḥusayn [Jehān-sūz] in some month of the year 546[/1151].

[11b] Ibn-al-Aṯīr (d. 1233), *al-Kāmil* IX,297 (Tornberg)/VIII,211–212 Beirut, *s.a.* 425/1034:	[11c] Ṣadr-ad-Dīn al-Ḥusaynī (wrote ca. 1225), *Zubdat at-tawārīḫ*, p. 35 (Nūraddīn):
Abū-Sahl [al-Ḥamdūnī]	Then Governor Abū-Sahl al-Ḥamdūnī together with Tāš Farrāš
headed for Iṣfahān and occupied it.	headed for Iṣfahān with an army that filled the length and breadth of the earth.
He drove out ʿAlāʾ-ad-Dawla who fled from him, lest he	They drove out of it King ʿAlāʾ-ad-Dawla Abū-Jaʿfar,

[5] This information is repeated twice by the Ottoman bibliographer Bağdatlı Ismāʿīl Paşa, *Hadiyyat al-ʿārifīn*, I,309.5–6 Bilge and İnal.

[6] Weisweiler 62 identified this person as the donor of a pious foundation for the ʿAzīziyya library in Marw (from Yāqūt, *Muʿjam al-buldān* IV,509, who also gives the *nisba* as Zanjānī instead of Rīḥānī in Bayhaqī).

be sought after, towards Īḏāj, which was then ruled by King Abū-Kālījār. After Abū-Sahl captured Iṣfahān, he pillaged (*nahaba*) the treasuries (*ḫazā'in*) and possessions (*amwāl*) of ʿAlāʾ-ad-Dawla.	and raided (*aġārā*) his treasuries (*ḫazā'in*) and palace (*dār*).
Avicenna was [then] in the service of ʿAlāʾ-ad-Dawla,	Master Avicenna (RIP) was vizier of King ʿAlāʾ-ad-Dawla,
and his books (*kutub*) were seized and carried (*ḥumilat*)	and the troops of Tāš Farrāš raided his library (*bayt kutub*) and transported(*naqalū*) most of his [own] writings as well as his books to the library (*ḫizānat kutub*)
to Ghazna where they were placed in its libraries (*ḫazā'in kutub*)	in Ghazna where they were collected
until the troops of the Ġūrid al-Ḥusayn ibn-Ḥusayn	until the retinue of the King of Jibāl, al-Ḥusayn ibn-al-Ḥasan,
put them [the libraries] to fire (*ilā an aḥraqahā*), as we shall mention.[7]	put it [the library] to fire (*ilā an aḥraqahā*).

[12] Ibn-Ṭufayl (d. 1185), *Ḥayy ibn-Yaqẓān* 3.4–4.3, 14.9–15.1 (Gauthier):

> You have asked me, noble friend, … to make you privy to whatever I am able to of the secrets of Eastern philosophy which Avicenna mentioned, making it known that "whoever wants the truth without indirection should seek [T9 § 4]" [this philosophy] and try earnestly to acquire it. …
>
> As for the books of Aristotle, Avicenna undertook in *The Cure* to interpret their contents, proceeding according to Aristotle's doctrine and following the method of his philosophy. In the beginning of the book, Avicenna stated explicitly that in his opinion the truth is something else, that he wrote *The* 118
> *Cure* according to the doctrine of the Peripatetics only, and that "whoever wants the truth without indirection" should seek his book on Eastern philosophy.

[12a] Abner of Burgos / Alfonso of Valladolid (d. ca. 1347).

> [Various references to "Eastern Philosophy" (*filosofi'a ha-mizraḥit, ph/filosofia oriental*) in four of his works, all taken from Ibn Ṭufayl's *Ḥayy ibn-Yaqẓān*.[8]]

[13a] Averroes (d. 1198), *Tahāfut at-tahāfut* 421.5–9 (Bouyges):[9]

> In our time we have seen many of the followers of Avicenna ascribe to him this view regarding this aporia, saying that he is not of the opinion that there

[7] Ibn-al-Aṯīr does not give any more details on the subject in his account of the sack of Ghazna, Vol. XI,108–109, Tornberg.

[8] As shown by Szpiech, who also provides translations of these passages. Twelve such passages are also translated in Zonta.

[9] Maurice Bouyges, ed., *Averroès. Tahafot at-tahafot*, Beirut: Imprimerie Catholique, 1930; cf. the English translation by van den Bergh I,254.

is something separate [*mufāriq*]. They say that this appears from what he says about the necessary existent in a number of passages, and that it is the import of what he set forth in his Eastern philosophy, adding that he called it Eastern philosophy only because it is the doctrine of the people of the East [*mašriq*, i.e., Ḫurāsān], for they are of the opinion that the divine is the celestial bodies, as Avicenna himself had come to believe.

[13b] ——, *Questions in Physics* VIII.7, p. 31 Tunik Goldstein:[10]

Among those who hold this opinion are many of the modern philosophers we have encountered who follow the doctrine of Avicenna. They think that this is the opinion of Avicenna, and that it is the opinion to which he inclined in the *Oriental Philosophy*, and that there is no being which is not a body, subsisting in itself, separate from the celestial bodies, which is itself a principle of those
119 bodies and what exists through them, as was the opinion of the Peripatetics. With all this, they think that this was the opinion of the Philosopher himself, and that what is to be found in his books is only by way of that concealment which was the custom of the ancient philosophers, who followed it because of the prevalence of ignorance.[11]

[13c] ——, *On the Separateness of the First Principle*, p. 98 Steel and Guldentops:[12]

That man [from North Africa (*terra barbarorum*) who was renowned for his study of Avicenna] thought that it was impossible to prove that there is some being separate from matter which is not a body nor in a body, and that this was the opinion of Avicenna. [That man] believed that that is what Avicenna demonstrated in a hidden fashion [*occulte*] in his Eastern Philosophy, in which he had uniquely explained the truth, and that the many things he wrote[13] in his books he did so in order to agree with his contemporaries.

---

[10] Helen Tunik Goldstein, *Averroes' Questions in Physics*, Dordrecht: Kluwer Academic Publishers, 1991.

[11] These remarks are based on Avicenna's own statements. See below, Chapter 5.3.

[12] This work is extant only in Latin translation, edited by Carlos Steel and Guy Guldentops, "An Unknown Treatise of Averroes against the Avicennians on the First Cause. Edition and Translation," *Recherches de Théologie et Philosophie Médiévales* 64 (1997) 86–135. I translate closer to the Latin (p. 98), with a view to the underlying Arabic text. The Latin title has *separatio*, which most likely translates the Arabic *mufāraqa* (cf. *mufāriq* in Averroes' *Tahāfut* cited above at Test. 13a), and this is to be understood as separateness, or even separability, rather than "separation", as in Steel and Guldentops. It is noteworthy that the translator of the Arabic of this treatise was the very same Abner of Burgos, or Alfonso of Valladolid (Steel and Guldentops 88–89), who is also responsible for the confusion about Avicenna's "Eastern" philosophy in his own works: see Szpiech.

[13] The Latin has *posita, posuit*, which most likely stands for Arabic *waḍaʿa*, to write, to put down in writing.

[14] Suhrawardī Maqtūl (d. 1191), *al-Mašāriʿ wa-l-muṭāraḥāt* 195 (Corbin *Opera* I):

> The quires [*karārīs*] which Avicenna attributed to the Easterners are extant separately in unbound form.[a] Although he attributed these quires to the East, they are the same as the precepts of the Peripatetics and common philosophy. The only difference is that he occasionally altered the form of expression, or proceeded in certain Corollary issues in a somewhat independent way which, however, neither deviates from his other books to any appreciable degree, nor establishes the Fundamental Principle of the East which was founded at the time of the sages in the era of Chosroes. This Fundamental Principle is the exalted subject and the philosophy of the elite [i.e., as opposed to the "common" philosophy of the Peripatetics].

[15] Faḫr-ad-Dīn ar-Rāzī (d. 1209), *Šarḥ ʿUyūn al-ḥikma* II,6 as-Saqā:

> Commonplace philosophers are in agreement that the divisions of practical philosophy are three and that those of theoretical philosophy are also three. Avicenna says the same thing in this book [i.e., *Elements of Philosophy*] and likewise in most of his books except in the *Eastern Philosophy* where he mentions that the divisons of practical philosophy are four and that those of theoretical philosophy are also four.[14]

[16] Ibn-Sabʿīn (d. 1270), *Budd al-ʿārif* 129 Massignon, 144 Kattūrah:[15]

> As for Avicenna, he engages in misrepresentation[16] and sophistry; a lot of noise is made about him but he is actually of little use: whatever he has written is good for nothing. He claims[17] to have attained the Eastern philosophy, but

a A variant manuscript reading has "incomplete" (*ġayr tāmma*) for "in unbound form" (*ġayr multaʾima*). Corbin *Opera* I,195 rightly prefers the latter, the *lectio difficilior*.

14 Faḫr-ad-Dīn manifestly had access to the first part of the extant *Easterners*, where this division is mentioned. See below Chapter 6.1, L50.

15 Text in Louis Massignon, *Recueil de textes inédits concernant l'histoire de la mystique en pays d'Islam*, Paris: Paul Geuthner, 1929, and in Ibn-Sabʿīn's *Budd al-ʿārif*, edited by Jūrj Kattūrah, Beirut: Dār al-Andalus and Dār al-Kindī, 1978. There is a French translation of the passage by Louis Massignon in "Ibn Sabʿin et la critique psychologique dans l'histoire de la philosophie musulmane," *Mémorial Henri Basset*, Paris: Paul Geuthner, 1928, 126, a free English translation by Rosenthal *Muslim Scholarship* 50b, and a German translation by Akasoy 301–302. I translate from Massignon's text, and give the few variants in the notes.

16 I.e., misrepresentation in the sophistical sense of making something wrong seem right. The term *tamwīh* was used in the translation literature as a synonym for *safsaṭa*, sophistry. The word does not mean "illusion" (Massignon).

17 Akasoy translates in the passive but this is hardly necessary. Ibn-Sabʿīn certainly did not have access to any book on the Eastern Philosophy by Avicenna, but derives this information from the Prologue to *The Cure* (T9, §4), just like Ibn-Ṭufayl—if not from Ibn-Ṭufayl's work itself and its spin-offs, like the writings of Abner of Burgos (Test. 12a above).

had he really attained it he would have been enveloped by its breeze, whereas he is in a fiery hole.[18] Most of his books are compilations deriving[b] from the books of Plato; what they contain of his own thought, on the other hand, is wrong, and what he has [himself] to say is unreliable. *The Cure*, which is his greatest book, is full of fumblings and opposes Aristotle, although his opposition to Aristotle is one of the reasons for which he is to be praised because he brought to light what Aristotle had concealed. His best work on Theology is *Reminders and Pointers* [*sic*] and what he expressed symbolically in *Ḥayy ibn-Yaqẓān*—with the reservation that everything that he mentioned in these books derives from concepts in Plato's *Laws*[c] and the sayings of the Ṣūfīs. Avicenna proceeded in this [symbolic and allusive] fashion for the sake of training[d] and research in philosophy,[19] two areas in which he is neither to be relied upon nor listened to.

[17] Ibn-Taymiyya (d. 1328), *ar-Radd ʿalā l-manṭiqiyyīn* 336:[20]

Avicenna also on occasion opposes the ancients on some of their doctrines. For this reason he says in his book called *The Cure* [T9, § 4] that he presents in the *Eastern Philosophy* what is established as truth according to his own view.

---

[b] "Compilations deriving:" reading *muʾallafatun wa-mustanbaṭatun* as in Kattūrah's edition for *muwallafuhu wa-mustanbaṭuhu* ("livres et théories" [!]) in Massignon.

[c] Read *Nawāmīs*, as in Kattūrah.

[d] The text should read, *wa-rakiba šibha ḏālika li-t-tamarrun* for *wa-rakkaba šibha ḏālika li-t-tamaddun* in Massignon, and *wa-rkb šibha ḏālika ʿalā t-tamaddun* in Kattūrah. Massignon translates, "Il les a combinées par esprit d'acculturation," and notes for "acculturation," "*tamaddun*: première apparition de ce terme qui signifie aujourd'hui 'civilisation' [!]." *Tamaddun* is also read here and translated as "sociology (politics)" by Rosenthal *Muslim Scholarship* 50b, and as "Zivilisation" (still in 2006) by Akasoy 302. But Arabic *tamaddun* in the sense of civilization is a modern calque on the European (Latinate) term which did not exist in Ibn-Sabʿīn's time. The reference here is to the condensed or symbolic and allusive style of philosophical instruction for the purpose of training (*tamarrun*, synonym of *riyāḍa*) the student in philosophical research; see the term as used in text L12, § 3, below and the discussion in Chapter 5.3.

---

[18] It is not clear what, if anything serious, Ibn-Sabʿīn meant by this Eastern philosophy to which he refers as something independent of Avicenna. He mentions it at least twice more in the *Budd al-ʿārif* (pp. 37 and 38 bottom), though the editor, Kattūrah, says (note on p. 37) that Ibn-Sabʿīn refers to it in his writings "a number of times" (*ʿiddat marrāt*). It is certain, though, that it has nothing to do either with Avicenna's work by that presumed title or with the historical Avicenna's notion itself. See the discussion by a puzzled Akasoy 304–305.

[19] This remark also is based on Avicenna's statements. See below Chapter 8.2 and 8.3.

[20] *Kitāb ar-Radd ʿalā l-manṭiqiyyīn*, Lahore: Idārat Tarjumān as-Sunna, 2nd printing, 1976.

[18] Ḥājjī Ḫalīfa (d. 1657), *Kašf aẓ-ẓunūn* I,685 ult. Yaltkaya and Bilge:

Eastern Philosophy by Avicenna.

III. Internal Evidence 120

[19] Contents of the work (*Mašriqiyyūn* 8.8–13):

> We do not intend to present in this book all the parts of theoretical and practical philosophy, but we wish to present only the following kinds of sciences: the instrumental science [i.e., Logic], the universal science [i.e., the first part of Metaphysics], Theology [i.e., the second part of Metaphysics], the fundamental part of Physics, and only as much of the practical science as is needed by the seeker of salvation. As for Mathematics, it is not a science about which there is disagreement, and the amount of it which we presented in *The Cure* is exactly what we would have presented here had we occupied ourselves with it—and similarly with the kinds of practical science which we did not present here.

[20] Manuscripts of the work.

There are extant what appears to be two portions of the work.

[20a] Logic. This is preserved in the following known manuscripts:[21]

1. Cairo, Ḥikma 6 M[uṣṭafā Fāḍil], ff. 116^{b}–138^{a}.[22] The title is given as "From *The Book of the Easterners*" (*min Kitāb al-Mašriqiyyīn*).
2. Cairo, Dār al-Kutub Ḥikma 213. This is copied directly from the preceding manuscript.
3. Istanbul, Ayasofya 4829, ff. 21^{b} bis–35^{a} (Arabic pagination). The text ends on p. 61.9 of *Manṭiq al-Mašriqiyyīn*.
4. Istanbul, Ayasofya 4852, ff. 34^{b}–80^{a}. The text ends on p. 61.9 of *Manṭiq al-Mašriqiyyīn*.
5. Mašhad, Riżavī I, 1/85. The text ends at the beginning of p. 37 of *Manṭiq al-Mašriqiyyīn*. (Mahdavī 93).
6. Tehran, Malik 2014. The text ends at the beginning of p. 37 of *Manṭiq al-Mašriqiyyīn*. (Mahdavī 93).
7. Tehran, Majlis-i Sanā 82, ff. 129–141.
8. Qum, Marʿašī 286, ff. 24–32.[23]

---

[21] I have been able to examine only the Cairo and the Istanbul manuscripts listed below. For the rest I am relying on information in the literature.

[22] See Gutas "Ṣiġnāḫī" 12b.

[23] For this and the preceding manuscript see Gutas "Eastern Philosophy" 169.

[20b] Physics. This part is preserved in the following known manuscripts:

9. Istanbul, Ayasofya 2403, ff. 1–127.[24]
10. Istanbul, Nuruosmaniye 4894, ff. 373^{b}–425^{b} (Arabic pagination).[25]
11. Istanbul, Ahmet III 2125, ff. 597^{a}–695^{a}.
121 12. Oxford, Bodleian Pococke 181 (= Hebrew 400 Uri = 1334 Neubauer); (Anawati 27, Mahdavī 270).
13. Leipzig 796 (DC 196), ff. 4^{a}–96^{b}: K. Vollers, *Katalog der Islamischen … Handschriften der Universitäts-Bibliothek zu Leipzig*, Leipzig 1906, 256–257.
14. Diyarbakır.[26]

b. *Title of the Work*

The title of the work is problematical. The question is whether the phrase "Eastern Philosophy" mentioned by Avicenna only seven times in all his extant works [Testimonia 1 and 2 above] refers to a title or is a mere designation of the kind of philosophy involved, i.e., "Eastern" as opposed to "Western" or even, perhaps, "Peripatetic." The occurrence of the phrase in the Prologue to *The Cure* is clearly a designation of the subject of the book: "this is my book *on* (*fī*) Eastern philosophy" [Test. 1]. The wording leaves little room for doubt, unless one were to suppose that the title was *On Eastern Philosophy* (*Fī l-falsafa al-mašriqiyya*), something which is not attested anywhere else. This is further corroborated by the fact that both Ibn-Ṭufayl [Test. 12] and Averroes [Test. 13], who apparently had access only to *The Cure*, understood the phrase to be a designation of Avicenna's philosophy.[27] Finally, it is to be noted that the phrase says, "Eastern *falsafa*,"

---

24 The contents of this manuscript are listed by G.C. Anawati, "Un manuscrit de la Hikma Mashriqiyya d'Ibn Sina," *MIDEO* 1 (1954) 164–165.

25 The contents of this manuscript are listed by Anawati, "Nour Osmaniyye" 381–386.

26 I am indebted to Fehrullah Terkan for informing me in a private communication (23 October 2012) that there is a further MS of the Physics part of the work in Diyarbakır discovered by Gürbüz Deniz.

27 Ibn-Ṭufayl's reference to the Prologue is evident from his verbatim quotation of it. Averroes does not refer to the Eastern philosophy in the context of the Prologue of *The Cure*, of which he was certainly aware, but as reported from a number of alleged followers of Avicenna in Spain. The fact that these followers are misrepresenting Avicenna's Eastern philosophy (especially in Test. 13c) indicates that Averroes did not have access to any book by Avicenna under that title. Furthermore, he understands the phrase to be a designation of Avicenna's philosophy because he quotes it as "*his* Eastern philosophy" (*fī falsafatihi l-mašriqiyya*) and not with the precise title [Test. 13a].

not "Eastern *ḥikma*" as in the references in the Commentary on the *Theologia*. If the phrase is to refer to the title, it has to be either one or the other; and since the wording speaks against it, the title of the work was not *al-Falsafa al-mašriqiyya*.

The six references in the Commentary on the *Theologia* from the *Fair Judgment* are more ambiguous; the phrase could refer either to a title or to the type of philosophy. The second alternative seems to be more likely. In the one instance in which Avicenna refers to "the books" and the "Eastern philosophy" [Test. 2], it is clear that he is juxtaposing two traditions since by "books" in such contexts Avicenna always meant books in the Aristotelian tradition.[28] He is therefore referring the reader here both to the Peripatetic philosophy and the Eastern philosophy. More significant, however, is the fact 122
that in two other passages where he would have been expected to refer to the book by its title, he uses two variant phrases. In his letter to an anonymous disciple (Bahmanyār, Test. 3), written, as we shall next discuss, about four years after the loss of the *Fair Judgment*, he talks about his books that were considered lost and refers to three of them by title; to what he had written on Eastern philosophy, on the other hand, he refers by the phrase "Eastern questions" [Test. 3]. Further on in the same letter he calls it a discussion on "Eastern Fundamental Principles" [Test. 4]. Neither of these can be the title of the book; they seem more like descriptions of its contents, and in any case there is no attestation for them.

The Shorter Bibliography (SB) also does not refer to the book by its title. In its first part, where the *books* (*kutub*) are listed (46.2–12 Gohlman)—as opposed to the *rasāʾil* in the second half (46.12–48.8 Gohlman)—the word *kitāb* is put before each title with the sole exception of the Eastern philosophy. What the SB says [Test. 9] seems to mean, "some texts about Eastern philosophy, totalling one volume (*baʿḍ al-ḥikma al-mašriqiyya, mujallada*)." Suhrawardī, who had access to the same part on logic extant today,[29] reflects the same vagueness about the work for which he does not seem to have a title either: "The quires which Avicenna attributed to the Easterners" [Test. 14]. Suhrawardī's designation, finally, is corroborated by the title in the oldest extant manuscript containing the part on logic: "From *The Book of the Easterners*" [Test. 20a, no. 1].

---

28 See, for example, the Autobiography (T3), § 6, last sentence, and the quotation from the Preface to the Physics of *The Cure* in Chapter 5.2, L38.

29 See the references given in Mahdavī 81–83.

The only two sources which make a title out of "Eastern Philosophy" are the Longer Bibliography (LB) and Extended Bibliography (EB) [Test. 10] on the one hand, which agree in calling it *The Book of Eastern Philosophy*, and Bayhaqī [Test. 11a] who, although he does not use the word *kitāb*, clearly understands it as a title. In view of the overwhelming evidence discussed above, it would seem that in both cases it can be assumed that the designation of the type of philosophy contained in those texts was transformed into a title for the book by these compilers themselves or their sources.

In sum, we have little information about the title of the book, if indeed it ever had a fixed one: given that it was never properly "edited" (*taḥrīr*) for circulation and was available in the drafts in quires written by Avicenna, it may have just been referred to as "the Eastern questions," the designation Avicenna uses in his letter to the anonymous disciple (Bahmanyār, Test. 3).[30] In any case, it is relatively certain that it was not *Eastern Philosophy*: neither *al-Falsafa al-mašriqiyya* nor *al-Ḥikma al-mašriqiyya*; it is best to use as its title *The Easterners*, since the weightiest evidence is provided by the Cairo MS Ḥikma 6M[31] and Suhrawardī's statements. What is surprising, however, is not so much that we are little informed in general about the title of the book, but that we are little informed about it from Avicenna himself. The significance of this will be discussed below (Section e).

123 c. *Dates of Composition and Loss*

In a preceding section (W6) we saw that Avicenna wrote the Prologue to *The Cure* shortly after he had written both *The Cure* and *The Easterners*, in that order. In that Prologue he also made no mention of the *Pointers and Reminders*, something which would have been quite inconceivable had it been already written, for the *Pointers and Reminders* presents philosophy

---

30 Reisman *Avicennan Tradition* 230 and 223n64 suggests that the term *masāʾil*, "questions," here refers to the incomplete nature of the drafts. But if the "Eastern questions" here refers to *The Easterners*, and if the composition of this book was definitely completed by December of 1028 (see next section), this cannot be the case, even if the letter to the anonymous disciple was written in 1030, as Reisman contends, let alone in 1034, as I argue, because the surviving half of the text (see section d below) is quite finished, even polished.

31 As noted by Nallino 459n2, the title *Manṭiq al-mašriqiyyīn* (*Logic of the Easterners*) is an invention of the publisher of the volume; it does not occur in the manuscript. See Gutas "Ṣiġnāḫī" and the introduction to T8, above. Unfortunately this concocted title is retained and repeated by S.H. Nasr in Nasr and Aminrazavi 268.

"as it is naturally [perceived] (T9, §4)," without any regard to Aristotelian conventions, even more so than *The Easterners* does. Similarly, in the Introduction to *The Easterners*, where he brought into mutual relationship, as he had done in the Prologue to *The Cure*, these two works with the *Appendices* (T8, §7), Avicenna made no mention of *Pointers and Reminders*. It is equally difficult to imagine that Avicenna would not have mentioned the *Pointers*, had it been written, in the introduction to a work which was, just like the *Pointers* (T10, §§5–6), addressed to his closest disciples (T8, §7).[32] Furthermore, as already mentioned at the end of W6, the Prologue refers to Avicenna's work on Eastern philosophy as readily available and in circulation, whereas in the Letter to an Anonymous Disciple (Bahmanyār = *Mubāḥaṯa* II), written about 425/1034, Avicenna said that even before then he had put the texts on Eastern philosophy away "so as no one would look at them" [T11, §1]. This would also indicate the posteriority of *Pointers and Reminders* since it suggests that it supplanted *The Easterners*. The relative order of composition, therefore, is, *The Cure, The Easterners*, the Prologue to *The Cure, Pointers and Reminders*.

Since we know that *The Salvation* was composed right after the completion of *The Cure* (W7), there remains to consider the relative place in this sequence held by the *Fair Judgment*, which was composed in 420/1029 and lost in Muḥarram 421/January 1030 (see below, W10). The question is whether it antedates *The Easterners* or not. Since there is no independent evidence for the composition of *The Easterners*, the argument can only be based on the sequence of tendencies exhibited by Avicenna in these 124
works. The Prologue to *The Cure* again plays a pivotal role in establishing this sequence. It is quite certain, from above and the earlier discussion (W6), that both *The Cure* and *The Easterners* were already in existence when

32 This by itself invalidates the objections to my late dating of the *Pointers* by Michot ("Réponse" 161) and Reisman (*Avicennan Tradition* 223) on the basis that Avicenna mentions in a letter to Bahmanyār that the book is for his eyes and those of Ibn-Zayla only and not to be shown to everybody—implying thereby to Abū-Qāsim al-Kirmānī (see the discussion below, W11)—and that therefore even if it had been written Avicenna would not have mentioned it. *The Easterners* also is to be shown "only to ourselves—I mean to whose who are to us like ourselves" (T8, §7), but Avicenna has no problem mentioning it—indeed, referring to it—elsewhere, most prominently in the Prologue to *The Cure* (T9, §4). Despite his difficulties with al-Kirmānī and their negative impact on his career, Avicenna wrote in order to be published and be read by everybody, and he would not have deliberately concealed a book such as the *Pointers*, of which he was manifestly proud; see the discussion on Avicenna's methods and styles of composition below in Chapter 8 and the Coda.

the Prologue to *The Cure* was written. The Prologue, however, also clearly implies the *Fair Judgment*, because it juxtaposes two ways of stating the same truth—one, the Eastern way, without indirection, and the other, in the Peripatetic mold, aporetic and more expansive (T9, § 4). If this implication was actual, i.e., if the *Fair Judgment* had already been written, we should have expected to see it mentioned in the Prologue; its absence indicates that the implication was potential and perhaps even the prime mover behind the composition of the *Fair Judgment*. Having made the juxtaposition in the Prologue, Avicenna was asked, or himself felt compelled, to explain himself, and hence the division of "scholars into two groups, the Westerners and the Easterners" (T12, § 3), and the resulting commentaries in the *Fair Judgment*. If that is so, putting the known absolute dates next to the relative sequence just established, we arrive at the following absolute chronology of the composition of Avicenna's later works:

until 1027:	*The Cure* completed (W6)
	Jūzjānī writes his Introduction to *The Cure* (T7)
1027:	*The Salvation* (W7)
1027–Dec. 1028:[33]	*The Easterners* (W9)
	Prologue to *The Cure* (T9)
Dec. 1028—June 1029:	*Fair Judgment* (W10)
after mid-1030 (and possibly by 1034):[34]	*Pointers and Reminders* (W11)
1037	Avicenna dies

This chronology is absolute in the sense that it is based on no external evidence but solely on the internal evidence of the works in question and the unimpeachable reports of the living participants: Avicenna's and his disciples' private letters and the Biography by Jūzjānī. One item that has been contested, the date of composition of *Pointers and Reminders*, is also beyond dispute: as argued above, it is inconceivable that, had it been written before December 1028, by which time *The Easterners* and its Introduction (T8) had been composed, Avicenna would have been silent about it either in that Introduction or in its contemporary Prologue to *The Cure*. Any other arguments based on external evidence, which will be discussed

[33] On the basis of the argument just given, it is fair to assume that the *Fair Judgment* was not begun until after the *Easterners* was completed. Besides, this is also clear from the many references in the *Fair Judgment* to the *Easterners* as something already in existence: cf. Test. 2 above.

[34] See the discussion that follows.

below in W11, are inevitably trumped by these considerations. As for the beginning of its composition, I suggested in the table above that it took place after the middle of 1030 because of the historical circumstances in which Avicenna found himself. After the Ghaznavid Masʿūd's raid on Iṣfahān in January 1030, ʿAlāʾ-ad-Dawla, together with Avicenna, moved to Ḫūzistān in the south where they stayed until the death of Masʿūd's father, Maḥmūd, in May of that year. ʿAlāʾ-ad-Dawla, benefiting from the destabilization generated by this event, occupied Rayy in that summer and only later returned to Iṣfahān (see the discussion in W10 below). Not that Avicenna could not write while on the move, as the example of the composition of *The Salvation* shows, but it may be fair to assume that he could have started on the ambitious project of *Pointers and Reminders* only after his subsequent return to Iṣfahān. The chronology given above can thus be taken as established.

Dating the loss of four particular books by Avicenna, however, is more complicated. These books are, *The Easterners, Fair Judgment, Throne Philosophy*, and *Pointers and Reminders* (Test. 3 above). One date is absolutely established, the loss of *Fair Judgment* in January 1030 when Masʿūd's troops rifled Avicenna's saddle bags during their incursion in Iṣfahān (see below W10 for a discussion of all the evidence). The question is when the other three books were lost, whether, that is, at the same time as the *Fair Judgment* or on another occasion. There are two kinds of evidence for these events. The first consists of reports by historians writing anywhere between one and two centuries after the fact, and the other of references by Avicenna and his disciples. The three reports by historians that survive (Test. 11 above) partly overlap and partly diverge significantly, but Reisman made a strong case that the two later ones by Ibn-al-Aṯīr and al-Ḥusaynī ultimately derive from Bayhaqī and reproduce Bayhaqī's error in dating the loss of all four of the books at the time of al-Ḥamdūnī's and Tāš Farrāš's incursion in Iṣfahān (in 1034) and not to Masʿūd's attack in January 1030.[35] But this is reading too much in the slippery account in the *Tatimma* and being unduly unfair at least to Ibn-al-Aṯīr if not also to the presumed author of the *Zubdat at-tawārīḫ*, al-Ḥusaynī. In reality, the one mistake that Bayhaqī actually makes (Test. 11a.i) is saying that the *Fair Judgment* was lost when al-Ḥamdūnī (with Kurds = Tāš Farrāš) attacked Iṣfahān (in 1034), because we have it on good

[35] Reisman "Stealing Avicenna's Books", and especially p. 113 (cf. Reisman's presentation of the three accounts in parallel columns on p. 99), much expanding the earlier discussion of this subject in his *Avicennan Tradition* 208–212.

authority from both Jūzjānī (Biography 80.5–7 Gohlman) and the disciple writing from Rayy (Ibn-Zayla? T13, § 2) that this happened during Masʿūd's attack (in January 1030). Bayhaqī was misled by Avicenna's letter to the anonymous disciple (Bahmanyār, Test. 3 above) where Avicenna talks about the loss of the aforementioned four books (cf. Reisman 99–100). For when Bayhaqī comes in his paraphrase of the Biography to the point where Jūzjānī talks about the loss of the *Fair Judgment*, he is reminded of that letter and is moved to report on the survival of the two other lost books mentioned by Avicenna there, *The Easterners* and *Throne Philosophy* (he says nothing about the fourth book, *Pointers and Reminders*, because Avicenna also mentions in the letter that a copy had survived and Bayhaqī well knew that it was in circulation). Now either Bayhaqī had independent information that *The Easterners* and *Throne Philosophy* were lost during al-Ḥamdūnī's attack or he did not and he simply assumed it (or made it up?); in either case, his mistake consisted only of lumping the losses of all books together on that occasion on the basis of his reading of Avicenna's Letter to Bahmanyār. This reading is erroneous, as I will discuss below, but it says nothing about whether there was one or two occasions of such losses. For we have independent information about the loss in January 1030, and if there is also independent information about another loss in 1034 during al-Ḥamdūni's attack, then the matter is settled.

This is provided by the two reports by Ibn-al-Aṯīr and al-Ḥusaynī which are close to each other in wording as in contents, as the parallel presentation of the reports shows (Test. 11b and 11c above), but quite different from what Bayhaqī says; in all likelihood they both go back to a common source, which can hardly be Bayhaqī. The main thing they have in common with Bayhaqī is that they too situate the loss of the books to al-Ḥamdūnī's attack on Iṣfahān, but the attack itself in 1034 was well known, and it is corroborated by Jūzjānī who reports on it and the ensuing flight of Avicenna and ʿAlāʾ-ad-Dawla to Īḏāj (also mentioned by Ibn-al-Aṯīr) in the south of Iṣfahān (Biography 82.2–7 Gohlman and note 108). The association of the loss of books with this attack is of course in Bayhaqī, but we do not know if this is the first such report or who else may have had it. We know very little about the sources of these histories (Reisman goes through the list of them and cf. also Bosworth's article "Akẖbār al-dawlat al-Saljūqīya" in *EIr* I,712–713) and possess even fewer, and in these circumstances arguments from silence (like those by Reisman, p. 108) do not carry much weight. But the story about the plunder of the books (Ibn-al-Aṯīr) or the library (al-Ḥusaynī) of Avicenna and their transportation to Ghazna is something about which Bayhaqī is silent, and we would have to impute an unacceptable amount of imaginative fabrication on the part of ibn al-Aṯīr,[36] if not on both, if we are to claim that they derive this from what Bayhaqī says. As for the story in all three reports about the burning of the library in Ghazna, this may or may not be all attributable to the motivations of Bayhaqī (admirably analyzed by Reisman 114–122), but it has nothing to do with the loss of Avicenna's books in Iṣfahān. What is important is that if Ibn-al-Aṯīr and al-Ḥusaynī are not dependent on Bayhaqī, which seems to be the case, we have independent evidence for the loss of some books by Avicenna during al-Ḥamdūni's attack in 1034.

The external reports by the historians, therefore, if they do not actually support, they do not preclude either the possibility that Avicenna's books may have been lost on at least two occasions towards the end of his life—that some of them were lost also on an earlier occasion is certain from other reports mentioned below. But the second set of evidence, statements by Avicenna and his disciples, make it a certainty. In general terms, Jūzjānī reports in the Introduction to *The Cure* that Avicenna "suffered from successive (*tawātarat*) misfortunes, and disasters (*ġawā'il*, pl.) destroyed his books" (T7, § 2); even if this Introduction was written before the loss of the particular books we are discussing, it describes a pattern in Avicenna's life. But for the books in question we have the explicit testimony of Avicenna himself. In the letter to the anonymous disciple (Bahmanyār, Test. 3 above) he says specifically (a) that the books that were lost on the occasion on which the *Pointers and Reminders* was lost were *The Easterners* (the "Eastern qustions") and *Throne Philosophy*, (b) that what was lost was "not voluminous," and (c) that it would be easy to rewrite what was lost. All this means definitely that the *Fair Judgment* was *not* among what was lost: Avicenna does not include it in the list of the books lost (a), he says that what was lost was not voluminous, while the *Fair Judgment* was twenty volumes (b), and from what he says next it is clear that rewriting it would *not* have been easy (c). When Avicenna mentions next the *Fair Judgment*, after the particle *balā* (equivalent to the German *doch* and the French *si*), it is not for the purpose of reporting on its loss, but to negate his own previous negative statement that what was lost "was not voluminous" and that it would be easy to rewrite it: to the contrary of the present loss of the "Eastern questions" and *Throne Philosophy*, he says, the previous loss of another book on a different occassion was of the

36 Reisman "Stealing" 100 and note 25 is too quick, in his efforts to discredit Ibn-al-Aṯīr, to blame him for "confusing his dates" because of a date given in error as 429 instead of 427. This, of course, has nothing to do with Ibn-al-Aṯīr but is merely a scribal error in some manuscript reading *tis'a* for *sab'a*.

Fair Judgment, which *was* voluminous and whose rewriting would indeed require work. Thus the *Fair Judgment* was not lost together with the three other books (cf. above, T11, note 6), and this evidence trumps the external evidence of the reports by the historians, however that is understood.

A final piece of evidence further to support the fact (by now) that Avicenna's writings were lost on more than one occasion comes again from Avicenna himself, in his letter to one of his disciples (Bahmanyār or Jūzjānī) known as *Repudiating charges of imitating the Qurʾān* (*al-Intifāʾ*, GPW 3), i.e., leveled at him by al-Kirmānī. In the course of the letter he mentions having composed a number of homilies (*ḫuṭab*) on various religious subjects which he describes in some detail, and that "these sermons were lost among my other belongings" (*wa-hāḏihi l-ḫuṭab qad ḍāʿat fī-mā ḍāʿa min al-asbāb*, Michot "Riz" 105 line 45 text, 113 translation). In the Letter to the Anonymous Disciple (Bahmanyār) cited in the preceding paragraph, Avicenna says nothing about the loss of homilies, *ḫuṭab*—he talks only about the "Eastern qustions" and *Throne Philosophy*—, and in any case, the contents of the sermons which he describes in this letter have little, if anything, in common with the two works that were lost on the other occasion. Clearly Jūzjānī was not exaggerating when he said in the Introduction to *The Cure* cited above (T7, § 2) that Avicenna suffered successive losses of his books.[37] The question is whether the evidence allows us to date them with relative certainty.

We have no direct evidence to say exactly when the three books other than the *Fair Judgment* were lost. The political and military situation in the Jibāl after the coming of the Ghaznavids was very unsettled and at any time the occasion for such "disasters" may have arisen. Thus the identification of the loss referred to by Avicenna in this letter to the anonymous disciple (Bahmanyār) with the pillage of Abū-Sahl in 1034 mentioned by all three historical reports is not absolutely certain, but neither is it subject to serious doubt, given that they say nothing to contradict it and given the exodus of Avicenna from Iṣfahān on that occasion and his flight to Īḏāj. *The Easterners* was therefore most probably lost during the attack on Iṣfahān by al-Ḥamdūnī in 1034.

[37] Reisman *Avicennan Tradition* 178 would like to date all the losses to that one event of Masʿūd's sack of Iṣfahān in January 1030. But as Michot "Riz" 84 rightly observes, Avicenna's flight from Hamaḏān to Iṣfahān with Jūzjānī, "his brother, and two slaves, disguised as Sufis" and having "suffered hardships on the way" (Biography 62.4–5 Gohlman) would naturally be one occasion when Avicenna could have lost his "belongings."

One final consideration confirms the absolute chronology given in the table above. If all the books by Avicenna had been lost in January 1030 when Masʿūd invaded Iṣfahān, as Reisman argues (cf. his chronology in *Avicennan Tradition* 212 and 304), then we must accept that he must have written all his major works of the last phase of his life after *The Cure* (i.e., *The Salvation, Philosophy for ʿAlāʾ-ad-Dawla, The Easterners, Fair Judgment, Pointers and Reminders*, and quite a few other shorter essays besides—all in all exceeding twenty-five volumes) in a period of only three years (1027–1029), while for seven years after January 1030 and until his death in 1037 he must not have written anything other than a few pages of responses in the *Discussions* and the three page final essay on the rational soul (T14). This rather defies credibility.

d. *Contents and Transmission*

Avicenna intended to include the following sections in this book, in the order given below [Test. 19]:

1. Logic
2. Metaphysics
   a. Universal Science
   b. Theology
3. Physics (partial)
4. Ethics (partial)

The inversion of the order between Physics and Metaphysics follows the precedent set in the *Philosophy for ʿAlāʾ-ad-Dawla* (W8). Putting Logic and the Universal Science in close proximity is consistent with Avicenna's basic view of their substantive relationship (Chapter 6.1, 6.4), which is now expressed, breaking the traditional mold, also in terms of the structure of the work. In the *Pointers and Reminders* which was to follow, Avicenna innovated again by adopting a two part format, with Physics and Metaphysics intermingled in the second part.[38]

[38] The format Logic-Physics-Metaphysics, with the disregard for Mathematics and Practical Philosophy which was established by Avicenna, was as a whole adhered to in subsequent philosophical discourse, but the breakdown of the conventional structure of philosophical treatises which was also initiated by Avicenna here was continued and much expanded in later philosophical (and, *mutatis mutandis*, theological) tradition. See on this subject the fundamental *Summae* and other articles by Heidrun Eichner listed in the Bibliography.

The history of the transmission of the text is apparently complicated and cannot be discussed without a study of the available manuscripts. From the
125 evidence presented above, it would seem that Avicenna had stored most of the book, and that it was these parts that were pillaged [Test. 3], taken to Ghazna, and burned in 545/1150–1151 [Test. 11b]. If this is true, then it would mean that the sections that were not stored were those that survive today, namely the part on Logic from beginning to the section corresponding to the Prior Analytics, and the part on Physics. On the other hand, Bayhaqī reports that *The Easterners* in its entirety was carried to Ghazna and lost [Test. 11a]. If this is the case, then the parts that are now extant must have been copied earlier by Avicenna's disciples; and by the same token, it might be possible to identify in the future other passages from the book that may have survived either in direct or indirect transmission.

The extant part on Logic, which was by and large a new composition on the subject, was known to subsequent philosophers; this is apparently the part to which Suhrawardī refers as Avicenna's Eastern "quires" [Test. 14], and other quotations have been traced to it.[39] As for the part on Physics, it is based on the corresponding sections in *The Cure*, which it occasionally edits and rewrites to conform to Avicenna's intention to present "philosophy as it is naturally [perceived]" without taking into account the historical development of the ideas [T9, §4].[40] Avicenna, finally, never rewrote the work after it was lost.

e. *The Place of Eastern Philosophy and the Easterners in the Development of Avicenna's Philosophy*

Starting with his very first works, *The Compilation* (W2) and *The Available and the Valid* (W3), and continuing with the works of his transition period, *The Provenance and Destination* (W4) and the "Lesser" *Destination* (W5), Avi-

---

39 See the references in Corbin *Opera I* 195 and Mahdavī 81–83.

40 For a description of Avicenna's method of composition in this work see Gutas "Eastern Philosophy." Mahdavī 270–271 notes that there is correspondence of contents and order of chapters with *The Cure*, as well as direct quotations from it. Assessments by others, on the other hand, are based merely on the misconception that the Eastern philosophy must be different in content from Avicenna's other works on physics, which it is not. See, for example, Corbin *Opera I* xxxix: "... rien dans le texte même ne vienne expliquer expressément ce titre [*al-ḥikma al-mašriqiyya*]. L'ouvrage contient ... un examen de tout le contenu habituel de la Physique." This is echoed by Fakhry 151n92: "A book entitled *Oriental Philosophy* exists in manuscript form (see, e.g., Ayasofia Ms, No. 2403, and Oxford, Pococke 181) but differs little in content or arrangement from his other conventional works." For similar assessments by earlier scholars see Anawati *Mu'allafāt* 27.

cenna began increasingly to follow a course independent from the transmitted formats of exposition and discussion in the Graeco-Arabic Aristotelian tradition. The former set of works broke with tradition by being not commentaries or detailed discussions of a specific issue, but comprehensive expositions of all the philosophical sciences according to the Aristotelian classification; the latter combined under the rubric of Metaphysics subjects previously discussed separately in De anima and Metaphysics—the Metaphysics of the Rational Soul. In the Prologue to *The Cure* (W6) Avicenna portrayed himself as a conscious reformer of the Aristotelian tradition, effecting a synthesis between its verifiably true contents and his own elaborations. The texts on Eastern philosophy and the Easterners represent a further, but temporary, stage of this development. 126

Avicenna had a progressive concept of philosophy, according to which philosophers revised and superseded the achievements of their predecessors (see Chapters 4–5 below); as for himself, he was conscious both of his growing independence from Peripatetic models of presentation—the "indirection" he mentions in the Prologue to *The Cure* [Test. 1]—and of his development of Peripatetic philosophy through his Discovery and Verification of Fundamental and Corollary Principles. It seems clear that as Avicenna was writing *The Cure*, he became forcefully aware that many of the issues dealt with in the praxis of philosophy were discussed merely for historical reasons, i.e., because they had traditionally formed a part of the discussion, not because they had any intrinsic or real value. In the close to thirty years of philosophical work that preceded the completion of *The Cure*, Avicenna developed an approach, or perhaps, more accurately, a philosophical *modus operandi*, which vested him with authority in philosophical matters—witness Jūzjānī's reasons for seeking him out and his acquiescence to the composition of *The Cure* in the form desired by Avicenna (T7, §§1, 3). This approach presented a synthesis, on the basis of concerns current in his own time and place, of thirteen centuries of philosophical praxis. Although this synthesis frequently accommodated the historical aspect of many questions treated, its significance, or rather, its *raison d'être*, resided precisely in the treatment, within the larger framework of the tradition itself, of essential issues that were of relevance to Avicenna in his specific setting. It was therefore inevitable that the disparity between the historical and essential aspects of this synthesis would be felt, and it was this, the essential, aspect of his work as a whole (what Avicenna calls in the Introduction "the fundamental elements of true Philosophy," *ummahāt al-ʿilm al-ḥaqq*, T8, §6) that Avicenna wished to designate by a different name in order best to project this disparity.

127 The name that Avicenna chose reflected appropriately his background in the *Mašriq* (East) of the Islamic world, i.e., Ḫurāsān, and the tradition of philosophy he generated was accordingly the Eastern philosophy, that is, the Ḫurāsānī school of Aristotelian philosophy.[41] This is precisely how certain philosophers in Spain who claimed to be Avicenna's followers understood it, and they communicated this understanding to Averroes [Test. 13]; but most significant of all, this is also how it was understood by the founder of Illuminationism, Suhrawardī, who described accurately, but perhaps with a certain understatement of Avicenna's achievement, the disparity in Avicenna's synthesis: "The only difference is that he occasionally altered the form of expression, or proceeded in certain Corollary issues in a somewhat independent way" [Test. 14]. To claim that Avicenna was the precursor of Suhrawardī in this direction, i.e., in the understanding of Eastern philosophy, first, contradicts Suhrawardī himself, and second, implies that Avicenna thought of Eastern philosophy as establishing "the Fundamental Principle of the East which was founded at the time of the sages in the era of Chosroes" [Test. 14]. This is decidedly not the case.

What is striking about Eastern philosophy and the Easterners, on the other hand, is that Avicenna stopped referring to them after a certain point, probably around 422/1031. There is not a single mention of them either in *Pointers and Reminders*, which, significantly, refers to *The Cure*,[42] or in what

---

[41] The geographical reference of *mašriq* and *mašriqiyya* (East, Eastern) has already been indicated, perhaps not forcefully enough, by Pines "Philosophie Orientale" 15–16n6. The point needs emphasizing: *Mašriq* means Ḫurāsān. Among the many references that could be cited in addition to those offered by Pines, four are most relevant and explicit. (a) The geographer Maqdisī discusses Ḫurāsān under the clime of *al-mašriq* (*Aḥsan at-taqāsīm*, M.J. de Goeje, ed., Leiden 1906, 260 ff.). (b) ʿĀmirī, himself from Ḫurāsān and working in Buḫārā at the very moment when Avicenna was astounding his elders with his competence in the Qurʾān and literature, identifies *al-Mašriq* with Ḫurāsān in his comparison of ʿIrāqīs and Ḫurāsānīs: "The best thing for a man is to be an Easterner [*mašriqī*] in substance and an ʿIrāqī in form, for in this fashion he combines the solidity of Ḫurāsān with the elegance of ʿIrāq, avoiding the uncouthness of Ḫurāsān and the frivolity of ʿIrāq;" quoted in the *Muntakhab Ṣiwān al-ḥikma* 2844–2846 Dunlop and translated in Rowson 6; see also Rowson's references in note 10. (c) The same identification is also made in the anonymous chronicle of the ʿAbbāsid revolution, written in the 11th, i.e., Avicenna's century. The ʿAbbāsid Muḥammad ibn-ʿAlī is reported to counsel his Kūfan activist (*dāʿī*), Bukayr ibn-Māhān, for the preparation of the revolution with the following words: "You have done right [to wait for the proper time to rise up]; you should [first] go into Ḫurāsān because our political power is Eastern [*fa-inna dawlatana mašriqiyya*; cf. F. Rosenthal s.v. "Dawla" in EI^2 II,178];" *Arabskii Anonim*, ed. P. Griyaznevitch, Moscow 1967, f. 250^b, 9. (d) In the Graeco-Arabic translation literature, the word ἀνατολαί (*anatolai*, the East) was translated as *bilād Ḫurāsān*! (Ullmann *Geheimwissenschaften* 436).

[42] In three places in the first part on Logic: *Išārāt* I.5.2 end, 49/111; I.5.4 middle, 52/115; I.8.1, 76/157.

is most probably his very last work, *On the Rational Soul* (T14), which deals with the subject Avicenna considered most significant. Even more to the point, there is no reference to them, or a discussion of any text belonging 128
to them, in his voluminous comments and responsa which are extant in the collections made by his disciples known as the *Discussions* and *Notes* (W12 and W13). The few passages from the *Discussions* in which they are mentioned are either fragments from the original *Fair Judgment*, or from personal letters incorporated in the *Discussions* in the process of transmission. The only exception is the "Eastern demonstrative proof" requested by (apparently) Bahmanyār [Test. 5], which, if anything, may date from the time when Avicenna was composing *The Easterners*, though even if so, it is astounding that there are no more similar requests. It is true that a sizable amount of the Eastern texts was lost and Avicenna could not easily refer to them, but this seems hardly relevant: what is significant is that he stopped mentioning the Easterners even as a concept.

The reason for this appears to be that Avicenna's designation of his own revision and extrapolation of Aristotelian philosophy as Eastern did not meet with general approval, or that the concept itself did not generate any interest among his colleagues and disciples, and he decided to abandon the idea. It is true that, following a course of Withholding Knowledge from those not prepared to receive it—an idea current in both the Aristotelian and Islamic traditions (see Chapter 5.3)—he may not have made the Eastern texts readily available to his companions (as he says in a letter, he had packed most of the Eastern texts away "so as no one would look at them" [Test. 3]), but it is also obvious that enough portions of them circulated among his closest disciples to ensure that the concept of Eastern philosophy did become known to those for whom it was intended (those who were to Avicenna like himself, T8, § 7): witness the survival, despite the adverse historical circumstances [Test. 3, 9–11], of these very texts.

Furthermore, judging from Avicenna's own lack of insistence, it appears that he himself considered the matter so unimportant as to relinquish the notion. When he came to write *Pointers and Reminders*, a book in which he attained the highest degree of independence from Aristotelian models of presentation, he desisted from any mention of the Easterners. What he presented there was neither Peripatetic nor Eastern philosophy but, as he claimed, just the truth and philosophical points: "Dear Friend: I have churned for you in these Pointers the cream of truth (*al-ḥaqq*) and have fed you choice morsels of philosophy (*ḥikam*) in pithy sayings" (T10, § 6).

In this light, the much debated question about the identity of the Easterners and Avicenna's meaning by it loses its mystery, for it becomes clear

that infinitely more has been made of the Easterners in contemporary Western scholarship than among Avicenna's immediate circles. Jūzjānī makes no mention of it in the Biography either as a concept or a book (*The Eastern Philosophy* as a title appears only in the Shorter, Longer, and Extended Bibliographies [Test. 9, 10], SB 16, LB 47, and EB13; see the Tetrapla chart in the
129 Appendix), and as far as I am aware nothing has come to light in the little that has become available from the works of Avicenna's disciples. It is true that, as discussed in W6, Jūzjānī had more orthodox Aristotelian inclinations and hence one would expect him to downplay the importance of the concept of the Easterners, but had it been a real issue in the last decade of Avicenna's life, or had Avicenna himself defended it strenuously and incontrovertibly, it is impossible to assume that it should have left no traces in the literature. Jūzjānī is not alone in this regard. In his memoirs, the disciple writing from Rayy (Ibn-Zayla?) recounts the genesis and execution of the *Fair Judgment* in terms similar to those of Avicenna himself (T12), but leaves completely aside any mention of Easterners or Westerners. What Avicenna did in that book, the disciple says, was to examine "all divergences of exegesis" by *anonymous* exegetes of the books of Aristotle (T13, § 2), not by "Westerners" and "Easterners." Bahmanyār, finally, in the introduction to his *Taḥṣīl*, which he describes as the "gist of the philosophy which Avicenna revised," mentions that he will follow the arrangement of Avicenna's *Philosophy for ʿAlāʾ-ad-Dawla* and that he will include in it subjects (*maʿānī*) from Avicenna's published (*ʿāmma*) works as well as matters which they discussed in their conversations. "To this," he says, "I will add the Corollary Principles which I have Validated through my theoretical analysis and which are analogous to Fundamental Principles" (p. 1 Moṭahharī). There is not a single word about Eastern philosophy.

Subsequent philosophical tradition in Islam east of al-Andalus is just as mute about an Eastern philosophy of Avicenna. Apart from the testimonia collected above, which are in any case mostly of a bibliographical nature, there is hardly any mention of the subject.[43] But the situation is different

[43] The two instances on the basis of which Goichon ("Philosophie" 29) seriously raises the question whether it was customary during Avicenna's lifetime or shortly thereafter to call his philosophy "Eastern" do not bear closer scrutiny. The fact that Niẓāmī ʿArūḍī calls Avicenna "the philosopher of the East" (*ḥakīm al-mašriq*; *Chahār maqāla*, M. Qazwīnī, ed. [E.J.W. Gibb Memorial Series 11], Leiden/London 1910, 71.15) certaintly means "the philosopher of Ḫurāsān," as Pines already mentioned (see note 26 above). As for the title in the MS Ayasofya 2403 (and the other manuscripts listed in Test. 20b), it does actually refer to the Eastern texts.

with the Andalusians. The single most misleading factor for Western scholarship has been Ibn-Ṭufayl's statement that in Avicenna's opinion "the truth is something else" (*al-ḥaqq ʿindahu ġayru ḏālika* [Test. 12]), i.e., something other than Aristotle's doctrine. This is patently wrong because no native speaker of Arabic would derive this sense from Avicenna's Prologue to *The Cure* (T9, §4). The problem here, however, is Ibn-Ṭufayl's, not Avicenna's, and what needs to be done is to realize that Ibn-Ṭufayl deliberately chose, for his own purposes, to misinterpret Avicenna's Prologue, not to account for Avicenna's "other truth" by dubbing it "Oriental". Andalusians like Averrroes [Test. 13c] and Abner of Burgos [Test. 12a] were misled by Ibn-Ṭufayl into thinking of Avicenna's "oriental philosophy" as something mystical, just as was Mehren in his editorial decisions, who, by choosing to use Ibn-Ṭufayl's 130
subtitle as his own, gave printed legitimacy to the myth of Avicenna's mystical oriental philosophy (see the introduction to T9).[44]

In the terms in which it has gained notoriety in contemporary scholarship, therefore, the *concept* of Avicenna's Eastern philosophy is a non-issue.[45] In the context of Avicenna's own work its significance lies in displaying his attitude toward his work during a specific and limited period of his career; this attitude is by no means unique, however, because variants of it are observable in other stages of Avicenna's philosophical activity (Chapter 7). As for the *texts* on Eastern philosophy and the Easterners, the loss of most of them, and especially of the *Fair Judgment*, is deplorable only to

---

44 On Ibn-Ṭufayl's manipulations and Abner's misunderstandings of the question of Avicenna's Eastern philosophy see Gutas "Eastern Philosophy" and Szpiech.

45 The history of Western scholarship on the "Oriental" philosophy of Avicenna is a comedy of errors that deserves separate treatment. Among the handful of serious studies, the most sober and best documented assessment was that by Pines, although he still thought that Avicenna was referring to an ancient, but imaginary, tradition, and could only explain it by assuming Avicenna to be playing games ("Philosophie Orientale" 29, 32). For the most part, however, the interpretations that were offered in the last two centuries range from the ridiculous (Massignon's discovery of the oriental philosophy in the symbolic letters of Avicenna's *Nayrūziyya*, "Avicenne et les influences orientales," *La Revue du Caire* 141 [1951] 10–12) to the phantastic (Nasr's *philosophia perennis*), and tell more about their authors than about Avicenna. As a matter of fact, the theories and approach of Henry Corbin have spawned an independent school of "Oriental" philosophy which does not even claim to deal in particular with Avicenna. The major representative of this school appears to be Corbin's hierophant, Christian Jambet, with his book, *La logique des Orientaux. Henry Corbin et la science des formes*, Paris: Editions du Seuil, 1983, now generalized to encompass all of philosophy in the Islamic world, *Qu'est-ce que la philosophie islamique?*, Paris: Gallimard 2011 (cf. my review in *Philosophy East and West* 64.4, 2014). The history of such interpretations is briefly presented by R. Macuch, "Greek and Oriental Sources of Avicenna's and Sohrawardi's Theosophies," *Graeco-Arabica* [Athens] 2 (1983) 9–22.

the extent that we have been deprived of the opportunity to admire more instances of the acuity and perspicacity with which a great mind confronted another through the encrustations of thirteen centuries of philosophical history (for examples see Chapter 8.4). In substantial terms nothing has been lost except variant reformulations of positions taken in other works, extant, but sadly, neglected.

Work 10. *Fair Judgment* (*al-Inṣāf*) [GS 11] and, related to it, *Marginal Glosses on De anima* (*at-Taʿlīqāt ʿalā Ḥawāšī Kitāb an-Nafs*) [GS 11c]

Avicenna's commentaries on the text of Aristotle's works and the Ps.-Aristotelian *Theologia Aristotelis* (Plotinus, *Enneads* 4–6), known under the general title of *Fair Judgment* given to them by their author, are extant only in relatively few fragments. These commentaries share the characteristic of frequently referring to the Easterners, a subject which had become, even by the
131 time of their publication in 1947 (Badawī *Arisṭū*), a scholarly cause célèbre. Because there already existed an area of debate for which they provided fresh information, they have been considered almost exclusively in this connection and used in the further clarification of the question of the Eastern philosophy. As a result, the fundamental, and procedurally prior, issue of the transmission of these fragments received only incidental attention. Here I will concentrate on this issue since the question of the Easterners was discussed in the preceding Section (W9).

Fragments of this work are extant both in direct and in indirect transmission. We are able to derive information about its direct transmission both from internal and external evidence, that is, from the manuscripts themselves in which it has been preserved and from the reports about its fate by Avicenna and later authors. The indirectly transmitted fragments are recovered from passages quoted by later authors.

a. *Testimonia*

I. Statements by Avicenna

[1] Letter to an Anonymous Disciple (Bahmanyār) (T11, § 1):

> You expressed sorrow at the loss of *Pointers and Reminders*, but I think that a copy of this book has been preserved. As for the Eastern questions, I had packed them up—no, most of them—[as they were] in their quires so as no one would look at them, and I had also written down on slips of paper

some passages from the *Throne Philosophy*; it is these which got lost. They were not voluminous, however (although they did treat many subjects and were quite comprehensive), and it would be easy to rewrite them. But yes, the *Fair Judgment*, on the other hand, could not but be extensive, and rewriting it would require work.

[2] Letter to Kiyā (T12, § 3):

I had composed a book which I called *Fair Judgment*. I divided scholars into two groups, the Westerners and the Easterners, and I had the Easterners argue against the Westerners until I intervened to Judge Fairly when there was a real point of dispute between them. This book had contained approximately twenty-eight thousand questions. I commented clearly on the difficult passages in the essential texts up to the end of the *Theologia Aristotelis*, despite the fact that the *Theologia* is somewhat suspect, and I talked about the oversights of the commentators. I wrote it in a short period of time—[a work] 132
which, had it been transcribed clearly, would have comprised twenty volumes. Then it was lost in the course of some rout, since there was only the first draft. Investigating it and these controversies was a pastime; after completing something I am working on [at present], I will occupy myself with rewriting it, although even thinking about rewriting is oppressive. But it had contained a precise exposition of the weakness of the Baġdādīs, and of their deficiency and ignorance. At the present moment it is impossible for me [to rewrite it]: I do not have the free time for it.

II. Statements by Others

[3] Memoirs of a Disciple (Ibn Zayla?) Writing from Rayy (T13, § 2):

In the year when the horsemen of the late Sultan overran these lands, Avicenna was prompted for some reason to occupy himself with a book which he called *Fair Judgment*. It contained commentaries on all the books by Aristotle, among which he even included the *Theologia* [*Aristotelis*], about whose contents he brought out matters that had never been taken into account. He examined all divergences of exegesis and Judged every question and every philosopher by bestowing Fairly praise or blame, and appreciation or deprecation. God only knows the number of problems and solutions, and Corollaries based on Fundamental Principles, which resulted, although the period [in which the book was composed] was from the middle of the month of Dey to the end of the month of Ḫordād in [less than] a year! It came to more than six thousand folios written in a crowded hand and ten thousand folios written in a straight hand; it relieved him, however, of what he needed to communicate, and left him manifestly cheered. The number of issues he discussed as lemmata about which he traced where previous statements were wrong, mistaken, deficient, or corrupt, was over twenty-seven thousand. But before all this was transcribed into a clean copy, he was hindered by a military rout in which all his belongings and books were carried off at the gate of Iṣfahān. When he returned to Rayy, he was urged to rewrite all that, but he found this repugnant, since doing all over again something that has just been completed is onerous.

[4] Biography 80.5–7 Gohlman (Bio 20):

> The Master also wrote *Fair Judgment*, but on the day when Sultan Masʿūd
> 133 arrived at Iṣfahān, his troops plundered the Master's baggage. The book was among them, and no trace of it has been found.

[5] Shorter Bibliography (SB 7) 46.5 Gohlman:

> *Fair Judgment*, twenty volumes.[1]

[6a] Longer Bibliography (LB 5) 92.5–7 Gohlman:

> *Fair Judgment*, twenty volumes. Avicenna commented in it on all the books of Aristotle and Judged Fairly between the Easterners and the Westerners. It was lost during Sultan Masʿūd's plunder.

[6b] Extended Bibliography (EB 7) Bayhaqī *Tatimma* 187 Shafīʿ:

> *Meting and Obtaining Fair Judgment.*

[7] Longer Bibliography (LB 84) 108.5–6 Gohlman:

> Commentary on Aristotle's *De anima*. It is said to be from the *Fair Judgment.*

[8] Bayhaqī *Tatimma* 56.1–4/67.15–68.2:

> Then Governor Abū-Sahl al-Ḥamdūnī along with a group of Kurds [troops] plundered the personal effects of the Master, among which were also his books. Of the *Fair Judgment* only some quires were [later] found, but then ʿAzīz-ad-Dīn al-Fuqqāʿī az-Zanjānī[2] claimed [the following] in some month of the year 545[/1150–1151]: "I bought a copy of it in Iṣfahān and took it to Marw." God knows best.

[9] Suhrawardī Maqtūl, *al-Mašāriʿ wa-l-muṭāraḥāt* 360.5–6 (Corbin *Opera I*):

> The author of *The Cure* mentions in the surviving parts of a draft of his called *Meting and Obtaining Fair Judgment* (*al-Inṣāf wa-l-intiṣāf*) ....

[10] Ḥājjī Ḫalīfa, *Kašf aẓ-ẓunūn* I,183 Yaltkaya and Bilge:

> *Meting and Obtaining Fair Judgment*, by Avicenna, who died in 428[/1037].[3]

---

[1] This information is repeated by Bağdatlı Ismāʿīl Paşa in the *Hadiyyat al-ʿārifīn* I,308 Bilge and İnal.

[2] See above, W9, Test. 11a.i.

[3] Ḥājjī Ḫalīfa gives *al-Inṣāf wa-l-ittiṣāf* for the title, but since it appears that he had no source for this information other than Suhrawardī [Test. 9], I translate the latter's original version.

[11] Muḥammad ad-Daylamī, *Maḥbūb al-qulūb* 120 (Lithograph Bombay 1317):

> The philosopher Alexander of Aphrodisias: … All the Peripatetics, and especially Avicenna in the *Fair Judgment*, honor and praise him.

III. Manuscripts of the Work 134

For the manuscripts of the work see the Inventory in the Appendix. The Cairo manuscripts are described in Gutas "Ṣiġnāḫī" 10–13. The single most important among them is the MS Dār al-Kutub Ḥikma 6 M[uṣṭafā Fāḍil]. It is by far the oldest and the best and, by all appearances, the archetype from which all of the rest derive except for the Bursa manuscript. The information which this manuscript provides about the contents and survival of the work will be discussed below in Section c.

b. *Dates of Composition and Loss*

The point of reference for the establishment of these dates is the Ghaznavid Masʿūd ibn-Maḥmūd's attack on Iṣfahān. Three independent sources provide complementary information in this regard. Avicenna notes in the Letter to Kiyā [Test. 2] that he wrote the book in a short period of time. The anonymous disciple writing from Rayy (Ibn Zayla?) specifies in his letter [Test. 3] that the *Fair Judgment* was written between the tenth and the (following) third Persian months, from Dey to Ḫordād, of the year in which "the horsemen of the late Sultan overran these lands." "These lands" must be taken to refer to the area in northern Iran known as Jibāl, which included both Rayy, the assumed location of the author of the letter, and Iṣfahān, Avicenna's center of operations for approximately the last twelve years of his life. Although the history of these lands during this time is quite complicated and replete with military incursions, the one campaign which qualitatively distinguishes itself from the rest is the Ghaznavid Maḥmūd's occupation of the area, and particularly of Rayy, in the spring of 420/1029.[4] Now for the year 1029, according to the Persian calendar, the end of the third month, or the 30th of Ḫordād 398, corresponded to the 7th of June, while the middle of the previous tenth month, or the 15th of Dey 397, corresponded to the 19th of December of 1028.

The assumption of this date as the year of composition of the book well accords with the developments next reported in our sources. Least

---

[4] Detailed events and references are given by Bosworth "Kākūyids" 76.

explicit of all is Avicenna himself who says in the Letter to Kiyā [Test. 2] that the first draft of the work, the only copy available, "was lost in the course of some rout." The disciple writing from Rayy adds [Test. 3] that before Avicenna could transcribe his first draft into a clean copy, it was carried
135 off in an incident near, or "at the gate of Iṣfahān" (*ʿalā bāb Iṣfahān*).[5] In the biography of Avicenna, Jūzjānī gives further details about the same incident: "On the day when Sultan Masʿūd arrived at Iṣfahān, his troops plundered the Master's baggage" [Test. 4]. After occupying Rayy, Sultan Maḥmūd sent his son, Masʿūd, to subjugate the local princes in the area. Masʿūd first turned westwards toward Daylam and Azerbayjan, and after his successes there, headed south and entered Iṣfahān in Muḥarram 421 /January 1030.[6] ʿAlāʾ-ad-Dawla, the ruler of Iṣfahān, was forced to evacuate the city, and Avicenna, his vizier and physician, who accompanied him in all his travels, doubtless went along with him. The *Fair Judgment* must have been lost during this exodus.

ʿAlāʾ-ad-Dawla and his entourage retreated southwards to Ḫūzistān. Barely three months later, however, in Jumādā I 421/May 1030, Maḥmūd died in Ghazna and Masʿūd had to leave Jibāl and travel east in order to tend to the question of succession. Availing himself of this temporary destabilization of the situation, ʿAlāʾ-ad-Dawla moved north again and even occupied Rayy during the same year.[7] Continuing with the assumption that the physician accompanied his master wherever he went, Avicenna must have been in Rayy later that year. It was during this stay that his disciples in Rayy urged him to rewrite the *Fair Judgment*, and it is these meetings and discussions which the disciple writing from Rayy is recounting in his memoirs. Avicenna himself was later to refer to this sojourn in Rayy (T11, § 7), something which Jūzjānī leaves totally unmentioned in the Biography.

On the basis of a report by the historian Ibn-al-Aṯīr, Gohlman suggested that the attack on Iṣfahān referred to by Jūzjānī in the Biography (and hence the loss of the *Fair Judgment*) is not that which took place in Muḥarram 421/January 1030, but rather the later one which occurred in 425/1034.[8]

---

[5] The expression *ʿalā bāb Iṣfahān* may also mean "at the court of Iṣfahān", in which case it will have to be assumed that Masʿūd's troops had entered Avicenna's quarters in the palace.

[6] Bosworth "Kākūyids" 76.

[7] Bosworth "Kākūyids" 77; George C. Miles, *The Numismatic History of Rayy*, New York: American Numismatic Society 1938, 187–189; cf. Gohlman 135n106.

[8] Gohlman 135–136n106; 136n108. Before Gohlman, both Pines "Philosophie Orientale" 5 and Weisweiler 62 had suggested the year 1034 as the date of the book's loss.

Ibn-al-Aṯīr's testimony, together with the concordant one by al-Ḥusaynī, the purported author of *Zubdat at-tawārīḫ*, are important about the fate of Avicenna's *Nachlass*.[9] Gohlman identified the transferral of Avicenna's books from Iṣfahān to Ghazna by Masʿūd's commander, Abū-Sahl al-Ḥamdūnī, with the pillage near Iṣfahān of Avicenna's saddle bags containing the *Fair Judgment*. This identification cannot be maintained for a number of reasons. First, there is the inherent dissimilarity in the details of the two inci- 136
dents: one talks about the wholesale transportation of Avicenna's books from ʿAlāʾ-ad-Dawla's treasuries and libraries in Iṣfahān to Ghazna, the other describes the incident of the plunder of Avicenna's saddlebags near Iṣfahān. Second, Jūzjānī is quite specific in the Biography that the incident occurred "on the day when Sultan Masʿūd arrived at Iṣfahān." This happened only in 421/1030; in 425/1034 the battle against Iṣfahān was directed by Abū-Sahl while Masʿūd himself was in Ghazna. Third, and perhaps most important, is the report about Avicenna's visit to Rayy *after* the loss of the book. During the sack of Iṣfahān in 425/1034, Avicenna was sick with colic, as described in detail by Jūzjānī [Gohlman 83–87]. He was obliged to flee south to Īḏāj with ʿAlāʾ-ad-Dawla[10] in that state, where apparently his condition deteriorated. He was *carried back*, to Iṣfahān when the situation there stabilized, and he recuperated sufficiently to resume his administrative duties [Gohlman 87]. In the letter to Kiyā [T12, § 4], he informs his addressee that he had been sick for a year and some months; this would date his (partial) recuperation sometime in 427/1036. He never fully recovered, and after a number of relapses he died the following year [Gohlman 87–89]. Between 425/1034 and his death in 428/1037, there are thus few opportunities when he was physically well enough to undertake the journey; in addition to that, he could not have abandoned Iṣfahān for political reasons as well. ʿAlāʾ-ad-Dawla was in Iṣfahān, as a matter of fact, preparing an attack against the Ghaznavid garrison in Rayy, the attack which took place in 429/1037–1038 shortly after Avicenna's death.[11] Avicenna must have therefore visited Rayy before his sickness (and Abū-Sahl's attack on Iṣfahān) in 425/1034, and the only time it was politically feasible for him to do so after the loss of his book was, as mentioned above, in the company of ʿAlāʾ-ad-Dawla in 421/1030.

---

[9] Testimonium 11b–c, W9, and see the discussion there. Cf. the account in Bosworth "Kākūyids" 77–78.

[10] Cf. Bosworth "Kākūyids" 77–78.

[11] Bosworth "Kākūyids" 78–79.

To recapitulate: The *Fair Judgment* was drafted approximately between 19 December 1028 and 7 June 1029, and this first and only draft was destroyed by Masʿūd's soldiers who pillaged Avicenna's saddlebags in January 1030.

c. *Contents and Survival of the Work*

The *Fair Judgment* was a detailed commentary on the Aristotelian corpus, including the *Theologia Aristotelis*, in which Avicenna came to grips with the
137 very texts and did not merely present their teachings in his own words. There is sufficient testimony to this effect both from Avicenna himself [Test. 2] and others [Test. 3], as well as from the extant portions of the work. In a way it was the counterpart of *The Easterners*. There he presented his own revision of philosophy in the Aristotelian tradition without taking "into account … the views of colleagues in the discipline" [T9, §4]; here he juxtaposed the transmitted texts with his elaborations.

The work was long. The disciple writing from Rayy (Ibn-Zayla?) says [Test. 3] that in a crowded, i.e., small, hand (presumably Avicenna's or his scribe's) it came to six thousand folios, which means, considering that it was written in about six months, that Avicenna composed an average of thirty-three folios (sixty-six pages) each day. This may or may not be realistic, but in the absence of any other information it is pointless to speculate on the matter.

With one exception, all of the extant portions of the *Fair Judgment* survive in the Cairo MS Ḥikma 6M which can be dated to the first half of the 6th/12th century and which appears to have served as the archetype for most of the subsequent copies now known. The scribe of the manuscript, ʿAbd-ar-Razzāq as-Ṣiġnāḫī, was a third generation student of Avicenna and an expert bibliographer of his works.[12] His testimony on this matter can be trusted, and the information he provides in the manuscript about the transmission of the *Fair Judgment* accordingly merits special attention.

The exception is the collective manuscript (*majmūʿa*) of Avicenna's works which was discovered in Bursa by Jean (Yaḥyā) Michot ("Recueil avicennien"), Ḥüseyin Çelebi 1194, dated to 675 / October 1276–May 1277. From a comparison of its readings with the Cairo manuscript, it appears relatively clear that it does not depend on the latter but that they both draw from a common source.[13] But the Bursa manuscript contains only two texts from

[12] See his brief biography by Bayhaqī *Tatimma* 124–125/130–131 = Meyerhof 178, and cf. Gutas "Ṣiġnāḫī" 8–9.

[13] An omission by homoioteleuton in the Cairo MS of a whole line of text, extant in

the *Fair Judgment*, whereas the Cairo one contains four; it would thus seem, provisionally at least, that ʿAbd-ar-Razzāq was the one who collected all the disparate fragments in his collective manuscript, whereas the scribe of the Bursa manuscript had independent access to two of those disparate sources.

The four texts in ʿAbd-ar-Razzāq's manuscript which may be considered to have belonged to the *Fair Judgment* are, in the order in which they occur therein, a commentary on Book *Lambda* of the *Metaphysics*, two recensions of a commentary on the *Theologia Aristotelis*, and a set of glosses on *De anima*. They were published from this manuscript by Badawī *Arisṭū*.

i) *Metaphysics* (pp. 22–33 Badawī). The title of the commentary on the *Metaphysics* reads as follows: "From the book *Fair Judgment*: Commentary on Book *Lambda*, by Avicenna."[a] ʿAbd-ar-Razzāq here explicitly ascribes the text to Avicenna and indicates that it is an extract from *Fair Judgment*. In actual fact, however, the text is reported in the third person: most of the major sections begin with the introductory phrase, "He [Avicenna] said,"

---

[a] F. 138[b], 1: *wa-min kitāb al-inṣāf, šarḥ ḥarf kitāb* [*sic*] *al-lām li-š-Šayḫ ar-Raʾīs Abī ʿAlī Ibn Sīnā* = Badawī *Arisṭū* 22. Badawī tacitly transposes the order of the words to read, *kitāb ḥarf*. The Bursa MS, according to Michot "Recueil Avicennien" 125, drops the word *kitāb* and reads, *šarḥ ḥarf al-lām*. All the references in parentheses after the citations in what follows are to Badawī *Arisṭū*.

---

the Bursa MS, appears quite conclusive. In the commentary on Book *Lambda* of Aristotle's *Metaphysics*, 1072b14–24, the Cairo MS omits (f. 140[a], line 10 = Badawī *Arisṭū* p. 27.10) the text in angular brackets which is found in the Bursa MS (f. 121[a], lines 14–15): *wa-kayfa wa-naḥnu naltaḏḏu bi-idrāki* ⟨*l-ḥaqqi ltiḏāḏan lā yumkinu waṣfuhu, fa-kayfa iḏā kāna l-ḥaqqu miṯla ḏālika*⟩ *l-ḥaqqi wa-naḥnu maṣrūfūna ʿanhu*. I am indebted to Yahya Michot for sending me a copy of this commentary from the Bursa MS, and to Jules Janssens for drawing my attention to this passage and sending me a page of the philological comments he and his collaborators are writing on it. — The sentence omitted in the Cairo manuscript referring to the "indescribable" (*lā yumkinu waṣfuhu*) intellectual pleasure of contemplating the truth is without doubt authentic (and thus not somebody's gloss that was at some point inserted in the source of the Bursa manuscript) because it is a central element in Avicenna's elaboration of the layers and nature of intellection from his middle period through the end of his life. The pleasure to be derived from intellection was expressed very clearly in Alexander's commentary on Book *Lambda* (extant in Arabic in Averroes's long commentary, *Tafsīr* III,1619.4–8 Bouyges), from which Avicenna would seem to be inspired. Avicenna himself talks of the "indescribable" emotive pleasure of intellection in *Provenance and Destination* 119 Nūrānī (*lā tūṣafu*) and then again in *Pointers* II.9.20, 205/364 (*lā yufhimuhā l-ḥadīṯu*), for a discussion of which see Gutas "Absence of Mysticism" 363–369.

and in one case a comment by Avicenna is preceded by the descriptive phrase, "[Avicenna] criticized Aristotle and the commentators and said" (23.21). This means that the text as we now have it was copied by ʿAbd-ar-
138 Razzāq not directly from Avicenna's draft but from an extract made by a disciple, who provided the editorial introductory phrases. The fragment is also preserved in the Bursa MS Ḥüseyin Çelebi 1194, ff. 119^{a}–123^{b} (Michot "Recueil Avicennien" 125).

A preliminary study of the "paraphrase-commentary," as he called it, has been conducted by Janssens "Livre Lambda."

ii) *Theologia Aristotelis* (pp. 37–74 Badawī). The commentary on the Ps.-Aristotelian *Theologia* is extant in two partially overlapping recensions. ʿAbd-ar-Razzāq entitled them respectively as follows: "Commentary on *Theologia*, from *Fair Judgment*, on the authority of Avicenna;" "Exegesis of the Book *Theologia*, from *Fair Judgment*, on the authority of Avicenna."[b] The Bursa MS Hüseyin Çelebi contains only the former of the two (ff. 123^{b}–128^{a}), as it appears from the information provided by Michot "Recueil Avicennien" 125–126. Another manuscript which appears this time to contain the "Exegesis" is in the Bodleian at Oxford, Marsh 536, ff. 69^{b}–84^{b}; its precise contents and relationship to the former two remains to be investigated. Badawī published the two recensions from the Cairo MS selectively, omitting the overlapping sections—and the valuable textual information they contain (for publication details see Gutas "Ṣiġnāḫī" 12b–13a). Recently Janssens discovered extensive quotations from this commentary in the metaphysical part of Lawkarī's major philosophical summa, *Bayān al-ḥaqq bi-ḍamān aṣ-ṣidq* (Janssens "Lawkarī" 14–24).

The use of the preposition *ʿan* ("on the authority of") in the titles by ʿAbd-ar-Razzāq in the Cairo MS is significant. The preposition, used in the reporting of the traditions of the Prophet (*ḥadīṯ*), indicates that the two recensions ultimately derive from the text of Avicenna through an unspecified number, in this case, of intermediary transmitters. ʿAbd-ar-Razzāq found the two recensions to be slightly divergent in their wording and did not know which one, if either, represented Avicenna's very words; he therefore used the preposition to alert the reader to this fact. This being the case, the extant texts of the two recensions are in all likelihood disciples' notes taken down

---

[b] F. 142^{a}, 15: *fī šarḥ Uṯūlūjiyā, min kitāb al-inṣāf, ʿan aš-Šayḫ ar-Raʾīs Abī ʿAlī al-Ḥusayn b. ʿAbd Allāh Ibn Sīnā* (cf. Badawī *Arisṭū* Introduction (46). 1–2); f. 146^{a}, 7: *Tafsīr kitāb Uṯūlūjiyā, min al-inṣāf, ʿan aš-Šayḫ ar-Raʾis Abī ʿAlī Ibn Sīnā* = Badawī *Arisṭū* 37.

from lectures given by Avicenna (according to Reisman *Avicennan Tradition* 203n125, the disciple was Ibn-Zayla), or copies from Avicenna's original draft by two different disciples, or possibly copies of each other at some unspecified remove. Their precise relationship will have to be determined by the future editor, after due consideration of the contents of the various manuscripts and the citations in subsequent authors, more of which will be doubtless unearthed.

iii) *De anima* (pp. 75–116 Badawī). ʿAbd-ar-Razzāq gives the following title for this commentary: "Glosses by Avicenna in the Margins of Aristotle's *De anima*."[c] This title, in which ʿAbd-ar-Razzāq does not mention the *Fair Judgment* at all, can only be interpreted literally. Even if we had no knowledge of ʿAbd-ar-Razzāq's bibliographical expertise, it would be difficult to explain why anybody would invent such a title. The inference, then, seems to be that Avicenna wrote these comments in the margins of his own copy of Aristotle's *De anima*, and that this copy subsequently passed in the hands either of one of his disciples or of ʿAbd-ar-Razzāq, who transcribed these notes cleanly and consecutively, omitting the Aristotelian text. The transmission of these glosses thus differs qualitatively from that of the preceding two parts from *Fair Judgment*: they are the *ipsissima verba* of Avicenna, copied from his own manuscript (indicated by ʿAbd-ar-Razzāq's express *min kalām aš-šayḫ*), while the latter are transmitted through the editorial filter of disciples' notes (indicated by the introductory phrase inserted in the commentary on *Lambda* and the preposition *ʿan* in that on *Theologia*). The *Marginal Glosses* 139
on De anima, therefore, is *not* part of the *Fair Judgment*, at least as far as ʿAbd-ar-Razzāq knew, while the Longer Bibliography of Avicenna's works (LB 84), which dates from before 1192 (see the Tetrapla chart in the Appendix) and lists a commentary (*šarḥ*) on *De anima* which was "said to be from the *Fair Judgment*" [Test. 7], can hardly derive this information from anywhere else but a manuscript, and indeed most likely from a direct or indirect knowledge of ʿAbd-ar-Razzāq's manuscript.[14]

---

[c] Literally, "Glosses in the Margins of Aristotle's *De anima*, from what Avicenna said," f. 154[a], 1: *at-taʿlīqāt ʿalā ḥawāšī kitāb an-nafs li-Arisṭāṭālīs, min kalām aš-Šayḫ ar-Raʾīs Abī ʿAlī Ibn Sīnā* = Badawī *Arisṭū* 75.

---

[14] Pines "Philosophie Orientale" 10n3, and Finnegan "Porphyrius" 196 assumed that the *Marginal Glosses* were part of the *Fair Judgment*, while Frank "*De Anima*" 235 and note 4 cogently argued that they are, in fact, marginalia.—Two other references to a commentary

However, it is clear that these marginal glosses share with the *Fair Judgment* the same style, nature, and method (discussed in detail in Gutas "Glosses"). They were written either immediately before the *Fair Judgment* (and after *The Easterners*, to which Avicenna repeatedly refers) and directly occasioned the *Fair Judgment* by whetting the appetite of Avicenna's students for a similar but more extensive composition, or immediately afterwards, in partial compensation for its loss. I would tend to favor the former alternative, if only because the political situation immediately following the incursion of the Ghaznavids in the area, as described above in Section (b), was little conducive to such activities; but there can be no certainty in this matter.

---

on *De anima* by Avicenna turn out, upon closer inspection, not to be to the *Marginal Glosses*. First, Avicenna himself says in the *Immolation* (*Aḍḥawiyya*) *Destination* (Lucchetta *Epistola* 153) that he discussed the substantiality of the soul in numerous treatises, "and especially in our commentary (*šarḥ*) on Aristotle's *De anima*." This would seem to be a reference, following Avicenna's practice earlier in his career (see Chapter 7), to the De anima part of *The Available and the Valid* (see W3), or perhaps even to *The Cure*. In any case, however one dates the *Aḍḥawiyya*, it is unlikely that Avicenna would have referred at all to his marginal glosses in his copy of *De anima*, which never seem to have circulated independently in his lifetime, and even if he did, that he would have referred to them as a "commentary." The second is a case of bibliographical muddle. In the hastily compiled first edition of his *Bibliyografya* (1937), Ergin reported (p. 22, no. 103) on the existence of a Persian *Šarḥ Kitāb an-nafs li-Arisṭāṭālīs* in the Istanbul MS Ahmet III 3447, without giving any folio numbers. He also provided the incipit and explicit of the text, but there is nowhere any indication that the work is by Avicenna—one infers it simply because Ergin listed it as no. 103 in the first section of the bibliography containing Avicenna's works (*İbni Sînanın* [*sic*] *Eserleri*). Brockelmann picked this up in his 1937 *Supplement* (*GALS* I,817, no. 21a), gave it an imaginary title (*at-Taʿlīqāt ʿalā k. an-nafs li Arisṭū*), and added that it was printed in "Stambul 1298." In his turn, Anawati *Muʾallafāt* 149–150 (1950), no. 87, repeated the information from both Ergin and Brockelmann, including the Persian incipit and explicit, and only added the folio numbers of the Ahmet III 3447 MS as 709[b]–736[a]. Mahdavī (1954) 279, no. 177, gave the title, incipit, and reference to Anawati only, and without mentioning any manuscripts, stated this to be a Persian translation by Afḍal-ad-Dīn Kāšānī of Aristotle's work. He added that it was printed in Tehran, without details, although it was he himself who had published this Persian translation two years previously, together with Mojtabā Mīnovī: *Moṣannafāt-e Afḍaladdīn ... Kāšānī*, Vol. 2, Tehran 1331Š/1952, pp. 389–458. In the second edition of his *Bibliografya* (1956), in which Ergin benefited from Mahdavī's work, he simply dropped the entry. Now the Persian work in question here, with the incipit and explicit given in Ergin, is not the *De anima* of Aristotle but a late antique paraphrase of it edited and studied by Arnzen *Paraphrase*. Arnzen, however, who gives quite a complete list of MSS containing Kāšānī's translation (pp. 42–51, 677–680), does not list the Ahmet III 3447 MS. To add to the mystery, Reisman "ARCE" 139, who gives a corrected list of contents of this MS, for ff. 709[b]–736[a], which, according to Anawati contain Kāšānī's Persian translation of the *De anima* paraphrase, has the entry, *al-Ajwiba ʿan masāʾil Abī Rayḥān al-Bīrūnī*, a work for which neither Anawati nor Mahdavī list the Ahmet III MS! And finally, the identity and whereabouts of Brockelmann's ghost publication published in "Stambul 1298" remains as much a mystery as ever.

The evidence provided by ʿAbd-ar-Razzāq's manuscript of the *Fair Judgment* thus leads to the following conclusions. The only parts of the work available to him were the commentary on *Metaphysics Lambda* and two recensions of a commentary on the *Theologia Aristotelis*. He had access to these parts not in Avicenna's original draft or a manuscript copied from it, but indirectly in the form of notes and extracts by a disciple or disciples, made from Avicenna's original draft or his lectures. In contradistinction to this, he had direct access to the marginal glosses which Avicenna himself made to the *De anima*, independently of the *Fair Judgment*. It is very likely that he owned the very manuscript used by Avicenna.

The fragments saved from extinction by ʿAbd-ar-Razzāq also found their way in the writings of subsequent authors. Mahdavī cites numerous such 140
references. To these should be added Šahrastānī's *Religions and Sects*, which copies almost the entire surviving parts of the commentary on the *Metaphysics Lambda*,[15] and Ġazālī's (?) *Maʿārij al-quds*, which incorporates sections from the commentary on the *Theology*.[16] Doubtless more will be identified as research progresses. But so far, the fact that all the identified fragments from the *Fair Judgment* quoted in later authors are also those extant in ʿAbd-ar-Razzāq's manuscript would tend to indicate that this manuscript (or its source) was solely responsible for their survival. For the reasons given by Avicenna himself [Testimonia 1, 2, 3], he never rewrote the *Fair Judgment*. The copy said to have been bought by Zanjānī in Iṣfahān in 1150 [Test. 8], if not the freshly written manuscript of ʿAbd-ar-Razzāq itself, would appear to have been an early transcription of it.

Work 11. *Pointers and Reminders* (*al-Išārāt wa-t-tanbīhāt*) [GS 9]

The *Pointers and Reminders* is Avicenna's last philosophical summa, written sometime between 421–425/1030–1034. The knowledgeable compiler of the Longer Bibliography (LB 95; see the Appendix) says that it is "his last work, which he would Withhold [from others],"[1] and this is clearly borne out

---

[15] Šahrastānī presents the entire text as "the theory of Aristotle" (*raʾy Arisṭūṭālīs*), *Milal* 312.19–320.4 Cureton. Cf. Janssens "Lambda" 404.

[16] See Janssens "*Maʿārij al-quds*" 39–40.

[1] This is probably the correct text, given in the Istanbul MS Üniversite 4755, f. 217^{b}, *Kitāb al-Išārāt wa-t-tanbīhāt wa-huwa āḫir mā ṣannafa wa-kāna yaḍinnu bihi*, as opposed to the fuller text in Ibn-Abī-Uṣaybiʿa (preferred by Gohlman 96.3, who in addition omits *mā*).

by the analysis given above under W9c. This information must have been widely known soon after Avicenna's time, and it appears in ʿAbd-al-Laṭīf al-Baġdādī's (d. 1234) *Two Pieces of Advice* (*Kitāb an-Naṣīḥatayn*), who may or may not have been echoing the Longer Bibliography (if he had access to independent information about the late dating of the *Išārāt*), but who clearly referred to Avicenna's own words in his opening and closing remarks in the book (T10, § 5, also given below): "He wrote it at the end of his life after his great works; he aggrandized and glorified it, and admonished that it not be shown to everyone and that it should be safeguarded like a most precious pearl."[2]

An earlier dating has been suggested by both Michot and Reisman. On the basis of an anonymous and highly ambiguous reference in one of the letters in the *Discussions*, which Michot "Réponse" 158–161 (1997) thought was to the *Pointers*, he dated the work to around 406/1016 (repeated in Michot *Abū Saʿd* 32*); but this date cannot stand for the many detailed reasons given by Reisman *Avicennan Tradition* 215–219 and "New Standard" 564–565.[3] Upon consideration of further evidence from the *Discussions* and other private writings of Avicenna, along with Reisman's arguments, Michot later changed his mind and dated the *Išārāt* this time to 415/1024–421/1030 (Michot "Riz" 94 and note 51), eventually agreeing with Reisman, and again on the basis of materials from the *Discussions*, in dating it to "between 418–421/1027–1030" (Reisman *Avicennan Tradition* 221–224) and "peu après 418/1027" (Michot *Astrologie* 33*n2). Reisman's result depends on his dating of the Letter to an Anonymous Disciple (Bahmanyār = *Mubāḥaṯa* II), which mentions the loss of the *Išārāt*, to 1030: since, Reisman claims (p. 222), a substantial portion of the *Mubāḥaṯāt* materials precedes this Letter, the *Išārāt* must have been written before 1030. I presented above (W9) the historical evidence which supports dating the Letter to 1034; and if that is so, then the "considerable amount of correspondence" referred to by Reisman could have taken place between 1030 and 1034, during the period of composition of the *Išārāt*.

In this discussion about the chronology of Avicenna's works, the private correspondence of Avicenna and his disciples naturally offers crucial evidence, but we should distinguish between relative and absolute chronology

---

[2] MS Bursa Hüseyin Çelebi 823, f. 95ᵃ: *Waḍaʿahu fī āḫir ʿumrihi baʿda taṣānīfihi l-kibār wa-ʿaẓẓamahu wa-faḫḫamahu wa-waṣṣā allā yuṭlaʿa ʿalayhi kullu aḥadin wa-an yuṣāna ṣiyānata d-durri n-nafīs.*

[3] Cf. also the remarks on this early dating of the *Išārāt* in the reviews of Michot's *Abū Saʿd* by J. Janssens in *Arabica* 49 (2002) 396–397, and R. Wisnovsky in *Journal of the Royal Asiatic Society*, III. ser., 12 (2002) 364.

and the evidence each relies upon: the former is more easily extracted from these documents, but it can be used for the absolute chronology only when it can be correlated with independently established dates. In the present case, Michot and Reisman succeed in establishing relative chronology only, and I argue that the sequence of composition of the works by Avicenna which is established in W9 above takes precedence over the relative dating, which should be adjusted to that sequence, not the other way around. But doubtless more research is needed in all the private writings of Avicenna—his correspondence and the *Discussions* as well as the *Notes*—before we can determine with greater precision the absolute chronology.

The *Pointers and Reminders* marks the culmination of Avicenna's philosophical career because it achieves the greatest possible extrapolation from Aristotelian models of presentation, surpassing the stage reached during his period of Eastern philosophy, and it provides a concrete and magnificent example of his concept of the praxis of philosophy which proceeds by Deriving Corollaries on the basis of Fundamental Principles through the help of syllogistic procedures highlighted by Guessing Correctly the middle terms (*ḥads*). As he says in the Prologue to the first part on Logic,

> O you who are zealous to Ascertain the truth: I have exposed to you in these Pointers and reminders Fundamental Principles and essential elements of philosophy; if sagacity takes hold of your hand [to guide you], it will become easy for you to Derive Corollary Principles from the former and work out the details of the latter. [T10, § 2]

Avicenna chose to write the entire work by using the indicative method of Pointers (Chapter 8.3) in order to ensure that the knowledge it contains be Withheld from those unworthy to receive it. As is usual in historical developments, a confluence of both personal and historical factors led to his choice. Avicenna's long-standing feud with the elder statesman and philosophaster, Abū-l-Qāsim al-Kirmānī, is well attested in the various documents in the *Discussions* and other private writings by Avicenna, and has been studied to a considerable extent by Michot *Abū Saʿd* and "Riz", and by Reisman *Avicennan Tradition*. The feud went beyond mere philosophical disagreement and sunk to levels of personal animosity and slander. In the letter known as *al-Intifāʾ* (GPW 3), Avicenna reports that the charge was made that his use of literary consonance in some of his works was allegedly imitative of the Qurʾān; the person to whom reference is made as having slandered Avicenna is not named in the letter, but it can hardly be anyone else but the said Abū-l-Qāsim (see Michot "Riz" and especially p. 114 for the calumny). Avicenna was thus understandably leery of having the *Išārāt*, a work in an allusive and elevated style making full use of all artistic devices, including consonance, be shown to Abū-l-Qāsim. In a letter to Bahmanyār included in the *Discussions* (*Mubāḥaṯa* I) he thus explicitly forbids it:

> As for the *Pointers*, the copy of it [*an-nusḫa minhā*, definite, i.e., in your possession] is not to be published (*tuḫraj*) except orally and [this] after conditions are stipulated only for the sake of its defense [i.e., against misuse],[4] [namely,] it is not possible for any outsider to ask to see it and look at it with you; as a matter of fact, it is not possible that anyone look at it except you and Abū-Manṣūr ibn-Zayla. As for the riffraff and [shit-]eaters and anyone who is not worthy of the truth and of respect, there is no way to present those propositions [in the *Pointers*] to them.[5]

Clearly the feud had been exacerbated to the point of *ad hominem* attacks and name-calling. But whatever personal reasons Avicenna may have had for the choice of style, they were subsumed to his particular purpose of communication and expressed in the traditional and collective language of the teaching of philosophy only to worthy and industrious students (Chapter 5.3), and in this respect also the work constitutes the culmination of a tendency long developing in the Aristotelian tradition. As Avicenna says in the Prologue to the second part of the *Pointers* on Physics and Metaphysics,

> What follows are Pointers to Fundamental Principles and reminders of essential elements. Whoever finds them easy will be able to gain insights through
> 141 them, while he who finds them difficult will not benefit even from the most obvious of them. We rely on God for success. Here I repeat my admonition and restate my request that the contents of these parts be Withheld as much as possible from those who do not meet the conditions I stipulated at the end of these Pointers. [T10, §§4–5]

This method of teaching depends on providing hints and guidelines to the student, rather than ready-made arguments, who is then expected to elaborate the entire theory on his own. This is what the two words of the title, Pointers and reminders, refer to.[6] In addition to these words Avicenna also used, though not as frequently, a number of others in order to describe as best as possible the nature of each statement. When a theory, for example, is to be censured, the statement introducing it is labelled *taḏnīb*; when a statement completes a preceding one it is called a *takmila*, etc.

---

[4] The Arabic has *mukāfaḥatan*, which I take it to be short for *mukāfaḥatan ʿanhā*, like *mudāfaʿatan*, as in the *Lisān al-ʿArab*, s.v. Cf. Michot, who has, "qu'à titre de prevention."

[5] *Mubāḥaṯāt* §2 Bīdārfar; cf. the translation of this passage in Michot "Réponse" 155 and Reisman *Avicennan Tradition* 206.

[6] See Chapter 8.3. Cf. Goichon *Directives* 68–69 and Michot *Astrologie* 27*-31* for a discussion of these terms. In the *Pugio Fidei* of Raymond Martin, the title appears in Latin as *Liber Inuitationum et excitationum*: d'Alverny "Notes" 358.

The arrangement of the contents of the work still follows the traditional order of Logic, Physics, Metaphysics, although Physics and Metaphysics are interwoven to form the second part. Each part contains ten chapters. Those of Logic are called *nahj*, "method," "path," and those of Physics and Metaphysics are called *namaṭ*, "form" (i.e., kind of subject matter or exposition).[7]

Because of its succinctness, the work was apparently felt to be in need of oral exposition and hard work in order to be understood even during Avicenna's lifetime; in subsequent philosophical tradition it was subjected to repeated commentaries.[8] It appears that it was responsible, more than any other work by Avicenna, first, for keeping interest in philosophy alive if only because it challenged the talents of the best commentators, and second, for establishing as normative the tripartite form of presentation of philosophy as Logic, Physics, and Metaphysics. It seems ironical, though perhaps true, that what Avicenna wished to accomplish through external means by giving a new name, Ḫurāsānī or Eastern, to his revision of the Aristotelian tradition was finally achieved through the inherent power and fascination of the *Pointers and Reminders*.

Work 12. *Discussions* (*al-Mubāḥaṯāt*) [GS 14]

The *Discussions* is a collection of philosophical correspondence between Avicenna and Bahmanyār (and indirectly, Abū-l-Qāsim al-Kirmānī) on the one hand, and between Avicenna and Ibn-Zayla on the other, all dating from the last (Iṣfahān) period of Avicenna's life. Bahmanyār initially collected the majority of texts related to this correspondence, which was subsequently enlarged as more texts became available for inclusion. The collection was eventually named *Discussions, al-Mubāḥaṯāt,* after the turn of the sixth/twelfth century at the earliest. With time, additional materials, which do not belong to the original correspondence and are called "accretional" by Reisman, were included in the collection. The various recensions of the work which exist in sundry manuscripts, the different contents of both the core and accretional materials, and their chronological order are listed and studied in Reisman *Avicennan Tradition.*

---

[7] See Goichon *Directives* 247 note 1, and the explanation of Faḫr-ad-Dīn ar-Rāzī mentioned there.

[8] See the list given in Mahdavī no. 27; their study has hardly begun. As the wise and learned Georges Vajda put it, "Le jour [est] sans doute très lointain, où un Corpus Commentariorum Avicennae sera mis en chantier;" in his "*Muḥākamāt*" 32.

The significance of the *Discussions* is both philosophical and biographical. The exchange of questions, answers, renewed questions and repeated responses refines our understanding of many a philosophical point in Avicenna's mature thought, while the occasional personal and historical references in the correspondence provide valuable biographical information for Avicenna and his contemporaries.

Work 13. *Appendices* (*al-Lawāḥiq*) and *Notes* (*at-Taʿlīqāt*) [GS 12b and 12a]

Avicenna conceived of the work which he consistently called in all his writings *Appendices* (*al-Lawāḥiq*) in the course of his composition of *The*
142 *Cure*. Since his intention in *The Cure* was to provide an expository summa of the philosophical sciences in his own words, as already discussed (W6), it appears that he initially envisaged the *Appendices* as a kind of notebook which would include what *The Cure* could not, namely his comments on the Aristotelian and other authoritative texts themselves. His brief reference to the *Appendices* in his Epilogue to the Sophistics part of *The Cure* (T6B, § 7), written around 414/1024, points to that direction. The same applies to his expositions of the works on astronomy and music in the mathematical section of *The Cure*: at the beginning of the former he says that he will follow Ptolemy's *Almagest* but not subsequent works because a thorough treatment of those will be found in the *Appendices*, while at the end of music he says that the *Appendices* will contain "many Corollary elaborations and additions (*tafrīʿāt wa-ziyādāt*)."[1] It is probable that in this way Avicenna also hoped to satisfy the requests of his companions who would rather see *The Cure* itself take the form of commentary (cf. W6).

Subsequently, Avicenna's attitude toward the *Appendices* gradually evolved. In the book on *Animals* in the Physics part of the *The Cure*, which is also the last part of that work that he wrote, around 1027 (W6), he does refer to the *Appendices* for a prospective fuller discussion of an Aristotelian passage,[2] but he also adds that it would include "the fullest possible

---

1 Mahdavī 159, 165.

2 The Aristotelian passage quoted by Avicenna, at the end of which this reference is made, is, "Aristotle said: 'They think that the substance of the brain is sensitive and that it has the sense of touch, but this is not so, but rather it [the brain] is like the marrow in the bones';" (*Ḥayawān* 222.18–19 Muntaṣir et al.). This appears to refer to *Parts of Animals* 656a17–18 and more generally to the discussion of the brain and the marrow in chapters 6–7 of Book Two.

commentary" on a subject that he treats in *The Cure*, namely that the soul, despite its various faculties, is essentially one and that its primary association is to the primary bodily organ (the heart).[3] At the end, he came to the point where he considered the *Appendices* a commentary on *The Cure* itself (see the discussion in Chapter 7): in its Prologue, written well after it was completed, he described as follows their mutual relationship:

> Then I thought it appropriate that I should write another book to follow this one [*The Cure*]. I have called it *Appendices*, and it will end with my life, finding its termination in whatever will have been completed every year. It is like a commentary to this book, Providing Corollaries to its Fundamental Principles and elaborating upon its briefly expressed concepts. [T9, § 3]

Despite Avicenna's definite description of the work and his explicit mention of the title, paradoxically no work by him has been preserved under this title. This fact appears also to have puzzled Avicenna's bibliographers and scribes of the manuscripts of his works. Among the former, Jūzjānī does not mention such a book in the Biography or that he ever saw it, the Shorter Bibliography (SB) does not list it at all, while the Longer Bibliography lists it only on the authority of Avicenna's statement in the Prologue of *The Cure* just cited (T9, § 3), not on the basis of independent knowledge of manuscripts of it in circulation: "The *Appendices*; he mentioned that it is a commentary on *The Cure*" (see LB 2 in the Tetrapla in the Appendix). The EB 5 merely lists it without comment. Among the latter, the scribe of the Leiden manuscript Golius Or. 184, copying Avicenna's essay *Instruments of Astronomical Observation* (GMath 4), says that this essay should be considered as an appendix to the Astronomy of *The Cure* and therefore as part of the *Appendices* (*wa-sabīluhu* [*sic*, for *sabīluhā*, with reference to *maqāla*] *an yuḍāfa ilā lawāḥiq ʿilm al-Majisṭī min Kitāb al-Lawāḥiq*).[4] By this reckoning, however, every separate essay by Avicenna on a discrete subject discussed in *The Cure* could also be considered as part of the *Appendices*. The question needs to be investigated further in the context of the transmission of Avicenna's entire works.

---

[3] He says, *Ḥayawān* 225.3–4 Muntaṣir et al.: "You will find the books of the *Appendices* (*kutub al-Lawāḥiq*) to contain the fullest possible commentary on the subject that the soul is one and that its primary association (*taʿalluq*) is with a primary organ." The plural reference to the "books of the *Appendices*" may indicate that Avicenna conceived of the work as being in many parts. Avicenna actually investigates this subject at the end of the *De anima* part of *The Cure* (*Nafs*, Book Five, chapters 7–8, especially pp. 263–264 Rahman).

[4] See the facsimile of the manuscript in Sezgin 49b; printed in Wiedemann 86, and also 83; reprinted in his *Gesammelte Schriften*, Frankfurt: Institut für Geschichte der Arabisch-Islamischen Wissenschaften, 1984, II,1122 and 1119. Cf. the comments by Reisman *Avicennan Tradition* 42.

There exists instead a collection of materials that meets Avicenna's description to some extent, and it has been transmitted under the title of *Notes* (*Taʿlīqāt*). The transmission and compilation of this work is extremely complicated, given its nature. As in the case of the *Discussions* (W12), it can be properly understood only after a detailed study and comparison of the numerous manuscripts in which it is extant, together with other relevant works by Avicenna. Here only the major issues and problems can be stated.

143 The *Notes* is a collection of discrete paragraphs of varying length discussing, paraphrasing, and especially commenting upon different subjects in Avicenna's Logic, Physics, and Metaphysics; passages in particular from the Metaphysics and Logic of *The Cure* and the Metaphysics of the *Philosophy for ʿArūḍī*, as well as from some other works, have been identified (Janssens "*Taʿlīqāt*"; Mousavian, Appendix 587–614). References to and quotations of these passages are properly introduced by the words, "we have said" (*qawlunā, qulnā*), as one would expect since Avicenna is the presumed author, but also by the words, "his saying," "what he means by his saying" (*qawluhu, maʿnā qawlihi*), which would point to reporting, and even commenting, by a second person—at the very least a context of live discussions is indicated which lends the work a flavor of oral teaching.[5] The fact that some of these notes are transmitted in some manuscripts under the (false) name of Fārābī, and that they on occasion suggest doctrinal positions not exactly consistent with Avicenna teachings,[6] strengthens the possibility that a second person may have been involved in their compilation. One recension of the *Notes*, to be mentioned presently, identifies it as having been transmitted by Bahmanyār, whose role would thus be consistent with that in the transmission of the *Discussions*, though his involvement in the *compilation* of the *Notes* remains questionable.[7]

More tellingly, the highly reliable Longer Bibliography (LB 41) records what would appear to be an earlier version of the title, *Kitāb at-Taʿālīq*, and adds a significant comment, whose text is transmitted in two ways: the Istanbul MS Üniversite 4755 has (f. 316[a]), "*Book of Notes*, which [Avicenna] wrote down in the presence of/in discussion with Ibn Zaylā" (*K. at-Taʿālīq, ʿallaqahu ʿinda Ibn Zaylā*), while the text in Ibn-Abī-Uṣaybiʿa reads, "*Book*:

5 See Janssens "Structuration" and "*Taʿlīqāt*" for detailed documentation.
6 See Janos, Appendix One, 383–396.
7 See the comments by Reisman *Avicennan Tradition* 195n95.

Notes, which [Avicenna's] disciple Abū-Manṣūr Ibn-Zaylā wrote down from him" (*K. Taʿālīq, ʿallaqahu ʿanhu tilmīḏuhu Abū Manṣūr ibn Zaylā*). The difference in the two versions depends on the reading *ʿinda* vs *ʿanhu*, which is clearly a scribal variant misreading of the one word for the other—I would estimate *ʿinda* ("in the presence of/in discussion with") to be the original reading since it is the more difficult one—but whichever one is chosen, the context of oral discussion or dictation between Avicenna and Ibn-Zayla is clearly established, corroborating Janssens' findings. Tentatively it would thus appear that the *Notes* arose as a result of live discussion and teaching between Avicenna and primarily Ibn-Zayla—so far there is little evidence to indicate that others may have been involved—and that the texts, though they "reflect a genuine Avicennian way of thought and ... none is in flagrant contradiction with the basic doctrine of" Avicenna,[8] were transcribed by Ibn-Zayla and hence present the appearance and possibly also nature of mixed authorship. These texts may have passed also in the possession of Bahmanyār, who would have transmitted them, as Lawkarī informs us in one recension (mentioned below). The main difference between the *Notes* and the *Discussions* would thus be that the *Discussions* were written responses to written questions by Bahmanyār and Ibn-Zayla (and Abū-l-Qāsim al-Kirmānī)—an investigative philosophical correspondence, so to speak—whereas the *Notes* had a primarily oral context with commentatorial purpose, and possibly did not involve directly Bahmanyār.[9] There is some transfer of passages from the *Discussions* to the *Notes*, but the transfer is not a simple extraction of passages from the one for inclusion in the other, "but rather takes the form of a reworking of questions and responses into the narrative style that is characteristic of the" *Notes*.[10] The inclusion of comments by Avicenna on his own works in the *Notes*, finally, comments which Avicenna may have originally intended for the *Appendices*, as he informs us, may also explain, in the end, the absence of a work entitled *Appendices* in the manuscripts, as it was (posthumously?) transformed or incorporated into the *Notes*.[11]

---

8 Janssens "*Taʿlīqāt*" 210.

9 Reisman *Avicennan Tradition* 51n63 put it succinctly: "By and large, the materials [that eventually constituted the *Mubāḥaṯāt* and the *Taʿlīqāt*] were distinguished [by the recensors] on the basis of genre: segments of expository analysis formed the *Taʿlīqāt*, while questions and responses formed Kitāb al-Mubāḥaṯāt. But it was initially a shared pool of material."

10 Reisman *Avicennan Tradition* 247, and see also Janssens "Structuration" 110n4.

11 "Future research may lead to the identification of parts of *at-Taʿlīqāt* as Ibn Sīnā's *al-Lawāḥiq*;" Reisman *Avicennan Tradition* 247.

The *Notes* has been transmitted in four recensions.[12] The first, that of ʿAbd-ar-Razzāq in the Cairo manuscript Ḥikma 6M,[13] is merely a consecutive and apparently haphazard transcription of all the notes (though Janssens "Structuration" 111 and n8 would see them as structured around the problematics of God's knowledge of particulars). In the second, the notes are presented in roughly the same order, but they are numbered individually from 1 to 990 and prefaced with a table of contents. The "editor" of this recension and author of the table of contents is identified in at least two of the manuscripts as Lawkarī. The Istanbul MS Ahmet III 3204 contains the following note: "Table of contents of the *Notes*, transmitted from (*riwāya*) Bahmanyār on the authority of (*ʿan*) Fārābī and Avicenna. ... This table was prepared by Lawkarī in the year 503[/1109]."[14] The third recension is represented by late Iranian manuscripts in which the individual notes are rearranged according to subject matter and grouped into Logic, Physics, and Metaphysics.[15] The fourth recension, finally, consists of extracts from these notes on specific subjects, circulating independently in the manuscript tradition under various titles and, in some cases, attributed to Fārābī.[16] The interrelationship of these recensions and the transmisison and authorship of some of those notes attributed to Fārābī are questions that have yet to be studied.

---

[12] I follow the more accurate description offered by El-Khodeiri "Opuscules" 344–345; Mahdavī 61–64 and Janssens "*Taʿlīqāt*" 201–202n3 disregard the fourth recension of extracts and recycled segments from the *Taʿlīqāt*, which may in the end provide valuable information on the collection, contamination, and transmission of the text. What Mousavian 6 (European numbers) identifies as a fourth "configuration" (i.e., recension), is actually an abridged variant of the first.

[13] See Gutas "Ṣiġnāḫī." This recension was published by Badawī *Taʿlīqāt* (1973).

[14] Badawī *Taʿlīqāt* 9, Mahdavī 62. The oldest manuscript containing this recension, Ayasofya 2390 (dated 521/1127), also has the table of contents and the remarks about Bahmanyār and Lawkarī: cf. El-Khodeiri "Opuscules" 344, Janssens "*Taʿlīqāt*" 202n3, Mousavian (97) and (154). Mousavian claims to have published this recension, on the basis of the MS Ayasofya 2390.

[15] This recension was published by ʿUbaydī *Taʿlīqāt* ([1]2002, [2]2008). Mousavian (34)–(35) notes that there is a medieval Persian translation of this recension (uniquely extant in MS Berlin 3364), which he used for his edition of the second recension in the Ayasofya 2390 manuscript.

[16] See the examples given by El-Khodeiri "Opuscules" 345. The *Notes* published in Hyderabad (*at-Taʿlīqāt*, 1346/1927) under the name of Fārābī are excerpts from the ᶜAbd-ar-Razzāq recension of Avicenna's *Notes*, *Taʿlīqāt* 16.2–193.19 Badawī. See Michot "Taʿlīqāt," and El-Khodeiri "Opuscules" 346–347. Mousavian (19)–(24) and 4–5 (European numbers), however, thinks that the *Taʿlīqāt* attributed to Fārābī is actually by him and is preparing an independent edition of it.

Chronology of Avicenna's Major Philosophical Works 145

and of Other Texts Discussed in Chapters 1 and 2

Period	Date	Work
EARLY PERIOD		*Compendium on the Soul* (W1)
		Philosophy for ʿArūḍī (W2)
		The Available and the Valid, Piety and Sin (W3)
	~ 389/999	Correspondence with Bīrūnī
TRANSITION PERIOD	403/1013	*The Provenance and Destination* (W4)
	404/1014	The "Lesser" *Destination* (W5)
MIDDLE PERIOD	414/1023	*The Guidance*
	~ 411–418/ ~ 1020–1027	*The Cure* (W6)
		Jūzjānī's Introduction to *The Cure* (T7)
	~ 418/ ~ 1027	*The Salvation* (W7)
		Philosophy for ʿAlāʾ-ad-Dawla (W8)
PERIOD OF EASTERN PHILOSOPHY	~ 418–420/ ~ 1027–1029	*The Easterners* (W9); lost in 425/1034
	~ 420/ ~ 1029	Prologue to *The Cure* (T9)
	420/1029	*Fair Judgment* (W10); lost in Muḥarram 421/Jan. 1030
		Marginal Glosses on *De anima* (W10)
	~ late 421/ ~ late 1030	Memoirs by a Disciple Writing from Rayy (T13)
		The Autobiography (T3)
LATE PERIOD	~ 418–428 / ~ 1027–1037	*Discussions* (W12); *Notes* (W13)
	~ 421–425 / ~ 1030–1034	*Pointers and Reminders* (W11)
	425/1034	Letter to an Anonymous Disciple (Bahmanyār) (T11)
	~ 427/ ~ 1036	Letter to Kiyā (T12)
	~ 428/ ~ 1037	*On the Rational Soul* (T14)

NOTE. Works for which no date is given cannot be dated absolutely (see Chapter 2, Introduction). In each period, these works are listed chronologically according to their relative order. The sign (~) before a number means approximately.

PART TWO

AVICENNA'S RECEPTION OF THE ARISTOTELIAN TRADITION

AVICENNA'S INTELLECTUAL UPBRINGING: THE AUTOBIOGRAPHY AND ITS INTERPRETATION

1. Avicenna's Studies. The Curriculum

Following Aristotle's general discussion in *Metaphysics* E1, the Alexandrian scholars of late antiquity erected an elaborate schema of classification of his works in which individual treatises corresponded to a field of study. The result of this process was that the classification of *Aristotle's* works became, in effect, a classification of all the sciences, and hence of *all human knowledge*. This classification, whose function was initially and preponderantly descriptive and pedagogical, but which later also acquired normative value on the assumption that it reflected ontological reality as well, was transmitted, mostly via Syriac, into Arabic, and became, with variations depending on the background and orientation of each scholar, the basis in medieval Islam of the classification and instruction of the Greek, as opposed to the native Muslim, sciences.[1] Both the theory of education and the curriculum of higher studies in these sciences which were prevalent in the Greek Aristotelian tradition became in this fashion integrated into Islamic intellectual life.[2]

[1] The venerable subject of the classification of the sciences in Islam has attracted much scholarly discussion and is therefore treated quite summarily here. A thorough survey of the Syriac and Arabic literature and its Greek antecedents, with full bibliography, is available in Hein. The *sui generis* arboreal (*mušajjar*) classification by Ibn-Farīġūn (4th/10th century) has been studied by H.H. Biesterfeldt, *Die Zweige des Wissens. Theorie und Klassifikation der mittelalterlich-islamischen Wissenschaften in der Darstellung des Ibn Farīġūn*, Habilitationsschrift, Ruhr-Universität Bochum, 1985.—For a study of the dual function—descriptive and normative—of the late antique classification of the sciences and its transmission into Arabic see Gutas "Paul the Persian," Section III. Useful summary reviews of the contents of the Muslim "encyclopedias" exhibiting each author's division of the sciences can be found in Peters 104–120 and, with emphasis on Muslim theology (*kalām*), in Louis Gardet and Georges C. Anawati, *Introduction à la théologie musulmane*, Paris: Vrin, 1948, 101–124. Various aspects of encyclopedism in the Islamic tradition are discussed in the articles collected, with further bibliography, in Gerhard Endress, ed., *Organizing Knowledge. Encyclopaedic Activities in the Pre-Eighteenth Century Islamic World*, Leiden: Brill, 2006.

[2] A general account of the formation of the Aristotelian tradition and its transmission

As a fairly standard representative of this classification I summarize below *The Categories of the Philosophical Sciences* (*Kitāb fī Aṣnāf al-ʿulūm al-ḥikmiyya*) by Abū-Sahl al-Masīḥī, a distinguished physician and companion
150 of Avicenna himself (and reportedly also one of his teachers of medicine).[3] Abū-Sahl's classification has the distinction of providing a relatively full syllabus of a course in these sciences. Presented in the order in which Abū-Sahl says these sciences ought to be studied, his account is the following:[4]

> A. Logic: Enables one to distinguish between truth and falsehood in the sciences that follow. Books by Aristotle:
>
> 1. *Categories*. Commentaries by ʾllynws,[5] Simplicius, Abū-Bišr Mattā ibn-Yūnus, Fārābī.
> 2. *De Interpretatione*. Commentaries by ʾllynws, Abū-Bišr, Fārābī.
> 3. *Prior Analytics* (*K. al-Qiyās*). Commentaries by ʾllynws, Abū-Bišr, Fārābī.
> 4. *Posterior Analytics* (*K. al-Burhān*). Commentaries by Themistius, Abū-Bišr, Fārābī.

---

and reception into Arabic can be read in Peters, especially pp. 1–22, 69–134. See also Gerhard Endress, "L'Aristote arabe: réception, autorité et transformation du Premier Maître," *Medioevo* 23 (1997) 1–42.

[3] The chronology and the events of Abū-Sahl's life, as well as his precise relation to Avicenna, require further investigation. See the collection of the known facts about his life and works, with further bibliography, in the entry "ʿIsā b. Yaḥyā Masiḥi Jorjāni, Abu Sahl" by David Pingree in *EIr.* XIII,609–610, and the summary account in Daiber "Khwārazm" 286–289. It is certain, however, that they were both in Gurgānj at the court of the Ḫwārizmšāh ʿAlī ibn-Maʾmūn (reigned 387/997–399/1009); Abū-Sahl's essay was written upon the request of Abū-l-Ḥusayn as-Sahlī, the minister of ʿAlī ibn-Maʾmūn in Gurgānj at the time of Avicenna's arrival there after leaving Buḫārā (T3, §14). That Abū-Sahl was in fact Avicenna's teacher of medicine in Buḫārā is simply stated by Ibn-Abī-Uṣaybiʿa, without any details (see T3 note 18).—The text of *Aṣnāf al-ʿulūm* survives in a unique manuscript, Leiden Acad. 44, ff. 2^b–12^a, from which it was published by M.-T. Dānešpažūh, "[ʿIsā b. Yaḥyā,] *Aṣnāf al-ʿulūm al-ḥikmiyya*," in *Taḥqīqāt-e Eslāmī*, Tehran 1370Š/1991, 211–220. I am grateful to Hans Hinrich Biesterfeldt both for bringing the existence of this treatise originally to my attention and providing me with a copy of the manuscript, and to Lukas Muehlethaler for a copy of the publication.

[4] Since the purpose of the following summary of Abū-Sahl's work is not to comment on it, the information it contains about the works of Aristotle, other authors, and their commentaries is to be compared in every instance with the bibliographical and biographical references provided by Francis E. Peters, *Aristoteles Arabus*, Leiden: E.J. Brill, 1968 (along with the additions made to it by H. Daiber in his review in *Gnomon* 42 [1970] 538–547), the entries on Aristotle's works in *DPhA*, M. Ullmann in his *Medizin* and *Die Natur- und Geheimwissenschaften im Islam* (Leiden/Köln: Brill, 1972), and the appropriate volumes of *GAS*.

[5] On this still unidentified commentator see the entry "Alīnūs (Allīnūs)" by A. Elamrani-Jamal in *DPhA* I,151–152, who does not cite the evidence in Abū-Sahl's text. It is thus established that this person did in fact write commentaries on the first three books of the *Organon* which were translated and available to scholars.

5. *Topics*. Commentaries by Yaḥyā ibn-ʿAdī, *Tracing the Topoi* by Themistius.[6]
6. *Rhetoric*. Commentary by Fārābī.
7. *Sophistics*. No commentaries are available.
8. *Poetics*. [No commentaries are mentioned by Abū-Sahl.]

Particular Sciences 151

B. Mathematics: Theoretical (*ʿilmī*) particular sciences. Propaedeutic to Physics and Metaphysics.

1. Geometry. The fundamental texts are those by Euclid, Archimedes, Apollonius.
2. Arithmetic. The fundamental texts are [*Introduction to*] *Arithmetic* [by Nicomachus of Gerasa], the arithmetical parts in Euclid, books on Indian arithmetic and algebra.
3. Science of the stars:
   a) Astronomy. Ptolemy's *Almagest*. Commentary by Nayrīzī. Books on *mutawassiṭāt*. Books on *Zīj* by Ḥabaš, Battānī, Nayrīzī.
   b) Astrology. Not being a demonstrative science, it does not belong among those enumerated here, but rather with interpretation of dreams, (bird) divination, physiognomy.
4. Music. Ptolemy's *Harmonics*, elaborated upon by Kindī. Fārābī wrote an exhaustive book on the subject.[7]
5. Optics. Books by Ptolemy and Euclid.

C. Non-mathematical: Applied (*mihnī*) mathematical particular sciences.

1. Mechanics. It is properly an applied, rather than a theoretical science.
2. Medicine. Books by Galen. Medical handbooks (*kunnāšāt*) by Paul [of Aegina], Ahrun, [Masīḥ] ad-Dimašqī, Ibn-Sarābiyūn, Rāzī's *al-Jāmiʿ al-kabīr* [*al-Ḥāwī* = *Continens*].
3. Agriculture.
4. Alchemy.

[6] *Taʿaqqub al-mawāḍiʿ*. The *Fihrist* (249.23 Flügel) reports that "Themistius commented on the *topoi* of the book," which appears to be a reference to the same book as that mentioned by Abū-Sahl. Avicenna himself is credited with an essay of a similar title, *Tracing the Dialectical Commonplace* (*Taʿaqqub al-mawḍiʿ al-jadalī*; see GL 13), which may depend on Themistius. This remains to be investigated (cf. Peters *Aristoteles Arabus* 22).

[7] In the historical process whereby the classification of Aristotle's works was transformed into a classification of all the sciences, the subjects of the quadrivium (arithmetic, geometry astronomy, music) were integrated into the schema as part of the mathematical sciences. The textbooks indicated by Abū-Sahl here as the fundamental ones had already achieved this status in late antiquity. See Henri I. Marrou, *A History of Education in Antiquity*, G. Lamb, trans., New York: The New American Library, 1964, 243–251.

Universal Sciences

D. Physics: Books by Aristotle:

1. *Physics*. Commentaries by Alexander, Themistius, Philoponus.
2. *De caelo*. Commentary by Themistius.
3. *De generatione et corruptione*. Commentaries by Alexander, Philoponus.
4. *Meteorology*. Commentary by Alexander.
5. *De animalibus*. No commentary is available.
6. *De plantis*. Not the book by Aristotle himself, but the epitome (*muḫtaṣar*) made by Nicolaus [of Damascus] is the only one that is available.
7. *De anima*. Commentary by Themistius. Alexander wrote a large treatise on the subject.
8. *De sensu et sensato*. It is attributed to Aristotle but does not seem like what he would say (*wa-laysa yušbihu kalāmahu*). No commentary is available.[8]

152 E. Metaphysics:

1. Metaphysics, by Aristotle. Commentary by Themistius on Book *Lambda*. Kindī wrote a short exegesis for the entire book which he called *The Inclusive Philosophy* (*al-Falsafa ad-dāḫila*).[9]

Practical Philosophy

F. Ethics: These sciences should be both practiced and studied. As practiced, they precede the theoretical parts of philosophy just enumerated. As objects of study, they follow them.[10]

1. Ethics. *Nicomachean Ethics* by Aristotle.
2. Politics. Letters on Politics by Aristotle.[11] Politics by Plato.
3. *Oeconomics*. (L5)

Avicenna's philosophical formation took place in this tradition, in the intellectually active capital of the Sāmānids, Buḫārā, where he spent the consequential years of his life, approximately from age six to twenty-two.[12] In

[8] For the transmission of this work in Arabic see Hansberger, who is also referring (note 3) to her prospective edition of the Arabic text. One must acknowledge Abū-Sahl's erudition and critical acumen in realizing the non-Aristotelian character of the Arabic text of this work that he had in front of him: as Hansberger has concluded (p. 143), "it is an adaptation that is … characterised far more by Neoplatonic and Galenic than by Aristotelian ideas."

[9] Cf. *Fihrist* 255.27–28 Flügel.

[10] The twofold application to ethics derives from the late Alexandrian discussions about the starting point of philosophical studies, which distinguished between a "pre-philosophical morality" and the study of philosophical ethics. See Gutas "Starting Point."

[11] Presumably the alleged correspondence between Aristotle and Alexander is meant. For this epistolary cycle and its contents see D. Gutas, "On Graeco-Arabic Epistolary 'Novels'," *Middle Eastern Literatures* 12 (2009) 61–72.

[12] It is relatively unimportant when Avicenna began his studies; he may have started when

the Autobiography he gives us a detailed account of the subjects he studied, with his age at each stage and his few teachers. The systematic nature of his presentation can be best elicited when this information is tabulated as follows:[13]

Age *Subjects*

[6?]-10 A. [ELEMENTARY EDUCATION]

1. Qur'ān and [Arabic] literature with anonymous teachers.
2. Hears Ismāʿīlī doctrines about the soul and the intellect from his family and an Ismāʿīlī missionary but does not accept them. 153
   They invite him to do so by talking [and talk?] about philosophy, geometry, and Indian arithmetic. [As a result?] his father sends him to study
3. Indian arithmetic with a greengrocer.

[10?]-16 B. [SECONDARY EDUCATION]

1. Islamic jurisprudence with Ismāʿīl az-Zāhid; practices law.
2. [Philosophical sciences]
   a. [Logic:] Porphyry's *Eisagoge* and the *Organon*: a literal reading with Nātilī; in detail and with commentaries by himself.
   b. [Mathematics:]
      i. Euclid's *Elements*: Book I.1–6 with Nātilī, the rest by himself.
      ii. Ptolemy's *Almagest*: Book I.1–8 with Nātilī, the rest by himself.
   c. Physics by himself.
   d. Metaphysics by himself.
3. Medicine by himself; practices medicine.

16–17.5 C. [UNDERGRADUATE EDUCATION]

1. [Philosophical sciences]
   a. Logic by himself.
   b. Mathematics by himself.

---

he was four or five or six. In the *Canon of Medicine* (Gruner 379, §735) he recommends that instruction of children start at six, and on the analogy of the Autobiography, it may be possible to read into this an autobiographical reference. The year of his departure from Buḫārā, on the other hand, can be established only after the problems associated with the chronology of his life, as discussed in the introduction to Chapter 2 above, have been solved. In any case, he says in the Autobiography (T3, §12) that he was still in Buḫārā when he was twenty-one. A similar amount of time for studies is also specified in sources deriving from the Greek tradition. See the references in T2 note 8, above. With Avicenna's period of study is to be compared the approximately twenty years that it took in average for a student in Nīšāpūr in the 10th–11th century to study Prophetic Traditions. See R.W. Bulliet, "The Age Structure of Medieval Islamic Education," *Studia Islamica* 57 (1983) 105–117.

[13] Words and numbers in square brackets indicate my conjectures and explanatory additions not found in Avicenna's text. See also the notes to the translation of the Autobiography.

c. Physics by himself.
d. Metaphysics by himself and with the aid of Fārābī's *On the Purposes of the Metaphysics*.

[17.5]-18 D. [GRADUATE EDUCATION]

[Philosophical sciences:] "Books of the ancients" in the royal library of Nūḥ ibn-Manṣūr. Dissertation: *Compendium on the Soul* (W1)

18 End of his studies.

21 E. ["HABILITATION":] *The Compilation* or *Philosophy for ʿArūḍī* (W2), containing,

1. Theoretical sciences:
   a. Logic.
   b. Physics.
   c. Metaphysics.

[2. Practical sciences:
   Ethics. (apparently not included)]

154 [22?] F. [Precursor of *The Cure* and *Fair Judgment*, in two books:]

1. Theoretical sciences:
   The Available and the Valid (W3), containing Logic, Mathematics, Physics, Metaphysics;
2. Practical sciences:
   Piety and Sin (W3), containing ethics.

The progression of Avicenna's education is clear enough from the above tabulation: reduced to this skeleton outline, the Autobiography appears as a transcript of studies and a curriculum vitae. His educational career is readily divisible into four stages (which I have taken the liberty of identifying with those current in our culture for purposes of easy reference and highlighting), and culminates with the composition of two works which establish him in the world of learning[14] and which can therefore be seen as the final two stages, the dissertation and "habilitation."

From the point of view of his philosophical training that interests us here, the salient aspects of his report are the following: Avicenna says that he began his education with studies in Qur'ān and literature, along with which he may have also learned grammar. During his tutelage under the greengrocer he could have learned no more than arithmetic,[15] and it is doubtful

---

14 Cf., for example, what Jūzjānī says in his introduction to *The Cure* (T7, §1) with §13 of the Autobiography.

15 He learned "Indian computation" (*ḥisāb al-Hind*); see note 8 to the Autobiography (T3).

that this can be counted as a formal study of Arithmetic, the branch of the philosophical science of mathematics. His brush with Ismāʿīlism during this time (if not by the time he was ten, certainly not long afterwards, judging by the chronology implicit in the presentation), much discussed and even more misinterpreted, is significant not for telling us what he learned from it but for the purpose for which he chose to include it in the Autobiography, to be analyzed below (Chapter 3.3E). Conspicuous in its absence is any mention of having studied Islamic sciences other than the mandatory Qurʾān (like Prophetic Tradition/*ḥadīṯ*, or Qurʾānic interpretation/*tafsīr*, a field in which he later wrote several essays), but in the absence of information to the contrary, not much can be made of this. The upshot of the account of his elementary education, therefore, is that he studied subjects preparatory for the philosophical sciences—language, literature, and arithmetic—and not subjects that have nothing to do with philosophy, like *ḥadīṯ*. This impression is further corroborated by the fact that his rejection of the Ismāʿīlī account of the soul and the intellect—subjects eminently philosophical—indicate a predisposition toward philosophical critical thinking.

Avicenna's first contact with a formal science, however, the Autobiog- 155
raphy continues, was with jurisprudence, an ostensibly non-philosophical subject. Were it not for jurisprudence, his secondary education would have consisted exclusively of the philosophical sciences (including medicine; cf. Abū-Sahl's classification above). And yet the particular way in which he first mentions jurisprudence indicates that he intended this to be understood differently. To quote him again:

> Then Abū-ʿAbdallāh an-Nātilī, who claimed to be a philosopher, came to Buḫārā. My father had him stay in our house, and he occupied himself with my education. *Before* his arrival, I used to occupy myself with jurisprudence, attending frequently Ismāʿīl az-Zāhid about it. I was one of the most skillful questioners, having become familiar with the methods of posing questions and ways of raising objections to a respondent in the manner Customary with these people. *Then* I began to study the *Eisagoge* with an-Nātilī, and when he mentioned to me the definition of "genus," viz. "what is predicated of many things differing in species, in answer to [the question] 'What is it?'," I surprised him in Verifying this definition with something whose like had never been heard. He was extremely amazed at me and cautioned my father that I should occupy myself with nothing else but Philosophy. [T3, § 5; emphasis added]

For the only time in the entire account of his studies, Avicenna abandons here the strictly chronological sequence of events. He first introduces his teacher, Nātilī, "who claimed to be a philosopher," thus announcing the beginning of his formal studies in philosophy, but then immediately he interrupts his narrative to interject his previous study of Islamic jurisprudence, taking care to point out his expertise in posing questions and raising objections to opponents. With this background, Avicenna continues, he had his first contact with logic, and not only was he able to grasp immediately its central concepts, but he also improved upon the analyses given by his teacher. The implication that he was able to do so *because* of his previous studies in jurisprudence, given the structure of the paragraph cited above, is inevitable.

The question, however, is what precisely Avicenna had in mind here, and what he meant by jurisprudence in this context. First of all, it is to be noted that he brings up the issue of having studied jurisprudence only in association with Prophyry's *Eisagoge*, not independently as he did with the subjects he had studied in his elementary education. If we are to look at the possible connection between the *Eisagoge* and jurisprudence, we discover the following: the *Eisagoge* deals, as is well known, with the *quinque voces* (the five predicables) for the purpose of analyzing the ten categories and assigning definitions, all subjects treated extensively in Aristotle's *Topics* (Books I–VII). The *Topics*, however, also deals (Book VIII) with "the methods of posing
156 questions and ways of raising objections to a respondent," namely, dialectics. Since then Avicenna is presenting the practice of *Islamic jurisprudence* in the same terms as those used to describe the practice of dialectical argumentation in Aristotle's *Topics*,[16] it seems clear that he is implying here that he was able to analyze the question "What is it?" so brilliantly on account of his previous training in a dialectical discipline, jurisprudence. This in turn is consistent with his position about the usefulness of dialectics: as he says in the Topics of *The Cure*, when we learn the *topoi* from which we may discover the arguments for every problem, acquire the instruments that lead to their discovery, and know how to use them, then we acquire practice which is "the ability to perform a given kind of acts frequently and well."[17] In this particular case Avicenna had practice, as he mentions, in asking questions—which is, in any case, the basis of dialectical disputation[18]—and hence his expert analysis of the definition of genus in the *Eisagoge*. By mentioning Islamic jurisprudence in connection with the *Eisagoge*, Avicenna meant to refer not to the subject matter of jurisprudence, which is properly

[16] For the terminology of dialectics used by Avicenna in this passage see note 12 to the translation of the Autobiography (T3).

[17] *Jadal* 48.12–14 Ahwānī.

[18] *Qiyās* 537.5–11 Zāyid.

a non-philosophical discipline, but to its method, which he understands and describes in terms of Aristotelian dialectic.

This is as to be expected. Avicenna would set, in the context of the philosophical sciences, little store by the subject matter of jurisprudence (and theology, *kalām*): the statements of religious leaders upon which it is based can yield only "jurisprudential syllogisms (*qiyāsāt fiqhiyya*) which are actually either enthymemes (*ḍamāʾir*) or examples (*miṯālāt*) that belong among dialectical arguments at best or rhetorical ones at worst."[19] The subject matter of jurisprudence and theology is thus of no interest to a philosopher except as examples of premisses constituting generally accepted beliefs (*mašhūr*), while their dialectical method forms part of the general subject discussed in the *Topics*.

For his secondary education, then, Avicenna lists in the Autobiography only the philosophical sciences which he studied: dialectic as a preparatory subject, then the rest of the Organon, then Mathematics, Physics, Metaphysics, and the particular discipline of medicine. This is not to imply that he did not study jurisprudence as an Islamic science; he may very well
have—as a matter of fact, it is certain that he did—but what is of relevance 157
here is that he is not reporting on that *prima intentione* in the Autobiography, just as he said nothing about having studied Islamic sciences other than Qurʾān and literature in his elementary education. His concern is to give an account of his education in the philosophical sciences, not of everything that he ever studied. We shall return to this subject below.[20]

Avicenna's higher education, undertaken this time entirely on his own, was devoted exclusively to the philosophical sciences, again according to the late antique Alexandrian / Islamic philosophical curriculum: Logic, Mathematics, Physics, Metaphysics. His particular difficulty with Aristotle's *Metaphysics*, largely misunderstood by contemporary scholarship, was resolved with the help of Fārābī's brief essay on the book's purpose.[21] After finishing

---

19 *Qiyās* 555.7–556.3 Zāyid. In a short essay entitled, "On the Supernal Bodies" (*Fī l-Ajrām al-ʿulwiyya*, GP 6) he says, in effect, "It is possible that the discipline called 'theology' (*kalām*) in this age of ours may be close to the rank of dialectic, falling short of it only a little" (*Tisʿ Rasāʾil* 41.5–7).

20 A related historical question on this issue concerns the extent to which the study of the principles of jurisprudence in Avicenna's time had already incorporated Aristotelian dialectical methods in order to provide the young Avicenna with the the training which he claims he had. If it had, then the Autobiography is a significant document for the history of the development of *uṣūl al-fiqh*. If not, then Avicenna is reading back into his early training his position about the usefulness of dialectical training mentioned above.

21 This subject is fully discussed below, Chapter 6.1.

his "undergraduate" studies, Avicenna capped his philosophical training by spending some time (at most six months) in the library of the physicians in the palace of the Sāmānid ruler, where he read "books by the ancients" unknown to many people and never seen subsequently even by him. He was, he says, eighteen years old at that time.

Avicenna thus reports in the Autobiography that he studied the philosophical sciences following the order of the classification in the late antique Alexandrian / Islamic Aristotelian tradition, and that he studied these sciences in three successive stages at increasingly advanced levels. Thanks to Abū-Sahl al-Masīḥī's little essay outlined above, we can also be relatively certain about the very books which Avicenna read, "both their essential parts and commentaries" (T3, § 6). As is evident from Abū-Sahl's comments about some works for which no commentaries were available, he must have included in his list only books in circulation in Gurgānj at that time, and hence presumably in broader Ḫurāsān as well.

The very systematic nature of Avicenna's presentation of the *actual* course of his studies, however, and its close correspondence to the *theoretical* classification of the sciences as found in works like that of Abū-Sahl, raise the question of the extent to which the subjects Avicenna says he studied and the order in which he says he studied them really reflect historical reality. The problem is, in other words, whether Avicenna presented a stylized
158 Autobiography in which the chronology of events is bent to fit the theoretical classification of the sciences. In the absence of outside corroboration, the issue cannot be resolved, insofar as there seems to be a "chicken-and-egg" situation: the classification of the sciences in the Aristotelian tradition influenced actual educational practice which in turn is presented in an autobiographical account reproducing that very classification in order to promote it. However, the exact historical sequence of events in Avicenna's studies is not as important as the point which his account intends to make and the tendentiousness it seems to exhibit: philosophy *ought to be* studied, and in his case, it *was* studied, as taught in the Aristotelian tradition and according to its division of the parts of philosophy.

Equally important as Avicenna's adoption of the late antique Alexandrian classification of Aristotle's works as the philosophical curriculum to be (or actually) followed is his embracing of the concomitant view, as mentioned at the beginning of this section, that this classification represents not only the work of Aristotle or the Philosophical Sciences alone, but *Knowledge* itself, *al-ʿilm*. Consistently in the Autobiography, but elsewhere in autobiographical passages as well, Avicenna uses the word, with the definite article, to refer to the Philosophical Sciences, thereby equating

scientific knowledge with Knowledge/Philosophy as classified in the Aristotelian tradition. In the Autobiography, this occurs every time Avicenna uses the singular word absolutely, *al-ʿilm*,[22] and the same is true with the plural in the general expressions, "these sciences" (*hāḏihi l-ʿulūm*), and "all the sciences" (*jamīʿ al-ʿulūm*).[23] Jūzjānī continues in this vein in the very first sentence of the Biography: "There was in Jurjān ... aš-Šīrāzī who loved these sciences" (*hāḏihi l-ʿulūm*), i.e., the philosophical sciences.[24] A misunderstanding of this fact has led to numerous mistranslations of these crucial passages in the Autobiography.[25] Avicenna's position with regard to this key term, however, was evident to subsequent Muslim scholars familiar with the Aristotelian/philosophical tradition. The percipient Faḫr-ad-Dīn
ar-Rāzī (d. 606/1209) says in the beginning of his commentary on Avicenna's 159
Pointers and Reminders that the philosophical sciences alone constitute real knowledge.[26]

2. Avicenna's Studies. Methods of Learning: Guessing Correctly (the Middle Term) (*Ḥads*)

If the Aristotelian curriculum, the Philosophical Sciences in their late antique Alexandrian classification, represents in the estimation of Avicenna absolute Knowledge, *al-ʿilm* as such, the question that has to be considered next is how this knowledge can be acquired, or more specifically, how Avicenna says he acquired it. The subject of the principles of Avicenna's epistemology appears upon closer inspection of his works to be so central to his thought, and he himself speaks so frequently about it both in theoretical and

[22] Gohlman 22.4 (T3, § 5 middle), 24.7 (§ 6 end), 26.5 (§ 8 beginning), 34.6 (§ 10 beginning), 38.1 bis (§ 11, second sentence), 38.4 (*hāḏā l-ʿilm*, § 12); see further T8, § 3 beginning, and § 6 middle; T12, § 2 beginning.

[23] Gohlman 30.4 (T3, § 8 end), 36.8 (§ 11, first sentence), 38.8 (§ 13), 40.5 (§ 14).

[24] Gohlman 44.3–4.

[25] "These sciences" for which Baraqī had an inclination, for example (T3, § 13), has been misinterpreted to refer to the Muslim sciences previously mentioned in the text, i.e., jurisprudence, exegesis, Ṣūfism. But when so understood, the sentence would make little sense: someone who favors the Muslim sciences cannot merely have an "inclination" for the same sciences. The contrast intended here is between the Muslim sciences, which Baraqī cultivated, and the Greek sciences, for which he had a liking. This is further evident by the subjects of the two books he commissioned from Avicenna: see W3 in Chapter 2.

[26] Reference in Rosenthal *Knowledge* 245. Rosenthal's book should be consulted in this connection for an evaluation of Avicenna's use of the term *ʿilm* in the wider Islamic context.

autobiographical terms, that it has to be seriously considered as the *via regia* to his philosophical system. The Autobiography provides again the starting point for the investigation.

This unique document makes strange reading today primarily because of a number of statements which have been consistently felt by virtually all interpreters to exceed all bounds of good taste in their apparent conceit, even after due allowance has been made for cultural and temporal divergences. I need only mention here Misch's use of the word "befremden" ("to estrange") thrice in a single page to describe two such statements.[27] The result of this feeling of estrangement has been to neglect to examine the purpose of Avicenna in making them, and consequently to misinterpret them.

These statements are the following: (a) Avicenna evokes amazement by mastering the Qur'ān and "a great deal of literature" by the age of ten (§ 2); (b) at this early—and one would think, impressionable—age, his "soul" rejects the Ismāʿīlī theories about the soul and the intellect (§ 3), and (c)
160 he is extremely skillful in dialectical disputation (§ 5); (d) Nātilī is amazed at his analysis of the definition of "genus" and at his conceptualization of logical problems (§ 5); (e) Avicenna claims that Nātilī had no real knowledge of geometry and astronomy (§ 6); (f) he says that "medicine is not one of the difficult sciences" and masters it "in a very short time" (§ 7); (g) he studies and masters the Philosophical Sciences (the Aristotelian curriculum) all by himself by the time he is eighteen years old (§ 11); and (h) he remarks twice that he has not learned anything new since the completion of his "undergraduate" and "graduate" education (§§ 8, 11). The intention of all these statements is certainly to draw the reader's attention to his precocity, but the ulterior motive for doing so is not conceit, vainglory, or seeking acclamation, but the desire to make a philosophical point, namely, to provide an illustration for his epistemology.

---

27 Georg Misch, *Geschichte der Autobiographie*, Frankfurt: G. Schulte-Bulmke, 1962, III.ii, 1003. This quite unscientific attitude to Avicenna's statements in the Autobiography is frequently based on a Eurocentric perspective, as exemplified, e.g., by Reuben Levy, a by no means superficial scholar of the Islamic world. In a paper read before the Cambridge University History of Medicine Society on 27 November 1956, entitled "Avicenna—His Life and Times," he expressed himself as follows: "It is obvious that we are here dealing with a prodigy, and one who was by no means unconscious of his own powers. But I have often remarked in such parts of *The East* as I have visited that there is not that reticence about personal accomplishments to which *we* are accustomed *here normally*. Formal modesty is *there* regarded as an affectation, and may in fact well be so. Clearly Avicenna did not *suffer* from it." (*Medical History* 1 [1957] 250–251; emphasis added.) Statements such as these are rather common in Western scholarship on Avicenna.

The most explicit passage in Avicenna's philosophical works in which autobiographical material is used for the purposes of illustration is the one from his *Philosophy for ʿAlāʾ-ad-Dawla*, translated in Chapter 1 as Text 2. It first presents his theory of instruction and Guessing Correctly the middle term (*ḥads*) as the ways of acquiring knowledge (§§1–3) and then ends with a paragraph (§4) so exactly parallel to the Autobiography as to merit closer scrutiny.

In this passage Avicenna states that although knowledge of intelligible matters, which is knowledge of the middle terms of syllogisms expressing the propositions known, is acquired in two ways, through Guessing Correctly the middle term and instruction, the latter is nevertheless ultimately reducible to the former since, as he puts it, the (theoretical) first person to acquire such knowledge had necessarily only Correct Guesses at his disposal. The significance which this formulation lends to the concept of *ḥads* as *the* way of acquiring knowledge should be explicitly appreciated and analyzed since it makes it the final arbiter over instruction, and consequently conditions the stand toward philosophical tradition (i.e., knowledge transmitted through instruction) which a philosopher who has learned by himself through Guessing Correctly the middle terms will adopt and how he will perceive the relation of his own philosophy to the transmitted knowledge. The basis of the present study is an investigation of the implications of this core theory of Avicenna for his philosophical system.

In order to analyze and trace the development of Avicenna's theory of *ḥads* it will be necessary to present first in chronological order the significant passages from his works relating to the subject.[28] At the expense of some redundancy, it will be useful to repeat some of the passages already presented in Chapter 1, for the methodologically sound reason, I believe, of 161
reading these passages in close succession and contextual proximity.

[1] From *Compendium on the Soul* (T1) (L6)

2. This faculty [the rational soul as material intellect], which exists in the entire human species, does not in itself possess any intelligible forms, but these rather come about within it in one of two ways. The first is through

28 The following passages do not exhaust all those discussing *ḥads* in Avicenna's works. I have omitted some of Avicenna's other discussions (e.g., *Mabdaʾ* 115–117 Nūrānī = ff. 200^{a-b} MS Ambrosiana 320 [Hammer]; *Hidāya* 293–294, §184 ʿAbduh; *Taʿlīqāt* 141.9–12 Badawī), which do not contribute anything beyond what is offered in the selections below. For a fuller discussion see Gutas "Intuition and Thinking."

divine inspiration [*ilhām ilāhī*], without any process of learning or utilization of the senses, as is the case with self-evident intelligibles [*al-maʿqūlāt al-badīhiyya*] ....

3. The second way is to acquire [them] through syllogisms and Discover [them] through demonstration ....

4. [Another aspect of the second way in which intelligibles come about in the rational soul:] In some people, keenness of mind [*yaqaẓa*] and contact with the universal intellect [*al-ittiṣāl bi-l-ʿaql al-kullī*] may so predispose the rational faculty as to free it from having recourse to syllogisms and deliberation [*rawiyya*] in order to become cognizant [*taʿarruf*]; inspiration [*ilhām*] and revelation [*waḥy*], rather, are sufficient sustenance for it. This specific property of the rational faculty is called sanctification [*taqdīs*], in accordance with which it is then called sanctified spirit [*rūḥ muqaddas*]. None shall gain the enjoyment of this rank except prophets and messengers of God.

[2] From the "Lesser" *Destination* = *The Cure* = *The Salvation*[29] (L7)

1. The acquisition of knowledge, whether from someone else or by oneself, is of varying degrees. Some people who acquire knowledge have greater facility for forming concepts [*taṣawwur*] than others because their predisposition [viz., the material intellect] which precedes the predisposition we have mentioned [viz., the intellect *in habitu*] is more powerful. If such is the private state of an individual,[30] then this powerful predisposition is called Guessing Correctly [*ḥads*]. This predisposition may be so strong in certain people that they do not need great effort, or training and instruction, in order to make contact with the active intellect—or rather their predisposition for this is so strong that it is as if they were in actual possession of the second predisposition [i.e., the intellect *in habitu*]; indeed it seems as if they know everything of themselves. This is the highest degree of this predisposition. In this state the material intellect ought to be called "sacred intellect" [*ʿaql qudsī*], being of the genus of intellect *in habitu*, except that it is so lofty that it is not something shared by all people. It is not unlikely that some of these actions pertaining to the "sacred spirit" [*ar-rūḥ al-qudsī*, i.e., the material intellect as "sacred
162 intellect"] because of their powerful and overwhelming nature are forced to overflow[31] into the imagination which then reproduces them also in terms of perceptible and audible linguistic images in the way in which we have previously indicated.

---

[29] Ahwānī *Aḥwāl* 122.6–123.9 (does not contain the first paragraph) = *Nafs* 248.9–250.4 Rahman = *Najāt* 272.3–274.4 / 339.2–341.9. I have noted only the significant variants among the three largely verbatim identical versions. Cf. the translation by Rahman *Psychology* 35.25–37.5, which I adopted with numerous modifications, and his commentary on pp. 93–95.

[30] The text of *The Salvation* reads, "if such a person is predisposed to acquire perfection in his private state."

[31] "Are forced to overflow" = *tafīḍu fayaḍānan*: in context, this would seem to be the meaning of the *mafʿūl muṭlaq*, rather than "overflow completely" or "forcefully".

2. What verifies this is the evident fact that the acquisition of intelligible matters[32] comes about only when the middle term of a syllogism is obtained. This middle term may be obtained in two ways: sometimes through Correct Guessing, which is a mental act by means of which the mind Discovers [*yastanbiṭu*][33] the middle term all by itself—acumen [*ḏakāʾ*] being the power of Correct Guessing[34]—and sometimes through instruction, the origins of which are [again] Correct Guessing, since doubtless everything is ultimately reduced to [knowledge derived from] Correct Guesses [*ḥudūs*] handed down by those who first Discovered them to their students.

3. It is possible, therefore, that Correct Guessing may occur to a man by himself, and that the syllogism may be constructed in his mind without a teacher. This varies both quantitatively and qualitatively; quantitatively, because some people have had a greater number of Correct Guesses of middle terms; and qualitatively, because some people Guess Correctly faster. Now since this variation is not restricted by any [arbitrary] boundary but is always susceptible to increase and decrease, and since its lowest point is reached in people who are wholly incapable of Guessing Correctly, its highest point as well must be reached in people who Guess Correctly regarding all or most problems, or[35] in people who can Guess Correctly in the shortest time possible.[36] Thus there might be a person whose soul has been rendered so powerful [*muʾayyad an-nafs*] through extreme purity and intense contact with intellective principles that he blazes with Correct Guessing (i.e., with the ability to receive them[37] in all matters from the active intellect), and the forms

---

[32] *The Destination* adds, "previously unknown."

[33] I would guess that the term *istinbāṭ* (Discovery), which repeatedly occurs in Avicenna's discussions of *ḥads*, may ultimately reflect the Greek *heuresis*, current in the commentatorial tradition. Cf. the texts of Themistius and Philoponus quoted below, L14 and following (*In An. Post.* 41.6 and 333.6, 9, respectively).

[34] This parenthetical aside is a reference to the Aristotelian definition of "acumen," *anchinoia*, *ḏakāʾ*. See the discussion below.

[35] *The Cure* reads, "and."

[36] The variation in Guessing powers among humans, Avicenna means to say, has only natural boundaries, namely the absolute idiot and the perfect prophet. It is therefore not unlimited, as Rahman translates ("these differences are unlimited"). Within these two termini, on the other hand, no arbitrary limit can be imposed on the variation of the levels of human sagacity. This variation is the foundation of Avicenna's proof of prophecy, a feature which appears in most analyses of prophecy in subsequent philosophical and theological discussions in Islam. Avicenna insists on this point here clearly in order to allow for the possibility that every human being may be a candidate for prophethood, and not only those so designated by tradition and the religious scholars. Cf. his concluding statement in this passage.

[37] This is the reading in *The Cure*, *qabūlan lahā*, "the ability to receive them," i.e., the intellective principles. The text in the "Lesser" *Destination* and *The Salvation* reads, *qabūlan li-ilhām*, "the ability to receive the inspiration," but Avicenna at this stage of his career would not be using the term *ilhām* to describe *ḥads*. If *ilhām* is a real variant (and not a scribal or reader's emendation), it might be an earlier reading, most likely in the *Destination*, taken over mechanically in *The Salvation*, but emended in *The Cure*.

of all things contained in the active intellect are imprinted on him either at once or nearly so. This imprinting is not an uncritical reception [of the forms] merely on Authority [*irtisāman lā taqlīdiyyan*], but rather occurs in an order which includes the middle terms: for beliefs accepted on Authority
163 concerning those things which are known only through their causes possess no intellective certainty. This is a kind of prophethood—indeed its highest faculty—and the most appropriate thing is to call this faculty "sacred faculty" [*quwwa qudsiyya*]. It is the highest level of human faculties.

[3] From *The Shorter Summary on Logic = The Salvation*[38] (L8)

Acumen [*ḏakā'*] is the power of predisposition to Correct Guessing. Guessing is a motion toward hitting upon [*iṣāba*] the middle term when that is the unknown, or hitting upon the major term once the middle term has been found.

[4] From *The Cure*[39] (L9)

As for the discussion of Mind, craft, comprehension, wisdom, Acumen, and Guessing Correctly, most of it would more appropriately take place in other sciences, in the areas of Physics and Ethics, although their definitions should be given here.

Mind [*ḏihn*] is a faculty of the soul that is ready and predisposed to acquire terms [of syllogisms] and ideas. Comprehension [*fahm*] is a complete readiness this faculty has to conceptualize whatever comes to it from others. Guessing Correctly [*ḥads*] is an accurate and spontaneous [*min tilqā'i nafsihā*] movement of this faculty toward tracking down the middle term, as, for example, when one sees that the moon is bright, according to its phases, only on the side that faces the sun, and his Mind tracks down a middle term by means of Guessing, namely, that the cause of its brightness comes from the sun. Acumen [*ḏakā'*] is accurate Guessing [*jūdatu ḥadsin*] by this faculty, taking place in an infinitesimally short period of time. Thought [*fikra*] is the movement of the human Mind toward the principles of the problems [whose solution is sought] in order to work down from them to the problems.

[5] From *Philosophy for 'Alā'-ad-Dawla* (T2) (L10)

1. It is a fact that unknown [intelligible] things are acquired by means of the middle term [of a syllogism]. The middle term can be obtained either through quickness of comprehension, in that Guessing Correctly pours [it] into the soul (and that is due to the soul's disposition to be affected by the active intellect), or from a teacher.

---

[38] This *Logic* is the earlier work of Avicenna which Jūzjānī says Avicenna incorporated in the logic part of *The Salvation* (see Chapter 2, W7, and GS 6a in Section B of the Inventory in the Appendix) = *Najāt* 137.8–10/169.5–7. The section where this definition of *ḥads* occurs corresponds to the part on the Posterior Analytics.

[39] *Al-Burhān* 259.12–20 'Afīfī, corresponding to Aristotle's *Posterior Analytics* 89b7–20. This revised translation is taken from Gutas "Intuition and Thinking" 4–5.

2. Guessing Correctly [the middle term] is likewise of two sorts: one comes about slowly and after delay, the other at once. ...

3. ... [A]mong people [a] there is the person who needs a teacher for most things, being completely incapable of any Correct Guesses—or even worse, he might be incapable of understanding even with a teacher; [b] there may be a person who knows most things by Guessing Correctly [the middle term] and has slight need for a teacher; and [c] there may also be a person, though rarely, who can attain whenever he wishes the sciences from beginning to end in the order in which Guessing Correctly [the middle term] occurs, without a teacher and in very little time. This is because he has made excellent contact with the active intellect so that he has absolutely no need of reflection [*andeša*], and therefore believes that [this knowledge] is being poured into his heart from one place—and perhaps this is what the truth is. It is from this person that the basis of instruction for humans must come.

4. One must not be amazed at this. We ourselves have witnessed a person who was not at this rank [of the prophet] and would learn things after reflection and hard work, but who nevertheless dispensed with excessive hard work through his strong [aptitude for] Guessing Correctly [the middle terms]. His Correct Guessing in most things corresponded with what is found in books, and consequently he did not have to endure the hard work of excessive book reading.

[6] From *Pointers and Reminders*[40] (L11) 164

[In this account of the faculties of the rational soul, Avicenna added to the philosophical presentation of the concepts he was discussing their symbolic equivalents from the famous Light Verse in the Qur'ān (24:35).[41] In Arberry's translation, the Light Verse reads as follows:

---

40 *Išārāt* II.3.10, 126–127/242–243. There is a French translation of the entire third *namaṭ* by the European editor of the text, Forget "Chapitre inédit," and of this passage at 27–28; cf. also the translation in Goichon *Directives* 324–327, and the discussion and references in her *Distinction* 321–325.

41 For Avicenna's symbolic method see below, Chapter 8.2. Avicenna first provided in a tentative fashion the correspondences between the Light Verse and the function of the rational intellect in *The Provenance and Destination* (*Mabda'* p. 117 Nūrānī; MS Ambrosiana ff. 200^{b}–201^{a}). This interpretation proved popular in subsequent centuries and it appears, with variations, in a number of contexts. Ġazālī used it fully in his *Miškāt* (for which see Treiger *Inspired Knowledge* 74–78), and it figures prominently in philosophical and theological pseudepigraphs, like the Ps-Avicennan *Proof of Prophecy* (*Fī Iṯbāt an-nubuwwa*; see GM-Ps 2 in the Inventory in the Appendix), and the Ps.-Farabian treatise entitled "Elevated Discourse on the Principles of Physics," where different correspondences are given for each of the items in the allegory with the aim of substituting, for the obscure philosophical correspondences which Avicenna provides, concepts taken directly from mainstream Islamic tradition. See N. Lûgal and A. Sayılı, "Fârâbî'nin Tabiat ilminin kökleri hakkında yüksek makaleler kitabı," *Belleten* 15 (1951) 81–122, at 105.

God is the Light of the heavens and the earth;
the likeness of His Light is as a niche
wherein is a lamp
(the lamp in a glass,
the glass as it were a glittering star)
kindled from a Blessed Tree,
an olive that is neither of the East nor of the West
whose oil wellnigh would shine, even if no fire touched it;
Light upon Light.]

Pointer.

1. Among the faculties [of the soul] there are some which it possesses in accordance with its need to perfect its substance as actual intellect.

2. The first is its faculty with a predisposition toward the intelligibles. People sometimes call it "material intellect;" (it is the "niche").

3. This is followed by another faculty that comes to the soul once it has attained the primary intelligibles, by means of which it is then prepared to acquire [*iktisāb*] the secondary intelligibles, either, if it is very weak, by means of Thought [*fikra*] (which is "the olive tree"), or, if it is stronger than that, by means of Guessing Correctly (which is also "the oil"). [This faculty] is then called "intellect *in habitu*" (which is "the glass"). At its sublime and consummate level, it is a sacred [*qudsiyya*] faculty, "whose oil wellnigh would shine, even if no fire touched it."

4. Next there come upon the soul another faculty and perfection. The perfection: the intelligibles come about actually in [the soul], observed and represented in the Mind. This is the "Light upon Light." The faculty: the soul is able to bring about whenever it wishes the intelligible, which has been acquired but is no longer [actually] present, as if it were [actually] being observed, without needing to re-acquire it. This is "the lamp." This perfection is called "acquired intellect," and this faculty is called "actual intellect."

165 5. What brings [the intellect *in*] *habitu* into complete actuality, and also the material [intellect] into [the state of intellect *in*] *habitu* is the active intellect. It is the "fire."

Reminder.

6. Perhaps you now wish to find out about the difference between "Thought" [*fikra*] and "Guessing Correctly." Listen:

7. Thought is a certain motion of the soul among concepts, having for the most part recourse[42] to imagination. It looks for the middle term (or, in case it

[42] "Having recourse to:" *mustaʿīna bi-*. Faḫr-ad-Dīn ar-Rāzī reads in the *Lubāb al-Išārāt* (Cairo 1355, p. 72), *mustaġniya bi-*, "managing with (?)". He criticizes Avicenna for introducing imagination in the process of Thought on the grounds that imagination is of particulars while Thought in search of middle terms is of universals.

cannot be located, [it looks for] anything analogous to it which might lead to a knowledge of the unknown), by surveying the stock [of ideas] (or whatever is analogous to it) stored inside. Sometimes it reaches what is sought and sometimes it falls short.

8. Guessing Correctly occurs when the middle term presents itself [*yatamaṯṯalu*] to the Mind all at once, either as a result of a search and desire [for it] but without any [corresponding] motion [of the soul], or without any desire and motion. The middle term is a means to something [i.e., the conclusion; see next selection, § 2]; that, or something like it, presents itself [to the Mind] along with the middle term.

> [There follows Avicenna's standard argument (similar to that in No. 5, above) for the existence of the "sacred intellect" on the basis of the varying degrees of Correct Guessing among men.]

[7] From *Discussions*[43] (L12)

1. Question in the hand of [Bahmanyar or Ibn-Zayla]: The intellective faculty cannot avoid using Thought [*fikra*] when learning and remembering—and worse, even when intellecting that it has intellected! So how will it be able to perceive after the separation [of the soul from the body upon death], when this faculty [of Thought] ceases to exist?

2. Answer in the hand of [Avicenna]. God forbid that it [the intellect] should have to use the Cogitative faculty [*mufakkira*] which searches for the middle term! The reason for this is that learning occurs in two ways: One is by way of Guessing Correctly, which consists of the middle term occurring to the Mind without search and thus being obtained, along with the conclusion [of the syllogism]; the second is through contrived means [*ḥīla*] and [after] search.

3. Guessing Correctly is a divine effluence [*fayḍ*] and an intellective contact [*ittiṣāl*] taking place without any act of acquisition at all. Some people may reach such a stage [of consummate Correct Guessing] that they almost have no need of Thinking [*fikr*] in most of what they learn, and possess the sacred faculty [*quwwa qudsiyya*] of the soul.

> 3a.[44] When the intellective faculty [i.e., the rational intellect] desires an intelligible form, by nature it entreats the donor principle [i.e., the active

---

43 *Mubāḥaṯāt* §§ 234–238 Bīdārfar 106–107 = § 467 Badawī *Arisṭū* 231. This revised translation is taken from Gutas "Intuition and Thinking" 14–15.

44 I insert paragraphs 3a and 3b from *Discussions* §§ 254–255 Bīdārfar = § 468 Badawī, instead of listing them separately, because they pertain to the same subject and are best read in conjunction with this passage in entry [7]; in the Ṣiġnāḫī recension of the *Discussions*, as a matter of fact, they are consecutive. See the translation, notes, and discussion of these two paragraphs, numbered as [16], in Gutas "Intuition and Thinking" 24–26.

intellect]. If the form flows upon it by way of Correct Guessing, then it is spared the trouble; otherwise it has recourse to movements of other faculties whose nature it is to prepare it to receive the effluence. This is on account of a special influence which they [the other faculties] have upon the [rational] soul and of a similarity between the [rational] soul and some of the forms which exist in the realm of effluence [i.e., the celestial spheres]. Thus it acquires after much trouble what [otherwise] would not have been acquired except through Correct Guessing.

3b. If by "Thinking faculty" [*al-quwwa al-fikriyya*] is meant the one that searches, then it is the rational soul as the intellect *in habitu*, especially when its purpose with going beyond the [state of intellect] *in habitu* is to attain perfection [i.e., attain the state of acquired intellect]. But if what is meant by it is the faculty that presents the forms and is in motion [i.e., the Cogitative/Imaginative faculty, *al-mufakkira/al-mutaḫayyila*, in the animal soul, lodged in the middle part of the brain, which blends and separates forms, ideas, and images], then this is the Imagining faculty insofar as it is in motion upon the instigation of the intellective faculty.

166 4. When the soul has reached a sublime stage, acquired the excellent [sacred] faculty, and separated from the body, it attains whatever is attained There, where all distractions vanish, faster than through Guessing Correctly: the intellectual world presents itself to the [soul] according to the essential, not temporal order of the terms of propositions and of the intelligibles, and this takes place all at once.

5. There is need for Thinking [*fikr*] [in this world] only because the soul is turbid, or because it has had little training [*tamarrun*] and is impotent to attain the divine effluence, or because of distractions. Were it not for this, the soul would obtain certain knowledge about everything to the farthest reaches of truth.

[8] From *On the Rational Soul* (T14) (L13)

3. … The [rational] faculty is prepared to acquire the secondary intelligibles either by means of Thinking, which is an act of finding what ⟨results from⟩ these primary intelligibles by [their] composition and combination [to form definitions and syllogisms], or by means of Correct Guessing, which is the representation of the middle term in the faculty all at once and without Thinking or considering. By "middle term" I mean the cause which makes acknowledging the existence or non-existence of a thing necessary—i.e., the evidence which justifies the judgment—and this sometimes comes about following search and a desire to attain the intelligibles, and sometimes initially, without desire or search; and whenever the evidence is attained, so is invariably that for which the evidence is provided. …

6. The bliss [of the rational soul] comes about when its substance is rendered perfect, and this is accomplished when it is purified through knowledge of God and works for God. …

7. Its purification through knowledge of God consists of its attainment … all the intelligibles … whenever it wishes without needing to acquire them, and thus to have all the intelligibles present in it in actuality [and] … there ensues [an automatic] practicing of the theoretical philosophical sciences.

8. Purification through works is accomplished by methods mentioned in books on Ethics and by assiduous performance of religious duties, both legal and traditional … .

9. Now it has become clear in the physical sciences that personal qualities and habits follow the temperament of the body … . There is thus no doubt that temperament is subject to change, in which case qualities of character are also subject to change thereby; and it is for this reason that the performance of the exercises mentioned in books on Ethics is specified. Whenever a person's temperament is balanced, his qualities of character are easily refined; his balanced temperament is thus influential in this process. … The closer a temperament is to a balanced state, the more is a person predisposed to develop excellent traits in both his knowledge and his works.

10. It has also become clear in the ⟨Physical⟩ sciences that the celestial bodies are not constituted from a mixture of these four elements but are totally lacking in these opposites. Furthermore, it is only the involvement with these opposites that hinders the reception of the divine effluence … . The closer, therefore, a temperament is to a balanced state, the more is a person predisposed to receive this effluence. … [W]hen a person expends all his efforts to purify [his rational soul] through knowledge, acquires the propensity for contact with the divine effluence, … has a balanced temperament, and lacks these opposites which hinder his reception of the divine effluence, then there comes about in him a certain similarity to the celestial bodies … . When the association of the soul with the body is severed through death … after the soul has acquired excellent traits in its knowledge and works, and the obstacle that hindered it from receiving the divine effluence in its totality ceases to exist, … then the soul will receive the divine effluence, will have revealed to it whatever was hidden from it before the separation, and there will come about it a similarity with the abstract intellects which are the principles of the causes of beings, since all the truths are revealed to these intellects.

Avicenna derived and developed his theory of Correct Guessing directly from Aristotle's brief, and almost incidental, discussions of *eustochia*, "hitting correctly upon the mark" (and the related concept of *anchinoia*, "acumen") in the *Posterior Analytics* and *Nicomachean Ethics*.[45] In the former

[45] For other passages where Aristotle uses the words *eustochia* and *anchinoia* see Barnes 202 and H. Bonitz's *Index Aristotelicus*, Berlin 1870, s.vv. Apparently independently from each other, Goichon (*Directives* 177n2) and Rahman (*Psychology* 94 and *Prophecy* 31 and 66n9) were the first to note that the passage in the *Posterior Analytics* formed the basis of Avicenna's theory of Correct Guessing. They both equate *ḥads* with *anchinoia*, however, something

167 work, Aristotle says (I.34, 89b10–11, 14–15), "Acumen [*anchinoia*] is a certain [talent for] hitting correctly upon [*eustochia*] the middle term in an inconsiderable time. … For seeing the extreme terms, one recognizes all the middle terms, which are the causes [*aítia*]." The Arabic translation available to Avicenna, that of Abū-Bišr Mattā ibn-Yūnus made from Isḥāq ibn-Ḥunayn's Syriac intermediary, read as follows: "As for Acumen [*ḏakā'*], it is a certain Correct Guessing taking place in a time that does not lend itself to search for middle terms. … For he who knows the two extreme terms knows all the ⟨intermediate⟩ causes."[46] The crucial term in the definition, *eustochia*, which in the Greek means literally "hitting correctly upon the mark" and metaphorically "quickness in guessing correctly," was thus rendered literally and accurately by *ḥusnu ḥadsin*, an expression that includes in Arabic both significations of the Greek.[47] The same literalness is also evident in the translation of "in an inconsiderable time" (*en askeptōi chronōi*) by "in a time that does not lend itself to research;" it reflects an etymological analysis of *askeptos* as interpreted by Philoponus, whose commentary on the *Posterior Analytics* was available in Arabic translation:

> "Aristotle said 'in an inconsiderable time' instead of 'instantaneously' [*en akariaiōi*] in order [to indicate] that the discovery [*heuresis*] of the middle term would come about without thinking [*skepsasthai*]."[48] (L14)

Apart from this aspect of the process of Correct Guessing that is made explicit by Philoponus (doubtless reflecting earlier practice), there is very

which, strictly speaking, is not correct. *Anchinoia* is rendered by *ḏakā'*, while it is *eustochia* that corresponds to *ḥads*. In her earlier *Lexique* (1938) and *Vocabulaires* (1939), Goichon had failed to see the connection between *ḥads* (§ 140) and *eustochia* in the definition of *anchinoia*. In the *Vocabulaires*, especially, she wrongly equated *ḥads* with *noēsis*. The same holds true of J. Bakoš, *Psychologie d'Ibn Sīnā (Avicenne) d'après son œuvre aš-Šifā'*, Prague 1956, II,201n145, who says that *ḥads* probably stands for *nous* or *noēsis*. In other discussions of the topic, even this relatively inaccurate association of *ḥads* with the Aristotelian *anchinoia* seems to be overlooked (Marmura "Ghazali's Attitude" 106 and 110n20).

46 *Manṭiq Arisṭū* II,406 Badawī = I,547 Jabr. Badawī fills in after *al-asbāb*, ⟨*al-mutawassiṭa*⟩ ("⟨the intermediate⟩ causes") because there is a tear in precisely this place in the Paris MS (Arabe 2346, f. 222[b]) and the word is not visible (http://gallica.bnf.fr/ark:/12148/btv1b8422956q/f456.image.r=arabe+2346.langFR). Jabr reads, *al-asbāb allatī hiya awsāṭ*, presumably on the basis of the Istanbul MS, but he does not so indicate in his note. On the basis of the space that is torn in the Paris manuscript and the ends of letters still visible, it appears that the reading was indeed *al-mutawassiṭa*.

47 The rendition of *eustochia* by *ḥusnu ḥadsin* is representative of what is called "etymological translation" or calque: *ḥusn* translates the prefix *eu-*, and *ḥads* translates *stochos*.

48 *In An. Post.* 333.8–9 (Wallies), *CAG* XIII.3. *Askeptos* in Greek means both "inconsiderate" and "unconsidered;" Philoponus interprets it to mean "in which no consideration takes place."

little elaboration in the extant commentatorial tradition. Themistius, for example, only states the obvious: "Acumen is a certain analysis of the conclusion [of a syllogism] into its [constituent] propositions and the quick discovery [*heuresis*] of the middle term."[49]

In the *Nicomachean Ethics*, Aristotle tries to discriminate among various intellectual virtues and argues as follows (1142a32–b6):

> "We must grasp the nature of excellence in deliberation [*euboulia*] as well—whether it is a form of knowledge, or opinion, or [a talent for] hitting correctly upon the mark [*eustochia*], or something else. Knowledge it is not .... Nor is it hitting correctly upon the mark; for this both involves no reasoning [*logos*] and is something that happens quickly, whereas men deliberate a long time— 168
> as a matter of fact, the saying goes that one should carry out quickly the conclusions of one's deliberation, but should deliberate slowly. Again, acumen [*anchinoia*] is different from excellence in deliberation; acumen is a sort of hitting correctly upon the mark."[50] (L15)

The Arabic translation of this passage, which Avicenna read, has not been preserved;[51] but it is clear from the commentaries extant in Greek that not much of substance was added in the commentatorial tradition to Aristotle's own discussion. An Arabic translation of a lost Greek summary of the *Ethics* would seem to indicate the extent of elaboration or interpretation Aristotle's enumeration of the intellectual virtues had undergone. These faculties are listed there as follows:

> Acumen [*ḏakāʾ*], memory, intellection [*ʿaql*], quickness of comprehension [*surʿat al-fahm*], ease of learning [*suhūlat at-taʿallum*; *sic lege*]. Acumen is the speed with which the soul moves to construct a syllogism quickly and easily. ... Quickness of comprehension is the predisposition of the soul to perceive .... Ease of learning is sharpness of comprehension which readily perceives theoretical matters.[52] (L16)

The only significant elaboration of the Aristotelian concept of intellectual virtues in subsequent Greek thought appears to have occurred in the

---

49 *In An. Post.* 41.5–6 (Wallies), *CAG* V.1.

50 Translation adopted, with modifications, from D. Ross, *The Nicomachean Ethics of Aristotle*, Oxford 1954 [World's Classics], p. 149.

51 The section of the unique Fez manuscript containing the Arabic translation of the *Nicomachean Ethics* V.9-VI. 13 (1136a25–1144b30) is missing; see D.M. Dunlop's edition of the text, edited by A.A. Akasoy and A. Fidora, *The Arabic Version of the* Nicomachean Ethics, Leiden: Brill, 2005, 330 and note 224.

52 Text in ʿAbdurraḥmān Badawī, *Al-Aḫlāq, taʾlīf Arisṭūṭālīs*, Kuwayt: Wikālat al-Maṭbūʿāt, 1979, 407. For the work and the author see M.C. Lyons, "A Greek Ethical Treatise," *Oriens* 13–14 (1960–1961) 35–57; this passage is discussed on p. 51.

medical tradition, where they were associated with the humoral constitution of the body and were provided with a quantitative dimension. Toward the end of his extremely influential work, *That the Faculties of the Soul Are Consequent upon the Temperaments of the Body*, Galen says the following:

> In the thinking part of the soul, that which is consequent upon the temperament of the body is quickness of comprehension [*anchinoia*/*sur'at al-fahm*] and stupidity [*mōria*, *jahl*], and a higher or lower degree of that.[53] (L17)

In the medical tradition, in other words, acumen was directly related to the temperament of the body, depending on which a person would have more or less of it.

169 From these passages it is evident that the following concepts, mentioned repeatedly in the passages of Avicenna quoted above, went into the making of his theory of Correct Guessing: Correct Guessing is a function of acumen; it occurs spontaneously and without thinking; it hits accurately upon the middle terms, which are the causes of, i.e., explain, the extreme terms; it is associated with quickness of comprehension and, most significantly, with ease of learning; acumen, furthermore, is a function of the temperament, or humoral constitution, of the body, according to which people have more or less of it. All these concepts were present in a discrete form both in the text of Aristotle and, to a lesser extent, in the elaborations in the subsequent commentatorial tradition on the *Posterior Analytics* and *Nicomachean Ethics*,[54] as well as in the mainstream medical tradition represented by Galen; what is not present in any of them, however, is an indication that these elements were integrated into a comprehensive epistemology as in Avicenna.

In addition to the Aristotelian tradition, it has been suggested that a possible background of Avicenna's theory of Correct Guessing is provided by

---

[53] Biesterfeldt 43.1–2. I am citing the Arabic translation because this is what Avicenna read. The Greek text is in I. Müller, *Galeni Scripta Minora*, Leipzig: Teubner, 1891, II.79.1–2. It is probable, though far from certain, that the Galenic passage may go back to Poseidonius. W. Theiler seems to think so, because he included it among the Stoic philosopher's fragments, in *Poseidonios. Die Fragmente*, Berlin/New York: De Gruyter, 1982, frg. 423, p. I.344 top, and cf. the commentary on p. II.361.

[54] The commentatorial tradition in both Greek and Arabic on this subject is relatively scanty and little studied. An authoritative judgment would require more extensive research, though at this stage the statement made above appears warranted. See further below the arguments for Avicenna's development of the theory of Correct Guessing on his own. For the Greek and Arabic commentaries on these two works see the entries in *DPhA* I,498–499 and 520–524 for the former and *Supplément* 174–183 and 191–198 for the latter.

the development by the Stoics of the Aristotelian acumen (*anchinoia*) "in relation to their doctrine of revelation of the wise man."[55] The Stoic understanding of "acumen," however, is not specific enough to be of use in the present discussion; it does not refer to Guessing Correctly *the middle term* of a syllogism, the core of Aristotle's and Avicenna's position. It talks of acumen in the context of ethics, as a subcategory of "prudence" (*phronēsis*), one of the four primary virtues: acumen (*anchinoia*) is the knowledge whereby one can discover on the spot "the appropriate act" (*to kathēkon*).[56] Avicenna, on the other hand, is not interested in the ethical but the epistemological function of the concept of *ḥads* (*eustochia*, not *anchinoia*). He uses it mainly in the psychological part of his physical treatises to describe the operation whereby the rational faculty acquires the secondary intelligibles. Furthermore, as in every instance of an alleged Stoic theory in Arabic philosophy, the problem that has to be solved first is to establish the material (i.e., textual) means whereby that Stoic theory was transmitted into Arabic, a problem that has not yet been satisfactorily and comprehensively addressed.[57] 170
It would thus seem that for reasons both of substance and textual transmission, the Stoic doctrine of acumen played no role in the development of Avicenna's theory of Intuition.[58]

There is, on the other hand, a Muslim dimension to the issue that ought not to be overlooked. A number of terms used to denote non-cogitative methods of acquiring or possessing knowledge have a long history of serious discussion in most disciplines of Islamic intellectual life. Foremost among these are *waḥy* (revelation), *ilhām* (inspiration), and *badīha* (self-evident knowledge),[59] all of which Avicenna uses in their traditional meanings in his

---

[55] Rahman *Prophecy* 31. Rahman's further reference (66, note 9) to Plutarch's concept of the intellection of the divine as a sudden illumination is too general an idea to be relevant here.

[56] *Stoicorum Veterum Fragmenta*, J. von Arnim, ed., Leipzig 1903, III.64.15–28.

[57] See the discussion of this problem in Gutas, "Pre-Plotinian Philosophy." With regard to Avicenna, Rahman *Prophecy* 45ff. suggests that the Stoic doctrine of sympathy, which he credits with constituting "the basis of Avicenna's doctrine of revelation, prayer, and miracles," was taken over by Plotinus, and hence, one would assume, was available in Arabic in the form of the *Theologia Aristotelis*. Be that as it may, this still does not account for the way in which the Stoic doctrine of acumen allegedly reached Avicenna.

[58] Except perhaps whatever may be due to Poseidonius as transmitted by Galen. See note 53 above.

[59] These concepts were widely discussed by philosophers one or two generations older than Avicenna, like Abū-Sulaymān, Yaḥyā ibn-ʿAdī, Tawḥīdī. See the references in Kraemer 148–150; cf. further Tawḥīdī *Muqābasāt*, Ḥasan as-Sandūbī, ed., Cairo 1347/1929, 238–239, and *al-Imtāʿ* I.106 Amīn and az-Zayn; see also these words in *EI*[2].

very first essay, the *Compendium on the Soul* (T1, §§2, 4), but without, as yet, the philosophical congruousness and specificity he was later to accord to them and to others, like *fiṭra*,[60] in the mature epistemology he built around the concept of Guessing Correctly the middle term (*ḥads*). There are finally, the theories of Fārābī, which, insofar as we are able to read and study them in his extant writings, appear to have provided the initial stimulus and basic orientation to Avicenna's thoughts on this subject.[61]

The confluence of all these factors briefly indicated above formed the background against which Avicenna developed his doctrine of Guessing Correctly the middle term (*ḥads*). The specific ingredients are directly traceable to the Aristotelian writings, complemented by the medical tradition; the urgency and high significance of concepts like inspiration and revelation are due to the Islamic context; and the general orientation of the philosophical discussion and its location within the theory of the soul, and not, as in Aristotle, in logic or ethics, are adopted from Fārābī. But the synthesis of these diverse elements into a coherent and consistent account is original to Avicenna, if only because it is clear that he did not formulate this theory from the very beginning of his philosophical career.

171 In his very first treatise, the *Compendium on the Soul*, his treatment of the two ways of acquiring the intelligibles is markedly divergent from that in all his later works. First of all, Avicenna makes the distinction between the two ways of acquiring the intelligibles on the basis of the *objects* acquired. The first way, which he says occurs through "divine inspiration," results in the acquisition of the primary intelligibles, while the second way, through syllogistic reasoning, results in the acquisition of the secondary intelligibles—in fact, as it became clear from T1, §3, of all the contents of logic and theoretical philosophy as classified in the Aristotelian tradition. Avicenna was later to make the distinction between the two ways of acquiring the *secondary* intelligibles on the basis, first, of the *provenance* of the knowledge, (self/teacher), and second, of the intellective *function* yielding the knowledge (Guessing Correctly the middle term/Thinking), while relegating the acquisition of the primary intelligibles not to the instrumentality of divine

[60] For the traditional understanding of *fiṭra* in the Qur'ān and Ḥadīṯ see J. van Ess, *Zwischen Ḥadīṯ und Theologie*, Berlin / New York: De Gruyter, 1975, 101 ff.; see also the related article "Fiṭra" by D.B. Macdonald in *EI*². Avicenna used *fiṭra* as a technical term to refer to the natural operation of the mind in its various functions, including estimation, and it is not any kind of *ḥads* which, always in Avicenna, is Guessing Correctly the middle term. Cf. Griffel 17–18n56 and see the discussion in Gutas "Empiricism" Section V.

[61] See Rahman *Prophecy* 11–20, 30–31.

inspiration (or, eventually, of the active intellect) but to the spontaneous and natural operation (*fiṭra*) of the intellect in its transition from the material status to that of *in habitu*.[62]

Next, in Avicenna's description of the second way in passage [1] above, the body of what was later to become his theory of *ḥads* is perceptible, but its soul, *ḥads* itself, is missing. He says that (secondary) intelligibles are acquired either through syllogistic reasoning or, in the case of some keen-minded people, through inspiration and revelation. It is easy to see in this the origins of the later Thinking/Guessing Correctly dichotomy, but the mechanism, or common feature, whereby two completely different methods will yield the same result, i.e., the same intelligible, is not specified, nor is their mutual relationship explained.

Finally, because of the problems with the theory just described, there is a tentativeness in the presentation and imprecision in its technical vocabulary. Avicenna is manifestly repeating here material both from the Islamic tradition (knowledge through inspiration) and from the philosophical tradition (knowledge through demonstration), but he does not attempt to integrate this disparate material in the resultant formulation. Instead, he relies on the indefinite semantic field denoted by traditional epistemological terms—both philosophical and Islamic—to do the work for him. It is no accident that in the very short passage [1] we find the indiscriminate use of almost all the Arabic terms employed in discussions of the theory of knowledge: revelation, inspiration, self-evident knowledge, sense-perception, learning, thinking, keenness of mind, and demonstration. This makes for hazy presentation and overall bad philosophy. Avicenna, who was intensely interested in the subject, must have quickly realized the deficiencies of his first formulation, and in one of the few instances which belie his statement that he had never learned anything new in philosophy since his early years, he made a substantial change in his theory. In an apparently 172
unprecedented move, as we saw above, he made Aristotle's concept of "hitting correctly upon the middle term" the focus of his argument and thereby lent cohesion and wide applicability to his theory.

We are not in a position to determine how early Avicenna hit upon this solution to the problem. The latter part of the section on De anima from his "habilitation," *Philosophy for ʿArūḍī*, and the entire *The Available and the Valid*, where *ḥads* would presumably have been discussed, have not been

[62] See Hasse 33 and Gutas "Empiricism" Section V.

preserved (see W2 and W3). The first extant work which contains this theory fully articulated is his psychological essay culminating in the eschatology of the rational soul, the "Lesser" *Destination* (W4), and Avicenna must have been so satisfied with it that he incorporated it verbatim first in *The Cure* and later in *The Salvation* (passage [2]). In subsequent works, Avicenna modified and refined it to a certain extent, but in essence it remained the same.

The great merit of this theory lies in the fact that, first, it enables Avicenna to combine into one the two seemingly disparate ways of acquiring the secondary intelligibles, the "demonstration" and "revelation" or "inspiration" of passage [1], by making the common feature of both cognitive processes the discovery of the middle term, and second, it integrates this process firmly into the function of the intellect *in habitu* (passage [7], § 3b), a philosophically well defined stage of the rational soul's relation to the intelligibles. The mechanism of acquiring the intelligibles is thus fully explained, "revelation" and "inspiration" are demystified and adapted to this mechanism, incongruities in terminology are eliminated or explained away (as, e.g., in T14, § 10), and the whole account is made not only to fit neatly in the theory of the soul as developed in the Aristotelian tradition, but also to harmonize and interrelate the various branches of this philosophical tradition: psychology provides the framework within which epistemology, through logic, reproduces ontology which posits psychology. In other words, the agent engaged in intellection (the intellect/ psychology), the process of intellection (Guessing Correctly the middle term/ epistemology), the method of intellection (syllogistic reasoning, the middle term/ logic), and the objects of intellection (the intelligibles/ ontology) are interdependent and mutually explanatory elements unified in a coherent and systematic theory.

Once the essentials of this theory were formulated in the "Lesser" *Destination*, Avicenna occupied himself in subsequent works with further clarifying and rendering more precise the central concept of the theory of Correct Guessing. The first and most important modification came from Avicenna's awareness of the implications of what it means to acquire knowledge by or of oneself. Initially he had held that the major difference in the acquisition of knowledge depends on the provenance of knowledge, oneself or
173 a teacher (passage [2], § 1), while he assumed the variations of acquiring knowledge by oneself to be of relatively secondary importance ([2], § 3), though of course crucial for establishing the possibility of the existence of a prophet. But Avicenna's own admission that instruction is ultimately reducible to the first teacher's Guessing Correctly the middle term ([2], § 2) forced him to look closer into the implications of what it means to acquire knowledge by oneself, and into his own exposition of the *rate* of

having Correct Guesses, from very fast to very slow, and eventually led him to an understanding that it is not the provenance of the acquired knowledge that is the essential difference but rather the process of the acquisition itself, whether, that is, it is one of learning and acquisition or spontaneous. Avicenna thus restricted the concept of Correct Guessing to apply to spontaneous and immediate perception of the middle term, while he used the term Thinking to describe the second, deliberative and time consuming way, and thus redefined the two ways of acquiring the intelligibles. In this final formulation instruction is not mentioned; he assumed that it would be considered a variant form of the second, acquisitive process. Second, this modification in the definition of the two ways—Thinking and Guessing Correctly the middle term—required a concomitant modification in the description of the psychic mechanism involved. The initial broad understanding of *ḥads*, capable of variations in its rate, described it as a mental *motion* in search of the middle term (passage [4]); in the final version of the theory, mental motion is relegated to the process of Thinking ([6], §7) while *ḥads* becomes a *state* of the mind wherein the intelligibles present themselves all at once ([6], §8; [7], §2; [8]). This leaves room for the discussion of the way in which this state is acquired, and in this fashion ethics and religious law, as well as dreams and medicine (passage [8] and see Chapter 3.3) are integrated in the theory.[63]

Once the absolute centrality of the concept of Guessing Correctly the middle term (*ḥads*) not only in Avicenna's epistemology but also in his philosophical system as a whole is recognized and duly appreciated, it clarifies a number of problems that have chronically plagued the understanding of his philosophy and hampered the reading of his philosophical works.

i) The Autobiography, first of all, can now be read in its proper light: it is not the self-congratulatory bombast of a megalomaniac but a concrete illustration, drawn from observed facts, of the philosopher's theory of knowledge, that of *ḥads*. In this light, the apparently vainglorious statements in the Autobiography enumerated at the beginning of this section are seen as specific instances of Guessing Correctly the middle term by a "powerful soul" and, although more will be said about them in what follows, lose their problematic and "estranging" aspect.

---

[63] For the details in the development of Avicenna's ideas on this subject see Gutas "Intuition and Thinking."

ii) This theory has numerous implications for the status of Knowledge/*al-ʿilm* (or Philosophy, as we saw at the end of the preceding Section), in gen-
174 eral, and of philosophy in the Aristotelian tradition in particular. First of all, since this Knowledge, when acquired by *ḥads*, means that "the forms of all things contained in the active intellect are imprinted" on man's intellect *in habitu* (passage [2], § 3 middle), which is then called "acquired intellect" and is "like a polished mirror upon which are reflected the forms of things as they are in themselves without any distortion" (T14, § 7), and since "the forms of all things as they are in themselves," or the intelligibles, contained in the intellects of the celestial spheres (including of course the active intellect, the last in the emanative series) represent ontological truth, the way things are (T14, § 10 end), there is necessarily a one-to-one correspondence between this Knowledge and ontological truth; i.e., the object of this Knowledge is ontological reality as it is in itself, and ontological reality is included, completely and exhaustively, in this Knowledge.

Secondly, since the intelligibles contained in the active intellect are imprinted on the human intellect "in an order which includes the middle terms" ([2], § 3) and "according to the essential, not temporal order of the terms of propositions and of the intelligibles" ([7], § 4), not only do the *contents* of this Knowledge correspond, one-to-one, to ontological *reality*, but the *progression* of this Knowledge also corresponds to the *structure* of reality. *The structure of reality is therefore syllogistic.*

Thirdly, since this Knowledge acquired through Correct Guessing "in most things correspond[s] with what is found in books" ([5], § 4), and since when one "stands face to face" with the contents of this Knowledge—the forms of things as they are in themselves—one engages automatically in "the theoretical philosophical sciences" ([8], § 7), this Knowledge is also identical with Philosophy in all its subdivisions as found in books. And since Avicenna was formed in and worked with the philosophical sciences in the Aristotelian tradition, the conclusion that has to be drawn from the above is that for Avicenna, truth, or ontological reality, or the forms of things as they are in themselves, or the intelligibles contained in the intellects of the celestial spheres, collectively comprise absolute Knowledge, which corresponds to Philosophy, or more specifically to the Philosophical Sciences as classified in the Aristotelian tradition, and the structure of this reality corresponds to the progression of the intellect in acquiring the Knowledge whose object this reality is, and this progression is syllogistic, according to Aristotelian logic.

The bond that unites these different parts of the equation, or their point of contact (or "interface"), is Avicenna's theory of *ḥads*, bridging the gap

between pedagogy, epistemology, and ontology. In Avicenna, the Alexandrian tendencies to transform the classification of Aristotle's works into a classification of all knowledge, and the descriptive and normative functions 175
of this classification become synthesized into a coherent system logically interconnected.[64]

iii) The identity between absolute Knowledge as acquired by Guessing Correctly the middle term and philosophy as actually stated in books written in the Aristotelian tradition, however, is not complete. As Avicenna prudently says in [5], § 4, from *Philosophy for ʿAlāʾ-ad-Dawla*, his "Correct Guessing [of the middle terms] in *most things* corresponded with" the Aristotelian books; and the illustration of his powers of *ḥads* in the Autobiography implies that for the things for which no such correspondence existed, it was his *ḥads* which, by its very nature, provided the correct Knowledge. Thus, although he says in the Introduction to *The Easterners* that the Peripatetics are "the sect ... most worthy of ... Adherence" (T8, § 3), through his emphasis on *ḥads* in the Autobiography he claims to be independent from slavish adherence to a philosophical school tradition and to have pursued absolute Knowledge embodying truth. By the same token, because of this slight disparity between the contents of philosophy in the Aristotelian tradition and of absolute Knowledge as acquired by Guessing Correctly the middle terms, he can also claim, in the Introduction to *The Easterners*, on the one hand to have overlooked insignificant differences between the doctrine of the Peripatetics and his own knowledge acquired through *ḥads*, and on the other to have "perfected what they meant to say but fell short of doing" (T8, § 3).

iv) The theoretical position of directly Guessing Correctly the middle terms as a means for philosophical Knowledge other than the one through the study of books in the Aristotelian tradition, and his experience, as described in the Autobiography, of having studied the philosophical sciences without having "to endure the hard work of excessive book reading" ([5], § 4) also explain the veiled remark in the Introduction to *The Easterners* (T8, § 2) that he acquired knowledge "from a direction other than that of the Greeks." This "direction" is, of course, *ḥads*. As he explicitly says toward the end of the same Introduction (§ 6), this true Knowledge/Philosophy (*al-ʿilm al-ḥaqq*), i.e., the forms of things as they are in themselves and as contained in the

[64] In this regard also Avicenna perfects the systematization of these tendencies already effected by Fārābī. See Gutas "Paul the Persian" 259.

active intellect, "was Discovered by someone who examined a lot, reflected long, and Guessed nearly perfectly [middle terms]."[65] And finally, for additional corroboration, there is the express testimony of Avicenna's disciple and philosophical correspondent, Bahmanyār, who says that Avicenna mastered "in the prime of his youth" all the philosophical sciences through his "*ḥads* without the need for long thinking and instruction."[66]

The same dual access to this Knowledge, book learning and the highest levels of the means made available by Guessing Correctly the middle
176 term, is also mentioned elsewhere by Avicenna, and in particular in the closing lines of what I consider his last work, *On the Rational Soul* (T14, § 11): "I
happened to write at the beginning of my career … a summary treatise …
about the soul … by following the method of those who engage in philosophy through research (*ahl al-ḥikma al-baḥṯiyya*); whoever wishes to find out
about the soul should study this treatise because it is appropriate for students who do research. But God Almighty 'guides whomsoever He will' to
the way of those who engage in philosophy through direct experience (*ahl
al-ḥikma aḏ-ḏawqiyya*)." The first method is that of "excessive book reading" ([5], § 4), of actually setting up syllogisms and following through by
means of Thinking to their conclusions, as we shall discuss in the next Section; the second is that of Guessing Correctly the middle terms and gaining
such familiarity with the intelligibles as to experience the highest levels of
intellectual pleasure, available to those "whose soul has been rendered …
powerful through extreme purity and intense contact with intellective principles" ([2], § 3 middle), and hence the invocation to God. The terms used
here by Avicenna are different, but the meaning is the same.

[65] The obsession with an imaginary "oriental philosophy" of Avicenna has prevented many a sagacious reader of this Introduction from seeing its connection with both the Autobiography and the passage from the *Philosophy for ʿAlāʾ-ad-Dawla* (T2). The only scholar to have noted this connection, in the form of an afterthought, was Goichon in her article "Philosophie" 31–32, note 36. Her purpose in that article, however, was to identify the non-Greek direction (*jiha*) from which Avicenna acquired his knowledge with an alleged scientific and experimental tradition in the East, and she consequently failed to recognize the reference to *ḥads* and the overall significance of the very passage she was referring to. Another scholar who also recognized the association of the epistemology implied in Avicenna's Autobiography with *ḥads* was A.F. El Ahwany (al-Ahwānī), "Théorie de la connaissance" 26, but he failed to develop the argument beyond a general exposition of the subject indicated in his title. Most of Ahwany's presentation was retold with some "mystical" elaboration by Salvador Gómez Nogales, "El misticismo persa de Avicena y su influencia en el misticismo español," *Milenario de Avicena* [Cuadernos del Seminario de Estudios de Filosofía y Pensamiento Islámicos, 2], Madrid: Instituto Hispano-Arabe de Cultura, 1981, 76–79.

[66] *At-Taḥṣīl* 817 Moṭahharī.

v) The eventual formulation of the theory of *ḥads* in full had thus two aspects: one was the dual access to Knowledge/Philosophy through hard work by Thinking and through *ḥads*, and the other was the classification of people according to their capacity for *ḥads*. Since people differ in this capacity, some being well endowed and others totally lacking in it, the question that faces the philosopher wishing to impart this Knowledge is to select his audience and express himself accordingly, since it is the quality of the audience that will determine the method of exposition that the author will have to follow. This is another factor that needs to be considered in an understanding of Avicenna's use of different methods of exposition in his various works. The subject will be discussed fully in Chapter 8.

3. Avicenna's Studies. Methods of Learning: Study

Avicenna states in the *Philosophy for ʿAlāʾ-ad-Dawla* (T2, § 4) that his aptitude for Guessing Correctly the middle term was not such as to enable him to learn, like the prophets, without any study. He had to spend time with "book reading" and other methods in order to supplement this deficiency 177
and reach full understanding of the philosophical sciences. In the Autobiography he describes in great detail the methods by which he studied and learned. These are (in order of importance after *ḥads*) logic, prayer, dreams, and, what we might call pharmacological means, wine drinking. Conversely, understanding through *ḥads* and these auxiliary processes implies a rejection of rote memorization, traditional Authority (*taqlīd*), and Partisan Adherence to it (*taʿaṣṣub*), and a corresponding reliance on independent Verification (*taḥqīq*) and Determination of Validity (*taḥṣīl*). We shall next discuss these methods and the way in which they are related to and help advance the function of *ḥads*.

A. *Logic*

During the year and a half which Avicenna devoted to his "graduate" studies, he says that he reread all the parts of philosophy (Logic, Mathematics, Physics, Metaphysics) as follows:

> I put together in front of me [sheaves of] scratch paper, and for each *argument* that I examined, I recorded the *syllogistic premisses* it contained, the way in which they were composed, and the *conclusions* which they might yield, and I would also take into account the *conditions of its premisses* [i.e., their modalities] until I had Ascertained that particular problem. Every time I was at a loss about a problem, concerning which I was unable to find the

> *middle term* in a syllogism, I would repair on its account to the mosque and worship, *praying* humbly to the All-Creator to disclose to me its obscurity and make its difficulty easy. At night I would return home, set the lamp before me, and occupy myself with reading and writing. Whenever I felt drowsy or weakening, I would turn aside to drink a cup of *wine* to regain my strength, and then I would go back to my reading. Whenever I fell asleep, I would see those very problems in my *dream*; and many problems became clear to me while asleep. So I continued until all the Philosophical Sciences became deeply rooted in me and I understood them as much as is humanly possible. [T3, § 8; emphasis added]

Avicenna was led to study and analyze Aristotelian philosophy in this fashion primarily by Fārābī's essay on *The Agreement between Plato and Aristotle*, which was to have an immense influence on his philosophical *modus operandi*.[67] Quite apart from its origins, however, the description of his studies above corresponds closely with Avicenna's overall method in logic. In order to explain precisely the procedure followed by Avicenna and identify
178 each stage of his process of learning it is indispensable to appreciate this fact.[68] Avicenna studied the philosophical sciences argument by argument,

[67] See the passage from Fārābī's essay translated below, Chapter 5.3, L43, and the discussion of Avicenna's methods of composition in Chapter 8.

[68] This has been ignored by all students and translators of Avicenna's Autobiography. As a consequence, their versions of the above passage and its interpretation have suffered to a greater or lesser degree. In what follows I will not refer to the mistranslations and misunderstandings of other scholars; this is a task for the future editor and student of both the Autobiography and Biography. There is a perversity in the way in which the very explicit words of Avicenna have been misinterpreted. As an extreme example I may mention the comments of A. Soubiran, *Avicenne* (Paris: Lipschutz, 1935), p. 33, who says, after citing the above passage, the following: "Cette manière d'acquérir la connaissance par la pénétration mystique [!] (kashf) était de la plus grande importance pour Avicenne et il en reparlera dans différents passages du Nadjat." He then adds the following note: "Il ne faut pas la confondre avec la 'connaissance intuitive' que la philosophie thomiste attribue à l'intelligence angélique—'atteinte de la vérité, d'un simple coup d'œil, sans l'aide du raisonnement'. St. Thomas, Summa Theologica." Soubiran is doubly mistaken. Not only is 'connaissance intuitive,' in the form of Correct Guessing given to it by Avicenna, precisely the thing he is referring to here (as already discussed in the previous Section), but also the words of Aquinas are themselves indebted to the theory of Avicenna. This example, though extreme, is nevertheless quite prevalent in secondary works on Avicenna. See also for example, B. Carra de Vaux, *Avicenne* (Paris: Félix Alcan, 1900), p. 299: Avicenna and philosophers like him were "hommes de grand cœur qui n'ont pas cru amoindrir l'estime dans laquelle ils tenaient la raison, an avouant qu'elle est bornée, et en admettant au-dessus d'elle une certaine possibilité de connaître intuitivement, qui a donné à leurs âmes le moyen de s'élancer dans les régions mystiques." There is not a single word about the primary function of Correct Guessing, namely, the Discovery of the middle term. This passage is translated and endorsed by Wickens "Aspects" 64.

analyzed its parts, and entered them in what we would call index cards—in itself an indication of an extremely systematic approach. Avicenna defines "argument" (*ḥujja*) as follows:

> Something which is set up (*yatarattabu*) first as a given, and through which something else *then* becomes known by being acknowledged as true (*ʿalā sabīl at-taṣdīq*), this thing, whatever its form (*kayfa kāna*), is called "an argument." [Kinds of] arguments are the syllogism, induction, analogy, and other things.[69] (L18)

Avicenna thus examined in the sciences he studied *all* arguments, regardless whether these were in the form of a syllogism, induction, or analogy; in other words he examined every passage in which an author professed to progress from the known to the unknown. All such arguments are composed of propositions which are called premisses, since "a premiss is a proposition that has become part of a syllogism or of an[other kind of] argument."[70] Avicenna then discriminated among the different kinds of arguments and entered into his "index cards" *only* the syllogistic propositions, i.e., the premisses of syllogisms. This is perfectly understandable since a syllogism is the only argument—or reasoning process—that leads to certainty: "its condition is not that its propositions should be admitted *so that* it can become a syllogism, but rather its condition is that it be such that, *should its propositions be admitted*, another statement must necessarily follow from them."[71] 179
Avicenna then noted the way in which the premisses were composed[72] and the conclusions that may be derived from them. What he did, in effect, was to identify and classify the premisses as follows: he recognized three primary classes of propositions according to their composition (*tarkīb*), i.e., structure: predicative (A is/is not B) and conditional, which is subdivided into conjunctive (if … then) and disjunctive (either … or). These are all further subdivided, amounting to a total of thirty-eight compositions.[73] So far,

---

69 *Madḫal* 18.6–9 Anawati et al. Cf. a fuller account of the three kinds of arguments named in Goichon *Directives* 191–194, Inati *Logic* 129–131.

70 *Išārāt* I.7.1, 65/138 = Goichon *Directives* 193, Inati *Logic* 130.

71 *Išārāt* I.7.1, 65/139 = Goichon *Directives* 193–194, Inati *Logic* 131.

72 Reading in the passage in the Autobiography *tarkībahā* for the transmitted *tartībahā* (Gohlman 28.1), which would mean "their arrangement." Gohlman translates "their classification," and refers (note 25, p. 122) to the classification of syllogisms given by Goichon *Lexique* No. 611, pp. 340 ff. But that which is composed or classified in this passage in the Autobiography is not syllogisms but *premisses* (propositions).

73 See Goichon *Lexique* No. 586 and the references given there. For *tarkīb* see ibid. p. 305. The reference to the *Manṭiq al-mašriqiyyīn* on that page is paralleled in *The Cure*, *ʿIbāra* 32–33 El-Khodeiri.

then, Avicenna had established whether an argument was a syllogism or not, the composition of each individual premiss of each syllogism, and the conclusions that would be acceptable in each case—in other words, he established the *theoretical* validity of each syllogism. There remained to examine the admissibility of its premisses in order to ascertain the truth, or objective validity *in reality*, of its conclusion, since as we saw above the latter is admissible only if the former were. This Avicenna did by duly taking into account (the term he uses is *urāʿī*) "the conditions of the premisses" (i.e., of the propositions) of the syllogism. In *Pointers and Reminders* he explains as follows the conditions of the propositions:

> In the predication, conjunction, and disjunction [that obtains in the predicative, conjunctive, and disjunctive propositions, as classified above according to their composition], you should take into account [*turāʿī*, the same word as that used in the Autobiography]: (a) the state of the relation. For example: if one says, "J is a father," one should take into account [the question], "Whose [father]?" In the same manner [you should also take into account], (b) the time, (c) the place, and (d) the circumstance. For example, if it is said, "Everything that moves changes," one should take into account that [this is so only] as long as it moves. Similarly one should also take into account (e) the state of the part and the whole, and (f) the state of the potentiality and actuality; for if it is said, "Wine intoxicates," one should take into account whether potentially or actually and whether a little portion or a large amount. Failure to consider these qualifications [*maʿānī*] is one of the causes of much erring.[74] (L19)

180 This refinement of Aristotle's modal syllogistic,[75] apparently fully developed in Avicenna's later years,[76] enabled him to test the ontological truth value of propositions, and hence to claim, as he does in the Autobiography, that he "had Ascertained that particular problem." The difficulties that Avicenna encountered in this method of study, a method whose goal was nothing

---

74 *Išārāt* I.3.10, 31/83–84 = Goichon *Directives* 132, Inati *Logic* 89.

75 The six "conditions" enumerated above were not the only ones specified by Avicenna; in the fifth chapter (*nahj*) of *Pointers and Reminders*, in the discussion of contradiction, he mentions at least two more, subject and predicate, as Ṭūsī points out in his commentary (*Išārāt* I,299–304 Dunyā). For the question of the "conditions of propositions" see Goichon *Directives* 50–68 and "Unité" 292–304 and especially 300–301. Also cf. her notes in *Directives* 132, 153–154. The precise relation of Avicenna's "conditions" to Aristotle's analysis of the modality of contingency, and the extent of Avicenna's refinement of the latter remain unclear; cf. I.M. Bochenski *Ancient Formal Logic*, Amsterdam: North Holland, 1963, 58 and Goichon *Directives* 63 and 53. For studies of Avicenna's modal logic see Thom 65–80, Lagerlund, and Street, with further bibliography.

76 Goichon *Directives* 132n2; 52–53.

less than to arrive at logical *and* ontological truth—to "prove" reality—by means of syllogistic reasoning, were invariably related to finding the middle term of a syllogism. This is as it should be. The middle term is the only term that does not appear in the conclusion of a syllogism, which consists of the minor (the subject) and the major (the predicate) terms; and any argument which was presented in the texts Avicenna read merely as a conclusion, without the syllogism that it presupposed, could be analyzed[77] and verified only with the help of the middle term, indispensable for the reconstruction of the syllogism. The process that enables one to alight all at once on the middle term is, as extensively discussed in the preceding Section, Guessing it Correctly (*ḥads*).

The passage in the Autobiography just analyzed is the most comprehensive description of Avicenna's method in studying philosophy, but it is not alone. The same account is also referred to in the passage from the *Philosophy for 'Alā'-ad-Dawla* (T2, §4), and is given in summary form in the Introduction to *The Easterners*:

> We ... measured all that [the Peripatetics bequeathed], word for word, against the sort of science which the Greeks call logic ... and we thus came to know what could bear such a confrontation and what resisted it. For each thing, we sought its manner [in which it was argued for], with the result that whatever is true was [actually shown to be] true, and whatever is false was [actually shown to be] false. ... [T]he fundamental elements of true Philosophy, which was Discovered by someone who examined a lot, reflected long, and Guessed nearly perfectly [middle terms]. [T8, §§2, 6]

The correspondence with the passage in the Autobiography is apparent. Measuring Peripatetic philosophy against the yardstick of logic is a less technical way of describing Avicenna's operation with the "index cards"; the 181
manner of argumentation for each thing which he sought reflects his classification of premisses according to their composition and his consideration of their conditions or modalities; and both long study and developed aptitude for Correct Guessing of middle terms are needed to attain the teachings of philosophy that are true.

Avicenna applied this method of logical analysis to his own compositions and commentaries, and taught it to his students who repeatedly asked him about it. The disciple writing from Rayy (Ibn-Zayla?) gives a succinct account of Avicenna's advice on logical procedure (T13, §§5–7, 10), advice

77 Cf. Avicenna's directions for analyzing a syllogism in *Najāt* 81/94–95.

which Avicenna himself also followed. His elaborations on points of detail about the syllogistic process as well as his application of this method in some of his works will be discussed below, in Chapter 8.4.

B. *Prayer*

Avicenna's prayers and frequent visits to the mosque when he was unable to discover the middle term in a syllogism are mentioned in the Autobiography not as an expression of his general piety (as frequently stated),[78] but rather as an indication of the salutary effect, in medical terms, which prayer has on the constitution of the body that leads to enhanced aptitude for Guessing middle terms Correctly. The connection between prayer and other forms of religious ritual was best described in Avicenna's last essay *On the Rational Soul*,[79] as presented above:

> Purification through works is accomplished by methods mentioned in books on Ethics and by assiduous performance of religious duties, both legal and traditional, such as observances relating to [the functions of] the body, one's property, and to a combination of the two. For being restrained at the places where religious law and its statutes place such restraints, and undertaking to submit to its commands, have a beneficial effect on subjugating the soul that "incites to evil" [and thus transforming it] into the rational soul which is "at peace," i.e., making the bodily faculties of the soul, the appetitive and the irascible, subservient to the rational soul which is "at peace." Now it has become clear in the physical sciences that personal qualities and habits follow the temperament of the body .... The closer, therefore, a temperament is to a balanced state, the more is a person predisposed to receive this effluence ... by which I mean the inspiration coming from the Lord, occurring all at once and revealing some intellective truth. [T14, §§ 8–10]

In the preceding Section on *ḥads* we saw precisely what these "intellective truths" comprised: "Guessing Correctly is a divine effluence (*fayḍ*) and an intellective contact .... The intellectual world presents itself to the [soul] according to the essential, not temporal order of the terms of propositions and of the intelligibles, and this takes place all at once" (L12, §§ 3–4). The

[78] By Gardet 29, for example, among many others: "son autobiographie semble témoigner de certaines habitudes de piété personnelle." His analysis of prayer on pp. 135–138 fails to see the role of Guessing middle terms Correctly in the process and concludes that prayer leads to "connaissance mystique" (p. 138).

[79] An essay *On Prayer*, transmitted in the manuscripts under Avicenna's name, shares some common points with Avicenna's genuine views on the subject, but some additional elements make its authenticity highly suspect. Cf. Eichner "Prayer" and see the discussion in the Appendix under GM-Ps 3.

connection between prayer and middle terms is thus as follows: prayer con- 182
centrates the mind and allows the rational soul to become dominant; when the rational soul dominates passions and lusts it becomes pure; when it becomes pure, it is ready, or predisposed (i.e. through the enhanced powers of Guessing Correctly) to acquire the divine effluence, i.e., to Discover the middle terms; so when the philosopher performs his prayer he acquires the effluence which comprises the intelligibles "in an order which includes the middle terms" (L7, § 3).

This is then the process whereby prayer is effective, and it is this process to which Avicenna wishes to point by mentioning in the Autobiography his praying habits in connection with the middle terms. More generally, however, prayer, and other acts of worship are ancillary to the epistemological process and preparatory because they purify the rational soul and render it receptive to the divine effluence, "the intellective matter," i.e., the world of the intelligibles which are known to the heavenly intellects of the spheres and are structured in syllogistic order, complete with middle terms.

At the time when Avicenna was studying, he may not have held this particular understanding of the efficacy of prayer, since the specific reference to prayer in connection with middle terms in the Autobiography is meaningful only in the context of Avicenna's theory of *ḥads* as it developed later (and hence the Autobiography is not "historical" in this sense). There is, however, no doubt that he held elevated forms of prayer in high esteem very young; already in the introduction of his first work, the *Compendium on the Soul,* he speaks with respect of the Greek tradition according to which Asclepius would cure people merely through their prayers. The very reference to Asclepius indicates that he was familiar with a wide range of Greek sources, and presumably he had access to a number of Neoplatonic works in
which the philosopher's prayer was discussed.[80] His general orientation with
regard to the efficacy of philosophical prayer thus would seem to have been 183

80 Richard Walzer discussed briefly some of the possible Greek antecedents of Avicenna's view of prayer in "Platonism in Islamic Philosophy," in *Recherches sur la tradition platonicienne* [*Entretiens Hardt* III], Geneva 1957, 220–224; reprinted in his *Greek into Arabic*, Oxford: Bruno Cassirer, 1962, pp. 248–252, and, with modifications, in German translation in *Antike und Orient im Mittelalter*, ed. Paul Wilpert [*Miscellanea Mediaevalia* I], Berlin: De Gruyter, 1962, 192–195. Cf. also his references in his *Greek into Arabic* 229n2. For Neoplatonic theories and practices of theurgy, as Avicenna would have known about them through the work of the commentators, see D. Baltzly, "Pathways to Purification: the Cathartic Virtues in the Neoplatonic Commentary Tradition," in H. Tarrant and D. Baltzly, eds., *Reading Plato in Antiquity*, London: Duckworth 2006, 169–184.

influenced by the Greek tradition, but the particular elaboration and significance that he imparted to the subject, and its association with Guessing middle terms Correctly, were his own contribution. This development constitutes a significant achievement in the way in which Avicenna was able to integrate prayer—and the ordinances of revealed religion in general—into the very operation of the process of logical analysis and epistemology.

C. *Dreams*

The same epistemological operation induced through philosophical prayer, viz., the acquisition by the rational soul of the intelligibles from the active intellect "according to the essential, not temporal order of the terms of propositions and of the intelligibles" (L12, § 4), also lies behind Avicenna's statement that "many problems became clear to me while asleep" (T3, § 8).[81] According to Avicenna, as a matter of fact, human souls can acquire "something from the unseen" (i.e., forms of particulars relating to things on earth that are present in, i.e., thought by, the souls of the celestial spheres) when a person is asleep.[82] The reason for this is that the imaginative faculty is less likely to be distracted by the calls of the other faculties during sleep, and thus more open to receive the divine effluence. Few of the representations depicted by the imaginative faculty during sleep, however, are those of the

[81] The popular notion of veridical dreams was discussed—and rejected—on philosophical terms by Aristotle in his *De divinatione per somnum*. This brief essay formed a part of the collection later known as *Parva Naturalia*, whose transmission in later Greek and especially Arabic Aristotelianism is extremely complicated. The extant Arabic version of the *De divinatione* in particular appears to be highly interpolated; see Hansberger and the discussion, with a few representative texts, in Gätje *Psychologie* 81–92, 130–139. For a comprehensive presentation of Islamic philosophical dream interpretation, with references to the Greek sources, see Gätje "Traumlehren." For a "folklore" of dreams of philosophers and by philosophers in Islamic philosophical circles immediately preceding Avicenna see the reports in the *Ṣiwān al-ḥikma* about Abū-Sulaymān as-Sijistānī (2852 ff. Dunlop), translated and discussed by Kraemer 124–125. *The Early Muslim Tradition of Dream Interpretation* is presented by John C. Lamoreaux, Albany: SUNY Press, 2002.

[82] "Experience and syllogistic reasoning are in agreement that human souls may acquire something from the unseen in the state of sleep," *Išārāt* II.10.8, 209/374 = Goichon *Directives* 506 = Inati *Mysticism* 95. What Avicenna formulates succinctly in this passage is set forth at great length and in detail in the second section of the fourth book of the De anima of *The Cure*, *Nafs* 173.9–182 Rahman. For a concise presentation of Avicenna's theory of dreams see *Philosophy for ʿAlāʾ-ad-Dawla*, *Ṭabīʿiyyāt* 131–135 Meškāt = II.82–84 Achena and Massé. For *ġayb* and *muġayyabāt* in Avicenna see Gutas "Imagination" 338–339 and "Absence of Mysticism" 359–365.

"effluence (*fayḍ*) from the supernal realm upon the soul;"[83] mostly they have
to do with a person's concerns while awake. But the sleeper whose rational soul is strong, has a balanced temperament, and is not distracted by
the imagination and the other senses, both external and internal, "perceives
the unseen things (*muġayyabāt*) by Ascertaining them either as they are in 184
themselves or through any images for them."[84] The use of the word Ascertaining (*taḥaqquq*) in this sentence is significant because it implies, as we
shall next discuss (Section E.i), that the perception is not only of the unseen
things themselves, but also of their syllogistic connections that justify the
logical progression from one to the other.[85] The process is thus similar to that
of hitting upon the middle term "out of the blue," i.e., Guessing it Correctly,
as Avicenna explains:

> There is not a single person who has not had his share of [veridical] dreams [while asleep] and perceptions [of the unseen] while awake, for the cause of the discrete ideas (*ḫawāṭir*) that occur all at once to the [rational] soul is nothing else but certain contacts [with the souls and intellects of the spheres], and one is conscious neither of these contacts [themselves] nor of that with which contacts have been made, either before or after them.[86] (L20)

D. *Wine Drinking*

Few incidents in Avicenna's life have enjoyed the notoriety of his report about drinking wine while working: it has attracted the religious condemnation of conservative Muslims and excited the romantic imagination of admiring Westerners. Avicenna, however, inserted it in his Autobiography neither to provoke the former nor to titillate the latter. He simply wished to make the pharmacological point, as a physician, that wine is a drug, and that when taken in moderation it enhances the physical capacity to think. Like so many other aspects of Avicenna's life and thought, his drinking wine has to be seen in its scientific, cultural, and social context.

In Greek medicine and materia medica, the varieties of wine and their effects were discussed at great length. When taken in moderation, wine

83 *Nafs* 179.6 Rahman; cf. Gutas "Imagination" 347.

84 *Nafs* 173.14 Rahman. For an analysis of the mechanisms whereby the human soul comes into contact with the supernal realm and receives information therefrom see Gutas "Imagination."

85 Cf. the use of the related term, *taḥqīq*, Verification, for the same purpose in the Prologue of *Pointers and Reminders*, T10, § 1, and note 1. The progression referred to here is that described in the previous Section, L7, § 3, and L12, § 4.

86 *Nafs* 174.1–4 Rahman. See the translation of this and related texts and the accompanying discussion in Gutas "Imagination" 347–349.

was considered to act beneficially on both the body and the soul. Generally speaking, it helped bring about a balance in the mixture of the bodily humors, and generated a mood of well-being and joy. Rufus of Ephesus specifically mentions that it made people work fast and with ease without feeling tired or exhausted.[87] In the *Canon of Medicine* Avicenna repeats most of the transmitted knowledge about the effects of wine and presents some additional material that is of relevance to this discussion. He first describes, in terms of humoral pathology, the beneficial effects on the body:

> Wine is also very efficient in causing the products of digestion to become disseminated through the body. It cuts phlegm and dissolves it. It extracts yellow bile into the urine and other [bodily wastes]. It renders black bile more slippery and able to leave [the system] easily. It subdues the harmful influence of this black bile by contrariety, and it breaks up all entanglements without the necessity of excessive and abnormal heating.[88] (L21)

There are two things to be noticed about this passage. First, by helping evacuate and counteract noxious humors, wine brings about a balance to, or "tempers", the humoral system. As we saw above, a balanced temperament is a precondition for the ability to have veridical dreams, and more generally, as Avicenna states in his last essay, "the closer ... a temperament is to a balanced state, the more is a person predisposed to receive this [divine] effluence" (T14, §10). Second, it subdues and evacuates black bile. This is extremely desirable in a thinker because prolonged thought produces in the body an excess of black bile, which not only destroys the humoral

[87] Despite its age, Francis Adams's *The Seven Books of Paulus Aegineta*, 3 vols., London: Sydenham Society, 1844–1847, still provides the most comprehensive overview of the entire Graeco-Arabic medical tradition. For wine see I,172–178, III,272–273. The great first century physician Rufus of Ephesus (Ullmann *Medizin* 71) wrote an independent treatise on wine which was translated into Arabic by Qusṭā ibn-Lūqā and apparently enjoyed great popularity. The surviving fragments were collected by Ullmann "Rufus;" see in particular fragment 1, pp. 33–35. The medical view of the effects of moderate wine drinking was also reflected in popular Greek literature, in the gnomologia, and thus available in Arabic from that direction as well. See, for example, a saying attributed to Orpheus (?) in Ḥunayn ibn-Isḥāq's *Nawādir al-falāsifa*, MS Munich 651, f. 39[a] (this section is omitted in Badawī's edition of the *Ādāb*, between pp. 61–62): "A little wine exercises the imagination" (*inna l-miqdāra l-laṭīfa mina š-šarābi riyāḍatun li-l-wahm*). This has further implications, yet to be investigated, for the connection of the effects of wine with the *ēthos* theory of music. Cf. the references in A. Loewenthal, *Honein Ibn Ishāk. Sinnsprüche der Philosophen*, Berlin: S. Calvary & Co., 1896, 85n2, and the translation of the saying by "Orpheus" on p. 86.

[88] *Al-Qānūn fī ṭ-ṭibb* I,169.24–26 (Būlāq numbers) al-Qašš and Zay'ūr; cf. Gruner 410, §802.

balance but could also lead to "black bile diseases," i.e., mental disorders and, in extreme cases, death.[89] Black bile diseases are, in contemporary terms, the "occupational hazard" of philosophers, to which, for example, Avicenna's contemporary and Baġdādī rival, Abū-l-Faraj ibn-aṭ-Ṭayyib, succumbed (T13, § 3). Wine restrains the development of such pathologies in the body.

Apart from assisting indirectly the process of thought and the soul's receptivity to the divine effluence by maintaining a balanced temperament,
however, wine also directly fosters mental activity. Avicenna elaborates on 186
this point in the following passage in the *Canon of Medicine* which appears to be his own contribution to the subject because it reflects his personal concerns:

> Wine does not inebriate quickly a person of powerful brain, for the brain is then not susceptible to ascending harmful vapors, nor does heat from the wine reach it to any degree beyond what is appropriate.[a] *His mind therefore becomes clear to a degree unequalled at other times.*[b] The effect is different on persons who are not of this calibre.[90] (L22)

The reference to Avicenna as the "person of powerful brain" is evident; in psychological terms it is identical with the "powerful souls" referred to in his treatises on the soul (e.g., T2).

From a strictly medical, or biological point of view, therefore, Avicenna considered wine to be responsible for increasing the brain's capacity for Guessing Correctly by causing a balanced temperament in general, expelling excessive black bile from the body, and clearing the mind. As in the case

---

[a] Reading *al-mulā'ima*, as in the Roman edition (1593), I,85.21.

[b] *Awqātan uḫrā* is the reading of the Roman edition (I,85.22); the Būlāq edition has "by other minds," *aḏhān uḫrā*.

---

[89] The most comprehensive extant treatise on black bile diseases (*melancholia*) is that by Isḥāq ibn-ʿImrān, which was written early in the tenth century and drew extensively from a similar work by Rufus; it is summarized by Ullmann *Medicine* 72–77. The extant fragments of Rufus's extremely popular and influential work were edited and translated by Peter E. Pormann, *Rufus of Ephesus On Melancholy* [SAPERE 12], Tübingen: Mohr Siebeck, 2008. See also the case history of a patient suffering from black bile disease, caused by "constant brooding over the intricacies of geometry," translated from another work by Rufus, in Ullmann *Medicine* 36–37. Avicenna himself reportedly treated the Būyid Majd-ad-Dawla for this disease (Biography 48–50 Gohlman).

[90] *Qānūn* I,169.26–28 (Būlāq numbers) al-Qašš and Zayʿūr; emphasis added. Cf. Gruner 410, § 803.

of the other epistemologically significant subjects, prayer and dreams, he is also credited with having written an independent essay on the *Benefits and Harms of Wine for Physical Regime*.[91]

From a cultural and social point of view, Avicenna could have had very few inhibitions about openly proclaiming his use of wine, as his continuing practice throughout his life indicates (Biography 78.4–5 Gohlman).[92] Whatever his feelings about the Šuʿūbiyya, he was certainly familiar with pre-Islamic—or allegedly pre-Islamic—Pahlavi wisdom material in which wine drinking in moderation is expressly stated to revive the spirit and lend intellectual acuity. Representative is the following passage from the Pahlavi *Answers of the Spirit of Wisdom*:

> Moderate drinking of wine ... digests the food, kindles the vital fire, *increases the understanding and intellect*, semen and blood, removes vexation, and ...
> 187 causes recollection of things forgotten. ... Work, which it is necessary to do
> and expedite, becomes more progressive.[93] (L23)

It is unimportant whether this material is originally Persian or itself ultimately derived from the same Greek medical tradition;[94] contemporaries and predecessors of Avicenna certainly thought it to be original, and this indicates the cultural background in which wine drinking has to be assessed. As a matter of fact, not only did the Pahlavi texts present this view of wine drinking as Persian, but Rufus himself mentions the same in his treatise on wine. He says that the Persians used to partake of wine when debating issues

---

[91] *Siyāsat al-badan wa-faḍāʾil aš-šarāb wa-manāfiʿuhu wa-maḍārruhu*, GMed 17. This is a brief one-page essay in the Istanbul MS Nuruosmaniye 4894 (see the Appendix) of a clearly medical nature, that is listed in a dubious manner only in the Extended Bibliography (EB 65, 66); its authenticity, and whether it draws upon any material from the *Canon* or the treatise by Rufus (note 87) have yet to be investigated.

[92] There is little need to repeat the well-known fact of the exceedingly wide-spread use of wine in the ruling circles of the Islamic East precisely at the time of Avicenna, and of the ubiquitous wine-drinking motif in Persian poetry. See, most succinctly, Ehsan Yarshater, "The Theme of Wine-Drinking and the Concept of the Beloved in Early Persian Poetry," *SI* 13 (1960) 43–53.

[93] Edward W. West, *Pahlavi Texts*, Part III [The Sacred Books of the East 24], Oxford: Clarendon Press, 1885, pp. 47–48; emphasis added. For the work see West's introduction and, more recently, J.C. Tavadia, *Die Mittelpersische Sprache und Literatur der Zarathustrier*, Leipzig: O. Harrassowitz, 1956, pp. 98–101. On this subject in general see B.M. Gai, "Wine in the Orient and Its Prohibition," *Indo-Iranica* 9.iii (1956) 31–33.

[94] There is a close correspondence between the contents of this passage and the treatise of Rufus; particularly significant is the mention of the "vital fire," the Greek *emphyton thermon* (*al-ḥarāra al-ġarīziyya*). See Ullmann "Rufus" 33, and especially note 47.

in which decisions had to be made or measures taken.[95] It is thus no coincidence that many inhabitants of the Persian provinces of the ʿAbbāsid Empire followed the Ḥanafī legal rite, which allowed the consumption of *nabīḏ*. This is dramatically confirmed by the report in the *Depository of Wisdom Literature* about Abū-Sulaymān as-Sijistānī himself:

> Although drinking wine (*šarāb*) is a controversial subject, he would partake of it on the grounds that he belonged to the Ḥanafī rite.[96] (L24)

The legal question of the permissibility of this practice was discussed not only by jurists but also by philosophers; Tawḥīdī reports how ʿĀmirī used to hold forth on the subject in philosophical terms.[97] By drinking wine Avicenna was thus engaging in a practice which was perfectly ordinary in his cultural, religious, and scientific milieu and which normally would not have merited special mention. The reason he does mention it is his desire to point to an aspect of it generally left unappreciated, its specific pharmacological use in the epistemological process.

E. *Independent Verification: taḥqīq and Related Concepts*

The various methods of acquiring knowledge described above are all complementary aspects of the same process, whose core is the rational soul's
contact with the active intellect, or Guessing and hitting upon the middle 188
term. When the soul is powerful enough and pure enough, Correct Guessing is automatic; otherwise there is need for Thinking, which is guided by the rules of logic. Prayer enables the philosopher to purify his soul and abstract himself from worldly preoccupations and thus render his intellect apt to Guess Correctly. When the body is asleep, worldly distractions are naturally diminished and, given the purity and strength of the soul and the balanced temperament of the constitution, contact of the rational soul with the souls of the celestial spheres is facilitated and takes the form of veridical dreams. Wine, finally, may be taken to assist materially this process by balancing the temperament and strengthening the intellectual power.

The Autobiography is the record of Avicenna's acquisition of knowledge in this fashion. It also contains *in nuce* the implications which such an epistemology had for Avicenna's conception of the relation of his philosophy

---

95 Ullmann "Rufus" 35, par. 22. Rufus is, of course, deriving his information from Herodotus (I.133), but Herodotus was not known in Arabic whereas Rufus was.

96 *Ṣiwān al-ḥikma* 2850–2851 Dunlop. Cf. Kraemer 123–124.

97 See the references in Rowson 5 and 19.

(Knowledge) to that of others. Three issues which he touches upon have a wider significance for his entire philosophical work.

i) *taḥqīq*/*taḥaqquq*; *taḥṣīl*; *istinbāṭ*. Acquiring knowledge in the fashion described above means establishing certain facts as absolutely true. This is because they have been verified not through the statements of an authority—whether a philosophical school or individual—but through detailed logical analysis and demonstration that includes the middle terms and hence reflects the syllogistic structure of the intelligible world. This process Avicenna called "Verification" (*taḥqīq*), "Ascertainment" (*taḥaqquq*), or "Validation" (i.e., Determination of Validity, *taḥṣīl*), and it centers around the Discovery of the middle term, what Avicenna consistently calls *istinbāṭ*, perhaps reflecting the Greek *heuresis*, as in the texts cited above in Section 2 on *ḥads*. The general understanding of *taḥqīq* along these lines was common in the theological discourse of Avicenna's times, in which *ḥaqqaqa* came to mean "to know validly," i.e., after an act of rational verification.[98] Avicenna appropriated this meaning and lent it precision by using it to refer to Verification after the process described above.

Avicenna also lent amplitude to the term *taḥṣīl* by understanding it to include the correction not only of logical inconsistencies in an argument but also of historical anachronisms. In other words, transmitted philosophical texts contain imperfections that are due not only to faults in the logical anal-
189 ysis but also to the historical context in which they were written. Determining their Validity thus includes also eliminating their time-bound fallacies (see T13, § 7 and L57, § 4). A scholar who acquires philosophical knowledge in this fashion, after Verifying it and Determining its Validity, is a *muḥaṣṣil*, a term which Avicenna uses to describe the most accomplished philosophers in the Aristotelian tradition, and in particular Alexander of Aphrodisias.[99]

In the Autobiography, Avicenna draws attention to his independent Verification of the truth, to his *taḥqīq*, in the presentation both of the details of

---

98 See the references in Richard M. Frank, "Moral Obligation in Classical Muslim Theology," *The Journal of Religious Ethics* 11 (1983) 217n14 (repr. in his *Texts and Studies III*, no. III): "What the author [al-Anṣārī] means here by 'to know validly' (*taḥqīqan*) is that the believer appropriates his belief and acquiesces to God's commands in an act of rationally-grounded conviction, not merely out of social conformity or the like."

99 See *Najāt* 35.5–6/40.10–11: "Among the later scholars who Determined the Validity [of philosophical knowledge], Alexander is the one who accomplished this the most" (*wa-minhum al-Iskandar wa-ʿiddatun mina l-muḥaṣṣilīna mina l-mutaʾaḫḫirīna mimman huwa ašadduhum taḥṣīlan*). Cf. Shehaby 7, and see note l (lower case L) to W1, above, for the meaning of *taḥṣīl*.

his studies and of their results. In the former case, there is a sharp distinction, in his account of his study of the philosophical sciences, between what he says he studied with Nātilī and what he learned by himself: while he is most meticulous in providing not only the *titles* of the books he read with his teacher but also the *chapters* of these books (see the tabulation in Section 1, above), he is general to the extreme when he talks about the subjects he studied by himself: "Then I began to study the books [of the Organon] *by myself* and consult the commentaries until I had mastered logic" (T3, § 5); "I occupied myself *on my own* with Determining the Validity of books on Physics and Theology, both their essential parts and commentaries" (T3, § 6, emphasis added). Such variation in bibliographic detail is certainly not accidental. It can only bespeak a concern on Avicenna's part to emphasize precisely *how little* of the philosophical sciences he learned on authority from a teacher and how much he acquired by independent Verification because of his personal predisposition.

As a result of this process of learning Avicenna is able to claim, twice in the Autobiography, that he had added nothing new to the knowledge of the philosophical sciences which he had acquired during his early studies (T3, §§ 8 end, 11). This is a natural implication of learning something through its Verification. The knowledge so acquired is perfect and complete because the Fundamental Principles (*uṣūl*) of a subject have been learned along with their causes, i.e., the middle terms, which provide intellectual certainty (cf. L7, § 3 end). Once such a state of knowledge about certain things has been reached, there is nothing that can be added to it. *It is the highest form in which Knowledge can be acquired.* Avicenna expresses this fact clearly in his letter to the anonymous disciple (Bahmanyār), written toward the end of his life (T11, § 8, emphasis added):

> With regard to matters upon which I have spent great effort, I have come to know things which *I have Verified and cannot be improved*, except that they
> are few. What I neither know nor have a way of knowing, on the other hand, 190
> is much indeed, but sometimes I have no hopes that about what I do not know I will ever come into possession of *new knowledge which I have not already achieved* by the assiduous research I have been engaged in, despite the fact that my dedication to the search for truth is unmatched. … [God] has granted me an *incessant certainty about Fundamental Principles* [*uṣūl*] which the seeker of salvation must without fail know, and a wide-ranging competence in subsequent areas.

In the Autobiography, therefore, Avicenna means that he added nothing new to whatever Fundamental Principles of philosophy he learned through Correct Guessing and study, i.e., to his knowledge of the structure of reality as contained in the active intellect and comprising Knowledge, not that he did not acquire, first, any additional knowledge about derivative, or non-essential, sciences, and second, a more profound and elaborate knowledge of the fundamental sciences.

This is clear, in the first place, from what he considers non-essential sciences in the Autobiography: the Islamic sciences (*tafsīr*, *ḥadīṯ*, *fiqh*), about which, as we saw in Section 1, he does not provide any information, and medicine, one of the "applied" philosophical sciences (according to Abū-Sahl's representative classification), which he says "is not one of the difficult sciences" (T3, § 7). These sciences are "easy" or not part of philosophical Knowledge because they do not offer or contain any philosophical Fundamental Principles which need to be Verified through demonstration;[100] a good memory, Avicenna seems to imply, is all that is required to learn them. Similarly, it is also clear from what we know about his later career that Avicenna did not mean to include these non-essential sciences among those about which he said he never learned anything new. Jūzjānī reports in the Biography that Avicenna did, in fact, study Arabic language and lexicography intensely for a period of three years later in his life, and that these studies culminated in his writing an Arabic lexicon or glossary entitled *The Language of the Arabs*;[101] that he improved his knowledge of medicine with experiments (Biography 72–74 Gohlman); and that he studied astronomy further and invented new instruments.[102] Avicenna himself says that he
191 wrote the Music part of *The Cure* "in a manner which was disclosed to [him] after long research and detailed theoretical analysis" (T9, § 5C).

Second, it is possible to gain a deeper understanding of the principles contained in the fundamental sciences by continuous study; this does not mean, however, that anything new has been added to the principles that have been Verified from the very beginning. Avicenna expresses this in the Autobiography when he says that at that time his understanding was more mature (T3, § 11)). How a more mature grasp of these principles comes about is described in the Introduction to *The Easterners* (T8, §§ 5,6):

---

100 In his own classification of the sciences, Avicenna explicitly calls these sciences "derivative," or "corollary" (*furūʿ*). See his *Aqsām al-ḥikma* (GS 1) in *Tisʿ Rasāʾil* 71.

101 Biography 68–72 Gohlman. The word *luġa* which occurs numerous times in this report clearly refers to lexicography (as Ullmann remarks in his review, 149), and not to "philology" (Arberry *Theology*, Gohlman), or "Grammatik" (Kraus "Biographie"). The extant fragments of this work (GL 17, ed. by Yarshater 1–31) leave no doubt: it is partly a dictionary of synonyms and partly a glossary of terms relating to Islamic religion and religious sects. These fragments ought to be compared with Abū-Ḥātim ar-Rāzī's *K. az-Zīna*.

102 Biography 80 Gohlman. See *GAS* VI,276 ff., and the references to Wiedemann's works.

> With regard to what was disclosed to us from the moment when we first applied ourselves to this field, we would expressly reconsider our position and examine anew whatever we thought repeatedly demanded closer scrutiny because an opinion was confusing to us and doubt crept in our beliefs, and we said "perhaps" and "maybe." But you, our friends, know what our position was at the beginning, at the end, and during the time between our first statement [on these matters] and the second. If we find this [to be] our case, then we should all the more trust in most of what we determined, judged, and emended, especially with regard to matters which are the greatest purposes and the ultimate goals which we have considered and reconsidered hundreds of times.

The "greatest purposes and ultimate goals" are the basic principles of the fundamental sciences, and especially what Avicenna was to call "the fruit" of Physics and Metaphysics, namely, as we shall discuss below, the theory of the Metaphysics of the Rational Soul. An example of this process of maturation in Avicenna's thoughts about a "greatest purpose" was provided in Section 2 in the discussion of his theory of *ḥads*, which he truly reconsidered numerous times.

ii) *taqlīd; taʿaṣṣub*. Closely related to and directly implied by the concept of *taḥqīq* are these two terms. If a person acquires knowledge through independent Verification, then obviously he is not Following Authority uncritically (*taqlīd*), i.e., without investigating reasons, and even less is he Adhering to this authority in a Partisan spirit and obstinately (*taʿaṣṣub*), i.e., despite manifest indications to the contrary.[103] Avicenna adopts these two concepts, 192
widespread in Islamic culture, and adds to the meaning of *taqlīd* a nuance that reflects his own interests. Not only does a philosopher that Verifies knowledge independently not accept it on Authority from *a person*, but he does not accept it wholesale even from the highest authority, *the active intellect*. Instead, he receives it from the active intellect in an order which

---

[103] These two concepts are widely used in Islamic culture. See, for example, J. Schacht's and N. Calder's articles "Taḳlīd" in *EI*[1] and *EI*[2], respectively, and A. Bausani, "Some Considerations on Three Problems of the Anti-Aristotelian Controversy between al-Bīrūnī and Ibn Sīnā," *Akten des VII. Kongresses für Arabistik und Islamwissenschaft*, Göttingen 1976, 78n8. A good example of the meaning of the latter concept as "Partisan Adherence to a school of thought or authority despite manifest indications to the contrary" is the following. The author of the *Ṣiwān al-ḥikma* (95–96 Dunlop) says that Ḥunayn ibn-Isḥāq "went too far in the Partisan Adherence he exhibited toward Galen's book on logic" (*fa-innahu aẓhara li-hāḏā l-kitābi taʿaṣṣuban ʿaẓīman tajāwaza fīhi l-ḥadd*) because all other logicians disparaged it. See also Goichon "Philosophie" 33 and note 38.

includes the middle terms of the syllogisms, i.e., the explanatory causes. This is what Avicenna means by non-Authoritative imprinting in *The Salvation*:

> ... The forms of all things contained in the active intellect are imprinted on him either at once or nearly so. This imprinting is not an uncritical reception [of the forms] merely on Authority [*irtisāman lā taqlīdiyyan*], but rather occurs in an order which includes the middle terms: for beliefs accepted on Authority concerning those things which are known only through their causes possess no intellectual certainty. [L7, § 3]

This is the reason why in the opening invocation of *Pointers and Reminders* he asks God "for inspiration with the truth *through its Verification*" (T10, § 1). The need for *personal* Verification and rational understanding beyond all Authority is paramount.

The Autobiography again provides numerous illustrations of Avicenna's aversion to *taqlīd* and *taʿaṣṣub*, and none more poignant (and ironically, more misunderstood) than his account of the Ismāʿīlī connections of his family. With regard to this notorious incident, it must be borne in mind that at the time Avicenna was writing the Autobiography, he was under no detectable obligation to mention the Ismāʿīlī doctrines taught in his house, or at least to mention them in the detailed way in which he did, and *then* to reject them. If he was an Ismāʿīlī, or had such inclinations, and wished to publicize the fact, he would not have expressly rejected their doctrines. If he was an Ismāʿīlī and wished to write an apology defending himself against charges of heterodoxy—charges of this nature which, as far as we know, were never made in his lifetime—he could have omitted the incident altogether; or, more to the point, he would not have drawn a cozy picture of his father *and* brother (notice the implicating of his brother, who even after the death of the father was moving in the same circles as Avicenna, since the latter wrote at least one work, *The Guidance* [*al-Hidāya*] apparently for him) having leisurely talks, manifestly without any secrecy, about the Ismāʿīlī doctrine of the soul and the intellect.[104] Avicenna was thus not an Ismāʿīlī, and he recounted these meetings to indicate that he disapproved at an early age of the way in which *they* (i.e., the Ismāʿīlīs;
193 the emphasis is in the Arabic) presented the theory of the soul and the intellect. The obvious implication is that the way in which he came to study it (by himself) and write about it is better. Another implication, quite sig-

[104] A very appropriate description of the atmosphere at these family meetings is that given by F. Rosenthal, "Autobiographie" 21: "ein anregendes Vaterhaus," "a stimulating home."

nificant in view of the importance attached in Arabic autobiographies and biographies to the intellectual associations of a scholar, is that Avicenna, in his very first encounter with an established speculative tradition and its instruction by *Authorized teachers* (the Egyptian proselytizer), exhibited a critical stand and independence of mind, i.e., he rejected *taqlīd* and *taʿaṣṣub*.

This independence is further emphasized, as we saw above, in the particular way in which he describes his philosophical studies: his unnecessarily disparaging remarks about the only teacher of philosophy he mentions, Nātilī; his pains—uncommon in the genre of Arabic autobiography—to record precisely how little he studied with him and how much by himself;[105] his singular failure to mention the names, if not of any teacher, then at least of the authors of the books he studied (with the only exception of Fārābī); and most importantly, his meticulous delineation of his methods of study on his way to truth, with references not only to Correct Guessing and logic, but also to dreams, prayer, and wine. All this betrays a concern and bespeaks a purpose to disclaim discipleship in any philosophical school and to direct attention to his autonomous Verification of matters that ought to be held true by all mankind. If he says in the Introduction to *The Easterners* that the Aristotelian tradition is most worthy of Adherence in a Partisan spirit (T8, §3), this is because, as we saw above, the teachings of this tradition most closely reflect the intelligible structure of the universe, which Avicenna Verified independently.

iii) *inṣāf*. The preceding considerations lead directly into the final implication which Avicenna's theory of *ḥads* had for his general philosophical orientation. If a person neither follows Authority uncritically nor Adheres to a set of doctrines in a Partisan spirit, but has instead acquired absolute Knowledge through independent Verification, then he is in a position to ascertain the degree of attainment of other philosophers precisely because he has an objective and absolute criterion wherewith to judge. This explains his statement upon completion of his "graduate" studies in the library of the Sāmānid ruler's physicians: "I read those books [of the ancients], mastered their teachings, and realized how far each man had advanced in his

105 There is no record that Avicenna studied medicine with him, as he did, apparently, with Abū-Sahl al-Masīḥī and Abū-Manṣūr al-Qumrī (T3, §7 and note 20, and above, Chapter 3.1, note 3), but he certainly, and tacitly, used Nātilī's revision of Dioscurides in his *Canon of Medicine*, as Ullmann *Dioskurides* 322–324 demonstrated.

science" (T3, §10). This is, again, no mere "intellectual arrogance,"[106] but fully consistent with the perspective of the Autobiography. Realizing the degree of others' attainments implies judging, and judgment can only be
194 properly passed by somebody impartial, like Avicenna, whose independent Verification of truth gives him the licence to judge. This attitude of Avicenna is also reflected in a report by Jūzjānī in the Biography (68.2–6 Gohlman):

> One of the remarkable things about the Master was that for the twenty-five years that I was his companion and servant, I never saw him, when he came across a new book, examine it from beginning to end; instead he would go directly to its difficult passages and complicated problems, look at what its author said about them, seek to ascertain the level which he had reached in the Philosophical Sciences and his degree of understanding. (L25)

The tendency to pass impartial judgment (*inṣāf*) on the basis of absolute Knowledge was exhibited by Avicenna also in writing. It formed the subject of his *Fair Judgment* (W10), and possibly also of the earlier *The Available and the Valid* (W3), works which aimed to measure the history of philosophical ideas against the yardstick of "the forms of all things contained in the active intellect" (L7, §3) as Correctly Guessed by Avicenna.

4. The Purpose and Date of the Autobiography

An autobiography is always a tendentious document, to be read only after the proper corrective measures against the slant of the author's perspective have been taken. By this I simply wish to draw attention to the fact, frequently overlooked (in historical, if not always in literary criticism), that autobiographies by their very nature reflect the author's perspective on himself and on his work *at a given moment in his career* and suggest the light in which the author wishes his life and work to be seen by his immediate posterity. I say immediate posterity because an author of an autobiography can only address and project the intended perspective to his contemporary and younger generations, whose thought patterns he knows and shares, and according to whose sensibilities he molds, consciously or unconsciously, his account. He has no control over the way in which later generations, in time as well as in place, will receive his account because with them he will have lost the common ground (cultural, semantic, semeiotic) that makes spontaneous communication at a certain expository level both viable and

[106] A view most explicitly expressed by Wickens "Aspects" 51.

intelligible. The reception of his work will be determined by critical sensibilities obtaining at the later time, not by his own, which shaped it in the first place. This is the major reason for the long series of misunderstandings in the history of literary interpretation in general, and of the interpretation of Avicenna's Autobiography in particular.

To these general observations regarding the analysis of an autobiography should be added the consideration of the particular tradition in which each was written. Pre-modern Arabic autobiography was predominantly of a factual nature, frequently rivaling the aridity and laconism of a *curricu-* 195
lum vitae. The main information imparted consisted of details about origins, early studies, names of teachers, travels, encounters with politicians and scholars, bibliography. This would tend to imply that in medieval Islamic culture, knowledge of a person's origins, teachers, and associates was considered *prima facie* sufficient to define completely that person. Autobiographies provided precisely that information, but—and this is endemic to the genre—with total discretion on the author's part with regard to its selection and quantity, the material that individuated it.[107]

Avicenna's account follows closely the traditional pattern of Arabic autobiography in providing succinct information about his origins, studies, and travels, and has by and large been received as such by scholarship, medieval and modern alike. The assessment first made by Ibn-Abī-Uṣaybiʿa (13th century) has been adopted, whether tacitly or explicitly, by both Muslim and Western scholars:

> Even though Avicenna is too famous to be mentioned [in a book on the biographies of physicians] and his virtues too manifest to be written down, he has nevertheless mentioned his personal circumstances and described his own life in a way that relieves others of describing it again. (II,1 Müller)
>
> (L26)

Such an assessment has caused the Autobiography to be received as if it were a mere information sheet and as if this, its ostensible, purpose coincided with and completely exhausted its real purpose.[108] Information it certainly

[107] Rosenthal "Autobiographie" 11, 19; and, with greater detail and nuance, Dwight F. Reynolds et al., *Interpreting the Self. Autobiography in the Arabic Literary Tradition*, Berkeley / Los Angeles: University of California Press, 2001, 241–249.

[108] In addition to reading the Autobiography merely as a *curriculum vitae*, scholars, both medieval and modern, added interpretations and inferences peculiar to their taste and times, and hence irrelevant but also misleading. For example, Bayhaqī (d. 565/1169–1170) infers from the Ismāʿīlī connection of Avicenna's father that he, Avicenna, "would occasionally study the *Rasāʾil Iḫwān aṣ-Ṣafāʾ*" (*Tatimma* 40.1–2/53.1), something which is decidedly *not* what

does provide, but how much information it provides, in which way and from what perspective, and which period of Avicenna's life this perspective reflects, are all essential questions that have never been asked.

The independently unverifiable nature of most of the facts offered in the Autobiography presents a difficulty that may not be resolved, although it can be procedurally obviated by assuming Avicenna not to have falsified or misrepresented facts but rather to have omitted some of them and cast the rest in a light consonant with his purpose.[109] In the preceding sections of
196 this chapter we have identified several such omissions and aspects of his purpose. Avicenna seems to have omitted or not to have adequately mentioned all the subjects he studied because he wished to concentrate only on the philosophical sciences which provide fundamental intellectual principles; he also apparently did not mention the names of at least his teachers in medicine in order better to project the image of an autodidact (T3, § 7 and note 18). His purpose in so doing was to indicate that he did not belong *by training* to any school of thought and that he was accordingly not beholden by a sense of loyalty or conditioning to defending it and perpetuating its traditions. What he learned, the implication is, was absolute Knowledge which, given the formal nature of the presentation of the course of his studies, should be studied in the order in which the philosophical sciences are classified in the Aristotelian tradition. The purpose, finally, of Avicenna's insistence on having learned most of these sciences by himself, of the numerous seemingly conceited statements enumerated above in Section 2, and of the references to his various methods of study, is to illustrate his central epistemological theory. At the same time that he is informing the reader about his studies in philosophy and fulfilling the requirements of the genre of autobiography (or, differently stated, in the guise of fulfilling the requirements of the genre), he is providing a concrete illustration for his theory of the twin methods of acquiring knowledge, Correct Guessing and study, with all the ancillary processes.

Another aspect of Avicenna's perspective on himself, which is complementary to the description of his purpose just outlined, is the striking resemblance which the Autobiography bears to the biography of Aristotle. Arist-

---

Avicenna says (see Gutas "*Maḏhab*" 323–324); Arberry "Avicenna" 17 deduces from Avicenna's teaching himself a "complete lack of qualified teachers" in Buḫārā at his time [!], something which is again quite far from the truth.

109 This assumption underlies the two critical studies of the Autobiography, Sellheim's review of Ergin, and Lüling's "Ein anderer Avicenna."

otle's biography was known in Arabic primarily in two versions: a translation of the biography of Ptolemy al-Ġarīb (P), and a tendentious account deriving from Greek philosophical circles in late antique Alexandria (A).[110] The following elements to be found in these two biographies are also present in Avicenna's Autobiography:

Aristotle	*Avicenna*	
Detailed information about parents and early life; his father was in the employ of King Amyntas. (P)	Detailed information about parents and early life; his father was in the employ of Prince Nūḥ ibn-Manṣūr.	
Father takes him to Athens, the capital, to study, at the age of eight. (A) (Note precise age.)	Father takes him to Buḫārā, the capital, to study, and he excels by the age of ten. (Note precise age.)	
Studies poetry, grammar, and rhetoric. (A)	Studies Qur'ān and literature.	
Refutes at this early age the Epicurean attacks on these subjects. (A)	Rejects at this early age the doctrines of the Ismāʿīlīs on the soul and the intellect.	197
After these preliminary subjects, he studies ethics, politics, mathematics, physics, metaphysics with Plato. (A)	After these preliminary subjects he studies logic, mathematics, physics, metaphysics by himself.	
Starts the study of these subjects at seventeen. (A) (Note precise age.)	Finishes the study of these subjects at eighteen. (Note precise age.)	
Plato calls him "the intellect."[111]	(He learns very fast because of his aptitude for Correct Guessing.)	
After Plato's death, travels to various places and works with various patrons: Assos, Mytilene, Macedonia, Athens, Chalcis. (P)	After his father's death, travels to various places and works with various patrons (names given in the Autobiography).	
Leaves Athens for Chalcis because of persecution, where he dies. (P)	Travels from place to place because "necessity led" him; persecution implied in the final poem of the Autobiography and substantiated in the Biography.	

110 For references and details see Gutas "Lives;" cf. L28 below.

111 Although this saying is neither in the *Ṣiwān al-ḥikma* version (A) of Aristotle's biographer nor in the extant form of Ptolemy's text, it was widely available in Arabic. Mubaššir, for example, incorporates it into his account: *Muḫtār al-ḥikam* 180.13–16 Badawī. See Gutas "Lives of Aristotle" 26, 28.

The two lives may have indeed been objectively parallel, but the similarities in presentation can hardly have been accidental. This becomes even clearer when Avicenna's precocity is compared with that of Aristotle in a well-known story in Ḥunayn ibn-Isḥāq's report about the gatherings of the philosophers for the purpose of instructing the Greek princes.[112] The report ends by stating the curriculum the students followed:

> Wise sayings, together with the Greek script, is the first thing that the philosopher teaches his pupil during the first year of instruction. After that he lets him go on to grammar and poetry and then gradually to law, arithmetic, geometry, astronomy, medicine and music. After that he studies logic and finally philosophy, namely the sciences of the heavenly phenomena. These are ten sciences which the pupil learns in ten years.[113] (L27)

With the exception of music, which Avicenna says he studied in order to write *The Cure* (T9, § 5C), the subjects enumerated in this passage are the *only* subjects Avicenna mentions by name as having studied. Conversely, the only subject in Avicenna's account that is added to this curriculum is, for obvious reasons, the Qur'ān.

The perspective of the Autobiography, therefore, is that of a philosopher
198 belonging to no school tradition, who established truth on his own by means of his Correct Guessing, equaling Aristotle in this regard, if not surpassing him, and whose independent Verification of the truth, which reproduces for the most part the philosophical sciences as classified originally by Aristotle, puts him in a position both to teach this more accurate version of the truth and to judge the philosophical attainments of others.

The question now remains: when did Avicenna have this perspective, i.e., when did he dictate his autobiography to Jūzjānī? The immediate reaction is to assume that he did so at the time in his life when the Autobiography breaks off, that is, soon after he met Jūzjānī in 1013.[114] The following considerations, however, make it clear that it was much later. The Autobiography has

112 See Gutas "Lives" 30–31.

113 Translation in Rosenthal *Classical Heritage* 73.

114 See, for example, Weisweiler 53, 57. Despite his original and perceptive—if not always acceptable—analysis, Lüling falls into this trap because, I assume, he unconsciously took the Autobiography to have been written in 1013. The reason he gives for Avicenna's concealing his motives for his travels is that he was a supporter of the last Sāmānid, al-Muntaṣir, and he found it inexpedient to publicize this support after the latter's fall, especially since al-Muntaṣir had attempted to install himself, with the help of Qābūs, in Rayy, where Avicenna later found refuge for a while. This assumes that the Autobiography was written at the time when it ends; for how important could it have been to conceal these motives much later when Avicenna was in Iṣfahān, and Rayy was no longer under the control of the Būyids?

the same purpose and perspective as some later autobiographical notes of Avicenna, notably in his Introduction to *The Easterners* (T8), in the *Philosophy for ʿAlāʾ-ad-Dawla* (T2), and in his Letter to Kiyā (T12). The same account of his early development and studies is given in *The Easterners* and the Autobiography, and the same claim is made in both that his philosophical position had not changed since the completion of his studies in his teens; the same claim to judging the degree of each philosopher's attainments is made in the Autobiography and in the Letter to Kiyā (in the latter the judgment took the form of a book, *Fair Judgment*), and the same and only philosopher, Fārābī, is singled out in both for praise as his only philosophical mentor. His independent Verification of the truth by means of Guessing Correctly, on the basis of which he can justify writing a book like *The Easterners*, is clearly alluded to in the *Philosophy for ʿAlāʾ-ad-Dawla* and plainly illustrated in the Autobiography; and it is the same basis that enables him to write about philosophy "as it is naturally [perceived]" (T9, § 4) without regard for predecessors, like Aristotle. Now these considerations clearly indicate that there is a congruence of themes and attitudes between these late works and the Autobiography, a congruence which, as Marmura rightly observes,[115] does not, by itself, *prove* temporal proximity. But if they are valid as a basis for argument—and there is no other basis that really presents itself if we wish at all to date the Autobiography—then it appears most likely that the Autobiography is contemporary with these works, written after the completion of *The Cure* and *The Salvation*, from *The Easterners* onwards, during the middle to late period of Avicenna's residence in Iṣfahān (1024–1037), that is, during the last decade of his life. It shares their concerns and tries to justify, or explain, them from a different approach. The Autobiography is thus both an apologia for and a protreptic to philosophy—Avicenna's philosophy.

115 Marmura "Avicenna's Thought" 335–336.

AVICENNA'S CONCEPTION OF THE HISTORY OF PHILOSOPHY

With modifications dictated by his purpose at every instance, Avicenna adhered to the classification of the sciences in the Aristotelian tradition in all his works. This applies both to his structuring of the polythematic philosophical summae and to his treatment of the division of the sciences itself, whether independently (as in *The Divisions of Philosophy*, *Aqsām al-ḥikma*, GS 1) or in other contexts.[1] This observation in itself is nothing new or particularly revealing: following the division of philosophy current in the Aristotelian tradition was the rule rather than the exception for Muslim scholars. What is noteworthy, rather, is the following: the elaborate classificatory schema of Alexandrian scholars in late antiquity presented an outline of the entire Aristotelian corpus, or, for that matter, of all philosophy; with the benefit of historical hindsight we can now see that by the same token it also presented a blueprint, or a table of contents, as it were, for a work that *would encompass* all philosophy. The Alexandrians and the tradition they had been reared in had noticed the systematic nature of Aristotle's thought. As stated by Jonathan Barnes (p. xii),

> we may allow that Aristotle's philosophy fails actually to present a grand system, without giving up the conviction that it is potentially and in design systematic; if the Aristotelian corpus is not, as it stands, an Encyclopaedia of Unified Science, it nevertheless forms—or was intended to form—the basis for such a large project. There are hints enough, scattered throughout Aristotle's writings, to show that he had a general conception of the range and classification of human knowledge, and that he saw his own voluminous researches in the light of that conception. And there are hints, less frequent but no less clear, that the theory of the *Posterior Analytics* was meant to provide the proper formal account and presentation of the finished system. In a perfect Aristotelian world, the material gathered in the corpus will be systematically presented; and the logical structure of the system will follow the pattern of the *Posterior Analytics*.

[1] As in the *Compendium on the Soul* (T1), for example, or in the Eisagoge part of *The Cure*, *Madḫal* 12–16 Anawati et al., or at the beginning of the Physics part of *Elements of Philosophy* (*ʿUyūn al-ḥikma*), etc.

But although the Alexandrians brought out the outline of the "perfect Aristotelian world," they were blind to the possibilities of the schema they had created, as were the Arabic philosophers to the potential of the system
200 they had adopted: for all of them each discrete item of the schema corresponded to a work by Aristotle which was the last word on the subject, admitting only of explicative commentaries in which differing viewpoints might be expressed through circumlocutions.[2]

It was only Avicenna, close to five centuries after the schema had been fully developed, who actualized the latent "summa" in the classification of the sciences and created a coherent account of human knowledge, an "Encyclopaedia of Unified Science," as called by Barnes, and indeed on the very basis of the *Posterior Analytics*. This revolutionary break with tradition on the part of Avicenna cannot be explained in a facile way by referring to his genius: he was preceded by no lesser philosophical minds in Islamic civilization. The reason rather ought to be sought in his conception of the history of philosophy in general and of the place of Aristotle and his commentators in it in particular; this will in turn facilitate the subsequent analysis (in Chapter 7) of Avicenna's attitude and approach to the Aristotelian tradition as well as his view of his own role in this historical process.

Avicenna did not develop his concept of the history of philosophy through a mere reading of the philosophers themselves; in this he was profoundly influenced by traditional views prevailing in the literature available to him. In the Neoplatonic school of Alexandria during the two centuries prior to the Muslim conquest, classroom discussions in the course on the prolegomena to Aristotle frequently centered on the key question of the degree to which Aristotle's philosophy was identical with Plato's, and on its corollary, the original contributions to philosophy by Aristotle.[3] These

---

[2] It is true that, as H.J. Blumenthal suggested, the later Greek commentators were "true to the aim of making Aristotle self-consistent through a knowledge of the whole of his philosophy" ("Neoplatonic Elements in the *De Anima* Commentaries," *Phronesis* 21 [1976] 71), but they accomplished their task through commentary on individual Aristotelian passages, and not through comprehensive exhibitions of a systematic nature and independently of the Aristotelian texts, like Avicenna. Philoponus, for example, presented himself in the preface to the *De anima* commentary as the defender of the true Aristotelian doctrine about the separability of the rational soul (*CAG* XV, 10–12 Hayduck) despite the fact that both some ideas which he lists in that passage and his commentary in general deviate significantly from Aristotelian teachings (cf. Blumenthal 70). An instance of the precise way in which Philoponus tacitly revised an Aristotelian text and its meaning on this subject I have examined in "Separability."

[3] Testimonia relating to this question have been collected by Düring 315–336; cf. also his

questions were not asked in a historical context about the development of philosophical ideas but in a context of introducing the student to Aristotle's philosophy, and they were preceded and followed by lectures on Aristo- 201
tle's life and works. Their purpose was to compare atemporally Plato and Aristotle and, given that the Alexandrian Neoplatonists had an Aristotelian orientation, glorify Aristotle. The answers that were given to these questions varied in detail and emphasis, and occasionally in substance: in the course of the last two centuries of Alexandrian scholarship a tendency is observed toward greater glorification of Aristotle and a corresponding minimization of Plato's achievements. This tendency is clearly reflected in the biographies of Aristotle used in classroom instruction, and is best illustrated by comparing two of them: the *Vita Marciana* (VM), which was in use in the school of Alexandria in the fifth century, and the so-called *Vita Vulgata* (VV), which was in use in the middle of the sixth century.[4]

VM	*VV*
I. (§ 28) We saw that Aristotle is a Platonist (*platonizein*) even where he contradicts Plato, for it is Plato who says that he cares little for Socrates but much for truth [*Phaedo* 91c]. …	
(§ 29) But perhaps Aristotle does not even fight against Plato's doctrines but only	(§ 8) Aristotle does not contradict Plato pure and simple, but those who have not understood Plato's doctrines. But even if he does contradict Plato himself, there is nothing improper (*atopon*) in that

notes on the appropriate passages in the *Vita Marciana* on pp. 112–113. The early positions up to the fourth century are discussed by George E. Karamanolis, *Plato and Aristotle in Agreement? Platonists on Aristotle from Antiochus to Porphyry*, Oxford: Oxford University Press, 2006. For an assessment of the later tradition see Lloyd P. Gerson, "The Harmony of Aristotle and Plato according to Neoplatonism," in *Reading Plato in Antiquity*, Harold Tarrant and Dirk Baltzly, eds., London: Duckworth, 2006, 195–221.

[4] The texts of *Vitae Marciana* and *Vulgata* are edited and studied by Düring 94–139. The former was also edited and annotated by Olof Gigon, *Vita Aristotelis Marciana*, Berlin: De Gruyter, 1962. Düring's thesis that these two *Vitae* are epitomes of Ptolemy's *Vita* is incorrect. See Gutas "Lives" 17–18. That the classroom discussions about Aristotle's original contributions to philosophy are reflected in these biographies is amply documented in Düring's Testimonia to his edition, pp. 101–103, §§ 28–30; p. 135, § 26; pp. 112–113.

against those who misunderstood them. …	because here too he follows Plato, (§ 9) for it was Plato who said that one should care more for truth than for anybody else. … (§ 10) Aristotle, then, did just that; and if he overturned what Plato said, here too he acted like him, not wishing to overlook truth. …
II. (§ 35) Aristotle added to philosophy more than what he selected from it. …	(§ 25) In philosophy, Aristotle transcended human standards by having missed nothing in its treatment; but he also fully erected (*katōrthōse*) [the edifice of] all philosophy by having added much to it out of his own acumen.[5]
202 III. (§ 40) Logic is Aristotle's discovery because he separated the methods of syllogisms from the syllogisms themselves (*tōn pragmatōn*).	(§ 26) He made additions to logic by distinguishing the rules from the subject matter (*apo tōn pragmatōn*) and by creating the demonstrative method. For his predecessors (*hoi palai*) knew how to use demonstration but were unable to construct demonstrative syllogisms, just like people who are unable to make shoes but know how to use them.
IV. (§§ 36–39) (Detailed enumeration of individual original contributions by Aristotle to ethics, physics, mathematics, and theology [!].)	(§§ 27–29) (Brief mention of Aristotle's original contribution to physics only. Aristotle did not contribute anything new to theology, though he did not miss anything, either; he did, however, show that divinity is incorporeal and impassive.)

In paragraph (I) above, VM is much more cautious than VV. Although the possibility that Aristotle contradicted Plato is entertained on the grounds of the Platonic dictum that truth should be dearer to one than adherence to a teacher's doctrines, it is quickly substituted by the assumption that Aristotle contradicted in reality only Plato's misinterpreters. The impression conveyed is thus that Aristotle only seemingly contradicted Plato, and that by adhering to Plato's real doctrines he was also adhering to truth. In VV the two parts of the same argument are reversed: it is first stated briefly that Aristotle fought only against Plato's misinterpreters, and then the hypothesis that he contradicted Plato himself is vigorously defended, with particular emphasis laid on truth, and not adherence to a teacher's doctrines, as the goal of philosophical activity. The implication here is that though both Plato

[5] The word for acumen here is *anchinoia*, the word defined by Aristotle as the *eustochia* (*ḥads*) of the middle term (*Post. An.* I.34). See Chapter 3.2.

and Aristotle strove after truth, Aristotle was closer to it since he had to overturn Plato's doctrines in order not to overlook it.

Paragraphs II–IV deal with the question of Aristotle's original contributions to philosophy. Again VM is more subdued and specific, VV more encomiastic and general. The number of specific contributions listed in VM (§ IV) is reduced in VV,[6] and Aristotle's accomplishments, assessed modestly in VM (§ II), are generalized in VV to include *all* philosophy, in a statement 203
that was to become axiomatic in the Arabic tradition: Aristotle erected fully the entire edifice of philosophy.

Paragraph III deserves special attention. It contains the most explicit mention of the claim that Aristotle was the first philosopher to distinguish and formulate the rules of syllogistic thinking. The issue was certainly raised before,[7] but it seems never to have been stated with as much clarity as in the writings of the sixth century Alexandrians, and indeed in terms borrowed from Aristotle himself. For strange as it may sound, it appears that it was Olympiodorus (d. after 565) who first[8] answered the question of Aristotle's original contribution to logic by implicitly referring to Aristotle's epilogue in the *Sophistici Elenchi* (183b16–184b8). This epilogue, of great importance for the history of the history of philosophy, on the one hand clearly states that Aristotle was the first to discover the methods of syllogism in general (184b1–6) and the discipline (*technē*) of dialectic and argumentation in particular (183b1, b35, 184a7–8), and on the other provides a historical blueprint for the way in which knowledge progresses (183b16–184a9): first, the particulars of a science are applied in practice without knowledge of its rules and principles; second, somebody discovers the basis of this science, but because the "beginning of anything is the most important and hence the most difficult," little progress is made by that person; future generations, finally, through

---

[6] The statement in VV that Aristotle contributed nothing new to theology (despite the fact that VV proceeds to add almost exactly the same material mentioned as original contributions in VM) is not discussed either by Düring or by Gigon *Vita Aristotelis Marciana* (in second preceding note). In all probability it is to be interpreted against the background of Christian sensibilities, which either were directly responsible for it or indirectly inhibited the compiler of VV from a more explicit statement. On this general issue see L.G. Westerink, *The Greek Commentaries on Plato's Phaedo, Vol. 1: Olympiodorus*, Amsterdam: North-Holland Pub. Co. 1976, 24.

[7] Philoponus (*In An. Pr.*, *CAG* XIII.2, p. 6.14) quotes Themistius who said that though Aristotle did not invent analytics as such, he nevertheless composed the Analytica by "crafting certain rules" (*technōsai kanosi tisi*).

[8] That is, as far as we know on the basis of the extant Alexandrian commentaries on Aristotle.

continuous elaborations (what Avicenna was later to call *tafrīʿ*, Deriving Corollary Principles), grant the discipline "amplitude" (*plēthos*). Aristotle says that he found rhetoric and "practically all the other disciplines" already at the third stage; but he himself claims the credit for advancing the syllogistic discipline from the first to the second stage "after many years of hard work at sedulous researches."

In the prolegomena to Aristotle's logic, and in the context of comparing Plato to Aristotle, Olympiodorus uses Aristotle's epilogue and particularly the cobbler metaphor (*CAG* XII.1, p. 17.37 ff.) to describe Aristotle's original contribution to logic. This passage was then incorporated in VV.

Aristotle's depiction of the progress of knowledge in historical terms in the epilogue of the *Sophistici Elenchi* also seems to have contributed to the development of a stylized conception of the history of philosophy. The (alleged) historical tripartite sequence—practice of a discipline, theory, elaboration—may be behind the introduction of the details about Aris-
204 totle's early education in VM (§ 4) and VV (§ 3), where it is mentioned that Aristotle, "while still young", had a liberal education, studying essentially rhetoric and poetry. I tend to believe that the rationale behind these additions—apart from the understandable desire to have Aristotle reflect in his education school practices contemporary with those of the compilers of the biographies—is the assumption that Aristotle had to reproduce, in his own education, the history of philosophy up to his time in order to be able to develop it further. This tendency is amplified and more visible in what is yet a later version of these *vitae*, preserved only in Arabic and found in the *Depository of Wisdom Literature*.[9] The passage reads as follows:

> When Aristotle became eight years old, his father brought him to Athens[10] and had him associate with the poets, grammarians, and orators that were there, as their student in order to learn from them. Aristotle acquired their knowledge in its entirety in nine years. …[11] When he completed his study of the disciplines of grammar, poetry and rhetoric, he turned to the science of

[9] *Muntaḫab Ṣiwān al-ḥikma* 680–682, 696–698 Dunlop. Mubaššir's *Muḫtār al-ḥikam* presents a parallel text (179–180 Badawī), obviously derived from the *Ṣiwān al-ḥikma*, but the precise relationship among these versions remains to be investigated. See the discussion of this passage in Gutas "Lives" 20–22.

[10] The Arabic translator adds here, "the city that was the gathering place of philosophers and sages."

[11] Here follows the report about Epicurus' attack upon these scholars and Aristotle's defense of them. Cf. Gutas "Lives" 22.

> philosophy[12] and desired to learn it. He became Plato's[13] student exclusively in order to learn from him. At that time he was seventeen years old. (L28)

This brief and necessarily limited survey of late antique Alexandrian conceptions of Aristotle's position in the history of philosophy reveals the following: Aristotle was the philosopher who sought the truth above all else; the syllogistic disciplines before him were practised but their theory was unknown, and it was he who discovered the rules and principles governing them and thereby laid the foundation of logic; Aristotle treated exhaustively all the branches of philosophy and through his own genius and original contributions set it on its feet (*katōrthōse*); and finally, if one were to judge from the elaborate classification of the parts of philosophy developed by the Alexandrian scholars, Aristotle organized philosophy, assigning each part to its proper place.

This picture of Aristotle's achievements and position in the history of
philosophy, most clearly present in the *Vita Vulgata*, was transmitted whole- 205
sale into Arabic. The details of this transmission are far from having been thoroughly studied, but we are informed adequately about its highlights, some of which, of particular relevance for Avicenna, are given below.

A major connecting link between the last generation of Alexandrian scholars and Arabic philosophy is Paul the Persian (fl. mid-6th century), whose works were known in the Syriac tradition and also partly translated into Arabic. In what appears to be the introduction of a treatise on the classification of the parts of Aristotle's philosophy,[14] he says the following:

> Prior to Aristotle, [the parts of] philosophy were dispersed like the rest of the useful things which God created, and with the exploitation of which He entrusted both men's natural disposition and the capacity he gave them for this purpose—[things] like medicaments which, found dispersed in the countryside and the mountains, result in useful medication when collected and combined. In a similar manner Aristotle collected the dispersed parts of philosophy, combined each part with what was conformable to it, and placed it in its [appropriate] place, so that he produced from it a complete course of treatment [*šifā'*] by means of which souls are cured of the diseases of ignorance. (L29)

---

[12] The parallel text in Mubaššir's *Muḫtār* (180.9 Badawī) enumerates the fields: "ethics, politics, physics, mathematics, metaphysics," i.e. the subdivisions of practical and theoretical philosophy.

[13] The Arabic translator adds, "his name means 'the broad one'."

[14] For this work and its transmission see Gutas "Paul the Persian" 233 ff.

The medical metaphor—philosophy is the medicine of souls—goes back to Aristotle himself and was in constant use throughout the history of Greek philosophy. In late antique Alexandrian Aristotelianism it was used as one of the possible definitions of philosophy and is found in the writings of scholars with which Paul was familiar.[15] It is tempting to see in Paul's description of Aristotle's oeuvre as a "course of treatment" (*šifāʾ*) that cures "the diseases of ignorance" the source of Avicenna's title for *The Cure* (*aš-Šifāʾ*). Avicenna says in his Prologue to *The Cure* that he collected the gist of all philosophical knowledge (T9, §1) and arranged it as he saw fit (§2) to produce a compendium which includes Fundamental Principles that "helped dispel the veils of fanciful notions" (§1); and in the actual execution of the work he follows the late antique Alexandrian blueprint of the classification of the parts of philosophy (Chapter 3.1), as did Paul in the rest of his treatise. The point cannot nor need be pressed any further; it is virtually certain, however, that such is the context that determined Avicenna's choice of a title.

The assessments of Aristotle's achievements and position in the history of philosophy which are given in the very popular Graeco-Arabic gnomologia are directly inspired by late antique Alexandrian texts like VV. The follow-
206 ing, probably by the great translator and physician Ḥunayn ibn-Isḥāq, are reformulations in elegant rhyming prose (*sajʿ*).[16] It is to be noted that the first one, intended to extol Plato, does so only by referring to Aristotle:

> Should you wish to see Plato on this august summit [which he occupies]
> and in this position of repute and exalted station,
> then look at his influence upon his disciple, Aristotle,
> for it was the latter who brought together into a whole the parts of philosophy,
> lifted it from its lowly states unto its lofty pinnacles,
> and reaped the fruit that all its custodians had sown.[17]

> Aristotle is the first teacher, the seal of the ancient philosophers,
> and the model of the learned men who followed their path.
> He classified [the parts of] philosophy and established it;
> he improved it and set it down accurately.
> He put logic at the beginning

[15] See Gutas *Wisdom Literature* A7 and the commentary, p. 385, and Py10 and the commentary, pp. 233–234.

[16] Gutas *Wisdom Literature* 216. The reference there to Dunlop is now to his edition of the *Muntakhab Ṣiwān al-ḥikmah*, pp. xvii–xviii.

[17] Gutas *Wisdom Literature* 117; cf. 332–333.

> and prepared a foundation for all of the other sciences.
> He thus became the medium through which the ancient philosophers
> were to benefit the future ones,
> and the means by which later philosophers
> were to procure the benefits of the earlier ones.
> Not only did he not restrict himself to pouring out upon later generations what the earlier ones had captured, but he even added to every kind [of knowledge] many times what they had produced, thereby rendering it more complete and more perfect.[18] (L30)

Similar encomia of Aristotle were common among Arabic authors, and their list could be expanded at will. Particular mention could perhaps be made of Ġazālī's comment, reproducing material that we saw in the *Vitae Marciana* and *Vulgata*, that Aristotle attacked all his predecessors, even Plato, because truth was dearer to him than his teacher.[19] This picture of the early development of philosophy and of Aristotle's achievements and position in the history of philosophy informed the writings of most Arabic authors, and it corresponds particularly closely with Avicenna's Introduction to *The Easterners* (T8, §1).[20]

The next question concerning Avicenna's understanding of the history of philosophy is to determine his view about the attitude which philosophers subsequent to Aristotle adopted, or should have adopted, toward 207
him. The disjunctive particle in the preceding sentence points to the two aspects of the question, one historical and the other procedural. This latter aspect is concerned directly with Avicenna's conception of the philosophical praxis, both in its general orientation (to be discussed in the next chapter), and its specific application (to be discussed in Chapter 8). Here we may look closely at the general background against which developed Avicenna's ideas on method and the philosophical praxis as stated, most comprehensively, in the Introduction to *The Easterners* (T8). In this regard, illuminating as well as fascinating is the debate about methods of inquiry and proper attitude toward authorities by two scholars from Rayy in NW Persia, both active about a century before Avicenna and known to him: the famous

[18] Gutas *Wisdom Literature* 159.

[19] Cited in Ġazālī's *Tahāfot al-falāsifat*, M. Bouyges, ed., Beirut 1927, 40: *Aflāṭun ṣadīq wa-l-ḥaqq ṣadīq wa-lākin al-ḥaqq aṣdaq minhu.*

[20] See also T6, where Avicenna paraphrases Aristotle's crucial epilogue of the *Sophistici Elenchi*. For further examples of Avicenna's understanding of the early history of philosophy along these lines see Booth 124, and Gutas "Paul the Persian" 259n70. For the development of this tendentious history of philosophy see also Gutas "Lives" 34n25.

philosopher and physician Abū-Bakr ar-Rāzī (Rhazes, d. 311/923 or 320/920), and the Ismāʿīlī theologian and missionary, Abū-Ḥātim ar-Rāzī (d. ca. 330/929). The debate is reported in the first person by Abū-Ḥātim in his *Signs of Prophethood* (*Aʿlām an-nubuwwa*) and hence the philosopher Abū-Bakr is made to have the worst of the argument, but it is his views that command our attention here.[21]

> Abū-Ḥātim: Tell me about the Fundamental Principle which you believe, namely your statement that these five—the creator, the soul, matter, space, and time—are pre-existent:[22] is this something on which the ancient philosophers agree or disagree with you?
>
> 1. Abū-Bakr: No, the ancients say various things on this matter, but through much research and theoretical investigation into their Fundamental Principles I have emended [their theories] and derived something which is the irrefutable and inevitable truth.
>
> Abū-Ḥātim: But how could the sagacity of these philosophers display such impotence and their doctrines vary when, by your own claim, they were assiduous scholars who had expended their zeal in philosophical investigations to the point that they mastered [even] the subtle sciences and became authorities in them and models [for others to follow]? [And how] can you claim that you achieved through much investigation into their writings [*rusūm*] and books what they failed to achieve when they are your leaders and you their follower, since you have studied their writings, investigated into their Fundamental Principles, and learned from their books? How is it possible, then, that the subject should be higher than the sovereign, and the led a more accomplished philosopher than the leader?
>
> 2. Abū-Bakr: On this issue I will now state something to you whereby you will
> 208 know that the matter is indeed as I have mentioned, and you will [be able to] recognize the true from the false on this subject. Know that when every succeeding philosopher expends his zeal in philosophical investigations, applies

[21] The text of the debate was first edited by Kraus "Raziana II" 44.4–46.22, and reproduced, with corrections, in his *Razis Opera Philosophica*, Cairo 1939, 300.21–303.19. The entire book was subsequently edited by Ṣalāḥ aṣ-Ṣāwī, *Abū Ḥātim al-Rāzī. Aʿlām al-nubuwwah*, Tehran 1397/1977; the text translated here appears on pp. 10.3–13.16. My translation is based on Kraus's second edition. The few insignificant variants presented in aṣ-Ṣāwī's edition have not been recorded. A freer English translation of the entire passage by G.E. von Grunebaum and M.G.S. Hodgson appeared in G.E. von Grunebaum, "Concept and Function of Reason in Islamic Ethics," *Oriens* 15 (1962) 1–17, at 8–11. There is also a French translation by Fabienne Brion, "Philosophie et Révélation," *Bulletin de Philosophie Médiévale* 28 (1986) 134–162, at 142–145.

[22] For a list of the sources about this theory by Rāzī and its provenance see Mehdi Mohaghegh, "Rāzī's Kitab al-Ilm al-Ilāhi [*sic*] and the Five Eternals," *Abr-Nahrain* 13 (1972–1973) 16–23.

himself with perseverance and assiduity to them, and researches issues that are controversial on account of their subtlety and difficulty,[23] he learns from his predecessors their knowledge, retains it, and supplements it with other things through his sagacity and numerous researches and investigations. This is so because, proficient now in the knowledge of his predecessors, he becomes aware of other useful ideas [*fawā'id*] and learns even more, since research, investigation, and assiduity necessarily result in additional and abundant material.

Abū-Ḥātim: But if what the successor supplements is in disagreement with [the theories of] his predecessors—just as you yourself disagree with your predecessors—then disagreement is not a benefit; on the contrary, disagreement is an evil, it increases blindness and strengthens falsehood, it is destruction and corruption—why, we find that the more you research and investigate the more are your opinions at variance and contradict each other! And when you set as a condition for yourself that the successor achieves what his predecessors did not—just as you claim that you achieved it and [as a result] disagreed with your predecessors—then you will not be safe [from the eventuality] that someone more assiduous than you will come after you, learn what you know and even more, achieve through his sagacity, assiduity, and investigation what you yourself never achieved, and invalidate your conclusions and disagree with your Fundamental Principles—just as you refuted your predecessors and disagreed with their Fundamental Principles when you asserted the pre-existence of your five [principles] and claimed that your predecessors are mistaken if they disagree with you, and just as some of you [philosophers] disagree with others. On the basis of this condition, then, corruption will become permanent in the world, truth will always be absent, and falsehood will be the order of the day. Those who disagree with you arrived at falsehood and strayed from the right course because disagreement [itself leads to] falsehood, and errors [cause] straying. On the basis of this assumption it will follow that you also will arrive at falsehood and stray from the right course since, on the analogy of your statement, your successor will produce a [new] useful idea and hit upon what you missed.

3. Abū-Bakr: This is neither falsehood nor straying from the right course because both the predecessor and the successor are striving in earnest; and when one makes earnest efforts and occupies himself with investigation and research, then he is on his way to truth because souls can become purified of the filth of this world and escape to the next only by means of philosophical investigation. And when one engages in such investigation and achieves something in it—be it even the slightest little bit—then his soul is purified of this filth and saved. If the common people who have caused the perdition of their souls in total ignorance of research had but engaged even in the

[23] "Subtlety and difficulty:" These ideas appear to have been taken from the treatise on *The Principles of the Universe* (*Fī mabādi' al-kull*), translated below, L34, § 3.

slightest philosophical investigation, this would have constituted their deliverance from this filth even if they had achieved very little.

209 Abū-Ḥātim: Didn't you stipulate that philosophical investigation means arriving at the truth and forsaking falsehood?

Abū-Bakr: Yes.

Abū-Ḥātim: And you also claimed that people perish through mutual enmity and disagreement.[24] On the basis of your claim, then, he who engages in philosophical investigation can increase only his [chances of] perdition because you have just affirmed that philosophers hold varying doctrines and that what you believe is in conflict with the views of your predecessors, and you have imposed upon yourself the condition that your successor may disagree both with you and with others. On the basis of this condition, then, the cause of perdition grows stronger day by day and falsehood and straying from the right course are on the rise.

4. Abū-Bakr: I do not consider this as falsehood or straying from the right course because he who is engaged in earnest [philosophical] investigation is the one who is in the right even if he does not reach the goal which I have just described to you, and because souls are purified only through investigation and research. This is all I am saying.

Abū-Ḥātim: Well, if you insist on this assertion and stubbornly refuse [to accept] the truth, then tell me what you think about the person who engages in philosophical investigation while at the same time he also believes in the laws of the prophets: will his soul be purified and do you expect him to be delivered of the filth of this world?

5. Abū-Bakr: How could he engage in philosophical investigation while he believes in these superstitions, is permanently involved in contradictions, and persists in his ignorance and in Following Authority?

Abū-Ḥātim: Yes, but did you not assert that the soul of the person who engages in philosophical investigation will be purified even if he does not delve into the subject but studies it "the slightest little bit"?

Abū-Bakr: Yes.

Abū-Ḥātim: This person, then, who does not delve into the subject but studies it a little is, in fact, imitating his predecessors and Following their Authority, and all he has learned is imitating disagreement and how to Follow Authority! So which superstition is greater than this, which other servility to Authority

[24] Abū-Bakr made this claim in a previous discussion recorded by Abū-Ḥātim. Abū-Bakr's argument was, in effect, directed against the belief that God chose certain peoples to whom He sent a prophet. If God is wise, Abū-Bakr argued, he would not have done this and thereby caused dissension and enmity among people which bring about their perdition. See Kraus "Raziana II" 38.

> can surpass it, and which ignorance is more immense than it? And what kind of purification of the soul is this, and what does it result in except in rejection of religious laws, disbelief in God and His prophets and messengers, entrance into apostasy, and upholding the doctrine which divests God of all attributes [*taʿṭīl*]?[25] Doesn't then this person deserve, more than anybody else, to be called ignorant, a Follower of Authority, and a believer in superstitions and disagreement?
>
> Abū-Bakr: When the discussion reaches this stage, one ought to keep silent. (L31)

It is to the credit of Abū-Ḥātim that, as far as we are able to judge, he seems 210
on the whole not to have misrepresented Abū-Bakr's ideas except, perhaps, for what might be ascribed to dramatic license. The views of Abū-Bakr presented here are consonant with what we know of his approach and theories from his other works.[26] The main points of his argument of particular relevance to our subject are the following.

Central to Abū-Bakr's argument is the concept of progress in the acquisition of truth. This lies at the root of his disagreement with the theologian Abū-Ḥātim for whom truth, by the very nature of what he is professing, was revealed complete all at once. At issue is the perennial problem of reason versus revelation, but neither of the two Rāzī's addresses the problem squarely, and they are hence arguing at cross purposes. For Abū-Bakr, then, truth is something that is acquired piecemeal and cumulatively by reason[27] in the march of history. Past philosophers, "the ancients," discovered Fundamental Principles (*uṣūl*, §1 above), and each succeeding generation of philosophers, after learning all that they had to teach them, added to their store of knowledge and supplemented it (§2 above). The individual doctrines of past philosophers are not sacrosanct; they are subject to criticism and rejection because the issues with which they deal are abstruse and the concepts fine and difficult (§2 above). For this reason what is required from a philosopher is zealous application, sustained research, and a keen mind. As a matter of fact, the disposition to and execution of research are the

25 For the doctrine of *taʿṭīl* in Islam see *EI*² s.v. "Tashbīh wa-tanzīh" (J. van Ess).

26 See in particular Arberry *Physick* and Kraus "Raziana I" 300–334.

27 Cf. Abū-Bakr's eloquent introduction to his *Spiritual Physick* (Arberry 20): "By reason we have comprehended matters obscure and remote, things that were secret and hidden from us; by it we have learned the shape of the earth and the sky, the dimension of the sun, moon and other stars, their distances and motions; by it we have achieved even the knowledge of the Almighty, our Creator, the most majestic of all that we have sought to reach and our most profitable attainment."

minimum requirements for a philosopher (§3 above), because his allegiance is to *discovering* the truth through personal endeavor (*ijtihād*) and not to following blindly the "truth" of an Authoritative predecessor (*taqlīd*).

This brief résumé does not exhaust all the ideas expressed in the debate, but enough has been said to indicate that Abū-Bakr's thoughts constitute the natural extension of the intellectual framework encountered in Alexandrian Aristotelianism in late antiquity and depicted especially in Aristotle's *Vita Vulgata*: a philosopher should care more for truth than for his predecessors, and in order not to overlook the truth he may have to contradict them (VV, §§9–10); in his work he should, like Aristotle, learn all that his teachers taught and add to it out of his own acumen (VV, §25). This is not to imply that there is necessarily an immediate connection between VV and Abū-
211 Bakr ar-Rāzī. The details of the transmission of Greek knowledge in Arabic are still far from having been thoroughly studied, and in the present case direct textual affiliation cannot be demonstrated (nor is it necessary); but it is incontestable that the same spirit permeates both, and also Avicenna's philosophy: the last part of §1 in the Introduction to *The Easterners* (T8) and §1 of the Prologue to *The Cure* (T9) are sufficient testimony.

Abū-Bakr ar-Rāzī and Avicenna were two very different philosophers with widely divergent systems; and yet they display the same attitude of critical inquiry toward past authorities, and the same dedication to hard work and independent thinking for the acquisition of truth. I attribute this to the fact that Abū-Bakr ar-Rāzī, like Avicenna, was an autodidact who was not educated in a philosophical school tradition and consequently, also like Avicenna, not beholden to reproducing the traditional school material. This may be further indicated also by the fact that they both wrote autobiographies whose main thrust seems to be a defense and exposition of their conduct as philosophers.[28]

With regard to the historical aspect of the question concerning the attitude toward Aristotle adopted by his successors, the information about post-Aristotelian philosophy available in Arabic was not plentiful. In general, no detailed report was available: the schools of Hellenistic and early imperial times—Stoics and Epicureans, Cynics and Neo-Pythagoreans—were mostly names chronologically not brought into relation with Aristotle,[29]

---

[28] For Abū-Bakr ar-Rāzī's Autobiography see Kraus "Raziana I."

[29] The most extensive historical information about philosophical schools in relation to the Peripatetics is the report by Ḥunayn in his *Nawādir* (*ādāb*) *al-falāsifa* (37–42 Badawī) which goes back to the Alexandrian Eisagoge complex (German translation in Merkle 36–40).

known primarily through snippets and sayings in gnomologia and doxographies,[30] while the Neoplatonists were either seen as commentators of Aristotle or, as in the case of Plotinus and Proclus, read under the name of Aristotle (Plotinus was little known by name[31] and Proclus only slightly more so). Those recognized by name were for the most part identified by an individual accomplishment in some area of specialization. Indicative of this notion is a tendentious history of Greek philosophy which survives in at least two apparently independent extracts, one in ʿĀmirī's *Al-Amad ʿalā l-abad* (composed in 375/985–986), and the other in Ṣāʿid al-Andalusī's (compiled in 460/1068) *Ṭabaqāt al-umam*. The ultimate provenance of this
history is certainly Greek, but the form in which it was available in Arabic 212
in the 4th/10th century was most likely shaped in Islamic circles, and it also appears that both ʿĀmirī and Ṣāʿid dealt relatively freely with their source. Of the two, ʿĀmirī's account is the more condensed, although at this stage of research it is difficult to assess the nature of interpolations in both authors and discriminate them from the passages original to the source.[32] The first five philosophers are given as Empedocles, Pythagoras, Socrates, Plato, and Aristotle. The two authors then continue:

Ṣāʿid	*ʿĀmirī*
These five are the masters of the Greek philosophers and those who attended to [all] the branches of philosophy. The Greeks have famous philosophers other than these, like Thales of Miletus, follower of Pythagoras, Democritus, who maintained in a work that bodies are dissolved into atoms, Anaxagoras, and others who were both the predecessors and contemporaries of Aristotle.	These five were the philosophers proper.[33]

[30] For the knowledge available in Arabic of these schools see Gutas, "Pre-Plotinian Philosophy" 4939–4973.

[31] See F. Rosenthal, "Plotinus in Islam: The Power of Anonymity," in *Plotino e il Neoplatonismo in Oriente e in Occidente* [Accademia Nazionale dei Lincei, Anno CCCLXXI, Quaderno N. 198], Rome: Accademia Nazionale dei Lincei, 1974, 437–446.

[32] This history of philosophy, its sources, and its relation to others available in medieval Islam (including Porphyry's *Philosophos Historia*) deserve further study. In his work on *al-ʿĀmirī*, Rowson suggests that (pp. 203–204) it was compiled by ʿĀmirī himself from existing material and that Ṣāʿid copied from his account. I tend to think that they both depend on a common source; the question remains open.

[33] Literally, "were characterized by philosophy," or "philosophy was predicated of them"

After Aristotle there was a group who followed his philosophy and commented upon his books. Among the most illustrious were Themistius, Alexander of Aphrodisias, and Porphyry. These three are the most learned in the books of Aristotle[a] and the most deliberate in their study of philosophical books. ...

The learned Greeks (*'ulamā'uhum*) who were famous in some [or: in one of the] philosophical sciences and attended to one of its parts are many. Among the celebrated in physical sciences
213 and medicine is Hippocrates, the master of the natural scientists and the most learned in the physical and demonstrative sciences. Galen collected the titles of his works—numbering more than a hundred—in a sizable bibliography, mentioned the order in which they are to be read, and gave advice on the way in which they are to be studied. ...

After them no one was called a philosopher but rather each person would be associated with a certain discipline or a way of life, like Hippocrates the physician, Homer the poet, Archimedes the geometer, Diogenes the cynic, and Democritus the natural scientist.[34]

I do not know of anybody after Aristotle more learned in physical science than these two excellent scholars, I mean Hippocrates and Galen.

['Āmirī's account contains instead a disparaging story about how Galen was ridiculed when he wished to be called a philosopher instead of a physician.[35] See what follows here.]

Among other physical scientists there are Asclepiades, Erasistratus, Lycus, Paul, etc.[36] ...

Among the mathematicians there was Apollonius. ... Euclid ... Archimedes ... Simplicius

---

[a] The text has *kutub faylasūf*, the books of a philosopher, instead of *kutub al-faylasūf*, the books of the philosopher (Aristotle), but it is certain that this is what is meant.

(*kānū yūṣafūna bi-l-ḥikma*). What is meant is that for one to be a philosopher proper and deserve the name of "philosopher," one must be proficient in all branches of philosophy. As Rowson 214 shows, this is stated explicitly by a younger contemporary of 'Āmirī, Miskawayh (*Al-Fawz al-aṣġar*, Cairo 1325/1907, p. 9); see also Rowson's further references.

[34] Text in Rowson 74.7–9. Cf. his translation in § 9.

[35] Text in Rowson 74.11–15; translation in § 10.

[36] The names are far from having been established (cf. Blachère's notes, 70n38), but this issue is not central to the present discussion.

... Poseidonius ... Hipparchus ... Ptolemy, the author of the *Almagest*.[37] ...

I know of no book written on a particular science, be it ancient or modern, which includes the entirety of that science and encompasses all its parts, other than three books: Ptolemy's *Almagest* on astronomy and the motions of the stars, Aristotle's book on logic [i.e. the entire *Organon*], and Sībawayh al-Baṣrī's *The Book* on Arabic grammar; for nothing is missing from each one of them: neither the Fundamental Principles [*uṣūl*] of the science nor its Corollary Principles [*furūʿ*], except what is of no significance. ...[38]

These people are the suns of the Greeks and their most resplendent stars in the skies. People have gained from their works, benefited from their lights, and been guided by their signs. After these the Greeks had numerous other philosophers whose judgment [subsequent] philosophers followed [*qallada*] and whose anecdotes they collected.[39]

... The Greeks undertook to
master disciplines which
are useful in producing
prosperity in the land,
and are beneficial in
promoting the well-being 214
of men—[disciplines]
like medicine, geometry,
astronomy, music, and
others. They composed
well-known books on them
which have been translated
into various languages and
which won the approval of
men of understanding in
the various nations, where
the Greeks have gained
high esteem.[40] (L32)

ʿĀmirī's version of the history of philosophy, including the disparaging story about Galen, are taken over by the compiler of the *Depository of Wisdom Literature* who then adds the following (*Muntaḫab Ṣiwān al-ḥikma* 88–93 Dunlop; emphasis added):

37 A host of other names given by Ṣāʿid is omitted here.

38 Cf. with this paragraph Avicenna's Prologue to *The Cure* (T9), and his overall plan in his works to write books which encompass the entirety of the philosophical sciences.

39 Text in Ṣāʿid al-Andalusī, *Ṭabaqāt al-umam* 27–31 Cheikho; French translation by Blachère 68–74.

40 Text in Rowson 76.17–20; translation adopted, with modifications, from § 15.

> After the ancients whom we have just mentioned, there appeared[b] some people who left the sound Fundamental Principles to[c] their predecessors, and thus occupied themselves with scrutinizing particulars in order to obtain a sound basis for some discipline. They confined their investigation to those perceptible[41] parts of that single discipline, and took most of their demonstrative proofs from the transmitted Fundamental Principles[d] with which the ancient theoreticians were occupied—one of them based his syllogisms on [arguments based on] "it is more appropriate" and "it is more like"[42]. Although they are excellent men, *they are unable to Verify the Fundamental Principles of their discipline*—I mean its first principles. They are people like Galen and Ptolemy, for each one of them occupied himself with empirical matters [*tajriba*] and with imitating the empiricists, and used syllogisms by forsaking Fundamental Principles and the premisses that are built on them. (L33)

215 The compiler of the *Depository of Wisdom Literature* then continues with a long tirade against Galen's deficiencies in logic.[43]

Reports such as the above betray their pro-Aristotelian bias and hence their affinity with the thought world of late antique Alexandrian Aristotelianism. The latter report in particular indirectly praises Aristotle by the implied comparison of the narrow specialization and logical incompetence of later philosophers with Aristotle's encyclopedic expertise (he treated *all* philosophy, *Vita Vulgata*) and superiority in logical analysis (he discovered the rules of logic, *Vita Vulgata*), qualities which a 'proper' philosopher, it is assumed, ought to have.

---

[b] Reading *naša'a* (line 88) with the Murad Molla MS and Badawī's edition, *Ṣiwān* 86.1.

[c] Reading *li-man* (line 88) with the Murad Molla MS and Badawī *Ṣiwān*, 86.2.

[d] Reading *al-uṣūl* for *al-awā'il*, as suggested by Dunlop in the apparatus.

---

[41] I.e., to empirical matters (*tajriba*, based on experience), as he is going to say later (line 93) about Galen and Ptolemy for medicine and astronomy. See Ullmann *Medizin* 98 for the empirical school, *aṣḥāb at-tajārib*.

[42] "It is more appropriate:" *a potiori*; cf. Joseph Schacht, *The Origins of Muhammadan Jurisprudence*, Oxford: Clarendon Press, 1950, 112, 124. "It is more like:" cf. Brunschvig 16.

[43] In his explicit remarks about Galen, Avicenna also shows little regard for the physician's abilities in logic, although it appears that Avicenna did benefit from his works on logic. See Shehaby 5–6; J.C. Bürgel, *Averroes "contra Galenum"* [Nachr. d. Akad. d. Wiss. in Göttingen, Phil.-hist. Kl., Nr. 9], Göttingen 1967, 263–340; F.W. Zimmermann, "Al-Farabi und die philosophische Kritik an Galen von Alexander zu Averroes," *Akten des VII. Kongresses für Arabistik und Islamwissenschaft*, A. Dietrich, ed., [Abh. d. Akad. d. Wiss. in Göttingen, Phil.-Hist. Kl., III. Folge], Göttingen 1976, 401–414; S. Pines, "Some Problems of Islamic Philosophy," *Islamic Culture* 11 (1937) 73n1; S. Pines, "Rāzī critique de Galien," *Actes du VIIe Congrès Internationale d'Histoire des Sciences*, Paris 1953, 480–487.

Even within the pro-Aristotelian tradition in the historiography of philosophy, however, the attitude adopted toward him was not always one of unadulterated adulation. Serious Aristotelians were aware of the problems in the Master's theories and adopted a critical, but constructive stand. In the epilogue of a treatise that was to have great influence on Avicenna, *On the Principles of the Universe*—a treatise which Avicenna, uncharacteristically for his later period, even cites by its title[44]—this very stand and the rationale behind it are described in detail. The treatise is essentially a discussion of *Metaphysics Lambda*, expounding the theory of the unmoved mover and the order of the universe.[45] The epilogue reads as follows:[e]

> 1. This, then, is how the universe is governed, according to what we have taken from divine Aristotle, by way of summary of the principles. For each one[f] of the things contained in the universe preserves its proper nature, while the activities which are proper to itself follow the eternity and order of the universe.
>
> 2. This theory [*ra'y*], in addition to the fact that it alone and no other is 216
> appropriate[g] to divine governance, is also the one to be heeded and acknowledged as true to the exclusion of other theories because of its conformity with and correspondence to observed facts in the world.[h] All people engaged in philosophy ought to act in accordance with this theory and prefer it in every case over others since it is[i] the most correct of the theories which have been held concerning God and the divine body. Among theories, it is the only one which preserves the continuity and order of things which originate from them and because of them [i.e., God and the divine body]. If it should appear to

[e] The text of one Arabic recension of *Fī mabādi' al-kull*, edited by Genequand 122–126, §§144–151, is an improvement over that by Badawī *Arisṭū* 276.6–277.6, though it disregards much of the broad base of evidence for the transmission of the text; see the review by Silvia Fazzo, *Rivista di Storia della Filosofia* 58 (2003) 384–387. It is controlled here according to the readings of the Istanbul MS Carullah 1279, f. 58[b]8–26 (C).

[f] Reading *fa-inna kulla wāḥidin* C, for *fa-inna li-kulli wāḥidin* in Genequand.

[g] Reading *dūna ġayrihi min al-ārā'i mulā'imun* C, for *dūna ġayrihi mulā'imun* in Genequand.

[h] Reading *fī l-'ālam* C, for *li-l-'ālam* in Genequand.

[i] Correcting to *iḏ kāna* for *iḏ kānat* C and Genequand (the subject is the preceding *hāḏā r-ra'y*; see the same sentence six lines below).

[44] In the Theology of *The Cure*, *Ilāhiyyāt* 392–393 Mūsā et al. = *Najāt* 436.11/635.7. For discussion and further references see Genequand 24–25, Endress 57–60, and especially Bertolacci *Reception* 443–447.

[45] Cf. Silvia Fazzo, "L'exégèse du livre *Lambda* de la *Métaphysique* d'Aristote dans le *De principiis* et dans la *Quaestio* I.1 d'Alexandre d'Aphrodise," *Laval Théologique et Philosophique* 64 (2008) 607–626.

someone that among the things that we have said there is something in need of greater and more detailed investigation, we should not, on account of some slight difficulty that might possibly appear in it, slacken our actual concern and efforts in the consideration of this entire theory, and distance ourselves[j] and feel alienated from it; on the contrary, as we adhere to this theory, we do have to show it to be correct, since it is the most excellent theory that has been held about God Almighty, and the one most worthy of Him. The right course is to aim to analyze[k] all the theories which are opposed to it and to revise whatever is defective or objectionable in them to the extent of our ability, after starting with the belief that it is really difficult to find a theory devoid of problems.

3. As for the reason for the divergence and opposition of theories, it is most probably among the following: it is either on account of the love for leadership and supremacy which inhibit the acquaintance and compliance with truth, or on account of the difficulty, fineness, and obscurity of the subjects under discussion, or on account of the weakness of *our* nature and our impotence to grasp truths. On account of this, however, we should not reject what we have come to believe and hold by way of theoretical and philosophical investigation; on the contrary, we should, in the main, believe in what has become clear to us after thorough examinations, and first investigate a subject in its own right and attempt to acquaint ourselves with its real nature—as people do with matters that concern them most intimately—and then investigate any of its problems about which there are doubts and solve them. We should not aim, on account of a few problems, at lengthy expositions and prolixity lest we thereby obscure the sense and hide its validity, but we should rather
217 relate acknowledging the truth[l] of what we previously thought doubtful to such kinds of knowledge as are themselves beyond doubt, and not reject it.[m] (L34)

Striking in this epilogue is the reasoned and educated defense of both Aristotle and the philosophical method of rational inquiry. Aristotle's theory of the workings of the universe is defended not by an *ipse dixit* argument, but by its objective merits: "its conformity with and correspondence to observed facts in the world" (§ 2). But theories, and especially of such profound and difficult matters, are seldom without problems; the proper

---

[j] Reading *wa-an nab'uda 'anhu* C, for *wa-an nanfira minhu* in Genequand.

[k] Reading *li-ḥall*, as in C, perhaps to be corrected to *ilā ḥall*; for *qaṣada ilā* see further below, last line of p. 124 Genequand.

[l] Reading *at-taṣdīq* as in Badawī's edition, and apparently all the manuscripts except C (Genequand's apparatus omits to register the manuscripts having this reading) for *li-t-taṣdīq* in C and Genequand. See the next textual note.

[m] The structure of this sentence is, *bal* (*yajibu an*) *naṣila t-taṣdīqa bi-mā* ..., as is also clear from the Syriac version of Sergius of Rēšʿaynā, last sentence in the text in Fiori 143.

attitude, therefore, is not to reject the entire theory, but to try and solve these problems and refine the theory. Secondly, knowledge is acquired through philosophical investigation into matters. Through human vainglory or mere incompetence, or even through the very difficulty of the subject matter itself, different opinions arise. Disagreement, however, is salutary rather than debilitating because it should lead to renewed and invigorated research into the the very principles of a subject and eventually to the solution of individual problems. The apologetic attitude perceptible in these arguments, and especially in the second one, is directed against the position that a variety of opinions about a theory invalidates the theory itself. This position was traditionally held by adherents of a revealed doctrine, like Abū-Ḥātim in the debate with Abū-Bakr ar-Rāzī cited above, and is thus but a corollary of the central discussion of reason versus revelation. In the case of *On the Principles of the Universe*, the polemic is in all probability addressed to Christians, and might thus point to late antiquity as the date in which the treatise took the form in which we find this version of it in Arabic.[46] From the very beginning of the pagan/Christian dialogue, a standard argument of the Christian

---

[46] The attribution of this treatise to Alexander of Aphrodisias, despite whatever Alexandrian elements it may contain (cf. Fazzo's article cited in the preceding note), is questionable. A late antique date, at least for this epilogue, is also indicated by the appellation of Aristotle as "divine" (§1), something which is attested, according to the *TLG*, not in any of the extant Greek works by Alexander of Aphrodisias but only once in Themistius (and this not in his professional paraphrases or public orations, but in the "private" funeral oration for his father, 234d Petavius-Harduinus, English translation by R.J. Panella, *The Private Orations of Themistius*, Berkeley, etc: University of California Press, 2000, 53), only once in Simplicius (*In Phys., CAG* IX,611.8, and cf. p. 31n23 by the translator, who remarks on the uncommon nature of this appellation even among Neoplatonists: J.O. Urmson, *Simplicius. Corollaries on Place and Time*, Ithaca, N.Y.: Cornell University Press, 1992), and once in the lives of Aristotle (*Marciana, Vulgata, Latina*: see Düring 107). A reference to Alexander in Eusebius, *Praeparatio evangelica* VI.9.1, is questionable. In addition, some version of this treatise is extant also in a fifth-sixth century Syriac translation by Sergius of Rēšʿaynā, in which neither is it attributed to Alexander of Aphrodisias nor is Aristotle called "divine" in that passage or anywhere else (text and French translation by Fiori 143 and 157–158). Furthermore, there are various versions in Arabic, while an entire section on intellection in the longer Arabic version is considered even by Genequand (17 and 34) an "interpolation" in what he claims is the original text of Alexander. For a critical and precise presentation of this cluster of texts, see Endress 41–49. The *Mabādiʾ al-kull* is clearly a multi-layered text with a very complicated transmission history and in need of thorough analysis before questions of authenticity and attribution to Alexander are settled; it should not be forgotten that works by Proclus and Philoponus are also attributed to Alexander in Arabic. It is hoped that the translation and commentary of both the Arabic and Syriac versions announced by Silvia Fazzo and Mauro Zonta (*DPhA Supplément* 67, § 24, and in her review, cited above in note e, p. 387) will go a long way toward accomplishing these goals for this very important cluster of texts.

apologists against the validity of philosophical ideas was the disagreement among philosophers as opposed to the single belief of the Christians. A few lines of the apologist Tatian will serve as an example:

> Philosophers ... dogmatize one against the other. ... They have, moreover, many collisions among themselves; each one hates the other; they indulge in conflicting opinions, and their arrogance makes them eager for the highest places (par. III). You who receive from your predecessors doctrines which clash with one another, you the inharmonious, are fighting against the harmonious (par. XXV). But with us [the Christians] there is no desire of vainglory, nor do we indulge in a variety of opinions (par. XXXII).[47] (L35)

The epilogue of *On the Principles of the Universe* provides an answer to the kind of objections to philosophical investigation raised by the likes of Tatian and Abū-Ḥātim in both Christianity and Islam.

218 Avicenna's conception of the history of philosophy, the position occupied by Aristotle in it, the attitude toward him adopted by his successors, and the proper approach of philosophical inquiry was formed against an intellectual background outlined by the passages selected above, a background which in its essentials was an extension of the thought world of Aristotelianism in late antique Alexandria. This conception is clearly reflected in all his personal writings where he explicitly mentions the subject and especially in the introduction to *The Easterners* (T8). It also provides one of the keys for our approach to his philosophy and to reading his works.

---

[47] *Address to the Greeks*, translated by J.E. Ryland in *The Ante-Nicene Fathers*, A. Roberts and J. Donaldson, eds., Vol. II, New York: The Christian Literature Company, 1890, 66b, 76a, 78a.

AVICENNA'S CONCEPTION OF THE PRAXIS OF PHILOSOPHY

The understanding of the history and development of philosophy which Avicenna acquired from the Aristotelian tradition provided the starting point and the context for his own philosophical activity and his self-consciousness as a philosopher. It helped him crystallize his thoughts about the philosophical praxis, or what it is to "do" philosophy, and by extension, about how all philosophers should proceed.

The starting point of all philosophical praxis is acknowledging the fact that the knowledge to be acquired and then communicated is the Knowledge possessed by the intellects of the spheres, the Knowledge, that is, which reflects ontology, and has a syllogistic structure. This Knowledge presents a closed system: it contains all the knowledge there is. But "what is known to mankind is limited" (T11, §7) because the human intellect is associated with a body which hinders its acquisition of this Knowledge. Only "when the association of the [rational] soul with the body is severed through death" will the soul "receive the divine effluence [containing Knowledge], will have revealed to it whatever was hidden from it before the separation, and there will come about for it a similarity with the abstract intellects which are the principles of the causes of beings, since all the truths are revealed to these [celestial] intellects" (T14, §10). While still associated with the body, the human soul can acquire the Knowledge, however partially, by philosophy. The goal of the *praxis* of philosophy is therefore to actualize in the human intellect the Knowledge of the celestial spheres, while the *history* of philosophy is the record of the progressive acquisition by humans of parts of this Knowledge. Thus, although the Knowledge to be acquired in itself and on a transcendent plane is a closed system and hence static, on a human level and in history it is evolutionary. This idea of progress in the acquisition of Knowledge which Avicenna inherited from the Aristotelian tradition informed both the orientation of his philosophical praxis and his prescription of it.

1. Objective Method: Fundamental Principles and Corollaries

Following the spirit of philosophical inquiry indicated by the attitudes of Abū-Bakr ar-Rāzī and the epilogue of *The Principles of the Universe*, Avicenna
220 repeatedly specified in his works that "doing" philosophy consists, essentially, of two operations: discerning the Fundamental Principles (*uṣūl*) of the Knowledge and Working Out Corollary Principles on their basis (*tafrīʿ*). The first philosopher to have done so and to have set the course for the future was Aristotle: he distinguished the parts of the sciences one from the other, he classified them, he perceived the truth in many things, and he discerned sound Fundamental Principles in most sciences (T8, §1). Subsequent philosophers were not as successful, as we saw in the preceding section, in establishing with the same precision such Principles; Avicenna, however, could claim for himself that God had granted him "an incessant certainty about Fundamental Principles which the seeker of salvation must without fail know, and a wide-ranging competence in subsequent areas" (T11, §8). What Aristotle's successors, and by implication, all philosophers, should do, is

> gather the loose ends [Aristotle] left, repair any breach they find in what he constructed, and Supply Corollaries to Fundamental Principles he presented. (T8, §1)

This is precisely what Avicenna claims to have done in the Prologue to *The Cure*: he presented the Fundamental Principles which he established as true and he Supplied their Corollaries (T9, §1). Even so, and despite his keen awareness of the validity of what he had done, the sense of historical evolution and of progress in the acquisition of Knowledge never left Avicenna. Toward the end of his life he could write with perfect candor to a disciple (Bahmanyār):

> With regard to matters upon which I have spent great effort, I have come to know things which I have Verified and cannot be improved, except that they are few. What I neither know nor have a way of knowing, on the other hand, is much indeed, but sometimes I have no hopes that about what I do not know I will ever come into possession of new knowledge which I have not already achieved by the assiduous research I have been engaged in, despite the fact that my dedication to the search for truth is unmatched. [T11, §8]

And in the same spirit he could exhort posterity in his last major work to continue with the search for truth along the lines he prescribed:

> O you who are zealous to Ascertain the truth: I am bestowing upon you in these Pointers and reminders Fundamental Principles and essential elements

> of philosophy; if sagacity takes hold of your hand [to guide you], it will become easy for you to Derive Corollary Principles from the former and work out the details of the latter. [T10, § 2]

The two concepts of Fundamental Principles and Working Out Corollaries on their basis (*uṣūl, tafrīʿ*) are therefore central in Avicenna's conception of the praxis of philosophy and used throughout his works. They are, however, 221
by no means original to him. They are primarily terms of Islamic jurisprudence, from which they have become completely integrated into common Arabic usage in all areas. A particularly apposite example is their use in an irreverent poem about hashish:

> The jurist says to me, while in my eyes
> there are allusions [to intoxication] more telling than evidence itself,
> Given the most eminent Fundamental Principles of relaxation, upon which basis
> would you Derive its Corollary states? And I replied, On the basis of hashish.[1] (L36)

In philosophical terminology, these two words were in use long before Avicenna. In the preceding chapter we saw them employed by Abū-Bakr ar-Rāzī for much the same purpose; and even before Rāzī the great Ḥunayn ibn-Isḥāq used them to describe precisely what it was that the ancient philosophers had done:

> The ancients provided Fundamental Principles for philosophy, Worked Out its Corollary principles, and spread it far and wide …[2] (L37)

Avicenna was thus following the mainstream tradition in this regard; his main contribution was to employ these terms with consistency and rigor and make them an integral part of his conception of the philosophical praxis. An excellent example is provided by his letter to Kiyā (T12, §§ 1–2) in which he describes in detail his analysis of Aristotle's *De anima*, *Physics*, and *De caelo*, and offers suggestions about how to proceed to build upon their teachings. As for the specific epistemological aspect of the procedure, it is intimately associated with Correct Guessing (*ḥads*), which helps a

---

[1] The last two lines of the poem in Arabic, quoted in Franz Rosenthal, *The Herb*, Leiden: Brill, 1971, 28n5, read as follows: *uṣūlu l-basṭi awjahahā ʿalā mā / tufarriʿuhū fa-qultu ʿalā ṣ-ṣaḥīḥi*. The pun here depends on the nickname for hashish, *ṣaḥīḥ*, which is also the title of Buḫārī's famous collection of *ḥadīṯ* (Prophetic Traditions), one of the *uṣūl* on the basis of which jurists derived legislation for individual cases.

[2] *Nawādir* (*ādāb*) *al-falāsifa* 37 Badawī (= MS Escorial 760, f. 2^b; cf. Merkle 36): *al-qudamāʾ … aṣṣalū l-ḥikmata wa-farraʿūhā wa-aḏāʿūhā*.

philosopher Discover the First Principles and Supply the Corollaries (T10, § 2 and note 3), subjects that have already been discussed.

2. Social Contextuality: Customary Practice

Avicenna exhibited great originality, on the other hand, by identifying another aspect of the philosophical praxis, which lent it fullness and co-
222 gency. Granted that perceiving Fundamental Principles and elaborating Corollaries are the two major operations that a philosopher has to perform, the fact nevertheless remains that each philosopher is grounded in historical circumstances and has been schooled in ways which determine his outlook and his position vis-à-vis the philosophical praxis itself. What Avicenna came to realize with great perspicacity, in other words, was the *contextuality* of the philosophical praxis and the inevitable distortions that result therefrom even if the philosopher avoids blind and uncritical Adherence to a sect (*taqlīd, taʿaṣṣub*) and proceeds by Principles and Corollaries. Doubtless Avicenna was alerted to this aspect of philosophizing by his own experience as described in the Autobiography, that is, by the development of his theory of *ḥads*. It enabled him to claim access to, and certainty in absolute Knowledge on his own and without a teacher, i.e., outside the historical process. Engaging in philosophy in history, however, entailed following habits of thought acquired from teachers and predecessors, from a tradition of instruction, which in turn generated a potential conflict between one's own ideas and those inherited. Hence there are two subjective issues involved, whose resolution is necessary before the philosophical praxis can proceed objectively by Principles and Corollaries. Acquired habits of research and study have to be brought into full consciousness and, if necessary, broken, while deferential attitudes toward tradition should not result, out of fear of creating schisms, in its accommodation by means of pretexts or deliberate disregard of past errors. For the philosophical praxis to yield results, the effects of a philosopher's contextuality have to be neutralized.

Avicenna came gradually to a realization of these issues.[3] The first note of independence, of his self-awareness of his contextuality and his attempt to counteract it, is struck in the very first page of *The Cure* that he wrote, the

[3] The evolution of Avicenna's independent attitude toward the Aristotelian tradition will be discussed in greater detail in Chapter 7; here it is sufficient to present his exposition of these issues.

introduction to the Physics, where he explains his statement to Jūzjānī and the other disciples (W6) that he did not wish to write commentaries:[4]

> We frequently see that when those who discuss the Philosophical Sciences [*al-mutakallimūn fī l- ʿulūm*] undertake to refute some feeble statement or turn to explicate a problem whose truth can be observed at a short distance, they exhaust every effort, Verify every part, and set forth every argument; but when they set out on a difficult matter and reach some ambiguity, they 223
> pass it over completely. As for ourselves, we hope that beyond this there is a way countering, and a course opposite theirs; we shall do our best to spread what is right from our predecessors and leave unmentioned what we think they neglected. This is then what prevented us from writing commentaries on their books and exegeses on their texts, since we were not sure that we would not eventually get to places in which we[a] think they were negligent, and we would therefore be compelled to either undertake to excuse them, or devise arguments and pretexts for them, or refute them openly. But God spared us all this and allotted to it a group of people who worked hard and wrote exegeses on their books. If anybody desires to understand their *words*, these commentaries will guide him and these exegeses will suffice him; but whoever actively strives for Knowledge and what [those words] *mean* [*al-maʿānī*], he will find them set down in those books [on Philosophy by our predecessors], and he will also find some of the results of our research, despite our young age, in these books[b] which we wrote and collectively called *The Cure*.[c] (L38)

There is an incipient awareness of the dangers of customary procedures here. The practice has been, Avicenna says, to concentrate on the process of commenting itself, on the words of the philosophical text, and overlook the purpose for which commentaries are written, namely, understanding the concepts behind the words, the substance of the issue. If he were to write commentaries, he would have to deal with the same issues already determined by his predecessors and in the same way as they did, and the only

---

[a] Reading *naẓunnu* with Mahdavī for *yuẓannu* (?) in Zāyid's text.

[b] Reading *fī hāḏihi l-kutubi*, as in some manuscripts and Mahdavī, for *fī hāḏā, al-kutub* in Zāyid's text.

[c] Reading *Kitāb aš-Šifāʾ majmūʿan* with Mahdavī for the misprint in Zāyid's text.

---

[4] Translation from *as-Samāʿ aṭ-ṭabīʿī* 3.8–4.9 Zāyid, controlled with the quotation of the opening page in Mahdavī 146.2–14. The indiscriminate edition in McGinnis *Physics* p. 2 has not been taken into consideration. Although Avicenna opens this introduction by stating that he has already presented the "gist" (*lubāb*) of logic, it is clear that this is merely in anticipation of what he intends to do. It is impossible to characterize the actual Logic of *The Cure* as "the gist," especially since, as Jūzjānī remarks, "the Logic grew longer" than anticipated (T7, §6).

alternatives would then be either to accommodate tradition and devise pretexts, or to spend time refuting it. In neither case would the real purpose, discussing the substance, be served. As Avicenna's disciple writing from Rayy (Ibn-Zayla?) put it, the commentaries of other scholars and especially of Ibn-aṭ-Ṭayyib are noted for their "scant attention to the meaning [*al-maʿānī*, of the text commented upon], the narrow scope of exposition, the dubious argumentation that fails to convince, the use of rhetorical and sophistical methods in the demonstrative sciences, and the inconsistent procedures. … Avicenna [would not write such refutations] because he keeps himself above engaging in arguments about everything and everybody" [T13, §4].

As Avicenna continued writing *The Cure*, the implications for the philosophical praxis of following tradition were becoming increasingly apparent to him. By the time he came to write the part on Music, he stated his views in a synoptic fashion. In its introduction he mentioned that he was going to deviate from the accepted method of presenting that subject, and justified
224 his originality by stating the numerous mistakes that have been caused in the history of philosophy by blind imitation of models and lack of independent and critical thinking:[5]

> [Presenting music in the traditional manner] is the practice of those who cannot distinguish one science from the next and separate the essential from the accidental. Their philosophy, which was the first to appear, was inherited undigested, and they were imitated by people inferior to the man who attained [the level of] revising philosophy and reached [the method of] detailed and Verified analysis.[6] Many a careless error has been caused by imitation, many an inadvertent thought has been covered by high opinion of the ancients and thus met with approval, many a Customary Practice [*ʿāda*] obstructed truth, and many an accommodating stance [*musāʿada*] has diverted [thinkers] from reflection!
>
> We have expended great efforts to observe the truth itself and turn a deaf ear to the lures of Customary Practices [*ʿādāt*] to the extent of our ability and good fortune, even though we were actually on our guard for the most part rather than at all times, and caution saved us from error in the majority of cases rather than in all. We therefore need our colleagues to correct what we have been remiss in and failed to achieve. (L39)

[5] *Mūsīqā* 4.1–8 Yūsuf.

[6] By the first philosophers Avicenna would seem to be referring to the Pythagoreans, especially since he says that the traditional manner of presenting music which he rejects included a discussion of the theory of *ēthos*. The man who revised philosophy, of course, is Aristotle, whose example Avicenna is following in proceeding by Verification.

In the Introduction to *The Easterners* (T8), finally, which can fairly be
called Avicenna's manifesto of the philosophical praxis, all these points are
taken one by one. The acquisition of Knowledge in history is piecemeal;
Aristotle was the first to discern Fundamental Principles in most sciences,
but his statements and those of the ancients are in need of addition, correction, and revision (§1). The philosophical praxis consists of establishing
Fundamental Principles and Working Out the Corollaries; but this should
be done only after the philosopher has become conscious of his historical
contextuality and has rejected sectarian opinion, his own fancy, Customary
Practice, and personal habit (§1). Otherwise, there is the danger of accommodating tradition and consequently failing to exercise his own mind and
reflect on the problems (§1). But even if such a level of awareness is reached
there is the further danger, to which Avicenna confesses to have succumbed,
of accommodating tradition and devising pretexts for it out of a desire to
avoid confrontation and the creation of schisms (§§3, 5). This can be over-
come only by the personal courage of the philosopher. He should have no
personal fear about appearing to contradict majority opinion (§4), and he
should have no fear about truth itself lest it be misunderstood (§5); these
two problems, which cannot be overlooked, can be resolved by adopting
appropriate methods of composition (Chapter 8, below). He should have the
strength of his convictions, especially if his personal experience assures him 225
of having reached Knowledge through Correct Guessing (§§2, 6); he should
therefore discard traditional molds, restate the issues on his own terms, and
present Knowledge as it is in itself (§6). This, indeed, is his duty as a philosopher: having come from within the tradition and Adhered to it in a Partisan
spirit, he commands the respect of his colleagues, and his works are held in
high esteem; he is therefore in the best position to teach them the truth and
save them from their faults. But neither can he do otherwise; the very Partisan attachment to doctrines now discredited in his eyes, which originally
made him sought after among his colleagues, lowers his self-esteem and
forces him to communicate the true Philosophy he has Discovered through
Correct Guessing (§6).

3. Social Contextuality: Withholding Knowledge

A significant factor that determined Avicenna's understanding of the praxis of philosophy was the attitudes about communication and withholding of knowledge which he inherited from tradition and his immediate milieu.[7] The idea of teaching one's philosophy only to those prepared to receive it traversed a long path in ancient and medieval intellectual history and is to be encountered in almost every aspect of it. Here we are specifically concerned with its manifestation in the Aristotelian tradition, within which Avicenna squarely placed himself.

Beginning with discussions on the difference between Aristotle's popular works ("exoteric") and his school treatises ("acroatic"), a long succession of Aristotelian scholars debated continuously the question whether Aristotle taught in the latter what he withheld from the former. Positions were taken on both sides of the question, but the focal point of the argument revolved around the issue of Aristotle's style in the acroatic works, or the
226 method he used in them to present his philosophy.[8] The sources that were used for the conduct of this debate included, in addition to whatever evidence could be produced from the scientific works of Aristotle himself, the pseudepigraphic "correspondence" of Aristotle. One such exchange of letters, allegedly between Alexander and Aristotle, has been preserved both in Greek and, in a derivative form, in Arabic, and was known to Avicenna. The Greek is found in Gellius's *Noctes Atticae* and reads as follows:[9]

> Alexander to Aristotle, best wishes.
> You did not do well to have publicized your acroatic works. For in what respect are we to be different from others, if they are going to share with us all the works in which we have been instructed? I personally would have much preferred to be distinctive with regard to acquaintance with or capacity for the best. Greetings.
>
> Aristotle to Alexander the King, best wishes.
> You wrote to me about the acroatic works, stating your belief that they should be kept secret. You should know, however, that, though publicized, they are

---

[7] The canard raised by Leo Strauss and his followers, that allegedly ancient and medieval philosophers concealed their true beliefs and doctrines out of fear of persecution by their societies, has no historical basis and has been properly debunked. See the discussion in Gutas "Historiography" 19–24. For an overall assessment see Rudolph p. XIX.

[8] The texts of this debate, lasting from the first century BC well into Byzantine times, were collected and discussed by Düring 426–443.

[9] Gellius 20,5,11–12 (Marshall) = M. Plezia, *Aristoteles, Privatorum Scriptorum Fragmenta*, Leipzig: Teubner, 1977, 28 (with exhaustive references to previous literature).

> not public: for they are intelligible only to those who have attended our lectures. Greetings, King Alexander. (L40)

In Mubaššir's *Muḫtār al-ḥikam*, after passing through an unknown number of stages, this exchange is reproduced in the following form:[10]

> Plato reproached Aristotle for the philosophy he had publicized and the books he had written. Aristotle made the following plea in his defense: "As for the practitioners and students[11] of philosophy, they ought to make copies of it;[d] but as for its enemies and those who refuse to have anything to do with it, they will never have access to it on account of their ignorance of its contents and their distaste for it, and of their shying away from it because it is too difficult for them. Thus, although I have made this philosophy public, I have surrounded it with impregnable fortifications—so that the foolish cannot scale its walls, the ignorant cannot gain access to it, and the wicked cannot lay their hands on it—and I have ordered it in such a way that is of no consequence to philosophers but does not benefit lying detractors." (L41)

Such discussions eventually led, in late antique Aristotelianism, to the formulation of the doctrine that Aristotle deliberately cultivated obscurity in
his works. This doctrine became incorporated in classroom instruction, and 227
was included among the ten points that were necessary for a student to study as an introduction to the works of Aristotle.[12] They formed the prolegomena of every commentary on the *Categories*, and as such were transmitted wholesale into Arabic. This introduction was available to Avicenna in the numerous translations of the commentaries on the *Categories*, a perfect specimen of which is preserved in Ibn-aṭ-Ṭayyib's adaptation of such a

[d] "They ought to make copies of it:" *fa-yanbaġī an yansaḫūhā*. The correct reading is found in the Ahmet III manuscript, a photograph of which is reproduced in Rosenthal *Classical Heritage*, facing page 45. Badawī has the impossible *yunjisūhā* [?], while Lippert reads *fa-lan yanbaġiya an yubḫasūhā* and translates, "so ist est nicht nötig, dass wir ihnen etwas vorenthalten."

[10] *Muḫtār al-ḥikam* 184.5–10 Badawī = J. Lippert, *Studien auf dem Gebiete der griechisch-arabischen Übersetzungslitteratur*, Braunschweig 1894, 9.2–7 = MS Istanbul Ahmet III 3206, f. 90[a], 1–7. Cf. the translation by Lippert, p. 18, and by M. Plezia, *Aristotelis Epistularum Fragmenta cum Testamento*, Warsaw 1961, 49. A version of this exchange appears in *Iṯbāt an-nubuwwāt* (p. 48 Marmura, English translation by Marmura in Lerner and Mahdi 116) which, even if not by Avicenna, was composed in his circles. See the discussion in the Appendix, GM-Ps 2.

[11] "Practitioners and students," literally, "sons and heirs."

[12] The ten points are presented in a summary form and with full references to the extant Greek texts by L.G. Westerink, *Anonymous Prolegomena to Platonic Philosophy*, Amsterdam: North-Holland, 1962, xxvi–xxvii, and in Düring 445–449.

commentary,[13] and in Fārābī's summary of the ten points, known under the title *Prolegomena to the Study of Aristotle's Philosophy*, which may be translated here because of its brevity:

> Aristotle used an obscure way of expression for three reasons: first, to test the nature of the student in order to find out whether he is suitable to be educated or not; second, to avoid lavishing philosophy on all people but only on those who are worthy of it; and third, to train the mind through the exertion of research.[14] (L42)

This tripartite etiology of Aristotle's obscurity was well known among Arabic authors writing on Greek philosophy. It was incorporated, for example, in a work not engaged at all in commenting upon the *Categories*, in ʿĀmirī's *Afterlife*.[15] Even more significant for the influence it was to exercise on Avicenna, however, is a passage from Fārābī's *The Agreement between Plato and Aristotle*[16] which presents a significant aspect of the tendentious
228 history of philosophy that developed in late antique Aristotelianism[17] and was received in early Islam. It manifestly derives from sophisticated elaborations of the dogma of Aristotle's obscurity that we find in the commentatorial tradition, for it informs the reader not only *why* Aristotle was obscure, but also *how*; it specifies in great detail the procedures whereby Aristotle

[13] Published from the unique Cairo manuscript Dār al-Kutub, Ḥikma 1M, by Cleophea Ferrari, *Der Kategorienkommentar von Abū l-Farağ ʿAbdallāh ibn aṭ-Ṭayyib*, Leiden: Brill, 2006. Ibn-aṭ-Ṭayyib's preface to this chapter is translated, from this manuscript, by Rosenthal *Classical Heritage* 70–72. The discussion of the reasons of Aristotle's obscurity is on ff. 7^{b}–8^{a} = pp. 13–14 (Arabic), 102–103 (German summary) in Ferrari's edition, and cf. the discussion on pp. 45–49. In this section, as in the entire commentary, Ibn-aṭ-Ṭayyib follows very closely, even to the reproduction of the poetic quotations, his Greek source, which must have been a variation of the text of Elias, *In Aristotelis Categorias* (*CAG* 18.1) 124.25–127.2.

[14] Fārābī, *Mā yanbaġī an yuqaddama qabla taʿallum falsafat Arisṭū*, in *Mabādiʾ al-falsafa al-qadīma*, Cairo 1328/1910, 14 = Dieterici *Abhandlungen* 54 (text) = Dieterici *Abhandlungen* 89 (translation). The standard three reasons given by Elias for Aristotle's obscurity, and reproduced by both Fārābī and Ibn-aṭ-Ṭayyib, with the respective terms used, are, testing the student (*dokimasia, istibrāʾ, imtiḥān*), training him (*gymnasia, riyāḍa, riyāḍa*), and withholding philosophy from the unworthy (*krypsis, li-allā tubḏala l-falsafa, li-kay-mā lā taẓhara asrāru l-falsafa*).

[15] Rowson 88–89, and see also Rowson's comments on pp. 262–263.

[16] The authorship of this work is disputed in modern scholarship. See the summary by Rudolph of the arguments in favor and against in Rudolph 402. Avicenna, however, thought the work to be by Fārābī: he refers to it in his correspondence with Bīrūnī, Nasr and Mohaghegh 40.12–13.

[17] See the references in Gutas "Starting Point" 122n11.

allegedly managed to conceal his innermost ideas behind a fortress of words impenetrable to the non-philosopher. It is translated here in full:[18]

> 1. It is also stated that there is disparity between the methods of Plato and Aristotle in recording the sciences and writing books and treatises. This is because formerly Plato used to refrain from recording anything of the sciences and depositing it in the depths of books except only in pure hearts and "well-pleasing" minds. But when he feared for himself that he would become heedless and forgetful, and that what he had discovered, hit upon, and achieved with his thought would be lost, inasmuch as he sought to amplify his knowledge and philosophy and expatiated upon them,[e] he selected symbols and allegories with the purpose of recording the various aspects of his knowledge and philosophy in a way that only those deserving of them, and those worthy of comprehending them, would come to know them after inquiries, research, examination, effort, instruction, and sincere need.
>
> 2. As for Aristotle, his method was to speak clearly, elucidate, record, arrange in order, communicate, uncover, expound, and to treat exhaustively everything for which he could find a way.
>
> 3. These two methods are apparently disparate. And yet, the person who researches the Aristotelian sciences, studies his books, and applies himself with perseverance to them, knows full well the different methods he used to render things inaccessible, cryptic, and intricate, despite his express intent to expound and elucidate. Among these [methods] are the following:
>
> > i. In many of the syllogisms which he presents in the fields of physics, metaphysics, and ethics, it is found in what he says that he omits the necessary premiss. The commentators have pointed out the passages where this occurs.
> >
> > ii. He omits many conclusions [of such syllogisms], and he also omits one of the two [terms of the conclusion] and offers only the other. For example,

[e] Reading *ḥaytu staġzara ʿilmahu wa-ḥikmatahu wa-tabassaṭa fīhimā* for *istaqarra … fīhā* in Martini Bonadeo. The reading *istaġzara*, clearly the *lectio difficilior* and also parallel to the following *tabassaṭa*, is attested in the Diyarbakır and British Library MSS (D and M), though Martini Bonadeo registers in her apparatus *istaġraza* for them which, if correct, is manifestly a misplacing of the point (with credit due to Dieterici for reading it correctly). For the 10th form of the verb, meaning to make or seek to make ample, enrich, see Lane (under *mustaġzir* only) and Dozy. The passage cited by Dozy, *wa-mā stuġzira bi-miṯli l-ʿadli*, a statement by Jaʿfar b. Yaḥyā the Barmakid, is found, before Ṯaʿālibī, in Ibn-Qutayba's *ʿUyūn al-aḫbār, Kitāb as-sulṭān*, vol. I,13.7 (Cairo 1930 etc.). All manuscripts seem to have *fīhā* for what I write as *fīhimā*, but this is a common scribal error.

[18] Text in Martini Bonadeo 42.11–44.9, based on the superior Diyarbakır manuscript and improving the previous edition by Dieterici *Abhandlungen* 5–7 (text). Cf. also Martini Bonadeo's notes on pp. 104–117.

in his 'Epistle to Alexander on the Constitutions of Particular Cities,' he says: "He who chooses justice in [civic] intercourse deserves to be set apart by the governor of the city when it comes to [meting] punishments." The complete form of this statement is the following: "He who prefers to choose justice over injustice, deserves to be set apart by the governor of the city when it comes to [meting] punishments and rewards;" i.e., "He who prefers justice deserves to be rewarded, just as he who chooses injustice deserves to be punished."

iii. He mentions two premisses of one syllogism, but follows them with the conclusion of another; or he mentions some premisses, but follows them with the conclusion of the consequents of these premisses. He did this, for example, in the *Analytica Priora* [A. 32, 47a27] when he mentioned the parts of substance to be themselves substances.

229 iv. He discusses at great length and presents multiple particulars about something evident in order to create the impression that he treated [the issue] exhaustively and with great effort; but then he passes over something obscure without discussing it at length or defining it fully.

v. The order, arrangement, and plan of his scientific works [i.e., Aristotle's "esoteric" or school treatises extant today] are such that make one think that these are his peculiar characteristics, from which it is impossible for him to deviate. But when his [exoteric, i.e., published] epistles are examined closely, it is found that his presentation of the subjects in them is structured and ordered according to plans and arrangements which differ from those in the ["esoteric"] books. It is sufficient for us [to mention here] his well-known letter to Plato in response to what Plato had written to him, reprimanding him for recording [things in] books and classifying the sciences, and making them public in his complete and thorough works. Aristotle explicitly says in this letter to Plato, "Although I have recorded [in writing] these well-guarded philosophical sciences which are Withheld [from others], I have nevertheless arranged them in a way that will be accessible only to their adherents, and expressed them in ways that will be comprehended only by their practitioners."

4. It is therefore evident from what we have described that what leads to the presupposition of a disparity between the two methods is two states of affairs [i.e., not recording vs. recording philosophy in an inaccesible way], apparently contradictory but [in fact] united by a single intent [i.e., making philosophy inaccesible to the unworthy]. (L43)

Avicenna studied Fārābī's treatise, and this passage in particular, with great care and applied its teachings in his efforts to understand the Aristotelian texts. In his responses to the physical questions posed to him by Bīrūnī he explicitly refers to Fārābī's treatise by title (p. 40.12–13 Nasr and Mohaghegh, as already mentioned); the description of his method of study in the Autobiography (T3, § 8) is directly inspired by the above passage (Chapter 3.3A), and the epilogue of his work, the "Lesser" *Destination* (T5), is conceived and worded by constant reference to the same passage. When he came to write his detailed analytical commentaries on Aristotle, as in the *Fair Judgment*, for example, he followed closely (as we shall see in Chapter 8) Fārābī's description of Aristotle's method of composition.

With regard to the problem of communicating philosophical knowledge, Avicenna's attitudes were thus shaped in part by the ideas he found in the Aristotelian tradition. This knowledge was to be communicated in writing lest it be forgotten, but it was to be communicated in an obscure style in order to conceal it from those unworthy of it, and in order to test and train the students. The stylistic devices whereby this obscurity was to be achieved consisted essentially of peculiarities in the arrangement of the works and the omission of various steps in the syllogistic process; the philosopher
would pay no attention to the arrangement, and he will easily supply these 230
steps, while the unlettered would be baffled by both and turn away from philosophy altogether.

Native Arabic and Islamic tradition developed analogous attitudes toward the problem of communicating knowledge quite independently of the Greek tradition. Although the subject of knowledge in Islam has been treated extensively,[19] it is necessary to elaborate here on the particular aspect of it that is our concern.

As in the Aristotelian tradition, there also developed in Islamic culture a two-sided approach to the question of disseminating knowledge. On the one hand, knowledge of all sorts, but frequently knowledge of a specific kind, was to be passed on and taught absolutely by the person who possessed it; withholding it was to be considered a sin and forbidden. On the other hand, the reverse position maintained that knowledge was to be given only to those worthy to receive it, lest it be ignored, debased, or lost. The terms that were universally used in this context were *ḍanna bi-* (and its various synonyms, like *baḫila bi-* and *šaḥḥa bi-*), "being stingy about" or "withholding" knowledge, and its antonym, *baḏala*, "lavishing," in the case of those deserving (*al-ahl*), and "squander", in the case of the unworthy (*ġayr al-ahl*).

The locus classicus of the term *ḍanna bi-* is the Qurʾānic *hapax legomenon*, *wa-mā huwa ʿalā l-ġaybi bi-ḍanīn* (81:24), "Neither does he [Muḥammad] withhold [knowledge of] the Unseen," where the "Unseen" was invariably

19 Rosenthal *Knowledge*.

interpreted as the Qur'ān. There is a variant reading of *ẓanīn* for *ḍanīn* among the early generations of Qur'ānic readers,[20] and there is the further problem that the preposition *ʿalā* should have been *bi-* (i.e., *wa-mā huwa bi-l-ġaybi bi-ḍanīn*). Whatever the original reading and its meaning in the time of Muḥammad, however, the entire Islamic tradition which preferred the reading *ḍanīn* interpreted it uniformly as meaning "being stingy about." Two representative interpretations may be offered from those collected by Ṭabarī in his commentary, both on the authority of early and reliable Qur'ānic scholars. "From Qatāda: 'This Qur'ān is the Unseen. God gave it to Muḥammad, lavished it upon him (*badalahu*), taught it to him, and summoned to it. God did not withhold it from Muḥammad'." "From Ibn-Zayd: '… God sent it [the Qur'ān] through Gabriel … to Muḥammad. Gabriel transmitted what had been consigned [to him] by God to Muḥammad, and Muḥammad transmitted what had been consigned [to him] by God and Gabriel to mankind. Not one of them [i.e., God, Gabriel, Muḥammad] withheld, suppressed, or fabricated [anything]'." Ṭabarī himself preferred *ḍanīn* because, he said, it was the reading of all the Qur'ānic manuscripts.[21]

231 These interpretations create a chain of transmission of *religious* knowledge and stipulate that no link in that chain is to hold back or fabricate any part of it. The same sentiment about the transmission of religious knowledge is sounded in a Prophetic Tradition reported by Ġazālī. The Prophet is reported to have said that there are two kinds of religious scholars of the Islamic community: those who, having been given knowledge by God, lavish it upon (*badala*) people and accept no payment in return, and those who, having also been given knowledge by God, withhold it (*ḍanna bi-*) from mankind and accept payment in return. The former will be rewarded on the Day of Judgment and the latter will be severely punished.[22] Withholding knowledge for the sake of gain was thus associated with "studying for this world" and counted among the major sins. It was so listed by Ḏahabī in his *Book of Major Sins*.[23]

---

[20] A consonantal alternation known as *ibdāl* in Arabic philology and much discussed; see Shady H. Nasser, *The Transmission of the Variant Readings of the Qur'ān*, Leiden: Brill 2013, 172 and note 39.

[21] Ṭabarī *Tafsīr* (Būlāq), Cairo 1321, XXX,45.

[22] Ġazālī *Iḥyā'*, Book I, *Bāb* 6, *fī āfāt al-ʿilm* = p. I,46–47, Būlāq 1312; I,55, Cairo 1334. This *ḥadīṯ* is found in none of the canonical collections, but this fact is insignificant. The *ḥadīṯ* is important for conveying a widely held belief, though it seems, not practice, that knowledge ought not to be withheld for the sake of personal gain.

[23] References in Rosenthal *Knowledge* 315, where the subject of the "Personal Failings of Scholars" is treated in detail.

Withholding *secular* knowledge, presumably for the sake of self-aggrandizement, also met with disapproval. There is the parabolical story of a lexicographer who wrote a dictionary of unparalleled richness, but who was "stingy about it" (*ḍanna bi-*) and did not allow his students to copy it. "He thus," says Azharī who reports the story, "saw no good come out of his work during his lifetime." But even after his death, the story continues, the book was jinxed, for it fell in the water while being transported across a river and was lost. Azharī concludes with the inevitable moral: "Withholding knowledge (*aḍ-ḍann bi-l-ʿilm*) is not praiseworthy and no good comes out of it (*wa-lā mubāraka fīhi*)."[24] In the same spirit Aristotle is credited in the *Depository of Wisdom Literature* with having said, "Withholding the knowledge (*ḍannu r-rajuli bi-l-ʿilm*) and philosophy which bring one close to happiness is one of the cruelest acts and greatest sins."[25]

The complementary position to this approach to disseminating knowledge, viz., that it should be divulged only to those deserving it and capable of understanding it, also found its authority among the sayings of the Prophet and other respected personalities in Islamic culture. A few Traditions in 232
the collection of none other than Buḫārī present the Prophet as favoring suppression of *religious* knowledge (i.e., of *ḥadīṯ*) from those who might misunderstand and misapply it.[26] In Avicenna's Andalusian contemporary Ibn-ʿAbd-al-Barr's *Comprehensive Exposition of Knowledge and Its Excellence*, where various statements on this subject are collected,[27] the Prophet's statement takes the following generalized form: "Forgetfulness destroys knowledge, and transmitting it to the undeserving (*ġayr ahlihi*) causes its loss." The famous logion of Jesus from Matthew 7:6, "neither cast ye your pearls before swine," figures prominently in such discussions, and is retold in numerous variations ascribed both to Jesus and others.[28] One version in

24 Al-Azharī *Tahḏīb al-luġa* (Cairo 1964–1967) I,25. See the story and references in J.A. Haywood, *Arabic Lexicography*, Leiden: Brill, 1965, 95–96. The author of the lost dictionary (*K. al-Jīm*) is reported to have been Šamir al-Harawī (*GAS* VIII,191), but Haywood rightly questions the attribution. In the *Marātib an-naḥwiyyīn* of ʿAbd-al-Wāḥid ibn-ʿAlī al-Ḥalabī (Cairo 1974, p. 145), which Haywood does not cite, a similar story is told of Abū-ʿAmr aš-Šaybānī's *K. al-Jīm*.

25 *Muntaḫab Ṣiwān al-ḥikma* 766 Dunlop.

26 Buḫārī, *aṣ-Ṣaḥīḥ*, I,45–46 (L. Krehl, ed., *Le recueil des traditions Mahométans par … el-Bokhâri*, Leiden: E.J. Brill, 1862; *bāb* 48 and 49 of *kitāb al-ʿilm*). See the summary in Rosenthal *Knowledge* 81–82.

27 Ibn-ʿAbd-al-Barr, *Jāmiʿ bayan al-ʿilm wa-faḍlihi*, Cairo 1968, I,130–133.

28 For further variants and references see D. Gutas, "Classical Arabic Wisdom Literature: Nature and Scope," *JAOS* 101 (1981) 78, note 67. Cf. also Rosenthal *Knowledge* 259.

Ibn-ʿAbd-al-Barr will serve as an example: "It is related on the authority of the Prophet, God bless him and grant him peace, that he said: 'My brother Jesus, peace be upon him, rose among the Israelites to deliver a sermon and said: "O Israelites, do not give wisdom (*ḥikma*) to the undeserving (*ġayr ahlihā*) lest you wrong it, and do not keep it from the deserving lest you wrong them".'" Ibn-ʿAbd-al-Barr then goes on to quote with great approval a few verses from an anonymous poet, which may not be irrelevant in the present context:

> Am I to strew pearls [in prose] among grazing droves,
> Or string them [in verse] for heedless sheep?
> Haven't you seen how I have been wasted in the worst of lands?
> I will not squander sayings/words like pearls among them!
> If ever the Merciful should cure me of the long hardship I am in,
> And I come across people worthy of knowledge and wisdom,[29]
> I will spread [my pearls], benefiting them, and gain their love;
> Otherwise I will keep [my pearls] stored with me, concealed. (L44)

This poem is significant because it illustrates the association that was made in Islamic culture between withholding knowledge and another widely held concept, "evil times:" a regular aspect of the "complaint about the times" at every age was that interest in knowledge had waned, and that there
233 was hardly anybody left able to understand and appreciate the knowledge transmitted to him.[30] In such circumstances, as our poet says, it is better to withhold knowledge.

The two attitudes in Islamic culture about communicating or withholding knowledge were complementary and converged on an unexpressed principle, the intention of the person in withholding it. All knowledge, and especially religious knowledge, was to be communicated except if the potential teacher knew that by communicating it some harm would ensue. The harm could be directed either to the knowledge itself (it might be lost if entrusted to dull minds), or to the person communicating it (he might be considered foolish, or called a liar, or attract abuse), or to the person receiving the knowledge and hence to society at large (he might misunderstand and misapply the contents of the knowledge).[31] If the intention

[29] It is impossible to convey in English the breadth of the Arabic words *ʿulūm* and *ḥikam*; the former suggests at the same time "different kinds of knowledge" and "sciences," the latter "maxims," "wisdom," and "different kinds of philosophical sciences."

[30] See the discussion of the "complaint about the times" in Franz Rosenthal, "*Sweeter than Hope*", Leiden: Brill, 1983, Chapter I, and particularly pp. 49–51.

[31] A good example of such potential harm of divulging knowledge to the unworthy is

of the potential teacher was to avoid causing any of these harms, then withholding knowledge was acceptable. If, however, his intention was gain, self-aggrandizement, or any worldly pursuits in general, then withholding knowledge was a sin. This state of affairs was satisfactory as long as knowledge was to be communicated orally, and there were few able and willing students (the "pure hearts" of Plato as reported by Fārābī in the passage above, L43, §1) to receive it. But the deteriorating state of the world (*fasād az-zamān*) made it increasingly evident that such students were no longer in sufficient supply—hence the need to consign knowledge to writing without at the same time also making it widely accessible and subject to the harms from which one wished to protect it. These are precisely the problems Avicenna referred to in *The Provenance and Destination* and *The Destination* (T4, §3; T5, §2). The Aristotelian tradition provided at this point the answer by stating the ways in which one could "publicize knowledge without making it public," and Fārābī, summarizing centuries of development, enumerates the ways.

The Greek and Islamic attitudes towards the communication of knowledge were thus largely complementary, and it was this cluster of ideas that formed the background against which Avicenna's views about the subject were shaped.

To recapitulate: There are three major aspects to Avicenna's understanding of the philosophical praxis, all dictated by the reality of the human
condition that the acquisition of Knowledge, that is, doing philosophy, is 234
a historical process. The first is theoretical and procedural. Knowledge is acquired by establishing Fundamental Principles and Working Out the Corollaries by syllogistic means. This centers on the Discovery of the middle term, which again is twofold. The middle term can be discovered either after study and thought or instantaneously by Guessing it Correctly. In terms of their intellectual development, this is the only avenue available to humans to evade the constraints of history. In the search for the middle term, because of the attendant requirements for prolonged study on the one hand and natural endowment for Correct Guessing on the other, this avenue is, understandably, limited to few individuals, prophets and accomplished philosophers.

provided by Buḫārī. The Prophet did not want his statement, that a mere pronouncement of the *šahāda* would protect one from Hell, become widely known lest people rely on the *šahāda* only and stop doing good deeds (*Ṣaḥīḥ* I,46 Krehl). See Rosenthal *Knowledge* 82.

The second and third are social. Since the acquisition of knowledge has to be done in a certain social context and by following the teachings of previous philosophers, incidental, but nonetheless deciding, considerations are operative. The teachings are transmitted in a certain tradition, and this tradition, by its very nature generates sclerotic attitudes which eventually hamper, rather than assist, the philosophical praxis. The "lures" of Custom and tradition have therefore to be avoided. The teachings are also transmitted in a society that has developed its own conventions, religious or cultural, of communicating the highest realities to the ignorant and dull multitudes. These conventions, because expressed in largely symbolic forms—the only forms of communication intelligible to the multitudes—may seem to contradict the outward sense of most of the pronouncements of the philosophers expressing realities as they are in themselves, and if exposed to them, the multitudes will misunderstand them, ignore the conventions which bind society together, and cause harm. The pronouncements of the philosophers have therefore to be Withheld from the multitudes, or presented in such a fashion that will be unintelligible to them. Philosophical Knowledge has therefore to be communicated in a couched manner, and the process of acquisition of knowledge by the philosopher has accordingly to take this into consideration and unravel the allusive manner of exposition engaged in by previous philosophers.

PART THREE

AVICENNA'S INTEGRATION OF THE ARISTOTELIAN TRADITION

THE RESOLUTION OF THE MAJOR POINTS OF CONFLICT WITH THE ARISTOTELIAN TRADITION

The Aristotelian tradition which Avicenna received and its teachings which he inherited were not homogeneous, nor were its various parts mutually compatible. The problems that presented themselves to him were endemic to the transmitted material and they ranged widely in origin: some were already to be found in the texts of Aristotle himself—the "loose ends" and "breaches" Avicenna refers to in the Introduction to *The Easterners* (T8, §1)—others were created by generations of commentators, both Greek and Arabic, in their "efforts to understand what [Aristotle] accomplished best and in Partisan Adherence to some defective theories he originated" [*idem*], and still others had their origin in the vicissitudes of the transmission of this tradition, both from Greek into Arabic and subsequently within Arabic intellectual history. The latter category includes distortions and misrepresentations of this tradition that are due not only to textual corruption or terminological debates (like the one about the term *manṭiq*/logic to be discussed below in Section 5), but also to Neoplatonic pseudepigraphs associated in Arabic with the Aristotelian tradition, and in particular the Plotinian *Theologia Aristotelis*. Content as previous philosophers and commentators may have been either to gloss over these problems or treat them discretely and individually, Avicenna laid before him the task of reconciling the divergent tendencies of thirteen centuries of philosophical history[1] in the context of the Aristotelian system as homogenized and reflected in his own understanding of absolute truth. His efforts in this direction are perfectly consonant with his awareness of the historical dimension of the progress of philosophy and its acqusition, as evidenced in his conception of the history and praxis of philosophy previously discussed. His identification, appreciation, and proposed solution of these problems shed light on his general approach to philosophy and on his purpose as a philosopher.

[1] Avicenna was fully aware of the thirteen centuries separating him from Aristotle; see T6B, §7, and below, Coda, note 11.

Avicenna himself directs us to the areas where these major problems lie. He opens *The Easterners,* which aims to present Philosophy/Knowledge "as it is naturally [perceived]" (T9, §4) i.e., systematically and not historically,
238 with the following words: "We have resolved to compile a treatise on matters about which researchers have disagreed" (T8, §1). At the end of the first section after this introduction, he states that the areas in which these disagreements are to be found are Logic, the Universal Science and Theology parts of Metaphysics, the fundamental parts of Physics, and that part of Ethics "which is needed by the seeker of salvation." Mathematics and the rest of the practical sciences, he adds, are not contested subjects (Testimonium 19 in Chapter 2, W9).

Avicenna provides the same information about the areas of disagreement in the Prologue to *The Cure,* which was written shortly after the passage above (see W6). Here, however, he presents them in a positive light by calling them matters which he treated through his own reflection, and omits any reference to practical science "in anticipation," as he says, "of a comprehensive and separate book" he intended to write on the subject:

> There is nothing of account to be found in the books of the ancients which we did not include in this book of ours .... To this I added some of the things which I perceived through my own reflection and whose Validity I Determined through my own theoretical analysis, especially in Physics and Metaphysics—and even in Logic ... [T9, §2]

A detailed comparison between Aristotelian logic, physics, and metaphysics and those of Avicenna is clearly beyond the scope of the present study and possibly not feasible with our present knowledge of his philosophy; but neither is it Avicenna's intention to draw attention in the passages above to differences of detail of which there would be many and not worth specific mention. This is indicated by the fact that Avicenna almost invariably presents his different viewpoint on matters of detail tacitly, while he makes a point to attract the reader's attention to divergences concerning significant issues in Metaphysics, Physics, and Logic.

1. The Contents of Metaphysics

Hardly a scholar who dealt with Avicenna's biography at some length failed to mention with amusement and awe his striking story in the Autobiography about his study of the *Metaphysics*:

> Ultimately I reached Theology [*al-ʿilm al-ilāhī*]. I read the *Metaphysics* [of Aristotle] but did not understand *what* it contained and was confused about

> the author's *purpose* to the point that I reread it forty times and consequently memorized it. In spite of this I still did not understand it or *what was intended by it* .... I bought ... Fārābī's book *On the Purposes of the Metaphysics*. I returned home and hastened to read it, and at once the *purposes* of that book were disclosed to me [T3, § 9; emphasis added].

The reaction to this report has been twofold. Some scholars have been 239
content simply to summarize it (with varying degrees of accuracy) or refer to it, as if it were self-explanatory and in need of no further comment other than, in some instances, an expression of amazement. Representative of this reaction is the following:

> An autobiographical tradition points out [Avicenna's] debt to al-Fārābī, whose *Intentions of Aristotle's Metaphysics* unraveled for him the secrets of that work, which he read forty times and almost memorized, we are told, without grasping its sense.[2]

Others have expressed some doubts about taking the story at its face value, on the basis that Fārābī's work referred to by Avicenna, in its extant form, could hardly have had the effect described. The following is an eloquent representative of this view:

> [Fārābī's] treatise on the *Metaphysics* ... was printed in eight pages at Hyderabad in 1927. ... The text as we have it is in truth exceedingly slight, and one is bound to suspect that what we possess is very far from the complete original, for it would constitute a most slender guide to the mysteries of metaphysical speculation.[3]

Both approaches make two fundamental mistakes. One is not to read Avicenna's words carefully: he does not say that he did not understand the *sense* of the book, but its *purpose* and why it contained what it does. This is why upon reading Fārābī's essay he says that he understood not the concepts and the ideas of the book but its purposes. To assume that Avicenna meant that he could not understand the sense of the work requires one to accept

---

[2] Fakhry *History* 147 ([1]1970), repeated unaltered in both subsequent editions, p. 128 ([2]1983) and p. 132 ([3]2004). Even more serious students of Avicenna fall into this category, e.g., Goichon *Directives* 16. Examples can be multiplied at will. Among the most amusing summaries of Avicenna's story is that given by Philip Hitti, admittedly not a historian of philosophy: "A copy of the Metaphysics ascribed to Aristotle fell into [Avicenna's] hands and floored him" (*Makers of Arab History*, New York: St. Martin's Press, 1968, 205–206).

[3] Arberry "Life and Times" 18. Through a later remark (1977), Goichon also expressed herself in this fashion: "Il est peu vraisemblable que celui que publia Dieterici [i.e., his edition of Fārābī's *Aġrāḍ*] apportât un grand secours à Avicenne;" review of Gohlman 98.

the blatant contradiction, of which neither approach seems to be aware, between Avicenna's precocity in everything else and his dullness with regard to the *Metaphysics*.

The second mistake is not to read Fārābī's essay carefully—or at least to read it in the light of the first erroneous assumption: for it is obvious that to someone incapable of understanding the sense of the *Metaphysics* Fārābī's essay is of absolutely no help (hence Arberry's suspicion of a lost fuller commentary).

240 Avicenna's problem evidently was not with the ideas analyzed by Aristotle in the *Metaphysics* but with its purpose, and specifically with the classification of the subject matter discussed therein under the heading of "Theology." The precise areas of his difficulty can be appreciated after a closer look at the first half of Fārābī's essay in order to formulate the questions to which Fārābī provides the answers.[a]

> 1. Our intention in this treatise is to indicate the purpose contained in the book by Aristotle known as *Metaphysics* and the primary divisions which it has, since many people have the preconceived notion that the import and contents of this book consist of a treatment of the Creator, the intellect, the soul, and other related topics, and that the science of metaphysics and Islamic theology[4] are one and the same thing. For this reason we find most of those who examine [this book] perplexed and astray, since we[b] find most of the discussion in it devoid of any such purpose—even worse, we[b] can find no discussion specifically devoted to this purpose except in the eleventh chapter, the one designated with the letter *Lambda*.
>
> 2. Furthermore, there exists[c] no discussion by the ancients commenting in the proper manner on this book (as is the case with the other books [by Aristotle]), but at most there is the incomplete commentary on Chapter *Lambda* by

---

[a] The following translation of the first part of Fārābī's *Maqāla fī aġrāḍ ... mā baʿda ṭ-ṭabīʿa* is based on the edition of Dieterici (D), *Abhandlungen* (text) 34.6–36.19, after comparison with the text printed in Hyderabad 1349 (H), pp. 3–6. Neither edition is satisfactory and in a few places the transmitted readings are questionable. Dieterici's edition is based on two manuscripts, British Library Or. 425 (D/B) and Berlin Landberg 368 (D/L), the first of which appears to be related to the manuscript used for the Hyderabad edition (Rāmpūr 70). In the absence of a critical edition, certainly a desideratum, I have simply followed what appeared to me the best reading, indicating significant variants in the notes. For a complete English translation, analysis, and references to all previous literature see Bertolacci *Reception*, Chapter Three, 65–103.

[b] H reads here "he" or "they," i.e., those who are perplexed.

[c] H reads, "we can find."

---

[4] *ʿIlm at-tawḥīd*, i.e. "the science dealing with the profession of God's oneness," a synonymous designation of *kalām*. See Gardet in *EI*² s.v.

Alexander [of Aphrodisias], and the complete one by Themistius. As for the other chapters, either they have not been commented upon, or rather [the commentaries] have not survived to our times since upon examination of the books by later Peripatetics it may be assumed that Alexander did, in fact, write a commentary on the entire book. For our part, we wish to point out the purpose of the book as well as the purpose of each one of its chapters.

3. We say: Some sciences are particular and others are universal. Particular sciences are those whose subject matter is *some* beings [*mawjūdāt*] or *some* imaginary objects [*mawhūmāt*], and which study specifically the accidents[d]
proper to them. For example: physics studies one being, namely, body, inso- 241
far as it changes, moves, and is at rest, and insofar as it possesses[e] the first principles and consequent characteristics of that [i.e., change, motion, and rest]. Geometry studies dimensions insofar as they admit the qualities that are proper to them and the ratios that are present in them (both the first principles and the consequent characteristics; and insofar as this is so).[f] Arithmetic does the same with number, and medicine with human bodies insofar as they are healthy or ill. The same applies for other particular sciences. None of them studies anything that is common to all beings.

4. Universal science studies what is common to all beings (like existence and oneness), its species and consequent properties, things which are not specific accidents of each individual object studied by the particular sciences (like priority, posteriority, potentiality, actuality, perfection, imperfection, and similar things), and the common first principle of all beings, which [alone] ought to be called by the name of God. There ought to be [only] one universal science, for if there were two, then each one of them would have a subject matter proper to it; but the science which has a subject matter proper to it and which does not include the subject matter of another science is a particular science; therefore both sciences would be particular; but this is contradictory; therefore there is [only] one universal science.

5. Theology [*al-ʿilm al-ilāhī*] ought to belong to this [universal] science because God is a principle of absolute being, not of one being to the exclusion of another. That part of [the universal science], then, which includes providing the principle of being[g] ought to be itself Theology. Furthermore,[h] because these categories [*maʿānī*] are not proper to physical objects but are loftier than them in their universality [*ʿumūman*], then this [universal]

---

[d] H reads, "the purposes," *aġrāḍ*.

[e] D/L reads "they are" (*mā hiya*) for "it possesses" (*mā lahu*), in which case the sense would be, "and insofar as they [presumably change, motion, and rest] are the primary principles and consequent characteristics of that [i.e., the body]."

[f] The text is rather uncertain here. H omits the entire text in parentheses.

[g] H reads, "existence," *wujūd* for *mawjūd*.

[h] All manuscripts (D/B, D/L, and H) have a conjunction here (*fa-li-anna, wa-li-anna*), which Dieterici omits.

science is loftier than physics and after physics, and should therefore be called the science of meta-physics [*mā baʿda ṭ-ṭabīʿa*].

6. Although mathematics is loftier than physics—since its objects are abstracted from matter—it ought not to be called metaphysics because its objects are abstracted from matter in imagination [only], not in [actual] existence: actually they exist only in natural things.

7. Of the objects of this science [of metaphysics], some have no existence at all, be it imaginary or actual, in natural things; and not only has the imagination abstracted them from natural things, but their being and nature are totally[i] abstracted. Others exist in natural things even though they can be imagined as abstracted from them; they do *not*, however, exist in natural things *essentially*
242 (i.e., not in such a way that their being could not be independent of them and that they would be things whose subsistence would depend on the natural things), but are found [only][j] with things, natural and non-natural, which are separable either in reality or in imagination. The science, therefore, which deserves to be called by this name [of metaphysics] is this science, and it alone, all other sciences excluded, is meta-physics.

8. The primary object of this science is absolute being[k] and what is equivalent to it in universality [*ʿumūm*], namely, the one. But since the knowledge of contrary correlatives [*mutaqābilāt*] is one,[5] theoretical inquiry into privation and multiplicity is also included in this science. Then after examination of these subjects, [this science] inquires into matters which are as species to them, like the ten categories of an existent being, the species of the one (like the individual one, the specific one, the generic one, and the analogic one, and the subdivisions of each one of these), and similarly the species of privation and multiplicity. [This science] then [inquires] into the consequent properties of being (like potentiality and actuality, perfection and imperfection, and cause and effect), the consequent properties of unity (like identity[l], similarity, equality, coincidence, parallelism, analogy, etc.), and the consequent properties of privation and multiplicity, and then into the first principles of each one of these. After further ramifications and subdivisions, it arrives at the objects of the particular sciences. It expounds the first principles of all the particular sciences and the definitions[m] of their objects. Here this science ends.

---

[i] Reading *innamā* with D for *annahā* in H. For the *laysa ... faqaṭ bal* construction in this sentence see M. Ullmann, "Nicht nur ..., sondern auch ...," *Der Islam* 60 (1983) 3–36. I am also grateful to Manfred Ullmann for a private communication on the structure of this sentence.

[j] This sentence also has a *laysa ... bal* construction; cf. Ullmann "Nicht nur" (in the preceding note) no. XXXIV. Dieterici disregards this construction.

[k] H reads "existent," *mawjūd*, for "being," *wujūd*.

[l] Bertolacci *Reception* 69n8 suggests reading *huwahuwiyya* for *huwiyya* here.

[m] "Definitions:" *ḥudūd*; Dieterici translates, "Abgrenzungen."

---

[5] I.e., knowing one correlative implies knowing the other.

> [Fārābī's text then concludes with brief descriptions of the contents of each one of the books of the *Metaphysics*, A and N excluded (cf. Bertolacci *Reception* 70–71).] (L45)

Fārābī's essay, whose succinctness conceals its importance for the history of metaphysics, provides answers to a number of interrelated questions that may have proved problematical for Avicenna. His formulation of these answers helps us locate Avicenna's problems and analyze their provenance.

Fārābī states that many people are baffled by Aristotle's *Metaphysics* because they expect it to deal with God, the intellect, and the soul, and because they assume metaphysics and Islamic theology to be identical. Upon actual study, however, they find these subjects to be discussed only in one of its books, the famous *Lambda*, and consequently, the implication is, they do not know what to make of the remaining books. Avicenna's great joy when he read this paragraph can only mean that he labored under the same mistaken preconception. This raises the question of the provenance of this preconception.

The early history of philosophy in Islam displays two main tendencies, 243
or lines of development.[6] One is associated with Kindī and his school, and the other with the Aristotelians of Baġdād, Abū-Bišr Mattā, Fārābī, and their followers. Since Fārābī is representative of one line of development, it is reasonable to seek the "many people" who Fārābī says have this misconception among representatives of the other line.

The tendency of identifying metaphysics with Islamic theology was initiated by Kindī, the first thinker who resurrected philosophy as an independent discipline in its new Arabic speaking environment. In the opening chapter of his treatise significantly entitled *On First Philosophy*, he presents an apologia for the study of philosophy and argues, through deliberate simplification, that the noblest part of philosophy contains the subjects discussed by Islamic theology:[7]

> It is true that whoever resists acquiring knowledge of the real nature of things and calls it unbelief is devoid of religion, because knowledge of the real nature of things [which has just been given as the definition of philosophy, the noblest part of which, first philosophy, studies the First Truth] includes knowledge of God's Lordship and Oneness, knowledge of virtue, and all the

---

[6] For the rebirth of philosophy in ninth century Baġdād and the early developments see Gutas "Origins."

[7] Ed. Abū-Rīda, I,104.6–13; ed. Rashed and Jolivet 15.8–14. Cf. the translations by Rashed and Jolivet 14 and by Adamson and Pormann 13.

> knowledge of everything useful and of the way to it, and of staying away from everything harmful and guarding against it. It is the acquisition of all this which the true messengers brought from God, for the true messengers brought precisely confirmation of the Lordship of God alone, adherence to virtues pleasing to Him, and relinquishment of vices opposed to them both absolutely and relatively.[n] (L46)

What is cited here as being included in philosophy, and by implication (through what preceded in the text), in the noblest part of philosophy, is, significantly, *only* the subjects regularly dealt with in Islamic, and indeed, Muʿtazilī, theology, namely, professing the oneness of God (*tawḥīd*), and commanding right and forbidding wrong (*al-amr bi-l-maʿrūf wa-n-nahy ʿan al-munkar*).[8] This simplified and apologetic presentation of the contents of metaphysics is deliberate, as I said above, because Kindī proceeds in the main body of the treatise to discuss that part of metaphysics that deals with being as such, not with the unmovable and eternal first cause.[9] More explicit
244 in its identification of metaphysics and theology is Kindī's description of the *Metaphysics* in his introductory essay to the works of Aristotle:[10]

> Aristotle's purpose in his book called *Metaphysics* is:
>
> a) to expound, among the things which are neither connected nor united with matter, those which subsist without matter but are found associated with something material,[o] and

[n] The pronoun in the transmitted reading *wa-īṯārihā* in genitive construction after *tark* would normally refer to the vices—i.e., *atat … bi- … tarki r-raḏāʾili … wa-īṯārihā*, i.e., *wa-bi-tarki īṯāri r-raḏāʾili*: "relinquishment of vices opposed to virtues both in themselves (= absolutely) and relinquishment of liking, or preferring, the vices (= relatively)." Taking the pronoun to refer to the virtues, as suggested by Rashed and Jolivet 15 note to line 14, and translated both by them and by Adamson and Pormann 13, would be redundant because Kindī already mentioned that the prophets brought adherence to virtues (*bi-luzūm al-faḍāʾil*). A.L. Ivry (in "Al-Kindī's On First Philosophy and Aristotle's Metaphysics," *Essays on Islamic Philosophy and Science*, G.F. Hourani, ed., New York: Albany, 1975) apparently read *wa-āṯārihā* and translated (p. 23), "and in their effects."

[o] Abū-Rīda emends the transmitted text here to read, *al-ašyāʾ al-qāʾima bi-ġayri ṭīna* ⟨*wa-*⟩ *l-mawjūda*, in which case the meaning would be, "among the things which are neither

[8] In the thorough treatment of the subject by Michael Cook, *Commanding Right and Forbidding Wrong in Islamic Thought*, Cambridge, Cambridge University Press, 2000 (for the Muʿtazilites see Chapter 9), there may be room for a more nuanced study of the subject in Arabic philosophy (cf. pp. 494–502).

[9] Cf. Ivry 16–17.

[10] Guidi and Walzer 403.8–11, 418 = Abū-Rīda 384.7–10. Cf the translation in Adamson and Pormann 295.

> b) to declare the oneness of God, and to expound His most beautiful names and that He is the efficient and perfecting cause of the universe [or, of all], God of the universe, and governor of the world[, governing it] with His perfect management and complete wisdom. (L47)

It is to be noted that Kindī specifies two subjects studied in metaphysics. The second is completely identifiable with Islamic theology, and is made to include even an exposition of God's "most beautiful names" (*al-ibāna ʿan asmāʾihi l-ḥusnā*)! What Kindī intended by the first, though, is more difficult to establish.

Textual difficulties aside, it seems clear that Kindī wished to include in metaphysics the study of things which, though not subsisting through matter and neither connected nor united with it, nevertheless exist in association with it. There are, I think, three possible alternatives about the referents of these "things;" they could be either the objects of mathematics (the "mathematicals," number), or universal concepts such as being, unity, etc. (being and its "consequent properties" as specified by Fārābī above, § 8), or the soul and the intellect in the Neoplatonic sense. Which of these alternatives is the "correct" one depends on the point of view from which Kindī's description of the first subject of metaphysics is approached.

(a) Seen from the point of view of Kindī's *sources* upon which his *On the Number of Aristotle's Books* is based, the objects of metaphysics which are found in association with matter must be probably understood to refer to the universal concepts of the Aristotelian tradition, however broadly these are taken. Despite the fact that the sources of Kindī's treatise had a "decidedly Academic [i.e., Platonic] orientation,"[11] the subject treated in it was, after all, the works of Aristotle, and formulations of Peripatetic origin 245
to express the contents of the *Metaphysics* could not (or need not) have been avoided, as is evident from the high degree of congruity between Kindī's description of the first subject of metaphysics cited above (L47, §a) and the statement of Fārābī (L45, § 6), a solid representative of the Alexandrian Aristotelian tradition.

connected nor united with matter, those which subsist without matter ⟨and⟩ those which are found with something material."

[11] Guidi and Walzer 378.

(b) Seen from the point of view of *Kindī himself*, it seems that this alternative, and the one about mathematicals as the objects of metaphysics found in association with matter, are to be excluded. Judging by the extant portion of his *On First Philosophy*, it is evident that his concern centers on a discussion of the One in Neoplatonic terms and by means of the "via negativa." Universal concepts and even number theory are indeed part of the discussion, but not for their own sake; they only serve to expound better what the One is or is not. But a discussion of the One, or God's oneness (*tawḥīd*), belongs, according to Kindī's description, to the part of metaphysics dealing with God, especially since the One, or God, cannot be described as existing "in association with matter." The extant portion of *On First Philosophy*, therefore, deals with the theological part of metaphysics, and the lost second part, if it ever existed, must have dealt with the intellect and the soul.

Circumstantial evidence for this assertion can also be found in the *Epistles of the Sincere Brethren* (*Rasāʾil Iḫwān aṣ-Ṣafāʾ*), which apparently employed a common source with Kindī on this subject,[12] where "knowledge of the substance of the soul" is said to be the first step of the study of the Theological Sciences (*al-ʿulūm al-ilāhiyya*).[13] In the extant first part of *On First Philosophy*, Kindī has a brief section dealing with the soul and the intellect,[14] but it also appears to be incidental to the main discussion of the One. It would not be unlikely to assume that the subject was treated on its own merit in the second, lost part of the treatise.

(c) More important—and conclusive—than these conjectures is the evidence provided by the *traditional understanding* of Kindī's position by his direct and indirect disciples. They understood the object of metaphysics to be the study of the One, intellect, and soul according to Neoplatonic emanationism, and they practically, though not explicitly, identified metaphysics and Islamic theology. Particularly relevant in the present discussion are two men, one of whom, Ibn-Farīġūn, was a third generation student of Kindī, and the other, Ḫwārizmī, was apparently schooled in the same tradition which was active in the tenth century in the Eastern provinces of the Caliphate.

---

12 See Ivry 21 and note 69, and the references given there.

13 *Rasāʾil Iḫwān aṣ-Ṣafāʾ* I,76 (Beirut ed.); cf. Ivry 21.

14 Ed. Abū-Rīda 154.10 ff. = ed. Rashed and Jolivet 85.7 ff. See Ivry 183 ff.

Ibn-Farīġūn's description of the contents and purpose of metaphysics in 246
his arboreal encyclopedia of the sciences merits quotation in full:[15]

> 1. No science is more majestic than this science [metaphysics] for three reasons:
>
> > a) It is a science which investigates the cause of things, while all other [sciences] investigate caused things; the science [investigating] the cause is of higher rank.
> >
> > b) It is a science which investigates an object that is the ultimate goal, namely, the Lordship of the Creator—He is exalted—because Lordship is the ultimate attribute whereby He can be described with reference to "majesty and splendor."[16]
> >
> > c) It is a science which investigates its object [i.e., Lordship] by means of the faculty of the intellect alone, without any recourse whatsoever to the faculties of sense perception and imagination.[p]
>
> 2. Whoever does not fully master these three sciences [i.e., physics, mathematics, metaphysics] is not a philosopher but [merely] a natural scientist or a mathematician. [Metaphysics] is a simple [homogeneous] science and does not admit the division which is characteristic of compound things, since composition pertains to bodies[q] first and acts of imagination second; thus whatever is not affected by bodies and acts of imagination in being perceived, [is perceived] through the intellect only.
>
> 3. The purpose of investigating these three sciences is
>
> > a) to acquire knowledge, as human need requires, about what one should believe concerning the Divinity, Lordship, and Oneness;
> >
> > b) to make the attainment of these [objects of belief] by means of premisses, based on the intellect (and not on sense-perception or imagina-

---

[p] Reading *wa-l-wahm* for *wa-l-ʿaql* in the MS, which is patently a mistake; cf. *al-awhām* in the following three lines in the MS.

[q] Reading *al-ajsām* for *al-ajnās* in the MS; cf. the following line, *al-ajsām wa-l-awhām*.

---

[15] Ibn-Farīġūn, *Jawāmiʿ al-ʿulūm*, MS Istanbul Ahmet III 2768, f. 73[a], reproduced in the Publications of the Institute for the History of Arabic-Islamic Science [Series C, Facsimile Editions, Vol. 14], Frankfurt 1985, p. 145. For all the available information on Ibn-Farīġūn see Hans Hinrich Biesterfeldt in Rudolph 167–170, 246–247.

[16] The reference here is to the Qurʾān 55:27: "All that dwells upon the earth is perishing, yet still abides the Face of thy Lord, majestic, splendid" (Arberry). In this passage majesty and splendor are indicated as subsidiary attributes of God as Lord (*rabb*), and Ibn-Farīġūn, who found Lordship (*rubūbiyya*) stated as the object of Metaphysics by Kindī (above, L46), sees a scriptural endorsement for the ancient science of metaphysics as the study of God's Lordship.

tion) and derived from logic, which are instilled by God, in order that Authority be not Followed uncritically [*taqlīd*];

c) to follow a proper course toward rational understanding by means of these premisses, taken from things whose soundness is agreed upon because of [what they are in] themselves; and

d) to make the other two sciences [physics and mathematics] the means of attaining the truths of this science [metaphysics].

4. The utmost that a seeker of this science can reach is to find out [*yaʿrifa*] that created things are gradated in a way required by the Creator's wisdom,
247 and that some of them are the final goal of others, some the movers of others, and that some are related to others ⟨as some others are related⟩ to the Mover[r] who originates qualified beings by means of [his] pure oneness to which no multiplicity, or change, or alteration ever attaches. (L48)

Ibn-Farīġūn clearly omits any mention of "universals," or "being-as-such"—Aristotle's first philosophy—from his discussions of metaphysics. Its object is, he says, the cause and ultimate goal of things (§ 1a, b) (which is the same thing depending on which end of the scale of emanation God is viewed from); its method is logic (§ 3b), which is a function of the intellect (§ 1c, 3b, c), because the intellect is the only faculty able to perceive objects subsisting neither in matter nor in imagination, i.e., God (§ 2); its preparatory sciences are physics and mathematics (§ 3d); and its purpose is to acquire knowledge about God (§ 3a) and how He relates to the rest of the created world (§ 4). The focal point of metaphysics is therefore God as the object of knowledge and the intellect as the means of knowledge. Discussing these subjects will inevitably entail an understanding of the "order" created by God, the scale of being referred to in § 4, which is the Neoplatonic scheme of emanation from the One to intellect, to soul, and to nature.

In his classification of the sciences, Ibn-Farīġūn discusses metaphysics and Islamic theology separately and without explicitly referring to the question of their connectedness, but his formulation of their description makes it clear that with respect to their object and method they are to be seen as complementary and interrelated, if not absolutely identical, sciences. Islamic theology (*kalām*), which he classifies as a science interpreting (*taʾwīl*) the concepts (*maʿānī*) of the Qurʾān, he defines as follows:[17]

---

[r] The MS has *min al-baʿḍ wa-nisbat baʿḍihā ilā baʿḍ ilā l-muḥarrik*; I read *wa-nisbata baʿḍihā ilā baʿḍin ⟨ka-n-nisbati mina l-baʿḍi⟩ ilā l-muḥarrik*.

---

[17] MS Istanbul Ahmet III 2768, f. 68^{b} (p. 136 of the facsimile edition).

> The discipline, called *kalām*, of those who interpret [*al-muta'awwilīn*] the oneness of God [*at-tawḥīd*], [His] attributes [*aṣ-ṣifāt*], and the principles of religion [*uṣūl ad-dīn*] that must be believed in. Their purpose is to investigate these principles. (L49)

Scholars of the three religious sciences—theologians (*mutakallimūn*), jurists (*fuqahā'*), and traditionists (*aṣḥāb al-ḥadīṯ*)—Ibn-Farīġūn continues, should beware in their method of the following:

> Their love for [uncritical] acceptance of Authority[s] should not induce them to believe in the soundness of reports occurring in the traditions [*āṯār*] that contradict reason/intellect [*'aql*], which is the fair balance [*mīzān*] by means of which everything disputed or doubtful is weighed.

The high degree of congruence between Ibn-Farīġūn's description of *kalām* 248
and metaphysics is obvious. *Kalām* studies the Qur'ānic data about the oneness of God and his other attributes by means of the intellect, which is here specifically designated as "the fair balance" (*al-mīzān al-'adl*), a well established synonym for logic (see Section 5 below). Metaphysics studies the same thing (including the Qur'ānic description of God)[18] in the same way. The only perceptible difference between the two would be in their stated purposes: the former's is to investigate the principles of religion (Islam), the latter's simply to acquire knowledge about God, although in their essence both purposes would seem to coincide. At most one could say that the two sciences are different only to the extent that *kalām* is *Islamic* metaphysics.

Ḫwārizmī, like Ibn-Farīġūn, discusses *kalām* and metaphysics in two separate chapters, the former among the Muslim sciences, the latter among the foreign. His treatment of *kalām*, which he does not define, is restricted to definitions of a number of conventional terms (*muwāḍa'āt*) used in Islamic theology, and consequently does not allow us to judge the extent to which he intended this science to be seen as corresponding to metaphysics.[19] Conversely, his description of metaphysics is most explicit. Under the subjects which it covers he lists God, whose specific attribute he says is "the necessary

---

[s] The next word or two (*wa-annahum* ⟨...⟩?) seem to be either corrupt or missing in the manuscript.

---

[18] See note 16.

[19] *Mafātīḥ al-'ulūm* 22–23 van Vloten; see C.E. Bosworth, "A Pioneer Arabic Encyclopedia of the Sciences," *Isis* 54 (1963) 104. Ḫwārizmī's remark that these terms are discussed differently by philosophers and geometers cannot be assessed without a clear understanding of which philosophers and geometers he is referring to.

existent" (*wājib al-wujūd*, a concept Avicenna was to make the center of his discussion of God, see Section 3 below), intellect (active and material), soul (universal and general), and nature.[20] These are precisely the subjects which Fārābī says (L45, § 1) are thought to constitute "the import and contents" of Aristotle's *Metaphysics*.

The philosophical tradition established by Kindī and continued by scholars active in the Islamic world east of Baġdād thus showed two distinct tendencies in its understanding of Aristotelian metaphysics. One was to consider it as dealing solely with the One and the stages of emanation from both the ontological and epistemological points of view, and the other was largely to identify it with the autochthonous science of Islamic theology. Whether the first was developed in order to justify the second, or the first was already present in the sources of the tradition and as a result led to the
249 second one, are historical questions of considerable significance that will have to be studied in the future; what they indicate, though, is a trend in the earliest philosophical school in Islam, perhaps existing already in the last phase of antiquity, to emphasize the theological aspect of Aristotle's *Metaphysics* at the expense of that dealing with first philosophy, being-as-such.

Fārābī belonged to a different tradition, one that descended directly from the last Aristotelians of the Alexandrian school.[21] As a representative of mainstream Aristotelianism he objected to these two tendencies in the older, and presumably more dominant, philosophical school of Kindī, and wrote his essay *On the Purposes of Aristotle's Metaphysics* in reaction to them and in order to point out that metaphysics and Islamic theology are *not* the same, and that the subject of metaphysics is not merely the One and the Hypostases. The first point is stated explicitly in his *Enumeration of the Sciences* in which Islamic theology (*kalām*) is defined not as a *theoretical* "investigation of the principles of religion," or of the One and His attributes (Ibn-Farīġūn), but as an *apologetic* discipline whose purpose is to defend the opinions and actions of the founder of one's religion.[22] Its method is not demonstration (the "logic" meant by Ibn-Farīġūn), but dialectics, rhetoric, and sophistry.[23]

---

[20] *Mafātīḥ al-ʿulūm* 134–135 van Vloten; Bosworth "Encyclopedia" 107–108 (preceding note).

[21] Fārābī rightly claims this for himself in the sketch of his philosophical pedigree. There is much independent evidence to support this claim. See Gutas "Paul the Persian" 255 and notes 58, 59, and Gutas "'Alexandria to Baghdad'".

[22] *Iḥṣāʾ al-ʿulūm* 100 Gonzalez Palencia = Lerner and Mahdi 27.

[23] Dialectics and rhetoric (*jadal, ḫiṭāba*) are mentioned by Fārābī in his *Book of Religion*

The sharp variation which the two traditions, Kindī's and Fārābī's, exhibit in their view of the relation of metaphysics and theology is excellently illustrated by a textual variant in the transmission of a text by ʿĀmirī, a second generation student of Kindī. Faithful to his tradition, ʿĀmirī identifies Theology, as a branch of metaphysics, with religion, apparently unwittingly (and hence all the more significant for our purposes). In the introductory chapters of his *On the Afterlife* (*Al-Amad ʿalā l-abad*), he says of Pythagoras the following: "Having learned geometry from the Egyptians, he then learned physics and Theology (*al-ʿulūm al-ilāhiyya*) from the companions of Solomon. These three sciences—that is, geometry, physics, and the science of religion (*ʿilm ad-dīn*)—he then transferred to the land of Greece."[24] No more than a few decades later, the compiler of the *Depository of Wisdom Literature* (*Ṣiwān al-ḥikma*), who had distinct affinities with the tradition of Fārābī as represented by Abū-Sulaymān as-Sijistānī,[25] copied this passage 250
word for word but with one exception: for "the science of religion" (*ʿilm ad-dīn*) he substituted "Theology" (*al-ʿilm al-ilāhī*).[26]

Avicenna was born and raised in the eastern parts of the Islamic empire where Kindī's tradition was most flourishing, as the provenance of the personalities just discussed indicates; he pursued his "graduate" studies in Buḫārā in the very library of the Sāmānids in which ʿĀmirī most likely composed and probably deposited his *On the Afterlife*.[27] As Fārābī noted in his essay (L45, § 2), "proper," i.e., Peripatetic, commentaries on the *Metaphysics* were scanty. The autodidact Avicenna could not help but approach the book with the misconceptions described by Fārābī, and be duly perplexed.

The problem, as it was presented to Avicenna, was essentially a historical one, though it was solved for him by Fārābī's explanations in terms other than historical. It centered, primarily, on the question whether there is a dichotomy in Aristotle's teaching between metaphysics as Theology (*theologikē*), the study of the unmoved mover, and metaphysics as first philosophy, the science of being-as-such (*on hēi on*), or, alternatively put, if there is both a "metaphysica specialis" and a "metaphysica generalis" in

(*Kitāb al-Milla wa-nuṣūṣ uḫrā*, ed. Muhsin Mahdi, Beirut 1968, 47–48); sophistry (*muġālaṭa*) in the *Enumeration of the Sciences* (*Iḥṣāʾ al-ʿulūm* 106 Gonzalez Palencia = Lerner and Mahdi 30).

24 Rowson 70–71, text and translation (slightly modified).

25 See Wadad al-Qāḍī, "*Kitāb Ṣiwān al-ḥikma*: Structure, Composition, Authorship and Sources," *Der Islam* 58 (1981) 115–119; G. Endress in Rudolph 199.

26 *Muntaḫab Ṣiwān al-ḥikma* 57 Dunlop.

27 Cf. Rowson 6–7, 28.

Aristotle.[28] Aristotle, first of all, used a number of terms to designate the science he was engaged in in the *Metaphysics*, notably "first philosophy," the science of "being-as-such," and twice "the science of divinity," or "Theology," *theologikē* (*scil. philosophia* or *epistēmē*). To the terms employed by Aristotle there was added another one, metaphysics, in the course of the transmission of his books.[29]

Second, the Alexandrian scholars of the school of Ammonius, who provided the immediate background for Arabic philosophy, viewed all these terms as referring to a single science and a single subject matter, but in their explanations of each one of these terms they highlighted different aspects of
251 it and thus generated the impression of a polythematic science.[30] They also clearly emphasized the theological aspect over the rest because they began their commentaries by saying that the purpose (*skopos*) of the *Metaphysics* was "to theologize" (*theologēsai*).[31]

Third, additional considerations were inevitably involved in Arabic philosophy through the mere fact of translation and the semantic field of the subject as it was discussed in Arabic. In the translation of the *Metaphysics*, the expression *philosophia theologikē* was rendered (etymologically for *theo-logikē*) as "philosophy treating of divinity" (*al-falsafa ... al-ilāhiyyat al-qawl*),[32] which became current in Arabic in a smoother form as *al-ʿilm al-ilāhī*, "the science of divinity," or "Theology." This expression, however, though perhaps clear to the few schooled in Aristotelian philosophy, was ambiguous to the educated Arabic speaking thinker. Literally it means "the knowledge/science pertaining to the deity," which theoretically could be interpreted either as 'God's knowledge,' or 'man's knowledge of God,' or 'the science dealing with God.'[33] Arabic theological discourse had well defined

---

[28] The problem has been intensively discussed by contemporary scholarship for more than a century now; for a brief history of the discussion with bibliographical references see Bertolacci *Reception* 112–113, with further references in Bertolacci "Autobiography" 259.

[29] *Metaphysics* E.1, 1026a29; K.7, 1064b3; see further references in Bertolacci *Reception* 111–112. For a discussion of the Greek word *theologia* used in this sense, apparently a Platonic/Aristotelian neologism, see W. Jaeger, *The Theology of the Early Greek Philosophers*, Oxford 1967 (1947), 4 ff. The use of the term in early Christianity is traced by F. Kattenbusch, "Die Entstehung einer christlichen Theologie," *Zeitschrift für Theologie und Kirche* 11 (1930) 161–205.

[30] Convincing arguments about their unified view of metaphysics were advanced by K. Kremer, *Der Metaphysikbegriff in den Aristoteles-Kommentaren der Ammonius-Schule*, Münster 1960. The issue is discussed extensively on pp. 5–9, 197–199, 209–216.

[31] See, e.g., Asclepius' notes of Ammonius' lectures (*apo phōnēs*), *CAG* VI.ii, 1.7–8, 1.18–19.

[32] Averroes *Tafsīr Mā baʿd aṭ-Ṭabīʿa* 707.5–6 Bouyges.

[33] As a matter of fact, Kindī, who *was* trained in Aristotelian terminology, exploits this

terms to cover all these meanings,[34] but whichever meaning was taken, the educated guess of an Arabic speaker, and especially a Muslim, unfamiliar with technical Aristotelian phraseology, would be to assume that it had something to do with theology as understood in an Islamic context.

These three aspects of the problem of the subject matter and terms of metaphysics were present the very moment the work was translated into Arabic. To them there was added, in the course of the development of Arabic philosophy in the school of Kindī, the identification of Aristotelian metaphysics with Islamic theology, as previously discussed. This was the state of the problem as addressed by Fārābī. His essay on the purposes of the *Metaphysics* is thus significant for the history of philosophy on two counts: it reformulates the problem on the basis of late antique Aristotelianism in Alexandria and, eliminating the incrustations due to the Islamic tradition, states the various aspects of the problem as they appear in the new Islamic context; and it paves the way and provides the theoretical foundation for the eventual synthesis worked by Avicenna.

The effect of Fārābī's essay on the philosophy of Avicenna was, by the 252
latter's own admission, decisive. It alerted him to the fact that Theology is only a part of metaphysics, not the entire subject, and that metaphysics also includes the study of "being-as-such," i.e., the universal science, and provides the first principles of the other sciences. In other words, Fārābī's essay gave Avicenna information about the three ways in which Aristotle himself described the subject of metaphysics and which were discussed in the historical development of the Aristotelian tradition: metaphysics as the study of "being-as-such," as "first philosophy," and as Theology (*theologikē*). In this light Avicenna could identify what he had earlier thought to be the entire Metaphysics as only one of its three parts, the Theological one, and add to it the other two parts, thus accounting for all the contents of Aristotle's *Metaphysics*. The purpose of the book Avicenna had read forty times became clear to him thanks, indeed, to Fārābī's essay, his indebtedness to

ambiguity precisely in order to effect a fusion between Aristotelian metaphysics and Islamic theology. In his bibliographical essay on the books of Aristotle he uses the expression *al-ʿilm al-ilāhī* to refer not to the Aristotelian science but to God's knowledge given to prophets, who acquire it without effort: Guidi and Walzer 395 (text), 409 (translation).

34 For a discussion of the terms used to cover "God's knowledge" and "man's knowledge of God," see Rosenthal *Knowledge* 108 ff. and 129 ff. The terms for Islamic theology were, of course, *ʿilm al-kalām* and *ʿilm at-tawḥīd*.

which is apparent in his first work, *Compendium on the Soul*, written shortly after the fateful encounter with the crier in the bookseller's quarter (T3, § 9). Avicenna follows in that work closely Fārābī's description of the contents of Metaphysics, and even occasionally his very words.[35] The contents of the Theological part he specifies as follows:

> [B. Theology: (iii) Natural Theology] Establishing the first creator, the first created, and the universal soul; the way in which creation occurs; the rank of the intellect with respect to the creator, of the soul to the intellect, of sublunar matter and the forms to the soul, and of the spheres, stars, and generated beings to matter and form; and why there is such a stark divergence in priority and posteriority among them. [T1, § 3 IV B iii]

Avicenna's sensibilities had been shaped in the philosophical tradition of Kindī, however, and he accordingly considered the Theological part to be the noblest and best, later calling it "the fruit" of Metaphysics (T4, § 1 end), in a passage strongly reminiscent of that of Kindī cited earlier (L46).

To this understanding of the contents of Metaphysics Avicenna added, with increasing finality, yet a fourth dimension, which was gained not so much from formal Islamic theology as from general Islamic belief, and which dealt with the subject of the survival of the rational soul and all that implied. This final category, which I call the Metaphysics of the Rational Soul, will be discussed separately in the following section.

The result of these developments was the most comprehensive view of metaphysics until Avicenna's time, one that incorporated all the devel-
253 opments within the Aristotelian tradition, Islamic theology, and broader Islamic tenets. This view categorized the contents of metaphysics into two broad divisions, each of which had again two relatively clearly discernible aspects: the first major division was the Universal Science, the two aspects of which were the study of being-as-such and its consequent properties, and first philosophy as the science that provides the principles of the other sciences; the second category was Theology, whose two aspects were natural theology and the Metaphysics of the Rational Soul.

The above classification of the contents of metaphysics is already present, as we saw, in the very first work of Avicenna, the *Compendium on the Soul*, and can be seen in all his subsequent works with varying degrees of sharpness. In the "Lesser" *Destination* he talks of the universal science and the first philosophy as synonyms, and distinguishes it from the "Theological

[35] Cf. T1, § 3.iv, with the text of Fārābī translated above, L45, § 8.

discipline."[36] In the Introduction to *The Cure* he mentions that the discussion of the categories properly belongs to the "philosophical" (as opposed to the "Theological") discipline, i.e., universal science or first philosophy (T9, § 2), while he refers to the Theological, *al-Ilāhiyyāt*, part of *The Cure* as "the science that belongs to metaphysics" (T9, § 5D). His precise words in this passage (*al-ʿilm al-mansūb ilā mā baʿda ṭ-ṭabīʿa*) are understandable only in the context of our preceding analysis: Theology, *al-ilāhiyyāt*, is not the *entire* metaphysics, but only a part that belongs to it.

The same understanding of the contents of metaphysics is also evident in Avicenna's formal classification of the sciences. In what must be considered a relatively early treatise, *The Divisions of Philosophy* (*Aqsām al-ḥikma*, GS 1), he presents as follows the divisions of metaphysics:[37]

	I. *Fundamental Divisions*
[A. Universal Science:]	
[i. Being as such:]	1. Universals
[ii. First Philosophy:]	2. Principles of the sciences
[B. Theology:]	
[iii. Natural Theology:]	3. God and His attributes
	4. Celestial beings
	5. Divine providence and governance of all
	II. Derivative Divisions 254
[iv. Metaphysics of the Rational Soul:]	1. Revelation and prophecy
	2. Destination and Afterlife

In *The Easterners*, where Avicenna finally decides to discard outward adherence to the transmitted forms of Aristotelianism, he breaks with tradition (he decides not to follow "a course of accommodation" with the Peripatetics, as he phrases it in the Introduction of the work, T8, § 5) and states explicitly

[36] At the beginning of the thirteenth chapter of the *Destination*, Avicenna says that the first principles of the sciences are known "from the universal science, which is called first philosophy (*al-ʿilm al-kullī allaḏī yusammā falsafatan ūlā*);" at the end of the preceding chapter he had just stated that knowledge of the first cause, the One, is verified through "the Theological discipline" (*aṣ-ṣināʿa al-ilāhiyya*); Ahwānī *Aḥwāl* 113–114.

[37] For this treatise see Jean Michot, "Les sciences physiques et métaphysiques selon la *Risālah fī Aqsām al-ʿulūm* d'Avicenne," *Bulletin de Philosophie Médiévale* (Louvain-la-Neuve), 22 (1980) 62–73. In the table below, the entries are Avicenna's designations; my additions are in square brackets, [...].

what had been latent in his earlier formulations: he makes the two primary parts of metaphysics, Universal Science and Theology, into two independent divisions of the theoretical sciences, thus raising their number from three to four:

> It is Customary to call the Knowledge of the first part [of the theoretical sciences] Physics, of the second part Mathematics, of the third part [dealing with things totally separate from matter and motion] Theology, and of the fourth part [dealing with things sometimes associated with matter] Universal [Science], even though this [fourfold] division is not conventionally used (*mutaʿāraf*).[38] (L50)

The problem of the contents of metaphysics and the classification of its parts thus generated a major point of conflict between Avicenna's understanding of philosophy and the form of the question as transmitted in the Aristotelian tradition and Islamic theology. His works represent repeated efforts to resolve the problem in satisfactory ways and integrate the results in his comprehensive system.[39]

2. The "Fruit" of Physics: Metaphysics of the Rational Soul

The most significant area of conflict between Avicenna and the Aristotelian tradition stems from his singular preoccupation with the subject of the survival and fate of the rational soul. The sources of this subject, as encountered by Avicenna, are diverse. They derive, to name but the most prominent, from Aristotelian noetics and the fateful concept of *nous thyrathen*, endlessly debated throughout the centuries and elaborated upon in late antique
255 tradition,[40] with accretions from Plotinian concepts of the contact of the

[38] *Manṭiq al-Mašriqiyyīn* 7.5–7. For the meaning of *mutaʿāraf* see Lane 2017a and Dozy II,118b.

[39] His solution to this problem in *The Cure* is discussed with acumen and in great detail by Bertolacci *Reception*.

[40] The history of Aristotelian noetics has been traced, with particular emphasis on Avicenna, by É. Gilson, "Les sources gréco-arabes de l'augustinisme avicennisant," *Archives d'Histoire Doctrinale et Littéraire du Moyen Age* 4 (1929) 5–149. Working only with the Latin Avicenna, Gilson was unable to see the significance of the theory of Guessing Correctly the middle term (*ḥads*), to which he devoted little attention (pp. 73–74). The late Greek, Arabic, and Scholastic theories of the active intellect are also briefly sketched by P. Wilpert, "Die Ausgestaltung der aristotelischen Lehre vom Intellectus agens bei den griechischen Kommentatoren und in der Scholastik des 13. Jahrhunderts," in *Aus der Geisteswelt des Mittelalters* [Beiträge zur Geschichte der Philosophie und Theologie des Mittelalters, Suppl. III.1], Münster 1935, 447–462; and by R. Walzer, "Aristotle's Active Intellect ποιητικός in Greek and Early Islamic Philosophy," *Plotino e il neoplatonismo in Oriente e in Occidente*, Rome 1974, 423–436.

soul with the One, also transmitted independently to Avicenna through the *Theologia Aristotelis*; from Neoplatonic emanationist cosmology and its implications for divine providence, which provided a scale for the ontological rank of the rational soul and lent concreteness to the subject of its final Destination; and most immediately, from basic Islamic tenets, which provided the proximate social context of the subject and determined to a large extent the way in which the issues were to be formulated. Avicenna grappled continuously with the problem of harnessing these divergent traditions and bringing them systematically within the compass of a single theoretical science in the Aristotelian classification. He discussed them repeatedly, depending on the focus of his interest, in three sciences, Metaphysics, the De anima part of Physics, and Ethics, and in his summae he included them in a fourth subdivision of the Metaphysics which he originated, the Metaphysics of the Rational Soul (see the end of the preceding section).

Just as Avicenna's theory of *ḥads* provided a process whereby the different sciences were interrelated (Chapter 3.2), so also the theory of the rational soul, the substance whose function Guessing Correctly the middle term is, provided the subject matter where they converged. The study of the different aspects of the rational soul unites several branches of philosophy and appears as the primary purpose and goal of all philosophical praxis. Avicenna explained succinctly and eloquently in his last essay, *On the Rational Soul*:

> [The] rational soul is a substance subsisting by itself, and is imprinted neither in a human body nor in any other corporeal entity.... [It] comes into existence together with the body, not before, but it does not perish when the body perishes and dies; it survives, rather, as it was, except that it attains, after its association with the body is severed, either bliss and pleasure or misery and pain.
>
> [Its] bliss comes about when its substance is rendered perfect, and this is accomplished when it is purified through knowledge of God and works for God. Its purification through works for God consists of (a) its being purged of vile and wicked qualities of character, (b) its being far removed from blameworthy attributes and evil and offensive habits by following reason and religious law, and (c) its being adorned with good habits, praiseworthy qualities of character, and excellent and pleasing traits by following reason and religious law.
>
> Its purification through knowledge of God consists of its attainment a disposition (*malaka*) of its own, by means of which it is ready to call all the intelligibles to presence whenever it wishes without needing to acquire them, and thus to have all the intelligibles present in it in actuality, or in a potentiality

> 256 that is as close to actuality as possible. The soul then becomes like a polished mirror upon which are reflected the forms of things as they are in themselves without any distortion, and whenever it stands face to face with them having been purified through knowledge, there ensues [an automatic] practicing of the theoretical philosophical sciences.
>
> Purification through works is accomplished by methods mentioned in books on Ethics and by assiduous performance of religious duties, both legal and traditional, such as observances relating to [the functions of] the body, one's property, and to a combination of the two. For being restrained at the places where religious law and its statutes place such restraints, and undertaking to submit to its commands, have a beneficial effect on subjugating the soul that "incites to evil" [and thus transforming it] into the rational soul which is "at peace," i.e., making the bodily faculties of the soul, the appetitive and the irascible, subservient to the rational soul which is "at peace." [T14, §§ 5–8]

The study of the rational soul thus involves both the theoretical sciences, Metaphysics (the knowledge of God and the intelligibles) and Physics (De anima), and the practical sciences, Ethics and religious law. The rational soul is the meeting point of philosophical theory and praxis because when it becomes "like a polished mirror," there ensues an automatic practicing of the philosophical sciences. The science that engages in this study, the Metaphysics of the Rational Soul, is thus the highest stage of the philosophical sciences.

From the very beginning of his philosophical career Avicenna had a clear understanding of the questions that were to be treated by this science. He lists them twice in his first work, the *Compendium on the Soul*:

> [Metaphysics of the Rational Soul:] Getting to know divine governance, the nature of the universe, the providence of the First One, prophetic revelation, the sanctified and Lordly spirit, and the supernal angels; attaining the real meaning of the doctrines denying polytheism and the anthropomorphism of the creator; attaining knowledge about the reward in store for the virtuous and the punishment for evildoers, and about the pleasure and pain befalling souls after their separation from the body. [T1, § 3.IV.B.iv.]

At the end of the work, he states the subjects that remain to be discussed:

> Among the subjects associated with this investigation [on the soul] that still remain to be done is to state how the souls exist in the bodies, the purpose on account of which they exist in them, and the eternal pleasure, never-ending punishment, or temporary punishment—which will end after the lapse of some time after the separation from the body—that will visit them in the Hereafter, and to discuss the concept called by specialists in religious law "intercession" and the nature of the four angels and carriers of the Throne. However, had it not been Customary to separate the investigation of these subjects from the investigation we have been conducting, out of

> respect and veneration for the former, and to offer the present investigation
> first as an introduction to the other and in order to establish the framework
> of discussion, I would have followed these chapters with the rest of the 257
> discussion on the other subjects to complete the matter. Had I not been wary
> of becoming tiresome through prolixity, on the other hand, I would have
> dismissed the dictates of Customary Practice.[41]

Avicenna is clear about the issues to be discussed, but there is a wavering about the precise *philosophical* science in which they are to be discussed: they are listed in this work both under Metaphysics and as "subjects associated with this investigation," i.e. De anima. There is no question, however, of treating them in another, *non-philosophical* science, according to established practice; Islamic theology, *kalām*, may provide the terms in which these questions are posed, but they have to be treated in a way different from that of *kalām*, because according to Avicenna *kalām*, as we saw above (Chapter 3.1 and note 19), is a dialectical discipline not conducive to the acquisition of demonstrative truth.

Avicenna's first philosophical summa, the *Philosophy for ʿArūḍī* (W2), does not contain a final section on the Metaphysics of the Rational Soul; but since it is not extant in its complete form, it is impossible to say whether Avicenna had already decided, after his hesitation in the *Compendium on the Soul*, to include the subject in a summa of the Aristotelian system and classify it under Metaphysics. The next work that may have contained such a section, *The Available and the Valid* (W3), is similarly lost, although it would appear that at that stage of his early career Avicenna treated the subject in the context of the practical sciences (Ethics and Politics) in his *Piety and Sin* (W3). Avicenna's reference to the latter work in *The Cure* clearly indicates that it was largely devoted to this cluster of ideas: "divine punishments descending upon corrupt cities and tyrants, ... the reason for ... praying, almsgiving, etc., as well as for the occurrence of wrongdoing and sin" (L1). It would also seem, however, that Avicenna soon abandoned the idea of treating the Metaphysics of the Rational Soul in Ethics because the subjects that he discussed in *Piety and Sin* reappear later in the tenth book of the Metaphysics of *The Cure* and, significantly, are also treated, under the heading "The Inner Meanings of Signs" (*asrār al-āyāt*), at the end of the Metaphysics part of his last major work, *Pointers and Reminders* (see the chart below).

---

41 Landauer 372 (text), 418 (translation); cf. van Dyck *Offering* 93.

This explains the reason why throughout his philosophical career Avicenna evinced little interest in the traditional practical sciences—Ethics, Oeconomics, and Politics—as understood and treated in the Aristotelian tradition. Although the transmission of his works on practical philosophy is fragmentary and confused, the material that is available for study indicates that he dealt with the subject perfunctorily. Such is the impression gener-
258 ated by chapters 4 and 5 in the tenth book of the Metaphysics of *The Cure*, his most extensive extant treatment of the subject, as well as by a perusal of what remains of his ethical writings, possibly fragments from *Piety and Sin*, a hodgpodge of quotations from Fārābī and other earlier ethical writings (see W3 above and GPP1 below in the Inventory in the Appendix). Since he saw the core of the philosophical theory and praxis in the study of the rational intellect, he found the subjects of divine providence, the influences of the celestial spheres upon this world (the "signs") and the rational soul's relation to them, and the real purpose of religious ordinances more germane to his central concern than the enumeration of vices and virtues or human social organizations.

Avicenna came to the realization that the Metaphysics of the Rational Soul thematically belongs with Natural Theology when he identified the former as the "fruit" of Physics and the latter as the "fruit" of Metaphysics, and decided to write an independent work on the subject that would combine both subdivisions of what was later to become the Theological part of Metaphysics. This was *The Provenance and Destination*, the first of many treatments of this subject he had originated.[42] In its introduction he described the work as follows:

> This treatise of mine contains the fruits of two great sciences, one of which is characterized by being about metaphysical, and the other physical, matters. The fruit of the science dealing with metaphysical matters is that part of it known as *theologia*, which treats [the subjects of] Lordship, the first principle, and the relationship which beings bear to it according to their rank. The fruit of the science dealing with physical matters is the knowledge that the human soul survives and that it has a Destination. [T4, §1]

When Avicenna came to discuss the Metaphysics of the Rational Soul in his philosophical summae, which implied a conscious classification of the subject among the other sciences, his wavering finally disappeared and he

[42] Later Islamic tradition was fully aware of Avicenna's innovations in this matter. See the assessments of his achievements offered by the Mālikī al-Imām al-Māzarī and the Ḥanbalī Ibn-Taymiyya cited below in the Coda, L92 and L93.

decided to treat it as the second section of the Theology part of Metaphysics, thus following his initial impulse evident in his first work, the *Compendium on the Soul* (T1, § 3.IV). Avicenna explicitly stated in *The Cure* that this subject is the domain proper of Metaphysics: "The subject of the Destination (*maʿād*) of the soul ought not to be discussed in the context of Physics but only in the context of the philosophical discipline (*aṣ-ṣināʿa al-ḥikmiyya*) where the things that are separable [from matter] are investigated."[43]

The first extant and dated summa that discusses the subject is *The Guidance*, although the *Elements of Philosophy*, which may antedate it, does end with a very brief section on the rational soul, its pleasure and future happiness.[44] *The Guidance*, which was written in 414/1023 while Avicenna 259
was imprisoned in the castle of Fardajān (Gohlman 60.7), has a full section on the Metaphysics of the Rational Soul. It is essentially the same as that included in the later summae, *The Cure* and *Pointers and Reminders*, and it is instructive to compare their contents in order to demonstrate the continuity of Avicenna's thought and dispel the misconceptions about his alleged progressive "mysticism," especially in the *Pointers and Reminders*.[45]

Guidance, III.4–6		*The Cure*, IX.6–7, X.1–5 *The Metaphysics of the Rational Soul*		*Pointers*, II.7–10	
		IX.6	Providence	7	b) Providence
4.2	Good and evil		The problem of evil		c) Evil
		7	Destination of soul;		a) Destination
6	Bliss;		its bliss and misery;	8	Bliss
	description of real happiness through knowledge		real happiness is the perfection of the rational soul through knowledge.	9	Knowledge that leads to bliss: the state of acquired intellect; the soul becomes like a polished mirror.[46] Details on those who attained this state.

43 *Nafs* 238.5–7 Rahman. This philosophical discipline is Theology, since it investigates things separable from matter, the definition given to Theology in the *Easterners* (*Manṭiq al-Mašriqiyyīn* 6–7).

44 *ʿUyūn al-ḥikma* 59.13–60 Badawī.

45 *Hidāya* 280–308 ʿAbduh; *Ilāhiyyāt* 414–455 Mūsā et al. (English translation in Marmura *Metaphysics* 339–378); *Išārāt* II.7–10, 176–222/319–391 = Goichon *Directives* 435–526.

46 The position which this controversial chapter of the *Pointers* occupies in Avicenna's philosophy is clearly indicated by the place Avicenna assigns to the person who has attained knowledge of God and whose soul became like a polished mirror in *On the Rational Soul* (T14, § 7), a work written after the *Pointers*.

Guidance, III.4–6	*The Cure*, IX.6–7, X.1–5 *The Metaphysics of the Rational Soul*	*Pointers*, II.7–10
4.1 Celestial effects on the world	X.1 Celestial effects on the world:	10 Inner meanings of signs: a) abstinence
5.1 Knowledge: *ḥads*		
5.3 Knowledge: revelation	inspiration	
5.2 Knowledge: dreams	dreams	c) dreams
4.3 Miracles		b) miraculous powers
4.4 Prayer	prayer	
	celestial punishment	
5.4 Prophecy	prophecy	d) prophecy
	astrology	
		e) evil eye etc.
	2 Proof of prophecy	
	3 Acts of worship	
	Practical Philosophy	
	4 Politics	
	Oeconomics	
	5 The Caliphate	
	Legislation	
	Ethics	

260 Avicenna wrote a number of monographs on the various aspects of the Metaphysics of the Rational Soul, ranging from essays strictly on the theory of the soul, Theology, and prophetology, to essays on the genre he originated, Provenance and Destination, and including those dealing with specific instances of the interplay between providence (the arrangement of the universe) and the rational soul.

There is one final aspect of this subject which Avicenna again approached innovatively. Part of the "fruit" of Ethics that belongs to the Metaphysics of the Rational Soul is also the matter of legislation by the prophet. Although the epistemological aspect of prophecy belongs to the De anima part of philosophy and to the discussion of *ḥads*, the applied aspect of laying the religious law that will serve, when followed, to purify rational souls, belongs to the practical sciences. For this reason Avicenna abandoned the traditional tripartite classification of the practical sciences in *The Easterners* and introduced a fourth subdivision, "the discipline of legislating" (*aṣ-ṣināʿa aš-šāriʿa*),[47] which would overlap with the Metaphysics of the Rational Soul but

[47] *Manṭiq al-Mašriqiyyīn* 7–8. See the detailed discussion of the subject by Kaya "Prophetic Legislation."

treat the subjects dealt in it from a practical science prespective. Many of the treatises listed in the Inventory in the category of the Metaphysics of the Rational Soul display this approach.[48]

To recapitulate: The material which Avicenna inherited from the last stages of Aristotelianism in late antiquity contained accretions from centuries of philosophical debates about the central subject of the separability of the rational soul and its relation to the divine. These accretions were heavily influenced by Plotinian and, later, general Neoplatonic ideas about the contact of the intellect with the One, the downward procession (i.e., emanationist cosmology, divine providence, and celestial influences), and the upward progression (i.e., prayer, purification, and theurgy). The fact that these discussions in late antiquity were taking place within a progressively Christian environment that had similar concerns which may have affected the formulation of many of these problems also played its role. With the emergence of Islam, the same concerns were expressed in terms and concepts drawn from the Islamic revelation. Philosophers in the Aristotelian tradition, from late antiquity until the time of Avicenna and including Fārābī, treated these issues, to the extent that they felt compelled 261
or inclined to discuss them, discretely, each in its own place within the rigid classificatory system of the sciences, and dissociated from each other despite their substantive coherence. This was the Customary Practice (*ʿāda*) of doing philosophy which Avicenna so frequently decried (L39, above and Chapter 5.2). Islamic philosophers like Kindī and ʿĀmirī, who attempted to accommodate the subject more in the direction of Islamic theology, did so at the risk of abandoning the philosophical rigor of the Aristotelian system—and were duly castigated by Avicenna himself (Chapter 7). What Avicenna attempted to do was to unify, as demanded by the subject itself, the loose ends and discrete discussions of the Aristotelian tradition by breaking the constricting classificatory mold, without at the same time sacrificing the sharpness and rigor of the philosophical analysis of the tradition. He was able to do so by concentrating on the one concept in the entire system that could act as the common denominator, the rational soul, and on its supreme function, Guessing Correctly the middle term, as the factor that could unite the various sciences, and by classifying the study of the rational soul and the

[48] See the introduction to the section in the Appendix on the Metaphysics of the Rational Soul, E, for further details also about the significance of this category of works for Avicennan pseudepigraphy.

related issues as the fourth, and highest, subdivision of Metaphysics (after being-as-such, first philosophy, and natural theology). In the revised Aristotelian system that he presented he could indeed claim that he "perfected what they meant to say but fell short of doing" (T8, § 3). History bore out his claim because after him Aristotelianism in the Islamic East became Avicennism.

3. Physics or Metaphysics: Prime Mover versus Necessary Existent

Another major point of conflict with the received tradition concerning Metaphysics revolved around the question of method in discussing and establishing the existence of the First Cause and First Mover. This conflict also had a historical origin. It stemmed from the two variant positions held by the original Aristotelian tradition and by the philosophical tradition of Kindī and his followers (above, Section 1), namely, the arguments for the First Mover by way of motion and by way of the concept of the Necessary Existent (*wāǧib al-wuǧūd*), respectively. The former is the explicit position of the Aristotelian texts;[49] the origins of the latter, on the other hand, are complex.[50]

Before Avicenna, the concept of the Necessary Existent developed in Islamic theology (*kalām*) as part of the general discussion of the attributes (*ṣifāt*) of God. The great Muʿtazilī theologian, the Judge ʿAbd-al-Jabbār, whom Avicenna probably met during his brief stay in Rayy between 403/1013
262 and 405/1015 (W6),[51] refers to it in his theological summa, *al-Muġnī*.[52] The encyclopedist Ḫwārizmī includes it in his description of metaphysics as one of the attributes of God (above, Section 1). The two older contemporaries of Avicenna, ʿĀmirī and Miskawayh, who attempted a synthesis of Greek philosophy and Islamic theology, also refer to it in their works. Miskawayh mentions it among the attributes of God:

> [E]xistence is essential for the First Creator, since He does not receive it from something else .... But if existence in Him is, as we say, essential, then it is

---

[49] See the discussion and detailed analysis in Bertolacci "Proof."

[50] See the detailed tracing of the background of this concept in Wisnovsky *Metaphysics*, Chapters 11–14.

[51] See George F. Hourani, *Islamic Rationalism*, Oxford: Oxford University Press, 1971, 6–8, and especially Dhanani.

[52] *Al-Muġnī fī abwāb at-tawḥīd wa-l-ʿadl*, Cairo 1962 ff., IV,250 f., XI,432.13 ff.

> impossible to imagine Him as nonexistent, and He is therefore necessary of existence (*wājib al-wujūd*). And what is necessary of existence is perpetual (*dā'im*) of existence, and what is perpetual of existence is eternal (*azalī*).[53] (L51)

ʿĀmirī mentions it in his *Afterlife* as part of the discussion on the attributes of God by "Empedocles":

> The Creator's existence is not like that of any of the existents of this world. For things existing in the world have an existence which is real [only] contingently, that is, it depends on creation, while His essence exists necessarily [*wa-ḏātuhu wājibu l-wujūd*], without depending on creation.[54] (L52)

It is clear that the concept of the Necessary Existent was very much in circulation in the Eastern parts of the Islamic world during Avicenna's philosophical formation, and that it was precisely because of these influences that it held such a significance for Avicenna as to create a conflict with the older and much more established Aristotelian argument by way of motion. The position and implications of the concept in Avicenna's philosophy, as well as its background, are now fairly well known and in no need of repetition.[55] What is significant in this context is that in the philosophical discourse immediately preceding Avicenna, an accommodation was reached whereby the two approaches, though both included within philosophy, were relegated to different areas of study: one was said to be the way of the Physicist, the other of the Theologian. This accommodation is evident in the work of Abū-Sulaymān as-Sijistānī, also an older contemporary of Avicenna:

> The most appropriate inquiry concerning the first mover is that in which 263
> discussion of Physical theory is combined with Metaphysical theory. ... Let us then state in what way this is so. Inquiry concerning the conjunction of effects with causes has two aspects; the first, insofar as it ascends through the connection of one to the other to their cause; and the second, insofar as the permeation of the power of the cause in its effects [is considered]. Inquiry in the first mode belongs to the Physicist, and in the second mode to the Metaphysician [i.e., *qua* student of Universal Science]. There exists also

---

53 *Al-Fawz al-aṣġar* 15 f. Quoted and translated in Rowson 233.

54 *Muntaḫab Ṣiwān al-ḥikma* 110–111 Dunlop = Rowson 78, and cf. the translation in Rowson 79.

55 Among the earlier studies see the foundational work by Goichon *Distinction*, especially pp. 165 ff. and 335 ff., and also Finianos *Être*, especially pp. 239 ff. Most recently see the comprehensive work by Wisnovsky *Metaphysics* and the state of the art presentation of the issue by Bertolacci "Distinction."

> a third mode unconcerned with relation, namely, inquiry into the essence apart from affinities and relationships. The discussion of this belongs to the Theologian.[56] (L53)

Avicenna initially adopted this accommodation. In *The Provenance and Destination* he first presented the argument for the Necessary Existent and then followed it by presenting the argument by way of motion. He connected the two by means of the following explanatory section, which displays a concern to justify his non-Aristotelian procedures:

> Section: Indicating which method of exposition the one just followed is; starting anew with the customary method; describing the difference between the two ways.
>
> We have established the Necessary Existent [*al-wājib al-wujūd*] neither by way of its acts nor by way of its motion. Syllogisms served neither as proof nor as pure demonstration (of the First there can be no pure demonstration because it has no cause), but were rather syllogisms resembling demonstration since they were inferences [*istidlāl*] drawn from the fact that existence requires something that is necessary. …
>
> We will now present the well-known way of establishing the First. This is by way of inference, and especially [that drawn] from motion. We will follow the method used by Aristotle in his two books dealing with universals, one of which, *Physics*, treats of the physical universals, and the other, *Metaphysics*, treats of the metaphysical universals.[57] (L54)

In his *Notes* he identifies, like Abū-Sulaymān, the areas of philosophy which follow these respective methods:

> The Physicists arrive at establishing the First Mover by means of their explanations about the necessity of an incorporeal and infinite power which moves the celestial sphere; they ascend to the First Mover starting with nature.
>
> The Theologians follow a different way. They arrive at establishing the First Mover from the necessity of existence and [the position] that the First Mover must be one and not many. They explain that existing things proceed from it and that they belong to the concomitants of its essence, that the celestial
> 264 motion moves out of a desire for it, seeking to imitate its perfection, and that it is impossible that its perfection not be specific to it or that there be a perfection above its perfection, for had this been possible, then whatever possessed that higher perfection would have been first.[58] (L55)

[56] *Maqāla fī l-muḥarrik al-awwal*, in Badawī *Ṣiwān* 372.3–4, 375.12–19. Translation adopted with modifications from Kraemer 285, § 6.1.1 and 291, § 6.4.1.

[57] *Al-Mabdaʾ wa-l-maʿād* 33–34 Nūrānī.

[58] *Taʿlīqāt* 62.14–19 Badawī = § 470 ʿUbaydī.

In his later period, Avicenna renounced the approach of the Physicists. Although he copied most of *The Provenance and Destination* in *The Cure* and *The Salvation*, he omitted the section translated above and the sections following it which present the arguments for the First Mover by way of motion (W4). More directly, however, he attacked the approach in the *Fair Judgment*:

> Avicenna found fault with Aristotle and the commentators. He said: It is bad [*qabīḥ*] to arrive at the First Real by way of motion and by way of the fact that it is the principle of motion, and [then] to undertake from *this* [position] to make it into a principle for the essences, because these people offered nothing more than establishing it as a mover, not that it is a principle for what exists. How utterly incompetent that motion should be the means of establishing the One, the Real, which itself is the principle of every being!
>
> Avicenna says that the fact that they make the first principle into a principle of the motion of the celestial sphere does not necessarily entail that they should [also] make it into a principle of the substance of the sphere.[59] (L56)

His criticism of the Aristotelian tradition in this regard was tempered, however, by his appreciation of the fact, as he saw it, that the Physical method of proving the existence of the First Mover was only the apparent sense of the *Metaphysics*; its innermost meaning and implicit doctrine was, in fact, to establish the First Real by means of the Theological way.[60] This is what he taught his students, as recollected by the disciple (Ibn-Zayla?) writing from Rayy:

> We also heard him say, "It distresses me that the belief in the permanence of the first principle and in the permanence of its unity should be arrived at by means of motion and the oneness of the moved world, as if [Aristotle's] *Metaphysics* could not yield its riches concerning God Almighty except in this way! This is to be regarded as distressing not on the part of our contemporaries only, but also on the part of all their masters like them." He further said, "Had they comprehended the innermost ideas of the *Metaphysics* they would have been ashamed of this sort of thing and not felt compelled to maintain that the course to be adopted includes both the Physical approach and the Theological approach—something totally unfounded because this book [Aristotle's *Metaphysics*] is distinguished by the Theological approach alone." [T13, § 8]

Avicenna's criticism of the Aristotelian proof of the First Mover by means of motion and his concomitant theory of the Necessary Existent were among

---

59 *Commentary on Lambda*, in Badawī *Arisṭū* 23.21–24.1. See the discussion of Avicenna's objections to this Aristotelian theory in Brown, esp. 35 and 44–45.

60 See below, Chapter 8.3, L80.

265 the most important aspects of his metaphysical system.[61] They were also among the most sensational, and they were attacked at first not only by Islamic theologians like Ġazālī, but also by "purist" Aristotelians as represented later by Averroes.[62] But the concept of the Necessary Existent gained, through Avicenna's synthesis—or his resolution of the conflict between it and the proof by motion—a firm foothold and an integral part in Islamic intellectual history.

4. Logic or Metaphysics: The Problem of the Categories

The subject of the categories, both the doctrine and the eponymous book by Aristotle, had a long history of debate by the time it reached Avicenna. Various aspects of the doctrine had been discussed in earnest throughout the history of Greek philosophy, and Porphyry's *Eisagoge*, which was written precisely in response to the problems posed by the doctrine, set in sharper focus its precarious relationship with Metaphysics. The subsequent philosophical tradition of the Alexandrians assimilated and continued these discussions without, however, relinquishing the framework which classified the categories as part of Logic.[63] The history of philosophy as transmitted

---

[61] Wisnovsky *Metaphysics* 199 even goes so far as to claim that Avicenna's "distinction between necessary and possible existence, and specifically his equation of that which is necessary through another and that which is possible in itself" was "his big idea—the idea which he knew was his most original and which he reckoned would be his most influential," and that it "came to him at the very young age of 18."

[62] For Ġazālī's criticisms and Averroes' emendations of Avicenna's theory see van den Bergh I,170 ff. and 254; see also Chapter 2, W9, Testimonia 13a–c. Averroes, as a matter of fact, wrote a separate treatise in refutation of Avicenna's Theological proof of God; see Jamāladdīn al-ʿAlawī, *al-Matn ar Rušdī*, Casablanca: Les Editions Toubkal, 1986, 39 no. 81.

[63] The origins of the problems raised by the *Categories* and the ensuing discussions about language, universals, and ontology are succinctly presented by Robert W. Sharples, "Peripatetics," in *The Cambridge History of Philosophy in Late Antiquity*, Lloyd P. Gerson, ed., Cambridge: Cambridge University Press, 2010, 147–150. For Neoplatonic discussions of the problem of the categories as related to metaphysics see A.C. Lloyd, "Neoplatonic and Aristotelian Logic," *Phronesis* 1 (1955–1956) 58–72, 146–160; and the same author's briefer exposition in *The Cambridge History of Later Greek and Early Medieval Philosophy*, A.H. Armstrong, ed., Cambridge: Cambridge University Press, 1970, 319–322. There has been a spate of recent collective volumes assessing the significance of the *Categories* in subsequent philosophy, notably by Otto Bruun et Lorenzo Corti, eds., *Les Catégories et leur histoire*, Paris: Vrin, 2005; Lloyd A. Newton, ed., *Medieval Commentaries on Aristotle's* Categories, Leiden: Brill, 2008; and Sten Ebbesen, John Marenbon, and Paul Thom, eds., *Aristotle's* Categories *in the Byzantine, Arabic and Latin Traditions*, cited under Eichner "Categories".

to Avicenna thus contained the inherent contradiction of discussing the extra-logical foundations of Aristotelian logic within the context of Logic itself. Avicenna addressed the contradiction explicitly and was able, as a result, better to formulate his understanding of First Philosophy as part of Metaphysics. His introduction to the Categories of *The Cure* presents a detailed exposition of the subject, and the following paragraphs contain the gist of his argument:

> 1. After becoming acquainted with such matters as we described relating to simple terms [Eisagoge], and after becoming acquainted with names and verbs [De Interpretatione], the student of logic can move on to study propositions and their parts, syllogisms, definitions, and their kinds [Prior Analytics], the matters of syllogisms, demonstrative and non-demonstrative terms along with their genera and species [Posterior Analytics], without having any idea that there are ten categories and that they signify either themselves or what pertains to them through the simple terms.
>
> 2. Disregarding the ten categories causes no harm to speak of, nor would it be a weakness in logic for one to labor under the misconception that there is a greater or smaller number of categories; furthermore, knowing whether some matters should be described as genera is not any more incumbent upon 266
> him than knowing whether some others should be described as species. No; knowledge about how all these exist should be sought from First Philosophy; knowledge about the way in which the soul forms concepts of them should be sought from that part of Physics which is close to First Philosophy [De anima]; and the knowledge that they require terms which signify them should be sought from lexicography.[64]
>
> …
>
> 3. You should know something else, namely that the author of this book did not write it in order to provide instruction, but by way of convention [*waḍʿ*] and following transmitted Authority, for there is no way to gain a Verified knowledge of what is known in it by means of an exposition that is appropriate to logic [only; i.e., without involving First Philosophy].
>
> 4. You should know that everything with which they attempt to establish the number of these ten, that there is no [special] science of them [?], that one is distinct from the other, that each one of them has such-and-such a special character, that the last nine of them differ from the first in that they are accidents whereas it is substance, and similar things, are all declarations, altogether deficient, drawn from other disciplines. This is so because there is no way to know about such things except after a thorough examination, and there is no way to engage in a thorough examination except after attaining the level of science called First Philosophy.

---

64 Avicenna discusses this subject further in *Taʿlīqāt* 169.1–8 Badawī.

> …
>
> 5. What indicates that what I am telling you is the truth is that these subjects have been left out of Aristotle's *Categories*. Moreover, all of the Validating logicians were averse to seeing this book as an investigation into the natures of beings, but said that it is rather an investigation into beings [only] insofar as they are signified by simple terms. …[65] (L57)

Avicenna's disagreement with the Aristotelian tradition is stated in the first paragraph above: in order to study logic as an instrument for proceeding from the known to the unknown,[66] the student needs to know only about simple terms, i.e., the Eisagoge and the De Interpretatione, before moving on to the core of logic, propositions and syllogisms, i.e., the Analytics. The categories not only have no useful function in this methodical process, but sometimes may even cause harm by misleading people.[67] If the objects of the categories are to be studied in themselves, then they are to be studied, depending on the purpose of the approach, either in First Philosophy (ontology), or in De anima (epistemology), or in lexicography (semantics).

267 Avicenna developed this view of the categories apparently early. It seems that his difficulty with understanding the purpose of the *Metaphysics*, in addition to stemming from his inherited misconception that it dealt only with Theology, was also associated with the problem of the categories. Fārābī's essay *On the Purposes of the Metaphysics* thus not only solved his difficulty with regard to Theology, as discussed in the previous Section, but also helped him develop a better concept of the Universal Science and helped him locate there the study of the categories. For this reason, apart from *The Cure*, whose section on the categories is foreshadowed in the earlier *Middle Summary on Logic* (cf. Kalbarczyk), Avicenna never included a critical discussion of the categories in the logical parts of his summae. The trend is already evident in his first summa, *Philosophy for ʿArūḍī* (cf. Eichner "Categories"), and continues through his last major work, *Pointers and Reminders*; the only two works dealing with all the philosophical sciences in which the categories are mentioned, *Elements of Philosophy* and *The Guidance*, contain not a critical discussion but a very brief list of the ten categories.[68] As

---

[65] *Maqūlāt* 5.1–11, 6.9–16, 7.8–10 Anawati et al.

[66] See Avicenna's passages stating the instrumental nature of logic translated below in Section 5, L64–69. For Avicenna's understanding of the subject matter treated in logic see Sabra, with further analysis in Germann. See also Avicenna's further explanations in *Taʿlīqāt* 167 Badawī, second paragraph.

[67] *Maqūlāt* 8.11–15 Anawati et al.

[68] For *The Compilation*, see the discussion in Chapter 2, W2; for the other works see their

for *The Cure*, Avicenna takes care to point out that he is discussing them not because of their intrinsic worth but merely by way of following tradition: the Customary practice (*ʿāda*) and course of previous philosophers.[69] Interestingly enough, he projects the same motive to Aristotle himself, who he says was also following convention when dealing with the categories.

5. Logic as Organon: Naming Things and Naming Logic

One of the persistent problems in the reading of Avicenna's philosophical works concerns the name he wished to give to logic. In two notorious passages from *The Easterners* Avicenna makes the following remarks:

> a) "… the sort of science which the Greeks call 'logic' [*manṭiq*]—it is not unlikely that the Easterners may have another name for it." (T8, § 2)
>
> b) "It is customary at the present time and in these lands to call by the name of 'logic' [*manṭiq*] the science which is sought in order to serve as an instrument. Perhaps it has another name among other people, but we choose to call it now by this well-known name."[70] (L58)

Because *The Easterners* has been considered by some to represent Avicenna's true philosophical system—his "esoteric" doctrines—these passages in that book would then seem to imply that according to his true belief, 268
logic should be called by another name, and consequently that the contents of that differently called logic would be different from those in the traditional Aristotelian logic. And yet, the fact remains—a fact which has baffled a number of scholars—that the extant portions of that "Eastern" logic in *The Easterners* are not any different from the logic of Avicenna as we know it from his other works. The questions that have to be answered, therefore, are, what do the Easterners call logic and why, who are the "other people" in passage (b) above and how do they call logic, and is this logic any different from Avicenna's logic in his other works. To answer these questions it is necessary to investigate the meaning and context of signification, or naming things, in Islamic culture prior to Avicenna.

The subject of signification of words (i.e., signification in both its senses, "what words mean" and "how they indicate meaning") in the formative

---

contents in Chapter 2. The categories are listed in *ʿUyūn al-ḥikma* 2–3 Badawī and in *Hidāya* 72–76 ʿAbduh.

[69] *Maqūlāt* 8.10 Anawati et al.

[70] *Manṭiq al-Mašriqiyyīn* 5.16–18.

period of medieval Islamic civilization is of great importance, which only recently has begun to be investigated. Central to this subject is the problem of terminology, an issue that plagued Arabic speaking scholars and forced them to expend considerable efforts in trying to control it. The scholars had two causes to worry about. One was the natural tendency of each specialized discipline to develop its own technical terminology which then had to be explained to the uninitiated. Even in disciplines which Muslims considered autochthonous (viz. linguistic sciences, especially grammar, and religious sciences, and particularly the principles of jurisprudence and theology), and whose terminology was a natural extension of the native Arabic semantic field,[71] there came a time when the very nature of specialization and the requirements of highly nuanced arguments necessitated long discussions about the specific terminology of each discipline. Thus one finds, for example, Ibn-Ḥazm (d. 456/1064) providing a long list of legal terms in the introduction to his bulky volume on legal theory, *al-Iḥkām*.

The other cause for worry (and some confusion) was the language of the translated Greek philosophical texts, and especially of the Aristotelian *Organon*, with a "vocabulary whose specialized meanings and implicit sense and reflection of the way things are, originating in a differently articulated historical experience of life and the world, not only did not arise congenially out of native Arabic usage but were in many instances dissonant with it and awkwardly superimposed upon it."[72] By the fourth/tenth century therefore, an Arabic speaking intellectual had to contend with three separate levels
269 of Arabic: native and literary usage (to say nothing of topical and colloquial forms), the usage of the Islamic disciplines (with their various subdivisions), and the usage of the translations, itself not uniform but varying according to different periods and complexes of translations.[73] This terminological disarray was one dimension of the problem. These terms also referred to, or signified, concepts, and it was clearly felt that there was overlapping of both concepts and terms. Analysis of the process of signification thus constituted a second, theoretical dimension of the problem. A third dimension was the methodological: the analysis of signification could either follow a grammatical way which was essentially empirical and positive, or a dogmatic and formal (rational) way, based on Aristotelian logic. Finally there

---

71 See Frank *Beings* 3–5.

72 Frank *Beings* 4.

73 For the issues and problems involved, see the discussion in Gutas *Translation Movement* 141–150.

was yet a fourth dimension, more important than all the others: this was the immediate problem of applying the theory to the practice. Grammarians, theologians, and philosophers might well argue *ad infinitum* about their respective positions without tangible consequences; legal experts, however, could not indulge in this academic luxury. They had to establish the principles of legal theory in order to derive from them positive legislation.

The tension created by the interplay of all these dimensions, coupled with the emotions generated by the prevalent attitudes in favor or against "foreign sciences," explain the unprecedented preoccupation with linguistic science in the fourth/tenth century and its incorporation, as an essential element, in the epistemological chapters of all the works on grammar, theology, and jurisprudence.[74]

Each author approached the problem of terminology from his own perspective and tradition, but the general aim was to explain the specific vocabulary (and hence discipline) one was advocating in terms of common words and concepts. Operative was the accepted epistemological rule that the less obvious term can be defined by the more familiar one (cf. Aristotle's *Topics* 111a9ff.), the assumption being that the concepts to which these various terms—as well as the words in different languages—correspond are the same. One of the most explicit statements of this procedure comes also from the pen of Ibn-Ḥazm, who was a younger contemporary of Avicenna but
living in the antipodes of the Islamic world, al-Andalus. Reflecting the intel- 270
lectual ferment about linguistic science, he wrote about the year 420/1029 the following in the introduction to his treatise entitled, significantly, *An Approach and Introduction to Logic by Means of Common Terms and Examples from Jurisprudence*:[75]

> The philosophers of the past long before our time composed books in which they classified the different ways in which named things acquire names. All nations agree about the meaning of these names although they differ in

[74] See Versteegh *passim* for grammar, and Rosenthal *Knowledge* 208–239 for theology and jurisprudence. The brief sketch drawn here is intended merely to emphasize the importance of the subject. A detailed study of all these dimensions to assess the contribution of this "war of signification" among the various disciplines to the formation of the classical Islamic position is a major desideratum. For a preliminary study see Richard M. Frank, "Meanings Are Spoken of in Many Ways: The Earlier Arab Grammarians," *Le Muséon* 94 (1981) 259–319, reprinted in his *Texts and Studies I*, no. XII.

[75] *Taqrīb* 6–9 ʿAbbās. There is a pun in the title: *at-taqrīb li-ḥadd al-manṭiq* can mean either "bringing one near the border of logic" or "clarifying the definition of logic." For the title and the date of composition of the work see ʿAbbās's introduction, pp. a-j. See also Anwar G. Chejne, "Ibn Ḥazm of Cordova on Logic," *JAOS* 104 (1984) 57–72.

their actual expression, since [human] nature is one whereas choice varies. [Such books, Ibn-Ḥazm continues, are the eight books on logic by Aristotle. Many people, however, mistook them for heretical and misunderstood them because] the translation was complicated and full of uncommon and rarely used terms, [and it is well known that] not everybody can understand every expression. With God's help we intend to present the meaning of these in terms that are easy and straightforward. God willing, both laymen and specialists, and both scholars and ignorant people will be able equally to understand them to the extent that we have been able to grasp them and God has given us the power and ability. ... The reader should know that the usefulness of Aristotle's books is not for a single science only but for every science. Their usefulness in [the study of] the Qur'ān, the Traditions of the Prophet, and in legal decisions concerning what is religiously permitted or forbidden, and obligatory or indifferent, is among the greatest. (L59)

Ibn-Ḥazm then continues to mention the usefulness of logic in almost all sciences. The text of his book lives up to the expectations raised by the title: it is, in fact, a lucid introduction to the *Organon*, and the terminology of the translations is rendered more accessible to the Muslim reader by being interpreted with terms derived from the Muslim sciences of grammar, theology, and especially jurisprudence. The following examples are sufficient indication of the strong parallelism that Ibn-Ḥazm wants to draw between logic and jurisprudence. In the presentation of Aristotle's *De Interpretatione*, and as an introduction to chapters 5–14 of that work, he interprets the Aristotelian terms "necessary" (*wājib* = *anankē*), "possible" (*mumkin* = *dynaton*), and "impossible" (*mumtaniʿ* = *adynaton*) by the legal terms used to qualify religious acts, *farḍ*/*lāzim* ("duty"/"binding"), *ḥalāl*/*mubāḥ* ("permissible"/"indifferent"), and *ḥarām*/*maḥẓūr* ("forbidden"/"prohibited"), respectively.[76] Furthermore, the three kinds of "possible" (viz. remote, equal, and proximate, as they were classified in the
271 commentatorial tradition on the basis of statements like *De Interpretatione* 19a33 ff.[77]) are also given corresponding terms from the legal vocabulary: proximate possibility = *mubāḥ mustaḥabb* ("indifferent but recommended"), remote possibility = *mubāḥ makrūh* ("indifferent but disapproved"), and equal possibility = *mubāḥ mustawin* ("equally indifferent").[78]

---

[76] For the legal application of these terms see Joseph Schacht, *An Introduction to Islamic Law*, Oxford: Oxford University Press, 1964, Glossary.

[77] Cf. Fārābī's commentary on this passage in his *Šarḥ Kitāb al-ʿIbāra*, Wilhelm Kutsch and Stanley Marrow, eds., Beirut: Dar el-Machreq, ^{2}1971, 97 = F.W. Zimmermann, *Al-Farabi's Commentary and Short Treatise on Aristotle's* De Interpretatione, London: Oxford University Press, 1981, 91–92.

[78] *Taqrīb* 86 ʿAbbās.

Ibn-Ḥazm does not restrict himself to jurisprudence for his examples. Some other logical terms he explains by the corresponding terms from grammar and theology. The word "verb," for example, in *De Interpretatione*, chapter 3 (*rhēma*, literally, "What is said" of something, i.e., predicate[79]), was translated into Arabic by *kalima*, "word."[80] Ibn-Ḥazm explains: "By this word the philosophers mean what the grammarians call *nuʿūt*, 'descriptive [predicates],' and the theologians *ṣifāt*, 'attributes'."[81]

As further examples of this ubiquitous procedure for explaining technical terminology we may look at Fārābī in the Muslim East, the immediate background of Avicenna. The Aristotelian division of simple expressions into "name," "verb," and "instrument" Fārābī interprets as follows: "The 'verb' (*kalima*) the Arab grammarians know as the 'verb' (*fiʿl*), and the 'instrument' (*adāt*) they call the 'particle' (*ḥarf*) which comes in relation to a meaning."[82] Elsewhere he introduces the logical terms for "subject" and "predicate" by referring to the better known theological terms *ṣifa* and *mawṣūf*: "Logicians call the attributes (*ṣifāt*) predicates (*maḥmūlāt*) and the things qualified by an attribute (*mawṣūfāt*) subjects (*mawḍūʿāt*)."[83]

Two further examples may be given, specifically on the interpretation of the term *manṭiq*, which are of particular interest for the present discussion. The Arabic word *manṭiq* means "speech," and was for this reason selected by the translators "to serve as a literal and artificial translation of the technical 272
meaning of Greek *logos*"[84] ("speech"/"reason," among other meanings). The selection proved particularly discomfiting to later apologists of logic in Islam because it provided ammunition to the arguments of its opponents: if the science of logic, which, in addition to its reprehensibility for being a "foreign" science, means the science of "speech," and hence, of foreign—or in this case, Greek—speech, then it is worthless to a speaker of Arabic

---

79 This is the function of the Aristotelian *rhēma* in logic; cf. J.L. Ackrill, *Aristotle's* Categories *and* De Interpretatione, Oxford: Clarendon Press, 1963, 118. Ibn-Ḥazm's interpretation shows that he understood it in the logical sense. Cf. below, note 82, for Fārābī's understanding.

80 Isidor Pollak, *Die Hermeneutik des Aristoteles in der arabischen Übersetzung des Isḥāḳ ibn Ḥonain*, Leipzig: Brockhaus, 1913, p. 1, line 3. For the theory of the parts of speech in Greek as compared with that in Arabic see Versteegh, Chapter 3.

81 *Taqrīb* 80–81 ʿAbbās. For the concept of attributes in Islamic theology see Frank *Beings*.

82 D.M. Dunlop, "Al-Fārābī's Introductory Sections on Logic," *Islamic Quarterly* 2 (1955) 270.1–2, 278.4–6. Fārābī takes the word *rhēma/kalima* in its grammatical sense. See note 79 above.

83 Dunlop "Introductory *Risālah*" 228.11. For *ṣifa* and *mawṣūf* see Versteegh 71n6, and especially Frank *Beings*, references in Index, pp. 198–199, under *w/ṣ/f*.

84 Rosenthal *Knowledge* 203; for what follows cf. the entire section, pp. 203–208.

who needs only the grammar of his native tongue. In the debate between the grammarian Sīrāfī and the logician Abū-Bišr Mattā, this was precisely Sīrāfī's point at one stage of his argument. He says to Abū-Bišr: "You are not, then, inviting us to the *science* of speech (*manṭiq*), but to learn the Greek language."[85] Fārābī, the colleague of Abū-Bišr, is accordingly at pains to clarify the situation and explain to a non-Greek audience first the difference in essence or function between logic and speech and logic and grammar, and second the reason why (as he thinks) logic and speech share a common term:

> The discipline of logic is an *instrument* (*āla*) by which, when it is employed in the [several] parts of philosophy, certain knowledge is obtained of all which the theoretical and practical disciplines include. Apart from the discipline of logic, there is no way to be certain about the truth of anything among the things we seek to know. Its name [*manṭiq*] is derived from *nuṭq* ("articulation"[86]). This term [i.e., *nuṭq*] signifies in the opinion of the ancients three things: (1) the faculty by which man intellects the intelligibles ...; (2) the intelligibles which are produced in the soul of man by the understanding, and are called interior speech; (3) the expression by language of what is in the mind and is called exterior speech. This discipline, since it gives rules to the rational faculty for the interior speech which is the intelligibles, and rules shared in common by all languages for the exterior speech which is the expressions, and directs the rational faculty in both matters at once towards what is right and protects it from error in both of them together, is called *manṭiq*, logic. Grammar shares with it to some extent and differs from it also, because grammar gives rules only for the expressions which are peculiar to a particular nation and to the people who use the language, whereas logic gives rules for the expressions which are common to all languages.[87] (L60)

273 As a footnote to Fārābī's efforts to clarify the issue we may note the care taken by his student, Yaḥyā ibn-ʿAdī—already two generations after the

[85] Tawḥīdī *Imtāʿ* I,111.11 Amīn and az-Zayn; German translation by Gerhard Endress, "Grammatik und Logik. Arabische Philologie und griechische Philosophie im Widerstreit," in *Sprachphilosophie in Antike und Mittelalter*, Burkhard Mojsisch, ed., Amsterdam: B.R. Grüner, 1986, 244. Cf. Muhsin Mahdi, "Language and Logic in Classical Islam," in *Logic in Classical Islamic Culture*, G.E. von Grunebaum, ed. [First Giorgio Levi della Vida Conference], Wiesbaden: Harrassowitz, 1970, 66.

[86] There is no word in English that combines both meanings of the Greek *logos* and the Arabic *nuṭq*, i.e., the rational thought process and its outward expression. "Articulation" comes the closest to such a homonymy in that it indicates both the process of creating a coherent whole and a distinct utterance. It is in these two senses that it is used in this translation.

[87] Dunlop "Introductory *Risālah*" 227–228, 232–233. Dunlop's translation is slightly modified; emphasis added.

Sīrāfī/Abū-Bišr debate—to qualify the term *manṭiq*/logic: in a special essay on the subject, he calls it "*philosophical* logic" (*al-manṭiq al-falsafī*) as opposed to *Arabic* grammar (*an-naḥw al-ʿarabī*).[88]

This elaborate and solicitous presentation of the meaning of the term *manṭiq* represents one path taken by scholars and philosophers in their attempts to differentiate it from a linguistic science, Arabic grammar; another was to substitute for it a plain term or phrase and avoid the logic/speech issue altogether. This was taken by Ibn-Ḥazm. He says that among the powers given to man by God there is "the power, or faculty, of discernment (*quwwat at-tamyīz*) which the ancients have named *manṭiq*."[89]

The few examples cited above sufficiently adumbrate, I hope, what must otherwise be subjected to a detailed investigation: the coming of age, in the fourth/tenth century, of the Islamic sciences of grammar, jurisprudence, and theology, their encounter at a sophisticated level with the translations of Aristotelian philosophy in general and logic in particular, and the centrality of the question of signification—i.e. terminology—in all interdisciplinary discussions. The method followed by scholars in all disciplines—but particularly in philosophy because of the defensive position which Islamic public opinion had put it in this regard—in order to solve or at least remove some of the problems posed by terminological variety was to give for each lesser known term equivalents from other disciplines. The theoretical basis of this procedure was that concepts can be expressed with different words both in the same language or in two different languages. In these terminological exchanges the term "logic" itself as well as its subject matter presented particular problems which were met in the way described. This was also part of Avicenna's immediate intellectual background.

There is, finally, yet another aspect of this background that has to be considered in the assessment of the context in which Avicenna engaged in "naming things." He was apparently a native speaker of Persian,[90] and he

---

88 Text edited by Gerhard Endress, "Maqālat Yaḥyā b. ʿAdī," *Journal for the History of Arabic Science* 2.i (1978) 39; French translation by A. Elamrani-Jamal, "Grammaire et logique d'après le philosophe arabe chrétien Yaḥya ibn ʿAdī (280–364H/893–974)," *Arabica* 29 (1982) 1–15, and cf. his comments on p. 1.

89 Ibn-Ḥazm, *Al-Iḥkām fī uṣūl al-aḥkām*, Cairo 1345, I,4; cf. Rosenthal *Knowledge* 235.

90 Although there seems to be little doubt about Avicenna's ethnic origin (i.e., his mother tongue), it has been argued that he was a Turk. Apparently he knew some Turkish (in a small treatise on phonetics he refers to the velarized Turkish *l*), but we cannot tell how much or how well (*Asbāb ḥudūṯ al-ḥurūf* 23 Ḫānlarī, trans. in Semaan 54). The question is of no import for our purposes here where the relevant fact is that, other than in Arabic, he wrote only in Persian.

wrote a number of works in prose, and reportedly some poetry, in Persian.[91]
274 This was at a time when Persian began to reassert itself as a literary language in a literary movement with nationalistic overtones—called "linguistic *šuʿūbiyya*" by Goldziher—which aimed at establishing Persian as an Islamic language equal to Arabic.[92] Although Avicenna's contribution to this movement was significant if only in retrospect because of the works he wrote in his native language, there is no reason in the present discussion to analyze his conscious stand on this matter. Irrespective of his feelings about the Persian *šuʿūbiyya*, what is of interest here is rather the fact that he was at least bilingual and therefore in possession of the concomitant heightened awareness of linguistic relativity and of the problems regarding the relation between signifier and signified both in one language and in more than one.

In Baġdād, where most of the translation activity took place, the issue revolved around Arabic and Greek; in al-Andalus, Ibn-Ḥazm talks of Arabic and Latin; and in the East, the concern was naturally about Arabic and Persian. In their explanation of unknown or uncommon terms, scholars of Persian descent writing (in Arabic) for a Persian speaking audience followed the same method as their colleagues in other parts of the Muslim world: they gave Persian equivalents, or, as the case may be, better known Arabic words. Although numerous examples from Persian-born authors could be given,[93] we should here concentrate on Avicenna, who is no exception to the general rule. He follows the same procedure already very early, in *The Compilation* (W2). One of the sub-species of persuasive arguments in Aristotle's *Rhetoric* is argumentation through examples (*paradeigma*, 1356a–b), which Aristotle considers as the rhetorical counterpart of induction. The Arabic translation had, quite literally, *miṯāl*, "example," and *tamṯīl*, "presenting an example" or "argument by example." The purport of Aristotle's text is perfectly intelligible

[91] For his Persian works see Lazard 62–67, with full bibliographical references.

[92] The classic study of the Šuʿūbiyya movement in early Islam remains that of Ignaz Goldziher, *Muhammedanische Studien I*, Halle a. S.: Max Niemeyer, 1889, 147–216; English translation by C.R. Barber and S.M. Stern, *Muslim Studies I*, London: Allen & Unwin, 1967, 137–198. About the controversy in the fourth and fifth centuries and its relation to the development of Neo-Persian see Lutz Richter-Bernburg, "Linguistic Shuʿūbīya and Early Neo-Persian Prose," JAOS 94 (1974) 55–64, with full bibliographical references.

[93] For example, the Persian-born historian Muṭahhar Maqdisī, an older contemporary of Avicenna (wrote in 355/966; *GAS* I,337), gives both the Darī and Pahlavī terms for god in his *al-Badʾ wa-t-taʾrīḫ*: see the passages cited by Gilbert Lazard, "Pahlavi, Pārsi, Dari. Les Langues de l'Iran d'Après Ibn al-Muqaffaʿ," in *Iran and Islam* [Festschrift V. Minorsky], C.E. Bosworth, ed., Edinburgh: Edinburgh University Press, 1971, 383. Lazard's article should be consulted for the linguistic variety in Iran during this period.

in the Arabic translation, but Avicenna finds it possible to improve on the translation because there is a technical term in Islamic jurisprudence that corresponds more closely to the way he understood Aristotle's text. He says that certain legal scholars of his time call *tamṯīl* analogy (*qiyās*), a principle
which is rejected, he adds, in the legal schools of the Šīʿīs and the Ẓāhirīs.[94] 275
With remarkable consistency (cf. his own statement in the Autobiography, T3, § 8, last sentence) he returns to the same interpretation of *tamṯīl* in one of his last works, *Pointers and Reminders*. At the very beginning of his discussion on syllogisms, he presents induction (*istiqrāʾ*), argument by example (*tamṯīl*), and syllogism (*qiyās*) as the three kinds of argumentation in establishing something. *Tamṯīl* he again explains by referring to legal theory, and this time adds some further details:

> *Tamṯīl* (argument by example) is what our contemporaries describe as *qiyās* (drawing an analogy). It consists of seeking to judge a matter by the contrivance of a previous judgment on a similar matter. It is a judgment on a particular thing by means of something similar in another particular thing having a common basis [of comparison: *maʿnan jāmiʿ*[95]] with the first. Our contemporaries call the matter being judged upon "corollary" (*farʿ*, literally, "branch") and the matter it resembles "principle" (*aṣl*, literally, "root"). What they have in common they call "the basis and ground [of comparison": *maʿnan wa-ʿilla*].[96] (L61)

In the following example, from Avicenna's last essay (T14, § 1), he introduces the rational soul (that is, the distinctly and exclusively human part or aspect of soul) by mentioning its various names in different contexts of discourse and cultures and thereby illustrating the purpose behind this procedure: different words signify the same concept.

> Know that human beings alone, to the exclusion of all other living beings, posses a faculty highly capable of grasping the intelligibles. This faculty is sometimes called rational soul, sometimes "soul at peace," sometimes sacred

---

94 *ʿArūḍiyya* f. 36^a5–7 = p. 90 Ṣāliḥ. Cf. Anawati "Ḥikma ʿArūḍiyya" 174. Avicenna may have found the *tamṯīl* = *qiyās* correspondence in Fārābī, who says that "common people call *tamṯīl qiyās*" (Langhade and Grignaschi 63.11; cf. also p. 83.14 ff., where Fārābī contrasts *fiqh* and *kalām* scholars to logicians, *aṣḥāb al-manṭiq*, 85.4). Avicenna adds himself the legal details.

95 For the technical meaning of *maʿnā* and *ʿilla* in analogy see Brunschvig 16–17; see also Frank *Beings*, Glossary s.vv. p. 194; Versteegh 100–101.

96 *Išārāt* I.7.1, 64–65/138 = Goichon *Directives* 192 = Inati *Logic* 129–130; cf. Madkour 220–221. As Madkour notes, Avicenna derived this understanding of argument by example from Aristotle's discussion of *paradeigma* (translated in Arabic as *miṯāl*) in *Prior Analytics* 68b38–69a19. It is accordingly imprecise to render *tamṯīl* as "analogy," which is the meaning proper of *qiyās*.

> soul, sometimes spiritual spirit, sometimes commanding spirit, sometimes good word, sometimes word that unites and separates, sometimes divine secret, sometimes governing light, sometimes chief commanding light, sometimes true heart, sometimes core of the self [*lubb*], sometimes understanding [*nuhan*], and sometimes brains [*ḥijan*]. It exists in every single human being, young or old, adolescent or adult, insane or sane, sick or sound.[97] [T14, § 1]

276 It is in this context of the discussion of issues relating to interdisciplinary terminology, the signification of the same concept through words in different languages, and the logic/speech controversy, that Avicenna's references to other names of logic in the beginning of his *The Easterners* are to be analyzed. More specifically, however, the entire book exhibits a heightened and conscious concern with problems of terminology, and the two instances of "naming logic" cited at the beginning of this Section (and normally singled out for interpretation) are thus part of a more general pattern.

Avicenna's solicitude with terminology in *The Easterners* is evident at three levels:

a) The first level is informative or didactic. As in all expository works, and in accordance with established precedent, technical terms of the particular subject under discussion have to be introduced and explained. Avicenna does this frequently and with repeated reminders to the reader of the *conventional* nature of the practice of establishing names. Many times Avicenna introduces the term for a concept which has already been presented and defined with the words, "people *Customarily* call this …" (*min ʿādat an-nās/qawm*; *min ʿādatihim*; *jarat al-ʿāda*; *min šaʾn an-nās* [*Manṭiq al-Mašriqiyyīn* 16 ult.; 17.3; 20.2–4; 60.-5; 61.2; 61.6; 76.10 etc.]), and more specifically, "the observed practice of our contemporaries is to call this …"

---

97 See also the notes to T14 above. This procedure of naming something through its various names used in different contexts and cultures can be witnessed also in Avicenna's colleague (and possibly teacher of medicine) Abū-Sahl al-Masīḥī, who says the following in his treatise on the interpretation of dreams: (L62)

"Each group of people or nation calls this power [the active intellect] by a different name. The ancient Sabians call it "the nearest manager;" the Greek philosophers "divine effluence" and "divine providence;" the Syrians call it "the word" (which in Arabic is called "the divine presence" and "the holy spirit"); the Persians call it "light of lights;" the Manicheans call it "the good souls;" and the Arabs [i.e. Muslims] call it "angels" and "divine assistance." [All] these different names signify one and the same power" (text in Khan "Dreams" 291–292).

The contents of this treatise, falsely ascribed to Avicenna (see below in the Appendix, Section J, Spurious Works), are presented and discussed by John C. Lamoreaux, *The Early Muslim Tradition of Dream Interpretation*, Albany: SUNY Press, 2002, 69–76.

(*al-mašhūd min ahl az-zamān annahum yusammūna* [6.9]). It seems that this procedure by Avicenna is intended to accomplish three things: i) to introduce the novice to the current terminology; ii) to point out the fact that the current names do not constitute the primary, or "natural" appellation of the things named but the secondary and "conventional" one; and hence, iii) to deny exclusivity to these particular names for the science under discussion (logic) even within Arabic, and therefore leave the possibility open that other people—contemporary or not—may provide other names.

b) The second level is analytical and critical, and follows naturally from implication (iii) of the first. At this level Avicenna is interested in analyzing or determining the appropriateness of the terms already established and their correspondence to the signified. For example: when discussing the names given to the different kinds of propositions, he finds the term "predicative" (*ḥamlī*) appropriate for the propositions so designated and adopts it. He says: "This kind of proposition does have a name that is appropriate for it in accordance with the [sense of the] Arabic language, and therefore 277
let us call it as people do" [62.5]. When it comes to conditional propositions, however, he objects to the application of the term 'conditional' (*šarṭī*) to separative (i.e., "either … or") propositions, and would like to restrict it only to the connective (i.e. "if … then") propositions. He says: "In accordance with the [sense of the] Arabic language, the conditional proposition (*aš-šarṭiyya*) should have been the connective one (*al-muttaṣila*) only, since it has a condition (*šarṭ*) for a protasis and a result for an apodosis; but people call the separative proposition (*al-munfaṣila*) also conditional" [61.7–8; cf. Shehaby 215–216]. In order to avoid confusion, Avicenna then proposes to retain the term "separative" for the separative-conditional propositions and to substitute a new term, "tropical" (*majāzī*) for the connective-conditional propositions [62.6; cf. Shehaby 254n7]. This latter step brings us to Avicenna's concern with terminology at the next level.

c) The third level is institutive; that is, Avicenna is engaged in providing different terms for those judged inappropriate and instituting new terms for concepts not previously differentiated. We have just seen an example of the former practice; for the latter the following may be cited. When a term signifies a concept in such a way as to correspond exactly with its essence, this kind of signification, Avicenna says, "is the one which *we call specifically* 'that which signifies quiddity' or 'that which signifies what a thing is' [*wa-hāḏihi d-dalāla hiya l-maḫṣūṣa ʿindanā bi-smi* …: 15.10–11]." A universal affirmative proposition which is true not by "real necessity," i.e. logically, but by reference to what actually exists, "we call," Avicenna says "by *our own technical term* 'existential' [*wa-hāḏihi hiya l-musammāt bi-ṣṭilāḥinā wujūdiyya*: 79.3; cf. Goichon *Directives* 54–55 and 137n2]." Finally, and most important, Avicenna introduces in *The Easterners* a new theoretical science and a new name for it. As we saw above, the traditional division of theoretical sciences was into Physics, Mathematics, and Metaphysics. Following the hints provided by Fārābī's analyses, Avicenna adds a fourth, "universal science" [*ʿilm kullī*], and says, "It is Customary to call the Knowledge of the first part [of the theoretical sciences] Physics, of the second part Mathematics, of the third part Theology, and of the fourth part Universal [Science], even though *this* [*fourfold*] *division is not conventionally used*" [*wa-in lam yakun hāḏā t-tafṣīl mutaʿārafan*: 7.5–7; cf. L50 above].

This three-level solicitude of Avicenna with terminology needs to be studied in the broader context of contemporary discussions on the same subject in all intellectual disciplines in Islamic culture. For our purposes here it is sufficient to note its function. The avowed purpose of *The Easterners* is to "include the fundamental elements of true Philosophy" [T8, § 6], that is, to
278 present "philosophy as it is naturally [perceived]," without consideration of the approaches historically taken by other philosophical schools [T9, § 4]. This requires—for various reasons—a corresponding independence, or at least critical stand, in the choice of terminology, and Avicenna is well aware of that.

The general background of the discussions about the signification of terms and the specific context of Avicenna's book *The Easterners* leave little room for ambiguity in the interpretation of his statement in the Introduction [T8, § 2], "the sort of science which the Greeks call logic—it is not unlikely that the Easterners may have another name for it ..." The very felicitous turn of phrase, "the sort of science which the *Greeks* call logic," by denying, as discussed above [par. (a.iii) in this Section], exclusive possession of this science by the Greeks, establishes logic as a science in its own right, independent of national origins and predilections. To a reader contemporary with Avicenna and raised in the intellectual context described in the preceding pages, this could only appear as a reference to and a repudiation of at least three positions: that of the school Aristotelians, the likes of Abū-Bišr Mattā, who would claim the superiority (indeed, the infallibility, as Sīrāfī would say) of the Greeks and especially Aristotle in this science; that of the traditional scholars in the Islamic sciences (especially in grammar and jurisprudence) who, like Sīrāfī, would deny logic/*manṭiq* ("the science of speech") a supranational existence independent of the rules of the language

in which it is expressed; and that of the fundamentalists who, as Ibn-Ḥazm says, would see in logic a “foreign science,” the beginnings of heresy and atheism.[98] To the same reader, the second part of Avicenna’s statement, the notion that different groups of people call one and the same thing (i.e. a signified) by different names appeared as a commonplace. Not only did people speaking different languages name things differently, but also people speaking the same language, as illustrated above. The change of name, finally, suggested by Avicenna’s statement could again only indicate, in the context of his avowed independent approach to subject matter and terminology alike in *The Easterners* and of the second level of his concern with terminology discussed above, that he found the term *manṭiq*: “speeech/logic” inappropriate for the science it signified. This again would not appear as particularly novel to the contemporary reader. The problems raised by the choice of this term to signify the science in question formed the core of the Abū-Bišr/Sīrāfī debate, and philosophers had been at pains ever since to solve them either through elaborate explanations, like Fārābī, or through direct substitution of another, more appropriate term, like Ibn-Ḥazm. Avicenna here clearly chose the second alternative, the only difference being that he presented 279
the alleged substitute term not as a discrete description of the science as practiced by the Greeks, but as an integral part of Philosophy itself, regardless of its historical origins.

The alternate term to which Avicenna alludes in the Introduction but does not actually cite is given a few paragraphs later. In the classification of the sciences which follows immediately after the Introduction, Avicenna divides the principal sciences into two large categories, the informative and the instrumental. “It is customary at the present time and in these lands,” he continues, “to call by the name of *manṭiq*/logic the science which is sought in order to serve as an instrument (*āla*). Perhaps it has another name among other people, but we choose to call it now by this well-known name” [L58]. It is in the same vein, critical of transmitted terminology, that Avicenna also mentions the division of theoretical sciences into four instead of three (above, par. c and L50), a division which is not, as he says, “conventionally used.” He ends, finally, the chapter on the classification of the sciences by saying that he will not treat in *The Easterners* all the sciences mentioned, but only

---

98 Cf. Rosenthal *Knowledge* 205–206.

> the *Instrumental Science* (*al-ʿilm al-ālī*), the Universal Science (*al-ʿilm al-kullī*), Theology (*al-ʿilm al-ilāhī*), the Fundamental Principles of Physics (*al-ʿilm aṭ-ṭabīʿī al-aṣlī*), and only as much of the practical science as is is needed by the seeker of salvation [i.e. that part of it that falls within the Metaphysics of the Rational Soul; see Ch. 6.2]. As for the science of Mathematics, it is not a science about which there is disagreement [among philosophers], and had we cared to present it here we would have presented of it exactly as much as we did in *The Cure*—and similarly with the kinds of practical science which we did not treat here. We now turn to the presentation of *the Instrumental Science, which is* Logic/*manṭiq* [*Manṭiq al-Mašriqiyyīn* 8.9 ff.; emphasis added]. (L63)

It is important to note in this passage that the term "instrumental science" is first given by itself and *instead of logic*, along with the other sciences according to Avicenna's own classification and terminology; only at the end of the paragraph does he use both terms when introducing the following chapter, in which he repeats the identification: "This science which points to the way how to proceed [from the known to the unknown] is the instrumental science, logic/*manṭiq*" [10.14]. It thus seems certain that the more appropriate term for logic which Avicenna had in mind was "the instrumental science." There is nothing extraordinary or surprising in this; the logical works of Aristotle were known collectively as the *Organon* in Greek, and Avicenna is consistent with the genuine and original Aristotelian tradition. What he is objecting to are the accretions to the concept "logic" brought about in the Arabic tradition through the equivocity of the term *manṭiq* and
280 the concomitant confusion that logic has somehow to deal with utterances, grammar, and syntax.[99]

Avicenna is also consistent with himself: from his earliest works onwards he repeatedly described logic as an instrument. A partial list of these descriptions is instructive [the order of the following passages is approximately chronological; emphasis is added]:

> 1. *The Compilation* (*ʿArūḍiyya*), f. 1^{b} (p. 32 Ṣāliḥ) = Mahdavī 79: (L64)
>
> Whoever wishes to become a man of knowledge must necessarily acquire first the *instrument* (*āla*) which will guide his mind and prevent[t] him from accepting falsehood and lies concerning matters in which he ought to believe or[u] according to which he ought to act. This is logic/*manṭiq*.

---

[t] Reading *al-māniʿati* for *al-māniʿatihi* in the MS, Ṣāliḥ, and Mahdavī.

[u] Reading *aw yanbaġī* for *an yanbaġī* in the MS and Mahdavī; Ṣāliḥ omits this phrase!

---

[99] Avicenna's objection is most clearly stated in *The Cure* (*Madḫal* 22.13 ff. Anawati et al.).

2. *Logic Epitomized* (*al-Manṭiq al-mūjaz*), Mahdavī 221: (L65)

... One must first prepare an *instrument* (*āla*) that will protect the human mind from error. ... This instrument is logic (*manṭiq*), and the first person who discovered it is Aristotle the Greek philosopher.

3. *The Guidance* (*Al-Hidāya* 64 ʿAbduh): (L66)

Logic/*manṭiq* is a science whereby one can know the way in which a [desired] combination (*ʿaqd*) can be obtained from an existing combination. [This description is more technical than most and refers to the syllogistic process of logic. Although the word 'instrument' is not used, the instrumental nature of the process is evident.]

4. *The Cure* (*Madḫal* 15.19–16.5, 16.10–12 Anawati et al.): (L67)

If philosophy is considered to deal with the investigation of things only insofar as they exist in themselves or as *mere* concepts in the mind, then the science [which inquires into the quantity, quality, and method of looking at the accidental properties acquired by concepts in the mind *in order that we move from the known to the unknown*][100] will not be a part of philosophy; but insofar as this science is useful [in the conduct of the investigation], it will be an *instrument* (*āla*) for philosophy. If philosophy is considered to deal with every theoretical investigation and from every aspect, then this science will be both a part of philosophy and an *instrument* (*āla*) for the other parts of philosophy. ... This sort of theoretical inquiry is the one called logic/*manṭiq*. It is a theoretical inquiry into the matters we mentioned insofar as it leads from them to knowledge of the unknown and their accidents only insofar as these matters are as described.

5. *The Salvation* (*Najāt* 3/4): (L68)

Logic/*manṭiq* is an *instrument* (*āla*) which protects the mind from error regarding the concepts we form and what we acknowledge as true,[101] and which leads to true belief by providing means and methods for its access.

6. *Pointers and Reminders* (*Išārāt* I.1.1, 2–3/39; cf. Goichon *Directives* 79–80 = 281
Inati *Logic* 47): (L69)

The purpose (*murād*) of logic/*manṭiq* is to be for man a *normative instrument* (*āla qānūniyya*) which, when taken into account (*murāʿātuhā*, cf. above, Chapter 3.3A), will protect him from going astray in his thinking. By 'thinking' I mean here what happens when a man resolves to transit from matters present in the mind ... to matters absent in it. ... Logic/*manṭiq*, then, is the

[100] The translation of this passage is somewhat expanded to provide the referents of the pronouns used by Avicenna. The description of logic in square brackets given in the quotation is taken from p. 15.14–17. For a discussion of this passage see Sabra "Logic" 751–752.

[101] The reference here is to *taṣawwur* and *taṣdīq*, the two aspects of all knowledge. See T3 note 15.

> science whereby are learned the different kinds of transitions from matters actually existing in man's mind to those whose acquisition is desired. …

In these passages, although it is possible to observe a progression in the description of the instrumentality of logic, from vague references to its prevention of error and its use in right belief and action, to specific mention of the aspects of the thought process as it advances from the known to the unknown—a progression that deserves closer study—the instrumental nature itself of logic is never questioned or abandoned. And in *The Easterners,* where Avicenna expresses himself in a language which he least allows to be conditioned by traditional impositions and connotations, he does not simply use the word "instrument" (*āla*) as part of the definition of logic/*manṭiq*, but as a *substitute* for it in the relative construction "instrumental science" (*ʿilm ālī*). This then must have constituted for Avicenna the essence—and name—of logic.[102] But again there is nothing novel or surprising in this. In the Prologue to *The Cure* Avicenna explicitly says that the difference between it and *The Easterners* is one not of substance but of form (T9, § 4), and this is also true in the present case: in *The Cure* itself, in the psychological part, he uses the expression "the instrumental discipline" (*ṣināʿa āliyya*) to refer to logic [*Nafs* 259.10 Rahman]. This, however, passes almost unnoticed because it is an incidental reference and Avicenna does not wish to make a point about it; in *The Easterners*, though, it is precisely this point that he wishes to make, and he accordingly invites all the possible attention to his avowed deviation from tradition.

In this light, it is possible to understand better Avicenna's "cryptic" remark that "it is customary at the present time and in these lands" to call it [logic] *manṭiq*, but perhaps other people may have another name for it (L58). The way the sentence is phrased has created the false impression that Avicenna meant that another people at another place and time developed a science,
282 *parallel* to what Greeks call logic, and named it differently. But this impression is totally unwarranted by what we know of Avicenna's understanding of the history of philosophy and specifically of logic. As discussed in Chapter 4, for him logic was discovered by the Greeks, and more precisely by

---

[102] Commentators on Avicenna, who were quick to grasp semantic nuances, were quite aware of this. In his commentary on the *Išārāt* in the description of logic translated above (L69), Ṭūsī explains "normative instrument" by referring to the passage in *The Easterners*: "Logic is both a science in its own right and an instrument in relation to the other sciences. For this reason Avicenna designated it elsewhere [i.e., in *Manṭiq al-Mašriqiyyūn* 8 ult., 10.14] as 'the instrumental science'" (*Šarḥ* I,117 ult. Dunyā).

Aristotle (as Avicenna himself mentions in the passage from the *Logic Epitomized* cited above, L65). There is no question of a rival science and a rival people, but only of a rival name. The logic discovered by Aristotle spread to other nations, which naturally gave the science a name in their own language. Available to Avicenna in this regard was Ḫwārizmī's encyclopedia of the sciences written in 977 AD, about the time Avicenna himself was born. Ḫwārizmī says about logic:[103] "This science is called in Greek *lōgikē*,[v] in Syriac *malīlūṯā*, and in Arabic *manṭiq*." Avicenna himself suggests *tarāzū*, "scales," for Persian in his *Philosophy for ʿAlāʾ-ad-Dawla* (Mahdavī 102). But foreign words for logic cannot be what Avicenna intended in that passage; it would be pointless as well as useless to Avicenna who was writing *The Easterners* in Arabic. Since he says that he chose not to use the other name, this means that he considered it for the book he was writing. He must therefore be referring to *Arabic* terms used by other people at other times and places, and, in view of the preceding discussion, terms referring to instruments: the word *āla* itself was used by the philosophers[104] and so was *mīzān* ("scales")[105] and *mikyāl* ("measure"),[106] to name but a sample;[107] *mīzān*, furthermore, was also current in the Ismaʿīlī tradition.[108] In an extended discussion on logic as the "indispensable instrument for the philosophical sciences," Avicenna himself uses the terms *mīzān*, *mikyāl*, and *miʿyār* ("gauge"),[109] but in the final analysis it appears that he opted in *The Easterners* for the generic term *āla*, "instrument," to stand for logic.

The motives behind Avicenna's attempts to suggest a different name for logic are thus to be sought, in a wider context, in the history of the controversy surrounding technical terminology in general and the equivocal term *manṭiq* (speech/logic) in particular, and, in the context of his own researches, in his critical attitude in *The Easterners* toward traditional Aristotelianism and terminology, and in his concomitant efforts to restructure

---

v Thus to be read, for *lwġyʾ* in the text.

---

103 *Mafātīḥ al-ʿulūm* 85 van Vloten.

104 E.g., Fārābī, see above; Abū-Sulaymān as-Sijistānī in Kraemer 144, etc.

105 E.g., by Abū-Bišr Mattā; Tawḥīdī *Imtāʿ* I,109.12 Amīn and az-Zayn; Fārābī *Iḥṣāʾ* 23 Gonzalez Palencia.

106 E.g., Fārābī *Iḥṣāʾ* 23 Gonzalez Palencia.

107 See also Rosenthal *Knowledge* 204–205, where most of the authors cited there lived after Avicenna.

108 See the references in van Ess *Īcī* 285.

109 *Qiyās* 11.12–13 Zāyid.

philosophy as transmitted in the Aristotelian tradition (cf. his unorthodox
283 division of the theoretical sciences) and present a new synthesis (see Chapter 2, W9). Nallino 456n4 had suggested that Avicenna's purpose was to avoid conservative opposition to logic by avoiding the stimulus to such opposition, the word *manṭiq*, but this consideration hardly seems to have been prominent in Avicenna's mind if only because he proceeds to use "this well-known name" anyway.

Avicenna's half-hearted suggestion that "instrumental science" be substituted for "logic/*manṭiq*" found acceptance, paradoxically, by the posthumous ostensible detractor of his philosophy, Ġazālī.[110] This was in a way to be expected. Avicenna had wished to propound philosophy in *The Easterners* "as it is naturally [perceived]," which meant according it a systematic rather than a historical treatment with references to various views, and this required that he establish, to the extent necessary, an alternative philosophical terminology that would avoid, if only by its sheer novelty, referring to controversial issues that were extraneous to Avicenna's purpose. If the term *manṭiq* was controversial because of its speech/logic equivocity, Avicenna was not only unwilling to defend it because of the unnecessary confusion it entailed regarding the proper domains of logic and grammar, but he positively suggested that he would just as well do without it—like other people at other times and places—were it not for the fact of its wide use. But for an ostensible *opponent* of philosophy, such a terminological dispute among philosophers could be viewed with impunity as splitting hairs. Ġazālī could therefore safely appropriate the alternate terminology suggested by Avicenna and leave the term *manṭiq*, with all its problems and the opprobrium by the self-styled "orthodox" that might accompany it, to the philosophers, Avicenna included. In practice Ġazālī does this by using the term *manṭiq* very sparingly: he employs instead the terms suggested by Avicenna and others, and most conspicuously and self-consciously in the titles of four of his books dealing specifically with logic: *The Gauge of Knowledge* (*Miʿyār al-ʿilm*), *The Scales of Action* (*Mīzān al-ʿamal*),[111] *The Touchstone*

[110] Ġazālī attacked Avicenna from a self-serving "orthodox" position. Avicenna's suggestion found acceptance only by Suhrawardī Maqtūl, who attacked Avicenna from an illuminationist position: in the introduction to *Philosophy of Illumination* (*Ḥikmat al-išrāq*) Suhrawardī refers to logic, with which he will deal, he says, only cursorily, exclusively as "the science which is the instrument" (*al-ʿilm allaḏī huwa l-āla*; Corbin *Opera* II,13.9–11).

[111] Whatever the final verdict about the authenticity and attribution of the extant work known as *Mīzān al-ʿamal* (cf. G.F. Hourani, "A Revised Chronology of Ghazālī's Writings," JAOS 104 [1984] 294–295), the fact remains that Ġazālī himself announced it under this title at the end of his *Miʿyār al-ʿilm* 348 Dunyā.

of Theoretical Inquiry (*Miḥakk an-naẓar*), *The Accurate Balance* (*Al-Qisṭās al-mustaqīm*). Ġazālī's full awareness of the existence of separate sets of terms for individual disciplines and of terminological issues may be illustrated in the following passages from the introductions to his *Precipitance of* 284
the Philosophers (*Tahāfut al-falāsifa*) and *The Gauge of Knowledge*, in which it is seen that his choice of words can only be conscious and deliberate, and not merely intended for rhetorical or stylistic effect. Ġazālī says that he wrote *The Gauge* for two reasons. One is "to instruct people in the methods of thinking and theoretical inquiry." Since people frequently stumble when dealing with abstract concepts (*maʿqūlāt*), he continues, "I have composed this book as a gauge (*miʿyār*) for theoretical inquiry and reflection, a scale (*mīzān*) for research and cogitation, a hone (*ṣayqal*) for the mind, and a whetstone (*mišḥaḏ*) for the faculty of thought and reason."[112] The second reason is to enable people "to study what we set down in *The Precipitance of the Philosophers*, because we debated with them in their own language and addressed them in accordance with their technical terms (*iṣṭilāḥāt*) which they conventionally employ in logic (*manṭiq*); in this book, then, these terms are explained."[113] It is to be noted that in the process of stating his first purpose for writing the book—which is, in effect, to instruct people in logic—Ġazālī never uses the word *manṭiq* itself; he uses it only when stating his second purpose, and there it is explicitly attributed to the philosophers. The intended implication seems to be similar to that of Avicenna in the Introduction to *The Easterners*: there is an instrumental science which teaches how to think correctly; the (Greek) philosophers call it *manṭiq*, others call it differently. Indeed, the fact that others have different name(s) for it is used in an implicit argument by Avicenna to indicate that it is not the exclusive property of the (Greek) philosophers. The creation of such an opinion was desirable to Avicenna because he wanted to sever the identification in people's minds between logic and Greek logic and thereby win acceptance for his own logic that he believed to be a revision of Greek logic, i.e., that of the Aristotelian school tradition. Ġazālī wanted to sever the same identification but for the different purpose of winning formal acceptance for logic as an instrument in theological studies. And if it is considered that Ġazālī's logic was, in all its essentials, that of Avicenna, then we could perhaps state with

---

112 *Miʿyār* 59 Dunyā. This accumulation of names of similar instruments is common with Ġazālī. See i.a., Rosenthal *Knowledge* 204 note 5, and the last paragraphs of Ġazālī's *Miʿyār* 347–348 Dunyā.

113 *Miʿyār* 60 Dunyā.

relative certainty that Ġazālī was in this respect Avicenna's collaborator and mouthpiece, through whom Avicenna's logic was advertised and ensconced in Islamic culture through the use of Avicenna's method of presenting his logic under a different name, that suggested in *The Easterners*.

With time, however, as the dissociation between logic and Greek logic—
285 through Avicenna's and Ġazālī's efforts—took root in public opinion, and as the term *manṭiq* ceased to evoke connotations of the old logic/speech controversy, 'the instrumental science' became once more *manṭiq* in Islamic culture. It is true that logicians continued to be occasionally called 'scholars who use the scales' (*mīzāniyyūn*)[114] but this never proved a serious challenge to the regained supremacy of *manṭiq*.

114 Cf. Max Horten, *Die spekulative und positive Theologie im Islam nach Razi und ihre Kritik durch Tusi*, Leipzig: Otto Harrassowitz, 1912, 268.

CHAPTER SEVEN

THE EVOLUTION OF AVICENNA'S ATTITUDE TOWARD ARISTOTLE, THE ARISTOTELIAN TRADITION, AND HIS OWN WORK

Avicenna saw himself as belonging essentially in the Peripatetic tradition. Not only does he himself say that the Peripatetics were the philosophical school most worthy of Partisan Adherence (T8, § 3), but it is also clear that he had very little patience with philosophical traditions other than the Peripatetic. His Prologue to the Sophistics of *The Cure* well summarizes his position:

> [Those who] attempted to slander the Peripatetics and to find fault with books on logic as well as those who built on their basis ... propagated the delusion that philosophy is [only] Platonic, wisdom [only] Socratic, and that among the ancients only the earliest, and among philosophers only the Pythagoreans possessed knowledge. [T6A, § 2]

Avicenna's dismissal of non-Aristotelian philosophical traditions is based on two factors, one personal and the other traditional. First, as is evident from the above passage, any philosophical system not based on logic, and hence on the Verification of truths by means of syllogisms and the Discovery of middle terms primarily by Guessing them Correctly, is by its very nature not valid. Second, as discussed in Chapter 4, Avicenna derived his conception of the history of philosophy from the late antique tradition of Alexandria which presented Aristotle as the pinnacle of philosophy, perfecting all the tendencies previous to his time.

Only in the case of Plato is there a noticeable evolution in Avicenna's attitude. Although he criticized Plato's theory of vision in two passages in his early writings,[1] he still followed tradition initially and called him "divine" (*ilāhī*),[2] and subscribed to the Neoplatonic theory of the basic agreement

---

[1] Landauer 354.5; *Answers to Bīrūnī* 40.9 ff. Nasr and Mohaghegh. Avicenna's defense of the Aristotelian theory of vision is discussed in its historical context by David C. Lindberg, *Theories of Vision from al-Kindi to Kepler*, Chicago: University of Chicago Press, 1976, 43–52.

[2] "Divine Plato" appears in the "Lesser" *Destination*, Ahwānī *Aḥwāl* 108.4, and is not excised in the reproduction of this passage in the much later *Salvation* (*Najāt* 313.6/391.10). This is due to the style of composition of the *Salvation*, a collage of earlier texts put together without editing; see above, Chapter 2, W7 and note 2, and below, GM 3 in the Appendix.

between him and Aristotle, claiming that their divergence was only appar-
287 ent.[3] By the time he came to write the Logic of *The Cure*, however, he abandoned his lip service to traditional forms of expression and spoke in condemnatory, yet fair terms about Plato:

> It is proper, then, that the truth be told: if the extent of Plato's achievements in Philosophy is what came down to us of him, then his wares were paltry indeed and philosophy in his time had not matured to the point of reaping. Whoever affects allegiance to him, having at his disposal only the amount of knowledge about Plato that has been transmitted to us, does it either out of envy for Aristotle or out of a foolish notion that the prior in time is also in a discipline prior in rank. The truth, however, is the opposite.[4] [T6B, § 8]

In particular, Avicenna criticized severely the Platonic theory of ideas, following Aristotle.[5] One of the many arguments that he used is that "it is impossible for one selfsame idea [*maʿnan*, i.e., Platonic form existing in reality] to exist in many [things]," because if this same idea exists in both Zayd and ʿAmr, "then whatever occurs to this [idea] in Zayd would necessarily occur to it when in ʿAmr."[6] But this is absurd, because in that case, Avicenna argues in the *Dānešnāme*, the idea that would appear as knowledge in Plato would appear as ignorance in someone else. In the *Ilāhiyyāt* of *The Cure*, Avicenna used the standard names of Zayd and ʿAmr as examples, common in all Arabic theoretical discourse; in the later *Dānešnāme*, he used the name of Plato instead, in a mocking reference to his theory of ideas.[7] Avicenna's attitude to Plato thus developed from traditional respect to ironic dismissal. As for Platonists, finally, both Greek—what he knew of them—and Muslim—like Abū-Bakr ar-Rāzī—Avicenna had nothing but contempt from the very beginning.[8]

---

3 *Answers to Bīrūnī* 40.10ff. Nasr and Mohaghegh, where Avicenna expressly refers to Fārābī's *Jamʿ* as proof of the congruity of the two philosophers.

4 For an example of a specific point on which Avicenna criticizes Socrates and Plato see Booth 124.

5 See now the detailed treatment by Arnzen *Platonische Ideen* 86–99.

6 *Ilāhiyyāt* 208.10–12 Anawati and Zāyid = Marmura *Metaphysics* 158–159.

7 *Dānešnāme, Ilāhiyyāt* 41 Moʿīn = Achena and Massé I,159–160. Achena and Massé, who perspicaciously remark on this (I,42), say that "Avicenne ironise ainsi la théorie des Idées Platoniciennes."

8 For Greek Platonists see Marmura "Critique of Platonists." For Abū-Bakr ar-Rāzī, Avicenna spoke in the most deprecatory terms about him already in his debate with Bīrūnī (*Answers to Bīrūnī* 13.10–13 Nasr and Mohaghegh): "He bit more than he could chew in his attempts to deal with Theology and he even exceeded his abilities when lancing abscesses (reading *fī baṭṭi l-ḫurāji*, as in MS U and suggested by Michot *Astrologie* 58n; for the expression see *GALex* II,287.8) and examining urine and feces—he certainly disgraced himself and exhibited his ignorance in what he endeavored and aimed to do."

Avicenna's attitude toward Aristotle never changed in its essence but only in its expression. It was transformed from the traditional adulation to critical appreciation and respect. In his early works he refers to Aristotle in traditional terms as "the Philosopher" (*al-faylasūf*),[9] "the philosopher Aristotle,"[10] and in at least one case, "Aristotle, the Greek philosopher."[11] Later, Aristotle becomes "The First Teacher" (*al-muʿallim al-awwal*),[12] and Aristotle's works "the first teaching" (*at-taʿlīm al-awwal*).[13] The shift in emphasis from "philosopher" to "teacher" would seem to be consistent with Avicenna's overall development toward seeing Knowledge not as the possession of one specific discipline, philosophy (as opposed to other subjects), or of one specific nation, but as universal because it reflects ontological reality. Aristotle was simply the first person to have taught this knowledge intelligibly in accordance with its inherent structure and Fundamental Principles, as Avicenna says in the Introduction to *The Easterners* (T8, §1). *Al-muʿallim*, "teacher," therefore means "he who dispenses Knowledge, *al-ʿilm*," in the sense understood by Avicenna, and Aristotle was the first to have done so, according to the conception of the history of philosophy bequeathed to 288
Avicenna by late antique Alexandrian Aristotelianism. This perception of Aristotle by Avicenna, along with the concomitant belief in human progress in the acquisition of this Knowledge by Working out Corollary Principles on the basis of the Fundamental Principles discovered by earlier thinkers, enables Avicenna on the one hand to have a reverential but critical attitude toward Aristotle, and on the other to claim for his own discoveries a new stage in the serial acquisition of Knowledge. Thus Avicenna may both state in the *Philosophy for ʿAlāʾ-ad-Dawla* that Aristotle "is the leader of the wise and the guide and teacher of philosophers,"[14] and criticize him on specific details in the roughly contemporary *Fair Judgment*.[15]

---

[9] E.g., in *al-Mabdaʾ wa-l-maʿād* 29, 34, 61, 68, 85 Nūrānī.

[10] E.g., in *Compendium on the Soul* 354.4, 360.14 Landauer.

[11] In *al-Manṭiq al-mūjaz*, quoted in Mahdavī 221.

[12] E.g., in all the passages from the *Mabdaʾ* cited in note 9, above, which Avicenna copied in *The Cure* and later in *The Salvation*, he changed "the Philosopher" to "The First Teacher:" *Najāt* 394.6/581.9, 435.7/634.1 (= *Ilāhiyyāt* 392.4), 435.17/634.12 (= *Ilāhiyyāt* 392.9). Avicenna continued referring to Aristotle as "the First Teacher" until the end of his career: *Išārāt* I.5.4, 52/115 = Goichon *Directives* 166, Inati *Logic* 114.

[13] E.g., *Jadal* 38.1 Ahwānī, *Ilāhiyyāt* 332.4 Mūsā et al., and throughout *The Cure*.

[14] *Dānešnāme, Ilāhiyyāt* 111 Moʿīn = Morewedge 76 = Achena and Massé I,215. Avicenna makes this remark just before giving a paraphrase of Aristotle's *Metaphysics* Lambda, 1072b24–26.

[15] E.g., in the few pages from the commentary on Lambda from the *Fair Judgment* which have survived, Avicenna openly criticizes Aristotle twice: Badawī *Arisṭū* 23.21 and 30.23.

This was Avicenna's view of Aristotle as the investigator of absolute Knowledge. But his attitude toward Aristotle was also affected by his understanding of the contextuality of the philosophical praxis. Aristotle, Avicenna thought, was circumscribed, like any philosopher, by his time and place, and was accordingly constrained on the one hand to heed tradition and Customary Practices in his communication of Philosophy, and on the other to take into consideration the fact that he had to Withhold knowledge from the unworthy (see Chapter 5). Avicenna was himself acutely aware of these two problems and he projected them unto Aristotle. He claimed that Aristotle was merely following Authority and Customary practices by discussing the Categories in Logic (Chapter 6.4), and he further maintained that Aristotle would occasionally present his arguments by intimation and implicitly (L80) and Work out Corollaries in a concealed manner (T12, § 1). This understanding of Aristotle was also influenced by tradition (Chapter 5.3), but it became more significant for Avicenna as he increasingly began himself to follow this model of the philosophical praxis.

In his earlier writings Avicenna shows a respect for the transmitted tradition and, more importantly, a respect for and adherence to the manner and method of philosophical discussion. This is evident (a) in his treatment of the major philosophers in the Aristotelian tradition and (b) in his use of the accepted philosophical jargon, as well as (c) in his adherence to traditional forms of exposition and (d) in his description of his own
289 works. In his later works the tradition becomes internalized and integrated rather than reproduced, and it is synthesized into the systematic scholastic philosophy of Avicenna which was forever to replace Aristotelianism in Islam.

(a) With regard to the major Aristotelian philosophers, Avicenna initially followed tradition and presented their views for the most part eponymously, and refrained from open criticism even when he preferred the views of one commentator over those of another. In *The Present*, for example, an early work very close in its ideas to his *Compendium on the Soul*, Avicenna mentions that "scholars and philosophers"—using the neutral terms *al-ʿulamāʾ wa-l-ḥukamāʾ*—disagreed on the subject of the incorporeal subsistence of the soul. He cites, following accepted procedure in philosophical discussion, Alexander of Aphrodisias (*al-Iskandar al-Afrūdīsī*, a form of the name never repeated by Avicenna in his later writings), who denied it, and Themistius, who accepted it, and says that both of them traced their doctrine to Aristotle himself. He then merely states that the view of Themistius is the correct one

without any comment, and proceeds with his argument.[16] Avicenna went even so far in his adherence to Peripatetic tradition as to defend prominent philosophers against their own statements and to attempt to save the appearances. He devised, that is, "pretexts" and excuses for them (T8, § 3 and L38). In his youthful debate with Bīrūnī he compares the latter's rejection of the Aristotelian theory of the eternity of the world to that of John Philoponus, but then proceeds to add that Philoponus "pretended to the Christians to display disagreement with Aristotle on this matter; but whoever examines his commentary on the last part of *De Generatione et Corruptione* and his other books will perhaps not fail to see that Philoponus agreed with Aristotle on this issue."[17] In his defense of Philoponus, Avicenna is clearly working within the tradition: it would seem that his argument was suggested to him by the passage in Fārābī's account of the transmission of philosophy, in which the Christians of Alexandria are said to have forbidden the teaching of logic beyond the end of the assertoric figures in *Prior Analytics* (i.e., I,7) "since they thought that that would harm Christianity."[18]
Much later, toward the end of his life, Avicenna was openly critical of Philo- 290
ponus's *Contra Aristotelem* and called it "a book which is apparently cogent but essentially weak" (T12, § 2).

Apart from such specific examples, however, it is evident from the whole tenor of Avicenna's debate with Bīrūnī that he saw himself fully within the Aristotelian tradition, defending it with numerous references to the works of Aristotle and the commentators, as well as to his own works, which he clearly viewed as belonging in the same field of philosophical endeavor.[19]

In Avicenna's later writings there is decreasing reference by name to scholars in the Greek tradition and a concomitant increase in qualifying descriptions when they are referred to at all. The implication of this new attitude is clear. Avicenna does not see himself, or does not wish to project

---

16 In *Majmūʿ rasāʾil* 15 Mūsawī, published under the title *Risāla fī s-saʿāda wa-l-ḥujaj al-ʿašara* (GM 6).

17 *Answers to Bīrūnī* 13.7–10 Nasr and Mohaghegh. It is to be noted that the term Avicenna uses here for "pretend" is *mawwaha*, a word used to refer to sophistical misrepresentation. Bīrūnī rejected Avicenna's argument in no uncertain terms: "God forbid that such pretense [misrepresentation, *tamwīh*] should be attributed to John Philoponus! More deserving so to be described is rather Aristotle, who decorates his blasphemies with beautiful ornaments!" (51.13–14). In his reply, Maʿṣūmī reiterated Avicenna's argument in a more elaborate form (69.12–70.5), advising Bīrūnī to read the other books by Philoponus, not just his *Contra Aristotelem*.

18 Gutas "Alexandria to Baghdad" 164.

19 See, e.g., *Answers to Bīrūnī* 23.12–14; 25.4–6; 25.9–12; 28.11–29.1; 35.4–7 Nasr and Mohaghegh.

himself, as belonging to the same philosophical tradition, defending and supporting his predecessors as he had done in the earlier writings. Instead, he presumes to judge and rank the previous Peripatetic philosophers, adopting the stance of an independent overseer. This is the same attitude we have seen earlier expressed in the Autobiography with regard to the accomplishments of each scholar.

An illustration of the tendency of Avicenna's new attitude is provided by a passage from his discussion of the celestial movers. The passage was first written in *The Provenance and Destination*, and then copied in the Metaphysics of both *The Cure* and *The Salvation*. They compare as follows:

	Provenance	*Cure/Salvation*
	a) Each celestial sphere has a proximate mover proper to itself, ... according to the opinion of the Philosopher, Alexander, Themistius, and the Peripatetic scholars. ...	a) Each celestial sphere has a proximate mover proper to itself, ... according to the opinion of the First Teacher and the Validating Peripatetic scholars[20] after him. ...
	b) The Philosopher established the number of the moving spheres according to the knowledge of his time	b) The First Teacher established the number of the moving spheres according to the knowledge of his time ....
	c) Alexander explained as follows in his treatise *On the Principles of the Universe*	c) One of his followers who speaks more to the point explained as follows in his treatise *On the Principles of the Universe* ....
291	d) Themistius explained as follows ....[21]	d) He who expressed well the books of the First Teacher by way of epitome—although he could not delve deeply into the ideas[22]—explained as follows ....
	e) [Omits.]	e) These two are the First Teacher's closest ancient disciples who followed the right course.[23] (L70)

[20] The *Salvation* reads, "the Validating scholars of Peripatetic philosophy."

[21] *Al-Mabda' wa-l-ma'ād* 61–62 Nūrānī.

[22] Cf. the similar assessment of Themistius by a modern scholar, Octave Hamelin, *La théorie de l'intellect d'après Aristote et ses commentateurs*, Edmond Barbotin, ed., Paris: Vrin, 1953, 39: "Ses [Themistius's] développements [on the text of Aristotle] gardent toujours ce caractère littéral qui fait de lui un interprète utile et sûr pour l'intelligence verbale d'Aristote, mais pauvre en aperçus profonds sur la pensée du maître."

[23] *Ilāhiyyāt* 392.8–10, 392.15–393.5 Mūsā et al.; *Najāt* 435.15–436.17/634.11–635.15.

The evolving attitude of Avicenna, clearly demonstrated in the above passages, to distance himself from membership in the company of the Aristotelian commentators entails two consequences for his work. First, when his purpose was to comment on the tradition, it enabled him to present himself as the impartial judge of the accomplishments of previous scholars. This development reaches its culmination in his book by the very title, *Fair Judgment*. In the extant fragments (see W10), the commentators are mentioned by name, and in each case, in the apposite words of the Disciple (Ibn-Zayla?) writing from Rayy, Avicenna "Judged every question and every philosopher by bestowing Fairly praise or blame, and appreciation or deprecation" (T13, § 2). Themistius, for example, is mentioned twice in the *Commentary on Lambda*, once with praise and once with blame; in the *Marginal Glosses on De anima* he is mentioned both times with blame.[24] Alexander is mentioned four times in the *Marginal Glosses*, and commended in only one of these.[25] Second, when Avicenna's purpose was expository, he could dispense almost completely with referring to any predecessors. This development culminates in the *Pointers and Reminders*, in which no philosopher is ever mentioned for his doctrines by name, with the sole exception of Porphyry who is severely criticized;[26] even Aristotle is mentioned once as "the First Teacher,"[27] once as "the author of logic,"[28] and referred to once again as "the master of the Peripatetics" in a passage which sets itself apart from the rest of the books because it is described neither as a "Pointer" nor as a "reminder," but specifically as a "reference" (*istišhād*).[29] All the other references to the commentators are very vague, and even the customary formula "the Validating scholars" (*al-muḥaṣṣilūn, ahl at-taḥṣīl*) is rarely used.[30]

The evolution of a similar critical tone can be observed in Avicenna's 292
attitude toward Muslim thinkers as well. *The Provenance and Destination* again contains passages which have either neutral or no references to predecessors in the Islamic tradition, but which reappear in *The Cure* and *The Salvation* with critical comments inserted. The scholars that come under such attack are ʿĀmirī and Kindī:

24 Badawī *Arisṭū* 26.23, 31.4, 98.18–19, 116.10–11.
25 Badawī *Arisṭū* 78.22, 101.17, 106.1, 114.6.
26 *Išārāt* II.7.10, 180/326 = Goichon *Directives* 448.
27 *Išārāt* I.5.4, 52/115 = Goichon *Directives* 166, Inati *Logic* 114.
28 *Išārāt* I.9.1 81/166 = Goichon *Directives* 225, Inati *Logic* 149.
29 *Išārāt* II.6.28, 167/308 = Goichon *Directives* 416. For these terms see W11.
30 *Išārāt* I.9.2, 81/167; II.1.4, 92/191 = Goichon *Directives* 226, 253.

Provenance	*Cure*	*Salvation*
a) We still have to consider something else: it is possible to imagine that the various objects of desire [which move the spheres] are bodies rather than separate intellects, ...	We still have to consider something else: it is possible to imagine that the various objects of desire [which move the spheres] are bodies rather than separate intellects,	We still have to consider something else: it is possible to imagine that the various objects of desire [which move the spheres] are bodies rather than separate intellects, ...
	... as was thought by	as was thought by Abū-l-Ḥasan al-ʿĀmirī,
	one of the foremost[a] modern philosophasters in muddling philosophy, since he did not understand the purpose of the ancients.	the foremost of the modern philosophasters in muddling philosophy, since he did not understand the purpose of the ancients.
We say that this is impossible	We say that this is impossible	We say that this is impossible ....[31]
b) Some people who are scholars/philosophers say	Some people who claim affiliation with scholars/philosophers say	Some people who claim affiliation with scholars/philosophers say ....[32] (L71)

In this last example Avicenna does not specify any names; Ṭūsī provides it in his commentary:

> "i.e., al-Kindī and his followers."[33]

(b) With regard to philosophical jargon, in his earlier writings Avicenna manifestly presents himself as a philosopher writing in the Graeco-Arabic

---

[a] The reading, rather than *al-fadm*, "sluggish," would seem to be *al-qudm/al-qudum* or *al-qadm/al-qadam*, both meaning "prior, foremost" and, by extension, "bold, audacious" (cf. *Lisān al-ʿArab*, root *qdm*; also in these meanings it has passed into Persian usage, which is significant for Avicenna: see Steingass 958); it has the better attestation in the manuscripts of both the *Šifāʾ* and the *Najāt*. This is also what the medieval Latin translator read, who renders it *praecipuus* (see Bertolacci *Reception* 545), indicating that he preferred the meaning "foremost;" this fits the context better than "audacious" as I had suggested earlier. The text of the Cairo edition of the *Ilāhiyyāt* (399.10 Mūsā et al.) is accordingly to be corrected.

---

[31] *Al-Mabdaʾwa-l-maʿād* 66 Nūrānī = *Ilāhiyyāt* 399.8–11 Mūsā et al. = Najāt 444.13–17/645.1–6. Cf. Rowson 28.

[32] *Al-Mabdaʾ wa-l-maʿād* 84 Nūrānī: *qawm min ahl al-ʿilm* = *Ilāhiyyāt* 413.1 Mūsā et al.: *qawm min al-muntasibīn ilā ahl* [thus to be read] *al-ʿilm* = *Najāt* 463.12/666.1: *qawm min al-muntasibīn ilā ahl al-ʿilm*.

[33] Ṭūsī in *Šarḥ* III,234 Dunyā.

philosophical tradition. In many instances he quotes the titles of Aristotle's books, and an occasional technical term, in Greek rather than Ara- 293
bic: *ṭūbīqā* (*Topica*),[34] *Rīṭūrīqā* (*Rhetorica*),[35] *Fw'īṭīqā* (*Poetica*),[36] *Māṭāfūsīqā* (*Metaphysica*),[37] *fanṭāsiyā/banṭāsiyā* (*phantasia*),[38] This practice is continued in, or perhaps, more accurately, is allowed in most cases to be transferred to, the re-presentation of earlier texts in *The Cure* with diminishing frequency. At other times in *The Cure*, the Greek word may be offered but only after the Arabic equivalent has been given, almost as if to ensure that the reader, more familiar with the Greek term, know which Arabic word it corresponds to. By late works such as *The Easterners* and *Pointers and Reminders*, the practice ceases to exist. The terminology used by Avicenna, whether the traditional one in Aristotelian philosophy or neologistic (as discussed in Chapter 6.5), is allowed to stand on its own and the reader is expected to identify the referents.

(c) There is a similar development toward independence in Avicenna's adherence to the outward forms of presentation and classification of philosophy in the Aristotelian tradition. In his very first work, *Compendium on the Soul*, he discusses only those subjects that the tradition considers appropriate for inclusion in a work on the soul, despite the fact that he would have wished to investigate related questions on the Metaphysics of the Rational Soul (Chapter 6.2). He dutifully expresses his respect for tradition:

> Among the subjects associated with this investigation that still remain to be done is .... However, had it not been Customary to separate the investigation of these subjects from the investigation we have been conducting, out of respect and veneration for the former, and to offer the present investigation first as an introduction to the other and in order to establish the framework of discussion, I would have followed these chapters with the rest of the discussion on the other subjects to complete the matter.[39]

In subsequent works, starting already with *The Provenance and Destination* of his transition period, Avicenna gradually leaves traditional forms of presentation and reaches, with the *Pointers and Reminders*, a stage of high emancipation from Customary Practices.

---

34 *'Arūḍiyya* f. 10^{a} = 47 Ṣāliḥ; Ahwānī *Aḥwāl* 55.8.

35 *'Arūḍiyya* f. 34^{a} = 87 Ṣāliḥ.

36 *'Arūḍiyya* f. 45^{b} = 105 Ṣāliḥ.

37 *Answers to Bīrūnī* 23.14 Nasr and Mohaghegh.

38 *'Arūḍiyya* f. 79^{b}-2 = 157 Ṣāliḥ; Ahwānī *Aḥwāl* 120.8.

39 Landauer 372 (text), 418 (translation).

(d) A concomitant development to the change in Avicenna's adherence to transmitted forms of exposition is the marked difference in the way in which he refers to his own books in his early and later periods. Until the compilation of *The Cure*, Avicenna refers to his previous works as commentaries, interpretations, compendia, or epitomes of the books of Aristotle. In *The*
294 *Provenance and Destination*, for example, he expresses himself numerous times as follows: "we have Verified and elucidated this in our precise exposition (*talḫīṣ*) of *Posterior Analytics*;" "we have elucidated this matter in our precise exposition (*talḫīṣ*) of *De Caelo* and *Physics*."[40] More explicit is the prologue to his *Logic Epitomized* (*al-Manṭiq al-mūjaz*), a work that apparently dates from this period:

> The first person who discovered [logic] is Aristotle, the Greek philosopher. We have written many books commenting [*mašrūḥa*] in great detail on the discipline of logic, and we have also written a number of epitomes and compendia [*jawāmiʿ wa-muḫtaṣarāt*] ....[41] (L72)

In his later period, Avicenna changes his practice altogether. He stops referring indiscriminately to all his earlier works as compendia or summaries of Aristotle's books; he no longer refers to Aristotle's books for documentation but rather to his own—he mentions Aristotle's books only when there is a historical point to be made;[42] and he refers to *some* of his previous works as "commentaries" only when they are clearly in the nature of a direct commentary on Aristotelian texts, like the *Fair Judgment*, not when they are general expositions of Knowledge like *The Cure*. The best illustration of his change of orientation is in the way he describes in two instances his own *Appendices*. In the Sophistics of *The Cure*, written around 414/1024 (W6) and before the completion of the entire work, he says that in the *Appendices* he expects to elaborate on some details of Aristotle's text that were not very explicit (T6B, §7), clearly implying that he planned that work to be a commentary on *Aristotle's* philosophy. About six years later when he wrote the

[40] *Al-Mabdaʾ wa-l-maʿād* f. 142a MS Ambrosiana 150 Sup (320 Hammer) = p. 35 Nūrānī, where the text reads differently and omits *fī talḫīṣinā*; p. 38 Nūrānī. For *talḫīṣ* = precise exposition (*diorismos* in Greek), interpretation, see the references in *WKAS* II, 1.428b–429a.

[41] *Al-Manṭiq al-mūjaz*, quoted in Mahdavī 221.

[42] In the extant fragments of the *Fair Judgment* and the *Marginal Glosses on De anima*, he refers numerous times to his *Easterners* by invoking the Easterners; in *Pointers and Reminders*, written after *The Easterners* was lost, he refers to *The Cure* for documentation (e.g., *Išārāt* I.5.2, 49/111 = Goichon *Directives* 161, Inati *Logic* 112), and again, in the same work, to the *Prior* and *Posterior Analytics* of Aristotle when discussing the historical aspect of a question (*Išārāt* I.9.2, 82/167 = Goichon *Directives* 226–227, Inati 150).

Prologue to the completed work, he describes the *Appendices* this time as a kind of "commentary to [*The Cure*], Providing Corollaries to its Fundamental Principles and elaborating upon its briefly expressed concepts" (T9, § 3). *The Cure* thus supplanted Aristotle's texts as the closest approximation to Knowledge, and therefore as the text to be commented upon.

The shift in Avicenna's attitude toward his own work in relation to the Aristotelian tradition is also apparent in the evolution of his general statements of purpose in the various introductions to his successive works. In the 295
introduction to *The Provenance and Destination* (T4, § 1), he states that his purpose is to expound the doctrines of the *Peripatetic* philosophers. In the prologue of the Physics of *The Cure*, the first part of the work to be written (W6), he says that he will write about Physics

> in the manner established by our opinion and arrived at by our theoretical investigation. The arrangement on this occasion will correspond to that followed in Peripatetic philosophy.[43] (L73)

Here Avicenna expresses his ideological independence from the Peripatetics but maintains his contextual affiliation. In the Prologue to the entire *Cure*, written after the work had been completed, there is yet another shift. Instead of writing about Peripatetic philosophy, he says (T9, § 1), his book contains "the Fundamental Principles contained in the philosophical sciences attributed to the *ancients*" as well as his own thoughts. There is no mention of a specific name at this point; later on (§ 5B) he says, interestingly enough, that with regard to physics he "was mostly unsuccessful in pursuing a course parallel to the systematic treatise and the memoranda of Aristotle, the paradigmatic master in this discipline." In the Introduction to *The Easterners* all direct affiliation with the Aristotelian tradition is expressly rejected; Aristotle merely provided the foundation and the direction, but Avicenna's purpose is to build beyond it, not to expound it or explain, as formerly, its hidden meanings. In *Pointers and Reminders*, finally, there is no historical context whatsoever in the very brief prologue, and extremely limited mention of any predecessors in the entire work. The purpose is merely to provide, to those able to understand, Pointers and reminders about Knowledge, regardless of pedigree, and as contained in the active intellect and acquired by Avicenna through study and Correct Guessing of middle terms.

---

43 *As-Samāʿ aṭ-ṭabīʿī* 3.5–6 Zāyid; Mahdavī 145; McGinnis *Physics* 1.

As Avicenna's awareness of his personal contribution to the history of philosophy grew and he developed a progressively more precise conception of the praxis of philosophy, and as he increasingly stopped seeing himself in the traditional mold of philosopher, i.e., a mere commentator on the Aristotelian texts, a self-perception shared by *all* philosophers after Plotinus, Greek and Arabic alike, he started coming into his own and speaking in his own voice as a philosopher—another Aristotle, as we saw in the implications of his structure of the Autobiography (Chapter 3.4). This shift in self-perception entailed a concomitant shift in his attitude to Aristotle and the Aristotelian tradition, and inversely proportional to it. The more he emanci-
296 pated himself from the traditional mold of philosopher/commentator and saw himself as the most accurate communicator of Knowledge/Philosophy, the more critical he became of the Aristotelian tradition and the less willing to spend time repeating their theories which he considered erroneous and refuting them. His focus shifted to presenting Knowledge independently of tradition and Customary practices, with scant attention to theories which by then had become, to him, irrelevant, outdated, or misguided, and with even less concern for the names of individuals who had held them. Once he had integrated in his mind the Aristotelian tradition with all the conflicting views, his purpose, which was never fully historical, became completely systematic. The evolution of his attitude toward Aristotle and the Aristotelian tradition is therefore of significance in assessing the concomitant evolution of his purpose in the praxis of philosophy.

THE ELABORATION OF METHODS

1. The Evolution of Avicenna's Methods of Communication

The development of Avicenna's different methods of composition runs parallel to the evolution of his attitude toward Aristotle and the Aristotelian tradition. With increasing awareness of independence from that tradition there came a corresponding independence of style and experimentation with different approaches and methods of communication.

Initially Avicenna saw himself as a commentator on the Aristotelian texts, and his style was accordingly expository, reformulating the accepted doctrines as transmitted. In the transition period of his literary activity, the need to incorporate in his works material not readily treated in the tradition—primarily subjects that belong to the Metaphysics of the Rational Soul—led Avicenna to approach the work of composition by following not so much the contents of the tradition as the doctrine about Aristotle's presumed obscurity which stood in need of explication. This enabled Avicenna to write about what he perceived to be the "fruits" of Physics and Metaphysics while claiming to be expounding the "innermost ideas stored in the depths" of Peripatetic books and "Withheld from explicit mention" (T5, §1; cf. T4, §3). In his mature period, and with increased self-confidence, Avicenna abandoned this approach and reverted to the expository method. Only this time the philosophical doctrines, which include the material introduced in the preceding period under the guise of decoding Peripatetic obfuscation, were presented as the work of Avicenna's own synthesis of what was best in the tradition with his own thoughts, and without reference to the authority of the tradition (T9, §1; T7, §3). In the following period, Avicenna attempted to set up his revised systematization of philosophy as a separate philosophical school native to his place of origin, Ḫurāsān (the East), and to delineate its identity sharply by explicitly contrasting it with the Aristotelian tradition. This innovation by Avicenna found little response in his immediate milieu; despite the wide receptivity shown to his revised systematization, the drastic break with the Peripatetic tradition indicated by its new name was not appreciated. In his last period, finally, Avicenna actively used the Peripatetic doctrine of deliberate obscurity and treated philosophy in such a way that would Withhold it from those unworthy to receive it.

298 This brief summary highlights the course of Avicenna's approach to communicating philosophical knowledge only as represented in the major works of each period. Throughout most of his life, however, or at least from his mature period onwards, Avicenna was continuously preoccupied with elaborating methods of composition and with fashioning the means of presentation to fit the audience he was addressing in each particular case. Almost all of his works were written for patrons who requested them from him. In the main we do not know the reactions, or the extent of satisfaction felt by the commissioners of his works when they received the finished product; Avicenna, however, certainly knew about it. Glimpses of such reactions we get, for example, from the attitude of one of his closest disciples, Jūzjānī, upon seeing the completed *Cure*. As discussed in Chapter 2 (W6), it seems obvious that he was not entirely pleased with it, in the sense that it did not meet his preconceived idea of what a commentary, or—be it—even an exposition of Aristotle's works ought to have been. In this connection we should not forget that as Avicenna's attitude toward Aristotle and the Aristotelian tradition was evolving and he developed an increasingly independent attitude toward it, we cannot expect his disciples and followers, let alone his calumniators or opponents, to have doffed ingrained attitudes of servility and slavish imitation of Aristotelian models. The opposition to Avicenna's neoteristic approach must have therefore been considerable even from his more attached disciples, as is evident from numerous passages of Avicenna himself where he expresses his impatience with such people. It was only his stature and renown that enabled him to continue working along these lines, and the personal cult surrounding him that arose early and was followed by those not so strongly attached to the Aristotelian tradition, that ensured the propagation and survival of his works.

Another indication of a reaction to a commissioned piece is provided by the possibly apocryphal story that ʿAlāʾ-ad-Dawla himself, his great protector and patron, understood nothing from the *Philosophy* which Avicenna condescended to write in Persian for his very edification.[1]

Considerations such as these, along with Avicenna's deep appreciation of the contextuality of the philosophical praxis (Chapter 5.2, 5.3), made him think seriously about the manner in which he was going to write his works

[1] Achena and Massé 19.

depending on the people to whom they were being addressed, and led him to elaborate three main distinct methods of communicating Knowledge, each with variations of its own. These are, a) the symbolic; presentation by means of symbols and allegories; b) the indicative; presentation by way of Pointers; i.e., allusion, suggestion, and implication; and c) the demonstrative or expository; presentation by means of syllogisms and syllogistic 299
argumentation with varying degrees of fullness. A fourth method, which can be called the mnemonic because it consisted of presentation in verse for easy memorization (like his *rajaz* poems on logic and medicine), will not be discussed here insofar as it is an ancillary subcategory of the expository method.

2.1. The Symbolic Method: Symbol and Allegory

Avicenna's symbolic method is directly derived from his theory of prophecy and its association, through the work of Fārābī, with the Greek traditions about allegorical writing.[2] Representative of the latter is the following passage from Galen's epitome of Plato's *Republic* (?), a work widely available in Arabic translation:

> The masses [*jumhūr an-nās*] are unable to understand the sequence of demonstrative argumentation and are therefore in need of symbols [*rumūz*] whereby they can be aided; (by "symbols" Galen meant the reports about the rewards and punishments in the Hereafter). We see today, for example,

---

[2] Since the question has been raised, it is necessary to state here the precise meaning of "symbol" and "allegory." The question was raised by Corbin and later by Bausani, who attempted to establish a highly subjective difference between the two terms. Bausani quoted Corbin with approval: "Corbin seems to me perfectly right when he writes: 'Symbol is there to announce something which cannot be expressed otherwise: it is the only possible expression of the thing symbolized; allegory is a more or less artificial figuration of generalities or abstractions that can be perfectly expressed and known by other ways'" (A. Bausani, "Continuity and Break in the Literary and Cultural Tradition of Iran," *Proceedings of the 26th International Congress of Orientalists*, New Delhi 1968, vol. II, p. 187 bottom). This is quite inaccurate and misleading, at least in English (and in French and Italian, I am sure). Contemporary English usage defines symbol as "something used for or regarded as representing something else; a material object representing something, often something immaterial;" and allegory as "a symbolic narrative" (*The Random House College Dictionary*, revised edition, New York 1979). As it can be readily appreciated, the criterion of whether the thing symbolized can be expressed in other ways or not does not enter into the definition; it was only relevant to Corbin's obsession with what he perceived to be the allegedly ineffable Iranian spirituality. In what follows I will be using the words in their dictionary sense.—Avicenna's theory of prophecy was initially discussed by Rahman *Prophecy*, and more recently by Gutas "Über die Seele" and by Afifi al-Akiti, with references to further bibliography.

> that the people who are called Christians have taken their faith merely from symbols and the miraculous, and yet they may be thought to behave like true philosophers: their lack of fear of death, namely, and of what they will encounter after it is something which we may witness every day. The same also applies to their abstinence from sexual intercourse: for some of them, not only men but also women, actually spend their entire lives refraining from sexual intercourse, while others have reached such a point of self-control in regulating their food and drink and in their intense desire for rectitude that they have in fact become not inferior to those who are truly philosophers.[3]
> (L74)

Avicenna stated his understanding of the function of allegory for the work of the prophet in explicit terms as follows:[4]

> [a] The prophet ... should let men know that they have a maker, one and omnipotent .... This will induce the masses [*al-jumhūr*] to obey the decrees put in the prophet's mouth by the deity and the angels. With regard to knowledge about God, however, the prophet ought not to involve the masses with anything beyond the fact that He is one, the truth, and has none like Himself. To lead them beyond this and demand that they believe in His existence as being not referred to in place, not subject to verbal categories, neither inside nor outside the world, or anything of this kind, is something that will tax them beyond their capacities, muddle their religion in their affairs, and immerse them in a state from which only the exceptional and rare person receiving the succour and success of God can be saved—for they can conceptualize these states in the right manner only with great strain, and few of them can form a mere concept of the real nature of this "oneness [of God]" and [His] "de-anthropomorphism;" before long, however, they will deny the truth of such an existence, fall into dissension, and devote their attention to discussions and analogical arguments that will divert them from performing the duties

---

[3] Galen's text is quoted in Abū-ʿĪsā ibn-al-Munajjim's *Chronography* as preserved in Abū-l-Fidā'’s *Historia Anteislamica*, H.L. Fleischer, ed., Leipzig 1831, 108, and in an abbreviated form in the *Muntaḫab Ṣiwān al-ḥikma* 209–211 Dunlop; see S.M. Stern, "Abū ʿĪsā Ibn Al-Munajjim's Chronography," *Islamic Philosophy and The Classical Tradition* [*Festschrift* Richard Walzer], S.M. Stern, A. Hourani, V. Brown, eds., Oxford: Cassirer, 1972, 453 and 466n53. This text, which may be one of two translations from the original Greek, has a complicated transmission history, which makes many details relatively unclear, including whether it comes from Galen's epitome of the *Republic* or the *Phaedo*. It has been much discussed in modern scholarship: see the presentation, with full references to previous studies, by Stephen Gero, "Galen on the Christians. A Reappraisal of the Arabic Evidence," *Orientalia Christiana Periodica* 56 (1990) 371–411.—The parenthetical sentence in the text explaining what Galen meant by "symbols" may be by Abū-ʿĪsā, though it could be earlier; see Gero 405n100.

[4] *Ilāhiyyāt* 442.10–443.12 Mūsā et al. = *Najāt* 500.5–501.17/710.16–713.5. Cf. the translations by Marmura *Metaphysics* 365–366, Lizzini *Metafisica* 1017–1019, with notes, and Bertolacci *Guarigione* 803–805.

of the body[a]—and it might even immerse them in opinions contrary to the welfare of society [*al-madīna*] and opposed to the imperatives of truth. As a result, their problems and doubts will multiply, and it will be difficult for any tongue[b] to control them. Divine wisdom is not easily acquired by everybody.

[b] It is not proper for any man to reveal that he possesses knowledge he is hiding from the common people [*al-ʿāmma*]. Indeed, he should not even permit an intimation of this. Rather, he should inform them about God's majesty and greatness through symbols [*rumūz*] and images [*amṯila*] derived
from things that for them are majestic and great, and present in addition to 301
that only this much, namely, that God has neither equal, nor companion, nor likeness. Similarly, he must establish for them the doctrine about the [final] Destination [of the soul] in a way that they will be able to conceive how it happens and that will reassure them, and he must strike images [*amṯāl*] for the eternal bliss and misery that they will understand and conceive. Of the true nature of these matters he should intimate to them only some general concepts: that it is something that "no eye has ever seen nor ear heard,"[5] and that there are pleasures that are great possessions and pains that are perpetual punishment.

[c] Know that God knows the manner in which good in these matters [is effected], and what God knows should accordingly be taken in the right manner[c] (as you have found out). There is nothing wrong if his [the prophet's] address contains symbols [*rumūz*] and Pointers [*išārāt*] inviting to philosophical research [*al-baḥṯ al-ḥikmī*] those naturally predisposed to theoretical investigation. (L75)

---

[a] The *Najāt* text reads *al-badaniyya* (of the body), while the *Šifāʾ* text has *al-madaniyya* (of the city). The city, however, is mentioned in the next sentence, while this long parenthetical aside aims to explain that by engaging in misguided theological discussions people are apt to forget (or disdain) physical acts of worship like prayer, fasting, etc., and thus fall into a state from which only God can save them.

[b] *ʿAlā l-lisān* (tongue) is the reading of the *Najāt*; the *Šifāʾ* has *ʿalā insān* (man). The intended meaning seems to be that such people cannot be restrained by advice and counsel and may thus have to be punished.

[c] I follow the *Najāt* readings, which give a better text than that of the *Šifāʾ*: *wa-ʿlam anna llāha taʿālā yaʿlamu* [the *Šifāʾ* adds *anna*] *wajha l-ḫayri fī hāḏā fa-yajibu an yuʾḫaḏa* [*Šifāʾ*: *yūjada*] *maʿlūmu llāhi subḥānahu ʿalā wajhihi.*

---

[5] This is a very popular tradition by the Prophet, cited in almost all canonical collections; see the references in Michot "Connaissance de l'âme" 490n87. As noted by Louis Gardet, *Dieu et la destinée de l'homme*, Paris: Vrin 1967, 336, it harks back to a letter by Paul, *I Corinthians* 2,9, which itself is a reference to Isaiah 64,3. For "The Ḥadīth and the New Testament" see the Excursus under this title by Ignaz Goldziher in *Muslim Studies*, S.M. Stern, ed., London: Allen & Unwin, 1967, II,346–362, and his article "Neutestamentliche Elemente in der Traditionslitteratur des Islam" in *Oriens Christianus* 2 (1902) 390–397; Goldziher does not discuss this particular ḥadīṯ/Paul/Isaiah text.

Several points need to be noted in this significant passage.

First, it establishes that the need for symbolical or allegorical communication derives from the fact that the masses (*al-ʿāmma*) are incapable, because of their stupidity, of understanding truth when stated in demonstrative or expository language. The only way in which they can understand it is when *the same truth* (and not another, mystical, or more profound, truth), or more precisely, a much simplified version of the same truth, reduced to the bare essentials, is expressed in terms of symbols and images to which they can relate and with which they are familiar from their everyday life.

Second, not only can the common people understand the truth only in this manner, but it is possitively deleterious to convey it to them in any other way because they will misunderstand and misapply it. They will not perform their obligatory acts of worship and other civic duties and thereby harm both their life in the Hereafter and society at large (L75, §a). This directly involves and explains Withholding the explicit truth from them, i.e., the entire constellation of ideas and attitudes associated with the concept of *ḍann* discussed in Chapter 5.3.

Third, not only would the common people misunderstand and misapply truth were they to be given it explicitly, but it is also harmful for them to perceive that it is actually withheld from them. It is therefore "not proper for any man to reveal that he possesses knowledge he is hiding from" them (§b). This is a second reason why they should be given the truth in symbols,
302 i.e., not only so that they can understand what is proper of it for them, but also to dispel their perception that somebody knows something which he is hiding from them.

Fourth, and most important, *the allegorical method of communication is inferior to the demonstrative and expository* because it is suited for and addressed to inferior minds. It merely gives them in symbols what it would have given them demonstratively had they been of greater understanding.

Fifth, the only use the allegorical method may have for superior minds is to invite them to "philosophical research," to the demonstrative method (§c). This is the third reason for communicating in symbols, corresponding to the training and testing of the students in the Aristotelian tradition, as mentioned in Chapter 5.3.

Sixth, finally, communication through various means—symbols, Pointers, demonstration—is part of the divine plan and intended to effect the greatest possible amount of good (§c).

On the basis of this understanding of the function and significance of allegorical communication, Avicenna both interpreted the Qurʾān and himself wrote allegorical works. In view of the great amount of scholarly effort that has been expended in trying, first, to understand the assumed "mystical" or "oriental" philosophy of Avicenna, and second, to prove that he actually did have one, it is necessary to present here in review our findings so far.

First of all, as we saw in Chapter 5.3 on the concept of *ḍann*, the numerous passages in which Avicenna mentions "Withholding knowledge" and "forbidding" his disciples to divulge his teachings to the unworthy do not indicate that he had a "secret," "mystical," or "esoteric" doctrine, separate from his "exoteric" Aristotelian teachings, which he wished to share only with the elect few. If anything, all they indicate is that he followed, to the contrary, Aristotelian tradition and Islamic attitudes in wishing to Withhold knowledge from mentally inferior people for fear that they would misunderstand and misapply it and hence cause damage to themselves and to society. There is no question here of *two* knowledges, one Aristotelian, the other not, one exoteric, the other esoteric, one for the elect, the other for the masses. Knowledge, as we have seen, is one, and that is the forms of things as contained in the active intellect, structured in a syllogistic manner, classified in the Aristotelian fashion, and best expressed, in a manner best suited to their structure, by the philosophy of the Aristotelian tradition. It is the *explicit* exposition of *this* Knowledge that has to be Withheld from the masses because they, unable to understand its syllogistic structure, will be corrupted by it, i.e., neglect their acts of worship and adopt ideas harmful to society. This Knowledge has to be communicated to them,
lest they perceive that something *is* being withheld from them, in sym- 303
bols. *The relevant discriminating factor here is social expediency, not doctrinal* 304
dichotomy.

Secondly, in all his works in which Avicenna either interprets a symbolically expressed text or himself composes an allegory, all he does is, as we just saw, to provide strict one-to-one correspondences between philosophical concepts and symbols. Again, the Knowledge to be communicated or the truth to be imparted is one, presented through different vehicles. There is no question of the allegories presenting a truth, or a doctrine, that is different, higher, or more profound, than the philosophical exposition. As a matter of fact, allegorical presentation is, if anything, inferior to demonstrative presentation, as already noted. For the demonstrative presentation includes the middle terms, or causes, of the extremes, and intellectual certainty can come about only when things are known through their causes. The most that an allegorical presentation can do is to induce the philosophically minded to engage in philosophical research, construct the syllogisms, and discover the middle terms, thus arriving at the same stage at which he would have been had he been given from the very beginning a demonstrative presentation rather than an allegory.

This correspondence in Avicenna's works between symbol and philosophical concept can be witnessed in numerous works. We saw above an example in the way in which he interpreted the Light Verse (Chapter 3.2): each element of the Qur'ānic metaphor corresponded to a specific philosophical concept. The Light Verse for Avicenna thus does not express a higher, or esoteric truth, but merely the doctrine of the intellect as developed in the Aristotelian tradition (including his theory of *ḥads*) and as
305 expressed in philosophical language numerous times throughout his works. The only difference is that everybody can understand the external meaning of the Light Verse (it is merely a picture), but very few can understand the epistemological theory indicated in the doctrine of the intellect expressed in philosophical terms.

Further examples of strict correspondences can be found, for example, in his last essay *On the Rational Soul* (T14, §10), where he explicitly makes the identification: "the intellectual substance which is the medium of the divine effluence ... is called 'angel' in the language of Revelation (*fī lisān aš-šarʿ*) and 'active intellect' in philosophical terminology."[6] In *Pointers and Reminders*, finally, when Avicenna refers the disciple/reader to the story of Salāmān and Absāl, he again provides the immediate correspondences and urges the disciple to work out and elaborate upon the rest of the symbolism:

> Salāmān is an image [*maṯal*] referring to yourself, and Absāl is an image referring to the stage [you have reached] in Knowledge [*ʿirfān*], if you are worthy of it.[7] Now analyze the allegory [*ar-ramz*], if you can.[8] (L76)

---

[6] Authors of pseudepigraphic works attributing them to Aviccenna picked up on this feature of his writing and used it to good measure, as in the spurious essay *On the Knowledge of the Rational Soul and Its States* (*Risāla fī Maʿrifat an-nafs an-nāṭiqa wa-aḥwālihā*) where the Farthest Sphere is said to correspond to "the Throne in the language of Revelation" (*wa-huwa l-ʿarš bi-lisān aš-šarʿ*; cf. Qur'ān 9:129), and the Sphere of the Fixed Stars to "the Footstool in the language of Revelation" (*wa-huwa l-kursī bi-lisān aš-šarʿ*; cf. Qur'ān 2:255); see the entry on this essay in Section J in the Appendix. The identification of the ninth heaven with the Throne was made elsewhere by Avicenna: see Gardet 140, where also further references to such correspondences can be found.

[7] "If you are worthy of it," *in kunta min ahlihi*; cf. the discussion of this expression in Chapter 5.3.

[8] *Išārāt* II.9.1, 199/355 = Goichon *Directives* 485. The term *ḥall*, "analyze," here, the opposite of *ʿaqd*, "tightening," is used in the literary criticism of proverbs; see the discussion in Gutas "Ibn Ṭufayl" 234.—Whatever the story of Salāmān and Absāl may have been, Avicenna clearly intended by it to symbolize the same epistemological progression, from the stage of

Ramz is here used in the sense of an aggregate of symbols, and hence allegory, which is to be "analyzed," i.e., identified and elaborated upon along the lines hinted at by Avicenna. The inducement is in full accord with one of the purposes for which Aristotle was said to have written in an obscure style, namely the training of students.

When Avicenna came to write his own allegories, the notorious *Ḥayy ibn-* 306
Yaqẓān and *The Bird*, he applied precisely the same method in constructing his symbols. For each philosophical concept there corresponds a symbol, and the demonstrative and expository presentation of a subject is reproduced in the allegories in the same sequence, albeit in symbols. This is expressly stated at the end of the Persian commentary and translation of *Ḥayy ibn-Yaqẓān* by a disciple (Jūzjānī?), written shortly after Avicenna's death, and addressed to their mutual patron, ʿAlāʾ-ad-Dawla:

> Know that, for each of the questions treated in this epistle [*Ḥayy ibn-Yaqẓān*], a mere indication has been given here. A complete exposition can be found in larger works. Avicenna—may the divine mercy be upon him!—has himself treated them in his *Cure*, a summary of which is found in the *Philosophy for ʿAlāʾ-ad-Dawla*.[9] (L77)

Following the advice of the commentator in this epilogue, Goichon in *Le Récit de Ḥayy Ibn Yaqẓān* compared all the concepts in *Ḥayy* "phrase for phrase and frequently word for word" with the works suggested and discovered the correspondences.[10] What she did, in fact, was to follow Avicenna's injunction and "analyze the allegory."

2.2. The Symbolic Method: Not Mystical Knowledge

Avicenna's exposition of his ideas in symbolic form, as just described, together with the issue of his "oriental" philosophy, as analyzed above (Chapter 2, W9), have led to the view in the West, beginning with Mehren at the

---

material intellect to that of acquired intellect, described in numerous works, as, for example, in his last essay *On the Rational Soul* (T14).

[9] Corbin *Recital* 380. The pious formula, "may the divine mercy be upon him," unless it is an addition by a later scribe, would indicate that Avicenna had died when the disciple wrote the commentary. Since ʿAlāʾ-ad-Dawla himself died in 433/1041, the commentary was written between 428/1037 and 433/1041; see Corbin *Recital* 128–130, also for the question of authorship.

[10] Goichon gave a preliminary report about this book, along with some interesting examples, in the 24th International Congress of Orientalists: "Le prétendu ésotérisme d'Avicenne dans le recit de Ḥayy Ibn Yaqẓān," *Akten des vierundzwanzigsten Internationalen Orientalisten-Kongresses*, Herbert Franke, ed., Wiesbaden: Franz Steiner Verlag, 1959, 299–301.

end of the nineteenth century, that Avicenna was a mystic, or, as put by the more discriminating adherents of this view, that Avicenna's theory of knowledge included an ineffable mystical cognition beyond intellection,[11] which is the real philosophical issue at hand. The question is resolved when one examines this very issue on the basis of Avicenna's texts.

Humans can know only to the extent to which they have receptors for different kinds of knowledge. Avicenna recognizes four such receptors: the external senses, the internal senses of estimation (*wahm*) and imagination (*taḫayyul*), and the intellect. Since a presumed mystical knowledge is of the transcendent supernal world, the external senses and estimation, which provide information about sensible objects in this world, clearly have nothing to offer. By contrast, the internal sense of imagination does ultimately provide information about the supernal world, but only about what Avicenna calls "the unseen" (*al-ġayb*), which incontrovertibly refers to the knowledge of particular past, present, and future events on earth, which is possessed by the souls of the celestial spheres and to which the human soul has access because of its congeneric similarity to them (*mujānasa*). The intellect, finally, knows through thinking and syllogistic means the intelligibles contained in the active intellect and the intellects of the spheres. Neither of these two ways of knowledge, through imagination and the intellect, is mystical, and since there are no more ways that humans can receive information or knowledge from the supernal world there is no place for mystical knowledge in Avicenna's philosophy.

However, Avicenna goes on to analyze the knowledge acquired by the human intellect of the intelligibles as contained in the active intellect, and states that in some cases it is accompanied by emotions of joy and pleasure. This happens when the intellect, through thinking and syllogistic means by Guessing Correctly the middle term, and if no other faculties of the external and internal senses distract it, acquires a certain intimacy (*alf*) and familiarity with the intelligibles which Avicenna describes as having an experience or direct vision (*mušāhada*) of them. *Mušāhada*, he says,

> is an intimacy (*alf*) on the part of the intellective faculty with the intelligible, without, however, the middle term ceasing to be present, but in which one has no need of recollection concerning what is to be done, nor is there any contention on the part of any inferior faculty; to the contrary, the inferior

[11] Best expressed in the questions raised by Marmura "Avicenna's Thought" 341b–342b.

> faculties are drawn upwards together with the intellective faculty. … *Mušāhada* is a disposition, and even though it is accompanied by the middle term it is as if it doesn't need it.[12] (L78)

This experience of the intelligible, with the intellectual pleasure that accompanies it, Avicenna began to call "taste", *ḏawq*, towards the end of his career (*Išārāt* II.8.8, 193/345). This is what he is referring to in his last essay *On the Rational Soul* when he talks about "those who engage in philosophy through direct experience," *ahl al-ḥikma aḏ-ḏawqiyya* (T14, § 11). But there is nothing mystical in this aspect of Avicenna's theory of knowledge. This experience of the intelligibles is also intellective knowledge that includes the middle terms, but "it is as if it doesn't need" them.[13]

To recapitulate: 1) The symbolic method of presentation consisted for Avicenna in presenting Knowledge in images (*amṯāl*) and symbols, either singly or in aggregates (*ramz/rumūz*), that corresponded one to one to the philosophical concepts in which this Knowledge was expressed when it reflected the syllogistic structure of the universe. By its very nature, this method of presentation was inferior to the demonstrative, and constituted the lowest possible way in which Knowledge could be communicated. It needs to be emphasized that the symbolic method did *not* communicate knowledge that was different, more true, or more profound than that communicated through the demonstrative method. 2) The symbolic method had for Avicenna four functions, two positive and two negative. a) Its main *positive* function was to impart to the common people, who are unable to understand syllogistic argumentation, *some* of the Knowledge, viz., that much of it as is necessary for their social and eschatological well-being, namely, about the creator, their immortal soul, and the hereafter. This method was 307
employed in Revelation, by prophets, and ancient philosophers. b) Its secondary positive function was, first, to ferret out, from among the people who first came into contact with a symbolic text, like that of the Revelation, those individuals with philosophical propensities so that they could then investigate this Knowledge from a demonstrative point of view, and second, once identified, to train them in analyzing the allegories, finding out the correspondences in philosophical terms, and Working Out Corollary

---

[12] *Mubāḥaṯāt* §§ 597, 726 Bīdārfar; translated in Gutas "Absence of Mysticism" 370.

[13] For a full presentation of the argument summarized here see Gutas "Absence of Mysticism" and cf. Treiger *Inspired Knowledge* 60–63.

Principles from the Fundamental Principles they could see symbolized. c) Its main *negative* function was to conceal from the common people a literal exposition of the same Knowledge because they would misunderstand it and cause damage to themselves and society. d) Its secondary negative function was to give the common people the impression that nothing was being withheld from them at the same time that the explicit exposition of the same Knowledge was concealed from them. The symbolic method of presentation by Avicenna is not to be confused with mysticism for the reasons stated and primarily because mystical knowledge is totally alien to his epistemology.

3. The Indicative Method: Pointers

Avicenna recognized two higher methods of communicating knowledge. At an earlier stage of his career, while composing the logic of *The Cure*, he differentiated them in this way in the Prior Analytics (*Qiyās* 15.13–17.1 Zāyid):

> Teaching is of two kinds: teaching which supplies knowledge of something whose nature it is not to be known—like one who teaches that the three angles of a triangle are equivalent to two right angles—and teaching which consists of reminding (*taḏkīr*) and readying/preparing [one for knowledge] (*iʿdād*). Reminding is bringing to mind (*bāl*) something which, once brought to mind, is not unknown. ... Readying [one for knowledge] is bringing to mind along with it [i.e., the thing to be taught] other things like it. Each of these [other things], when it is known, supplies no further knowledge beyond itself; but when [the first thing] is brought into the mind in proximity with these others[d], the two of them [together] supply knowledge that had not existed [before].[14] ... Most of what is found in [Aristotle's] *Peri Hermeneias* consists of reminding and readying, though some of it is argumentation and inference (*istidlāl*). (L79)

In his Letter to an Anonymous Disciple (Bahmanyār) in Rayy he described them as follows:

---

[d] Reading *uḫar* for *āḫar* in the text.

---

[14] In the *Discussions* (§ 600 Bīdārfar), and in connection with hitting upon the middle term, Avicenna explains this "readying" in a hunting metaphor with reference to this passage: readying/preparing (*iʿdād*) "a snare to track down whatever may happen to fly in the vicinity of the possible; the instruction provided in the book of syllogisms is instruction for preparing the snares and approaching the place where one expects [the middle term to lie];" see Gutas "Intuition and Thinking" 27, § 17.2.

> As for the questions which you asked me, they are significant questions about the Philosophical Sciences, and especially these particular ones. ... I have studied these questions carefully and I have found them to be the proper ones; some I have answered at sufficient length, others by means of Pointers, and still others perhaps I have been unable to answer at all. ... [At the end of the letter Avicenna repeats himself:]
>
> ... [T]his sort of investigation, i.e. an investigation with demonstrative methods, is appropriate for the loftiest Philosophical Science .... You should engage in more such discussions [with me] on anything you wish, because in them lies pleasure and benefit. Whatever I am able to bring to light I will do so either openly, or from behind a veil which acts as a useful kind of stimulus and drill for it [i.e., the question at hand]; whatever I am unable to do so, I will excuse myself and admit it, since what is known to mankind is limited. [T11, §§3, 7]

Of the two methods of composition described here, one is expository, following demonstrative methods, and of appropriate length, and the other is by means of Pointers (*išāra*), indications, and as though from behind a veil. The purpose of the former is to explain openly and thoroughly the problem; that of the latter is to prompt the student to further investigation and train him. The first is demonstrative, the second indicative.

Avicenna's thoughts about the distinction between these two methods were formed, or rather, crystallized by the passage in (what he thought as) Fārābī's *The Agreement between Plato and Aristotle* cited earlier (L43). 308
Properly, an argument should be presented along the lines described by Avicenna in the Autobiography: all the premisses stated, all conclusions analyzed, all middle terms discovered. As indicated in Fārābī's passage, however, Aristotle was said to have engaged in deliberate obfuscation in order to render his teachings inaccessible to the unworthy. The means his objective was incomplete and jumbled presentation of the same analytic argument; the unworthy would be confused by it, while the philosopher could easily supply the missing steps. Thus Aristotle could claim to have publicized his philosophy without making it public (L40).

One question that needs to be raised at this stage is why, if the purpose in writing in an obscure manner is to protect Knowledge from reaching the unworthy, philosophers did not write only in a symbolic manner. The answer is that the symbolic method is appropriate for the common people; when Knowledge has to be communicated to philosophers, however, the symbolic method is inadequate because it cannot convey, being inferior, the demonstrative argumentation which alone brings about certainty. The only way therefore in which both the demonstrative argumentation can be conveyed and Knowledge concealed from the common people is by presenting it in an obscure way as Aristotle did; by providing, that is, Pointers which will show the way to the unexpressed conclusion or premiss or middle term. The indicative method therefore has a second function which it shares with the symbolic, namely, concealment of Knowledge from the unworthy.

In his own works, Avicenna followed such an understanding of the indicative method both to expound what was thought to have been so written in the Aristotelian tradition and to present his own theories. In the former case, he expressly states this to have been his purpose in *The Provenance and Destination* and the "Lesser" *Destination*:

> I strive to clarify what they [the Peripatetic philosophers] obscured, proclaim what they concealed and suppressed, collect what they dispersed, and expand what they summarized [T4, § 3].

> In this essay ... I have ... "removed the cover," lifted the veil, and indicated the innermost ideas stored in the depths of books and Withheld from explicit mention. ... One cannot rely [on others] ... to examine the symbolically expressed passages [in these books] and interpret them (should symbolic expression have in fact been used) and to elaborate their succinct passages (should the author have in fact restricted himself only to a succinct exposition). [T5, §§ 1–2]

In both these passages Avicenna clearly echoes the description of the indicative method in Aristotle given by Fārābī (L43) and bases his procedure upon it. Avicenna maintained this understanding of the composition of Aristotle's
309 works throughout his life; when he mentions in the Letter to Kiyā, written shortly before his death, that Aristotle in the first book of *De anima* "Worked Out Corollary Principles in a concealed fashion" (T12, § 1), he is referring to this understanding. A further example, among the many that could be adduced, of his application of this method to exegesis is provided by his comments on a disputed Aristotelian passage, *Metaphysics* 1072a23–25, where the First Mover is established by way of motion. Avicenna criticized Aristotle and the commentators in the *Fair Judgment* for having adopted such a way of argumentation (Chapter 6.3), but when he was asked again about the matter in the *Discussions*, he exonerated the ancients of having committed a flagrant error by claiming that they employed the indicative method:

> Question: What is the real exposition of [the argument] that the First is a principle of being and substance? For the ancients explained that it is a principle of movement only.

> Answer in Avicenna's hand: Not quite; they engaged in an exposition that it is a principle of movement openly and explicitly [*wāḍiḥan wa-bi-l-fiʿl*], while they engaged in the other [exposition that it is a principle of being and

substance] by intimation and implicitly [*ka-t-taʿrīḍ wa-ka-š-šayʾ bi-l-quwwa*]. [Avicenna then goes on to provide a Pointer about how to proceed to elaborate upon their implicit argument.][15] (L80)

Avicenna also used the indicative method in the presentation of his own works throughout his life. In the relatively early *Logic Epitomized* he applied it primarily for its didactic function.

> In these pages [*ajzāʾ*] we wish to set forth by way of summary and *Pointers* [the discipline of logic] to those who desire to comprehend both its Fundamental and Corollary Principles.[16] (L81)

In general, it seems that Avicenna used Pointers for the purpose of obfuscation when dealing primarily with the metaphysics of the rational soul (Chapter 6.2), with those subjects, that is, which he identified in *The Cure* as appropriate for such a treatment by the prophet (L75): the attributes of God, resurrection, the Afterlife and the attendant misery or bliss, and related subjects like the acts of worship. And it is in connection with these subjects that later pseudepigraphic tradition exploited Avicenna's method to lend an air of mystery to his alleged teachings, as in the following passage from what in all probability is a spurious essay, *On Prayer* (GM-Ps 3), where the case is overstated:

> All the ordinances of religion are explicable along the lines we have set forth in the present treatise. We would have desired to set forth for you each particular act of worship [separately], but it was impossible for us to enter upon matters with which it is not proper for every man to be acquainted. We have accordingly prepared a clear and straightforward division [between outward and inward acts of worship], and a Pointer is sufficient for the liberal man.[17] (L82)

But for Avicenna the reason for obfuscation in these matters was, as already 310
mentioned, to prevent the common people from disobeying the ordinances of religion and causing harm to themselves and society, not to present an esoteric doctrine different from his "Peripatetic" philosophy.[18]

---

15 *Mubāḥaṯāt* § 862 Bīdārfar = § 290 Badawī.

16 Quoted in Mahdavī 221.

17 Mehren *Traités* III.42.7–10; translation adopted with modifications from Arberry *Theology* 63, and cf. Hourani "Destiny" 42–43.

18 Daiber "Limitations" misunderstands Avicenna's indicative method as having an *epistemological* (rather than a social and psychological) function which enables people to understand matters that allegedly reason cannot express (he identifies it with the mystics' statements to that effect), and objects to its obfuscatory role; however, as discussed in the previous

If the obfuscatory function of the indicative method was designed for the common people, then its didactic function was intended for the philosopher. In the passage from *The Cure* he described him as the person "naturally predisposed to theoretical investigation" (L75c); in the epilogue of *Pointers and Reminders* he added further details: he "whose heart [is] ... pure, his way of life straight, who abstrains from the sudden insinuations of the Whisperer [Satan], and who directs his attention to the truth readily and sincerely" (T10, § 7). All these descriptions easily remind one of the attributes Avicenna implicitly claims to possess in the Autobiography, and explicitly says are required of the person in search of Knowledge (Chapter 3.3). In short, they are the attributes necessary if one is to Guess Correctly and acquire Knowledge through the middle terms. This is so because the person who studies by means of Pointers has to do research in order to hit upon them, derive Fundamental Principles, and Work out Corollary Principles, as Avicenna says philosophy ought to be done. All these concepts are neatly encapsulated in Avicenna's last major work, which bears the very name of his indicative method, *Pointers and Reminders*:

> O you who are zealous to Ascertain the truth: I am bestowing upon you in these Pointers and reminders Fundamental Principles and essential elements of philosophy; if sagacity [cf. Guesing Correctly] takes hold of your hand [to guide you], it will become easy for you to Derive Corollary principles from the former and work out the details of the latter. [T10, § 2]

311 In his last major work therefore Avicenna decided to cast the entire Knowledge in the form of Pointers for those who are able to understand them. The Knowledge that is to be communicated is exactly the same as that in the other works, and the way in which this Knowledge is to be acquired by the reader is exactly the same as that which Avicenna says is the only way to acquire Knowledge: through syllogistic argumentation by hitting upon the middle terms and by Working Out Corollary principles, in order to reproduce, in the Knowledge acquired in one's intellect, the syllogistic structure of the universe. There is no separate Knowledge presented here, "esoteric" or "mystical;" it is the Knowledge of the Aristotelian tradition as integrated, systematized, and represented by Avicenna.

---

section, Avicenna did not have two different methods of communication for two different knowledges—one that reason could reach and another not—but different methods of communication for the same knowledge. See also the comments on this subject by Michot *Astrologie* 27*-29*.

4. The Demonstrative Method: Syllogism

The demonstrative method involves exposition by demonstrative proofs (*burhān*) and arguments; it follows, in its strictest form, detailed syllogistic reasoning, and in its loosest, clear and sequential presentation of thoughts and arguments. This is the method that has to be engaged in when the purpose of the investigation is Verification (Chapter 3.3E). Avicenna called this method demonstrative, and is the one in which he engaged in most of his works. Representative of his attitude and of his disciples' understanding of this method is the following passage from the *Discussions*:[19]

> Proof [*iṯbāt*] of the separate substance, according to the method employed in *Throne Philosophy* [*ʿalā ṭ-ṭarīqa al-ʿaršiyya*], in Avicenna's hand:
>
> The basic demonstrative method [*aṭ-ṭarīqa al-aṣliyya al-burhāniyya*] is the one described in *The Cure*, namely, that existence is in need of a first principle that exists necessarily, because existence is either contingent in itself or necessary in itself, and contingent existence ultimately derives from the necessary. (L83)

The disciples' reference to Avicenna's treatise *Throne Philosophy* is to his systematic presentation of the material mostly in syllogistic form, which Avicenna expressly calls in the introduction as the method of Verification and contrasts it with that of Following Authority.[20] Avicenna refers in turn to *The Cure* (*Ilāhiyyāt* 37 ff. Anawati and Zāyid) because the presentation there is more elaborate than the one in *Throne Philosophy*, which is called an "abridgement" (*iḫtiṣār*).

Throughout his works, Avicenna comes back to the same arguments and demonstrations numerous times, and depending on his purpose or the addressee of each work, he amplifies or reduces them. This does not entail 312
a change in the method itself, but merely an omission or addition of several steps of the argument. The fullness of the argument in the demonstrative method is not determined, as in the case of the indicative method, by the desire to be didactic or obscure, but purely by considerations of clarity of exposition and comprehensibility. If, within the scope of the work and the context of the particular argument, a certain length of presentation is

19 *Mubāḥaṯāt* § 900 Bīdārfar = § 264 Badawī.

20 Avicenna did write something which may be called *Throne Philosophy*, though the essay that has been transmitted by that title has problems of authenticity; see GM-Ps 1 in the Appendix. The extant text is analyzed in detail by Meyer "Thronschrift."

deemed adequate and sufficient, there is no need to encumber the argument with further steps that might detract from the flow of the overall presentation. This is clearly indicated by Avicenna in *The Provenance and Destination* in a parenthetical aside which, however, is left out in the parallel passages in *The Cure* and *The Salvation*:[21]

Provenance and Destination	*Cure/Salvation*
It is thus clear and evident that the celestial spheres have first principles that are neither corporeal nor forms of bodies, and that each sphere has among them a first principle that is proper to it, while there is a first principle that is common to all.	It is thus clear and evident that the celestial spheres have first principles that are neither corporeal nor forms of bodies, and that each sphere has among them a first principle that is proper to it, while there is a first principle that is common to all.
There are many syllogisms and demonstrative proofs [*barāhīn*] for this point [*maʿnā*], but in this book we have selected only those arguments [*ḥujaj*] which will not require us to employ many premisses and a long analysis but will be most easily comprehensible. This point, then, has been made clear.	
It is said that there is no doubt that there are simple, separate intellects	There is no doubt that there are simple, separate intellects ... (L84)

The majority of Avicenna's works thus apply the demonstrative method with greater or lesser strictness. Consistently presenting "many premisses" and making "close textual analyses" (T7, § 3), on the other hand, is the strictest possible way of applying the demonstrative method. It is also long and arduous. This is the way in which Avicenna studied the entire Aristotelian corpus (Chapter 3.3A), and possibly the way in which he wrote, while still in his early twenties, the lost *The Available and the Valid* (W3). He declined doing it all over again in *The Cure*, as he told Jūzjānī (W6), because its most appropriate application is in commentaries, and he did not wish to write
313 a commentary in *The Cure*. He used it therefore in the *Fair Judgment*, a

[21] *Al-Mabdaʾ wa-l-maʿād* 81 Nūrānī = *Ilāhiyyāt* 408.15–17 Mūsā et al. = *Najāt* 458.2–6/659.10–14.

commentary on the Aristotelian corpus, in order to enhance the areas of conflict and accord between his own systematization of the Aristotelian tradition and the various statements in that tradition stemming from specific stages in its long history. When this book was lost, it was natural for Avicenna to say that it would be difficult to rewrite it (T11, §1). When, finally, his disciples had questions about individual passages in his own books that were presented with lesser demonstrative rigor, he intended to use it in the comments on his own books, the *Appendices*.

Avicenna also taught the demonstrative method orally to his students, and the high standards that he set for them as well as himself can be readily appreciated from the candid memoirs of his disciple (Ibn-Zayla?) writing from Rayy (T13, §§4–7, 10). His specific injunctions to pay heed not only to the form of the syllogism but also to its contents, to the relations among terms, to the identification of premisses, etc., are all principles on the basis of which he himself used to study the works of Aristotle, as discussed in the analysis of the Autobiography (Chapter 3.3A), and which he applied in his own works that follow the strictest possible demonstrative method, notably his commentaries. The following two examples are taken from his *Marginal Glosses on De anima* and the *Fair Judgment*.

A. *Marginal Glosses on De anima 403a10–12*[22]

The Aristotelian text commented upon is the following, as Avicenna read it in translation:

> If any of the actions or affections of the soul are proper to it, it will be possible for it to be separate; but if there is nothing proper to it, then it will not be possible for it to be separate.[23] (L85)

In his paraphrase, Themistius says that the sequence from the first to the second premiss is logically necessary and adds that

---

22 Badawī *Arisṭū* 76.15–77.2, corrected from the readings of the Cairo MS Ḥikma 6M. For a detailed analysis of the passage in question see the Appendix in Gutas "Glosses."

23 Aristotle's text is translated from the Latin version of the Arabic translation that was available to Avicenna, as preserved by Averroes, in Crawford 18.1–4 (cf. the translation by Richard C. Taylor with Thérèse-Anne Druart, *Long Commentary on the De Anima of Aristotle. Averroes (Ibn Rushd) of Cordoba*, New Haven: Yale University Press, 2009, 16). The original Arabic text of the second premiss survives in the commentary by Avicenna (cited below), where it reads, *in lam yakun šay'un yaḫuṣṣuhā fa-laysa yumkinuhā l-mufāraqatu*, where *mufāraqatun*, an infinitive, "to be separate, separable," translates manifestly both the Greek infinitive *chōrízesthai* in 403a11 and the verbal adjective *chōristḗ* in 403a12.

this sequence is confirmed by a manifest axiom, namely, that nature creates nothing that is idle.[24] (L86)

314 In his marginal glosses, Avicenna criticizes Aristotle for not having confirmed the truth of, or verified, either one of the two premisses he cites; for not determining the relation between the two premisses; for using a dialectical premiss (the second one) in a demonstrative context; and criticizes Themistius for adducing a further argument from the unverifiable "axiom" about nature creating nothing idle:

a) [Aristotle] should have confirmed[e] each one of these two premisses, but neither did he do it, nor even pay any attention to it.

b) Aristotle had the first premiss which he cited followed by a second one neither as an exception [to it] nor as a conclusion. Had he wished, he could have exchanged their places without affecting the existing relation [between them].

c) The Easterners said: [Aristotle's] statement, "if there is nothing proper to it, then it will not be possible for it to be separate," is based on [the assumption] that something does not exist unless it acts and is acted upon, otherwise it would be idle. This is a statement [*kalām*] of the kind that is "generally accepted" [*mašhūr*; i.e. "endoxic" or dialectical][25], which is inappropriate[f] for the [demonstrative philosophical] sciences. For something may possess in itself a perfection that extends neither to others nor to itself from others, and hence it would not be *a priori* necessary that it should not exist.

d) As for their statement [i.e., of the commentators], "because it would be idle," it is a statement which resorts to a *petitio principii* when its Validity is Determined [*ḥuṣṣila*], because it is as if[g] one were saying, "otherwise, it would be something neither acting at all nor being acted upon at all," which is a tautology. [This minor premiss] needs to be followed by the major premiss, namely, "and whatever is like that, does not exist;" at which point the objection will be raised, from where does he know that? (L87)

In paragraph (d), Avicenna reconstructs as a syllogism the argument of Themistius, analyzes it, and refutes it. The statement which he imputes to

[e] Reading *yuṣaḥḥiḥa* with the Cairo MS for *tṣḥḥ* in Badawī.
[f] Reading *lā yaṣluḥu* with the Cairo MS for *lā yaṣiḥḥu* in Badawī.
[g] Reading *ka-annahu* with the Cairo MS for *kāna* in Badawī.

[24] R. Heinze, *Themistii Librorum de Anima Paraphrasis* [*CAG* V.iii], Berlin 1899, 6.32–33. The Arabic translation of this passage in Themistius has not been preserved; see M.C. Lyons, *Themistius Commentary on Aristoteles de Anima*, Norfolk/Oxford: Cassirer, 1973, 4–5.

[25] For Avicenna's understanding and classification of "endoxic" propositions (*mašhūrāt*) see Gutas "Empiricism" 397.

the commentators is actually that of Themistius, who in his paraphrase supplies "idle" as the midle term in this particular syllogism. Avicenna's reconstruction of it is as follows.

> Minor premiss: Whatever neither acts nor is acted upon at all is idle.
> Major premiss: Whatever is idle does not exist.
> Conclusion: Therefore, whatever neither acts nor is acted upon at all does not exist.
> Inference based on this conclusion: If the soul has no action or affection proper to it, it has no separate existence.

From this it becomes apparent that those who wish to maintain the separate existence of the soul by following the above argumentation will necessarily have to make separate existence of the soul a function of the soul's actions and affections. To this Avicenna expressly objects by saying that something may be in a state of perfection (i.e., completely actualized) without having
to be in communication with anything else (L87, §c). He therefore has to 315
maintain the separate existence of the soul independently of its actions and affections. To do this he must first refute the syllogism which claims that. He finds two faults with it: first, he says that the syllogism begs the question because the middle term of the syllogism as he reconstructs it, i.e., "idle," is nothing else but a synonym of the minor term in the minor premiss, "whatever neither acts nor is acted upon at all." The minor premiss thus becomes, in his words, "whatever neither acts nor is acted upon at all is something neither acting nor being acted upon at all," which is indeed a tautology. This causes the major premiss to be, "whatever neither acts nor is acted upon at all does not exist," which is identical with the conclusion, and therefore a *petitio principii* (begs the question).[26] Second, Avicenna disagrees with the major premiss itself. Themistius calls it "a manifest axiom" (L86), but Avicenna claims that this is a dialectical proposition (because it is an "endoxon," a generally accepted proposition) that cannot be used in demonstrative proofs.

B. *Fair Judgment. Commentary on Book Lambda*[27]

The Aristotelian text commented upon is the following (*Metaphysics* 1074a31–38):

---

[26] For *petitio principii, al-muṣādara ʿalā l-maṭlūb al-awwal*, see Goichon *Directives* 240n2, and Inati *Logic* 158n2.

[27] Badawī *Arisṭū* 29.19–21.

> That heaven is one is evident. For if there are many heavens, they will be like men .... Therefore, the unmoved first mover is one both in word and in number; therefore, that which is moved always in continuous movements ought to be one only; therefore, one heaven only.[28] (L88)

The argument in the garbled version of Usṭāṯ's translation available to Avicenna was relatively unclear. Avicenna used Themistius' commentary to gain a better understanding:

> If the universe is more than one, the first causes must be more than one. ... The first mover must be one both in definition and in number. The body in motion, if it moves continuously, must also be one. The universe therefore is one.[29] (L89)

Avicenna made the following comments in the *Fair Judgment*:

> Whereas Aristotle said, "the mover of heaven is one," he said, [in effect]:
>
> Heaven must be one, because,
> 316 had it been many, their first principles would have been many;
> but this is not possible;
> on the contrary, its first principle is one;
> it is thus evident from this that heaven is one.
>
> This is [a] true and strong [argument] when it is developed and completed. (L90)

Avicenna's students obviously asked him to elucidate and "develop" the argument further. Their question and his answer are recorded in the *Discussions*:[30]

> Completion of the statement that
>
> "Had heaven been many, their first principles would have been many;
> but this is not possible;
> on the contrary, its first principle is one;
> therefore, heaven is one;"
>
> and exposition [of the statement] that the single universe, despite the multiplicity of the parts it contains, must have a single principle. Avicenna's answer in his own hand: "That the first principle of all being is one is evident in a way that dispenses with the need to seek others. When the first principle is one, it is impossible that anything but a single order [proceed] from it. It is much

[28] The text of Aristotle is taken from Usṭāṯ's translation, Averroes, *Mā baʿd aṭ-Ṭabīʿat*, III.1683.4–1684.2 Bouyges.

[29] Badawī *Arisṭū* 19.10–13. Cf. S. Landauer, *Themistii in Aristotelis Metaphysicorum Librum Lambda Paraphrasis* [*CAG* V.v], Berlin 1903, 28.35–29.8.

[30] *Mubāḥaṯāt* § 631 Bīdārfar = § 347 Badawī.

> better to use this demonstrative proof, which is of the reason why [i.e., of the cause], than to use its converse, which is of the fact." (L91)

Avicenna develops and completes this argument by making here the following logical analysis of the syllogism implied in the Arabic translation of the Aristotelian passage 1074a31–32. He says in the *Discussions* that the better way to construct this syllogism is:

> (I) If the first principle is one, only one order proceeds from it; [a]
> but the first principle *is* one [this is proven independently]; [b]
> therefore only one order proceeds from it; [c]
> i.e., there is only one universe.

This syllogism, which is an exceptive syllogism of the first mood, is perfect (*kāmil*) and always valid, regardless whether the connection implied in the conditional premiss [a] is complete or incomplete (*ittiṣāl tāmm, ittiṣāl nāqiṣ*); or, in other words, regardless whether the antecedent and consequent of the conditional premiss are convertible or not.[31] Moreover, as Avicenna says in the *Discussions* passage, this syllogism provides a demonstration of the reason why[32] because the middle term, i.e., the exceptive premiss [b] does not only make the conclusion *logically* necessary and thus make us assent to the conclusion, but it also gives the reason why the minor term (i.e., "the first principle is one") and the major term (i.e., "one order proceeds from it") are *ontologically* connected. As Avicenna puts it, the middle term is 317
"the cause of the major term in itself" and "it is the cause of the existence of the major term in the minor."[33] In other words, the reason why when there is one principle there is only one universe is that from the one, *qua* one, only one thing proceeds.

The syllogism implied in the Arabic translation of the Aristotelian passage 1074a31–32, on the other hand, is the converse (*ʿaks*) of the perfect syllogism (I) discussed above. With regard to connective (conditional) propositions, Avicenna says that there are two kinds of conversion. "The one is the conversion *simpliciter*, and the other is the conversion *per contradictionem*." In the former "you turn the antecedent into a consequent, and the consequent into an antecedent," and in the latter "you put the contradictory

---

[31] For the discussion of exceptive syllogisms in Avicenna see *The Cure, Qiyās* 389–399 Zāyid = Shehaby 183–192; for complete and incomplete connection see ibid., 233–234 = 37–38, respectively.

[32] Cf. Aristotle's *Posterior Analytics* I.13.

[33] *Naǧāt* 104–105/128.4; cf. *Išārāt* I.9.5, 84–85/170–171 = Goichon *Directives* 231–234 = Inati *Logic* 154–155, and Goichon *Lexique* 22–23, no. 47.

of both the antecedent and the consequent."[34] When both conversions are effected, the perfect syllogism (I) becomes the syllogism which Avicenna thinks is implied by Aristotle:

(II) If heaven (= order) were not one (= were many), then its first principle would not be one (= would be many); [d]
but the first principle is one; [e]
therefore heaven is one. [f]

Depending on whether the connection implied in the conditional premiss [d] is complete or incomplete, this syllogism becomes an exceptive syllogism of the eighth or fourth mood, respectively. The conclusion of the fourth mood does not always necessarily follow, while that of the eighth mood does; and since Avicenna seems to approve of this syllogism in the passage from the *Fair Judgment*, it appears that he considered it to be of the eighth mood. But even so, the demonstration provided by this syllogism is of the fact, not of the reason why, because, according to Avicenna,[35] demonstration of the fact either gives the indirect (distant) cause or no cause at all, while demonstration of the reason why always gives the direct (proximate) cause; and in the present case, the syllogism does not give the cause, which is, as stated above, that from the one, *qua* one, only one thing proceeds. In other words, it is not because there are not many heavens that there are not many first principles (syllogism II, of the fact), but it is because there is one first principle that there is one heaven (syllogism I, of the reason why), even though both syllogisms are technically and formally valid. Avicenna's preference for the one over the other because of its contents, given their formal equivalence, underscores his insistence to his students, as recorded by the
318 Disciple (Ibn-Zayla?) writing from Rayy (T13, § 6), that they should concentrate on the matters of syllogisms rather than their forms.

Another technical point, which Avicenna may or may not have had in mind when calling syllogism (II) of the fact, is Aristotle's remark in the *Posterior Analytics* (I.13, 78b14–15) that a demonstration is of the fact in "cases in which the middle term has outside position."[36] In syllogism (II) above, the middle term [e], "the principle is one," is neither of the other two terms, "heaven is not one," and "the principle is not one," and hence it "has outside position." Syllogism (II), therefore, is syllogism of the fact.

[34] *Qiyās* 385 Zāyid = Shehaby 180.
[35] *Najāt* 119/145.
[36] Barnes 20. Cf. T13, § 5.

CODA

AVICENNA'S PHILOSOPHICAL PROJECT[1]

I

Avicenna came of age in the last quarter of the tenth century, a time when the philosophical and scientific activities in the Islamic world, and the Graeco-Arabic translation movement which they fostered and sustained, had been in progress for over two hundred years. The vast majority of Greek philosophical and scientific texts had already been translated into Arabic upon demand by those who engaged in these activities as both practitioners and sponsors, and in all intellectual fields works originally composed in Arabic developed research beyond the level of the translated texts.

The rationalist outlook which considered research on the philosophical curriculum (described above, Chapter 3.1) as a cultural good was developed in Baġdād, along with the beginnings of the Graeco-Arabic translation movement, in the second half of the eighth century during the first decades of the rule of the new Arab dynasty of the ʿAbbāsids.[2] It was to this outlook

[1] An abridged version of this chapter appeared in Adamson *Interpreting Avicenna* 28–47.

[2] The causes, history, and development of the Graeco-Arabic translation movement are discussed in detail in Gutas *Translation Movement*. The larger question of the structure of early ʿAbbāsid society and its ideological orientations that produced this rationalism has not yet been properly addressed by social historians. Consideration of the flux and flexibility of a society on the ascendant in the process of formation may be relevant. The Muslim community, although the motive force behind the historical developments since the Prophet, was, at the time of the early ʿAbbāsids, demographically the minority in the Near East; the vast majority were Christians and Zoroastrians, with sizable populations of pagans, Jews, and adherents of other, minor religions; even the Manicheans came back to Iraq, the land of their founder. With the major empires of the Byzantines and the Sasanians defeated, the nascent ʿAbbāsid society was not threatened from outside, while on the inside, the local populations, with all their diverse religions, acquiesced to Muslim rule—the only quarrels for political supremacy were intra-Muslim, i.e., among descendants of the various branches of the Prophet's family (the Umayyads, the ʿAbbāsids, the Šīʿites, etc.). In addition, the Muslim community's own ideological position was in the course of formation; there was as yet no established "orthodoxy" which would try to impose itself on the rest—as a matter of fact, the new ʿAbbāsid rulers followed, for their own political gain, a deliberate course of cultural

and the factors that brought it about, in the final analysis, that we owe the rebirth of philosophy in Arabic with Kindī early in the ninth century, after its extinction as living practice and instruction in Greek before the rise of Islam.[3] With the decentralization of political power that followed the gradual erosion of caliphal authority by the middle of the tenth century, there arose local dynasties in the vast Islamic empire, from al-Andalus to central Asia, which took over regional governing while acknowledging the caliph in Baġdād as the supreme overlord. A concomitant of the decentralization of power was decentralization of culture, and the several capitals of the local dynasties, from Cordoba to Buḫārā, began to imitate and rival Baġdād for intellectual and cultural supremacy, adopting the same tastes and fashions as those in the ʿAbbāsid capital.

Avicenna grew up in Buḫārā, the capital of the Persian-speaking dynasty of the Sāmānids (819–1005) in central Asia. As he informs us in his Autobiography (T3, §1ff.), his father was governor of nearby Ḫarmayṯan, and Avicenna as a young boy grew up in the company of the Sāmānid administrative elite. His education began early, as was customary, and continued throughout his teens. He studied the traditional subjects, the Qurʾān, Arabic literature, and arithmetic, and had a particular propensity for legal studies as well as medicine: he reports that he had started practicing both law and medicine by the time he was sixteen; but he also reports that at the same time he was studying repeatedly all the branches of philosophy at increasingly proficient levels.

His studies were crowned by advanced research in the royal library of the Sāmānids, which he describes as follows in the Autobiography (T3, §10–11):

> I was admitted to a building with many rooms; in each room there were chests of books piled one on top of the other. In one of the rooms were books

inclusion of all the various groups within society (and hence the translation movement). In this context, rationalism appears both to serve the purposes of irenic (i.e., non-revolutionary) co-existence and social progress within society, and to be not threatening to the hold on power of the dynasty and the elite, given the absence of political danger from abroad. Other factors would be complementary to the major conditions stated here.

[3] For the "general breakdown of [Hellenic] culture" in Byzantium during its "Dark Ages" see P. Speck, "Byzantium: Cultural Suicide?" in *Byzantium in the Ninth Century: Dead or Alive?*, in L. Brubaker, ed., Aldershot: Ashgate, 1998, 73–84 at 82, with references to his other works. For a survey of the paltry evidence for "Early Byzantine Philosophy," see K. Ierodiakonou and G. Zografidis in *The Cambridge History of Philosophy in Late Antiquity*, L.P. Gerson, ed., Cambridge: Cambridge University Press, 2010, 843–868. The rebirth of philosophy in Arabic is discussed in Gutas "Geometry" and "Origins."

> on the Arabic language and poetry, in another jurisprudence, and so on in each room a separate science. I looked through the catalogue of books by the ancients and requested those which I needed. I saw books whose very names are unknown to many and which I had never seen before nor have I seen since. I read those books, mastered their teachings, and realized how far each man had advanced in his science. So by the time I reached my eighteenth year I had completed my study in all these Philosophical Sciences. At that time my retention of Knowledge was better, but today my grasp of it is more mature; otherwise the Knowledge is the same, nothing new having come to me since.

Avicenna's description of the Sāmānid library and its contents, apart from its invaluable testimony about library science in central Asia in the tenth century, is a significant witness to the spread and dominance of the philosophical culture that was created in Baġdād in the first two centuries after its foundation in 762. It was this culture that provided Avicenna both with an intellectual orientation of rationalism within which to work, and the resources—the philosophical material—with which to carry out his research. It is important to realize this intellectual and social context in order to appreciate the direction of his work. There is no doubt that he was gifted, and not only because he says so himself—his awesome analytical powers are manifest; but mental prowess is only one half of the whole. The other half is availability of means.

On his testimony, therefore, there is little doubt that during his education (but also later in his career) Avicenna had access to everything that we know was translated from Greek,[4] and certainly to the entire intellectual production in Arabic since the beginning of Islam in all fields, and especially in philosophy and theology (*kalām*). Nevertheless, in order to avoid misunderstanding and desist from imagining non-existent sources, it should be borne in mind that by the ninth century Graeco-Arabic translation movement the vast majority of (pagan) Greek philosophical works had already mostly perished, and of what had survived—mainly the texts of the Aristotelian and Platonic traditions—not all were translated into Arabic. On the Greek side, therefore, to be specific, Avicenna mastered essentially the Aristotelian tradition: all the works of Aristotle that had been translated[5] and

[4] For a list of all the Greek philosophical works known to have been translated into Arabic see Gutas "Greek Philosophical Works Translated into Arabic," in *The Cambridge History of Medieval Philosophy*, Robert Pasnau, ed., Cambridge: Cambridge University Press, 2010, 802–814.

[5] Of the extant authentic works of Aristotle, the following are not known to have been translated into Arabic and were hence unavailable to Avicenna: *Movement* and *Progression of*

the whole range of commentators, from Nicolaus of Damascus, Alexander of Aphrodisias, and Themistius to the late antique Alexandrian philosophers, notably Philoponus. On Plato, on the other hand, Avicenna had partly peripheral information about his life and works, their order, and the subjects they treated, and partly access to paraphrases and summaries of some dialogues and to the synopses of some others by Galen. Of the authentic dialogues he had read none, for none had been translated in its entirety in Arabic.[6] From all that he knew about Plato he had come to the following assessment of Plato's philosophical worth (T6B, § 8):

> If the extent of Plato's achievements in Philosophy is what came down to us of him, then his wares were paltry indeed and philosophy in his time had not matured to the point of reaping. Whoever affects allegiance to him, having at his disposal only the amount of knowledge about Plato that has been transmitted to us, does it either out of envy for Aristotle or out of a foolish notion that the prior in time is also in a discipline prior in rank. The truth, however, is the opposite.

Of the other ancient schools of philosophy, finally, none had survived in any significant form until late antiquity, and neither did any of their works that would be available to the Arabic translators in the ninth century, even if interest in them had been forthcoming. Stoics, Epicureans, Sceptics, and Pythagoreans were known primarily through collections of the lives and sayings of the philosophers and, in the case of the Neopythagoreans, through the translation of a few works, some mathematical, some hortatory, and some spurious.[7]

Animals, *Eudemian Ethics*, most of *Magna moralia*, most of *Politics*, and from the collection later known as *Parva naturalia*, the brief essay (or the three even briefer essays, according to some), *On Youth and Old Age, Life and Death, and Respiration*. The *Constitution of Athens*, which has survived accidentally in a papyrus roll discovered at the end of the 19th century, was not available in medieval manuscripts even in Greek.

[6] For the knowledge of Plato and his works in Arabic see Gutas "Platon—Tradition Arabe," in *DPhA* Va,845–863. Even the *Timaeus*, Plato's most influential and widely diffused dialogue in the Middle Ages, was available in Arabic in bits and confusing pieces; for the knowledge of it that Avicenna would have had see Rüdiger Arnzen, "Plato's *Timaeus* in the Arabic Tradition. A Philological Study," in *Il Timeo. Esegesi greche, arabe, latine*, F. Celia and A. Ulacco, eds., Pisa: Plus, Pisa University Press, 2012. For Avicenna's attitude towards Plato see above, Chapter 7.

[7] For a survey of the information about these schools in Arabic see Gutas "Pre-Plotinian Philosophy."

II

Equally important as the availability of the Graeco-Arabic philosophical literature to Avicenna was the structure of this philosophical knowledge which he studied and internalized. The course of studies, or philosophical curriculum which he followed, as he reports in the Autobiography, is patterned according to the classification of the philosophical sciences in the Aristotelian tradition of Alexandria in late antiquity: logic comes first as the instrument, the *organon*, for the study of philosophy, followed by theoretical philosophy, which consists of physics (Aristotle's physical and zoological treatises), mathematics (the *quadrivium*: arithmetic, geometry, astronomy, music), and metaphysics (Chapter 3.1). This would be followed by practical philosophy (ethics, household management—i.e., oeconomics—, politics), but Avicenna does not say anything explicitly about having studied these subjects in the Autobiography, a point to which I will come back later.

The systematic presentation of the actual course of his studies in the Autobiography is important on a number of counts. In the first place, it raises the question whether the stylized curriculum that he presents is intended to alter the chronology of the events to fit the theoretical classification of the sciences. However, the historicity of his account is not so important—regardless of the order he followed in his studies during his teens, it is absolutely clear that he did, indeed, study the sciences in this curriculum—as the fact that this classification is presented in the autobiographical account as historical in order to validate and promote it. For it is significant to realize that Avicenna did not study these sciences as discrete entities, but as a structured whole.

Avicenna was in fact following a curriculum, based on a classification of the sciences and exhibiting an understanding of the philosophy of education, that was very influential in imperial and late antique times and throughout the Middle Ages in many languages. It largely set the framework both for the kind of knowledge in high learning that was to be translated and transmitted, and for the way in which it was to be studied. The ultimate origin of this classification and theoretical structure of the sciences was the edition of Aristotle's "esoteric" works (i.e., the extant school treatises), apparently by Andronicus of Rhodes, in the second half of the first century BC. In late antique times it was used for pedagogical purposes in instruction, in a classification that was used this time to reflect all knowledge, insofar as each part in this classification reflected a book by Aristotle. However, also by late antique times, this classification gained normative value in that it was seen to reflect actual reality: the sciences are so classified because the order of the universe is so arranged. All these aspects of the classificatory scheme were taken over into Arabic, where they were developed in particular by Fārābī, just as they were later taken over and developed by Dominicus Gundisalvi in Latin.[8] Avicenna was schooled—or schooled himself—in this curriculum with this understanding of the structure of knowledge and its correspondence to, or explication of, reality. In this tradition, doing philosophy meant being what we today call a scientist: the rational and logically verifiable understanding of the universe and its operation.

This traditional classification of the Aristotelian corpus and, by extension, of all philosophy, presented a blueprint for an all-encompassing book of knowledge, or "an Encyclopaedia of Unified Science" that was already hinted at in some later statements by Aristotle himself. "In a perfect Aristotelian world, the material gathered in the corpus [of his writings] will be systematically presented; and the logical structure of the system will follow the pattern of the *Posterior Analytics*."[9] Throughout the long history of Aristotelianism until Avicenna, followers and adherents never actualized this implicit comprehensive and systematic work of unified science, possibly because they thought the Aristotelian corpus had already achieved it—though other factors, yet to be investigated, were certainly also operative. They wrote commentaries instead, or monographs, clarifying or treating various points which better expressed what this implicit "encyclopaedia" in their minds contained. Avicenna broke the mold. He was the first philosopher ever to write about *all philosophical knowledge* (what he called simply *al-ʿilm*, Knowledge) within a single composition as a unified whole: he developed the *summa philosophiae*, as I will discuss later. The first goal of his philosophical project was thus clear. Philosophy, he felt, needed to be presented as a whole, to reflect both the interrelatedness and interdependence of all knowledge, and its correspondence with reality.

---

[8] See Gutas "Paul the Persian" and "Greek to Arabic" for detailed treatment of the subject. Most philosophers and scholars in Islamic civilization expressed themselves on the classification of the sciences along these lines, with variations in each case as the occasion arose; for a quick orientation see Hans Hinrich Biesterfeldt, "Medieval Arabic Encyclopedias of Science and Philosophy," in *The Medieval Hebrew Encyclopedias of Science and Philosophy*, S. Harvey, ed., Boston: Kluwer, 2000, 77–98, and "Arabisch-islamische Enzyklopädien: Formen und Funktionen," in *Die Enzyklopädie im Mittelalter vom Hochmittelalter bis zur frühen Neuzeit*, Ch. Meier, ed., München: Wilhelm Fink, 2002, 43–83. Avicenna himself has an essay on the very subject, *The Divisions of Philosophy* (GS 1).

[9] Barnes p. xii, cited above, Chapter 4.

III

The philosophical knowledge that Avicenna received in this fashion, though structurally presented as a unified whole, was neither internally self-consistent nor complete. From our vantage point and understanding of the history of philosophy from Aristotle to Avicenna, we can identify the diverging directions taken after the Hellenistic period by mainstream philosophy, i.e. the Aristotelian and Platonic traditions. There are discrepancies already within the surviving work of Aristotle (the uneasy relationship which Book Lambda has with the rest of the metaphysical books being a prime example), while the developments after Aristotle brought about shifts and changes on the original teachings in the hands of the commentators. Neoplatonists, on their part, in addition to effecting substantive elaborations of Platonic philosophy—partly with an eye to responding to or accommodating Aristotle, as in Plotinus, and partly largely independently of such concerns, as in Proclus—by late antiquity developed the "conception that Aristotelianism leads to and is completed by Platonism,"[10] thus introducing upon the trunk of the Aristotelian system an incongruous emanationist head, among other changes. This development is not unrelated to the power of the aforementioned Aristotelian curriculum to rationalize and integrate discrepant elements. At the same time, the view of the history of philosophy through an Aristotelian prism that it presents must be a significant factor in the reception of Aristotelianism as the main philosophical tradition in Arabic, as described above, and the favoring of the translation of some books over others. In addition, the philosophers preceding Avicenna in Islam, faced with the same problems as he, had effected their own partial adaptations and accommodations.

Avicenna had no way of knowing the particulars of this history of philosophy for the pre-Islamic period, but he was fully aware of Aristotle's philosophical project and could tell where it fell short, as we do, just as he could distinguish between it and what he would characterize as the subsequent developments and accretions, erroneous or not, in the hands of the "commentators," among whom he would count the Neoplatonists. As Avicenna came to realize and acknowledge, Aristotle, the architect of the system, was correct in most things but not in all; moreover, Aristotle had lived one thou-

---

[10] D'Ancona and Adamson in Peter Adamson, *The Arabic Plotinus*, London: Duckworth, 2002, 42.

sand three hundred and thirty years before him,[11] and knowledge, being cumulative over time, had advanced since then. More significantly, in Avicenna's opinion, successive generations of philosophers in Aristotle's footsteps had followed Customary Practice in defending and trying to explicate what Aristotle said instead of discovering the truth through critical thinking and philosophical analysis, and had added to and compounded the errors (Chapter 5.2). The second task of his philosophical project, then, Avicenna concluded, was to bring philosophy up-to-date.

IV

But just as much as Avicenna was aware of the unity of philosophy and its history, he was equally conscious of his own historical moment and social context, which was yet a third factor motivating his holistic efforts. He was convinced that if philosophy is what we would call today a scientific system explaining all reality, it must certainly also explain religion and other manifestations of the contact between humans and the transcendent, all parts of reality in his time. Starting from an empirical stand, as I will next discuss, Avicenna acknowledged that religious phenomena such as prophecy, miracles, eschatological beliefs, the efficacy of religious practices like prayer and fasting, and the insights of some mystics, were all real, just as he readily accepted the existence of other phenomena that we would call "paranormal," such as veridical dreams, prognostication of the future by soothsayers, the ability by some to effect telekinesis, the evil eye, etc. At the same time, however, he set out to understand the causes of these phenomena, explain how they happen, and describe the mechanisms of the human soul which bring them about. Previous philosophers writing in both Greek and Arabic had touched upon some of these subjects but none had done this effectively or completely. Avicenna dealt with these phenomena compre-

[11] It is important to realize that in medieval Islamic civilization there was available precise knowledge of chronology for those scholars who would have it, and that for them not everything coalesced in an inchoate *Jāhiliyya* period. Avicenna mentions this number in the epilogue of the Sophistics part of *The Cure* (T6, §7). Aristotle died in 322 BC. Assuming Avicenna is reckoning in solar years (which in this case he would, because he knew that transmitted chronologies, like the Alexandrian era from which he most likely derived this number, reckoned in solar years), he must have been writing in 1008 AD. By my reckoning above (see the chronology at the end of Part One), he had started writing *The Cure* around 1020. Avicenna says "approximately" (*al-mudda qarība min*) 1330 years had gone by since Aristotle. This is pretty accurate.

hensively within the parameters of the Aristotelian theory of the soul, which he greatly developed to accommodate the demands of this new subject, creating a veritable Metaphysics of the Rational Soul, as I have called it.[12] Thus if philosophy needed to be treated not piecemeal but comprehensively as an integral whole, and if it needed to be brought up-to-date through the elimination of its internal inconsistencies and anachronisms, it also needed to include within its compass the experience of reality of his time and place.

In this latter respect, Muslim intellectuals were keenly aware of Avicenna's achievement. The following assessments by two leading traditional scholars are representative. The first is by the greatly respected Mālikī jurist of Tunisia, al-Imām al-Māzarī (d. 1141), who reports the following:

> In recent times there was a philosopher, known as Ibn Sīnā (Avicenna), who filled the world with writings on philosophy, in which he was a great master. His superior ability in philosophy led him to attempt to derive the principles of religious doctrines from philosophy (*ḥāwala radda uṣūli l-ʿaqāʾidi ilā ʿilmi l-falsafa*). He proceeded in his efforts with great skill until he achieved what nobody had ever achieved.[13] (L92)

The second is by the great Ḥanbalī theologian, Ibn-Taymiyya (d. 1328), a keen observer of Islamic intellectual life and uncompromising critic, who offers the following evaluation of Avicenna:

> Avicenna's philosophical doctrines are a composite of the theories of his predecessors [the philosophers] and of what he himself innovated. ... Avicenna talked about matters which his predecessors did not discuss, their minds could not attain, and their sciences could not reach—matters like philosophical theology (*ilāhiyyāt*), the theory of prophecy, the return of the soul to its place of origin [after death], and subjects relating to Islamic law.[14] (L93)

It is significant that these two scholars who had a proper assessment of Avicenna's philosophical project and described it explicitly and accurately were a Mālikī and a Ḥanbalī respectively, members of the two juridical schools which, in the centuries after Avicenna, were the least prone to philosophize theology and adopt its language and methods. The adherents of all the other mainstream schools who did—the Šāfiʿīs, Ḥanafīs, and Šīʿites—did so implicitly, partly by openly criticizing philosophy while surreptitiously

---

12 Above, Chapter 6.2, and discussed in greater detail in Gutas "Rational Soul."

13 Quoted by Subkī, *Ṭabaqāt al-Šāfiʿiyya al-kubrā*, ʿAbdalfattāḥ al-Ḥulw and Maḥmūd aṭ-Ṭanāḥī, eds., Cairo 1969, VI,241. I am obliged to M. Cüneyt Kaya for bringing this passage to my attention.

14 From Ibn-Taymiyya's *ar-Radd ʿalā l-manṭiqiyyīn*, cited in Gutas "Heritage" 85.

adopting its methods and ideas (like Ġazālī),[15] and partly by interpreting Avicenna tendentiously to fit their views or otherwise misrepresenting his positions (like the majority in the Šī'ite tradition). In the former instance, there was created a philosophical theology among both Sunnīs and Šī'ites whose parameters have only now begun to be fully understood in recent research. In the latter, there developed a tradition that interpreted Avicenna's philosophy as having two sides: an exoteric aspect—he was the unchallenged representative of Peripateticism in Islam (*maššā'ī*)—and an esoteric and mystical one, based partly on Avicenna's allusive style and use of mystical terminology in some works (and in particular in his latest summa, the *Pointers and Reminders*), and partly on pseudepigraphic works that began circulating about a century after his death.[16] In Iran especially, where he was elevated to a most revered status also on account of his presumed Persian origins, he has been seen as the master of what has been incongruously called "gnosis" (*'irfān*), the origins of which allegedly go back to a pre-Islamic Persian spirituality.

In modern times and until quite recently, scholarship both East and West, partly following this latter tradition in its tendentiousness and partly on the basis of the European predisposition since the nineteenth century to view "orientals" as mystical and otherworldly, believed Avicenna to have a two-sided philosophy, one Aristotelian and logical, and another esoteric and mystical, representing his true teachings. But there is no basis to such an understanding of the historical Avicenna, as early scholars like Māzarī and Ibn-Taymiyya knew, and as more recent studies have shown.[17] Avicenna's philosophical project aimed at erecting a system that harmonized, rationalized, and completed, through personal verification on the basis of syllogistic logic, all the discrete traditions of Aristotelian philosophy and the Neoplatonic and other accretions that accumulated over the ages, while at the same time expanding it to incorporate analyses of all reality, including all manifestations of religious life and beliefs.

[15] See now the fundamental study of Ġazālī's "despoil-and-repackage technique" of appropriating philosophical ideas, and indeed on the crucial subject of noetics and prophecy, in Treiger *Inspired Knowledge* 103.

[16] For a discussion of Ṣūfī pseudepigraphy in works attributed to Avicenna see Reisman "Ps.-Avicenna Corpus II."

[17] For a critique of this understanding and a discussion of the question of Avicenna's alleged "mysticism" see in particular Gutas "Absence of Mysticism" and "Imagination." See also Adamson "Non-Discursive Thought" for the syllogistic nature of non-discursive thought in the human intellect, and McGinnis *Avicenna* for a comprehensive evaluation of Avicenna's rational philosophical system.

V

In the realization of his project, Avicenna from the very beginning concentrated above all else on the verifiability of the knowledge he set out to acquire. Verifiability depends on two interdependent factors for the person doing the verification: following a productive method and having the mental apparatus to employ that method and understand its results. The method Avicenna adopted already at the start of his career was logic, and the mental apparatus wherewith we know involved an understanding and study of the human soul. Thus logic and the theory of the soul as the basis for epistemology are the two motors driving Avicenna's philosophy. He wrote more, and more frequently, on these two subjects than on anything else.

Avicenna discovered logic early and, more importantly, realized that he was good at it. In the Autobiography he recounts how, when he must have been barely twelve years old, he stupefied his teacher by analyzing the definition of genus better than anything the teacher had heard, and that he was better at forming concepts (*taṣawwartuhā*) than his teacher (T3, §5, and the notes thereto). There is no reason not to take this report at its face value, but that is unimportant. The reference here is clearly to one of the most basic logical theories of Avicenna, namely, that all knowledge is either forming concepts (*taṣawwur*) by means of definitions—i.e., in good Aristotelian fashion, realizing the genus and specific difference of something—or acknowledging the truth (*taṣdīq*) of a categorical statement by means of syllogisms. The inspiration here is apparently the beginning of Aristotle's *Posterior Analytics*; Avicenna took this book seriously, following both the curriculum, in which this book was made the center of logical practice, and especially his two Peripatetic predecessors in Baġdād, Abū-Bišr Mattā and Fārābī, who made it the cornerstone of their philosophy and advertised its virtues.[18]

Acknowledging the truth of a categorical statement meant verifying it, and this could only be done by taking that statement as the conclusion of a syllogism and then constructing the syllogism that would conclude it. There being three terms in a syllogism, two of which, the minor and the major, are present in the conclusion, the syllogism that leads to that conclusion can be constructed only if one figures out what the middle term is that

[18] For the significance of the *Posterior Analytics* in philosophy in the Islamic world see Michael Marmura, "The *Fortuna* of the *Posterior Analytics* in the Arabic Middle Ages," in *Knowledge and the Sciences in Medieval Philosophy*, S. Knuuttila et al., eds., Helsinki: Acta Philosophica Fennica, 1990, I 85–103.

explains the connection between the two extreme terms. In other words, if we seek to verify the statement "A is C," we must look for a suitable B to construct a syllogism of the form, "A is B, B is C, therefore A is C." The significance of the middle term is also discussed in the *Posterior Analytics* (I.34), where Aristotle further specifies, "Acumen is a talent for hitting upon (*eustochia*) the middle term in an imperceptible time" (Barnes). Avicenna picked up on the very concept of the talent for hitting upon the middle term, literally translated in the Arabic version as *ḥads* (hitting correctly upon the answer, Guessing Correctly), and made it the cornerstone of his epistemology. This he did apparently for two reasons: it made the core of syllogistic verification by means of Guessing Correctly the middle term the one indispensable element of all certain intellectual knowledge, and it explained why people differ in their ability to apply this syllogistic method by presupposing that they possess a different talent for it, as with all human faculties. A third reason would be its transcendent implications, of which more later.

Avicenna actually tested in the course of his studies the validity of the heuristic capacity of syllogistic analysis and the central role which Guessing Correctly the middle term played in it. He makes a point to mention it in the Autobiography in a report which, again, must be taken at face value if only because it squares with his practice as it can be seen in his works. The entire paragraph is very telling about his method and approach in his project:

> The next year and a half [i.e., when he was between sixteen and seventeen and a half years old] I devoted myself entirely to reading Philosophy: I read Logic and all the parts of philosophy once again. During this time I did not sleep completely through a single night, or occupy myself with anything else by day. I put together in front of me [sheaves of] scratch paper, and for each argument that I examined, I recorded the syllogistic premisses it contained, the way in which they were composed, and the conclusions which they might yield, and I would also take into account the conditions of its premisses [i.e. their modalities] until I had Ascertained that particular problem. Every time I was at a loss about a problem, concerning which I was unable *to find the middle term in a syllogism,* I would repair on its account to the mosque and worship, praying humbly to the All-Creator to disclose to me its obscurity and make its difficulty easy. At night I would return home, set the lamp before me, and occupy myself with reading and writing. Whenever I felt drowsy or weakening, I would turn aside to drink a cup of wine to regain my strength, and then I would go back to my reading. Whenever I fell asleep, I would see those very problems in my dream; and many problems became clear to me while asleep. So I continued until all the Philosophical Sciences became deeply rooted in me and I understood them as much as is humanly possible. Everything that I knew at that time is just as I know it now; I have

> added nothing more to it to this day, such that I mastered Logic, Physics, and Mathematics (emphasis added, and cf. Chapter 3.2 above for a discussion of the details). (T3, § 8)

It is to be noted that the reference to the Aristotelian curriculum is there, while the method Avicenna says he used to study it is to look at every argument and verify its syllogistic validity. In essence this meant examining the texts of Aristotle, read in the order in which they are presented in the curriculum, and testing the validity of every paragraph. How he did this in practice, teasing out the figures and forms of syllogisms implied in Aristotle's texts, can be seen in numerous passages in his works.[19] By his eighteenth year, he had internalized the philosophical curriculum and verified it to his own satisfaction as a coherent system with a logical structure that explains all reality.

According to the scientific view of the universe in his day which he studied in the curriculum—Ptolemaic cosmology to which was attached Neoplatonic emanationism—all intelligibles (all universal concepts and the principles of all particulars, or as Avicenna says, "the forms of things as they are in themselves") were the eternal object of thought by the First principle, and then, in descending hierarchical order, by the intellects of the celestial spheres emanating from the First and ending with the active intellect (*al-ʿaql al-faʿʿāl*), the intellect of the terrestrial realm. Avicenna's identification of Guessing Correctly the middle term and his favoring it as the central element in syllogistic analysis gave structure to all intelligible knowledge and provides valuable insight into his philosophical project.

All understanding that involves syllogistic thinking—that is, that involves acknowledging the truth of a proposition, which is one half of all knowledge, the other half being forming concepts, as discussed above—must include the middle terms which explain a statement. Avicenna repeatedly states in numerous contexts that the intelligibles are thought of and understood by, or "imprinted" on the human intellect, "in an order which includes the middle terms" (L7, § 3). Now the intelligibles which the human intellect thinks are contained essentially in the intellects of the celestial spheres and in the active intellect, which are their locus (in the sense that they are constantly thought by them),[20] and by definition represent the way things are, ontological truth. And since, following the syllogistic process, the human intellect

---

19 Examples of his procedure are presented above, Chapter 8.4, and in Gutas "Glosses," Appendix.

20 There is no other place for the intelligibles to be essentially: Avicenna would not accept Platonic ideas for the same reason that Aristotle did not, the intelligibles cannot be stored in

thinks of the intelligibles contained in the active intellect in an order which includes the middle terms and thus in accordance with the order of the terms of propositions in a chain of mutually dependent syllogisms, not only do the contents of this knowledge correspond, one-to-one, to ontological reality, but the progression of this knowledge also must correspond to the structure of reality, which is accordingly syllogistic.

The establishment of the syllogistic structure of *both* all human theoretical knowledge *and* transcendent knowledge as thought by the celestial intellects enabled Avicenna to unify and integrate the different levels of its acquisition by the human intellect within a single explanatory model and accordingly de-mystify concepts like inspiration, enthusiasm, "mystical" vision, and revelation. At the basic level there is discursive thinking in which the intellect proceeds to construct syllogisms step by step with the aid of the internal and external senses, and acquires the intelligibles by Guessing Correctly the middle terms (something which in emanationist terms is described as coming into "contact" with the active intellect, to be discussed presently). At a higher level Avicenna analyzed non-discursive thinking, which takes no time and grasps its object in a single act of intellection, though the knowledge acquired is still structured syllogistically, complete with middle terms[21] (again, because in its locus, the active intellect, it is so structured, as just mentioned). Avicenna also discussed a facility for or habituation with intellection, which he called direct vision or experience (*mušāhada*) of the intelligibles. It comes about after prolonged engagement with intellective techniques through syllogistic means until the human intellect is not obstructed by the internal or external senses and has acquired a certain familiarity or "intimacy" with its object, "without, however, the middle term ceasing to be present." This kind of intellection is accompanied by an emotive state of joy and pleasure.[22] The highest level of intellection is that of the prophet, who, on account of his supremely developed ability to hit upon middle terms, acquires the intelligibles "either at once or nearly so … in an order which includes the middle terms."[23]

---

a body since they are immaterial, and they cannot be stored in the human intellect since, it being also immaterial, has no compartments: storing them in itself would mean actually thinking them, which manifestly the human intellect does not always do. Hence the active intellect and the intellects of the spheres function as the locus of the intelligibles in that they always actually think them. See the discussion in Gutas "Intuition and Thinking" 11–13.

21 Adamson "Non-Discursive Thought."

22 Gutas "Absence of Mysticism" 365–369.

23 A formulation of the issue with which Avicenna was very pleased, for he repeats it in at least three different works, cited above in L7, § 3.

This knowledge, which represents and accounts for reality and the way things are, also corresponds, Avicenna maintains, with what is found in books, i.e., with Philosophy, or more specifically, the Philosophical Sciences as classified and taught in the Aristotelian tradition. However, the identity between absolute knowledge in the form of the intelligibles contained in the intellects of the celestial spheres and philosophy as recorded in the Aristotelian tradition is not complete. Though Aristotelianism is the philosophical tradition most worthy of adherence, Avicenna says, it is nevertheless not perfect, and it is the task of philosophers to correct and amplify it through the acquisition of further intelligibles by syllogistic processes. It is this understanding that enabled Avicenna to have a progressive view of the history of philosophy and set the framework for his philosophical project. For although the knowledge to be acquired, in itself and on a transcendent plane is a closed system and hence static, on a human level and in history it is evolutionary. Each philosopher, through his own syllogistic reasoning and ability to Guess Correctly the middle terms, modifies and completes the work of his predecessors, and reaches a level of knowledge that is an ever closer approximation of the intelligible world, of the intelligibles as contained in the intellects of the spheres, and hence of truth itself. Avicenna was conscious of having attained a new level in the pursuit of philosophical truth and its verification, but he never claimed to have exhausted it all; in his later works he bemoaned the limitations of human knowledge and urged his readers to continue with the task of improving philosophy and adding to the store of knowledge (Chapters 4 and 5).

VI

The human intellect can function in syllogistic processes in an order which includes the middle terms and which are identical with those of the celestial intellects for the simple reason, as Avicenna repeatedly insists, that both human and celestial intellects are congeneric (*mujānis*) immaterial substances. However, their respective acquisition of knowledge is different because of their different circumstances: the human intellect comes into being in a potential state and needs its association with the perishable body in order to actualize itself, whereas the celestial intellects are related to eternal bodies and are permanently actual. Thus unfettered, their knowledge can be completely intellective because they perceive and know the intelligibles from what *causes* them, while the human intellect is in need of the corporeal senses, both external and internal, in order to perceive the *effect* of an intelligible from which it can reason syllogistically back to its cause. And this makes it necessary for Avicenna to have an empirical theory of knowledge, an informative précis of which is given in the following passage from his *Notes*:

> Perception belongs only to the soul, while to the sensory organ belongs nothing else but to have the sensation of the sensible object and to be affected by it. What indicates this is that the sensory organ may be affected by the sensible object but the soul may be inattentive, in which case the object is not sensed and not perceived. The soul perceives the sensible forms by means of the senses and it perceives their intelligible forms through the mediation of their sensible forms, since it comes into possession of the intelligible-ness (*maʿqūliyya*) of these forms from their sensible-ness (*maḥsūsiyya*)[24] and what is intellected of these forms matches that which is sensed of them, for otherwise it would not have been that which is intellected of *them*. It is not possible for man to perceive the intelligible-ness of things without the mediation of their sensible-ness on account of the deficiency of his [rational] soul and his need for the mediation of the sensible forms in order to perceive the intelligible forms. But as for the First and the separate intellects [of the celestial spheres], given that they are in their essence intellecting, they have no need, in order to perceive the intelligible form of something, for the mediation of its sensible form, nor do they come into possession of it from sensing it, but they perceive the intelligible form from its causes and occasions, which never change. As a result, what they intellect of that [thing] does not [itself] change for this reason.
>
> Every particular individual has an intelligible [form] which matches its sensible [form], and the human soul perceives that intelligible through the mediation of its sensible. The First and the separate intellects perceive the intelligible from its causes and occasions, whereas the attainment of different kinds of knowledge (*maʿārif*) by man comes about by way of the senses, and his perception of universals [comes about] by way of his sensation of particulars. Now man's soul can know potentially: the soul of the child is predisposed to have come about in it [i.e., the soul] primary [notions] and principles [of knowledge], which come about in [the child] without his having recourse, on their account, to the senses—no, as a matter of fact, they come about in him unintentionally and unawares; and the reason of their coming about in him is his predisposition for them. When the soul is separated from the body [after death] and has the predisposition to perceive the intelligibles,[25] then perhaps they will come about in it [the soul] without its having any need

[24] I.e., the fact of their being objects of the intellect and objects of sensation respectively.

[25] I.e., when a man has during his lifetime exercised his intellect and gained a facility in perceiving the intelligibles; see the discussion of this process and the eschatological significance of philosophical training for the human soul in Gutas "Intuition and Thinking" 29–31.

> for the sensory faculties which have left it—yes, they will come about in [the soul] unintentionally and unawares, as is the case with the primary [notions] coming about in the child. But the senses are the means by which the human soul comes into possession of different kinds of knowledge (*maʿārif*).[26]
>
> (L94)

Elsewhere, Avicenna specifies that man's predisposition for the primary notions and principles of knowledge which come to him unawares is itself actualized by the experience of particulars.[27] For human knowledge, therefore, the intellect functions as a processor of the information provided by the external and internal senses by forming it into intelligible concepts: they do not pre-exist in it. It is important to realize that this is not because the intellect does not have the constitution to have purely intellective knowledge, like the celestial spheres, but because its existence in the sublunar world of time and perishable matter precludes its understanding the intelligibles through their causes. Instead, it must proceed to them from their perceived effects. Once however, the soul has been freed of the body after death, and if it has acquired, while still with the body, the predisposition to perceive the intelligibles through philosophical training, then it can behold the intelligibles through their causes and become just like the celestial spheres, a state which Avicenna describes as happiness in philosophical terms and paradise in religious.

Avicenna's rationalist empiricism was broadly conceived to include, as it did later with John Locke, our immediate experience of ourselves, an empiricism, so to speak, of the self. Propositions based on experience (*mušāhadāt*), he said, are of two kinds, one based on sense perception and another on self-reflection (*qaḍāyā iʿtibāriyya*). These latter "are due to the observation of faculties other than sense perception, like our realization that we have thought, that we are afraid and angry, and that we are aware of our selves and of the acts of our selves."[28] "Self awareness," he further specified, "is innate to the self, being its very existence, and thus we do not need anything external with which to perceive the self, but the self is that with which we perceive its self."[29]

That empiricism, and especially empiricism of the self, was essential to

---

26 *Taʿlīqāt* 23 Badawī = 96–98 al-ʿUbaydī (§§11–13) = 30–32 Mousavian (§10). Translated and cited in Gutas "Empiricism" 412–413.

27 *Naǧāt* 101–102/121–122. See the discussion in Gutas "Empiricism" section V.

28 *Išārāt*, I.6.1, 56/124 = Goichon *Directives* 176 = Inati *Logic* 120.

29 *Taʿlīqāt* 161 Badawī = 125 al-ʿUbaydī (§72) = 484 Mousavian (§889). Cf. Black "Self-Awareness" and Gutas "Empiricism" section IV.

Avicenna's philosophical edifice can be gauged from the fact that he based it on the absolutely primary and irreducible empirical fact of existence.[30] We simply know that there is existence and that we exist, absolutely: not by acknowledging the fact at the end of a syllogism, not by forming a concept by identifying species and specific differences, and not by any sense, either external or internal; we simply know that there is existence: as stated in five simple words by Avicenna, *lā šakka anna hunā wujūdan* ("no doubt, there is existence").[31] This irreducible empirical fact is the basis for his argument for the existence of God—we exist, but contingently, therefore we may not have existed; but we do exist; therefore there must be a necessary existent that causes existence to exist—and for the existence of our immaterial and substantial rational souls—the flying man argument whereby we simply know that we exist apart from our body or any other external element. And from these two positions flows everything else.

Avicenna's rationalist empiricism is the main reason why he strove in his philosophy on the one hand to perfect and fine-tune logical method and on the other to study the human soul and cognitive processes at an almost unprecedented level of sophistication and precision. In section after section and chapter after chapter in numerous works he analyzes not only questions of formal logic but also the very conditions operative in the process of Guessing Correctly and hitting upon the middle term: how one can work for it and where to look for it, and what the apparatus and operations of the soul are that bring it about.[32] He charts in great detail the operations of all the senses, and especially the internal senses—common sense, imagination, estimation, etc.—and how they can help or hinder the intellect in hitting upon the middle term and perceiving intelligibles more generally. In order to enable the internal senses, which, being resident in the brain, are biological operations, to function in ways that support the intellect, Avicenna discusses behavior that can affect positively the humoral temperament of the body and bring it to a state of equilibrium so that the intellect can function unen-

---

30 Cf. Herbert A. Davidson, *Proofs for Eternity, Creation and the Existence of God in Medieval Islamic and Jewish Philosophy*, Oxford: Oxford University Press, 1987, 303, and Gutas "Empiricism" 415–417.

31 *Najāt* 383/566; cf. the translation of the entire passage in Marmura "Proof from Contingency" 350. Marmura (p. 339) calls the apperception of existence "an intellectual intuition of existence," but in the case of the proof of God from contingency based on existence, it is the proof itself that is intellective (as Avicenna says in *The Cure*: *Ilāhiyyāt* 21 Anawati and Zāyid, cited by Marmura on p. 339), not the apperception of its starting point, existence, which is empirical.

32 See the discussion in Gutas "Intuition and Thinking."

cumbered by extraneous considerations or hindrances. His references to prayer and wine drinking in the autobiographical passage cited above are intended to indicate these ancillary practices in the promotion of intellection (Chapter 3.3).

When, at the end of all these operations just described, the intellect Guesses Correctly a middle term or just perceives an intelligible that it had not been thinking about before, it acquires the intelligible in question (and hence the appellation of this stage of intellection, "acquired intellect," *al-ʿaql al-mustafād*), or, otherwise expressed, "receives" it from the active intellect which thinks it eternally and atemporally since it is, in effect, the locus of the intelligibles (as mentioned above, note 20). Avicenna calls this process of acquisition or reception a "contact" (*ittiṣāl*) between the human and active intellects. In the emanative language which he inherited from the Neoplatonic tradition, and which he incorporated in his own understanding of the cosmology of the concentric spheres of the universe with their intercommunicating intellects and souls, he referred to the flow of knowledge from the supernal world to the human intellect as "divine effluence" (*al-fayḍ al-ilāhī*). The reason that this is at all possible is again the consubstantiality of all intellects, human and celestial alike. Only, as already mentioned, because of their varied circumstances, the latter think of the intelligibles directly, permanently, and atemporally, while the human intellect has to advance from potentiality to actuality in time by technical means leading to the discovery of the middle term as it is assisted by all the other faculties of the soul and body.

The wording itself of this acquisition of knowledge by the human intellect—"contact with the active intellect," or receiving the "divine effluence"—has misled students of Avicenna into thinking that this "flow" of knowledge from the divine to the human intellect is automatic and due to God's grace, or it is ineffable and mystical, etc. But this is groundless; the "flow" has nothing mystical about it since it just means that the intelligibles, as constantly thought by the celestial intellects and hence resident there, are permanently available to human intellects who *seek* a middle term or other intelligibles at the end of a thinking process, including abstraction. Avicenna is quite explicit about the need for the human intellect to be prepared *and* demand to hit upon a middle term or actively seek an intelligible *in order to* receive it: "The active principle [i.e., the active intellect] lets flow upon the [human rational] soul form after form *in accordance with the demand by the soul*; and when the soul turns away from it [the active intellect], then the effluence is broken off."[33]

---

[33] Or, "as the soul itself demands," for the emphasized phrase: *al-mabdaʾu l-faʿʿālu yufīḍu*

The same applies to other forms of communication from the supernal world. In the case of the prophet, he receives all the intelligibles comprising knowledge complete with middle terms, as already mentioned, because his intellective capacity to Guess Correctly the middle terms and acquire the intelligibles is extraordinarily high, and this is coupled with an equally highly developed imagination that can translate this intellective knowledge to intelligible language and images (in the form of a revealed book) that the vast majority of humans can easily understand. But in addition to intelligible knowledge, the divine effluence from the intellects and the souls of the celestial spheres includes also information about events on earth, for all of which they are responsible: past, present, and future, what Avicenna calls "the unseen" (*al-ġayb*).[34] This information also can be received by humans in various forms—as waking or sleeping dreams, as visions, as messages to soothsayers—depending on the level of the humoral equilibrium of the recipient, the proper functioning of his internal and external senses, and the readiness of his intellect. Somebody whose internal sense of imagination or estimation is overactive, for example, may be hindered thereby in the clear reception of dream images so that his dreams would require interpretation, while someone else not so afflicted may get clearer messages; or the Turkish soothsayer who wishes to receive information about the future has to run long and hard in order to bring about such an equilibrium through the exertion, thereby preparing his intellect to receive the message,[35] etc.

The logistics of the reception of information from the supernal world thus varies in accordance with what is being communicated and who is receiving it, but in all cases the recipient has to be ready and predisposed to receive it. All humans have both the physical and mental apparatus to acquire intelligible or supernal knowledge and the means to do so, but they have to work for it, just as they have to prepare for their bliss in afterlife while their immortal rational souls are still affiliated with the body. There is no free emanation of the intelligibles on "couch-potato" humans, or after-life contemplation for them of eternal realities in the company of the celestial spheres (Avicenna's paradise). To have thought so would have negated the entire philosophical project Avicenna so painstakingly constructed.

ʿalā n-nafsi ṣūratan baʿda ṣūratin bi-ḥasabi ṭalabi n-nafs, wa- … iḏā aʿraḍat ʿanhu nqaṭaʿa l-fayḍu; in *The Cure*, *Nafs* 245–246 Rahman; emphasis added.

34 See in particular the discussion in Gutas "Absence of Mysticism," section III.

35 A case actually mentioned by Avicenna in the *Išhārāt*, II.10.23, 217/384–385.

There is a deeply ethical aspect to Avicenna's philosophical project, much as he may not have dwelled a lot upon the traditional parts of practical philosophy because, it seems, he considered it too self-evident and philosophically unchallenging.[36] Because our theoretical intellects—our selves—are consubstantial with the celestial intellects, it is our cosmic duty to enable them to reach their full potential and behave like the celestial intellects, i.e., think the intelligibles.[37] And because we (i.e., our essential core which identifies us and survives, our rational souls) are given a body and our materiality hampers our unencumbered intellection like that of the celestial beings, we have to tend to the body by all means, behavioral (religious practices, ethical conduct) and pharmacological, to bring its humoral temperament to a level of equilibrium that will help the function of the intellect. This is humanist ethics dictated by a scientific view of the world.

VII

If Avicenna's philosophical project involved putting together a unified theory of everything in which he would integrate in a self-consistent whole, based on Aristotelian logic, all parts of philosophy as traditionally transmitted, and which would represent all Knowledge and account for all reality, including religious reality, then the ways which he devised and employed to communicate this knowledge were no less global in their aspirations. To a large extent this is to be expected from a thinker who dwelled long and hard on the modalities of the transmission and reception of knowledge from all directions, transcendent and mundane, and was alive as much to the mechanics of every nuance of this process as to the range and subtleties of literary style.[38] But it is still amazing to witness the numerous compositional styles with which he experimented and the different registers of language that he used for each. This is not accidental or routine, but bespeaks the

---

36 In the introduction of the *Easterners*, he says that he will treat "only as much of the practical science as is needed by the seeker of salvation," i.e., the fourth part of practical philosophy containing the subjects discussed in the Metaphysics of the Rational Soul, while the rest of it, i.e., ethics, household management, and politics, will not be dealt with presumably because, just like mathematics, "there is no disagreement about it" (L63).

37 See the discussion of the "contemplative life" in Avicenna's philosophy in Lizzini "Vie contemplative."

38 Avicenna's sophisticated discussion and presentation in the Poetics part of *The Cure* of the garbled translation of Aristotle's *Poetics* is a masterpiece of literary analysis, to say nothing of his forgery, recounted in Jūzjānī's biography (Gohlman 68–73), of belletristic essays good enough to fool the experts of his day.

fact that communicating intelligibly this Knowledge, both to his contemporaries at their various levels of preparation and background *and* to posterity, was part of his philosophical project itself. More than most other indicators, this fact alone shows that Avicenna was the second philosopher after Aristotle to have as pronounced a sense of advancing philosophy to a qualitatively higher level and the corresponding need to communicate it broadly and systematically.[39]

At a very basic level, Avicenna brought to fruition a development that had been in progress for centuries, first in Greek and then in Arabic, by putting between the covers of a single book the entire philosophical curriculum: he developed the *summa philosophiae*. None had done this before him. In imperial and late antique times, philosophy was done primarily in the form of commentaries on Aristotle and Plato, with the occasional essay or book on a single subject. Avicenna's closest predecessor in this form of writing was Fārābī, though his two major works, significantly both entitled *Principles*,[40] are not written with the purpose to cover all the sciences, as does Avicenna, but present a synoptic and interconnected account of the universe—descending from the One and through the celestial spheres to terrestrial phenomena and then all the way down to social formations among humans—and omit sciences like logic and mathematics which are extraneous to his plan. In the case of Avicenna, however, the very first substantial philosophical work that he wrote, *Philosophy for ʿArūḍī* (*al-Ḥikma al-ʿArūḍiyya*, GS 2), is a summa of all the parts of theoretical philosophy, while mathematics, which is omitted, is nevertheless registered as something that should have been included.[41] And Avicenna went on to write *seven* more summae, ranging in length from a booklet he called *Elements of Philosophy* (*ʿUyūn al-ḥikma*) to the monumental *Cure*.[42]

---

[39] See above, Introduction to the First Edition.

[40] That is, *The Principles of the Opinions of the Inhabitants of the Virtuous City* (*Mabādiʾ ārāʾ ahl al-madīna al-fāḍila*), and *The Principles of Beings* (*Mabādiʾ al-mawjūdāt*). The first has been usually and erroneously referred to only as *The Virtuous City* or *The Perfect State* (Walzer), and the latter by its alternate title, of unknown provenance, *Governance of the City* (*as-Siyāsa al-madaniyya*), usually also mistranslated as *The Political Regime*. Cf. D. Gutas, "The Meaning of *madanī* in al-Fārābī's 'Political' Philosophy," in *Mélanges de l'Université Saint-Joseph* 57 (2004) 259–282, at 269–270.

[41] See above, Chapter 2, W2, also for a discussion of the omitted or missing parts on practical philosophy.

[42] In chronological order these are, *Philosophy for ʿArūḍī, Elements of Philosophy, The Guidance, The Cure, The Salvation, Philosophy for ʿAlāʾ-ad-Dawla, The Easterners* (or *Eastern Philosophy*), and *Pointers and Reminders*, GS 2–9.

The Cure (*aš-Šifāʾ*), which in the Cairo edition (1952–1983) runs to twenty-two large size volumes, contains the most extensive coverage of philosophy he ever wrote. In it he treated all subjects in the curriculum; its contents are listed above in Chapter 2, W6. The work is methodical and argumentative in its approach, discussing all aspects of an issue that had been raised since Aristotle, and is written in a fine expository prose that subsequently became the standard in philosophy.

Avicenna rewrote the summa, on what he considered the controversial subjects in philosophy—logic, physics, and metaphysics, thus bypassing the mathematical sciences and the traditional parts of practical philosophy—in *The Easterners* (or, *The Eastern Philosophy*), which he explicitly declared to be a doctrinal work intended to present the truth. The language is the same as in *The Cure*—indeed much of it is taken verbatim from that work—but the historical discussions are eliminated and many arguments are recast to follow the doctrinal rather than historical presentation. The different audiences—or the different interests of the same audience—to which these two works are addressed can be seen in their varied approaches to the subject, even as the doctrine presented in both is the same.[43] For a somewhat less philosophically adept, but equally serious, audience he wrote, upon their request, the short *Salvation*, a one-volume pastiche of previous expository writings of his that aimed to present, according to those who commissioned it, the indispensable minimum on logic, physics, mathematics, and metaphysics. Though strictly speaking not a summary of *The Cure*, given its components, it has often been treated as such.

Similar to *The Salvation* in its purpose and scope, and roughly contemporaneous, was the *Philosophy for ʿAlāʾ-ad-Dawla*, covering logic, metaphysics, and physics (in that order). Juzjānī added the parts on mathematics, as he had done with *The Salvation*. What is astonishing about this work, though, is that it is in Persian, the first philosophical work to be composed in neo-Persian. His final patron and protector, the Kākūyid prince ʿAlāʾ-ad-Dawla had asked for it in Persian in order to understand it better. In a single stroke, Avicenna fashioned modern Persian philosophical prose.

The earliest summa he wrote, the one commissioned by ʿArūḍī, was in his home town. We may be thankful to this gentleman insofar as he gave Avicenna an occasion to put together in a unified whole all the notes on the entire philosophical curriculum he had taken during his studies and alerted him to the fact that it can be meaningfully done. Only part of this

43 For a presentation of the contents and style of the work see Gutas "Eastern Philosophy."

summa survives, but there is enough of it to show that although it was a youthful work it was not amateurish, for not only Avicenna himself but other philosophers as well copied passages from it in later compositions (see above, Chapter 2, W2). This supports Avicenna's claim in the Autobiography to have mastered the whole structure of philosophy by his eighteenth birthday.

With the one-volume summa entitled *The Guidance*, written in his mid-career apparently for his brother while in political prison, according to al-Jūzjānī's biography, there is a perceptible change in the expository prose toward a more literary style. This tendency will find its full expression in his last summa, the *Pointers*.

In lapidary fashion he also wrote *The Elements of Philosophy*, a brief work on physics and metaphysics to which an earlier short précis of his on logic was at some point attached (see GS 3 in the Appendix)—sixty pages in Badawī's edition—which lives up to its title and which Badawī likened to Lombard's *Sententiae*. It is not known for whom or on what occasion he wrote it, but it is almost like an *aide-mémoire*, which may give a clue to its purpose. But it was subjected to a massive commentary of seven hundred and thirty pages by the great Ashʿarite theologian Faḫr-ad-Dīn ar-Rāzī (d. 1210)—a purposeless undertaking, one would have thought, insofar as anyone who had difficulty with its tersely expressed statements could have found them all expounded at great length by Avicenna himself in *The Cure*. But laconism, and the inevitable attendant obscurity, invite comment and preoccupation with an author's work, keeping it alive for generations. It is an effective technique to communicate one's thought to posterity.

That such a consideration may have actually been part of Avicenna's strategy of communication is shown by his very last summa, *Pointers and Reminders*. The work covers again logic, metaphysics, and physics but in two parts this time, with metaphysics and physics treated together in the second. It is written entirely in the allusive and suggestive style indicated by its title, a style expressly developed by Avicenna for this purpose. It consists of a presentation by means of discrete paragraphs, each of which is mostly labeled either "pointer" (*išāra*) or "reminder" (*tanbīh*). In the former, Avicenna presents the subject briefly, pointing to its various aspects, and in the latter he offers an equally brief reminder of a doctrinal point that would help the reader round out the argument for himself and come to an understanding of the philosophical issue at hand. The language is ornate, with frequent use of rare words culled from literature, while the syntax at times is complex to the point of obscurity, pushing the regular paratactic structure of Arabic to its limits. Later commentators, of whom there were many—as,

I would claim, was intended—regularly include in their comments lexicographic explanations and on occasion feel the need, like professors in an Arabic language seminar, to spend time parsing a particularly abstruse sentence. The whole is breathtaking and quite a tour de force; there is nothing like it in Arabic philosophical literature.

A topos in the introductions to the study of Aristotle in later Greek tradition, taken over also in Arabic, and intended to explain why Aristotle was difficult to understand, was that the philosopher had cultivated obscurity deliberately both in order to discourage the unworthy from taking up philosophy and to train students (Chapter 5.3). Avicenna taps into this tradition to justify and explain his procedure by pointers and reminders both in this work and in other contexts. To a certain extent this topos was part of the philosophical culture in Arabic to which lip service had to be paid[44]—historically though, there was never any question, in the two centuries of the Graeco-Arabic translation movement until Avicenna, of hiding philosophy from anybody; to the contrary, the efforts of philosophical authors were directed at popularizing philosophy in the intellectual arena. With the style of pointers and reminders, Avicenna hit upon the perfect formula to wed his philosophical system as exposed in detail in *The Cure* to a means of communicating it to the widest possible sophisticated audience in the Islamic societies of his time. The work was wildly popular and the subject of numerous commentaries through the centuries. *The Cure*, by contrast, though dutifully copied in many surviving manuscripts and diligently studied by all serious students of philosophy, had almost none for all parts but the metaphysics.

But Avicenna was not content to engage the attention of this wider public by means of his allusive pointers and reminders style. He wanted everybody to be exposed to his philosophy, so he also wrote allegories, consonant with his belief, otherwise widely shared by philosophers both in his time and before, that people vary in mental acuity and that those on the lower end of the scale who cannot understand the expository language of philosophy respond to information transmitted symbolically—which is, in essence, the reason why a prophet's highly developed internal sense of imagination

[44] A misunderstanding (and, in some cases, deliberate disregard) of the history and function of this topos in Arabic philosophical literature gave rise, in the second half of last century, to the notion that these philosophers expressed themselves cryptically out of fear of persecution by the religious authorities. The baseless nature of this notion is set forth by Oliver Leaman, "Does the Interpretation of Islamic Philosophy Rest on a Mistake?" *International Journal of Middle Eastern Studies* 12 (1980) 525–538, and Gutas "Historiography."

translates into symbols the intelligibles which it receives in syllogistic order containing the middle terms, and generates the holy texts of revelation. He wrote two of them, *Ḥayy Ibn-Yaqẓān* and *The Bird* (GM 7–8). Meticulous in their construction, he was careful to have every element in his allegory correspond precisely with a philosophical concept.[45] In the same vein he wrote some smaller treatises in which he explained certain theological concepts like the divine decree and predestination (*al-qaḍāʾ wa-l-qadar*), composed homilies in poetic prose on any number of religious subjects, and interpreted a number of verses from the Qurʾān (listed under GM and GPW in the Inventory in the Appendix). Philosophical interpretation of the Qurʾān had already started with the first philosopher, Kindī,[46] but Avicenna elevated it to new levels and effectively ensured its incorporation into mainstream Qurʾān interpretation (*tafsīr*), as the philosophical content of the huge commentary by the same Faḫr-ad-Dīn ar-Rāzī shows. In this fashion Avicenna brought philosophical ideas closer to the masses.

Equal in extent to the summae were two massive works, each in about twenty volumes, written in the age-old traditional style: the text of Aristotle followed by commentary. The first, *The Available and the Valid* (of philosophy, to be understood), was an early work, commissioned by a neighbor in Buḫārā, that has apparently completely disappeared (Chapter 2, W3 and GS 10); Avicenna says in the Autobiography that the neighbor never lent it to anyone for copying. The second, *Fair Judgment*, fared only slightly better; the first draft was lost in some military upheaval, and the few surviving sections would seem to come from disciples' notes (Chapter 2, W10). Despite their huge size, though, commentary writing is not what Avicenna readily did. Commentaries were the genre par excellence of philosophical writing in late antiquity, and this practice was continued in Syriac and then in Arabic with the Baġdād Aristotelians. Avicenna consciously broke the mold, as I already remarked—Jūzjānī asked him to write commentaries on Aristotle but he said that he would write about what he thinks is sound, and *The Cure* was born—and experimented with the different genres I have been enumerating. For the first of these commentaries we have absolutely no information other than its title, *The Available and the Valid* [*of Philosophy*], which itself

---

[45] This correspondence for *Hayy Ibn-Yaqẓān* was studied and presented in detail by Goichon *Ḥayy*.

[46] On philosophical interpretation of the Qur'ān by Kindī and Avicenna see Janssens "Al-Kindī: The Founder of Philosophical Exegesis of the Qur'ān," *Journal of Qur'ānic Studies* 9 (2007) 1–21, and Janssens "Qurān."

may imply a critical attitude on Avicenna's part. But in the case of the second of these commentaries, the *Fair Judgment*, it is clear that Avicenna engaged in it for a purpose other than the traditional, so that it was more of an adjudication than commentary. In this way, again, it set the stage for a new philosophical genre in Arabic that was to gain some traction in subsequent centuries, the *muḥākama*. In the *Fair Judgment* Avicenna divided philosophers into two camps, the Westerners (the traditional Aristotelians of late antiquity and Baġdād) and the Easterners (himself, working in Ḫurāsān in the East), and went along commenting on the Aristotelian text by judging fairly, he claimed, between the views of the two camps, but actually presenting in the most traditional of ways, for those who preferred commentaries, his own system, that of "the Easterners," or the "Eastern philosophy." It was in this vein that he also wrote *The Easterners*, indicating that this was the new appellation he wanted to give to philosophy (Chapter 2, W9). However, in this final regard, it appears that Avicenna met his contextual limits. This was too much neoterizing for his milieu to take; the complete break with tradition that this step would have entailed was not tolerated, and Avicenna in his final years tacitly disowned the idea of the Easterners, and wrote *Pointers and Reminders* instead.

In expository prose and in a more conventional style Avicenna of course composed monographs and essays on specific subjects, notably on the soul and its faculties and especially on the Metaphysics of the Rational Soul, in which he dealt with traditionally religious phenomena within the context of Aristotelian psychology, as mentioned above. But he also dealt with whatever other subjects came up or were requested of him, including an essay on phonetics, *On the Causes of the Articulation of the Letters* (GL 16).

Traditional educational practice in the Islamic world, from elementary school onward, heavily involved memorization of the texts to be learned, with the Qur'ān and the Prophetic traditions (*ḥadīṯ*) taking pride of place. The practice extended to all textbooks in school, including, for example, grammar books. Poetry, with meter and rhyme, is quintessentially memorizable, and accordingly it was not long before didactic poems—poems setting in rhyming verse the entire subject to be learned—became common in educational technique. The meter used in Arabic was the one called *rajaz*, which was not considered proper poetry by the specialists precisely because of its broad flexibility. In its most common form it consisted of six diambic feet in a line of two rhyming hemistichs. Avicenna, wishing to reach students of all ages and levels, composed an as yet unspecified number of poems in this meter, the most important among which is one on the entire Logic (GL 4) and another on medicine (GMed 27), which was commented upon by a number of scholars, notably Averroes. A brief poem attributed to him in 20 verses, known as the *Poem rhyming in ʿayn* (GP-Ps 4), on the descent of the soul into the body and its later ascent, became quite popular in subsequent tradition and was frequently commented upon. Even if almost certainly a peudepigraph, it nevertheless illustrates the wide appreciation and dissemination of such versified philosophical pieces.

Indicative of the vast capacity of Avicenna's mind and uncanny ability to mind every detail is his project, after the compilation of *The Cure*, to update it yearly with new discoveries and results in a work which he meant to call *Appendices*. This was apparently never written as such—or if some parts of it were they have been dispersed (GS 12b)—, though there are two collections of precisely such notes, comments, and responses to questions by students put together by disciples, circulating in the manuscript tradition under the titles of *Discussions* and *Notes* (GS 14 and 12a). No less important than *The Cure*, they provide significant information about the development of Avicenna's ideas on a number of problems during his last years.

Finally, and related to the preceding, is the considerable correspondence that has come down to us. These were occasional pieces, written usually in response to some crisis in his personal and professional relations (cf. Reisman "Patronage"). They can be called personal and controversial writings, but they frequently deal with real philosophical issues. More than anything else they provide a comprehensive view of the integral position that doing philosophy occupied among the intellectual and political elites of Avicenna's times.

Avicenna sought to express his new synthesis of philosophy in a way that would also respond to the philosophical concerns of his age and society, and this explains his experimentation with the wide variety of compositional styles listed above. He communicated with everybody, not only among his contemporaries but also with an eye to posterity. Perhaps the most telling indication of his success is that after him philosophers read no more Aristotle and Galen, but Avicenna. By the same token, however, he was responsible for the final integration and naturalization of Greek philosophical thought in Islamic intellectual life. His influence was colossal; it introduced a "golden" era in the Islamic world when philosophical activity reached unprecedented heights,[47] and it determined high intellectual culture for centuries to come.

---

[47] An assessment first made in Gutas *Translation Movement* 172, and then presented in detail in Gutas "Heritage;" see now Langermann.

APPENDIX

INVENTORY OF AVICENNA'S AUTHENTIC WORKS

PART ONE

TETRAPLA: SYNOPSIS OF THE FOUR LISTS OF AVICENNA'S WORKS

Introduction

Avicenna left behind a huge *oeuvre*, even by the standards of polygraphic authors in medieval Islamic civilization, but "the preservation and transmission of the written record of [his] philosophy proved to be a singularly disastrous affair."[1] The reasons are roughly known; I discussed some of them at the beginning of Chapter Two, above, and Reisman has added others, following his dramatic introductory sentence I just quoted. Briefly, Avicenna was what may be called a disorganized writer who kept clean copies neither of what he wrote for himself nor of the commissioned pieces; his itinerant life style was the cause of the dispersal of many of his works; he corresponded on philosophical matters with colleagues, students, and adversaries; he was involved in a number of social disputes which were partly caused by some of his homiletic works and which themselves occasioned some private correspondence; he wrote many occasional pieces for patrons which may have resurfaced at any time in subsequent centuries; his amanuensis Jūzjāni, who states that he joined him in order to bring some order into his writings, largely failed in this "noble intention" for reasons that are personal to Jūzjānī; and his works generated massive reactions among Muslim intellectuals, both positive and negative, and resulted partly in the fragmentation and re-publication of some of them, partly in the falsification of the text of some others, and partly in the creation of numerous pseudepigraphs. In a very real sense, "the study of the transmission of the works of Avicenna is intimately related to the intellectual history of the Islamic world in the three or four centuries after his death,"[2] a factor which cannot be ignored in such a study.

Establishing a complete and accurate catalogue of his authentic writings thus lies in the future. Essentially, three areas of research are available

[1] Reisman *Avicennan Tradition* 21.
[2] Gutas "Agenda" 53, which is to be consulted for details on the subject.

to this end, listed in diminishing order of significance and efficacy: (a) examination of the manuscripts that claim to contain works by Avicenna; (b) the medieval lists of his works; and (c) examination of the contents of these works for internal evidence of authenticity. Regarding (a), it is clear that much more time will elapse before all the extant manuscripts of Avicenna's works have been traced and scrutinized, let alone edited and studied, but with the material available in Mahdavī and subsequent studies, along with the examination of some manuscripts which in the meantime have been shown to be crucial in the transmission process, it is possible to arrive at some more secure interim conclusions.

(b) The medieval lists of Avicenna's works are bibliographies that were drawn up within two centuries of his death, and their compilers, demonstrably thorough and conscientious, scoured both manuscripts and the relevant literature for each entry. They inform us not only about what the compilers knew or thought was by Avicenna, but also, insofar as they drew on manuscripts of his works contemporary with them, about the works that were in circulation at their time. If, therefore, a title does not appear in any of them, this means either that the work in question, if authentic, came into circulation after all the bibliographies were compiled (i.e., by the middle of the thirteenth century), or that the work is pseudepigraphic. If the former is the case, it could have come about only if the descendant of a patron for whom Avicenna had composed a work, which existed only in that copy, found the manuscript and put it, or a copy of it, in circulation. But this, or the generic variation of this case—namely, that a manuscript of an authentic work would have lain concealed among someone's papers and come to light only after two centuries following Avicenna's death—is precisely what needs to be proven, and hence the significance of studying the manuscript transmission of the works. But even if a title appears in the bibliographies, and especially in the Extended Bibliography (for which see below), which is the youngest, authenticity is not guaranteed, for the work may have been forged before the bibliography was compiled—indeed Avicennan pseudepigraphy began already a century after his death—and hence the need for skepticism. Given these circumstances in the transmission of Avicenna's works, and especially his supremely dominant position in the philosophical developments after him, pseudepigraphy in his case is a significant factor that cannot be overlooked. In this regard, the early lists of his works have not been taken as seriously as they deserve though they provide valuable evidence, which will be presented below.

(c) Arguments in favor of or against authenticity on the basis of the contents of a work provide the weakest means for establishing or disproving it; unfortunately, it is also the method to which most common recourse has been had almost to the exclusion of the first two. Pseudepigraphers and forgers were as a rule quite familiar with Avicenna's authentic works and ideas, and, depending on their objectives and methods of working, they could produce treatises that looked and sounded genuine. Egregiously maladroit forgeries are of course easy to detect; but in cases where the objective was to present a particular doctrine by means of a mere tweak or slant of authentic Avicennan material, argumentation by mere analysis of contents offers little help by itself and needs to be supported by the evidence provided by manuscript transmission and the bibliographies.

Tetrapla

The complex of the Autobiography and Biography of Avicenna, along with the early lists of his works with which this complex is associated, is in need of renewed scrutiny and study, the pioneering edition by Gohlman (1974) having by now exhausted its usefulness. Nevertheless, and in anticipation of a truly critical edition and study of this complex, the information about Avicenna's works that these medieval bibliographies offer can be usefully summarized as follows and presented synoptically in the accompanying tetrapla chart.

There are, in essence, four separate sources which list the works of Avicenna. Preserved as they are in the extant manuscripts and not in the holograph copies of their respective authors, and after centuries of copying and recopying, they display different levels of revision, contamination, accretions, and adjustments, but they are recognizable as distinct attempts to catalogue his writings. The motivations of their authors, the sources they used, and the methods they followed in compiling them are in need of detailed study in order to extract fully and accurately the information they provide on the subject, but for our purposes the following notes will suffice to identify and evaluate them.

Group (a). *The Autobiography / Biography Complex* (*Autobio, Bio*)

This is naturally not a "catalogue" properly speaking, insofar as Avicenna's major purpose in composing or dictating the Autobiography to Jūzjānī was to provide a case history for his epistemological theory as I argued above (Chapter 3.4), while Jūzjānī's was to promote his own position and importance in furthering the achievements of the Master, but the way in which they are structured also includes organically a listing of Avicenna's works together with the surrounding circumstances that led to their composition (their *asbāb at-taʾlīf*, so to speak). This latter feature, eminently useful and thus apparently deliberate, is introduced by Avicenna himself, who reports on the context of three of his earliest literary efforts (*al-Majmūʿ*, *al-Ḥāṣil wa-l-maḥṣūl*, *al-Birr wa-l-iṯm*), and faithfully adhered to by Jūzjānī in the Biography. It was also followed to the extent possible, as we will see below, in the Longer Bibliography (LB).

The list of works in the Auto- / Biography Complex (thus for short henceforth) accordingly dates from the time of its authors (before 1037 for the Autobiography and before ca. 1050 for the Biography, around which time Jūzjānī may have died—the precise date being unknown), and is thus the most authentic and reliable. However, it is to be noted that it was not intended to be complete, given the purposes of its composition just mentioned and as is obvious from the mere twenty, both actual and implied, titles reported. Thus, for example, Avicenna says nothing about the treatises he composed for as-Sahlī while in Gurgānj (between 999 the earliest and 1012), before he met Jūzjānī, just as Jūzjānī does not mention, of all of Avicenna's major works, even the *Išārāt*!

The Complex is preserved in at least two recensions, one transmitted independently in the manuscripts and another as embedded in the biographical works of Ibn-al-Qifṭī and Ibn-Abī-Uṣaybiʿa. The particular problems that will need to be addressed in a future edition have been briefly sketched in Chapter One, T3, note a.

Group (b). *The Shorter Bibliography* (*SB*)

The transmission of the SB has the peculiar characteristic that it appears embedded in Jūzjānī's Biography only in the versions extant in the *ṭabaqāt* works of Bayhaqī, Ibn-al-Qifṭī (Q), and Ibn-Abī-Uṣaybiʿa (IAU) but not in the independently transmitted manuscripts containing the Auto-/Biography Complex. Thus in the *ṭabaqāt* works the SB appears as the work of Jūzjānī, but it is absent in his text of the Biography in the independent manuscripts which contain it. The text of the SB in Q and IAU, who wrote around the middle of the 13th century, is very similar, as will be discussed below, but it is quite divergent from that in Bayhaqī, whose *Tatimma* was completed a century earlier in 1159, in which case it is out of the question that the former are derived from the latter, and therefore that it was Bayhaqī who embedded the SB in the Biography. There must thus have existed before 1159 an independently circulating "fuller" version of the Auto-/Biography Complex which contained the embedded SB in Jūzjānī's Biography and which formed the source of both Bayhaqī and Q/IAU. This "fuller" version, however, does not survive independently in the manuscript tradition, to the best of my current knowledge.[3]

At the same time, however, there must also have existed the same Auto-/Biography Complex in a "shorter" version, without the SB embedded in Jūzjānī's Biography, which survives in the various manuscripts extant today. Since the earliest surviving manuscript of this "shorter" version is the Istanbul MS Üniversite A[rapça] Y[azma] 4755 which dates from 588/1192, this version was in circulation before that date.

The question is which version is the original, and who the compiler is. Naturally, if the "fuller" version is original, then clearly Jūzjānī is the author, and it must be dated some time after Avicenna's death in 1037 when the Biography was written. But there are problems with this view, which had been the prevalent one until Reisman called it into question in *Avicennan Tradition* 134–137. Essentially, as Reisman has argued, the SB is artificially and clumsily embedded in the Biography, breaking the flow of Jūzjānī's narrative, and it repeats titles which Jūzjānī has mentioned in the Biography just a few lines before, something which a listing of Avicenna's books organically belonging to that place would hardly do. In addition, also as Reisman has shown, the SB lists *al-Mubāḥaṯāt* among the titles, something which Jūzjānī could hardly have written since the collection of Avicennan materials known by this title and the title itself came into being after him. To this, one may add that it is difficult to envisage that, if the SB had been present in the Biography from the very beginning as part of what Jūzjānī wrote, someone would actually take it *out* and form the "shorter" Auto-/Biography Complex as extant in all the manuscripts. If the purpose was to *add* a longer and more complete bibliography at the end of the Biography, as it happens in these manuscripts of the Complex, this could have been done by literally adding those titles missing from the SB, or simply just adding the longer bibliography and disregarding the repetition of the titles, as IAU actually did and also as some scribes of some manuscripts of Bayhaqī's *Tatimma* also did—not by excising the SB from its allegedly organic place. For all these reasons, therefore, the SB was not compiled by Jūzjānī as part of the Biography but independently, and it was later added in that place of the Biography to form the "fuller" version.

---

[3] According to Reisman *Avicennan Tradition* 121 and note 29, the SB in the "fuller version" of the Complex extant in MS Tehran University 2441, f. 125^{b}, "apparently derives from the longer bibliography in later manuscripts of al-Bayhaqī's *Tatimma*."

But if Jūzjānī is not responsible for the SB as embedded in his Biography and if, by extension, he is taken not to be its author, it is nevertheless certain that the compiler was among the circle of Avicenna's disciples and Persian speaking followers. First of all, the SB is compiled according to a plan, in obvious imitation of the lists of works of Aristotle. The SB is divided into two sections according to genre, first the books (*kutub*) and then the shorter treatises (*rasā'il*). In addition, each book in the former section is provided with the number of volumes it covers. This mirrors the catalogue of Aristotle's books as given, for example, in Ptolemy al-Ġarīb's bibliography, which was known in Arabic. I mentioned above (Chapter 3.4) the apparently deliberate similarities between Avicenna's Autobiography and Ptolemy's life of Aristotle; SB follows suit in the presentation of Avicenna's works, and this could have come only from someone intimately familiar with Avicenna's life and legacy.

The earliest form of the SB that we can recover is that in Bayhaqī, and it appears that it must be quite close to the original, despite certain problems that it has. It contained at least 38 entries; Bayhaqī's copy has now 37, but the omission of the *Qawlanj* in it, which title we get from the SB as copied by Q and IAU, no. (13), must be due to a scribal error. What SB included was all the main works of Avicenna, or, perhaps put in another way, everything that was known to exist in the circles of his disciples not long after his death. What it does not include, in comparison with the Longer Bibliography (LB), which manifestly was compiled subsequently, is primarily (a) works in the form of correspondence, responses to questions, and occasional pieces, (b) works that had not yet taken their final shape, like the *Ta'līqāt*, (c) an occasional main work, like the *Aḍḥawiyya*, which may have lain in the possession of an obscure patron and had surfaced only in a later period, (d) works that began to circulate subsequently following the balkanization and fragmentation of some of his works, like the *Maqāla fī l-aḫlāq* (no. 54 in LB) which may be a segment of *al-Birr wa-l-iṯm*, and finally (e) pseudepigraphic works that began to appear about a century after his death.[4] The compiler tried to account for works in category (a) above by simply entering as his last item (no. 37) the generic description of "epistles on issues current between him and some contemporary scholars."

The original SB must have circulated widely, and it was at some point "revised" or "updated" in Arabic speaking circles, probably in Iraq or Syria.

---

[4] For the last two categories of works by and attributed to Avicenna, which present a particular problem to the restitution and study of his works, see Gutas "Agenda".

It is this "updated" version that was accessible to Q and IAU and which we find in their works. That the "updating" was done in Arabic speaking circles appears from the entry no. 30, which in Bayhaqī appears simply as *Fī n-nabḍ*, "On the Pulse." In Q and IAU, however, there is both a change in title, *Muḫtaṣar fī n-nabḍ*, and an editorial comment, *bi-l-ʿajamiyya*, "in Persian," which could only have come from an Arabic speaking reviser.[5] The updating apparently also introduced some errors, as in the number of volumes of some books. *The Cure*, for example (no. 4), is listed as being in 20 volumes in Bayhaqī but 18 in Q and IAU. The error must have come about not so much from a mistaken copying of a number as from actually counting the volumes to which the reviser had access. If we count the parts of *The Cure*, it has nine in logic, four in mathematics, eight in physics, and one in metaphysics, which makes 22 parts; thus 20 volumes would more easily accommodate these parts than 18. Similarly, *The Salvation* is listed as having three volumes in Q and IAU but only one in Bayhaqī. The mistake, in the revision this time, must have come about from counting the *parts* of the work which, if it excluded the mathematical part, would have come to three, representing logic, physics, and metaphysics, though each one of these could hardly amount to a "volume."

IAU has the same text as Q, both in terms of the order of the treatises and textual similarity. The only difference in the order is that *al-Inṣāf* is put in the third place between *al-Ḥāṣil wa-l-maḥṣūl* and *al-Birr wa-l-iṯm*, which must be clearly a scribal mistake; *al-Ḥāṣil* and *al-Birr* are two works that are closely related, mentioned by Avicenna himself in the Autobiography almost in the same sentence as having been composed for his neighbor Abū-Bakr al-Baraqī, so no bibliographer would have deliberately separated them and interposed the *Inṣāf*. In all likelihood *al-Inṣāf* must have been omitted from the list at some point, then added in the margin, and then inserted in the wrong place in the list between *al-Ḥāṣil* and *al-Birr*. However, in the LB *al-Inṣāf* is right after *al-Ḥāṣil* and *al-Birr* so it is likely that there is some contamination here.

The textual differences between Q and IAU are very slight, as registered in the notes of the Tetrapla synopsis. Regular errors in Q which occur also in IAU might lead one to surmise that IAU was copying from Q, or perhaps from Zawzanī (the author of the original work which Q abridged), rather than from an independent manuscript containing Jūzjānī's Biography with the SB. However, IAU differs from Q in that he includes both the SB and the

[5] However, this is not specified in SB 12, *al-ʿAlāʾī*, in Q and IAU.

LB, the former in its place in the Biography and the latter at the very end of his entry on Avicenna, introduced by the appropriate editorial comments. In Q the SB is introduced by its compiler with the words, *wa-hāḏā fihrist jamīʿ kutubihi*, "This is the list of all his books," which IAU reproduces omitting the word *jamīʿ*, "all," in anticipation of the fuller list, i.e., LB, that he planned to give at the end of his entry.

Group (c). *The Longer Bibliography* (*LB*)

The two earliest copies we have of the LB are the Istanbul MS Üniversite 4755 (siglum B in Gohlman), dated 588/1192, and the text in IAU, the final and fuller recension of which was compiled in 667/1268 (Q omits the LB). But it is clear that neither has the original text as it stood in the autograph of the compiler. They both derive from a common archetype stemming from that autograph, but at different levels of corruption and revision. It should be possible through their help to arrive at a text of LB that would be relatively close to the archetype. In general, B shows fewer corruptions in the first half of the list, but in the second it abridges the information a lot, writing only the bare titles. For example, for no. (50) in IAU, B no. 52 has only, *M. fī Tadāruk al-ḫaṭaʾ al-wāqiʿ fī t-tadbīr aṭ-ṭibbī*. By contrast, IAU has both a slightly divergent title and a statement about the addressee of the treatise: *K. at-Tadāruk li-anwāʿ ḫaṭaʾ at-tadbīr, sabʿ maqālāt, allafahu li-Abī-l-Ḥasan Aḥmad b. Muḥammad as-Sahlī*. Given the detailed information about addressees and sponsors of Avicenna's works which the B version of the LB has in the first half of the list, it is obvious that the addition about the addressee of this work that IAU found in his exemplar of the LB must go back to the archetype, but that the scribe of B omitted it. Similarly, for no. (53) in IAU = 56 in B, IAU has the full name of the dedicatee, *aš-Šayḫ Abū-l-Ḥasan Sahl b. Muḥammad as-Sahlī*, whereas B merely has the nisba, *as-Sahlī*, something that is highly unusual for the confusion that it might engender, especially given that this person would seem to be the brother of the dedicatee cited just a few of entries before at (50) in IAU = 52 in B. The reason for this change of style in B is unclear, though there is a strong possibility that the scribe was running out of space and tried to cram the last 45 titles on one page, f. 217^{b}. Accordingly he may have omitted the additional information in his exemplar about the dedicatees in order to save space.

When all the texts that comprise the complex of the Auto-/Biography and bibliographies are taken into consideration, it can be seen in general that Q and IAU have the least contaminated versions. Even B, though earliest in date of the extant manuscripts, is more corrupt than Q, for it includes the mention of Avicenna's beauty right at the beginning of Jūzjānī's Biography (Gohlman 45). As for the LB, with B and IAU being the earliest witnesses, and coming from different textual traditions, their agreement over the other, later manuscripts of the complex may be considered conclusive at this stage of our knowledge. For example, already at the very beginning of the LB, under the title *Lawāḥiq*, no. 2, the later manuscripts add *fī taṣānīfihi* after *ḏakara*, but IAU and B do not have it (Gohlman 90, line 5). It is unnecessary: the Bibliographer says about the *Lawāḥiq*, Avicenna "mentioned that it is a commentary on *The Cure*" (*ḏakara annahu šarḥ li-š-Šifā'*). Since he is talking about *The Cure*, it is obvious to the reader that the mention that the *Lawāḥiq* is its commentary is in that very book, which is right. The addition in the later manuscripts, *yaḏkuru fī taṣānīfihi*, is redundant, but also vague, if it is in the plural, raising the question in the reader's mind in which of his works Avicenna would mention that.

The compiler of the LB must also have belonged to the tradition of Avicenna's disciples and scholars who transmitted his works if only because it is clear that he had access to manuscripts stemming directly from that tradition. The Üniversite MS 4755 (B) contains notes that indicate that some of the texts copied in it came from Bahmanyār's exemplars (see for example the notes relating to the transmission of the *'Uyūn al-ḥikma*, given below in the Inventory at GS 3, GS 3a, and GL 2), while the LB itself lists a text that in all likelihood came from aṣ-Ṣiġnāḫī's codex (now in Cairo Ḥikma 6M; see further below). Some manuscripts of the LB introduce the catalogue with the words of the compiler himself, who is alleged to have written, "As for the catalogue of Avicenna's books which Jūzjānī mentioned in his Biography [i.e., SB], it contained some forty works. However, I have tried to collect whatever was written and I have set down in this catalogue whatever I found which, added to what Jūzjānī mentioned, comes to about ninety works" (Gohlman 90). This statement of intent does not occur in the Üniversite 4755 MS, something which makes its ultimate author questionable, but there is hardly any doubt that the compiler, whether he had actually written these words or not, did exactly that: he prepared a catalogue of Avicenna's books on the basis of Avicenna's works and their manuscripts he could locate, manuscripts which derived from the tradition of the philosopher's disciples and followers, to which he added bibliographical details he also found in the same tradition.

The same conclusion is reached by another piece of evidence which may be thought to refer to the compiler of the LB. One branch of the manuscripts containing Avicenna's essay in refutation of astrology (*al-Išāra ilā 'ilm fasād* *aḥkām an-nujūm*, GP 14) contains the following introduction by the scribe:[6] "Treatise on invalidating astrology, copied from an exemplar given to me as a present by the Šayḫ Abū-l-ʿIzz Ibn-Zayla, who said that it is the work of Avicenna. A part of the exemplar was in the hand of Abū-Manṣūr Ibn-Zayla, and what is said [in it] is close to what Avicenna would say, but I do not know whether it is Avicenna's work [written] for Abū-Manṣūr ⟨or⟩ not,[7] except that [Abū-l-ʿIzz] Ibn-Zayla said that it is Avicenna's work. Because it is attributed to him *I have added it to his works in its most appropriate place*." The last sentence, emphasized here, can only mean that its author, besides being a scribe copying Avicenna's treatises, was compiling a bibliography of Avicenna's works, and the only bibliography that includes this work on the refutation of astrology is the LB (no. 86): none of the others has it. If then this note is by the compiler of the LB, this means that he had access to material coming not only from Avicenna's disciple Bahmanyār but also from Avicenna's disciple Abū-Manṣūr Ibn-Zayla. The identity of this Abū-l-ʿIzz Ibn-Zayla remains unknown (Reisman *Avicennan Tradition* 197n104, Michot *Astrologie* 22*), but regardless whether he was a relative of Abū-Manṣūr or not, he had in his possession works by Avicenna copied by Abū-Manṣūr, which he passed on to the compiler of the LB.

The compiler seems to list the books in a roughly chronological order, following in the main Jūzjānī's biography, but it is also clear that he reports on the titles from the manuscripts he has seen as well as the dedications heading the treatises. In one instance he expressly mentions this: in the LB no. 9, for *al-Mabdaʾ wa-l-maʿād*, he says, "I found at the beginning of this book …" (*wajadtu fī awwali hāḏā l-kitāb* …). Thus he gives the titles according to what he finds in manuscripts, not listings in the earlier SB; as, for example, for LB 31 he has, *al-qaṣīda al-muzdawija fī l-manṭiq*, with further information about the dedicatee and alternate titles, whereas SB 25 merely has, *al-manṭiq bi-š-šiʿr*. Final attestation to the LB's independence from the earlier SB is that the compiler disregards the classification of Avicenna's books under the rubrics *kutub* and *rasāʾil* but has his own categories, adding *maqāla* in the list, which is not used in the SB.

Finally, the date in which the LB was compiled has an upper limit of 588/1192, the date of the Istanbul MS Üniversite 4755. The lower limit can

---

[6] Text in Michot *Astrologie* 1, note, French tranlation p. 21*; English translation in Reisman *Avicennan Tradition* 197.

[7] The text should read (as suggested by Reisman in his translation and Michot 21*n1), *wa-lā aʿlamu hal hiya taṣnīfuhu lahu* ⟨*am*⟩ *lā, illā annahu* …, with *taṣnīfuhu lahu* necessarily meaning, "his [Avicenna's] work [written] for him [Abū-Manṣūr ibn-Zayla]."

be estimated as being around the middle of that century. LB 84 lists the *Marginal Glosses on De anima*; if this text existed as comments in the margins of Avicenna's own copy of the Arabic translation of *De anima* and Ṣiġnāḫi first copied it into the clean copy in Cairo 6M, and if this was done around 1150,[8] then the LB was compiled by someone having access to the Ṣiġnāḫi codex or its copy, after 1150. Similarly, the compiler of the LB lists (no. 43) *al-Mubāḥaṯāt* under that title, which means that by his time the collection of this book with this title had already taken place.

Group (d). *The Extended Bibliography* (*EB*)

An extended, or padded, longer bibliography (EB), apparently containing some 115 items, is found at the end of the Avicenna entry in some manuscripts of Bayhaqī's *Tatimma*, edited by Shafīʿ separately at the end of his edition, 187–190. The date of the earliest extant manuscript that contains it, Istanbul Murad Molla 1408, is 639/1242 (cf. Reisman *Avicennan Tradition* 132), thus giving us an upper limit for this bibliography. Its compiler was working in the Persian speaking world (he reports on the Persian translation of some works, e.g., no. 36a), but beyond this his identity and the rationale of its compilation remain problematic. It is clearly intended to supersede the existing bibliographies, though it neither incorporates all the well established titles from the Biography and the SB, nor does it include all the additional titles in the LB. Instead, after an initial (but lacunose) run-through of the standard titles and some of those in the LB, it proceeds to list, both interspersed with the others and at the very end, numerous new titles, some of which correspond to those we find in manuscripts and some others which remain unidentified and are manifestly spurious. Also, no particular ordering principle in the listing of the titles can be detected at this time. It begins, properly enough, with *al-Majmūʿ*, and does follow it to a certain extent by the major works, though *al-Birr wa-l-iṯm*, which is everywhere else listed as third or fourth, occupies here slot no. 82, *al-Hidāya* is no. 48, the logic *Urjūza* is no. 62, and *Ḥayy b. Yaqẓān* no. 51. Nevertheless, the fact that some of the titles which it alone lists are also extant in manuscripts and are indubitably authentic indicates that it was compiled on the basis of manuscripts alleging to contain Avicenna's works. The reliability and accuracy of all these bibliographies, and the overall responsibility with which they were compiled, are indicated by the fact that of the hundreds of titles which they list only four,

8 See Gutas "Ṣiġnāḫī".

and these only in the EB, are so far completely unknown and unaccounted for: EB 17 *al-Istibṣār*, 32 *K. zubdat al-quwā l-ḥayawāniyya*, 67 *R. fī t-tuffāḥ*, and 90 *K. yūṣaf ẓafar al-Amīr ʿAḍud ad-Dawla*; all the rest can be identified and traced, and are listed in the Inventory.

Used with this understanding of their history and compilation, the bibliographies provide reliable information about both the authentic and the spurious works which had been in circulation at their time.

Tetrapla
Synopsis of the Four Lists of Avicenna's Works

Roman type indicates the actual titles of the books, as best as we can tell; *italic* what must be considered descriptions by bibliographers. For ready reference, I have added serial numbers, indicating the order in which the titles are listed, to all except to the LB entries in the Istanbul MS Üniversite 4755, which are numbered by the scribe of the MS himself or his source. The serial numbers in the SB group (b) are those in Bayhaqī's *Tatimma*, followed in parentheses by the serial numbers in Ibn-al-Qifṭī (Q) and Ibn-Abī-Uṣaybiʿa (IAU); the numbers in the LB group (c) are those in the Istanbul MS, followed in parentheses by the serial numbers in IAU, with the number of the repeated titles in IAU given after the equal sign. I have added all bibliographic comments on each title by the compiler of the LB as found in the Istanbul MS except those in which he repeats information from the Autobiography and Biography, and noted the most significant variants from the copy of the LB that was available to IAU. The letters and numbers in bold in the right margin are the serial numbers of the works given in the Inventory below (without the initial G[utas]). All the works listed in these bibliographies are included and accounted for in the Inventory that follows under the serial numbers in bold; only those works that are listed twice in the bibliographies are not given their serial number at the second occurrence.

Abbreviations: K(itāb), M(aqāla), R(isāla), v(olume).

(a) *Autobiography (before 1037), Biography (ca. 1050)	(b) SB in *Tatimma*, (Q, and IAU) (before 553/1159)[9]	(c) LB in MS Istanbul Üniversite 4755 = B, and (IAU) (before 588/1192)[11]	(d) EB in *Tatimma* (before 639/1242)[10]	Inventory numbers (G+)
	Kutub			
*1. al-Majmūʿ, al-Ḥikma al-ʿArūḍiyya	1. (1) al-Majmūʿ, 1v	6. (6) K. al-Majmūʿ, al-Ḥikma al-ʿArūḍ.	1. K. al-Majmūʿ	S 2
*2. al-Ḥāṣil wa-l-maḥṣūl, ca. 20v	2. (2) al-Ḥāṣil wa-l-maḥṣūl, 20v	3. (3) K. al-Ḥāṣil wa-l-maḥṣūl	4. K. al-Ḥāṣil wa-l-maḥṣūl	S 10
*3. al-Birr wa-l-iṯm	3. (3) al-Birr wa-l-iṯm, 2v	4. (4) K. al-Birr wa-l-iṯm	82. K. al-Birr wa-l-iṯm	PP 1
7. aš-Šifāʾ (Hamaḏān, Iṣfahān)	4. (4) aš-Šifāʾ, 20v (Q, IAU: 18v)	1. (2) K. aš-Šifāʾ	3. K. aš-Šifāʾ	S 5
4. al-Qānūn (Jurjān, Hamaḏān)	5. (5) al-Qānūn, 4v (Q, IAU: 14v)	7. (7) al-Qānūn fī ṭ-ṭibb	6. K. al-Qānūn	Med 1
3. K. al-Arṣād al-kulliyya (Jurjān)	6. (6) al-Arṣād al-kulliyya, 1v	10. (10) K. al-Arṣād al-kulliyya		S 6d
20. al-Inṣāf (Iṣfahān)	7. (7) al-Inṣāf,[12] 20v	5. (5) K. al-Inṣāf wa-l-ittiṣāf[13]	7. K. al-Inṣāf wa-l-intiṣāf	S 11
13. an-Najāt (Iṣfahān to Šābūr Ḫwāst)	8. (8) an-Najāt, 1v (Q, IAU: 3v)	15. (14) K. an-Najāt	8. K. an-Najāt	S 6
8. al-Hidāya (Fardajān in Hamaḏān)	9. (9) al-Hidāya, 1v	16. (16) K. al-Hidāya *fī l-ḥikma*	48. K. al-Hidāya	S 4
	10. (10) al-Išārāt,[14] 1v	95. (15) K. al-Išārāt wa-t-tanbīhāt[15]	11. K. al-Išārāt	S 9
1. al-Muḫtaṣar al-awsaṭ fī l-manṭiq (Jurjān)	11. (11) al-Muḫtaṣar al-awsaṭ,[16] 1v	8. (8) K. al-Awsaṭ *al-Jurjānī* fī l-manṭiq	16. K. al-Awsaṭ *al-Jurjānī*	L 1
			16a. al-Jadal *al-mulḥaq bi-*K. al-Awsaṭ	L 1
14. al-ʿAlāʾī (Iṣfahān)	12. (12) al-ʿAlāʾī, 1v	12. (13) K. al-ʿAlāʾī *bi-l-fārisiyya*	38. K. al-ʿAlāʾī	S 7
		14. (13) K. Dānešnāme[17]		S 7

9 The latest date on which the *Tatimma* was completed; see Reisman *Avicennan Tradition* 122n31.

10 The date of the earliest extant MS that contains it, Istanbul Murad Molla 1408.

11 The date of the earliest extant MS that contains it, Istanbul Üniversite 4755.

12 IAU misplaces *al-Inṣāf* after *al-Ḥāṣil wa-l-maḥṣūl*, which must be a scribal error; see the discussion above.

13 IAU omits *wa-l-ittiṣāf*.

14 Gohlman, in his table on p. 143, has the three titles in numbers 10–12 as missing in IAU (Müller). This is incorrect; they are all there.

15 B adds, *wa-huwa āḫir mā ṣannafa wa-kāna yaḍinnu bihi.*

16 Bayhaqī omits *al-Muḫtaṣar*, most likely because he has just cited the work a few lines previously.

17 The separate double listing of the book under two titles sandwiching the *Lisān al-ʿarab* in the Üniversite MS is apparently due to scribal error. In the correct version of the LB available to IAU, the full title is given properly (though slightly misprinted in the Müller edition): *K. Dānešnāme-ye al-ʿAlāʾī bi-l-fārisiyya.*

(a) *Autobiography (before 1037), Biography (ca. 1050)	(b) SB in *Tatimma*, (*Q*, and IAU) (before 553/1159)	(c) LB in MS Istanbul Üniversite 4755 = B, and (IAU) (before 588/1192)	(d) EB in *Tatimma* (before 639/1242)	Inventory numbers (G+)
10. al-Qawlanj (Fardajān in Hamaḏān)	(13) al-Qawlanj, 1v[18]	17. (17) K. al-Qawlanj	75. K. al-Qawlanj	**Med 3**
15. Lisān al-ʿArab (Iṣfahān)	13. (14) Lisān al-ʿArab, 10v	13. (12) K. Lisān al-ʿArab *fī l-luġa*	103 K. Lisān al-ʿArab	**L 17**
11. al-Adwiya al-qalbiyya (Hamaḏān)	14. (15) al-Adwiya al-qalbiyya, 1v	20. (19) K. al-Adwiya al-qalbiyya,	39. K. al-Adwiya al-qalbiyya	**Med 2**
	15. (16) al-Mūjaz, 1v	30. (30) K. al-Mūjaz *al-kabīr fī l-manṭiq*	22. al-Mūjaz *al-kabīr fī l-manṭiq*	**L 3**
	16. (17) *baʿḍ* al-Ḥikma al-mašriqiyya,[19] 1v	47. (46) K. al-Ḥikma al-mašriqiyya *wa-lā yūjadu tāmman*	13. K. al-Ḥikma al-mašriqiyya	**S 8**
	17. (18) Bayān ḏawāt al-jiha, 1v	29. (28) M. fī ʿUkūs ḏawāt al-jiha	23. K. Bayān ḏawāt al-jiha	**L 10**
2. K. al-Mabdaʾ wa-l-maʿād (Jurjān)	18. (20) al-Mabdaʾ wa-l-maʿād, 1v	9. (9) K. al-Mabdaʾ wa-l-maʿād *fī n-nafs*	18. K. al-Mabdaʾ wa-l-maʿād	**M 1**
6. al-Maʿād (Rayy)	19. (19) al-Maʿād, 1v	11. (11) K. al-Maʿād *al-aṣġar*[20]	36. K. al-Maʿād	**M 3**
			36a. *Tarjamat* K. al-Maʿād *bi-l-fārisiyya*	**M 3**
	20. (21) al-Mubāḥaṯāt,[21] 1v	43. (42) al-Mubāḥaṯāt[22]	10. K. al-Mubāḥaṯāt / ? 14. Muqtaḍayāt al-kutub as-sabʿa	**S 14**
5. Muḫtaṣar al-Majisṭī (Jurjān)[23]				**S 6d**
17. al-Muḫtaṣar al-aṣġar fī l-manṭiq (Jurjān) [the logic of *Najāt*]				**S 6a**

[18] Bayhaqī omits this entry, which is most likely a scribal omission at the level of the archetype of the extant manuscripts.

[19] Bayhaqī reads here *qudsiyya* instead of *mašriqiyya*, which must be an error of confusion; in the later EB found in the *Tatimma, qudsiyya* is actually a scribal misreading of *ʿaršiyya*; see LB 61 = EB 2 and 116, below.

[20] B adds after the title, *ṣannafahu bi-r-Rayy wa-huwa fi ḫidmat al-malik Majd-ad-Dawla*; IAU omits *al-aṣġar* and the words *wa-huwa fī ḫidmat*, thus making the work seem as having been dedicated to Majd-ad-Dawla.

[21] Bayhaqī reads here *Kitāb al-Muqtaḍayāt, mujallada*. In his entry on Nātilī, Bayhaqī 22/38 says that Avicenna mentions Nātilī in this book only. For this title see Reisman *Avicennan Tradition* 127–130.

[22] B adds, *bi-suʾāl Bahmanyār tilmīḏihi wa-jawābihi lahu.*

[23] This title and the following one, no. 17, are the only two titles in the Biography which are not taken up by any subsequent bibliography. See the discussion in the Inventory on work GS 6d under Astronomy and work GS 6a under Logic.

(a) *Autobiography (before 1037), Biography (ca. 1050)	(b) SB in *Tatimma*, (*Q*, and IAU) (before 553/1159)	(c) LB in MS Istanbul Üniversite 4755 = B, and (IAU) (before 588/1192)	(d) EB in *Tatimma* (before 639/1242)	Inventory numbers (G+)
	Rasā'il			
	21. (22) al-Qaḍā' wa-l-qadar	35. (34) M. fī l-Qaḍā' wa-l-qadar[24]	112. Mas'ala fī l-qaḍā' wa-l-qadar	**M 4**
	22. (32) al-Ajrām al-ʿulwiyya[25]	51. (49) M. fī l-Ajrām as-samāwiyya	49. R. fī Maʿrifat al-ajrām as-samāwiyya	**P 6**
19. R. fī Ālāt ar-raṣad (Iṣfahān) (Gohlman 80.3–4)	23. (23) al-Āla ar-raṣadiyya	55. (54) M. fī Āla raṣadiyya[26]		**Math 4**
	24. (24) Ġaraḍ Qāṭīġūriyās	57. (55) M. fī Ġaraḍ Qāṭīġūriyās		**L 7**
	25. (25) al-Manṭiq *bi-š-šiʿr*	31. (32) al-Qaṣīda al-muzdawija fī l-manṭiq[27]	62. Urjūza fīl-manṭiq	**L 4**
	26. at-Tuḥfa	34. (33) M. fī Taḥṣīl as-saʿāda, *wa-tuʿrafu bi*-l-Ḥujaj al-ʿašr (IAU: al-ġr)	26. K. at-Tuḥfa	**M 6**
	(26) *al-qaṣā'id fī l-ʿaẓama wa-l-ḥikma*	70. (68) *ʿIddat* (IAU: *ʿAšr*) *qaṣā'id wa-ašʿār fī z-zuhd wa-ġayrihi yaṣifu fīhā aḥwālahu*		**PW 7**
	27. (27) Fī l-Ḥurūf	22. (21) M. fī Asbāb ḥudūṯ al-ḥurūf wa-maḫārijihā[28]		**L 16**
	28. (28) Taʿaqqub al-mawāḍiʿ al-jadaliyya	48. (47) M. fī Taʿaqqub al-mawāḍiʿ al-jadaliyya	19. R. fī Taʿaqqub al-mawḍiʿ al-jadalī	**L 13**
		49. M. fī Ḫaṭa' man qāla inna l-kammiyya jawhar[29]	35a. M. fī Ḫaṭa' man qāla inna l-kammiyya jawhariyya	**L 8**

[24] B adds, *ṣannafahā fī ṭarīq Iṣfahān ʿinda ḫalāṣihi wa-harabihi ilā Iṣfahān*. This appears to be inaccurate. See the discussion in the Inventory on work GM 4.

[25] Q and IAU have *as-samāwiyya* for *al-ʿulwiyya*.

[26] B adds, *ṣannafahā bi-Iṣfahān ʿinda rujūʿihi wa-raṣadihi li-ʿAlā'-ad-Dawla*.

[27] B adds, *ṣannafahā li-s-Sahlī bi-Gurgānj wa-tuʿrafu bi-Mīzān an-naẓar wa-bi-l-Urjūza*.

[28] B adds, *ṣannafahā bi-Iṣfahān li-l-Jabbān*. IAU has an abbreviated title, *M. fī Maḫārij l-ḥurūf*.

[29] IAU omits this title.

(a) *Autobiography (before 1037), Biography (ca. 1050)	(b) SB in *Tatimma*, (Q, and IAU) (before 553/1159)	(c) LB in MS Istanbul Üniversite 4755 = B, and (IAU) (before 588/1192)	(d) EB in *Tatimma* (before 639/1242)	Inventory numbers (G+)
	29. (29) Muḫtaṣar Awqlīdis	68. (66) Muḫtaṣar K. Awqlīdis[30]		S 6b
	30. (30) Fī n-Nabḍ[31]	21. (20) M. fī n-Nabḍ *fārisiyya*	81. R. fī n-Nabḍ *bi-l-fārisiyya*	Med 5
	31. (31) Fī l-Ḥudūd	26. (25) K. al-Ḥudūd	41. al-Ḥudūd	L 6
	(33) al-Išāra ilā ʿilm al-manṭiq	37. (36) M. fī l-Išāra ilā ʿilm al-manṭiq	15. Išāra ilā ʿilm al-manṭiq	L 5
	32. (34) Aqsām ʿulūm al-ḥikma (Q, IAU om. ʿulūm)	38. (37) M. fī Aqsām al-ḥikma[32]	53a. Fī Aqsām al-ḥikma 53. Fī Aqsām al-ʿulūm	S 1 S 1
	33. (35) Fī n-Nihāya wa-l-lā-nihāya	40. (39) M. fī l-lā-nihāya	29. Fī t-Tanāhī wa-l-lā-tanāhī	P 3
	(36) ʿAhdun *katabahu li-nafsihi*	62. (60) ʿAhdun *ʿāhada llāha bihi li-nafsihi*	50. ʿAhdun *ʿahidahu li-nafsihi*	PP 1c
9. R. Ḥayy b. Yaqẓān (Fardajān in Hamaḏān)	34. (37) Ḥayy b. Yaqẓān	19. (18) R. Ḥayy b. Yaqẓān	51. R. Ḥayy b. Yaqẓān	M 7
	35. (38) Fī anna Abʿād al-jism ġayr ḏātiyya lahu			P 2
	36. (39) *al-kalām* Fī l-Hindibāʾ[33]	36. (35) M. fī l-Hindibāʾ	42. R. fī l-Hindibāʾ	Med 4
	(40) *lahu ḫuṭba* Fī annahu Lā yajūzu an yakūna šayʾun wāḥidun jawharan wa-ʿaraḍan[34]	91. (87 = 96) M. fī annahu Lā yajūzu an yakūna šayʾun wāḥidun jawharan wa-ʿaraḍan	35b. (M. fī Ḫaṭaʾ) man qāla inna šayʾan huwa jawharun wa-ʿaraḍun maʿan	L9
	(41) Fī anna ʿIlma Zaydin ġayru ʿilmi ʿAmrin	63. (61) M. fī anna ʿIlma Zaydin ġayru ʿilmi ʿAmrin	33. R. fī anna ʿIlma ʿAmrin ġayru ʿilmi Zaydin	L14
	(42) *rasāʾil lahu iḫwāniyya wa-sulṭāniyya*	71. (69) *Rasāʾil bi-l-fārisiyya wa-l-ʿarabiyya wa-muḫāṭabāt wa-mukātabāt wa-hazliyyāt*		PW4

[30] B adds, *aẓunnuhu al-maḍmūm ilā n-Najāt*. This would be based on what Jūzjānī himself says in his introduction to the Mathematics part of the *Najāt*, Mahdavī 234.

[31] Q, IAU: *Muḫtaṣar* (*fī*) *an-nabḍ bi-l-ʿajamiyya.*

[32] IAU has a longer title, *M. fī Taqāsīm al-ḥikma wa-l-ʿulūm.*

[33] IAU adds *ḫuṭab* before *al-kalām.*

[34] IAU omits *lahū ḫuṭba* and reads *jawhariyyan* and *ʿaradiyyan* for *jawharan* and *ʿaraḍan.*

(a) *Autobiography (before 1037), Biography (ca. 1050)	(b) SB in *Tatimma*, (Q, and IAU) (before 553/1159)	(c) LB in MS Istanbul Üniversite 4755 = B, and (IAU) (before 588/1192)	(d) EB in *Tatimma* (before 639/1242)	Inventory numbers (G+)
	37. (43) *masāʾil jarat baynahu wa-bayna baʿḍ fuḍalāʾ al-ʿaṣr*[35]	92. (88) *Masāʾil jarat baynahu wa-bayna fuḍalāʾ al-ʿaṣr* (IAU: *baʿḍ al-fuḍalāʾ*) *fī funūn al-ʿulūm*		**PW3.1**
	Additions			
	(44) K. al-Ḥawāšī ʿalā l-Qānūn			**Med 1b**
16. *Muʿālajāt ṭibbiyya* (*li-l-Qānūn*) (Iṣfahān) [Gohlman 72.9–74.1]		73. (71) *Qawānīn wa-muʿālajāt ṭibbiyya*		**Med 1a**
	(45) K. ʿUyūn al-ḥikma	28. (27) K. ʿUyūn al-ḥikma, *yajmaʿu al-ʿulūm aṯ-ṯalāṯa*	12. K. ʿUyūn al-ḥikma	**S3**
	(46) K. as-Šabaka wa-ṭ-ṭayr	25. (24) R. aṭ-Ṭayr *marmūza, yaṣifu fīhā ʿamalan yūṣiluhu ilā ʿilm al-ḥaqq*	31. *ar-R. al-mawsūma bi-ṭ-Ṭayr*	**M8**
		2. (1) K. al-Lawāḥiq, *ḏakara annahu šarḥun li-š-Šifāʾ*	5. K. al-Lawāḥiq	**S12b**
		18. (91) Muḫtaṣar fī anna z-zāwiya allatī (B: *om.* allatī) min al-muḥīṭ wa-l-mumāss lā kammiyya lahā		**Math 2**
		23. (22) R. ilā Abī Sahl al-Masīḥī fī z-Zāwiya *ṣannafahā bi-Jurjān*	54. Fī z-Zāwiya	**Math 1**
		24. (23) M. fī l-Quwā ṭ-ṭabīʿiyya ilā Abī Saʿīd (IAU: Saʿd) al-Yamāmī	77. R. ilā Abī l-Faraj al-Yamāmī	**Med 10**
		27. (26 = 98) M. fī Naqḍ R. Ibn aṭ-Ṭayyib fī l-quwā ṭ-ṭabīʿiyya[36]	78. R. fī r-Radd ʿalā M. li-Abī l-Faraj	**Med 11**
		32. (31 = 93) al-Mūjaz aṣ-ṣaġīr fī l-manṭiq *wa-huwa manṭiq ʿUyūn al-ḥikma*[37]	25. al-Mūjaz aṣ-ṣaġīr fī l-manṭiq	**S3a**

35 Q adds at the beginning *rasāʾil fī*, and Q and IAU read *al-fuḍalāʾ* omitting *al-ʿaṣr* at the end.

36 This is the correct title in B; IAU has a corrupt text: *M. fī taʿarruḍ risālat aṭ-ṭabīb fī l-quwā ṭ-ṭabīʿiyya.*

37 Not to be confused with the *Muḫtaṣar al-aṣġar fī l-manṭiq*, which is the one inserted in the *Najāt*. IAU (or his LB source) makes this mistake and calls this work, *fa-huwa manṭiq an-Najāt*.

(a) *Autobiography (before 1037), Biography (ca. 1050)	(b) SB in *Tatimma*, (*Q*, and IAU) (before 553/1159)	(c) LB in MS Istanbul Üniversite 4755 = B, and (IAU) (before 588/1192)	(d) EB in *Tatimma* (before 639/1242)	Inventory numbers (G+)
		33. (29) *al-Ḫuṭba* (IAU: *al-ḫuṭab*) *at-tawḥīdiyya fī l-ilāhiyyāt*[38]		**PW 6a**
		39. (38) R. fī Sikanjubīn	110. M. fī Sikanjubīn	**Med 6**
		41. (40) K. at-Taʿālīq *ʿallaqahū ʿinda* (IAU: *ʿanhu*) *Ibn Zaylā*	9. K. at-Taʿlīqāt	**S 12a**
		42. (41) M. fī Ḫawāṣṣ ḫaṭṭ al-istiwāʾ		**Math 5**
			57. Ajwibat ʿašr masāʾil	**S 14c**
		44. (43) ʿAšr masāʾil ajāba ʿanhā li-Abī r-Rīḥān al-Bīrūnī		**P 9**
		45. (44) Jawāb sitta ʿašrata masʾala li-Abī r-Rīhān	56. Ajwibat Abī r-Rīḥān al-Bīrūnī *anfaḏahā ilayhi min Ḫwārizm*	**P 8**
		46. (45 = 94) M. fī Hayʾat al-arḍ min as-samāʾ wa-annahā (IAU: kawnihā) fī l-wasaṭ	28. R. fī ʿIllat qiwām al-arḍ fī ḥayyizihi [*sic*]	**P 7**
		50. (48) al-Madḫal ilā ṣināʿat al-mūsīqā *wa-huwa ġayr al-mawḍūʿ fī n-Najāt*		**Math Ps-3**
			68. R. fī l-Mūsīqā *siwā aš-Šifāʾ*	**S 6e**
		52. (50) M. fī Tadāruk al-ḫaṭaʾ al-wāqiʿ fī t-tadbīr aṭ-ṭibbī[39]	40. Tadāruk anwāʿ al-ḫaṭaʾ	**Med 7**
12. *Ašyāʾ fī āḫir al-Majisṭī* (Iṣfahān) [Gohlman 64.8–9]		53. (51) M. fī kayfiyyat ar-raṣad wa-taṭābuqihi maʿa l-ʿilm aṭ-ṭabīʿī		**Math 3**
		54. (52) M. fī l-Aḫlāq	52. R. fī l-Aḫlāq	**PP 1b**
		56. (53 = 102) R. ilā s-Sahlī fī amr mastūr, ay al-kīmiyā	70. R. ilā Abī l-Ḥasan Sahl b. Muḥammad fī amr mastūr	**P-Ps 9**
		58. (56) ar-R. al-Aḍḥawiyya fī l-maʿād	71. R. al-Aḍḥawiyya	**M 2**
		59. (57) Muʿtaṣim aš-šuʿarāʾ *fī l-ʿarūḍ*[40]	? 45. K. fī š-Šiʿr	**L-Ps 6**
		60. (58) M. fī Ḥadd al-jism	? 27. R. fī Taḥarrī al-ajsām/aqsām	**P 1**

38 B adds, (*a*)*ẓ*(*unnuhu*) *hiya al-Kalima al-ilāhiyya wa-t-tasbīḥiyya*.

39 IAU has, *K. at-Tadāruk li-anwāʿ ḫaṭaʾ at-tadbīr, sabʿ maqālāt, allafahu li-Abī l-Ḥasan Aḥmad b. Muḥammad as-Sahlī*.

40 IAU adds, *ṣannafahu bi-bilādihi wa-lahu sabʿa ʿašrata sana*.

(a) *Autobiography (before 1037), Biography (ca. 1050)	(b) SB in *Tatimma*, (*Q*, and IAU) (before 553/1159)	(c) LB in MS Istanbul Üniversite 4755 = B, and (IAU) (before 588/1192)	(d) EB in *Tatimma* (before 639/1242)	Inventory numbers (G+)
		61. (59) al-Ḥikma al-ʿaršiyya, *wa-huwa kalām murtafiʿ fī l-ilāhiyyāt*	2. al-Ḥikma al-qudsiyya/116. K. al-Ḥikma al-ʿaršiyya	**M-Ps 1**
		64. (62) K. Tadbīr al-jund wa-l-mamālīk (B: mamālik) wa-l-ʿasākir wa-arzāqihim wa-ḫarāj al-jund (om. IAU) wa-l-mamālik		**Med 12**
		65. (63) Munāẓarāt jarat lahu fī n-nafs maʿa Abī ʿAlī an-Nīsābūrī		**P-Ps 7**
		66. (64) *Ḫuṭab wa-taḥmīdāt* (IAU: *tamjīdāt*) *wa-asjāʿ*		**PW 6**
		67. (65) Jawāb yataḍammanu l-iʿtiḏār ʿammā nusiba ilayhi fī hāḏihi al-ḫuṭab	72. R. ilā ... l-Jūzjānī fī l-intifāʾ ʿammā nusiba ilayhi min muʿāraḍat al-Qurʾān	**PW 3**
		69. (67) M. fī l-Ariṯmāṭīqī, (*a*)*ẓ*(*unnuhu*) *hiya llatī fī n-Najāt*		**S 6c**
		72. (70) Taʿālīq ʿalā Masāʾil Ḥunayn	108. Šarḥ Masāʾil li-Ḥunayn b. Isḥāq	**Med 8**
18. *Jawāb masāʾil ahl aš-Sīrāz fī l-manṭiq* (Iṣfahān) [Gohlman 78.5–8]		74. (73) ʿIšrūna masʾala saʾalahū ʿanhā ahl al-ʿaṣr	58. Ajwibat ʿišrīna masāʾil [*sic*]	**L15**
			59. Ajwibat ʿišrīna masāʾil [*sic*] uḫrā	**S-Ps 2a–b**
		75. (72) *Masāʾil ʿidda ṭibbiyya*		**Med 26**
		76. *Masāʾil tudʿā* al-Buḏūr[41]		**S 13**
		77. (74) *Masāʾil tarjamahā bi*-t-Taḏkīr		**S-Ps 4**
		78. (75) *Jawāb masāʾil kaṯīra* (B: *yasīra*)		**S-Ps 2**
		79. ʿUyūn al-masāʾil (IAU om.)		**S-Ps 1**
		80. (76) R. ilā ʿulamāʾ Baġdād yasʾaluhum al-inṣāf baynahu wa-bayna rajul Hamaḏānī yaddaʿī al-ḥikma		**PW 1**

[41] IAU omits this title, most likely through scribal error, since both this and the following entry begin with the word *masāʾil*.

(a) *Autobiography (before 1037), Biography (ca. 1050)	(b) SB in *Tatimma*, (*Q*, and IAU) (before 553/1159)	(c) LB in MS Istanbul Üniversite 4755 = B, and (IAU) (before 588/1192)	(d) EB in *Tatimma* (before 639/1242)	Inventory numbers (G+)
		81. (77) R. ilā ṣadīq yas'aluhu l-inṣāf baynahu wa-bayna l-Hamaḏānī allaḏī yaddaʿī al-ḥikma[42]		PW 2
		82. (78) *Jawāb li-ʿiddat masā'il*		S-Ps 2
		83. (79 = 101) *Kalām lahu* Fī Tabyīn mā'iyyat al-ḥuzn (IAU: al-ḥurūf!)	106. Fī Māhiyyat al-ḥuzn	PP-Ps 2
		84. (80) Šarḥuhu li-K. an-Nafs li-Arisṭū *wa-yuqālu innahū min al-Inṣāf*		S 11c
		85. (81) M. fī n-Nafs *tuʿrafu bi-l-*Fuṣūl		P 10
		86. (82) M. fī Ibṭāl aḥkām (B: ʿilm) an-nujūm		P 14
		87. (83) K. al-Mulaḥ fī n-naḥw		L-Ps 7
		88. (84) Fuṣūl ilāhiyya fī iṯbāt al-awwal	79. R. fī Iṯbāt al-mabda' al-awwal	M-Ps 13
		89. (85) Fuṣūl fī n-nafs wa-ṭ-ṭabīʿiyyāt		P-Ps 8
		90. (86) R. ilā Abī Saʿīd b. Abī l-Ḫayr fī z-zuhd	60. K. ilā Abī Saʿīd b. Abī l-Ḫayr	Spur.
			61. *K. āḫar ayḍan ilayhi*	Spur.
		93. (89) Taʿlīqāt *istafādahā Abū l-Faraj al-Hamaḏānī aṭ-ṭabīb min majlisihi* wa-jawābāt *lahu*	76. Fuṣūl ṭibbiyya jarat fī majlisihi	Med 9
		94. (90) *M. ḏakarahā fī* (IAU adds, *taṣānīfihi annahā fī*) l-masālik (IAU: mamālik) wa-biqāʿ al-arḍ		Math-Ps 2
		(92) Ajwiba li-su'ālāt sa'alahū ʿanhā Abū l-Ḥasan al-ʿĀmirī, wa-hiya 14 mas'ala		S-Ps 3
		(93 = 31) K. al-Mūjaz aṣ-ṣaġīr fī l-manṭiq		
		(94 = 45) K. Qiyām al-arḍ fī wasaṭ as-samā'		
		(95) K. Mafātīḥ al-ḫazā'in fī l-manṭiq		L-Ps 1
		(96 = 87) Kalām fī l-jawhar wa-l-ʿaraḍ		

42 B abbreviates: for *al-Hamaḏānī allaḏī yaddaʿī al-ḥikma* it has, *hāḏā l-Hamaḏānī*.

(a) *Autobiography (before 1037), Biography (ca. 1050)	(b) SB in *Tatimma*, (*Q*, and IAU) (before 553/1159)	(c) LB in MS Istanbul Üniversite 4755 = B, and (IAU) (before 588/1192)	(d) EB in *Tatimma* (before 639/1242)	Inventory numbers (G+)
		(97) K. Ta'wīl ar-ru'yā	74. K. at-Taʿbīr	**Spur.**
		(98 = 26) M. fī r-radd ʿalā M. aš-Šayḫ Abī l-Faraj b. aṭ-Ṭayyib		
		(99) R. fī l-ʿIšq, *allafahā li-Abī ʿAbdallāh al-faqīh*	43. R. fī l-ʿIšq	**M 5**
		(100) R. fī l-Quwā l-insāniyya wa-idrākātihā	34 (= 107). M. fī l-Quwā al-insāniyya wa-idrākātihā	**Spur.**
			105. Dafʿ al-ġamm	**Spur.**
		(101 = 79) Qawl fī tabayyun mā al-ḥuzn wa-asbābihi		
		(102 = 53) M. ilā Abī ʿAbdallāh al-Ḥusayn b. Sahl b. Muḥammad as-Sahlī fī amr mašūb [*sic*]		
			17. al-Istibṣār	**Unknown**
			20. K. al-Muhja (/ al-Bahja?)	**L-Ps 2**
			21. R. fī Iṯbāt an-nubuwwa	**M-Ps 2**
			24. R. fī s-Siyāsa	**PP-Ps 1**
			30. al-Jumal min al-adilla al-muḥaqqaqa li-baqā' an-nafs an-nāṭiqa	**P 12**
			32. K. zubdat al-quwā l-ḥayawāniyya	**Unknown**
			37. R. an-Nayrūziyya	**PW 4f**
			44. R. fī l-Ḥadaṯ	**P-Ps 1**
			46. R. ilā Abī l-Qāsim al-Kirmānī	**PW 4h**
			47. R. fī n-Nafs al-falakī [sic]	**M 3**
			55. R. al-ʿArūs	**M-Ps 9**
			63. R. fī l-Quwā l-jusmāniyya	**M 3**
			64. R. ilā Abī l-Faḍl	**PW 4e**
			65. R. fī š-Šarāb mujadwal	**Med 17**
			66. R. fī š-Šarāb ġayr mujadwal	**Med 17**
			67. R. fī t-Tuffāḥ	**Unknown**
			69. R. ila l-Baraqī	**Spur.**
			73. (*jawāb?*) *K. ilā baʿḍ al-mutakallimīn*	**P 4**

(a) *Autobiography (before 1037), Biography (ca. 1050)	(b) SB in *Tatimma*, (*Q*, and IAU) (before 553/1159)	(c) LB in MS Istanbul Üniversite 4755 = B, and (IAU) (before 588/1192)	(d) EB in *Tatimma* (before 639/1242)	Inventory numbers (G+)
			80. R. fī l-Fayḍ al-ilāhī	PP 1e
			83. Tafsīr *ba'ḍ suwar kalām Allāh*	PW 5
			84. *Rasā'il wa-kutub*	
			85. K. ilā Abī l-Qāsim al-Faḍl b. Maḥmūd	PW 4e or f
			86. Ta'ālīq fī l-manṭiq	S 12a: d
			87. K. ilā Abī l-Faḍl Māfīd b. Īrāmard	PW 4g
			88. *Qaṣā'id lahu*	PW 7
			89. al-Ma'ānī fī l-manṭiq	L-Ps 5a
			90. *K. yūṣaf ẓafar al-Amīr 'Aḍud ad-Dawla*	Unknown
			91. al-Imlā' fī l-manṭiq	L-Ps 5a
			92. R. fī Ma'nā ḥaqīqat Wa-ḍrib …	PW 5i
			93. R. fī Kayfiyyat inšiqāq al-qamar	PW 5j
			94. R. fī Kayfiyyat Aṣḥāb al-kahf	PW 5h
			95. R. fī n-Nafs	P 11(?)
			96. R. *ayḍan* fī n-Nafs	P-Ps 8
			97. R. *ayḍan* fī n-Nafs	P-Ps 8
			98. Nukat al-manṭiq	L 11
			99. R. Hamaj ar-ra'ā' ilā sākin al-qilā'	S 14e
			100. R. fī Ḍamm māḍiġ al-ḫarā'	S 14d
			101. Tadbīr al-manzil	PP-Ps 1
			102. Tadbīr al-musāfirīn	Med 13
			104. Dustūr ṭibbī	Med 1c
			107 R. al-Firdaws	Spur.
			109. R. fī l-Bāh	Med 14
			111. R. fī l-Faṣd	Med 15
			113. R. ilā Abī Ṭāhir b. Ḥassūl	PW 4c
			114. R. ilā Abī Ṭāhir al-mutaṭabbib fī ma'nā s-sirāj (?)	PW 4i
			115. M. fī Ḥifẓ aṣ-ṣiḥḥa	Med 16
			116 = 2. al-Ḥikma al-'aršiyya	

PART TWO

INVENTORY OF AVICENNA'S AUTHENTIC WORKS

Introduction

Mahdavī's fundamental *Fehrest* listed all the works attributed to Avicenna sequentially (nos. 1–242) and in alphabetical order by title, and offered for each work critical information for its identification and a listing of its manuscripts and publication record. The works were divided into two categories, the first including works of certain (*mosallam*) and probable (*moḥtamal*) attribution mixed together, and the second "works of doubtful attribution, misattributed works, and parts of authentic works extracted and renamed as independent works." The research that followed in the half century since its publication has enabled a better understanding of Avicenna's bibliography and made necessary an inventory of the *authentic* works by subject matter that will describe them more sharply, give a better idea of their number and range, and distinguish them from probable pseudepigraphic works whose authenticity remains very much to be verified. The aim is to focus research on two essential and related fields: the manuscript transmission of all works attributed to Avicenna—it cannot be stressed strongly enough and frequently enough how basic this is for a complete and accurate list of his works—and the history, modalities, and nature of the generation of Avicennan pseudepigrapha and forgeries.[1] Without a thorough understanding of these subjects, we can never hope to know fully not only the quantity and quality of Avicenna's works and ideas, but also the history of philosophy in the Islamic world during the three centuries after him, which is inextricably linked to the formation of a pseudepigraphic Avicennan corpus.[2]

The inventory of Avicenna's authentic works presented here is accordingly conservative. In essence, the default position taken is that a work is presumed pseudepigraphic unless it can be proven authentic beyond any

---

[1] Fundamental for laying the gound and setting the framework of the discussion are the two articles by Reisman, "Pseudo-Avicennan Corpus, I" and "Ps.-Avicenna Corpus, II".

[2] See on both these subjects Gutas "Agenda" 47–53.

reasonable doubt. The burden of proof is thus on the authenticators, and the usual caveat in its study that "we should always err on the side of caution in making arguments against authenticity" is not productive.[3] As stated in the introduction to the preceding part on the Tetrapla, the investigation of the authenticity of the attributed works is based on the manuscript transmission to the extent that this was accessible in the available literature and some manuscripts (notably the Istanbul MS Üniversite 4755), on the early bibliographies of his works as evaluated and presented synoptically in the Tetrapla, and only tertiarily and conjointly with the first two, on internal evidence from the works themselves or the analysis of their contents. It should be noted, however, that the works labeled "pseudepigraphic" in this inventory do not all share a uniform degree of falsification. Some are almost certainly forgeries, but others may contain a core of authentic Avicennan material which has been either edited or somehow altered to form a new text for some purpose, with variations in between. The label "pseudepigraphic" should therefore direct the attention of researchers to those works that need to be investigated in order to determine how much of their contents, if any, is genuinely Avicennan, and alert them to the fact that these works cannot be used indiscriminately in studies of Avicenna's thought without prior authentication.

The inventory is of the authentic works, and accordingly the manifestly spurious writings that crowd many manuscripts and have been registered as inauthentic already by Mahdavī are not taken into consideration; if a title is not mentioned in the inventory then it is to be considered spurious. Only a few of the titles that were included by Mahdavī among those that were certainly or probably by Avicenna, and which may still be so taken by researchers, have been registered in a separate section on spurious works at the very end of the inventory. The net result of this inventory has been to grant us a more precise understanding of the number and kinds of Avienna's works—reduce the fuzzy edges, so to speak, in this regard—and direct attention to those works that need it the most. The final tally will eventually come to fewer than one hundred works, once the pseudepigraphs in each category have been properly assessed and the titles in the categories of Avicenna's private and medical writings have been pruned of them. Closer to historical reality, this is still a very large number, though a far cry from the 276 listed by Anawati and even the 131 certainly or probably authentic of

[3] See Reisman "Pseudo-Avicennan Corpus I," and p. 11 for the quotation, as well as p. 15n32 for the opposite position.

Mahdavī, and it gives a better understanding of the subjects which attracted most the attention of Avicenna and his sponsors.

In the arrangement of the titles I have followed the classification of the sciences as given by Avicenna himself in the *Divisions of Philosophy* (GS 1 below), except for the section on Medicine, which I displaced to the very end instead of keeping it under the derivative works on Physics as classified by Avicenna, both because of its special status and length (at least 34 medical works are attributed to him in the manuscripts consulted) and in order not to enlarge disproportionately the number of the works on Physics. To this classification I added two sections, neither of which could have been, by its very nature, a part of Avicenna's *Divisions of Philosophy*: a first section on works comprising all or most of philosophy (summae), and a penultimate section on his private and homiletic writings. I have re-numbered the works in each category of writings in this classification, abandoning the serial numbers in Mahdavī, Anawati, and Ergin, which have become cumbersome, both in order to reduce the size of the numbers involved and to make future adjustments within each category easier to implement without affecting the entire series. To each number I prefaced the letter G (for Gutas) followed by the initials or abbreviation of the category involved, as follows:

S	Summae
L	Logic and Language
P	Physics
Math	Mathematics
M	Metaphysics
PP	Practical Philosophy
PW	Private Writings
Med	Medicine

Each category, numbered in capital letters (A, B, C ...), is divided into subcategories (again according to Avicenna's divisions) designated with a Roman numeral in capitals, and the works in each subcategory are arranged by genre—expository, commentary, versified, etc.—designated with a lower case Roman numeral. At the very end of the authentic works in each subcategory are listed the pseudepigraphic works as a final genre. The ensuing arrangement and classification can be seen in the Conspectus of Works below in Part Three of the Appendix.

Each work is introduced by the G-number, followed by its title in Arabic and English, using the standard abbreviations, *K*(*itāb*), *M*(*aqāla*), *R*(*isāla*), and by references to the numbers in Mahdavī (M) and Anawati (A) and to the serial numbers in the Tetrapla Bibliographies (Bio, SB, LB, EB). Then come the known alternate titles to the work, mostly as given by Mahdavī, followed by a brief discussion about the date of its composition, if known, and a discussion of its authenticity, if necessary.

The manuscripts that follow are listed according to Mahdavī, with additions from Reisman's *Avicenniana*, Daiber's *Collection IV*, and my random findings. With few exceptions I did not consult systematically any manuscripts or catalogues of manuscripts, both for lack of time and because the purpose of this book is not bibliographical, and the information I provide is as accurate and reliable as these sources I just mentioned, barring any mistranscriptions of my own. Thus although the listing of these manuscripts is far from complete, it seemed preferable to provide it, despite its shortcomings, for the convenience it offers of making them readily accessible in this introductory volume to reading Avicenna's philosophical works. The numbers of the manuscripts themselves are those given by Mahdavī, which include both catalogue numbers and shelf numbers in the respective libraries, something of which readers should be aware. The libraries themselves are entered under the city in which they are found, in alphabetical order. A list of the libraries by cities, and cities by country is easily accessible in *GAS* VI, 311–466, and *GAS* VIII, 296–312.

For printed versions and translations of a work into modern European languages I necessarily list the one that is available if there is only one, and the one that can be considered relatively more reliable when there are more than one, or the most recent one in which references to earlier ones can be found. For bibliographical inclusiveness the reader is referred to Janssens' bibliographies and to other, earlier, works such as Michot's *Destinée* pp. xiv–xxxii.

Beginning from soon after his death and to this very day, Avicenna's works have been translated into various Near Eastern languages and into Latin, but these translations necessarily could not be covered in the present inventory. For these languages the following should be consulted.

Persian. Mahdavī provides extensive coverage of the pre-modern translations into Persian. For modern translations, Janssens *Bibliography* 110–111 refers to Jonaydī 145–153. Mohammad Javad Esmaeili of the Iranian Institute of Philosophy, to whom I am greatly indebted, informs me that he will be providing a selective bibliography of Persian translations and publications on Avicenna on the web site of the Institute, www.irip.ir, which should be consulted.

Syriac. Takahashi.

Latin. Janssens "Latin Translations."

Hebrew. For medieval Hebrew translations see Freudenthal and Zonta; for modern Hebrew see Harvey.

Turkish. Kaya *Miras* 345–357.

Urdu. Urdu translations of Avicenna were mostly limited to his *Canon*; see Hakim Zill al-Rahman, *Qanun-i Ibn Sina aur us ke sharihin aur mutarjimin*, Aligarh: Aligarh University, 1986.

Avicenna's works, and in particular the *Išārāt*, were the subject of numerous commentaries, which again cannot be covered in this inventory. Mahdavī lists many of them. With Robert Wisnovsky at McGill as Principal Investigator, there is a *Post-classical Islamic Philosophy Database Initiative*, accessible at http://islamsci.mcgill.ca/RASI/pipdi.html, which plans to create a public database of the material its title indicates, including commentaries on Avicenna's works. It should be periodically consulted, as should Wisnovsky's forthcoming publications. In the meantime, see Wisnovsky "Philosophical Commentary" and Wisnovsky "Islamic Reception".

A. Summae (GS)—Works Comprising All Philosophy

i. *Classificatory*

GS 1. *M. fī Aqsām al-ḥikma* (M32, A4)—*The Divisions of Philosophy* / SB 32, LB 38, EB 53, 53a

Alternate titles: *Taqāsīm al-ḥikma wa-l-ʿulūm*, *Aqsām al-ʿulūm*, or *Aqsām al-ʿulūm al-ʿaqliyya*.

I follow the entry in the LB in the Istanbul MS Üniversite 4755; the same manuscript gives the title of the treatise itself as *K. Aqsām al-hikma wa-tafṣīlihā*, while the SB and EB also have *Aqsām al-ḥikma*. In the opening words Avicenna says that the anonymous person who commissioned this work from him had asked him "to point out the divisions of the intellectual sciences" (*qad iltamasta minnī an ušīra ilā aqsām al-ʿulūm alʿ-aqliyya*) and Mahdavī prefers this title for this reason, but these are the words of request by that person, not Avicenna's title, which is ubiquitously listed as *Aqsām al-ḥikma* (with slight variations).

This treatise, which appears to be relatively early in Avicenna's career, has been the subject of numerous studies; see Lizzini "Divisioni," with rich bibliography.

Daiber *Collection IV* 152–153 reports that MS Arab. V.293 in Lisbon, Academia das Ciencias, which contains this treatise (see immediately below), also has another work on ff. 1^{b}–6^{b}, a *R. fī Jamīʿ aqsām ʿulūm al-awāʾil*, which is attributed to Avicenna but which is different both from this treatise here and from Abū-Sahl al-Masīḥī's *Aṣnāf al-ʿulūm al-ḥikmiyya*. Its nature and authorship remain to be investigated. On the Lisbon MS see Adel Sidarus, "Un recueil de traités philosophiques et médicaux à Lisbonne," *ZGAIW* 6 (1990) 179–189.

MSS: **Baghdad**, Iraq Museum 594 pp. 128–142 (639H); **Bursa**, Hüseyin Çelebi 1194 ff. 152^{b}–155^{b}; **Cairo** I 250, Taymūr 1 Majāmīʿ, Ṭalʿat 339; **Gotha** 1158_{29}; **Hyderabad** II 1716; **Istanbul**, Ahmet III 1584_{13}, 3447_{50}, Ayasofya 4818_{6}, 4829_{20}, 4852_{2}, 4853_{25}, Carullah 1302_{1}, Esad Efendi 3688, Hamidiye 1448_{58}, Köprülü 868_{5}, 1605_{3}, 1628_{5}, Nuruosmaniye 4894_{9}, Pertev Paşa 647, Şehit Ali Paşa 2725, Üniversite 1458_{87}, 4711_{3} (579H), 4754_{4}, 4755_{5}; **Leiden** 1478; **Lisbon**, Academia das Ciencias, Arab. V.293 ff. 33^{a}–39^{a}; **London**, Brit. Lib. 430_{3}, 978_{13}, 980_{7}, 981_{10}; **Manchester** 384_{N}; **Manisa**, İl Halk Kütüphanesi 1705 ff. 1^{a}–15^{a}; **Meshed**, Riżavī I 3/102, IV 1/595–596; **Oxford**, Bodleian $H430_{3}$, $A980_{10}$; **St. Petersburg** A.M. 156; **Tehran**, Majlis 634_{38}, 866_{8}, 2761_{3}; Malik 2012_{3}, 2019_{2}, Miškāt 1149 ff. 43^{b}–45^{b}, Tangābunī 317_{6}.

Published: Kurdī *Majmūʿat ar-rasāʾil* 225–243; Šamsaddīn 261–272.

Translations: French, Anawati "Divisions"; Mimoune.

ii. *Expository Summae*

GS 2. *K. al-Majmūʿ* or *al-Ḥikma al-ʿArūḍiyya* (M62, 137, A10, 28, 29, 32, 65, 247)—*The Compilation* or *Philosophy for ʿArūḍī* / Autobio 1, SB 1, LB 6, EB 1

See the description above, Chapter 2, W2.

MS: **Uppsala** 364; excerpts and paraphrases of most parts are found in the works by Avicenna and others: see Chapter 2, W2 above.

Published: The entire manuscript was published by Ṣāliḥ (2007). The section on Rhetoric was published by Sālem *Rīṭūrīqā* (1950); cf. Langhade and Grignaschi 24. The concluding part of this section on Rhetoric, *al-Aḫlāq wa-l-infiʿālāt an-nafsāniyya* ("Natural dispositions and affections of the soul") was published, with a brief introduction and translation into French, by Remondon (1954). The section on Poetics was published by Sālem *Šiʿr* (1969). A part of the Poetics was translated into English by van Gelder and Hammond 26–28.

GS 3. *K. ʿUyūn al-ḥikma* (M93, A15)—*Elements of Philosophy* / SB (45), LB 28, EB 12

A lapidary treatment of philosophy, "comprising the three sciences," as the LB has it—i.e., Logic, Physics, and Metaphysics—it was subjected to a massive commentary by Faḫr-ad-Dīn ar-Rāzī. The work itself appears to have been generated by splicing together two independent parts, one on Logic and the other on Physics and Metaphysics.

To begin with, the section on Logic was originally composed independently and circulated under the title, *Shorter Epitome on Logic* (*al-Mūjaz aṣ-ṣaġīr fī l-manṭiq*, see below in the section on logic, GS 3a), and was later joined to the Physics and Metaphysics part to form the *ʿUyūn*. The Istanbul MS Üniversite 4755 (dated 588/1192) contains both works, the *Mūjaz* (ff. 1[b]–9[b]) and the *ʿUyūn* (ff. 44[a]–83[a], with logic on ff. 44[a]–53[a]), and indeed the two logical works are identical save for minor stylistic variations. On f. 53[a], at the end of the part on Logic of the *ʿUyūn*, the scribe notes in the margin that this part is actually *al-Mūjaz aṣ-ṣaġīr*, but that there were added in the *ʿUyūn* version, without specifying by whom, three sections (*fuṣūl*) to the Posterior Analytics (*K. al-Burhān*) segment.[4] This is accurate: in the Üniversite MS the *ʿUyūn* does have an additional three sections in the Posterior Analytics segment (ff. 51[a–b]) which do not appear in the *Mūjaz* text in the same

[4] Eichner "Universal Science" 73n10 makes a note of this on the basis of the information in Mahdavī.

manuscript. The edition of the *'Uyūn* by Badawī, p. 12 line 4, does not include these three sections.

Secondly, at the end of the entire work in the Üniversite MS, f. 83[a], the same scribe adds the following colophon: "I collated the *'Uyūn al-ḥikma* from [the part on] Physics and until here [i.e., the end of Metaphysics] with a copy at the end of which [there was written]: 'This is the last of what was dictated to me by Avicenna—may he live long!'; I think this was in the hand of Bahmanyār, but God knows best."[5] The detail in this note that only two parts were copied from that particular exemplar allegedly in the hand of Bahmanyār, rather than all three, would seem to confirm its authenticity; a later forger wishing to claim Bahmanyār's authority for the text he was copying would not have restricted himself to the two parts of Physics and Metaphysics only. If then the colophon is authentic and Avicenna dictated only these two parts to Bahmanyār (or any other disciple, even if we disallow Bahmanyār's agency), it would mean that these two parts together were thought of by Avicenna as an independent unit and not as part of a larger composition called *'Uyūn al-ḥikma*. This is further corroborated by the fact that Avicenna opens the part on Physics by giving a definition of philosophy (*ḥikma*) which is then followed by a classification of the philosophical sciences, something normally done at the very beginning of an entire work, as in the *Madḫal* of the *Šifā'* and the *Mašriqiyyūn*, and not of its second part, the Physics, which would have been the case had the *'Uyūn* been initially conceived as a tripartite work.

The question then is, who the person was to put the two parts together and call the work *'Uyūn al-ḥikma*. Considering the fact that for the compilation of the *'Uyūn*, three sections were added to the Posterior Analytics part of the Logic, as mentioned above, it would appear that this person was Avicenna himself; but if Bahmanyār was indeed the person to have received this text, he could himsefl have made the additions—either by himself or on the basis of materials he had received from Avicenna—and provided the title. Even a later scholar in the same tradition of Avicenna's disciples could have done it. This seems more likely, considering the fact that the earliest bibliographies do not mention the *'Uyūn*, neither Jūzjāni in the Biography nor the SB. It appears for the first time in the LB, thus before 1192, and then again in the expanded version of the SB as we find it in Ibn-al-Qifṭī and Ibn-Abī-Uṣaybi'a, thus before mid-thirteenth century (see the Tetrapla listing above). Accordingly, although there seems to be little doubt about the authentic-

[5] Text cited also in Reisman *Avicennan Tradition* 46.

ity of the work, the question about the person who put the parts together remains open.

So does the question about the time of the composition of the two parts, the Logic on the one hand and the Physics and Metaphysics on the other. As mentioned, there are no references in the bibliographies, and the work itself has no introductions or dedicatees to provide some guidance. If the association of the Physics and Metaphysics part with Bahmanyār is to be credited, then the earliest that Avicenna could have met Bahmanyār and dictated that part would be 404–405/1014–1015, when he was in Rayy serving the Sayyida and Majd-ad-Dawla, though this may be too early a date for their encounter.[6] As for the Logic part, it also appears relatively early, so the composition of these two parts may be tentatively placed during Avicenna's "Transition Period" (Chart at the end of Part One above), though there is no certainty. Further investigation into the doctrinal relationship of the contents to the dated works of Avicenna may provide a more secure answer.

Finally, a word about the meaning of the title. Arabic *ʿayn—ʿuyūn* in such titles does not mean "source" as is usually and mistakenly translated (cf. Badawī's Latin title to his edition, *Fontes sapientiae*), but "essence, best part, element," as in the titles of the well known works of Ibn Qutayba, *ʿUyūn al-aḫbār*, and of Ibn-Abī-Uṣaybiʿa, *ʿUyūn al-anbāʾ*.

MSS: **Bursa**, Hüseyin Çelebi 1194 ff. 41ᵇ–56ᵇ; **Cairo**, Ṭalʿat 387 Ḥikma; **Istanbul**, Ahmet III 3268_1 (580H), 3355_2, 3447_{15}, Ayasofya 4829_{33}, Carullah 1441_5, Feyzullah 2188_7, Hamidiye 1448_2, Köprülü 868_1 (Physics), Nuruosmaniye $4894_{91,108}$, Üniversite 4755_4 ff. 44ᵃ–83ᵃ (588H); **Leiden** 1446 (Logic); **Vatican** 977_7 (Logic).—Mahdavī 185 further reports that **Istanbul**, Şehit Ali Paşa 2725_{59}, and **Tehran**, Tangābunī 136 and Malik 2018 are not MSS of this work. Published: Badawī *ʿUyūn*.

GS 4. *K. al-Hidāya* (M130, A24)—*The Guidance* / Bio 8, SB 9, LB 16, EB 48

Avicenna wrote this book, according to Jūzjānī's biography (Gohlman 58–60), while imprisoned in the castle of Fardajān outside of Hamaḏān in 414/1023. In the brief introduction addressed to a "dear brother" (*al-aḫ al-ʿazīz*), who may be his real brother, ʿAlī, he says that he will include in the book "synopses (*jawāmiʿ*) of the philosophical sciences expressed as concisely and clearly as possible" (*bi-awjaz lafẓ wa-awḍaḥ ʿibāra*); the philosophical sciences he treats are, again, Logic, Physics, and Metaphysics,

6 Reisman *Avicennan Tradition* 192.

concluding with the Metaphysics of the Rational Soul (see the table given above, Chapter 6.2). The style, in addition to its brevity, is also literary and is distinguished by its avoidance of technical terms, to the extent possible given the nature of the subject, and by its use of metaphors. For example, the very first sentence of the work, the definition of logic reads as follows (p. 64 ʿAbduh): *al-manṭiq ʿilmun yuʿlamu/yuʿallamu(?) fīhi kayfa yuktasabu ʿaqdun ʿan ʿaqdin ḥāṣilin*: "Logic is a science in which one knows/is taught how to acquire a complex from an existing complex," meaning by "complex" the existing premises and the acquired conclusion. And the definition of the sophistical syllogism reads (p. 128 ʿAbduh): *wa-ammā l-qiyās as-sūfisṭāʾī fa-yuʿlamu/yuʿallamu li-yuḥḏara, lā li-yustaʿmala, ka-s-sammi*: "As for the sophistical syllogism, it is known/taught in order to guard against/be avoided, not to be used—like poison." It may be thought that Avicenna adopted a more literary style because he may not have had access to his philosophical books and notes in prison and was writing from memory; or that he expected his "brother" to appreciate and understand philosophy better if it were put in less technical terms which he would find more appealing—his real brother, it should be recalled, was the one who had responded to the Ismāʿīlī dāʿī together with their father when Avicenna was still a boy; or that, as Michot "Eschatologie" 138 suggested, he employed an extremely concise style as an exercise intended to distract and amuse him during his imprisonment. Perhaps all of these factors were operative; the result was that the *Hidāya* and its literary style prefigure the *Pointers* that was to come later.

MS: **Istanbul**, Nuruosmaniye 4894_6 ff. 5^b–16^b. Mahdavī notes that the Istanbul MS Ayasofya 2475_1, which is listed by Ergin and Anawati, is in fact the *K. al-Hidāya* by Aṯīr-ad-Dīn al-Abharī.

Published: ʿAbduh.

Translation: Italian, Metaphysics in Lizzini "*Guida*."

GS 5. *K. aš-Šifāʾ* (M84, A14)—*The Cure* / Bio 7, SB 4, LB 1, EB 3

See the description above, Chapter 2, W6.

MSS: The various parts of the work are found in the following MSS:

1. Complete or mostly complete (Logic, Physics, Mathematics, and Metaphysics; for details consult Mahdavī 170). **Aligarh** 110/30; **Bankipore** (Patna) 2223–2226; **Cairo**, Azhar 331, Dār al-Kutub 262 Ḥikma, 894 Ḥikma; **Istanbul**, Ahmet III 3263, Ayasofya 2442 (671H), Beyazıt (Umumi) 3969, Carullah 1424 (693H), Damat İbrahim Paşa 822, 823 (697H), Hekimoğlu Ali Paşa 857, Nuruosmaniye 2709, 2710 (666H),

Yeni Cami 770; **Leiden** 1445; **London**, India Office 474–477; **Oxford**, Bodleian Poc. 109–124 (601–604H) (according to Mahdavī 170, the Istanbul MS Fatih 3211 contains the 19th volume of this set of the complete work); **Tehran**, Millī 580, Miškāt 243, Sipahsālār 1438, 1439, 8331.

2. Logic, Physics, and Metaphysics. **Istanbul**, Ahmet III 3262, Hamidiye 795, Köprülü 894, Nuruosmaniye 2708, Şehit Ali Paşa 1748; **Leiden** 1444; **London**, Brit. Lib. Or. 7500; **Tehran**, Majlis 135.
3. Logic and Physics. **Cairo**, Dār al-Kutub 753 Ḥikma; **Istanbul**, Ahmet III 3261 (677H), Lâleli 2550, Yeni Cami 771; **London**, Brit. Lib. 1655 (576H); **Tehran**, Miškāt 241.
4. Logic and Mathematics. **London**, India Off. RB 114.
5. Logic and Metaphysics. **Istanbul**, Carullah 1425; **Paris**, 6829.
6. Physics and Mathematics. **Cairo**, Dār al-Kutub 675 Falsafa.
7. Physics and Metaphysics. **Cairo**, Taymūr 140 Ḥikma (535H); **Istanbul**, Carullah 1332, 1333, Nuruosmaniye 2711; **Oxford**, Bodleian 435 (571H); **Tehran**, Ṭabāṭabāʾī 865.
8. Logic. **Aligarh** 160/21, 84; **Beirut**, St. Joseph 372; **Berlin** 5044 (*fann* IV); **Calcutta**, Bengal 82 (*f.* IV), Būhār 284, 285, 286; **Istanbul**, Ahmet III 3445, Ali Emiri Efendi 1504 (674H), Aşir Efendi 207 (*f.* I–IV; 680H), Atıf Efendi 1565 (*f.* I–V), Carullah 1426 (*f.* V–IX), Damat İbrahim Paşa 824, Feyzullah 1206 (*f.* I–III), Hatice Sultan 208; Ragıp Paşa 909, 1461_{31} (*f.* V); Yeni Cami 773, 772 (628H); **London**, India Off. 4752; **Manchester** 379_{d} (*f.* III); **Paris** 6527; **Meshed**, Riżavī I 1/181 (*f.* V), 3/156, IV 3/260 (*f.* V), 261 (*f.* V); **Tehran**, Majlis 105 (*f.* V), Malik 1057, 4276 (*f.* I–II), Millī 91 (*f.* V), 117 (*f.* V), Ṭabāṭabāʾī 889 (*f.* I), 1296 (*f.* V).
9. Physics. **Aligarh** 110/24, 47; **Cairo**, Dār al-Kutub 172 Ḥikma (*f.* VIII), Ṭalʿat 342 Ḥikma, 402 Ḥikma, Taymūr 56 Ḥikma; **Calcutta**, Būhār 287; **Istanbul**, Atıf Efendi 1597, Ayasofya 2441 (*f.* I–VI), Beyazıt (Umumi) 3967 (*f.* I–II), Damat İbrahim Paşa 825 (650H), Feyzullah 1207, 1208 (*f.* V–VI), Halet Efendi 514, Hamidiye 796, Ragıp Paşa 866, Vehbi 1401 (*f.* VIII); **London**, Brit. Lib. Or. 2873; **Meshed**, Riżavī IV 1/872, 873, 874, 875; **Princeton** 861 (*f.* VI–VIII); **Tehran**, Majlis 137, Malik 1041, 1110, 1243, 1275, 2482, Millī 857 (*f.* VIII), 858 (*f.* VII–VIII), Sipahsālār 1436 (*f.* I–V), Ṭabāṭabāʾī 1022 (*f.* VII–VIII).
10. Mathematics. **Cairo**, Dār al-Kutub 675 Ḥikma; **Istanbul**, Ahmet III 3473, Ali Emiri Efendi 2850 (arithmetic only), Ayasofya 2720 (geometry and astronomy only), Fatih 3211, Feyzullah 1209 (arithmetic and music only); **London**, Brit. Lib. Or. 7368 (falsely ascribed to Fārābī; astronomy only; 628H), Or. 1190 (missing geometry; 485H); **Manchester** 379_{c}

(music only); **Oxford**, Bodleian Poc. 250; **Paris** 2484 (geometry only; 683H).

11. Metaphysics. **Aligarh** 110/40, 53; **Berlin** 5045; **Cairo**, Dār al-Kutub 144 Falsafa, 826 Falsafa, Ṭalʿat 363; **Istanbul**, Ahmet III 3447$_{55}$, Atıf Efendi 1596, Feyzullah 1445, Halet Efendi 513, Kılıç Ali Paşa 689, Lâleli 2546, Nuruosmaniye 4894$_{32}$, Ragıp Paşa 865, Üniversite 760; **Manchester** 378; **Meshed**, Riżavī I 1/172, 182, 183, 184, IV 1/876, 877, 878; **Mosul** XLIII 226; **Tehran**, Majlis 136, Malik 714, 715, 745, 1085 (509H), Miškāt 242, Sipahsālār 1435, 1437, Ṭabāṭabāʾī 862, 929, 1300, 1344.

Published: The complete Cairo edition (1952–1983) has the following parts.

- LOGIC. *Madḫal*: Anawati et al.; *Maqūlāt*: Anawati et al.; *ʿIbāra*: El-Khodeiri; *Qiyās*: Zāyid; *Burhān*: ʿAfīfī; *Jadal*: Ahwānī; *Safsaṭa*: Ahwānī; *Ḫiṭāba*: Sālem; *Šiʿr*: Badawī.
- PHYSICS. *as-Samāʿ aṭ-ṭabīʿī*: Zāyid; *as-Samāʾ wa-l-ʿālam, al-Kawn wa-l-fasād, al-Afʿāl wa-l-infiʿālāt:* Qāsim; *Maʿādin*: Muntaṣir et al.; *Nafs*: Anawati and Zāyid; *Nabāt*: Muntaṣir et al.; *Ḥayawān*: Muntaṣir et al.—Separately, there is the edition of *Nafs* by Rahman.
- MATHEMATICS. *Handasa*: Sabra and Maẓhar; *Ḥisāb*: Maẓhar; *Mūsīqā*: Yūsuf; *Hayʾa*: Madwar and Aḥmad
- METAPHYSICS. *Ilāhiyyāt 1*: Anawati and Zāyid; *Ilāhiyyāt 2*: Mūsā *at al.*

Translations (of complete or most of a book; for translations of segments see Janssens *Bibliography*):

- LOGIC. *ʿIbāra*, English, Bäck; *Qiyās*, partial English, Shehaby; *Ḫiṭāba*, partial German, Würsch; *Šiʿr*, English, Dahiyat.
- PHYSICS. *as-Samāʿ aṭ-ṭabīʿī*, English, McGinnis; *Nafs*, partial English, McGinnis and Reisman.
- MATHEMATICS. *Mūsīqā*, French, d'Erlanger II,103–245.
- METAPHYSICS. *Ilāhiyyāt*, English, Marmura; Italian, Lizzini, Bertolacci.

GS 6. *K. an-Najāt* (M118, A23)—*The Salvation* / Bio 13, SB 8, LB 15, EB 8

See the description above, Chapter 2, W7, where the composition of the Physics and Metaphysics parts is discussed. For the part on Mathematics, Jūzjānī says the following in his introduction to it:

> I had in my possession books by him [Avicenna] which were composed on the Mathematical sciences and were appropriate for it [the *Najāt*]. One of them was his book (1) *On the Principles of Geometry*, as an abridgment of the

> book by Euclid (*kitābuhu fī uṣūl al-handasa muḫtaṣaran min kitāb Awqlīdis*) ...; another was his book (2) *On Comprehensive Observations and Cognizance of the Structure of the Celestial Spheres*, as an abridment of the *Almagest* (*kitābuhu fī l-arṣād al-kulliyya wa-maʿrifat tarkīb al-aflāk, ka-l-muḫtaṣar min al-Majisṭī*); and another was his book (3) *Abridgment of the Science of Music* (*kitābuhu l-muḫtaṣar fī ʿilm al-mūsīqā*). I thought I would add these treatises to this book [the *Najāt*] in order for his writings to end in accordance with what he indicated in its introduction. But since I could not find on Arithmetic anything by him similar to these treatises, I thought I would (4) abridge his book on *Arithmetic* (*kitābuhu fī l-ariṯmāṭīqī*) into a [smaller] treatise ... and add it to [the *Najāt*].[7]

Jūzjānī is referring here to three books by Avicenna which were in his possession, and to another by him, which is an abridgment of a book by Avicenna. These books are all attested in the various bibliographies of Avicenna's works, drawing apparently on this passage. They are the following:

(1) The title Jūzjānī gives would be properly *Uṣūl al-handasa*, or even *Fī uṣūl al-handasa*, while "abridgment of the book by Euclid" is its description, as is obvious from the way in which the word *muḫtaṣar* is in the accusative. However, in both the SB 29 and the LB 68, it is the description that appears as the title, *Muḫtaṣar Awqlīdis*. The compiler of the LB indicates the provenance of the title from Jūzjānī's introduction cited above by commenting after the title, "I think it is the one added to the *Najāt* (*aẓunnuhu l-maḍmūm ilā n-Najāt*)."

(2) *Al-arṣād al-kulliyya wa-maʿrifat tarkīb al-aflāk*: This title appears in Jūzjānī's Biography 3 and in both the SB 6 and the LB 10, but in a shortened form, omitting the second half. However, the description that Jūzjānī adds to this title, as in the preceding one, *ka-l-muḫtaṣar min al-Majisṭī*, also appears in the bibliographies a second time as an independent title.

(3) *Al-muḫtaṣar fī ʿilm al-mūsīqā* appears in LB 50 as *al-Madḫal ilā ṣināʿat al-mūsīqā*, *Introduction to the Art of Music*, and in the EB 68 simply as *Treatise on Music*, but with the specification, "other than [the one in] the *Šifāʾ*," which is correct insofar as this earlier treatise was used in the *Najāt*.

(4) The title on Arithmetic mentioned by Jūzjānī, *Kitābuhu fī l-ariṯmāṭīqī*, must be the section on Arithmetic in the *Šifāʾ*, which Jūzjānī abridged to form the section on Arithmetic in the *Najāt*. Thus the title that

[7] Text in Mahdavī 234–235 and, in facsimile, in *Najāt* 399 Dānešpažūh, which offers a slightly better text. The entire introduction is translated in Ragep and Ragep.

appears in the LB 69, *Maqāla fī l-ariṯmāṭīqī*, again qualifed by the knowledgeable compiler as "I think it is the one which is in the *Najāt*" (*aẓunnuhu hiya llatī fī n-Najāt*), is strictly speaking the work of Jūzjānī, even if it is ultimately based on Avicenna's lengthier book on arithmetic in the *Šifā'*.

Finally, as also mentioned by Mahdavī 226, Jūzjānī used a translation of these same treatises to complete the Mathematics part of the *Dānešnāme* as well.

MSS: The various parts of the work are found in the following MSS:

1. Complete (Logic, Physics, Mathematics, and Metaphysics). **Cairo**, Muṣṭafā Fāḍil 25 Ḥikma (Anawati: only Mathematics part); **Istanbul**, Ahmet III 3448, Ayasofya 4829_{41}, Carullah 1345 (618H), Hamidiye 1448_{1}, Hatice Sultan 211, Köprülü 904, Nuruosmaniye 2718_{1}, Üniversite 678; **Meshed**, Riżavī IV 1/1054, 1055 (524H); **Tehran**, Millī 873.
2. Logic, Physics, and Metaphysics. **Cairo**, Ṭalʿat 394 Ḥikma, Taymūr 76 Ḥikma, 273 Ṭibb; **Calcutta**, Būhār 315; **Cambridge** 921; **Istanbul**, Atıf Efendi 1601, Damat İbrahim Paşa 936_{2}, Esat Efendi 1937 (603H), Köprülü 903, Ragıp Paşa 878, Selim Ağa 681, Yeni Cami 777; **London**, Brit. Lib. 978_{5}, 979; **Manchester** 379_{A}; **Oxford**, Bodleian 456_{3} (465H; cf. Reisman *Avicennan Tradition* 93n174); **Paris** 5104; **Tehran**, Khan 875, Malik 684, 1029, 1086, 1087, 4648, Sipahsālār 1443.
3. Various sections. **Cairo**, Ṭalʿat 364 Ḥikma (logic); **Cambridge** Suppl. 1480_{a} (physics); **Istanbul**, Ayasofya 2471 (mathematics, metaphysics), 2573 (logic); **London**, Brit. Lib. Or. 6572_{19} (geometry); **Oxford**, Bodleian 985, 1026 (music).—The Istanbul MSS Ahmet III 3447_{54}, Ayasofya 2349_{4}, and Nuruosmaniye 4894_{31}, contain fragments from the *Taʿlīqāt, Mubāḥaṯāt*, and also from the second *maqāla* of the Physics of the *Najāt* under the title *Lawāḥiq aṭ-ṭabīʿiyyāt* (Mahdavī 240, Reisman *Avicennan Tradition* 75).

Published: Kurdī *Najāt*; Dānešpažūh *Najāt*.
Translations: English, Logic part in Ahmed, section on the Soul of the part on Physics in Rahman *Psychology*; German, Music part in El Hefny.

GS 7. *Dānešnāme-ye ʿAlāʾī* (M72, A11, 13)—*Philosophy for ʿAlāʾ-ad-Dawla* / Bio 14, SB 12, LB 12, EB 38

See the description above, Chapter 2, W8.
MSS: **Berlin** P 55_{1}; **Calcutta**, (Bengal) I 1357, II 565, (Būhār) 215; **Hyderabad** I 334; **Istanbul**, Fatih 3312, Nuruosmaniye 2682; **London**, Brit. Lib. Add.

16659_3 ff. 255^b–348^b, Add. 16830, Or. 2361_3; India Off. 2218; **Meshed**, Riżavī I 1/98, IV 1/557; **Tehran**, Majlis 123, Malik 1025, 1026, 2009_2, 4648_3, Millī Pers. 43, Ṭabāṭabāʾī 1322, Tangābunī 74.—According to Mahdavī, the first two Brit. Lib. MSS, the Majlis and Millī MSS, and the first Malik MS are complete; the rest all comprise the Logic, Metaphysics, and Physics and lack the Mathematics, except for the second Bengal MS, which has only the Geometry, and the third Malik MS, which has only the Physics.

Published: Meškāt (Logic, Physics), Moʿīn (Metaphysics), Mīnovī (Mathematics).

Translation: French, Achena and Massé.

GS 8. *al-Mašriqiyyūn* (M63, 160, A12)—*The Easterners* / SB 16, LB 47, EB 13

See the description and MSS listed above, Chapter 2, W9, and in Gutas "Eastern Philosophy".

Published: Logic, in *Manṭiq al-mašriqiyyīn* 1–83 (based on the Cairo MS 6M); Physics, published in a doctoral dissertation by Ahmet Özcan, *İbn Sīnaʾ-nın el-Hikmetu'l-meşrikiyye adlı eseri ve tabiat felsefesi*, Marmara Üniversitesi Sosyal Bilimler Enstitüsü, İslam Felsefesi Bilim Dalı, Istanbul 1993.

Translation: English, the Introduction only, above, T8.

GS 9. *al-Išārāt wa-t-tanbīhāt* (M27, A3, 239)—*Pointers and Reminders* / SB 10, LB 95, EB 11

See the description above, Chapter 2, W11.

MSS: **Algiers** 1754_1; **Bankipore** 2338 (520H?); **Berlin** 5046 (647H), 5047; **Cairo** VI 93; **Escorial**^{2} 656 (724H); **Hyderabad** III 484; **Istanbul**, Ahmet III 1411_2, 3248_1, 3278, 3353_1, 3355_1, Atıf Efendi 1564_1 (650H), Ayasofya 2379, 2380, 2381, 2382, Carullah 1272, Damat İbrahim Paşa 809, Eyüp 1232, Fatih 3170_{2+7}, 3172_1, 3173, Feyzullah 1179 (583H), 1180 (691H), Halet 545, 546, Hamidiye 1448_3, Köprülü 869_1, Lâleli 2485 (640H), Nuruosmaniye 2653, 4894_{38}, Ragıp Paşa 822, Şehit Ali Paşa 1809, Selim Ağa 683_1, Yeni Cami 762; **Leiden** 1449 (614H), 1450 (690H), 1451, 1464_4 (the last three *namaṭ*s only); **London**, Brit. Lib. 978_6, Or. 5773; **Mosul** XX 270; **Rampur** I 379; **St. Petersburg** 87, 88; **Tehran**, Majlis 866_7 (*namaṭ*s 9–10 only), Millī 1015_1 (698H), Miškāt 288, Sipahsālār 8359_2; Ṭabāṭabāʾī 1307_4; **Uppsala** II 185; **Vatican** 1477_3 (*namaṭ*s 9–10 only).

Published: Forget (1892), Zāreʿī (2002).

Translations: Complete: French, Goichon *Directives*. Partial: Part One, English, Inati *Logic*; Part Two, 8–10, English, Inati *Mysticism*; Part Two, 8, French, Michot "Joie".

iii. *Commentaries and Notes*

GS 10. *al-Ḥāṣil wa-l-maḥṣūl* (M-, A-)—*The Available and the Valid* [*of Philosophy*] / Autobio 2, SB 2, LB 3, EB 4

See the description above, Chapter 2, W3. Not extant. In his works Avicenna refers to a Commentary on *Physics* (GS 10a, below under Physics), a Commentary on *De caelo* (GS 10b, below under Physics), a Commentary on *De anima* (GS 10c, below under Physics), and a commentary on *Metaphysics* (GS 10d, below under Metaphysics), all of which are in all probability parts of *al-Ḥāṣil wa-l-maḥṣūl*; there is no record whatsoever of any other commentary on the Aristotelian texts from his early period.

GS 11. *al-Inṣāf* (M35, A6)—*Fair Judgment* / Bio 20, SB 7, LB 5, EB 7

Alternate title: *al-Inṣāf wa-l-intiṣāf/ittiṣāf*.

See the description above, Chapter 2, W10. The surviving parts are as follows:

(a) *Šarḥ Kitāb al-Lām—Commentary on Aristotle's Metaphysics Lambda*
See Janssens "Lambda".
MSS: **Bursa**, Hüseyin Çelebi 1194 ff. 119b–123b (675H); **Cairo**, Muṣṭafā Fāḍil 6 Ḥikma, Dār al-Kutub 216 Ḥikma, Taymūr 86 Ḥikma.
Published: Badawī *Arisṭū* 22–33.

(b1) *Tafsīr Kitāb Uṯūlūjiyā*, (b2) *Šarḥ Uṯūlūjiyā—Exegesis* and *Commentary on the Theologia Aristotelis*.
For a bibliographical review see Maroun Aouad, "Théologie d'Aristote. G. Avicenne," in *DPhA* I,583–585.
MSS: **Bursa**, Hüseyin Çelebi 1194 ff. 123b–128a (675H); **Cairo** Muṣṭafā Fāḍil 6 Ḥikma, Dār al-Kutub 215 Ḥikma, 216 Ḥikma, Taymūr 86 Ḥikma, 102 Ḥikma; **Oxford**, Bodleian 980_7; **Tehran**, Majlis 1845 ff. 29–52, Tangābunī 335_2.—See Gutas "Ṣiġnāḫī" 12–13.
Published: Badawī *Arisṭū* 37–74 (cf. Gutas "Ṣiġnāḫī" 12–13).
Translation: French, Vajda "Théologie".

(c) *At-Taʿlīqāt ʿalā ḥawāšī Kitāb an-Nafs li-Arisṭūṭālīs—Marginal Glosses on Aristotle's De anima* / **LB 84**
Although this appears not to be part of the original *al-Inṣāf*, it is by style, contents, and approach similar; see Gutas "Glosses".
MS: **Cairo** Muṣṭafā Fāḍil 6 Ḥikma, Dār al-Kutub 214 Ḥikma, Taymūr 86 Ḥikma.
Published: Badawī *Arisṭū* 75–116.

GS 12a. *at-Taʿlīqāt* (M49, 163, 193, A8, 271, 89)—*Notes* / LB 41, EB 9, 86

See the description above, Chapter 2, W13.

The four recensions of the *Taʿlīqāt* are extant in the following MSS.

1. ʿAbd-ar-Razzāq recension: **Cairo**, Muṣṭafā Fāḍil 6 Ḥikma, Dār al-Kutub 2694 Ḥikma, Taymūr 67 Ḥikma; **Istanbul**, Ahmet III 3447_{52}, Ayasofya 2389, Feyzullah 2188_{2}, Köprülü 869_{3}, Nuruosmaniye 4894_{29}; **London**, Brit. Lib. 978_{7}; **Meshed**, Riżavī IV 1/416; **Tehran**, Khān 621, Majlis 2174, Malik 2007_{1}, Miškāt 261, Sipahsālār 2912_{11}.—Published: Badawī *Taʿlīqāt.*
2. Indexed (Lawkarī) recension: **Istanbul**, Ahmet III 3204, Ayasofya 2390, Köprülü 869_{2}, Nuruosmaniye 4894_{28}.—Published: Mousavian.
3. Recension arranged by subject: **Meshed**, Riżavī IV 1/415; **Tehran**, Khān 875, Millī 141_{4}.—Published: al-ʿUbaydī.
4. Partial recensions and extracts:
   (a) = GM-Ps 5: *Fawāʾid min Kitāb at-Taʿlīqāt fī sabab ijābat ad-duʿāʾ.* MSS: **Istanbul**, Ayasofya 4853, Nuruosmaniye 4894 f. 203^{b}.
   (b) Mahdavī 163 (p. 273), 193 (p. 285), 196 (p. 286), 211 (p. 292) and Reisman *Avicenniana* 14 and 51–52 refer to the following MSS as containing fragments which belong to the *Taʿlīqāt*: **Istanbul**, Ahmet III 3447_{51} ff. 315^{b}–326^{b}, Köprülü 1604 f. 72^{a}, Nuruosmaniye 4894 ff. 203^{b}–204^{a}, 565^{a}–569^{a}, Ragıp Paşa 1461; **London**, Brit. Lib. 1349_{3}; **Tehran**, Majlis I 1961, I 2937, I 1807, Miškāt 339 f. 62^{b}, 876, 1079 f. 89^{b}, Tangābunī 317_{21}.
   (c) See further El-Khodeiri "Opuscules" 345.
   (d) The EB 86 registers a title, *Taʿālīq fī l-manṭiq*, which may refer to an independent circulation of the logical part of the *Taʿlīqāt*, or a related collection. No manuscripts of it are known.

GS 12b. *Lawāḥiq* (M-, A-)—*Appendices* / LB 2, EB 5

See the description above, Chapter 2, W13.

I list the *Lawāḥiq* separately here because in conception it appears to have been different from what is now extant in the *Taʿlīqāt*. However, insofar as it existed only in conception, it cannot be given a separate number. But if it exists in actuality, then it appears to do so only as incorporated in the *Taʿlīqāt*, and hence it is given the same number with it.

GS 13. Masāʾil tudʿā *l-Buḏūr* (M-, A-)—Topics called *Seeds* / LB 76

The title *al-Buḏūr* occurs a number of times in the discussions between Avicenna and Bahmanyār, and the text itself appears to have been a collection of "'fragments' or philosophical 'jottings'." See the discussion in Reisman *Avicennan Tradition* 254–258. The collection of these texts itself may not have survived independently and was scattered among the papers of Avicenna after his death: there are certainly no known extant manuscripts. The compiler of the LB lists the title, but from the way that he does, "Topics/questions called *Seeds*," it appears that he did not have in front of him a manuscript with this title but that he derived the information about these texts from the same passages in the Avicenna and Bahmanyār correspondence as did Reisman. As for the word *buḏūr* itself, which is given differently in the manuscripts (cf. Gohlman 108.1 and the apparatus), the skeleton in the Istanbul MS Üniversite 4755 of LB is, الزور, with the first letter after the article unpointed, and the top part of the *zāʾ* a bit elongated above the line, possibly in a second attempt at revision by the same scribe, to look like a *ḏāl*, in which case this would be obviously *al-Buḏūr*.

iv. *Responsa*

GS 14. *K. al-Mubāḥaṯāt* (M105, A19, 257)—*Discussions* / SB 20, LB 43, EB 10

See the description above, Chapter 2, W12.

Due to the lengthy posthumous compilation process of the *Mubāḥaṯāt*, various passages from the material that eventually formed it appear independently in the manuscripts and also incorporated in pseudepigraphic compilations, like the Avicenna—Ibn-Abī-l-Ḫayr correspondence. Only those passages that have been signalled by title in the literature are listed below; an eventual scouring of all the Avicenna manuscripts will likely reveal more.

For the MSS of this work in its various recensions see Reisman *Avicennan Tradition*.

Published: (1) Independent (ʿAbd-ar-Razzāq aṣ-Ṣiġnāḫī) recension: Badawī *Arisṭū* 119–249; (2) Later recension: Bīdārfar.

Translation: French, partial, Michot "*Mubāḥatha III*".

The following independently transmitted passages under various concocted titles appear to belong to the *Mubāḥaṯāt* materials. This has still to be verified for the most part, while doubtless other such scattered fragments will be found in the manuscripts.

a. *Fī Masʾalat Kitāb an-Nafs* (M4h, A88)—*Question on De anima*

Alternate title: *aṣ-Ṣūra al-maʿqūla*.

This question (most likely by Ibn-Zayla) and answer from the *Mubāḥāṯāt* (§§ 707–709 Bīdārfar), with reference to the De anima part of the *Šifāʾ*, was

incorporated in the pseudepigraphic Avicenna—Ibn-Abī-l-Ḫayr correspondence. See Reisman *Avicennan Tradition* 139.
MSS: **Istanbul**, Hamidiye 1452_3, Nuruosmaniye 4894_{71}; **Tehran**, Miškāt 339_7.

b. ***Li-Kull ḥayawān wa-nabāt ṯabāt* (M4y, A-)—*Every Animal and Plant has Permanence***
This brief question and response pair from the *Mubāḥaṯāt* is also found in the pseudepigraphic Avicenna—Ibn-Abī-l-Ḫayr correspondence. See Reisman *Avicennan Tradition* 139.
MSS: **Berlin** Landberg 368 (Ahlwardt 5056) ff. 27^b–31^a; **Istanbul**, Ayasofya 4853 ff. 93^{a-b}, Nuruosmaniye 4894; **Tehran**, Miškāt 339_8 f. 62^a.
Published: ʿA. Nūrānī, ed., *Naṣīraddīn aṭ-Ṭūsī, Talkhis al-Muhassal, with Thirty Philosophical and Theological Treatises*, Tehran, 1980, 491–496.

c. ***Al-Ajwiba ʿan al-masāʾil al-ʿašr II* (M7, $A38_1$)—*Answers to Ten Questions II* / EB 57**
Alternate title: *al-Masāʾil al-ʿašr allatī waradat ʿalayhi fa-ajāba ʿanhā.*
Mahdavī 16 reports that the fourth question-answer pair occurs in the *Mubāḥaṯāt* (§ 426 Badawī), but the rest do not seem to be present there.
MSS: **Istanbul**, Üniversite 4755_{18} ff. 264^a–266^b; **Tehran**, Majlis 625_2.

d. ***R. fī Ḏamm māḍiġ al-ḫarāʾ* (M-, A-)—*Reproach of the Shit-eater* / EB 100**
Avicenna calls Abū-l-Qāsim al-Kirmānī by this name in at least two places in letters to Bahmanyār included in the *Mubāḥaṯāt*: *Mubāḥaṯa I*, 39,1 and note 15 Bīdārfar, and *Mubāḥaṯa III*, 69,4 Bīdārfar (see Michot "Réponse" 155 and 183, and cf. Reisman *Avicennan Tradition* 206). No such letter by this title is extant in the manuscripts, as far as I now know. It is likely that one of these letters of the *Mubāḥaṯāt* may have at one point circulated independently under this title registered in the EB.

e. ***Varia***
The same as in paragraph (d) above may apply to the immediately preceding title in the EB, no. 99, *R. Hamaj ar-raʿāʿ ilā sākin al-qilāʿ*, for Avicenna calls those unworthy to receive his philosophy "rabble" (*raʿāʿ*) in the same passage of *Mubāḥaṯa I*, but also "parasites" and "gnats" (*hamaj*) at the very end of the *Išārāt*, above T10 § 6 and note 8. No such letter by this title is extant in the manuscripts, but if it existed, it may well have been another passage from the correspondence in the *Mubāḥaṯāt*.
Mahdavī 133 (p. 259), 134 (p. 260), 194 (p. 285), 200 (p. 288), 202 (p. 289), 224 (p. 296) reports on some materials, some of which go under the name of Bahmanyār, which belong to the *Mubāḥaṯāt* and the *Šifāʾ*.

MSS: **Berlin** 5124; **Istanbul**, Ahmet III 1584_{20}, Ayasofya 4829_{10}, 4849_{4}, 4853, Hamidiye 1448_{25}, Köprülü 1589_{50}, Nuruosmaniye $4894_{39,74}$, Pertev 617, Ragıp Paşa 1461_{24}; **Leiden** 1484.

v. *Pseudepigraphs, to be authenticated*

GS-Ps 1. *ʿUyūn al-masāʾil* (M189, A16)—*Elements of* [*Philosophical*] *Topics* / LB 79

This collection of brief discussions of twenty-two philosophical topics in logic, physics, and metaphysics is attributed in the manuscripts to Fārābī, Avicenna, Abū-l-Barakāt al-Baġdādī, and others. It is quite certain that it is not by Fārābī, as demonstrated independently of each other by both Janos (Appendix One, 383–396) and Kaya "Şukûk". The LB lists it among the works of Avicenna—but only, apparently, in the copy of the LB preserved in the Istanbul MS Üniversite 4755, f. 317[b] margin[8]—while the text of the treatise is included in the same manuscript (ff. 285[b]–291[b]). The treatise has distinctive Avicennan features, again as demonstrated by both Janos and Kaya "Şukûk", who suggest Avicennan circles as the probable milieu of its composition. It is to be studied further in the context, and will contribute to an understanding, of the development of a pseudepigraphic corpus of Avicennan works within a century of his death, as is indicated also by its early attribution to him in the Üniversite MS.

MSS: See Kaya "Şukûk" 63–66.

Published: Dieterici *Abhandlungen* (text) 56–65.

Translations: German, Dieterici *Abhandlungen* (translation); Spanish, Manuel Alonso Alonso, "Las "ʿUyūn al-masāʾil" de al-Fārābī," *Al-Andalus* 24 (1959) 251–273.

GS-Ps 2. *Jawāb masāʾil katīra* / LB 78; *Jawāb li-ʿiddat masāʾil* / LB 82—*Answers to Many Questions*

Collections of a varying number of questions and answers under this or similar headings are contained in the manuscripts. From the title listings in the LB, manifestly the compiler's or a scribe's attempt somehow to describe the manuscript material in front of him, it is clear that these circulated early

[8] Gohlman 108, line 2, omits this title without registering in the apparatus that it appears in his MS B (the Üniversite MS), though he does list it in the Appendix, p. 152, in the column under MS B, with the correct serial number (79) it occupies in the LB in that MS.

in a loose fashion. Their nature, authenticity, and especially whether they are to be attributed to the *Mubāḥaṯāt* or the *Taʿlīqāt* are to be investigated.

a. *Al-Ajwiba ʿan al-masāʾil al-ḥikmiyya* (M10, A22)—*Answers to Philosophical Questions* / EB 59?
Alternate title: *al-Masāʾil al-ḥikmiyya wa-hiya ḫams wa-ʿišrūn masʾala suʾila š-Šayḫ ʿanhā.*

EB 59 lists another set of twenty answers, not twenty-five, which may or may not be related to this set. Manifestly Avicennan material—if it is Avicennan—circulated in the form of questions and answers and the manuscripts collected them under such generic titles.

MSS: **Bursa**, Hüseyin Çelebi 1194 ff. 128^a–131^b; **Istanbul**, Ayasofya 4829_4, 4849_{23} ff. 126^b–131^b, Nuruosmaniye 4894_{117}; **Lisbon**, Academia das Ciencias, Arab. V.293 ff. 26^a–32^b; **Tehran**, Majlis 599_2 ff. 103^a–115^b (570H), Tangābunī 324_1.

b. *Al-Ajwiba ʿan al-masāʾil* (M9, A21)—*Answers to Questions* / EB 59?
Alternate title: *al-Masāʾil al-iṯnā wa-ʿišrūn.*

See the preceding entry.

MSS: **Istanbul**, Pertev 617_8 ff. 26^b–39^b; **Tehran**, Miškāt 1149 ff. 345^b–352^b.

GS-Ps 3. *Al-Majālis as-sabʿa bayn aš-Šayḫ wa-l-ʿĀmirī* (M107, A20)—*Seven Sessions between the Šayḫ and al-ʿĀmirī* / LB (92)

An intriguing collection of forty-one questions and answers in seven sessions. The title in the sole known manuscript is as given above, while at the very end there is a reference to aš-Šayḫ Abū ʿAlī b. Sīnā. Thus both in the title and at the end the person in question is referred to only as aš-Šayḫ, and not as aš-Šayḫ ar-Raʾīs, which is the ubiquitous title of Avicenna. Each question and answer is introduced by *qāla s-sāʾil* and *qāla l-mujīb*, never with a name. This raises two problems: who the interlocutor of ʿĀmirī is, and who is asking and who responding. Whoever supplemented the LB before the middle of the thirteenth century—as the LB appears in IAU but not in the Üniversite MS—lists the title as, *Ajwiba li-suʾālāt saʾalahu ʿanhā Abū l-Ḥasan al-ʿĀmirī, wa-hiya arbaʿa ʿašrata masʾala,* making it clear that ʿĀmirī is the questioner. It is known that ʿĀmirī was in Buḫārā in 985–986, and he could have met Avicenna then. Avicenna was born much before the transmitted date of 980 (see Gutas "*Maḏhab*"), so he would have been in his mid to late teens during this meeting. But ʿĀmiri, who was born in 912, was much older than Avicenna, and the question remains whether it was he who would have asked the very young Avicenna rather than the other way around. Besides, the doctrinal content of the answers is much

more consistent with ʿĀmirī's views than Avicenna's (private communication from Cüneyt Kaya), so there would seem to be little doubt that ʿĀmirī is the respondent. In his *Amad*, where ʿĀmirī lists his works, he mentions explicitly that he wrote "answers to various [religious] questions" (Rowson 55), which would perfectly describe this discussion. But the identity of the questioner remains very much open. The unique manuscript that contains the text refers to ʿĀmirī's interlocutor as *aš-Šayḫ* (and not *aš-Šayḫ ar-Raʾīs*, as just mentioned), and if the discussion did indeed take place between the seventy-four year old ʿĀmirī and the teenager Avicenna, it is difficult to see how Avicenna would be referred to in this context as *aš-Šayḫ*. Furthermore, the unique MS of the text, Ragıp Paşa 1461, also contains materials from the *Mubāḥaṯāt* (see Reisman *Avicennan Tradition*, index), which would point to a provenance of the manuscript from circles transmitting the papers and works of Bahmanyār and Avicenna: in this context it is even more difficult to accept that Avicenna would be called by the scribes in these circles as simply *aš-Šayḫ* and not *aš-Šayḫ ar-Raʾīs*. There is, finally, the additional problem regarding the number of the questions; it may be that the person who supplemented the LB as we find it in IAU (or his source) had access to a collection of just fourteen of the forty-one questions. Cf. further Elvira Wakelnig in Rudolph 175.
MS: **Istanbul**, Ragıp Paşa 1461_{28} ff. 150^{a}–162^{b}.

GS-Ps 4. Masāʾil tarjamahā bi-*t-Taḏkīr* (M-, A-)—Questions which he entitled *Reminder* / LB 77

Only the LB lists this title, specifying that the text was given the title *at-Taḏkīr*. There are no other references to this title and no text with this title is known to exist in manuscript. In the *Išārāt* Avicenna uses the word to introduce three sections in the second half of the book, Namaṭ 2.8 and 6.41, *taḏkīr*, and 10.26, *taḏkira*. It is not known whether the *Išārāt* references are related to the naming with this title, whether by Avicenna himself or some compiler or forger, of whatever collection of texts this was.

B. Logic and Language (GL)

i. Logic

Avicenna wrote three kinds of works on logic: (1) general works comprising all or most parts of logic, as classified in the ninefold division of the Aristotelian Organon (Eisagoge, Categories, De Interpretatione, Prior Analytics, Posterior Analytics, Topics, Sophistics, Rhetoric, Poetics), (2) works on particular subjects and problems in logic, and (3) responses to logical questions posed to him by various correspondents. Of the general works, (1a) some he wrote especially for the larger summae of philosophy (listed above under GS), and (1b) some he wrote independently of the summae, though a few of those were subsequently embedded in the summae. These independent general works on logic tended to be occasional pieces, mostly written for sponsors who requested them from him, and they bear titles which by and large seem to be designations by bibliographers rather than the specific names that Avicenna himself may have given them. They survive in various forms and under various titles, which makes their identification and categorization somewhat difficult.

i. *General Expository*

GL 1. *Al-Muḫtaṣar al-awsaṭ fī l-manṭiq* (M108, A45)—*Middle Summary on Logic* / Bio 1, SB 11, LB 8, EB 16, 16a

Alternate titles: *al-Awsaṭ, al-Awsaṭ al-Jurjānī.*

As noted by Eichner "Universal Science" 73n9 and "The *Categories* in Avicenna" 80–85, and demonstrated by Kalbarczyk, this is not identical to the logic of the *Najāt* (contrary to the claim of Mahdavī 217). There are some sections which are indeed identical with it, and some which are similar, but the entire work is different. In many aspects the *Awsaṭ* is more detailed than the logic of the *Najāt,* and it contains only the first five books of the Organon, Eisagoge through Burhān, omitting Topics, Sophistics, Rhetoric, and Poetics. From the entry in the EB 16a, *al-Jadal al-mulḥaq bi-K. al-Awsaṭ,* it appears that at some point somebody added to the work a chapter on Topics, since the original lacked one, and that this chapter circulated independently. But there is no further information either on the author of this appendix or its fate; at present no such work is known in manuscript.

MSS: **Istanbul**, Carullah 1144_6, Hatice Sultan 213, Köprülü 869_4 ff. 126^a–189^b, Nuruosmaniye 2763 (528H), 4894_{54} ff. 253^b–303^a; **Tehran**, Miškāt 1149 ff. 148^b–203^a (Cat. 3:4, 2410–2411).

Published: The part on the Categories only in Kalbarczyk 326–349.

GS 6a. *Al-Muḫtaṣar al-aṣġar fī l-manṭiq* (M-, A-)—*Shorter Summary on Logic* / Bio 17

In the Biography Jūzjānī explicitly says (74.9–76.1 Gohlman) that this book, written in Jurjān, that is, in about 1013–1014, was the logic which Avicenna later included in the *Najāt*. Mahdavī 217–218 for some reason conflates this title with that of *al-Muḫtaṣar al-awsaṭ* (perhaps because they were both composed in Jurjān?) and says that the *Awsaṭ* is the one included in the *Najāt*. However, Jūzjānī's attestation in this regard cannot be impugned: he was intimately involved in the compilation and publication of the *Najāt* (see W7), and it is quite unlikely that he would have confused the titles *al-Awsaṭ* and *al-Aṣġar* or that he would have used two different titles to refer to a single work.

Further confirmation comes from Ibn-aṣ-Ṣalāḥ, who quotes from the *Awsaṭ*, a quotation which does not appear in the *Najāt* (see Nicholas Rescher, "Ibn al-Ṣalāḥ on Aristotle on Causation," in his *Studies in Arabic Philosophy*, Pittsburgh: University Press, 1966, 68, and Kalbarczyk 307–308). If the *Awsaṭ* were the logic of *Najāt* we should have found this quotation there.

The *Awsaṭ* and the *Aṣġar*, therefore, are two different compositions, and it was the latter, the *Aṣġar*, which was later included in the *Najāt*, that baffled the scholars in Šīrāz to whom Avicenna responded in the "historic" fashion described by Jūzjānī (76–80 Gohlman; below, GL 15).

The text of the *Aṣġar* is preserved in the *Najāt*, but there are no independent manuscripts of it recorded and no entries for it in SB, LB, or EB. However, given the confusion between the *Awsaṭ* and the *Aṣġar*, it may be that some manuscripts have not been identified as those of the *Aṣġar* because they were thought to be of the *Awsaṭ*.

Publication and translations: see above under GS 6.

GL 2. *Ar-Risāla al-Mūjaza fī uṣūl al-manṭiq* (M116, A31, 44)—*Epitome of the Principles of Logic*

Alternate titles: *Jawāmiʿ ʿilm al-manṭiq, ʿIlm al-burhān, Fī Uṣūl ʿilm al-burhān.*

In the oldest manuscript in which this work is preserved, Istanbul Üniversite 4755 (ff. 20[a]–43[b]), it contains two *maqālas*, the first on Eisagoge, Categories, and De interpretatione (so labeled in the headings of sub-sections), and the second on Prior Analytics (see Eichner "Universal Science" 73n10, also for the relation to the *Šifāʾ, Burhān*). At the end of this text there is the marginal note of the scribe: *Balaġati l-muqābalatu bi-n-nusḫati llatī nuqilat minhā wa-kānati l-ummu bi-ḫaṭṭi Bahmanyār tilmīḏi š-Šayḫi raḥimahumā llāhu, wa-ṣaḥḥat bi-ḥasabi ṭ-ṭāqati fī Muḥarram sanat 589.*

The title well reflects the contents: in the classification of the works of the Organon, the first four books, the Eisagoge through the Prior Analytics, were considered preliminary to demonstration and hence the principles of logic (*uṣūl al-manṭiq*), while the fifth, Posterior Analytics, represented demonstration (*burhān*), and the remaining four what protected demonstration (cf. Gutas "Paul the Persian"). And given the authority of the copy by Bahmanyār from which this treatise was copied, it appears beyond doubt that the original by Avicenna was precisely this text. In the Istanbul MS Nuruosmaniye 4894, f. 32ᵃ (and in Ahmet III 3447, according to Mahdavī), the end of this treatise is immediately followed by a text introduced as, *Bāb al-burhān min al-mūjaz*, as if it were its continuation. See below GL 12.

MSS: **Istanbul**, Ahmet III 3447_{64+65}, Nuruosmaniye 4894_{7} ff. 16ᵇ–57ᵇ, Üniversite 4755_{3} ff. 20ᵃ–43ᵇ (588H); **Tehran**, Miškāt 1149 ff. 204ᵇ–233ᵃ.

GL 3. *Al-Manṭiq al-mūjaz* (M114, A44)—*Logic Epitomized* / SB 15, LB 30, EB 22

Alternate title: *al-Mūjaz al-kabīr fī l-manṭiq*.

This is a brief essay on logic in three parts (*maqālas*):[9] (a) Preliminaries (*muqaddamāt*), covering matters in the Eisagoge and De Interpretatione; (b) Declaration of desired goals (*al-ifṣāḥ bi-* [sic] *l-ġaraḍ al-maṭlūb*), covering syllogisms and their figures (referring to Aristotle as "our ancient teacher," *muʿallimunā l-mutaqaddim*); and (c) Concluding matters (*tamām*), covering demonstrative, dialectical, rhetorical, sophistical, and poetic syllogisms.

MSS: **Istanbul**, Ahmet III 1548_{25}, Ayasofya 4829_{7} ff. 19ᵇ–26ᵇ, 4849_{19} ff. 88ᵃ–108ᵃ, Carullah 1441_{2}, Nuruosmaniye 4894_{118} ff. 543ᵃ–550ᵃ.

GS 3a. *Al-Mūjaz aṣ-ṣaġīr fī l-manṭiq* (M115, A43)—*Shorter Epitome on Logic* / LB 32, EB 25

This brief essay on all nine parts of logic was incorporated, with the addition of three paragraphs to the Posterior Analytics (*K. al-Burhān*) segment, into the *Elements of Philosophy* (*ʿUyūn al-ḥikma*; see above GS 3) as its Logic part.

MSS: **Istanbul**, Carullah 1260_{4}, Üniversite 4755_{1} ff. 1ᵇ–9ᵇ (588H);[10] **Leiden** 1446; **Vatican** 977_{7}.

9 Cf. Eichner "Universal Science" 73n10.

10 In the margin of the last page of this treatise (f. 9ᵇ) it is noted that this MS was collated with a copy from Avicenna's holograph: *qābaltu hāḏā l-Mūǧaza bi-nusḫatin* ⟨*bi-*⟩*ḫaṭṭi Hibatillāhi bni Ṣāʿidi bni t-Tilmīḏi l-manqūlati* [sic] *min ḫaṭṭi l-muṣannifi raḥimahu llāhu.*

ii. *General Versified*

GL 4. ***Urjūza fī ʿilm al-manṭiq*** **(M22, A25, 33)—*The Science of Logic, in verse* / SB 25, LB 31, EB 62**

Alternate titles: *ar-Rajaz al-manṭiqī, al-Qaṣīda al-muzdawija, Mīzān an-naẓar, al-Qaṣīda al-muṣarraʿa.*

A didactic poem in the metre known as *rajaz*, numbering 290 verses and covering all nine parts of the Organon.

MSS: **Escorial** 1561_{3}; **Hyderabad** III 732; **Istanbul**, Ahmet III 3447_{77}, Ayasofya 4829_{32}, Nuruosmaniye 4894_{125}, Üniversite 4755_{2}; **Leiden** 1458 (515H); **Lisbon**, Academia das Ciencias, Arab. V.293 ff. 44[b]–53[b]; **London**, Brit. Lib. 974_{47}; **Rampur** I 433, 712; **Tehran**, Malik 2019_{5}, Miškāt 1149 ff. 330[a]–333[b]; **Vatican** 977_{6}.

Published: Schmoelders 11–23 (Arabic numbers); *Manṭiq al-mašriqiyyīn* 1–18.

Translations: Complete: Modern Latin, Schmoelders 26–42. Partial: Section on the Categories, English, Gutas "Logical Works" 63–64.

iii. *Particular Expository*

GL 5. ***M. fī l-Išāra ilā ʿilm al-manṭiq*** **(M28, A37)—*Pointer to the Science of Logic* / SB (33), LB 37, EB 15**

Alternate titles: *Al-Išāra fī l-manṭiq; Taʿālīq al-manṭiq; Fī Masʾala min al-manṭiq.*

This is a brief discussion of the usefulness of logic (it is like *ʿarūḍ* and grammar), the categories, the five predicables, and the modal concepts of possibility and necessity. Probably an early work, it includes references to Aristotle, Plato, and Porphyry by name.

MSS: **Istanbul**, Ayasofya 4849 ff. 32[a]–33[a], 4853_{24}, Nuruosmaniye $4894_{37,109}$, Üniversite 4755_{17} ff. 261[a]–264[a].

GL 6. ***K. al-Ḥudūd*** **(M57, 186, A9, 90)—*Definitions* / SB 31, LB 26, EB 41**

Alternate titles: *al-Ḥudūd wa-r-rusūm*. The Istanbul MS Üniversite 4755 has the following title (f. 292[a]) and colophon (f. 305[b]): *Kitāb al-Ḥudūd wa-yuʿrafu bi-l-Mabāḥiṯ aṣ-ṣadīqiyya; tammat al-Mabāḥiṯ aṣ-ṣadīqiyya wa-hiya l-Ḥudūd*; see Reisman *Avicennan Tradition* 161n128.

A booklet of 72 brief definitions ranging from 'definition' to 'pre-eternity' (*qidam*).

MSS: **Berlin** 5375; **Cairo**, Taymūr 200 Majāmīʿ; **Escorial** 703_{9}; **Istanbul**, Ahmet III 3447_{44}, Ayasofya 2661_{2}, 2684_{5}, 4852_{5}, Carullah 1260_{6}, Fatih 3172_{2}, Hamidiye 1448_{33}, Kaptan Paşa 1262, Köprülü 868_{4}, 869_{9} ff. 225[b]–229[b], Nuruosmaniye 4894_{63} ff. 332^a–336^a, Ragıp Paşa 1461_{13}, Revan 2042_1, Üniversite 1458_{87}, 4390_1, 4711_2 (579H), 4754_3, 4755_{23} ff. 292^a–305^b; **Kabul**, Ṣiddīqī ff. 23^a–27^b (551H);[11] **Leiden** 1460, 1461, 1462, 1463; **London**, Brit. Lib. 978_{23}, India Off. 771; **Manchester** 384_0; **Meshed**, Riżavī I 3/101, IV 1/636, 637, 638, 639, 640, 641; **Oxford**, Bodleian 102_2, II 290_1; **Paris** 1338_8; **Rampur** I 390, 712, II 818; **Tehran**, Khān 875, Majlis 611_5, 634_{37}, 1061_{23}; Malik 2005_{10}, 2012_4, 2015_1, 2019_1; Miškāt 398_1, 1022_{14}, 1053_{43}, 1079_{25}, 1149 ff. 32^a–35^b, Ṭabāṭabā'ī 1231_{18}, 1373_{10}, Tangābunī 205_6, 308_2, 317_8.

Published: Goichon *Définitions*; al-Aʿsam (as in note 11) 229–263.

Translation: French, Goichon *Définitions*.

a. ***Al-ʿUqūl*** **(M186, A90 [?], 186)—*Intellects***

Alternate titles: *al-Fuṣūl, Taʿrīf ism Allāh wa-šarḥuhu.*

The part of *al-Ḥudūd* on the intellect (Goichon 11.1–13.12) circulated separately in a paraphrastic version and with additional material under these titles, as Mahdavī 282 recognized. The precise relationship of this text to the *Ḥudūd* has to be investigated. This provides a good case of the way in which Avicenna's authentic works were cannibalized, paraphrased, and recycled as independent and sometimes pseudepigraphic treatises.

MSS: **Istanbul**, Nuruosmaniye 4894 ff. 449^a–450^a, 4898_{86}; **Meshed**, Riżavī IV 1/667.—A90 lists the following two MSS, without providing incipits to identify them: **Hyderabad** III 730; **Rampur** I 712.

Published: Šamsaddīn 414–418.

b. ***Jumal al-ḥudūd*** **(M-, A-)—*Main Points of Definitions***

Michot "Recueil avicennien" 128 says that this collection of 124 definitions does not correspond to the *K. al-Ḥudūd*.

MS: **Bursa**, Hüseyin Çelebi 1194 ff. 156^a–158^b.

GL 7. *M. fī Ġaraḍ Qāṭīġūriyās* (M-, A-)—*On the Purpose of the* Categories / SB 24, LB 57

The reliable bibliographies SB and LB report such a title but it appears not to be extant in any known manuscript. Avicenna's critical attitude toward the *Categories* developed early and he evicted the subject from logic (Chapter 6.4 above). Incidental remarks in some other works aside, his most extensive discussion of the nature and purpose of Categories is in *The Cure*, which

---

11 Described by ʿAbdalamīr al-Aʿsam, *al-Muṣṭalaḥ al-falsafī ʿinda l-ʿArab, nuṣūṣ min at-turāṯ al-falsafī fī ḥudūd al-ašyā' wa-rusūmihā*, Cairo: al-Hay'a al-Miṣriyya al-ʿāmma li-l-kitāb, 1989, 128–134.

makes the loss of this particular work deplorable, unless it is an extract from *The Cure* itself which at an early stage (the SB was compiled before 553/1159) circulated independently under this title.

GL 8. *R. fī Ḫaṭa' man qāla inna l-kammiyya jawhar* (M67, A68)—*On the Error of Those Who Hold that Quantity Is Substance* / LB 49, EB 35a

Alternate title: *al-Kammiyya laysat bi-jawhar.*

As Mahdavī 97 points out, the subject treated here is related to the discussion of the categories in the third book of the *Ilāhiyyāt* of the *Šifā'*, and Faḫr-ad-Dīn ar-Rāzī has this treatise and the next in mind in *faṣl* 15 of book two of his *al-Mabāḥiṯ al-mašriqiyya* (I, 161).

MSS: **Istanbul**, Ayasofya 4849_{12} ff. 54[a]–55[b], 4853_{13}, Üniversite 4755_{21} ff. 283[b]–285[a] (588H).

GL 9. *R. fī Ḫaṭa' man qāla inna š-šay' jawhar wa-'araḍ* (M68, A59)—*On the Error of Those Who Hold that Something Can Be Substance and Accident Simultaneously* / SB (40), LB 91, EB 35b

This title is given by the Istanbul MS Nuruosmaniye 4894. It is a brief treatise on the subject indicated by the title. See the preceding entry.

MSS: **Bursa**, Hüseyin Çelebi 1194 ff. 143[a]–146[b]; **Istanbul**, Ayasofya 4853_{15} ff. 52[b]–58[a], Nuruosmaniye 4894_{36} ff. 201[b]–203[b]; **Princeton** (ELS) 308 ff. 12[b]–16[a]; **Tehran**, Majlis 599_{11} ff. 209[a]–216[a] (570H), Tangābunī 324_{5}.

GL 10. *Bayān ḏawāt al-jiha* (M42, A42)—*Explanation of the Modal Propositions* / SB 17, LB 29, EB 23

Alternate title: *Fī 'Ukūs ḏawāt al-jiha, Ḏawāt al-jiha.*

It is referred to in *Twenty Questions* (*mas'ala* 11).

MSS: **Cairo**, Muṣṭafā Fāḍil 6 Ḥikma ff. 168[b]–187[a], Dār al-Kutub 217 Ḥikma

GL 11. *An-Nukat fī l-manṭiq* (M125, A46)—*Subtle Points in Logic* / EB 98

Alternate titles: *al-Fuṣūl al-mūjaza, Ma'rifat al-ašyā'.*

Brief discussion of the "principles of syllogisms," which here are given as four: sense perception, estimation, faculty of conventional knowledge, i.e., of the endoxa (*al-quwwa at-ta'ārufiyya*), and the theoretical faculty, followed by a discussion of the kinds of propositions, categorical and conditional, both conjunctive (*muttaṣila*) and disjunctive (*munfaṣila*).

This is either a disjointed note or a fragment from a longer composition. It is to be dated rather early in Avicenna's career: his enumeration of the principles of syllogisms is much shorter than all of the other discussions of this topic in his later works, as is his unique appellation of the faculty perceiving the endoxa (*mašhūrāt*) as *al-quwwa at-taʿārufiyya*, never repeated in all his other discussions of the same subject (for which see Gutas "Empiricism", section II). It came into circulation by the middle of the thirteenth century (EB 98).

MSS: **Istanbul**, Ayasofya 4829_{14} ff. 57^{b}–58^{b}, 4849_{13} ff. 55^{b}–58^{b}; Nuruosmaniye 4894_{111}.

Published: in the margin of *Šarḥ al-Hidāya al-Aṯīriyya*, pp. 327–329, under the title, *Fī Maʿrifat al-ašyāʾ*, Tehran 1313.

GL 12. *Fī Uṣūl ʿilm al-burhān / Kitāb al-Mūjaz fī l-manṭiq* (M-, A-)—*On the Principles of Demonstration / Epitome of Logic*

The title *Kitāb al-Mūjaz fī l-manṭiq* is made up by scribes. In the Istanbul MS Nuruosmaniye 4894, f. 16^{v}, it appears as given here, in large red lettering. Immediately following this, however, there is a *basmala* and a *ḥamdala* and then the following title, also in red, *al-maqāla al-ūlā min ar-risāla al-mūjaza fī l-manṭiq; maʿānī kitāb Īsāġūljī* [*sic*]. What follows next is the text of *ar-Risāla al-mūjaza fī uṣūl al-manṭiq*, as given above under GL 2, which continues through to the end of the section on Prior Analytics, *qiyās*. Then follows another title in large red lettering (f. 32^{a}, last line), *Bāb al-burhān min al-Mūjaz li-š-šayḫ ar-raʾīs Abī ʿAlī b. Sīnā*, after which there is another *basmala* and then another title, in smaller letters but also in red (f. 32^{b}, top), *Fī Uṣūl ʿilm al-burhān wa-bayān anna kull taʿlīm wa-taʿallum min ʿilm sābiq*. At the end of this section on demonstration, the following sections, taken from *al-Majmūʿ/ al-ʿArūḍiyya*, are introduced also in small red letters, as follows:

- f. 46^{b}: *al-Qawl fī taʿrīf al-qiyās al-jadalī* (= *al-Majmūʿ* 47–79 Ṣāliḥ)
- f. 53^{a}: *Fī maʿānī tabkīt as-sufisṭāʾiyyīn wa taʿrīf wujūh al-muġālaṭa* (= *al-Majmūʿ* 81–85 Ṣāliḥ)
- f. 54^{a}: *Fī maʿānī Rīṭūrīqā wa-huwa Kitāb al-ḫiṭāba* (= *al-Majmūʿ* 87–98 Ṣāliḥ, ending in line 4 with the words, *bal bi-fāʿilātihā*).

From this it is clear that of the compound treatise presented in the Nuruosmaniye 4894 MS under the title *Kitāb al-Mūjaz fī l-manṭiq* (*Epitome of Logic*), only the part on *Burhān* is "original" in the sense that it is not copied from or does not constitute another treatise, as far as we can tell. The title itself of this part, *Fī Uṣūl ʿilm al-burhān*, may well indicate that it was intended to be a sequel to the preceding treatise, *ar-Risāla al-Mūjaza fī uṣūl*

al-manṭiq, though there is no certainty. No medieval bibliography mentions this or the preceding treatise, but it hardly matters. The authenticity of the *Burhān* part is established by its close relationship to the text of the *Burhān* in the *Šifāʾ*, as shown by Eichner "Universal Science" 73n10. The question of the author of this collage of disparate pieces into a treatise comprising all nine parts of logic remains to be investigated through consideration of all extant manuscripts. Mahdavī 223 suggests that it was Avicenna himself, but this seems unlikely, given the discussion above.
MSS. See the MSS listed under GL 2 above.

GL 13. *M. fī Taʿaqqub al-mawḍiʿ al-jadalī* (M48, A26)—*Tracing the Dialectical Commonplace* / SB 28, LB 48, EB 19

MSS: **Bursa**, Hüseyin Çelebi 1194 ff. 97[a]–101[a]; **Cairo**, Taymūr 200 Majāmīʿ; **Istanbul**, Ahmet III 1584_{26}, Ayasofya $4829_{8,23}$, 4849_{21} ff. 109[a]–115[a], 4852_{7}, Carullah 1441_{3}, Nuruosmaniye 4894_{115}, Üniversite 3328_{11}, Veliyüddin 2134_{15}.
Published: Dānešpažūh in Mohaghegh and Izutsu 61–77.

GL 14. *Fī Anna ʿilm Zayd ġayr ʿilm ʿAmr* (M-, A-)—*That the Knowledge of Zayd Is Other than the Knowledge of ʿAmr* / SB (41), LB 63, EB 33

This title, given in all the bibliographies, is not extant in any known manuscript.

iv. *Responsa*

GL 15. *Al-Ajwiba ʿan al-masāʾil al-ʿišrīniyya* (M8, A39)—*Answers to Twenty Questions* [*on Logic*] / Bio 18, LB 74, EB 58

Alternate titles: *ʿIšrūn masʾala fī l-manṭiq*, *al-Masāʾil al-ġarība*.

This logical correspondence may be dated to around 1026–1027 (Street) when scholars in Šīrāz asked the questions upon reading Avicenna's *Shorter Summary on Logic* (above, GS 6a), which was originally composed in Jurjān around 1013 and later incorporated in the *Salvation*. The questions cover material in *The Salvation* that corresponds to the subjects discussed in the *Prior Analytics* (see Street 99, with full listing of the questions). The *Twenty Questions* is a transitional text in the developing exposition of Avicenna's logic. It allows us to focus on the changes Avicenna made to the Aristotelian system that seemed strange to his contemporaries.
MSS: **Cairo** VI 104; **Istanbul**, Ahmet III 1584_{27}, Ayasofya $4829_{5,18}$, 4849_{22}, 4852_{6} ff. 93[b]–110[b], Carullah 1441_{4}, Nuruosmaniye 4894_{116}.
Published: Dānešpažūh in Mohaghegh and Izutsu 79–103.

v. *Pseudepigraphs, to be authenticated*

GL-Ps 1. ***Mafātīḥ al-ḫazā'in fī l-manṭiq*** **(M111, A-)—*Keys to the Trasures in Logic* / LB (95)**

Introductory piece on logic in eight "steps" (*martaba*), which seems to survive in the only manuscript listed below in Tehran. Mahdavī 219 reports that on the verso of the first page the scribe notes, in red letters, "*Mafātīḥ al-ḫazā'in*, by the Šayḫ ar-Ra'īs Abū-ʿAlī Ibn-Sīnā, God have mercy on him." The title is found among the additional entries to the LB listed by IAU, doubtless recording it from a manuscript, which means that it was in circulation before the middle of the thirteenth century.
MS: **Tehran**, Malik 2022_1.

GL-Ps 2. ***Al-Bahja fī l-manṭiq*** **(M41, A42)—*Splendor, on Logic* = ? *K. al-Muhja—Book of the Lifeblood* (?) / EB 20**

This appears to be a phantom work. It is listed only in the late EB as *K. al-Muhja*, without any further explanation. Ergin (first edition) no. 191 and Anawati record the existence of a title *al-Bahja fī l-manṭiq*, which on the face of it would appear to be the *Muhja* miswritten (or vice versa), in an enigmatic MS in Istanbul, Kaptan Paşa 1243. Ergin (second edition) 16, no. 41, repeats the entry without any further information. According to him, the Kaptan Paşa collection is in Eyüp. Sezgin in GAS VI,433 ff., however, does not list such a collection either independently or under Eyüp Camii.
MS: **Istanbul**, Kaptan Paşa 1243_{22} ff. 58^b–71^a.

GL-Ps 3. ***Al-Qiyās*** **(M4a, A35)—*Syllogism***

An answer allegedly by Avicenna on syllogism (*al-Qiyās*) is found in the pseudepigraphic correspondence with Abū–Saʿīd. Some of the answers in this correspondence derive from Avicennan material from the *Mubāḥaṯāt*, though apparently not this one, which in all probability is spurious; see Reisman *Avicennan Tradition* 141 note.
MSS: **Istanbul**, Hamidiye 1452_3, Nuruosmaniye 4894_{66} ff. 361^b–362^b, Pertev 617_{30}; **Tehran**, Miškāt 339_4.
Published: M.T. Dānešpažūh, "Pāsuḫ-i Ibn-i Sīnā bi-Šayḫ-i Abū Saʿīd Abī l-Ḫayr, az āṯār-i Ibn Sīnā, bā muqaddima va taṣḥīḥ," *Farhang-i Īrān Zamīn* 1.2 (1332/1953) 189–204.—See also Reisman "New Standard" 567n30.

GL-Ps 4. ***Fī Ḍabṭ anwāʿ al-qaḍāyā*** **(M37, A34)—*The Species of Propositions***

Alternate title: *al-Qaḍāyā fī l-manṭiq.*

A poem of seven verses, rhyming in *q*, on the fifteen species of propositions; not from Avicenna's *Urjūza*. The *rajaz* didactic poems of Avicenna normally rhyme only the two hemistichs of each verse, not the end of all verses, as is the case here. Also, its absence from all bibliographies and its presence only in three late manuscripts does not suggest authenticity.
MSS: **Istanbul**, Ahmet 3447_{36}, Nuruosmaniye 3427_{9}, 4894_{53}.

GL-Ps 5. ***Talḫīṣ al-Manṭiq*** **(M152, A27)—*Precise Exposition of Logic***

According to Mahdavī 267, this work is listed by Ergin (no. 47), by Brockelmann (no. 23a), and Anawati (no. 27), although the Fatih MS upon which Ergin relies does not attribute it to Avicenna, while the Tehran MS Millī gives the title *Iʿānat al-manṭiq* and attributes it to Nasafī.
MSS: **Istanbul**, Fatih 3170 (688H); **Tehran**, Millī 992_{20}.

a. ***Al-Maʿānī fī l-manṭiq; al-Imlāʾ fī l-manṭiq*** **(M-, A-)—*Subjects in Logic; Logic by Dictation* / EB 89, 91**
These titles are listed in the EB; they may refer to any of the preceding generic titles. There are no known manuscripts.

II. LANGUAGE

i. *Expository*

GL 16. ***Asbāb ḥudūṯ al-ḥurūf*** **(M25, A47)—*On the Causes of the Articulation of the Letters* / SB 27, LB 22**

Alternate titles: *Fī Maʿrifat ḥudūṯ al-ḥurūf, Maḫārij al-ḥurūf, Maḫārij aṣ-ṣawt.*

A treatise on the phonetics of the Arabic language composed upon the request of Abū-Manṣūr Muḥammad al-Jabbān, a philologist and littérateur at the court of ʿAlāʾ-ad-Dawla in Iṣfahān. It was accordingly written after 415/1024. It survives in two versions, one in a slightly more floral style than the other; their origination and their causes remain unresolved. Mahdavī reports that the Tehran MS Majlis 599_{5} contains both.
MSS: **Bursa**, Hüseyin Çelebi 1194 ff. 82b–86b; **Istanbul**, Ahmet III 3447_{7}, Ayasofya 2456_{5}, 4829_{25}, 4849_{2}, Fatih 5380_{8}, Hamidiye 1448_{10}, Hazine 1730_{32}, Nuruosmaniye 4894_{10}, Ragıp Paşa 1461_{25}, Üniversite 1458_{88}, 4711_{4}, 4755_{19},

Veliyüddin Efendi 3263_3; **Leiden** 1479; **London**, Brit. Lib. 978_{45}; **Marāġa**, pp. 432–442 Pourjavady; **Rampur** II 778; **Tehran**, Majlis 599_5 ff. 155^b–171^b (570H), 634_{27}, Malik 2005_8, 2007_{19}; Millī 9_7, Miškāt 367,[12] 1149 ff. 25^b–28^b.

Published: aṭ-Ṭayyān and ʿAlam print both versions; text reprinted, without the apparatus, in Sara.

Translation: English, Semaan; English, Sara.

GL 17. *K. Lisān al-ʿarab* (M104, A-)—*The Language of the Arabs* / Bio 15, SB 13, LB 13, EB 103

In the Biography, Jūzjānī reports that after a confrontation with the philologist Abū–Manṣūr al-Jabbān on questions of lexicography, Avicenna "wrote a book on lexicography, which he called *The Language of the Arabs*, the like of which had never been written on the subject. But he never transcibed it into a clean copy and the book remained in rough draft after his death, with nobody being able to figure out how to organize it" (Gohlman 72.5–8). Part of the text survives in a single manuscript, whose introduction by the compiler or a scribe echoes Jūzjānī's report: "Avicenna had composed a lexicographic work, which he called *The Language of the Arabs*, in a number of books, each book containing several [separate] themes (*funūn*). It is an extraordinary work, which he organized very well, except that he never finished it and never transcribed it from the rough draft into clean copy. He avoided listing the terms in the manner customary with lexicographers but instead stated clearly the significations they express (*muqtaḍayāt*) and the difference in meaning they express. I have seen a portion (*ṭaraf*) of this work in his hand, coming to some one hundred and thirty folios, but I was unable to make a clean copy and so made a selection of some sections and various remarkable entries."[13]

The transmission of this work is nebulous. Juzjānī does not say in whose possession the rough draft came after Avicenna's death and who the individuals were who could not figure out how to organize it. If it were the usual disciples to whom we owe the transmission of numerous works by Avicenna—Juzjānī, Bahmanyār, and Ibn-Zayla—then it would seem unlikely that the work would have disappeared altogether and then reappeared. The SB seems to know it well enough as to indicate that it was a work in ten volumes,

---

[12] Reisman *Avicenniana* 30n22 notes that the incipit and explicit of this treatise in this MS given by Dānešpažūh in his catalogue of the Miškāt collection do not resemble those of either version.

[13] Yarshater *Panj resāle* 7; cf. his Persian translation, p. 1.

but the version of the LB in the Üniversite 4755 MS, which derives from these disciples, does not know it at the end of the twelfth century (the compiler says that not a copy was to be found—*lā wujidat lahu nusḫa*), but a part of it, most likely what we have today, had reappeared by the middle of the next century: IAU, after copying the entry of the LB just cited, adds, "I came upon a part of this book, which has a strange arrangement" (*waqaʿa ilayya baʿḍu hāḏā l-kitāb, wa-huwa ġarīb at-taṣnīf*). It is not clear whether the first person pronoun here refers to IAU or his source. Moreover, it is also not clear why the author of the introduction in the extant text, who says that he had seen a part of the work in Avicenna's handwriting covering some 130 folios, could not copy that entire part but selected only a few pages to copy. These uncertainties may not be enough to cast doubt on the authenticity of the surviving fragment, but the questions remain.

The format the book took is indeed unusual, as stated by those who reported on it. It was structured according to key terms indicating a theme, and then words which fell under that category were listed and discriminated one from the other.

MSS: **Tehran**, Malik 2013. For other MSS containing parts of the text see Yarshater *Panj Resāle* 3–4.

Published: Yarshater *Panj Resāle* 7–18, with facsimile of the Malik MS 19–23.

a. *Qaḍāʾ Allāh taʿālā* (M4ṭ, A192)—*The Decree of God*

An extract from the *Lisān al-ʿArab*, it was incorporated in the pseudepigraphic Avicenna—Ibn-Abī-l-Ḫayr correspondence. See Reisman *Avicennan Tradition* 139.

MSS: **Cairo**, Ṭalʿat 197 Maʿārif ʿāmma, ff. 33^{a-b}; **Istanbul**, Ayasofya 4849_{26} ff. 133^{b}–134^{a}, 4853 ff. 94^{a-b}, Nuruosmaniye 4894_{119}; **Tehran**, Miškāt 339_{11} ff. 63^{b}–64^{b}, 876 ff. 51^{a}–52^{a}.

Published, with French translation: Michot *Abū Saʿd* 103–115.

ii. *Pseudepigraphs, to be authenticated*

GL-Ps 6. *Muʿtaṣim aš-šuʿarāʾ fī l-ʿarūḍ* (M-, A-)—*Poetic Guard (?), on Prosody* / LB 59

The LB, which lists this title, says that Avicenna wrote this treatise in his home country when he was 17. Not known to be extant, it would appear to be a concocted title deriving from the first patron of Avicenna, al-ʿArūḍī.

GL-Ps 7. *K. al-Mulaḥ fī n-naḥw* (M-, A-)—*Grammatical witticisms* / LB 87

Only the LB lists this title about which nothing else is known.

C. Physics (Natural Science) (GP)

I. *Physics and On the Heavens*

i. *Expository*

GP 1. *Kalām fī Ḥadd al-jism* (M56b, A-)—*On the Definition of Body* / LB 60

ʿAbd-ar-Razzāq aṣ-Ṣiġnāḫī's MS in Cairo, Ḥikma 6M, ff. 195^{b}–206^{a}, contains a treatise with this title attributed to Avicenna (see Gutas "Ṣiġnāḫī" 13b, no. 9). The LB has an entry with this title, which is most likely this treatise, and possibly even taken from ʿAbd-ar-Razzāq's manuscript or a descendant. It does not appear that the work survives in other known manuscripts, and Mahdavī p. 72 refers to it only on the basis of the information in Badawī's *Arisṭū* p. (48). In the introduction Avicenna says that he saw a treatise by the chief judge (*qāḍī al-quḍāṭ*) Abū-Naṣr al-Ḥusayn ibn-ʿUbayd-Allāh on the definition of body which he found not to be based on the rules of logic and he proceeds to discuss the subject.

GP 2. *Fī Anna abʿād al-ǧism ġayr ḏātiyya lahu* (M56, A56, 60, 64, 72)—*That the Dimensions of a Body Are not of Its Essence* / SB 35

Alternate titles: *Ḥadd al-jism, Istiḍāʾat al-jaww, aḍ-Ḍawʾ, aṭ-Ṭūl wa-l-ʿarḍ, al-Mušiff*.

The SB lists the title as given above, and the Leiden manuscript, the oldest extant (515/1121), provides the corroboration that it is the earliest used; the other titles given to the treatise over the centuries are later additions. The beginning of the text in the Leiden manuscript reads (as cited in Mahdavī 71), "A treatise by Avicenna in response to criticism for his opinion that the actual transparent (*al-mušiff*) does not contain light by which it is qualified, and that the body *qua* body need only have density, not any specific three dimensions."

MSS: **Hyderabad** III 730; **Istanbul**, Ahmet III 3447_{25}, Ayasofya 4829_{31}, Hamidiye 1448_{44}, Köprülü 1589_{10}, Nuruosmaniye 4894_{104}; **Leiden** 1477 ff. 89^{b}–94^{b} (515H); **Rampur** I 431, 712; **Tehran**, Miškāt 1074_{14}, 1149 ff. 325^{b}–327^{a}, Tangābunī 335_{3}.

GP 3. *Al-Ḥukūma fī ḥujaj al-muṯbitīn li-l-māḍī mabdaʾan zamāniyyan* (M64, A75)—*Judgment of the Arguments of Those Who Maintain that the Past Has a Temporal Beginning* / SB 33, LB 40, EB 29

Alternate titles: *Fī n-Nihāya wa-l-lā-nihāya, Fī t-Tanāhī wa-l-lā-tanāhī.*

An essay on the subject indicated by the title, which is mentioned by Avicenna in his introduction. It is in eleven sections, the first of which contains a detailed enumeration of the principles of syllogisms, as set forth in numerous other works (cf. Gutas "Empiricism" Section II), while the rest offer an evaluation of the syllogistic validity of the said arguments. For a summary of their contents see the article by Shlomo Pines referred to in Janssens *Bibliography* 52–53.

MSS: **Bursa**, Hüseyin Çelebi 1194 ff. 105^{b}–110^{b}, 164^{b}–166^{b}; **Istanbul**, Ahmet III 1584_{21}, 3447_{23}, Hamidiye 1448_{42}, Hazine 1730_{43}, Köprülü 1589_{42}, Nuruosmaniye 4894_{102}, Üniversite 4724_{2}, 4755_{10} ff. 186^{b}–203^{b} (588H); **Leiden** 1464_{12}; **London**, Brit. Lib. 426_{14}, 978_{37}, 1349_{14}; **Manchester** 384_{p}; **Meshed**, Riżavī IV 1/694; **Rampur** II 779; **Tehran**, Malik 2005_{11}, Miškāt 384_{4}, 1149 ff. 355^{a}–360^{a}, Tangābunī 317_{15}.

Published: Mohaghegh *Ḥudūṯ* 131–152.

GP 4. *R. fī l-Wusʿa* (M129, A68)—*On Space* / EB73

Alternate titles: *al-Faḍāʾ, R. fī l-Makān, K. ilā Baʿḍ al-mutakallimīn.*

A brief essay on the subject in response to a question posed to him by a theologian (*mutakallim*). It must have come into circulation relatively late, i.e., by the middle of the thirteenth century, for only the EB lists it; but since it is essentially a response sent to a specific person (a theologian), as we learn both from its first title in the EB and from its opening words (given by Dhanani), it would appear that a descendant of the original recipient eventually put it in circulation. Studied by Dhanani, there seems to be no doubt about its authenticity.

MSS: **Berlin** 2299; **Istanbul**, Ahmet III 3447_{19}; Ayasofya 4829_{1}, 4849_{11} ff. 50^{a}–53^{b}, 4853_{19}; Hamidiye 1448_{36}; Nuruosmaniye 4894_{25}; **London**, Brit. Lib. 978_{25}; **Tehran**, Tangābunī 79_{16+17}.

GP 5. *Jawhariyyat an-nār* (M11, A63)—*That Fire Is a Substance*

Alternate title: *al-Ajwiba ʿan al-masāʾil.*

A brief response to a question on the subject by Jaʿfar al-Kiyā, apparently the same person as al-Kiyā Abū-Jaʿfar Muḥammad b. al-Ḥusayn b. al-Marzubān. Avicenna refers to the *Physics* in the course of the discussion.

MSS: **Aligarh**, University Collection no. 125 ff. 2^{b}–3^{a}; **Baghdad**, Iraq Museum 952 pp. 165–169; **Hyderabad** 41 Majāmīʿ; **Istanbul**, Ahmet III 3447_{66}, Hazine 1730_{34}, Nuruosmaniye 4894_{94}, Pertev Paşa 617_{17}, Üniversite 4724_{12}; **Rampur** 76 Majāmīʿ; **Tehran**, Majlis 634_{14} pp. 41–42, Miškāt 1149 ff. 353^{a-b}.

GP 6. *Fī l-Ajrām al-ʿulwiyya* (M53, A53)—*On the Supernal Bodies* / SB 22, LB 51, EB 49

Alt. titles: *R. fī Jawhar al-ajrām as-samāwiyya*; *Bayān al-jawhar an-nafīs*; *Taʿrīf ar-raʾy al-muḥaṣṣal*; *Maʿrifat al-ajrām as-samāwiyya.*

A brief treatise on the nature and generation of the heavenly bodies and their influence on the world. The variant titles are again all derived from its opening words. It survives in two recensions, one more simple and briefer in its expression, the other more elaborate. Their relationship and origin remain to be determined. But the treatise appears to be very early, possibly even composed while Avicenna was still in Buḫārā (cf. Gutas "Agenda" 60–61).

MSS: **Baghdad**, Iraq Museum 952 pp. 110–129; **Bursa**, Hüseyin Çelebi 1194 ff. 110^{b}–115^{b}; **Cairo**, Taymūr 200 Majāmīʿ; **Istanbul**, Ahmet III 3447_{41}, Ayasofya 2456_{4}, 4829_{13}, 4849_{16}, 4853_{18}, Hamidiye 1448_{23}, Hazine 1730_{40}, Köprülü 868_{2}, 869_{8} ff. 220^{b}–224^{a}, Nuruosmaniye 4894_{60}, Ragıp Paşa 1461_{30}, Üniversite 4754_{9}, 4755_{6} ff. 92^{a}–102^{b} (588H), Veliyüddin 3263_{4}; **London**, Brit. Lib. 978_{36}; **Manchester** 384_{E}; **Tehran**, Majlis 634_{32}, Malik 2001_{8}, 2005_{6}, 2012_{5}, 2013_{10}, 2017_{5}, Miškāt 1149 ff. 28^{b}–31^{b}, Sipahsālār 1217_{39}, 2912_{52}, 8371_{8}.

Published: Kurdī *Majmūʿat ar-Rasāʾil* 257–279.

GP 7. *R. fī ʿIllat qiyām al-arḍ fī ḥayyizihā* (M91, A168)—*On the Cause of the Earth's Remaining in Its Position* / LB 46

Alternate titles: *Tanāhī l-ajsām*; *Qiyām al-arḍ fī wasaṭ as-samāʾ*, *M. fī Hayʾat al-arḍ min as-samāʾ wa-annahā fī l-wasaṭ.*

In the introduction Avicenna says that he wrote this treatise upon request by the vizier of the Maʾmūnids in Gurgānj, Abū-l-Ḥasan Aḥmad b. Muḥammad as-Sahlī (thus the name in all the MSS and sources relating to Avicenna, though biographers give the name as Abū-l-Ḥusayn as-Suhaylī; see Gohlman 124n41). The date of composition is thus after 389/999 and before 402/1012. The LB is the only Bibliography to list it, under the third title given above.

MSS: **Bursa**, Hüseyin Çelebi 1194 ff. 115^{b}–119^{b}; **Cairo**, Dār al-Kutub 47 Nujūm, Ṭalʿat 197 Mā baʿd aṭ-ṭabīʿa; **Dublin**, Chester Beatty 3045_{1} ff. 1–9^{a}; **Gotha** 1158_{23}; **Hyderabad**, Āṣaf. III 307; **Istanbul**, Ahmet III 1584_{23}, 3447_{29}, Esat Efendi 3688_{5} ff. 34^{b}–39^{b}, Hamidiye 1448_{51}, Köprülü 1589_{41}, Nuruosmaniye 4894_{96}, Üniversite 4724; **London**, Brit. Lib. 981_{11}, 1349_{8}; **Oxford**, Bodleian 980_{1}; **Rampur** I 394, 712; **Tehran**, Sipahsālār 2912_{73}, Tangābunī 317_{20}.

Published: Kurdī *Jāmiʿ* 152–164.

ii. *Commentaries*

GS 10a. *Tafsīr K. as-Samāʿ aṭ-ṭabīʿī* (M-, A-)—*Commentary on* [*Aristotle's*] *Physics*

In his treatise *On Love* (Mehren *Traités* III,18), which is an early work, Avicenna mentions that he explained in his commentary at the beginning of the first book of Aristotle's *Physics* (*fī tafsīrinā ṣadr al-maqāla al-ūlā min K. as-Samāʿ aṭ-ṭabīʿī*) how one cannot form concepts of caused intelligibles without first coming to know the true causes and especially the First Cause. Such an independent commentary is not mentioned in any bibliography, while it appears that it was Avicenna's habit early in his career to name his books with reference to those of Aristotle, a habit he discontinued later in life (see Chapter 7d). Accordingly it appears most likely that the reference here is to the Physics section of the twenty-volume work he wrote for Baraqī commenting on Aristotle, *The Available and the Valid* (GS 10), especially since it does not seem that by the time he had composed the treatise *On Love* (below, GM 5) he had written anything else that could be seen as a commentary on the *Physics*. See also below GS 10b and 10c under Physics and GS 10d under Metaphysics.

GS 10b. *Tafsīr as-Samāʾ wa-l-ʿālam* (M-, A-)—*Commentary on De caelo*

In the introduction to his *Risāla fī ʿIllat qiyām al-arḍ fī ḥayyizihā* (above, GP 7), Avicenna says that he wrote a commentary on Aristotle's *De caelo* also for the same patron, the vizier Abū-l-Ḥasan as-Sahlī, i.e., in Gurgānj (between 999–1012). His words are the following: *wa-qad šaraḥnāhu fī kitābinā l-mawsūm bi-Tafsīr as-Samāʾ wa-l-ʿālam bi-smi š-šayḫ al-jalīl* (MS Istanbul, Nuruosmaniye 4894, f. 482[a]), and *wa-qad šaraḥnāhu fī tafsīrinā li-Kitāb as-Samāʾ wa-l-ʿālam bi-smi š-šayḫ al-jalīl* (MS Istanbul, Hamidiye 1448, f. 627[b]). No work by Avicenna is reported under the title *Tafsīr as-Samāʾ wa-l-ʿālam* or survives in manuscript, so the question is which work this is. There are three possibilities:

(1) It is the De caelo part of his earlier work written in Buḫārā for his neighbor Baraqī, *The Available and the Valid* (GS 10), which Avicenna described as a commentary. Elsewhere Avicenna also refers to his *tafsīr* of Aristotle's *Physics, De anima*, and *Metaphysics* which seem to be references also to this book for Baraqī (GS 10a above and 10c below, in the section on the soul, and GS 10d under Metaphysics). However, Avicenna also mentioned in the Autobiography that Baraqī never lent it to anyone for copying, which implies that Avicenna himself

may not have had a copy. If this is true, at most it can be said that Avicenna rewrote from memory that commentary and gave it to as-Sahlī.

(2) It is an independent work entitled *Tafsīr as-Samāʾ wa-l-ʿālam*, more extensive and detailed than the *Risāla fī ʿIllat qiyām al-arḍ fī ḥayyizihā* as he says in the introduction, and written expressly for as-Sahlī who appears to have had a particular interest in the subject.

(3) It is the work which Avicenna later incorporated with some modifications into the *Šifāʾ* as its De caelo part, as suggested by Ragep and Ragep 7.

Avicenna wrote fast, often from memory, but just as often he was copying himself. Any one of the three hypotheses is possible, which further research may specify. However, since it appears that it is not identical with (3), even if it lay at its basis, and since it seems unlikely that Avicenna would have composed two independent commentaries on *De caelo*, possibility (1) seems to describe best the situation at this stage of our knowledge.

iii. *Responsa*

GP 8. *Al-Ajwiba ʿan masāʾil Abī Rayḥān al-Bīrūnī* (M5, A54)—*Answers to Questions Posed by Bīrūnī* / LB 45, EB 56

Alternate titles: *R. ilā Abī r-Rayḥān al-Bīrūnī, Jawāb masāʾil al-Bīrūnī, al-Asʾila wa-l-ajwiba*.

Bīrūnī completed his *al-Āṯār al-bāqiya* around 390/1000 in Jurjān, during the rule of Qābūs b. Vušmagīr to whom it is dedicated. In it he mentions that he had some "debates" (*muḏākarāt*) with Avicenna, to whom he refers as "the excellent young man" (*al-fatā al-fāḍil*).[14] By this time Avicenna was already in Gurgānj, in the service of the Maʾmūnids in Ḫwārazm, having left Buḫārā at least a year earlier in 389/999, and the debates (by correspondence?) with Bīrūnī are to be dated to this period. Bīrūnī himself had left Jurjān at some point around this time and returned to Ḫwārazm, and thus the historical evidence, though not precise enough to allow certainty,[15] does not preclude a personal meeting between the two men. Strohmaier "Dialog" [116]/343 briefly makes the plausible point that the text of the questions and

14 The dates of composition are figured by Eduard Sachau in his edition, *Die Chronologie orientalischer Völker von Albêrûni*, Leipzig: Otto Harrassowitz, 1923, pp. xxiii–xxv; the reference to Avicenna is on p. 257.

15 *Ibid.* xxxiv–xxxv.

answers that we have may be a transcript of an actual debate rather than a stylized subsequent composition. In any case, the dating of the exchange is not in doubt.

Mahdavī 11 claims a later date for this debate, thus postulating a second such exchange between the two men (since the first one is registered in Bīrūnī's *al-Āṯār al-bāqiya* which was completed in 1000), on the grounds that Bīrūnī addresses Avicenna as *al-ḥakīm*, which Mahdavī asserts Bīrūnī would not have used for the young Avicenna who was writing while still in Buḫārā. But Avicenna was born certainly before the transmitted date of 370/980,[16] and thus was roughly the same age as Bīrūnī, who was born in 362/972–973, if not even older; besides, titles of address in the courtly environment where such exchanges took place were always excessively polite and without reference to age.

MSS: **Baghdad**, Iraq Museum 594 pp. 88–91 (see Daiber *Naturwissenschaft* 7) (639H), 952 pp. 55–90; **Bursa**, Hüseyin Çelebi 1194 ff. 87^a–95^b; **Dublin**, Chester Beatty 3045_2; **Istanbul**, Ayasofya 4853_6, Feyzullah 2188_4, Nuruosmaniye 2715, Üniversite 1458_{85}; **Leiden** 1476 (515H); **London**, Brit. Lib. 978_{50}, 980_{15}; **Meshed**, Riżavī IV 1/1024_2; **Milan** 320_c; **Oxford**, Bodleian 980_2; **Princeton** (ELS) 308 ff. 3^b–12^b; **Rampur** II 816; **Tehran**, Majlis 599_3 ff. 119^b–153^b, 634_{24}, 1061_1, Miškāt 253_{22}, 1149 ff. 320^a–325^b, Tangābunī 317_{10}, 324_2.

Published: Nasr and Mohaghegh; Yāfī.

Translations: English, Berjak and Iqbal; German, partial, Strohmaier *Al-Bīrūnī* 49–65; German summary in Strohmaier "Dialog".

GP 9. *Al-Ajwiba ʿan al-masāʾil al-ʿašr I* (M6, A2, 38_2)—*Answers to Ten Questions I* / LB 44

Alternate titles: *ʿAšr masāʾil ajāba ʿanhā li-Abī r-Rayḥān al-Bīrūnī; Jawāb masāʾil ʿašr.*

Mahdavī 15 reports that at the beginning of the Tehran MS Ṭabāṭabāʾī 1367_9 the questioner is stated as being "Abū-l-Qāsim al-Jurjānī or al-Kirmānī," whereas the attribution to Bīrūnī in the Istanbul MS Ayasofya 4853 would appear to be copied from the proper Bīrūnī-Avicenna correspondence (above GP 8); cf. also Lucchetta "Dieci questioni" 102 and the articles by Türker cited in Janssens *Bibliography* 44. The LB identifies Bīrūnī as the questioner in the title, which would indicate that the confusion like the one seen in the Ayasofya MS occurred early. It appears quite unlikely that Bīrūnī was, in fact, the questioner.

16 Gutas "*Maḏhab*."

MSS: **Berlin** 5057; **Bursa**, Hüseyin Çelebi 1194 ff. 161[b]–164[a]; **Cairo**, VI 103, Taymūr 200 Majāmīʿ; **Istanbul**, Ahmet III $3447_{57,67}$, Ayasofya 2389_6, 4829_{21}, 4851_8, 4853_5, Feyzullah 2188_5, Hamidiye 1448_{11}, 1452_{13}, Köprülü 1602_3, Nuruosmaniye 4894_{132}, Ragıp Paşa 1461_{29}, Üniversite 1458_{84}, 4724_7, Veliyüddin 3181_9, 3263_6; **Leiden** 1475 (515H); **London**, Brit. Lib. 978_{35}, 980_{11}, Or. 6572; **Meshed**, Riżavī IV $1/667_2$; **Princeton** (ELS) 308 ff. 67[b]–70[b]; **Tehran**, Majlis 625_2, Malik 2013_{23}, Miškāt 422, 1149 ff. 318[a]–319[b], Sipahsālār 8371_{10}, 2912 ff. 50[b]–51[b], Ṭabāṭabāʾī 1367_9, Tangābunī 324_4.
Published: Türker; Türker's text repeated by Lucchetta "Dieci questioni" 122–132, with the addition of variants from the Tehran MS Majlis 625.
Translation. Italian: Lucchetta "Dieci questioni".

iv. *Pseudepigraphs, to be authenticated*

GP-Ps 1. *R. fī l-Ḥadaṯ* (M55, A61)—*On Origination* / EB 44

The treatise starts by defining *ḥadaṯ* as "something's coming to be after it had not existed" (*kawn aš-šayʾ baʿda an lam yakun*), and then defines pre-existence (*qidam*). Only the EB lists it.
MSS: **Gotha** 1158_{27}; **Istanbul**, Ayasofya 4849_{10} ff. 49[a–b], 4853_{12}, Nuruosmaniye 4894_{34}.

GP-Ps 2. *Masʾalatān* (M109, A71)—*Two Questions*

On the occupation of space by existents and the void.
MSS: **Istanbul**, Ayasofya 4853 ff. 39[a]–40[a], Nuruosmaniye 4894_{33}.

II. *Meteorology*

i. *Pseudepigraph, to be authenticated*

GP-Ps 3. *Al-Āṯār al-ʿulwiyya* (M24, A51)—*Meteorology*

Alternate titles: *al-Ajrām al-ʿulwiyya*, *Asbāb al-āṯār al-ʿulwiyya*

The titles all come from the beginning words of this very brief treatise on meteorology. Its ascription to Avicenna is problematic; none of the bibliographies mentions it, and it is certainly different from *al-Ajrām al-ʿulwiyya* (GP 6), with which it seems to be confused. From the published evidence it is not clear what the manuscripts have; the Escorial MS, according to the old catalogue by Miguel Casiri I,205b (*Bibliotheca arabico-hispana escurialensis*, Madrid 1760), appears to be attributing it to Naṣīr-ad-Dīn aṭ-Ṭūsī. Sezgin, *GAS* VII,301–302, who lists it as a work by Avicenna without argument, says (p. 293) that it is a very brief presentation of subjects dealt with in the Meteorology of the *Šifāʾ*. Mahdavī 29, however, rightly questions its authenticity.

MSS: **Escorial** 703_1 ff. 1–6 (926H); **Istanbul**, Serez 4094_4 ff. 49^a–50^b (925H), Yeni Cami 1181 ff. 254^b–255^a (560H).

III. *On the Soul*

i. *Expository*

GP 10. *K. fī n-Nafs ʿalā sunnat al-iḫtiṣār* (M120, A102)—*Compendium on the Soul* / LB 85

Alternate titles: *Mabḥaṯ ʿan al-quwā n-nafsāniyya, Hadiyya, al-Fuṣūl, ʿAšara fuṣūl.*

For description see above, W1.

MSS: **Istanbul**, Nuruosmaniye 4894_{84}, Üniversite 4711_1, 4755_7 ff. 103^a–125^b (588H); **Leiden** 1467; **London**, Brit. Lib. 426_{22}, 978_{31}; **Meshed**, Riżavī I 1/125; **Milan**, Ambrosiana 320_3; **Tehran**, Malik 2004_{15}, 2005_{12}, 2013_{14}, Miškāt 861_4, 1074_3, 1149 ff. 15^b–21^b, Tangābunī 267_2.

Published: Landauer; reprinted in van Dyck *Hadiyya*; Ahwānī *Aḥwāl* 145–178.

Translations: German, Landauer; English, van Dyck *Offering*.

GP 11. *R. fī l-Kalām ʿalā n-nafs an-nāṭiqa* (M122, A p. 165)—*On the Rational Soul* / EB 95 (?)

For description see above, Text 14.

MS: **Leiden** 1468 ff. 247^a–250^a (954H).

Published: Ahwānī *Aḥwāl* 195–199.

Translation: English, Text 14 above.

GP 12. *Al-Jumal min al-adilla al-muḥaqqaqa li-baqāʾ an-nafs an-nāṭiqa* (M52, A80)—*The Main Points of Verified Proofs on the Survival of the Rational Soul* / EB 30

Alternate titles: *Baqāʾ an-nafs an-nāṭiqa, Sabʿa min al-maqāyīs al-manṭiqiyya, an-Nafs an-nāṭiqa.*

This brief treatise offering seven arguments for the survival of the rational soul, in response to a question on the subject by "one of the chiefs" (*baʿḍ ar-ruʾasāʾ*), is transmitted in early manuscripts, as the Majlis 599 MS recorded by Mahdavī indicates (570H). It is also listed in the EB with exactly the same title as that given above, manifestly from a manuscript in the same tradition as that of the Majlis MS. Not much can be said about its authenticity without a study of the text itself, which remains unpublished, and its manuscript transmission. It is, however, also transmitted in the Istanbul MS Ayasofya 4853, which contains numerous scattered and loose pieces by Avicenna, some of which found their way in the *Mubāḥaṯāt* and *Taʿlīqāt* (Reisman *Avicennan Tradition* 50–53), and it would appear that this treatise was such an occasional piece in response to a question which achieved independent status in the manuscript transmission some time after Avicenna's death.

MSS: **Cairo**, Taymūr 200 Majāmīʿ; **Hyderabad** M 41; **Istanbul**, Ayasofya 4853_{9}; **Rampur** M 76; **Tehran**, Majlis 599_{12} ff. 216b–222b (570H); Malik 2007_{15}; Sipahsālār 1217_{16}, 2912_{61}, 8371_{9}.

GP 13. *Iḫtilāf an-nās fī amr an-nafs wa-amr al-ʿaql* (*R. ilā l-Kiyā*) (M12, A78, 108, 259)—*Dispute on the Subject of Soul and Intellect* (*Letter to Kiyā*)

Alternate titles: *Amr an-nafs wa-amr al-ʿaql, R. aš-Šayḫ Abī ʿAlī ilā l-Kiyā al-Jalīl Abī Jaʿfar Muḥammad b. al-Ḥusayn/al-Ḥasan b. al-Marzubān*; see further Reisman *Avicennan Tradition* 63–64.

An independent work on the subject, addressed to al-Kiyā Abū-Jaʿfar Muḥammad b. al-Ḥusayn/al-Ḥasan b. al-Marzubān, otherwise unknown, that is extant in three versions; see Reisman *Avicennan Tradition* 63–66, 258.

MSS: **Bursa**, Hüseyin Çelebi 1194 ff. 148b–149b; **Cairo**, Muṣṭafā Fāḍil 6 Ḥikma; **Gotha** 1158_{28}; **Istanbul**, Ayasofya 4849_{25} ff. 133a–134b, 4853_{14}, Nuruosmaniye 4894_{118}; **Leiden** 1485; **Tehran**, Majlis 634_{36}, Malik 2019_{7}, Sipahsālār 1217_{2}.

Published: Badawī *Arisṭū* 119–122.

Translation: French, Pines "Philosophie Orientale" 6–9; English, partial, above, T12.

ii. *Commentary*

GS 10c. *Šarḥ K. Arisṭūṭālīs fī n-Nafs* (M-, A-)—*Commentary on Aristotle's De anima*

Mentioned in the *Aḍḥawiyya* (*fī šarḥinā li-K. Arisṭūṭālīs fī n-Nafs*, 153 Lucchetta), it is in all probability a reference to the De anima part of *The Available and the Valid*. See above GS 10, GS 10a and 10b under Physics, and below, GS 10d under Metaphysics.

iii. *Pseudepigraphs, to be authenticated*

GP-Ps 4. *Al-Qaṣīda al-ʿayniyya* (M99, A93)—*Poem Rhyming in ʿayn*

Alternate titles: *an-Nafsiyya, al-Warqāʾiyya, al-Qaṣīda al-ġarrāʾ*.

A poem in the *kāmil* meter in 20 verses rhyming in -ʿī (i.e., the letter *ʿayn* and hence its name, the *ʿayniyya*) on the descent of the soul from its heavely abode to the body. Although it has been admitted as an authentic work by Avicenna, its spuriousness can hardly be doubted.[17] It is, first of all, not mentioned at all by name in any of the bibliographies, even if they do include general entries on "poems" by him (SB 26, LB 70). If one is to project the later popularity of the poem backwards into the century and a half after Avicenna's death (the period during which the bibliographies were compiled), it is difficult to see how it could have failed to be mentioned by any of them. Second, the main point of the poem, the fall of a pre-existing soul from the heavenly abode into the body at the time of birth is a distinctly Ismāʿīlī tenet which Avicenna rejected from his childhood: in the Autobiography he reports how as a child he would hear the Ismāʿīlī dāʿī and his father and brother discuss the account about the soul—manifestly its descent into the body—but his "soul would not accept it" (T3 § 3). Later he would erect his theory of the soul on the foundation stone of the soul's generation *simultaneously* with the body. Third, the very first commentary of it that exists is one by the Ismāʿīlī 5th Dāʿī Muṭlaq, ʿAlī b. Muḥammad b. al-Walīd (d. 1215),[18] who presents Avicenna as an Ismāʿīlī and gives no reference whatsoever to any of the works of Avicenna—as a matter of fact, as De Smet writes (11–12), Ibn al-Walīd comments on Avicenna not with the help of Avicenna but by invoking the authority of Ismāʿīlī sages like Kirmānī and al-Ḫaṭṭāb, and especially that of 'the excellent personality' (*aš-šaḫṣ al-fāḍil*), who is allegedly none other than one of the hidden Imāms who authored the *Rasāʾil Iḫwān aṣ-Ṣafāʾ*. And fourth, even if not by modern authors, the authenticity was in fact disputed by a Muslim scholar, aš-Šarīšī (d. 619/1222), precisely for the second reason given above. Furthermore, mainstream Avicennan commentators, like the one published by Carra de Vaux and discussed by De Smet 16–17, went through interpretive contortions to adjust the tenets of the poem to Avicenna's authentic views—even if on one point, namely the soteriological need of the soul for the body, the two are in agreement, as De Smet argues. In view of the above, the default assumption is necessarily that the poem is spurious and that its authenticity has to be proven.

---

17 In medieval times its authenticity was doubted by aš-Šarīšī, as will be discussed below, and in modern literature some scholars also raised objections; see Madelung 167n1.

18 Discussed and presented by both De Smet (2002) and Madelung (2005) unbeknownst to each other, though Madelung's essay was printed later.

Finally, on the basis of De Smet's discovery and analysis of Ibn al-Walīd's commentary, it is now possible to investigate the source of the fabrication of the poem: it would seem most likely that it was in fact generated in Ismʿāʿīlī circles—perhaps even in Yemeni Ṭayyibī circles, to whom Ibn al-Walīd belonged—some time before the end of the twelfth century.[19] It is significant that the scholar who disputed its ascription to Avicenna, the great Andalusian philologist and littérateur aš-Šarīšī, who traveled extensively in the Near East and had profound knowledge of Arabic poetry, was a contenporary of Ibn al-Walīd. He must have heard of the poem and its misattribution to Avicenna, which was apparently a recent development and had not yet taken firm root in Avicenna scholarship, and expressed his expert opinion on it along with numerous other comments on Arabic literature. His views are therefore more weighty than those of a mere observer or casual critic. The connection of this poem to Ismāʿīlī circles is further strengthened by its relation to another pseudepigraph, known as *Aḥwāl ar-rūḥ, The States of the Spirit* (M135, A98). The initial question in that work is, "Whence has the spirit descended (*habaṭat*) [i.e., into the body]," reminding one of the very first word of the *ʿAyniyya*. And the *Aḥwāl ar-rūḥ* has been convincingly tied to circles that produced the *Iḫwān aṣ-ṣafāʾ* by Michot "États de l'esprit". As for the motive behind the poem's fabrication in Ismāʿīlī circles, if this were to be assumed, it is most likely the same as that behind much of Avicennan pseudepigraphy: to claim for themselves some of the authority which the philosopher enjoyed, or alternately, to prove the universality of their message on the basis of Avicenna's alleged familiarity with Ismāʿīlism in that passage in the Autobiography referred to above. If Avicenna could not have been blind to dominant Ismāʿīlī ideas in his environment, even if only to refute them, as De Smet suggests, then neither could the Ismāʿīlīs be immune to the position of authority Avicenna's ideas gained soon after his death, and not claim some for themselves.

MSS: **Baghdad**, Iraq Museum 594 pp. 86–87 (639H); **Berlin** 5346; **Gotha** 1_{3}, 14_{26}, 1158_{20}, 1167; **Istanbul**, Ahmet III 3447_{47}, Ayasofya 4849, Hamidiye 1448_{7}, Ragıp Paşa 1461_{26}, Üniversite 4755_{14} (588H); **Leiden** 1471, 1473; **London**, Brit. Lib. 886_{13}; **Manchester** 453_{A}; **Paris** 2502_{8}, 2541_{3}, 3171_{13}; **Tehran**, Majlis 1768_{14}, Millī 884, 992_{2}.

[19] It is to be noted, as indicated in other contexts as well, that the growth of spurious additions to the works of Avicenna occurred around the middle of the twelfth century. See Reisman "Pseudo-Avicennan Corpus I" 14 and note 30.

For the commentaries, see the list in Mahdavī, and for the different recensions, further MSS, publications, and translations see the text and the references in De Smet. There is a venerable English translation by Arberry *Theology* 77–78, and a brand new and improved one by G.J. van Gelder, *Classical Arabic Literature*, New York and London: New York University Press, 2013, 73–74.

GP-Ps 5. *R. fī Infisāḫ aṣ-ṣuwar al-mawjūda fī n-nafs* (M36, A81)—*On the Disappearance of the Vain Intelligibles*

Alternate titles: *Fī Bayān aṣ-ṣuwar al-maʿqūla al-muḫālifa li-l-ḥaqq; Infisāḫ aṣ-ṣuwar baʿda l-mawt.*

The treatise is not mentioned in any bibliography. Michot “Disappearance” 96 reports that of the twelve manuscripts that he used for his translation only three attribute the work to Avicenna—his note 8 indicates that one manuscript ascribes it to “some of the philosophers.” According to its introduction, the treatise is dedicated to, or occasioned by a question from, an anonymous *al-ustāḏ ar-raʾīs*, a form of address not known to have been used for Avicenna. Michot does raise the possibility of its being a pseudepigraph, but nevertheless regards the “attribution to Avicenna as the most reasonable one” (“Disappearance” 96). Black, who devotes a study to the subject (“Fictional Beings”), assumes the authenticity of the treatise without even raising the question. There are, however, many philosophical problems with the treatise–“difficulties,” as Black calls them and proceeds to list them (435 and 446)–but instead of questioning its authenticity on their basis she prefers to pronounce Avicenna incoherent: “To admit an exception to this account of intellectual knowledge is to threaten the overall coherence of Avicenna’s epistemology. And yet this would seem to be precisely what Avicenna’s views on unreal forms require” (446).

MSS. **Berlin** 5345; **Istanbul**, Ahmet 3063$_{6}$, Nuruosmaniye 4894$_{73}$; **London**, Brit. Lib. 978$_{30}$; **Meshed**, Riżavī IV 1/38$_{7}$; **Tehran**, Majlis 634$_{13}$, Malik 2013$_{9}$,[20] Miškāt 1037, 1149 ff. 386^{b}–387^{b}, Tangābunī 79$_{18}$.—See also Michot “Disappearance” and “Disparition” for further MSS.

Published: Michot “Disparition”.

Translations: English, Michot “Disappearance”; French, Michot “Disparition”.

[20] The author is not mentioned.

GP-Ps 6. *Taʿalluq an-nafs bi-l-badan* (M4b, A83)—*Association of the Soul with the Body*

The core of this treatise may have been part of the exchange between Avicenna and Bahmanyār that eventually—and posthumously—formed the collection known as the *Mubāḥaṯāt*, but in the form that it survived, incorporated into the pseudepigraphic Avicenna—Ibn-Abī-l-Ḫayr correspondence, it is certainly spurious. It is listed in no bibliography, it is not known by any of Avicenna's followers or critics who studied his works intensively until Mullā Ṣadrā, all the extant MSS that contain it are dated in the sixteenth century and later, and most importantly, the treatise itself contains an explicit reference to the *Mubāḥaṯāt* itself, a title that came to be used for this collection long after Avicenna's death (Reisman *Avicennan Tradition* 141–144). The transmission history argues heavily against its authenticity, and Sebti "*Taʿalluq*", who claims it is by Avicenna himself as such, answers none of these questions but argues solely on the basis of its contents which she finds compatible with Avicenna's ideas.

MSS: **Istanbul**, Ayasofya 4851, Hamidiye 1452_{3}, Nuruosmaniye 4894_{67}, Pertev 617; **Tehran**, Malik 2007_{7}, Miškāt 339_{14} ff. 68^{a}–70^{a}, Sipahsālār 1216, 1217_{10}.

Published, with French translation: Sebti "*Taʿalluq*".

GP-Ps 7. *Munāẓarāt jarat lahu fī n-nafs maʿa Abī ʿAlī an-Nīsābūrī* (M-, A-)—*Disputations on the Soul with Abū-Alī an-Nīsābūrī* / LB 65

Only the LB lists this title. The disputant in question remains unidentified (cf. Gohlman 140) and no such text has surfaced in the manuscripts.

GP-Ps 8. *Fuṣūl fī n-nafs wa-ṭ-ṭabīʿiyyāt; R. fī n-Nafs* (M-, A-)—*Sections on the Soul and Natural Science; On the Soul* (thrice) / LB 89, EB 95–97

Only the LB lists the former title, which is a generic description by a scribe or the compiler for a collection of paragraphs on these subjects. Similarly the EB lists three consecutive items with the generic title *R. fī n-Nafs*. Unless one of them is a reference to GP 11 above, there is nothing specific to these titles, which must remain unidentifiable.

IV. *Astrology*

GP 14. *Al-Išāra ilā ʿilm fasād aḥkām an-nujūm* (M2, A52)—*The Pointer to Knowing the Fallacy of Astrology* / LB 86

Alternate titles: *R. fī Ibṭāl aḥkām an-nujūm, Fī r-Radd ʿalā l-munajjimīn, Fī Ibṭāl ʿilm an-nujūm.*

The title is given explicitly by Avicenna himself in the introduction as indicated above (p. 4.8 Michot); Michot wrongly "corrects" the reading *ʿilm fasād* of all the manuscripts to *fasād ʿilm*. But the essay begins with an epistemological introduction which frames the research that follows; the pointer, therefore, is not to the *fallacy* of astrology but to how one can *know* the fallacy of astrology—its fallacy is a given, as Avicenna says at the very beginning, like the science of amulets, scapulomancy, and other vile and degenerate sciences (Michot *Astrologie* 3, 51). The other alternate titles listed above are manifestly bibliographers' and scribes' descriptions. It is listed only in the LB, among the very last entries (see above the discussion of the LB in the introduction to the Tetrapla), though its authenticity cannot be seriously doubted, as convincingly argued by Michot.

Avicenna also says in the introduction that he wrote it for "one of my friends" (*baʿḍ aṣdiqāʾī*), who is to be identified, Michot suggests, with Abū-Manṣūr ibn-Zayla (*Astrologie* 20*-41*). The fact is that the scribe of some manuscript adds a note, repeated in some extant manuscripts, that he saw the text *in the hand* of Ibn-Zayla, which may raise the possibility that it is by Ibn-Zayla himself. With some reservations, Reisman *Avicennan Tradition* 196–198 concurs with Michot about the work's authenticity, though the question may be considered still open. From the references to Iṣfahān in it, the essay was written in all probability in that city during the last period of Avicenna's career (Michot *Astrologie* 31*).

MSS: **Istanbul**, Ahmet III 3447_{24}, Hamidiye 1448_{43}, Köprülü 1589_{9}, Nuruosmaniye 4894_{103}, Üniversite 1456, 1458_{27}; **Leiden** Warn. Or. 1020 (Cat. 1464_{13}) ff. 91^{b}–98^{a}; **London**, Brit. Lib. Or. 1349_{6}; **Tehran**, Majlis I 14473 ff. 53^{b}–61^{b}; **Tashkent**, Al-Bīrūni Institute NP 2385 (partial text).

Published, with French translation: Michot *Astrologie*.

V. *Alchemy*

All Arabic and Latin treatises on alchemy attributed to Avicenna are spurious (Ruska); his refutation of alchemy is quite categorical and well known (cf. Gutas "Empiricism," Section VIII). They will not be listed here. For a listing, with references to bibliography, see Ullmann *Geheimwissenschaften* 222–224, 251–252; discussion by Strohmaier "Écrits pseudépigraphiques" 45–46; more recent material can be found in issues of *Ambix*. Only the following alchemical work deserves special consideration.

i. *Pseudepigraph, to be authenticated*

GP-Ps 9. *R. fī Amr mastūr, ilā s-Sahlī* (M33, A154)—*On the Occult, to as-Sahlī* / LB 56, EB 70

Alternate titles: *R. fī Amr mastūr aṣ-ṣanʿa, al-Iksīr, al-Kīmiyā, Fī ṣ-Ṣanʿa.*

This title is remarkable because of its age. It appears listed in the LB and the text itself is included in the Istanbul MS Üniversite 4755, ff. 250^b–260^b, under the title given above. It was also "translated into Latin within 150 years of Ibn Sina's death" (Stapleton in Stapleton 42). It was accordingly in circulation and attributed to Avicenna before the end of the twelfth century. This has led a number of scholars to argue in favor of its authenticity, primarily on the basis that it was an early work by Avicenna, written for as-Sahlī in Gurgānj, and that he later changed his mind in the *Šifāʾ*.[21] Rather than for the question of its spuriousness—which appears quite beyond doubt—the treatise is important because its transmission history will shed light on the generation of Avicennan pseudepigrapha within a century of his death.

MSS: **Hyderabad** III 732; **Istanbul**, Ahmet III 1584_{17}, 3063_{3}, 3447_{8}, Nuruosmaniye 4894_{11}, Üniversite $1458_{5, 28}$, 4724_{8}, 4755_{16} ff. 250^b–260^b (588H), 6117; **Rampur** I 712; **Tehran**, Millī 9_{8}, Miškāt 1149 ff. 365^a–368^a.—See further Ullmann *Geheimwissenschaften* 223.

Published: Ateş; reprinted from Ateş, without the apparatus, in Anawati "Alchimie" 302–312.

Translation: English, Stapleton; French, Anawati "Alchimie" 313–326.

[21] Primarily the eminent historian of alchemy H.E. Stapleton (in Stapleton), the Turkish editor of the treatise, Ahmed Ateş, and G.C. Anawati, the latter cited with approval by Janssens *Bibliography* 58; see also Sezgin in *GAS* IV,7–9.

D. Mathematics (GMath)

Avicenna wrote relatively few works on the mathematical sciences (arithmetic, geometry, astronomy, music), thinking them little controversial,[22] though from all accounts he was clearly interested in the subject and tried to improve and emend the transmitted material. In general he seems to have worked on the subject during two periods in his life, first during his stay in Jurjān (ca. 1012–1013), the work from which period was incorporated by Jūzjānī into the *Najāt* and later translated into Persian by him for the *Dānešnāme*, and later in Iṣfahān in the course of the composition of the *Šifā'* (after 1024). Jūzjānī provides most of the information on the subject (see the texts in GS 6d below under Astronomy). For general studies of Avicenna's Mathematics see R. Rashed, al-Daffa and Stroyls, Djebbar, Ragep and Ragep, and Ardeshir.

I. *Geometry—Geodesy*

i. *Expository*

GS 6b. *Muḫtaṣar Awqlīdis* (*Uṣūl al-handasa*) (M-, A-)—*Compendium of Euclid* (*The Principles of Geometry*) / SB 29, LB 68

In the introduction to the Mathematics part of the *Najāt* and then again of the *Dānešnāme*, Jūzjānī says that he had in his possession abridgments made by Avicenna of the Geometry, Astronomy, and Music, and that he added these to the *Najāt* and, in Persian translation, to the *Dānešnāme* (text C cited below under Astronomy GS 6d). These were in all probability composed during Avicenna's stay in Jurjān (ca. 1012–1013), when Jūzjānī says he was studying the *Almagest* with him (Biography 44–45 Gohlman). The double descriptive title is given by Jūzjānī himself in that inroduction, and it would appear that both the SB and the LB list only one part of it from Jūzjānī: the compiler of the LB notes, "I think it is the one added to the *Najāt*" (*aẓunnuhu l-maḍmūm ilā n-Najāt*). It is not clear that the work circulated independently before its incorporation in the *Najāt*—i.e., whether anyone else other than Jūzjānī had a copy—and as far as is currently known, it exists only as part of the *Najāt* but not in any independent manuscripts. The one manuscript that bears this title, Istanbul Fatih 3211 (M219, A169), is actually the Geometry of the *Šifā'*, not the *Najāt*.

---

[22] As he says explicitly, *wa-ammā l-ʿilm ar-riyāḍī, fa-laysa min al-ʿilm allaḏī yuḫtalafu fīhi*, in *Manṭiq al-Mašriqiyyīn* 8.

Translation: Persian, by Jūzjānī, incorporated in the *Dānešnāme*, and in a French translation of the Persian in Achena and Massé II,91–136. Summary of contents in al-Daffa and Stroyls 79–88.

GMath 1. ***R. fī z-Zāwiya*** **(M80, A160)—*On the Angle* / LB 23, EB 54**

The LB states that Avicenna wrote this treatise in Jurjān (ca. 1013) for Abū-Sahl al-Masīḥī, and Mahdavī reports that the *explicit* of the text in the Istanbul MS Ayasofya 4849 confirms this (possibly the scribe of the MS himself drawing on the LB). See the study of its contents and background by Luther.

MSS: **Istanbul**, Ayasofya 4829_{11} ff. 47^b^–49^b^, 4849_{3} ff. 13^b^–22^b^, Nuruosmaniye 4894_{89} ff. 453^b^–457^b^, Pertev 617 ff. 126^b^–134^a^, Üniversite 4724_{14} ff. 92^a^–102^a^; **New Haven** Yale Ar. Suppl. 51, ff. 3^b^–39^a^ (partial); **Tehran**, Majlis-i Sanā 2252 ff. 104–120, Miškāt 1149 ff. 373^a^–376^b^.

Published: Mawāldī.

GMath 2. ***Muḫtaṣar fī anna z-zāwiya allatī min al-muḥīṭ wa-l-mumāss lā kammiyya lahā*** **(M-, A-)—*Compendium on That the Angle which Is Formed by the Circumference and the Tangent Has no Magnitude* / LB 18**

A treatise on the subject indicated by the title, which is separate from the preceding one, was commented on by Quṭb-ad-Dīn aš-Šīrāzī (see Luther 124–125, who identified it). Although no manuscript of it appears to be extant at present, it was manifestly in circulation in the twelfth and thirteenth centuries for aš-Šīrāzī to comment on it and for the compiler of the LB to include it in his list (as further testimony to the accuracy and reliability of the LB).

ii. *Pseudepigraphs, to be authenticated*

GMath-Ps 1. ***Fī Ṭūl Jurjān*** **(M-, A-)—*On the Longitude of Jurjān***

Reported and discussed by Bīrūnī in his *Taḥdīd al-amākin* (see Ragep and Ragep 5 and 7), this title is not listed in any bibliography and is not extant in any known manuscript. If not a part of the correspondence between the two men, its nature and authenticity remain to be verified.

GMath-Ps 2. ***M. fī l-Masālik wa-biqāʿ al-arḍ*** **(M-, A-)—*On Roads and Provinces* / LB 94**

Only the LB lists this work, which it presents as "a treatise which he mentioned in his works that it is on roads and provinces" (for the Arabic see the Tetrapla). There seem to be no other references to this title or the work in the manuscripts.

II. *Astronomy*

GS 6d. *Al-Arṣād al-kulliyya* (M-, A-)—*Comprehensive Observations* / Bio 3, SB 6, LB 10 (= *Muḫtaṣar al-Majisṭī* [M142/A171]—*Compendium of the Almagest* / Bio 5)

The titles and number of Avicenna's works on the *Almagest* are to be decided on the basis of the following evidence:

(A) Jūzjānī, Biography (44.4–8 Gohlman):
There was in Jurjān a man called Abū-Muḥammad aš-Šīrāzī … . I used to attend Avicenna [in the house bought for him by aš-Šīrāzī] every day and study with him the *Almagest* … . Avicenna composed for aš-Šīrāzī *Kitāb al-Arṣād al-kulliyya* [the book of *Compehensive Observations*]. He composed in Jurjān many [monograph-length] books [*kutub*], like the beginning of the *Qānūn* [*Canon for Medicine*] and the *Muḫtaṣar al-Majisṭī* [*Abridgment of the Almagest*] and many of the [smaller] treatises [*rasāʾil*].[23]

(B) Jūzjānī, Biography (64.5–66.2 Gohlman):
Avicenna occupied himself in Iṣfahān with finishing the *Šifāʾ* [*The Cure*], completing the Logic and the Almagest [Astronomy], since he had already abridged Euclid [Geometry], Arithmetic, and Music. In every book of the Mathematics he presented additional materials, the need for which he thought to be compelling. As for the Almagest [astronomy], he presented ten figures on the parallax, and at the end of *al-Majisṭī fī ʿilm al-hayʾa* [*The Almagest, On the Science of Astronomy*] he presented materials which were unprecedented. In Euclid [Geometry] he presented some problematic passages,[24] in Arithmetic some excellent [numerical] properties, and in Music some problems which the ancients had neglected.

---

[23] It is to be noted that Jūzjānī here is making a distinction between *kitāb*, a monograph-length book, and *risāla*, a smaller or article-length treatise. The same distinction is made in the SB, where there is first presented explicitly a listing of books, *kutub*, and then one of the treatises, *rasāʾil*. See the discussion above in the Introduction to the Tetrapla, Part One of the Appendix.

[24] IAU and Q both read *šubahan*, as does the text of al-Kāšī (Ahwānī *Nukat* 22.7) and the Istanbul MS Üniversite 4755, f. 313[a] bottom, where it is clearly vocalized. Gohlman's entry in the apparatus (p. 66, line 1) is unclear and omits references to manuscripts. Gohlman's reference to Dozy (though the same entry is also found in Wehr) for his rendering "geometrical figures" is misunderstood: *šabīh*, pl. *šubahāʾ*, by itself does not mean "geometrical figures" but only when followed by another word indicating the figure in question, while *šabīh* itself translates properly the Greek element -ειδής ("in the form of," "like") in words like "rhombo-id" and "trapezo-id."

(C) Jūzjānī, Introduction to the Mathematics of the *Najāt*:[25]

I had in my possession books by him [Avicenna] which were composed on the Mathematical sciences and were appropriate for it [the *Najāt*]. One of them was (i) *kitābuhu fī uṣūl al-handasa muḫtaṣaran min kitāb Awqlīdis* [his book on the *Principles of Geometry*, as an abridgment of the book by Euclid] ...; another was (ii) *kitābuhu fī l-arṣād al-kulliyya wa-maʿrifat tarkīb al-aflāk, ka-l-muḫtaṣar min al-Majisṭī* [his book *On Comprehensive Observations and Cognizance of the Structure of the Celestial Spheres*, as an abridment of the *Almagest*]; and another was (iii) *kitābuhu l-muḫtaṣar fī ʿilm al-mūsīqā* [his book *Abridgment of the Science of Music*]. I thought I would add these treatises to this book [the *Najāt*] in order for his writings to end in accordance with what he indicated in its introduction. But since I could not find on Arithmetic anything by him similar to these treatises, I thought I would abridge (iv) his book on *Arithmetic* (*Ariṯmāṭīqī*) into a [smaller] treatise ... and add it to [the *Najāt*].

(D) In the Bibliographies, the entry on *Kitāb al-Arṣād al-kulliyya* in passage (A) above (= Biography no. 3) is reproduced in SB 6 and LB 10.

All the evidence we have comes from Jūzjānī, with the exception of the entries in the SB and LB—and if the SB in the end is proven to be by Jūzjānī, then only the LB, which in any case depends on Jūzjānī. Jūzjānī himself was interested and competent in the mathematical sciences (cf. Wisnovsky "Jowzjāni" 83b–84a), had first-hand knowledge of the works Avicenna composed during their long association together, and, in the case of the *Almagest*, makes a point to inform us that he had studied the book together with Avicenna (passage (A) above). His testimony therefore in this regard can hardly be doubted.

In the information Jūzjānī provides, he mentions three titles of astronomical books, which have to be analyzed. These are:

1a) *Kitāb al-Arṣād al-kulliyya*, composed in Jurjān in 1012–1013 for Abū-Muḥammad aš-Šīrāzī, his patron and landlord. (A)
1b) The same title is listed in SB 6 and LB 10. (D)
1c) The same title in the Introduction to the Mathematics of the *Najāt*

[25] Text in Mahdavī 234–235 and, in facsimile, in *Najāt* 399 Dānešpaǰūh, which offers a slightly better text. The entire introduction is translated in Ragep and Ragep. According to Sezgin, *GAS* VI,281n3, the Cairo MS Ṭalʿat Riyāḍiyyāt 118, f. 69^b, begins with exactly the same words from Jūzjānī's introduction.

is listed and described as follows: *Kitābuhu fī l-Arṣād al-kulliyya wa-maʿrifat tarkīb al-aflāk, ka-l-muḫtaṣar min al-Majisṭī* (C). Jūzjāni says he incorporated this work into the *Najāt*. (C)

1d) The astronomy part of the *Najāt* begins and ends as follows: *urīdu an aḥṣura bayān al-arṣād al-kulliyya allatī ʿulima minhā l-aḥkām al-kulliyya fī hayʾat al-falak wa-taqdīr al-ḥarakāt ... . wa-qad balaġnā l-ġāyata min ġaraḍinā fa-l-naqṭaʿ al-maqālata* (*Najāt* 445[a]–475[b] Dāneš-pažūh).

2) *Muḫtaṣar al-Majisṭī*, composed in Jurjān in 1012–1013. (A)

3) *al-Majisṭī fī ʿilm al-hayʾa*, the astronomical part of the *Šifāʾ*, composed in Iṣfahān after 1024. (B)

The last item, the astronomical part of the *Šifāʾ*, presents no problems of identification. It was composed in Iṣfahān after Avicenna moved there in 1024, and it is accordingly not to be identified with item no. 2, the *Muḫtaṣar al-Majisṭī*, which Jūzjānī says expressly that it was composed in Jurjān (in 1012–1013, when Avicenna lived there). It is possible that in composing the astronomy for the *Šifāʾ* Avicenna used this earlier piece, but it is not likely, given that he rarely kept copies of his previous works. Also, Jūzjānī mentions in (C) that he, Jūzjānī, had kept a copy of *al-Arṣād al-kulliyya* but not of the *Muḫtaṣar al-Majisṭī* (which theoretically he could have offered to Avicenna to use). Besides, the astronomy of the *Šifāʾ* is a huge work (647 pages in the Cairo edition), and it cannot be labeled a *muḫtaṣar* as a title. It is true that Avicenna himself at the opening of the work calls it a "synopsis," *jawāmiʿ* (p. 15), and in closing he says he reached the end of what he "abridged," *mā ḫtaṣarnāhu*, of *al-Majisṭī*, but it is clear that these words are not used in their technical sense referring to a genre but in their literal sense indicating that Avicenna treated the contents of the entire *Almagest* selectively and not comprehensively.

The first item in the list above, *al-Arṣād al-kulliyya*, is also litttle problematic: it was composed in 1012–1013 in Jurjān, was added to the Mathematics part of the *Najāt* by Jūzjānī, and is extant in the manuscripts of this work. The one question relating to it is its precise title (even if the entire issue of the titles of Avicenna's works is in itself very complicated and in need of detailed study). In the Biography (A) Jūzjānī gives a short title, but in the introduction to the Mathematics of the *Najāt* (C) he expands the title and adds a descriptive phrase. Avicenna's opening words of the work help decide the issue. Avicenna says (no. 1d above), *urīdu an aḥṣura bayān al-arṣād al-kulliyya allatī ʿulima minhā l-aḥkām al-kulliyya fī hayʾat al-falak wa-taqdīr al-ḥarakāt*. The first part of this sentence is precisely the short title of the work given by Jūzjānī in the Biography (A). The second part, *allatī ʿulima minhā l-aḥkām al-kulliyya fī hay'at al-falak wa-taqdīr al-ḥarakāt*, is too long for a title and it is clear that Jūzjānī summarized it in the three words that say the same thing, *maʿrifat tarkīb al-aflāk*. It can be safely concluded that *al-Arṣād al-kulliyya* is as close to the original title as Avicenna would have given the work (had he indeed given it any title, given that it was presented to Abū-Muḥammad aš-Šīrāzī who had requested it from him).

The second title, *Muḫtaṣar al-Majisṭī*, is the problematic one. It was also composed in Jurjān in 1012–1013, but the way that it is presented by Jūzjānī almost in the same breath it appears that it is a different work from *al-Arṣād al-kulliyya* (see (A) above). It is also indubitably different from the astronomy part of the *Šifā'*, as just discussed. But it can hardly be thought that it is yet a third, and separate, abridgment of the *Almagest*, and indeed, composed in the same year as *al-Arṣād al-kulliyya* and in the same place. It thus appears that it is the same work as *al-Arṣād al-kulliyya*, but that Jūzjānī inadvertently presented it in the Biography as a separate work, an inadvertence which he seems to have remedied in the introduction to the Mathematics part of the *Najāt* where he calls *al-Arṣād al-kulliyya* a treatise that is *like* an abridgment of the *Almagest* (*ka-l-muḫtaṣar min al-Majisṭī*). All the other evidence we have corroborates this conclusion. *Al-Arṣād al-kulliyya*, first of all, is indeed a true *muḫtaṣar* of the *Almagest*: it covers the essentials of that work in nine sections, and it takes only 30 folios in the MS presented in facsimile by Dānešpajūh, and 10 in the Istanbul MS Ayasofya 4829 (ff. 223ᵃ–232ᵇ). Most importantly, the SB, LB, and EB do not list *Muḫtaṣar al-Majisṭī* at all, manifestly because they also consider it (and rightly so) as part of the *Najāt*: the *Muḫtaṣar al-Majisṭī* and *al-Muḫtaṣar al-aṣġar fī l-manṭiq* are the only two titles mentioned by Jūzjānī in the Biography which are not taken up by any of the bibliographies, SB, LB, and EB, clearly because they are part of the *Najāt*. There are, finally, no manuscripts of the *Muḫtaṣar al-Majisṭī*,[26] and it is not mentioned anywhere else. It is actually a description of *al-Arṣād al-kulliyya* which Jūzjānī inadvertently presented in the Biography as the title of an independent treatise. Accordingly, Avicenna wrote two works on the *Almagest*, a shorter and a longer one, the former incorporated in the *Najāt* and the latter in the *Ṣifā'* (nos. 1 and 3 above).[27]

---

[26] The MSS listed by Anawati no. 171 (pp. 232–233) either contain the astronomical part of the *Šifā'* or are by other authors; cf. Mahdavī p. 172 and 263, and Ragep and Ragep 6.

[27] The entries in Ragep and Ragep 4–5 and *GAS* VI.278–280 are accordingly to be adjusted.

MSS: *Al-Arṣād al-kulliyya* does not exist independently in any known MSS but only as integrated into the Mathematics part of the *Najāt*, for which see above, GS 6.

Published: Facsimile reproduction of MS Tehran, Dānešgāh 1348 in *Najāt* 443–475 Dānešpažūh.

Translations: A Persian translation by Jūzjānī himself was incorporated into the Mathematical part of the *Dānešnāme-ye ʿAlāʾī*, a French translation of which appeared in Achena and Massé II,137–191.

GMath 3. *M. fī Kayfiyyat ar-raṣad wa-taṭābuqihi maʿa l-ʿilm aṭ-ṭabīʿī* (M242, A173)—*On the Nature of [Astronomical] Observations and their Conformity with the Science of Physics* / Bio 12, LB 53

Alternate titles: *al-Maqāla al-aḫīra al-muḍāfa ilā mā ḫtuṣira min Kitāb al-Majisṭī; Ibtidāʾ al-maqāla al-muḍāfa ilā mā ḫtuṣira min Kitāb al-Majisṭī.*

This is a brief essay intended as a corrective and updated appendix to Avicenna's treatment of the *Almagest* in the *Šifāʾ*. He refers to it explicitly in the Prologue to *The Cure*, as does Jūzjānī in the Biography (Bio 12). Avicenna says (T9, § 5C): "After I finished this [the *Almagest*], I appended to it such additions as are necessary for the student to know in order to complete thereby [his study of] this discipline and bring astronomical observations into conformity with the laws of Physics." The compiler of the LB, to his credit, unearths this reference from this passage and adds it to his list (LB 53). Thus the title, which appears to be by this compiler or his source, is nevertheless the closest to Avicenna's description of what he intended to do in this appendix. His opening statement reads, "It is incumbent upon us to bring what is mentioned in the *Almagest* into conformity with what is intellectually perceived from the science of Physics, and to describe the way in which these [celestial] motions occur" (*yalzamunā an nuṭābiqa bayna l-maḏkūr fī l-Majisṭī wa-bayna l-maʿqūl min al-ʿilm aṭ-ṭabīʿī wa-nuʿarrifa kayfiyyat wuqūʿ hāḏihi l-ḥarakāt*). From this it is clear that the expression *kayfiyyat ar-raṣad* in the title corresponds to the phrase *kayfiyyat wuqūʿ hāḏihi l-ḥarakāt*, and accordingly the former means "on the nature of observations = on the nature of observed celestial motions." Other titles that are given to it, like that in the Cairo edition of the *Šifāʾ*, *Ibtidāʾ al-maqāla al-muḍāfa ilā mā ḫtuṣira min Kitāb al-Majisṭī mimmā laysa yadullu ʿalayhi l-Majisṭī*, are either lengthy descriptions by scribes of the contents or innovations.

For the contents see Ragep and Ragep 6.

MS: **Istanbul**, Ahmet III 3303_2.—In addition to the MSS of the Astronomy of the *Šifāʾ*, for which see GS 5, this essay is also independently transmitted, under various titles; see Ragep and Ragep 6.

Published: *Hay'a* 651–659 Madwar and Aḥmad.
Translation: English, forthcoming Ragep and Ragep 6.

GMath 4. *Al-Ālāt ar-raṣadiyya* (M1, A164)—*Instruments of Astronomical Observation* / Bio 19, SB 23, LB 55

Title in the MS: *M. fī ṭ-Ṭarīq allaḏī āṯarahu ʿalā sāʾir aṭ-ṭuruq fī ttiḫāḏ al-ālāt ar-raṣadiyya.*

In the Biography Jūzjānī reports as follows the occasion of this treatise: "In the course of his astronomical observations [in Iṣfahān], he invented instruments which had never before existed and wrote a treatise about them" (Gohlman 81.4–6).

MSS: **Bursa**, Hüseyin Çelebi 1194 ff. 101[a]–105[b]; **Leiden** Warn. Or. 184_8 (Cat. 1061), ff. 49[b]–62[a] (515H). Facsimile of the Leiden MS in Sezgin "al-Āla ar-raṣadiyya."

Published, with German translation and commentary, by Wiedemann, with further references in Sezgin "al-Āla ar-raṣadiyya" and in *GAS* VI,279, no. 5.

GMath 5. *M. fī Ḫawāṣṣ ḫaṭṭ al-istiwāʾ* (M-, A-)—*On the Characteristics of the Equator* / LB 42

This title, listed only by the LB, is not extant in any known manuscript. On the subject cf. Ragep and Ragep 8, no. 9.

III. *Arithmetic*

GS 6c. *M. fī l-Ariṯmāṭīqī* (M-, A-)—*On Arithmetic* / LB 69

In the introduction to the Mathematics part of the *Najāt*, Jūzjānī says that "since I could not find on Arithmetic anything by him similar to these treatises [i.e., the abridged presentations of Geometry, Astronomy, and Music he had written earlier], I thought I would abridge his book on *Arithmetic* (*Ariṯmāṭīqī*) into a [smaller] treatise ... and add it to [the *Najāt*]" (above, text C in GS 6d under Astronomy). The version of the Arithmetic that is found in the *Najāt*, therefore, and the Persian translation of it by Jūzjānī in the *Dānešnāme*, are actually by Jūzjānī himself and not directly by Avicenna, though it is clear that what Jūzjānī referred to by abridging Avicenna's book on *Arithmetic* was the Arithmetic of the *Šifāʾ*.

MSS: The listing of the title in the LB may be no more than a reflection of this report by Jūzjānī, though it may be also a reference to a manuscript of the work in circulation independently of the *Najāt*; two Cairo MSS are listed as containing the work and should be consulted: Dār al-Kutub 863_{13-14}

(ca. 850H) ff. 278[b]–290[a] and 290[b]–297[a], and Ṭal'at Riyāḍa 118_3 (1075H) ff. 69[b]–86[b].[28] The *Muḫtaṣar K. al-Ariṯmāṭīqī* in the Istanbul MS Ali Emiri Efendi 2850, listed by M221 and A170, is apparently the Arithmetic of the *Šifā'*.

Translation into Persian by Jūzjānī in the *Dānešnāme*, and a French translation of that in Achena and Massé II,193–219.—For a summary of the contents see al-Daffa and Stroyls 65–71.

IV. *Music*

i. *Expository*

GS 6e. *R. fī l-Mūsīqā* (M-, A165)—*Treatise on Music* / EB 68

This is the Music part of the *Najāt*, apparently in the possession of Jūzjānī, who added it to the Mathematics part of that work. It survives independently of the *Najāt*, as its publication indicates, and it must have circulated early as such, for the EB lists it as a separate treatise (*risāla*) on music and adds the comment that it is not the musical part of the *Šifā'*. The compiler of the EB must have been looking at a manuscript containing the work, for he does not call it a *muḫtaṣar*, as Jūzjānī does, and neither does it seem likely that he is referring to the *Madḫal* listed in the LB (below, GMath-Ps. 3).

MSS: The Hyderabad publication (Mūsawī *Majmū' Rasā'il*, treatise no. 7) is based on two MSS in India, listed by Anawati.

Publication: Mūsawī, treatise no. 7; *Najāt* 477–489 Dānešpažūh.

Translation: French, of the Persian translation by Jūzjānī, Achena and Massé II, 221–243.

ii. *Pseudepigraph, to be authenticated*

GMath-Ps 3. *Al-Madḫal ilā ṣinā'at al-mūsīqā* (cf. M232, A165)—*Introduction to the Science of Music* / LB 50

There exist two known works by Avicenna on music: a brief treatise (GS 6e above), composed independently and found in the possession of Jūzjanī, who calls it a "compendium" (*kitābuhu l-muḫtaṣar fī 'ilm al-mūsīqā*, text C in entry GS 6d above under Astronomy), later incorporated by him into the Mathematics of the *Najāt*; and a monograph on the subject, called "epitome" (*jawāmi'*) by Avicenna, which constitutes the Music part of the *Šifā'*. The LB,

[28] David A. King, *A Survey of the Scientific Manuscripts in the Egyptian National Library* [ARCE / Catalogs 5], Indiana: Eisenbrauns, 1986, 49, no. B82; cf. *GAS* VI,281n3.

however, lists the music part of neither the *Najāt* nor the *Šifāʾ* but only the title of *Madḫal* given above, and adds the comment that this essay is not the Music part of the *Najāt*. In light of the high reliability of the compiler of the LB, and of the fact that for two other mathematical parts of the *Najāt* he does make the comment that they belong to the *Najāt*, this comment of his about the musical work must be taken seriously. However, this *Madḫal* can hardly be the music of the *Šifāʾ* either, which is an extensive treatment of the subject and cannot readily be called an "introduction." Now the Music part of the *Najāt*, which also circulated independently, is called in the colophon of the Indian MS(S?) *imlāʾ aš-Šayḫ ar-Raʾīs ʿalā sabīl al-madḫal*, which is a scribal note of unknown origin. If this colophon has an ancient pedigree, it is likely that the compiler of LB saw it in the manuscript from which he was drawing his information and gave the treatise this title. However, for him to say specifically that this is not the Music of the *Najāt* means that he somehow checked that book and saw the difference. So the question remains and the *Madḫal* may be a separate treatise by Avicenna on music, to be investigated.

E. Metaphysics of the Rational Soul (GM)

Avicenna wrote no independent works on metaphysics as universal science (*metaphysica generalis*); all of them were embedded in larger works, and especially in his summae, the most extensive and elaborate of which, that in the *Šifāʾ*, "constitutes the first concrete replacement of this work [Aristotle's *Metaphysics*] with an original treatment on metaphysics, thus allowing metaphysics the possibility of an autonomous progress" (Bertolacci *Reception* p. viii). For a listing and brief descriptions, with bibliographical references, of the embedded segments on metaphysics in the summae listed above under GS, see Bertolacci *Reception* 581–591, Appendix C.

By contrast, Avicenna wrote much on the extended and "derivative" (*furūʿī*), as he called it in the *Aqsām* (above, Chapter 6.1), part of metaphysics which he originated and which he incorporated into the traditional one. It dealt with divine providence and the problem of evil, the afterlife of the human rational soul and its bliss or misery, and the communication of the human rational soul with its congeneric celestial intellects and the latter's effect on the former. It is this communication which on the one hand leads to prophecy, inspiration, veridical dreams, and the "miraculous" power of the human soul to act upon not only its own body but other bodies as well, and on the other makes the efficacy of prayer and other forms of religious practice ontologically possible and philosophically meaningful. This latter aspect of the communication between the celestial and human souls is, in the final analysis, what provides the ground for and sustains practical philosophy and its branches of ethics, household management, and politics.[29] All this Avicenna incorporated in the last part of the *Ilāhiyyāt* of the *Šifāʾ*, Books IX.6–7 and Book X, which ends, as just mentioned, with what is considered to be practical philosophy. It thus becomes clear that the subjects that Avicenna repeatedly identifies as those that are to be studied in the derivative part of metaphysics, which he originated, essentially overlap with those that are to be studied in the "discipline of legislating" (*aṣ-ṣināʿa aš-šāriʿa*), the fourth part of practical philosophy, which he also originated.[30]

[29] The foundation of practical philosophy in metaphysics Avicenna takes over from Fārābī, whose works on the subject in any case he copied in his early *al-Birr wa-l-iṯm*; see below, GPP 1.

[30] In the introduction to the *Easterners, Manṭiq al-Mašriqiyyīn* 8.1. See the tables of the contents of these parts in the various works by Avicenna above, Chapter 6.1 and 6.2, and in Kaya "Prophetic Legislation" 215 and the preceding discussion. Faḫr-ad-Dīn ar-Rāzī, a keen

This explains the perceived absence of practical philosophy in Avicenna's works. The part of the practical sciences that he was really interested in, which he eventually came to call the "discipline of legislating," he treated as the "derivative" part of Metaphysics, thus concealing it from our view. Given the fluctuations in Avicenna's appellation and categorization of this part of metaphysics/practical philosophy which he originated, and its philosophical basis on his concept of the rational soul, I have given it a new name, the metaphysics of the rational soul, as discussed above, Chapter 6.1–2.[31]

Because of the very nature of the subjects that were treated in the works falling in this category—subjects essentially relating to religious life—, they aroused great interest and inevitably gave rise to numerous pseudepigraphs. The authentication of these works thus constitutes a primary task for future research, which at this stage presents the following picture: some of these works which do not appear in the earliest bibliographies of Avicenna and have been transmitted in post thirteenth century tradition under his name can be seen either as (1) very early compositions by him, written before he met Jūzjānī whose express purpose was to register Avicenna's works, and which entered manuscript circulation much later, or (2) pseudepigraphs composed during a second wave of such activities in the thirteenth century and beyond, after the first wave of pseudepigraphs that began circulating over a century after Avicenna's death. If the first turns out to be the historical fact, it will require drastic re-evaluation of the extent to which Avicenna changed some of his views on crucial issues.

i. *Expository*

GM 1. *K. al-Mabdaʾ wa-l-maʿād* (M106, A195)—*The Provenance and Destination* / Bio 2, SB 18, LB 9, EB 18

For a description see above, Chapter Two, W4.

MSS: **Bursa**, Hüseyin Çelebi 1194 ff. 1^{b}–40^{b}; **Escorial** 703_{10}; **Istanbul**, Ahmet III 1584, 3225, 3247_{1}, 3268_{7} ff. 61^{a}–110^{a} (580H), Fatih 3217_{1}, Feyzullah 2188_{1}, Köprülü 869_{12}, Nuruosmaniye 4894_{65}, Ragıp Paşa 872 (625H), Üniversite

student of Avicenna's works, noted explicitly this innovation in his commentary on the *ʿUyūn al-ḥikma*: see above, Testimonium 15 in Chapter 2, W9.

31 Most recently presented in Gutas "Rational Soul." Apart from being Avicenna's own, this is a category whose distinctiveness and significance have been recognized. Wisnovsky *Avicenna's Metaphysics* 141 has called "an appreciation of the complex and dynamic cosmology of procession and reversion" crucial to an understanding of the metaphysics of the rational soul.

1630, 4390_{2}; **Leiden** 1464_{2}; **London**, Brit. Lib. 978_{33}; **Manchester** 384_{S}; **Meshed**, Riżavī IV 1/971, 972, 973, 974, 975, 976; **Milan** 320_{4}; **Tehran**, Majlis 634_{30}, Malik 2007_{8}, 2013_{21}, 2019_{4}, Miškāt 861_{5}, 1037, 1149 ff. 242^{b}–267^{b}, Sipahsālār 1217_{41}, 2912_{3}, Tangābunī 171_{2}, 308_{1}.

Published: Nūrānī.

Translation: Draft French translation with critical notes of variant readings based on ten MSS, by Michot *Livre de la genèse*.

GM 2. ***Al-Aḍḥawiyya fī l-maʿād*** **(M30, A200)—*The Immolation Destination (i.e., On the Destination, on the Occasion of the Feast of Immolation)* / LB 58, EB 71**

Alternate title: *al-Maʿād*.

The dedicatee, dating, and title of this treatise are problematical. The evidence that we have is as follows.

(a) As Mahdavī 39 reports, all the MSS which do mention a dedicatee in the exordium of the *Aḍḥawiyya* say that it was written for a certain aš-Šayḫ al-Amīn (or al-Amīr?) Abū-Bakr Muḥammad b. ʿUbayd or Abū-Bakr b. Muḥammad b. ʿUbayd/ʿAbdallāh. Apparently the same person is also mentioned in some manuscripts as the recipient of the *R. Nayrūziyya* (below, GPW 5k). This person remans unidentified.

(b) Bayhaqī *Tatimma* 33/48 says that Avicenna wrote the *Aḍḥawiyya* for the vizier Abū-Saʿd al-Hamaḏānī.

(c1) Jūzjānī in the Biography (Bio 6 = 50.1 Gohlman) says that Avicenna wrote the *K. al-Maʿād* in Rayy, before the death of Hilāl ibn-Badr, which took place in Ḏū l-Qaʿda 405/May 1015 according to Ibn-al-Aṯīr (Gohlman 127n63).

(c2) The scribe of the Istanbul MS Üniversite 4755 of Jūzjānī's Biography (Bio 6) adds, after the title *K. al-Maʿād* (f. 311^{b}), the word *al-aṣġar* in the margin, without any sign about the provenance of the correction. The same scribe, when he comes to copy the treatise (W5) *The State of the Human Soul/The Destination* (which he entitles, *Risāla fī n-nafs ʿalā ṭarīq ad-dalīl wa-l-burhān*), writes in the margin (f. 125^{b}), *hāḏā K. al-Maʿād al-aṣġar*,[32] thus identifying the treatise on *Maʿād* written in Rayy with the *State of the Human Soul* and not with the *Aḍḥawiyya*.

---

[32] Reisman "ARCE" 160 says that the marginal note is "in later hand," but it isn't. The shape of the letters and the color of the ink are the same as those in the main text as well as in numerous other marginal corrections made by the original scribe.

This means that in the MS tradition from which the scribe of the Istanbul MS copied his texts, a tradition which goes back directly to copies by Bahmanyār and Ibn-Zayla, the "lesser" *Maʿād* was identified with the *State of the Human Soul* and not with the *Aḍḥawiyya*.

(d) The Shorter Bibliography (SB) lists two books by the title *al-Maʿād*, one simply by this title, without specifying whether it is *al-aṣġar* or the *Aḍḥawiyya* (SB 19), and *al-Mabdaʾ wa-l-maʿād* (SB 18). The compiler of the Longer Bibliography (LB) repeats the two entries as in SB (LB 11 and 9) but complements the first title by saying (LB 11), *K. al-Maʿād al-aṣġar, ṣannafahu bi-r-Rayy wa-huwa fī ḫidmat al-malik Majd-ad-Dawla* (the correct text on f. 216^{b} in the Istanbul MS Üniversite 4755), thus identifying the *Maʿād* which Jūzjānī says was written in Rayy (Bio 6) with the *State of the Human Soul/The Destination*, as in the rest of the MS (above, c2). In addition, he *adds* later in LB 58 *al-Aḍḥawiyya fī l-maʿād* as a separate title, distinct from the "lesser" *Maʿād*. Thus the compiler of the LB, like the MS tradition of the scribe of the Istanbul MS, also did *not* identify the plain, or "lesser" *al-Maʿād* with the *Aḍḥawiyya*.

This evidence leads to the following conclusions. First, the dedicatee of the *Aḍḥawiyya*, who in all the manuscripts that include his name is called (above, a) Abū Bakr Muḥammad b. ʿUbayd (with small variations in the name), remains unidentified, though there can be little doubt about the authenticity of the name; he must have been some notable whose patronage Avicenna, in unsettled circumstances, was seeking to gain, to judge from the introductory address (Italian translation in Lucchetta *Epistola* 6–12, Michot *Abū Saʿd* 33*-34*). Bayhaqī says (above, b) that the *Aḍḥawiyya* was written for the Būyid vizier Abū-Saʿd al-Hamaḏānī, but this can hardly be entertained. Michot *Abū Saʿd* 27*-28* is willing to trust Bayhaqī's veracity, but he fails to realize that Bayhaqī, as Reisman rightly observed ("New Standard" 563n10), had no other independent source of information for his entry on Abū-l-Qāsim al-Kirmānī, where this identification occurs, than the very letter of Avicenna to Abū-Saʿd, which says nothing about the *Aḍḥawiyya*. It is a mystery from where Bayhaqī came up with the statement that Abū-Saʿd was the dedicatee, right after he stopped quoting Avicenna about the altercation he had with Kirmānī. But from wherever it was (if not off the top of his head), it cannot invalidate the very concrete manuscript evidence identifying Abū Bakr Muḥammad b. ʿUbayd as the dedicatee. In addition, there is great disparity in the form of address to the two individuals. Avicenna addresses Abū-Saʿd in the highly reverential form as *mawlāyā wa-raʾīsī wa-man anā ʿabduhu*, "my master and lord, whose slave/servant I am" (Michot

Abū Saʿd, p. 1 of the Arabic text), whereas Abū-Bakr he addresses simply as "*aš-šayḫ al-amīn*", and later adds that he hopes that Abū-Bakr will prove to be a "friend," *ṣadīq*. Thus the *Aḍḥawiyya* quite certainly was not addressed to the vizier Abū-Saʿd.

Second, there is the question whether the *Aḍḥawiyya* is the same as the treatise called *al-Maʿād* which Jūzjānī says was compiled in Rayy before 1015 (above, c1). The compiler of LB is definite that it is not, calling the second "the lesser *Destination*" to distinguish it from the *Aḍḥawiyya* which is the proper, or "larger" *Destination* (above, d), while the scribe of the Istanbul MS Üniversite 4755 just as definitely identifies the "lesser *Destination*" with *The State of the Human Soul*, which also bears in some manuscripts the title, *On the Soul, by Way of Proof and Demonstration*. The reliability of the LB has been discussed above. The Istanbul Üniversite MS, in addition, also derives from the immediate circle of Avicenna, with numerous bibliographical indications strewn throughout it (see Reisman *Avicennan Tradition* 45–49). The evidence they provide is thus weighty.

Third is the question of the date of composition of the *Aḍḥawiyya*. If it is not to be identified with the "Lesser" *Destination* which was written in Rayy before 1015, and the dedicatee remains unidentified, the question needs to be resolved by different criteria. Lucchetta *Epistola* p. XIV and XVII argues for a late date on the basis of its "mature" content and of references in it to what she considers to be *The Cure*, but these references are not so much explicit references specifically to that book than to Physics and Metaphysics as sciences. Michot *Abū Saʿd* 28* opts for an early date but that is because he identifies it with the "lesser *Destination*" mentioned above. The tendency I have identified above (Chapter 7) in Avicenna's later works not to refer explicitly to authorities would tend to indicate that the *Aḍḥawiyya* is an early work, since there are numerous authorities quoted by name, but the nature of the work is partly historical, in which Avicenna refers to various opinions concerning *maʿād*, and thus name dropping is to be expected. Nevertheless, the fact that he would refer to a specific book by Aristotle by its title (the *Metaphysics*, Lucchetta *Epistola* 107: *Arisṭūṭālīs fī-Mā baʿda ṭ-ṭabīʿa*), and that he would refer to his own "commentary" on *De anima* (Lucchetta *Epistola* 153: *fī šarḥinā li-kitāb Arisṭūṭālīs fī n-Nafs*; cf. GS 10c under Physics, above) tends to indicate that the work is an earlier composition. The dedicatory introduction, in which Avicenna describes the hard times he is experiencing, corroborates this view, for it points to an unsettled period in Avicenna's life when he had not yet arrived at the safe haven of ʿAlāʾ-ad-Dawla's court in Iṣfahān (see also Michot *Abū Saʿd* 33*-36* for a description of this period). This period was also posterior to Avicenna's youth in Buḫārā and even in Gurgānj, where he enjoyed the patronage of the Ma'mūnids and in particular of Abū-l-Ḥasan as-Sahlī. The *Aḏḥawiyya* can thus be dated with reasonable certainty to the middle years of Avicenna's activity in Jurjān, Rayy, and Hamaḏān, from 1012 to 1024.

The final question that needs to be resolved in this connection is the identity of the "Lesser" *Maʿād*, if it is clear that it is not the *Aḏḥawiyya*. To begin with the most reliable evidence, Jūzjānī reports in the Biography only on two titles dealing with the subject of the soul's Destination in the afterlife: *al-Mabda' wa-l-maʿād* written in Jurjān for Abū-Muḥammad aš-Šīrāzī (Bio 2), and just the plain title of *al-Maʿād*, written in Rayy (Bio 6); the LB further specifies, while Avicenna was in the service of Majd-ad-Dawla.[33] There has never been any doubt concerning the identity of the work with the fuller title, *al-Mabda wa-l-maʿād*, which is the well known work described above (GM 1). The question is the identity of the plain *al-Maʿād*. Among all the works of Avicenna, the only ones that have been, or can be, so entitled, are the *Aḏḥawiyya* and what is known with several titles: it has been discussed under the title *The State of the Human Soul* and was published by Ahwānī *Aḥwāl* 43–142 (below, GM 3). As Mahdavī 244 properly notes, the introduction plainly states that the work is about the survival and fate of the human soul, to which the sections on the various faculties of the soul serve as a prelude. As discussed in the second preceding paragraph above, then, if this plain *al-Maʿād* mentioned by Jūzjānī in the Biography is not the *Aḏḥawiyya*, then it can only be, by elimination, *The State of the Human Soul*. Which also means that, accordingly, Jūzjānī does not mention the *Aḏḥawiyya* in the Biography.

Chronologically the next bibliography to be compiled, the SB, follows the entries in Jūzjānī's biography closely. This compiler also just lists *al-Mabda wa-l-maʿād* (SB 18) and plain *al-Maʿād* (SB 19) only, and omits any mention of the *Aḏḥawiyya*.

Next comes the LB, whose compiler introduces two new elements in the listing of these works. He qualifies the plain *al-Maʿād* by calling it "lesser" (*al-aṣġar*) (LB 11), and adds a separate listing for the *Aḏḥawiyya* (LB 58), which means, as noted above, that he considered the two to be distinct. The adjective "lesser" is clearly a bibliographer's addition at some point in the

33 The text of the LB as printed in IAU (II.19.1) is wrong: "written in Rayy *for* Majd-ad-Dawla" (*ṣannafahu bi-r-Rayy li-l-malik Majd-ad-Dawla*); what the LB says in the text in the Istanbul MS Üniversite 4755, f. 216^b, is that it was "written in Rayy *while* Avicenna was in Majd-ad-Dawla's service" (*ṣannafahu bi-r-Rayy wa-huwa fī ḫidmat al-malik Majd-ad-Dawla*). Gohlman also is wrong in printing this phrase in the apparatus (p. 94.5) instead of in the text.

transmission to effect precisely this distinction, with the implication that the *Aḍḥawiyya* was considered to be the "greater" *al-Maʿād*, which, however, needed no additional special qualification since the descriptive *Aḍḥawiyya* was considered sufficient. The EB, finally, brings no additional information on the subject, as it repeats the listings in the LB.

For the only two works by Avicenna which can lay claim to the title *al-Maʿād*, therefore, the *Aḍḥawiyya* and *The State of the Human Soul*, Jūzjānī in the Biography and the compiler of the LB provide no information, while bibliographers and scribes working a century after Avicenna's death are unanimous in their verdict that it was *The State of the Human Soul* which was to be so identified, with the additional qualification that it was also the "lesser" *al-Maʿād*. For the early bibliographers, as for us, it would be counterintuitive to call the *Aḍḥawiyya* the "lesser" book, given that it is manifest to any casual observer, let alone the expert bibliographers of Avicenna's books, that the *Aḍḥawiyya* was the most comprehensive work on the subject.

A final problem in the identification of *The State of the Human Soul* as the "lesser" *al-Maʿād* is the absence of the *Aḍḥawiyya* from both Jūzjānī's Biography and the SB. If the *Aḍḥawiyya* was composed between 1012 and 1024, as suggested above, this period corresponds to the very beginning of Avicenna's association with Jūzjānī, and the latter should have been aware of this work and reported it. One possibility of its absence from the Biography and the SB is that Avicenna wrote it and gave it to his patron just before he met Jūzjānī—when he was already moving from one place to another in search of patronage (and the absence of information about the addressee may support this theory)—and thus Jūzjānī was not aware of it and would not have requested information about it, given that soon thereafter Avicenna wrote another work on the subject in Rayy, the "lesser" *Maʿād*. Another possibility would be that Avicenna wrote the work and sent it to his patron without keeping a copy, as it frequently happened, and Jūzjānī somehow missed the event, being otherwise preoccupied. The treatise surfaced after a generation or two among Avicenna scholars, also as it happened with other treatises, and it came to the attention of the compiler of the LB who registered it.

MSS: **Berlin** 2734; **Cairo**^{2} I 186; **Istanbul**, Ahmet III 3247_{2}, 3447_{14}, Ayasofya 4829_{28}, Hamidiye 1448_{20}, Hazine 1730_{29}, Nuruosmaniye 4894_{99}, Ragıp Paşa 1461_{6}, Revan 2042_{10}, Üniversite 1458_{79}, 4724_{6}, 4755_{15} ff. 219^{a}–250^{a} (588H); **Leiden** 1465; **London**, Brit. Lib. 978_{4}; **Manchester** 384_{1}; **Marāġa** pp. 365–402 Pourjavady; **Meshed**, Riżavī IV 1/353, 354; **Rampur** I 712; **Tehran**, Majlis 634_{25}, 1264_{6}, Malik 2003_{10}, Miškāt 422_{1}, 1074_{2}, 1149 ff. 387^{b}–395^{b}, Sipahsālār 8371_{3}, Ṭabāṭabāʾī 1280_{1}, Tangābunī 40_{1}, 79_{3}.

Published: Lucchetta *Epistola*; ʿĀṣī *Aḍḥawiyya*.
Translation: Italian, Lucchetta *Epistola*.

GM 3. *Al-Maʿād* [*al-aṣġar*] (*Ḥāl an-nafs al-insāniyya*) (M121, 207, A74, 77, 109, 199, 201)—*The* [*"Lesser"*] *Destination* (*State of the Human Soul*) / Bio 6, SB 19, LB 11, EB 36, 47, 63

Alternate titles: *R. fī n-Nafs ʿalā ṭarīq ad-dalīl wa-l-burhān; Fī n-Nafs an-nāṭiqa; Aḥwāl an-nafs; an-Nafs al-falakiyya* [Chapter 13]; *an-Nufūs* [Chapter 1]; *R. fī l-Quwā l-jusmāniyya* [Chapter 1].

If this treatise is the *Maʿād* mentioned by Jūzjānī (Bio 6), as argued in the preceding entry (GM 2), it was composed in Rayy shortly before 1015; it was discussed above, Chapter Two, W5.

In a welcome critical article ("Authenticité"), Sebti has recently questioned its authenticity and concluded that the treatise was composed after Avicenna by a compiler who extracted most of the chapters from the *Najāt* and added three new ones, chapter one, chapter thirteen, and the concluding piece, chapter sixteen. Sebti bases all her arguments on a criticism of the contents of the allegedly spurious chapters, which on occasion she finds going against the grain of the theses in the De anima of the *Šifāʾ*, but her major objection is "the lack of rigor" ("le manque de rigueur," pp. 334 and 352) in the argumentation of these chapters. Such internal criticism of relatively fine points—unless the forger has made egregious blunders—can hardly prove inauthenticity, as Sebti herself admits (p. 334), especially in a work which comes from the transition period of Avicenna's career and whose two contested chapters (one and thirteen) have passsed muster with an Avicennan expert (Michot *"Définition"* and "Prophétie"). Nevertheless, her caveat is well taken, for this treatise has a particularly complicated transmission history which needs to be investigated in detail. Apart from the question of its original title and whether it is to be identified with the *Maʿād* written in Rayy (Bio 6) and the great variety of titles under which it is transmitted, there is the fact that precisely these two chapters, one and thirteen, have in fact circulated independently with different titles (though always in the name of Avicenna),[34] and most significantly, this treatise, in the form in which we know it, was one of the main sources in the work that goes also under Ġazālī's name as *Maʿārij al-quds* (see Janssens "Maʿārij al-quds"). A minute examination of all these texts and their manuscript transmission is necessary before definite conclusions can be reached.

---

34 See below at the end of this entry.

For the time being, there are weighty arguments that the treatise as such, even if possibly interpolated in places, is the work of Avicenna and that it is the *Maʿād* which he wrote in Rayy while in the service of Majd-ad-Dawla. The concluding chapter sixteen (= T5), to begin with, is indisputably his work. It has the same tenor and message as the introduction to the *Provenance and Destination* (T4, § 3) with which it is roughly contemporary, and it uses a number of technical terms (capitalized in T5) in the sense in which it is common with Avicenna, while the exhortation in § 3 that the work be shown only to those worthy to receive it is part and parcel of the theme of Withholding knowledge cultivated by Avicenna also elsewhere and discussed above, Chapter 5.3.[35] Second, the contested chapters use certain technical terms and references to books and previous philosophers in ways that are typical of the early Avicenna. In chapter one, for instance, the author refers to the Aristotelian *Topics* (II,1 109a16–21, as identified by Michot *"Définition"* 248n42) by the transliterated name, *Ṭūbīqā* (Ahwānī *Aḥwāl* 55.8)—would a forger writing after Avicenna have used this Greek term, instead of *Jadal*, to refer to the *Topics*, and indeed to a precise passage of it? The same applies to the term *fanṭāsiyā/banṭāsiyā* for the internal sense instead of *ḥiss muštarak*, which is used in the contested chapter thirteen (120.1 and 120.8 Ahwānī) but also in the authentic chapter two (61.11 Ahwānī). Third—and this goes to the argument of Sebti as much as to that of Michot (*"Définition"* 240–241), who would see this *Maʿād* treatise as posterior to the *Najāṭ* and compiled from extracts from it—in the uncontested chapter eleven, but also in the *Najāt*, Avicenna refers to Plato as "the Divine" (*al-ilāhī*: 108.4 Ahwānī = *Najāt* 313.6/391.10). If this treatise *al-Maʿād* is posterior to the *Najāt* and extracted from it, this means that Avicenna incongruously still used the term "divine" to refer to Plato while compiling the *Najāt* in 1027 *after* he completed the *Šifāʾ*, in the Sophistics part of which he had declared Plato incompetent, as early as 1024, by maintaining that Plato's "wares were paltry indeed and philosophy in his time had not matured to the point of reaping" (T6B, § 8). Even more to the point is the fact that in the part of the *Šifāʾ* to which this passage in the *Maʿād* / *Najāt* corresponds, Avicenna avoided the confrontational tone with which he opens the chapter in the *Maʿād* and, without mentioning Plato or any other names, simply stated how the issue is to be conceived (*fa-ammā kayfiyyat taṣawwur hāḏā, fa-huwa anna l-ajsām al-ʿunṣuriyya …*, *Nafs* 261.8–9 Rahman). So this would mean not only that Avicenna called Plato "divine" after having called him philosophically

[35] Sebti "Authenticité" 352 fails to see these elements as indicated in the translation and annotation of T5 and assumes that the chapter makes claims of an "enseignement ésotérique"!

inconsequential, but also that after discussing a passage without reference to any particular philosopher in the *Šifāʾ*, he went on in the *Najāt* to discuss it in the context of an apparent disagreement between Aristotle and the "divine" Plato. All these elements are quite contradictory to the progression of Avicenna's practice and usage, as analyzed in Chapter 7 above. And finally, if this *Maʿād* is a collage of Avicennan pieces with the addition of two forged chapters, the question that still has to be answered is who would have created a pseudepigraph in such a complicated fashion (and why) as to *insert* a chapter between the twelfth and the fourteenth for seemingly very little, if any, gain in doctrinal change from authentic Avicenna—in pseudepigraphs, as a rule, the driving ideological motivation is usually readily perceptible. Nevertheless, a detailed investigation of the text and its transmission imposes itself.

MSS: **Alexandria** 3131; **Berlin** 5343; **Istanbul**, Ahmet III 3247_{3}, 3447_{38}, Feyzullah 2188_{6}, Hamidiye 1448_{21}, Köprülü 1605_{8}, Nuruosmaniye 4894_{128}, Ragıp Paşa 1461_{20}, Üniversite 1458_{12}, 4755_{8} ff. 125^{b}–169^{a} (588H); **Leiden** 1464_{3}; **Lisbon**, Academia das Ciencias, Arab. V.293 ff. 62^{b}–66^{a} (ch. 1 only); **London**, Brit. Lib. 978_{32}, 1349_{2}; **Meshed**, Riżavī IV 1/703, 704, 705, 706; **Rampur** 2955; **Tehran**, Majlis I 1807, Malik 2003_{7}, 2005_{13}, Miškāt 861_{8}, 1037_{7}, 1149 ff. 3^{b}–15^{b}, Sipahsālār 2912_{70}, Tangābunī 317_{22}.

Published: Ahwānī *Aḥwāl* 43–142.

Translations: Chapter 1, French, Michot "*Définition*"; Chapter 10, French, Guy Monnot, "La transmigration et l'immortalité," *MIDEO* 14 (1980) 149–166, at 156–158; Chapter 13, French, Michot "Prophétie"; Chapter 16, English, Gutas, above T5.

Independently transmitted parts:

Chapter 1: *R. fī l-Quwā l-jusmāniyya* (M207, A-)—*On the Bodily Faculties.* MS **Tehran**, Miškāt 367.

Chapter 1: *an-Nufūs* (M240, A109)—*Souls.* MS **Istanbul**, Ayasofya 2052.

Chapter 13: *an-Nafs al-falakiyya* (M239, A74)—*The Celestial Soul.* MSS **Istanbul**, Ayasofya 4829, 4849_{14}, Nuruosmaniye 4894_{112}.

GM 4. *Fī l-Qaḍāʾ wa-l-qadar* (M100, A193)—*On the [Divine] Decree and Predestination* / SB 21, LB 35, EB 112

Alternate title: *Fī l-Qadar.*

At the beginning of the treatise Avicenna says that he was returning from Šalamba,[36] "traveling on the highway to Iṣfahān" (*rākiban ǧadada Iṣfahān*).

[36] Šalamba was one of the main towns in the Dunbāwand (Damāwand) district (cf. V. Minorsky in *EI*², VI,744b), some hundred miles east of Rayy, and certainly a long way off

The compiler of the LB, however, adds after the title that Avicenna "composed the treatise on the way to Iṣfahān after his release and escape to Iṣfahān." Rather than stating a historical fact, this appears to be the compiler's own guess, associating this trip to Iṣfahān from Šalamba with Avicenna's flight from Hamaḏān to Iṣfahān in 414/1023 after his release from the castle of Fardajān, as Mahdavī 197 suggests. The compiler may have been led to this faulty association by the fact that Avicenna composed the *Ḥayy b. Yaqẓān* in Fardajān, and the figure of Ḥayy b. Yaqẓān figures proninently in this treatise on predestination. Mahdavī 197 further mentions that in the Istanbul MS Ayasofya 4852$_3$ it is written that Avicenna "composed it at the end of Muḥarram of the year 424 [/1033]" (without any indication about the source of this information), and suggests that if this date is correct, then the journey is to be identified with one of those Avicenna undertook from fear of Sulṭān Masʿūd's soldiers. In either case it would appear that the treatise was composed during Avicenna's Iṣfahān period at the end of his life, perhaps in the course of the trip Avicenna took to Rayy during 1030, as Michot *Abū Saʿd* 105*n1 suggests; though if the Šalamba mentioned at the beginning of the treatise refers to the actual town and is not a symbolic location somehow associated with the Ḥayy b. Yaqẓān figure that appears later, it is difficult to know what Avicenna was doing there at that time; one would more readily assume that it was a way station during his initial peregrinations on the way to Iran from Buḫārā after the fall of the Samanids.

MSS: **Bursa**, Hüseyin Çelebi 1194 ff. 57^b–63^b; **Cairo**, Ṭalʿat 197 Mā baʿd aṭ-ṭabīʿa; **Istanbul**, Ahmet III 3447$_{26}$, Ayasofya 4829$_{24}$, 4852$_3$ ff. 21^b–34^a, 4853$_{17}$, Esat Efendi 3688$_2$, Hamidiye 1448$_{45}$, Hazine 1730, Köprülü 869$_5$, Nuruosmaniye 2718$_{3,5}$, 4894$_{55}$, Revan 2042$_8$, Üniversite 1458$_{74}$, 4724$_5$; **Leiden** 1464$_{11}$; **Meshed**, Riżavī IV 1/684; **Tehran**, Tangābunī 317$_{11}$.

Published: Mehren *Traités* IV.

Translation: French, Sabri.

GM 5. *R. fī l-ʿIšq* (M90, A230)—*On Love* / LB (99), EB 43

Alternate title: *Iṯbāt sarayān al-ʿišq fī l-mawjūdāt.*

Avicenna says in the introduction that he wrote this essay for his colleague al-Maʿṣūmī, the same person who participated in Avicenna's correspondence with Bīrūnī (ca. 1000). Maʿṣūmī was an early companion of Avicenna and this treatise is accordingly among his early works, as is also

from Iṣfahān. The word Šalamba is in Mehren's text, without reference to variants in the manuscripts; Mahdavī, however, in the *incipit* of the work he provides, prints Šalīmar (!).

evident from the way in which he refers to his books (see above GS 10a and 10b under Physics). It was composed before Avicenna met Jūzjānī, which accounts for the absence of the title from the Biography and the SB (which, if not by Jūzjānī, is close to his work and tradition), and even from the LB, insofar as the title was added at the end of it apparently by Ibn-Abī-Uṣaybiʿa himself (or his immediate source) to complete the entries he found in his own copy of the LB. The title became integrated into the lists of Avicenna's works only by the middle of the thirteenth century, the time when the EB was compiled and Ibn-Abī-Uṣaybiʿa was writing.

MSS: **Bursa**, Hüseyin Çelebi 1194 ff. 75^{b}–82^{a}; **Istanbul**, Ahmet III 1584_{2}, 3447_{9}, Esat Efendi 3688, Hamidiye 1448_{12}, Hazine 1730_{44}, Kaptan Paşa 1262_{4}, Köprülü 1589_{36}, Nuruosmaniye 4894_{12}, Ragıp Paşa 1461_{10}, Üniversite 1458_{29}, 4390_{30}, 4711_{7} (579H); **Konya**, Yusuf Ağa 4989_{12}; **Leiden** 1480; **London**, Brit. Lib. 978_{1}; **Manchester** 384_{g}; **Meshed**, Riżavī IV 1/668, 669, 670; **Oxford**, Bodleian 980_{12}, II 290_{3}; **St. Petersburg**, University 94; **Tehran**, Majlis 634_{39}, 1061_{14}, 1768_{9}, Malik 2001_{14}, 2019_{3}, Millī 992_{1}, Miškāt 861_{9}, 871 ff. 152–153, 1079 ff. 130–140, 1149 ff. 396^{b}–400^{b}, Sipahsālār 1217_{14}, Tangābunī 79_{9}, 308_{3}.—Rundgren, Bell, and Anwar should also be consulted for information on MSS and discussion of contents.

Published: Mehren *Traités* III,1–27; ʿĀṣī *Tafsīr* 241–269; cf. Soreth.

Translations: English, Fackenheim; English, the fist section only, Rundgren.

GM 6. *R. at-Tuḥfa* (M43, A84)—*The Present* / SB 26, LB 34, EB 26

Alternate titles: *M. fī Taḥṣīl as-saʿāda wa-tuʿrafu bi-l-ḥujaj al-ʿašr; Fī s-Saʿāda; al-Ḥujaj al-ʿašr fī jawhariyyat nafs al-insān; R. fī n-Nafs wa-mā taṣīru ilayhi baʿda mufāraqatihā l-badan; al-Maʿād al-aṣġar.*

In his treatise *On Love* (GM 5), Avicenna refers to a *risāla* of his that goes by the title of *at-Tuḥfa, The Present* (*fī risālatinā l-mawsūma bi-t-Tuḥfa*: Mehren *Traités* III,14). To his great credit, Mahdavī 55 noted that Faḫr-ad-Dīn ar-Rāzī cites a lengthy passage from Avicenna's *Tuḥfa* in his *al-Mabāḥiṯ al-mašriqiyya* (Hyderabad ed., II,105.8–17: *qāla* [Ibn Sīnā] *fī Risālat at-Tuḥfa*), which Mahdavī then identified as a verbatim quotation from the essay printed in Hyderabad under the title, *R. fī s-saʿāda wa-l-ḥujaj al-ʿašr* (in Mūsawī *Majmūʿ Rasāʾil*, fifth *Risāla*, p. 14.6–18). This establishes the original title of the work and ensures its identification with the sundry other titles given to it by bibliographers and scribes over the centuries. It also helps in distinguishing it from other titles that go under the title of *al-Maʿād*. The valuable Istanbul MS Üniversite 4755, usually helpful in resolving bibliographical issues, in this case adds to the confusion, for the scribe adds, next to the main title of this treatise, *wa-tuʿrafu bi-l-Maʿād al-aṣġar*. But this can hardly be correct for the same scribe says the same thing about the original "Lesser" *Maʿād*, as discussed above (GM 2 and 3). It is important to note that the SB, which does list the *Tuḥfa* (no. 26), also lists the *Maʿād* separately (no. 19), which is identified with *al-Maʿād al-aṣġar* in the LB. This means that the very reliable SB did not consider the *Tuḥfa* to be identical with the *Maʿād* either. Besides, the identity of *Tuḥfa* with what is known as *al-Ḥujaj al-ʿašr* or *as-Saʿāda* is verified by the contents of the latter which correspond to what Avicenna says about it in the *ʿIšq*.

The *Tuḥfa*, then was composed before the *ʿIšq*, and it was addressed to an unspecified "brother."

MSS: **Bursa**, Hüseyin Çelebi 1194 ff. 67^{b}–75^{a}; **Hyderabad** I 732; **Istanbul**, Ahmet III 3447_{60}, Esat Efendi 3688_{6}, Fatih 3170_{13}, Hazine 1730_{42}, Köprülü 1602_{2}, Nuruosmaniye 4894_{80}, Pertev 617_{20}, Ragıp Paşa 1461_{15}, Revan 2042_{11}, Üniversite 1458_{83}, 4724_{15}, 4755_{9} (588H), Veliyüddin 3263_{5}; **Lisbon**, Academia das Ciencias, Arab. V.293 ff. 8^{b}–21^{a}; **Manchester** 384_{c}; **Marāġa**, pp. 226–243 Pourjavady; **Meshed**, Riżavī IV 1/1025; **Rampur** I 389; **Tehran**, Majlis 599_{13}, 625_{51}, Malik 2001_{13}, 2003_{9}, Miškāt 1074_{1}, 1149 ff. 376^{b}–381^{b}, Sipahsālār 8371_{4}.
Published: Mūsawī, no. 5.

ii. *Commentary*

GS 10d. *Tafsīr Mā baʿd aṭ-ṭabīʿa* (M-, A-)—*Commentary on the Metaphysics*

Referred to both by Avicenna and Ibn-Zayla (?), this appears to be part of *al-Ḥāṣil wa-l-maḥṣūl*. See the discussion and references above, W3, and, in the Inventory, GS 10, and GS 10a, 10b, and 10c under Physics.

iii. *Allegories*

GM 7. *R. Ḥayy b. Yaqẓān* (M65, 182, A219, 227)—*Ḥayy Ibn-Yaqẓān* / Bio 9, SB 34, LB 19, EB 51

Alternate title: *ar-Risāla al-marmūza, aṭ-Ṭabariyya.*

Jūzjānī states (Bio 9) that this work was composed in the castle of Fardajān outside of Hamaḏān where Avicenna was imprisoned shortly before his move to Iṣfahān; the date of composition is accordingly about 414/1023. Mahdavī 96 records the existence of another text with the title *Ḥayy b. Yaqẓān ʿalā bayān āḫar* in two Istanbul MSS, Ayasofya 4829_{34} ff. 150^{b}–159^{b}, and Nuruosmaniye 4894_{107}, also attributed to Avicenna but obviously spurious.

MSS: **Bursa**, Hüseyin Çelebi 1194 ff. 64^a–67^a; **Cairo**, Muṣṭafā Fāḍil 6 Ḥikma; **Istanbul**, Ahmet III 3268_4 (580H), 3447_{75}, Ayasofya 2456_1, 4829_6, 4849_{18}, Hamidiye 1448_{14}, Köprülü 869 ff. 190^b–195^a, 1605_2, Ragıp Paşa 1461_4, Revan 2042_{23}, Üniversite 1458_6, 4755_{12}, Veliyüddin 3263_{15}; **Leiden** 1464_9; **Lisbon**, Academia das Ciencias, Arab. V.293 ff. 74^b–80^b; **London**, Brit. Lib. 978_2; **Oxford**, Bodleian 456_2; **Tehran**, Majlis 1264_4, Malik 2005_3, Miškāt 1074_{15}, Millī 884_1.

Published: Mehren *Traités* I, with selected passages from Ibn-Zayla's commentary; Amīn 43–53.

Translations: Persian, executed either during Avicenna's lifetime or soon after his death, possibly by Jūzjānī; French translation of the Persian by Corbin *Récit* 1545–165, and English translation of Corbin by Trask, in Corbin *Recital* 137–150, reprinted in Nasr and Aminrazavi I,260–268; French, Goichon *Ḥayy*.

GM 8. *R. aṭ-Ṭayr* (M88, A229)—*The Bird* / SB (46), LB 25, EB 31

Alternate title: *Aš-Šabaka wa-ṭ-ṭayr*.

This allegory is not listed in the SB except as a subsequent addition which is found in Ibn-al-Qifṭī and Ibn-Abī-Uṣaybiʿa, with the title, *The Net and the Bird*. The LB does list it, and adds the qualification, "Epistle of *The Bird*, in symbols, in which he describes a procedure that will lead him to knowledge of the True." Some manuscripts of Bayhaqī list it together with *Ḥayy b. Yaqẓān* as one of the treatises Avicenna composed while imprisoned in the castle of Fardajān (Bayhaqī 50n8 Shafīʿ), but there is no independent verification of this. It would rather seem that the association was made by some scribes because of the similarity in style and content between the two works, something echoed by Corbin *Recital* 184 who says that the "two recitals, the one continuing the other, thus exemplify a single mode of vision; they correspond to the same psychic situation, the same mental projection."[37]

MSS: **Beirut**, St. Joseph 410_9; **Bursa**, Hüseyin Çelebi 1194 ff. 95^b–97^a; **Cairo**, Taymūr 290 Adab; **Hyderabad** II 1718; **Istanbul**, Ahmet III 3268_2 (586H), 3447_{74}, Ayasofya 2456_3, 4829_{38}, 4849_{17}, 4853_{21}, Esat Efendi 1234, Hamidiye $1448_{27,39}$, Köprülü 1589_{37}, 1605_1, Nuruosmaniye 3427, 4894_{79}, Ragıp Paşa 1461_{11}, Revan 2042_{22}, Üniversite 1458_{72}, 4755_{12}, Veliyüddin 3263_{14}; **Leiden** 1464_{10}, 2144; **London**, Brit. Lib. 978_{28}; **Manchester** 410_9; **Rampur** III 777;

[37] The arguments by Taghi 199–200, that the *Ṭayr* is a very late work, like the rest of her book are quite beyond comment. See the review by David C. Reisman in *JNES* 65 (2006) 59–62.

Tehran, Majlis 610_4, Malik 2001_9, 2005_4, 2012_6, 2017_6, Miškāt 1074_6, 1149 ff. 46^b–47^a.—Further MSS listed in Taghi 39–40.

Published: Mehren *Traités* II,42–48; ʿĀṣī *Tafsīr* 336–343.

Translations: French, Mehren *Traités* II,27–32. French translation, "on the basis of the Arabic text and of the two Persian renderings, Sāwajī's and Suhrawardī's" by Corbin *Récit* 203–209; English translation of Corbin by Trask, in Corbin *Recital* 186–192. English, Heath 164–168.

iv. *Versified*

GM 9. *Al-Jumāna al-ilāhiyya fī t-tawḥīd* (M51, A178)—*The Divine Pearl: On Professing the Unity of God*

Alternate title: *al-Qaṣīda an-nūniyya.*

An ode of 334 verses rhyming in *-nī* (and hence the alternate title, *Ode with the rhyme nūn*), on God and the emanated creation.

MSS: **Cairo**, Muṣṭafā Fāḍil 142 Majāmīʿ; **Istanbul**, Ahmet III 3355_3, 3447_{78}, Ayasofya 4829_{26}, Hamidiye 1448_6 ff. 350^b–359^b, Nuruosmaniye 4894_{93}, 3427_2; **Tehran**, Miškāt 1149 f. 234^b.

v. *Pseudepigraphs, to be authenticated*

GM-Ps 1. *Ḥaqāʾiq ʿilm at-tawḥīd* (*al-ʿAršiyya* ?) (M61, A179, 183)—*The Real Meaning of Theological Truths* (*Throne Philosophy* ?) / LB 61, EB 2, 116

Alternate titles: *al-ʿAršiyya, al-Ḥikma al-ʿaršiyya, Maʿrifat Allāh wa-ṣifātihi wa-afʿālihi.*

In his Letter to an Anonymous Disciple (Bahmanyār), Avicenna refers to a work with what appears to be a title (rather than a description of contents or method of discussion), *al-Ḥikma al-ʿaršiyya*, and says that some passages from it written on slips of paper were lost during the raid of 1034 (T11, §1). This was clearly a work in progress, as other indications also show (and discussed by Reisman *Avicennan Tradition* 228–230 and elsewhere), and it is not clear that the work was ever completed, if it survived the raid, or that it was rewritten, if it was completely lost, given that Avicenna died only a few years subsequently. Among the bibliographies of Avicenna's works, the LB 61 lists a treatise under the title *al-Ḥikma al-ʿaršiyya wa-huwa kalām murtafiʿ fī l-ilāhiyyāt* (*Throne Philosophy*, elevated discourse on theology). It is again unclear whether the compiler was looking at a treatise by that title in a manuscript in front of him and deduced the description therefrom, or was reporting on the basis of Avicenna's letter just mentioned. The EB does not add the descriptive phrase, but lists the title twice: once as *al-Ḥikma al-qudsiyya* (EB 2), which is manifestly a scribal corruption or misreading of *ʿaršiyya* as *qudsiyya* in unpointed Arabic (العرسيه—القدسيه), and once as an addition at the very end (EB 116) to compensate for its apparent absence, since *al-Ḥikma al-qudsiyya* at the beginning was taken to be different from *al-Ḥikma al-ʿaršiyya.*

Coming next to the manuscripts, Mahdavī 75 reports that some of them have a treatise entitled *Ḥaqāʾiq ʿilm at-tawḥīd,* and others have the same treatise under the title *al-ʿAršiyya.* In the introduction of this treatise though, the author explicitly mentions that it treats of the *ḥaqāʾiq ʿilm at-tawḥīd,* and there appears to be no mention of *ʿAršiyya* other than in colophons which would have been added by scribes and not reflect Avicenna's own words.

This treatise with the author's title, *Ḥaqāʾiq ʿilm at-tawḥīd,* was published in Mūsawī *Majmūʿ rasāʾil* in Hyderabad and by Hilāl, and preliminary research has raised serious doubts about its authenticity, as expressed by Reisman *Avicennan Tradition* 21n2 and as reported by Wisnovsky "Causes" 65n32 and 67n35. The question is thus threefold: whether the *ʿAršiyya* that Avicenna mentioned was completed or rewritten, whether the extant treatise with the title *Ḥaqāʾiq ʿilm at-tawḥīd* is by Avicenna, and whether the two are identical.

MSS: **Istanbul**, Ahmet III 1584$_{30}$, Ayasofya 4849$_{7}$ ff. 33^{b}–40^{b}, Ali Emiri Efendi 4822$_{4}$, Hazine 1730$_{31}$, Nuruosmaniye 4894$_{85}$, Üniversite 3328$_{12}$, Veliyüddin 3263$_{1}$; **London**, India Off. 4657; **Manchester** 384$_{F}$; **Oxford**, Bodleian 980$_{11}$; **Rampur** H 82; **Tehran**, Majlis 625$_{3}$, 634$_{26}$, Malik 2001$_{16}$, Miškāt 384$_{1}$, 1030 ff. 393–400, 1035$_{44}$, 1088, 1149 ff. 21^{b}–25^{b}, Sipahsālār 2912$_{25}$, 8371$_{6}$, Ṭabāṭabāʾī 1367$_{5}$, Tangābunī 205$_{5}$, 317$_{1}$.

Published. Mūsawī no. 4; Hilāl.

Translations. English, partial, Arberry *Theology* 25–37; German: Meyer, part translation part paraphrase.

GM-Ps 2. *R. fī Iṯbāt an-nubuwwa* (M3, A245)—*Proof of Prophecy* / EB 21

Alternate titles: *Fī Izālat aš-šukūk fī n-nubuwwa wa-taʾwīl rumūzihim wa-amṯālihim; Fī n-Nubuwwa.*

The authenticity of this work has been questioned by a number of scholars.[38] Marmura, who edited it, defended its authenticity on the basis of its

[38] Already in 1992 Davidson 87n56 had registered that he was "not convinced" of its authenticity. See further Afifi al-Akiti 201n36, and Treiger *Inspired Knowledge* 133n18. Eichner *"Prayer"* 173n8 also remarks on the deviant nature of the *Iṯbāt* though she considers it an early work (see further below).

ideas' "being Avicennian through and through" (*Nubuwwāt* p. viii) and stated that doubts about it have been raised "only because the Medieval Arabic biographical literature does not mention this treatise" (p. ix), though subsequently he discovered the listing in the EB 21 ("Rational Soul" 133n49). This means that the treatise came into circulation by the middle of the thirteenth century, but the doubts that have been raised are primarily on the basis of its contents. A sustained analysis has not yet been conducted; for the time being two examples of egregiously non-Avicennan content should suffice.

Avicenna's theory of the four levels of human intellection (or, as he says in the classic formulation in *The Cure, Nafs*, I,5, the four relations (*nisba*) that the intellect bears to the intelligibles), is well known; these are, the "material" (*hayūlānī*) or potential, dispositional (*bi-l-malaka*), actual (*bi-l-fiʿl*), and acquired (*mustafād*), with the active or agent intellect (*ʿaql faʿʿāl*) serving as the intellect of the sublunar or earthly realm which contains all the intelligibles. Avicenna repeats this theory, with the same terminology, in all his extant works except his very first treatise, the *Compendium on the Soul* (W1 and T1), in which the theory is the same though there is still uncertainty in young Avicenna's mind about the terminology: the third and fourth levels (or relations) of human intellection are variously called *ʿaql bi-l-fiʿl* but never *mustafād*, and the active intellect seems to be called "universal" (*ʿaql kullī*). In the *Proof of Prophecy*, however, in § 7 of Marmura's text, the third and fourth together (they are not discriminated) are described as follows: "[There exists in man] a third faculty, actually conceiving the forms of the universal intelligibles, which the former two faculties (the "material" and dispositional) follow, and the two [then] issue forth to actuality.[39] It is

[39] The Arabic of this relatively simple sentence reads, [*inna fī l-insāni*] *quwwatan ṯāliṯatan mutaṣawwiratan bi-ṣuwari l-kulliyyāti l-maʿqūlati bi-l-fiʿli taʾḫuḏu bihā l-quwwatāni l-māḍiyatāni, wa-ḫarajatā ilā l-fiʿli*. The initial *inna* clause is entered from line 1 of p. 43 (Marmura), for the enumeration of the three faculties on this page forms a syntactical unit. The clause beginning with *taʾḫuḏu bihā* is actually a relative clause (*ṣifa*) modifying the indefinite *quwwatan* at the beginning, with the next verb in the perfect, *wa-ḫarajatā*, introducing an independent sentence. Marmura's translation, "There is … a third power … of which the other two form a part when these have become actualized" (p. 114 Lerner and Mahdi), misconstrues both the structure of the sentence—there is no temporal clause here ("when … actualized")—and the meaning of *taʾḫuḏu bihā*: it does not mean "to become a part of something" but to follow, adhere, and adopt to the ways of something (Lane I,29a) or practice something (*GALex* I,80, and cf. Qurʾān 43:48). However, it is not clear that the reading *taʾḫuḏu* is actually in the text: five of the six manuscripts Marmura uses for the edition have different readings, which would imply that *taʾḫuḏu bihā* is the reading in the one manuscript that is not mentioned in that entry in the apparatus, the Bursa MS, but Marmura's apparatus is not clear. Rahman *Prophecy* 33 translates differently for he was using the text in the Cairo

called the acquired/active intellect." There are two problems with this sentence.

The first is textual. This third faculty, which ordinarily should be either the actual (*bi-l-fiʿl*) or the acquired (*mustafād*) intellect, is called here "active intellect" (*faʿʿāl*) in all the manuscripts inspected by Marmura except one, the Leiden MS Warn. 1020a, which has "acquired" (*mustafād*). Marmura prefers this reading, but this is difficult to defend stemmatically, for it would mean that the Leiden MS was copied from an exemplar that had the "correct" reading, and that all the other extant manuscripts, which are numerous, derive from a single subarchetype which had made the "wrong" correction from *mustafād* to *faʿʿāl*. But Marmura, who gives no details about the relationships of the manuscripts, groups them differently (p. x), though the Leiden MS cannot belong in the same family as those which read *faʿʿāl*. This question cannot be answered in the abstract but will need the study of the stemmatic relationships of all the manuscripts.[40] In any case, though, if the correct reading is indeed *faʿʿāl*, it cannot be Avicenna who wrote that, because the text makes the active intellect one of the three *human* intellects, which is impossible for Avicenna, at any stage in his career.

On the other hand, the reading *mustafād* may find support from § 21 in the text of Marmura which says, "the acquired intellect is the perfection of the material intellect and what brings it out (*muḫrij*) from potentiality to actuality," which is close to the statement in § 7 cited above. But even if the reading is *mustafād* (despite the stemmatic difficulties), it cannot be what Avicenna said either, for he never said that it is the *acquired* intellect that brings out the potential into actuality; that role is reserved for the active intellect or, in his early *Compendium on the Soul*, the universal intellect (*kullī*).

Furthermore, the author appears to be calling the estimative faculty the material intellect, though the text in this passage is quite corrupt and Marmura's reconstruction dubious (56.5–8). But in any case the material intellect is blamed for "clutching" (or "taking away", *bi-ḫalbihi*, Marmura) or "attracting" (*bi-jalbihi*) the *lubb*, which Marmura translates as "reason", and

---

1326/1908 edition of *Tisʿ Rasāʾil*, pp. 121–122, which for *taʾḫuḏu bihā* reads only *minhā*. An edifying, if shocking, example of the misinterpretations actually caused by the lack of critical editions of Avicenna's texts.

40 The Leiden manuscript Warn. 1020a, in particular, with its miswritten date of copying (408 for 804; see Lameer "*Ishārāt*" 210), its penchant for the "mystical" works of Avicenna, and its peculiar presentation of only the last three *anmāṭ* of the *Išārāt*, needs to have its compilation and transmission history studied in detail.

for causing the perdition of the individual. In the same vein, and further down from this passage just cited (59.8–9), the text says that the animal soul is the hell-fire (*al-jaḥīm*) and that it survives the death of the body eternally in hell (*an-nafs al-ḥayawāniyya ... tabayyana annahā l-bāqiya ad-dā'ima fī jahannam*).[41] Such nonsense could not have been written by Avicenna, even as a teenager, who in the *Compendium on the Soul* (Chapter 7 and p. 359 lower half, Landauer; T1, § 1) assigns disctinct functions to the animal soul and to estimation, as well as to the material intellect, that we know from his later works.

A second and major incompatibility with the thought of Avicenna is the interpretation of the Light Verse of the Qur'ān, in which the correspondences between the images and the faculties of the soul which are found in the *Iṯbāt an-nubuwwa* are mostly different—and almost senseless—from those given by Avicenna in the *Pointers*. The reader can make the comparison himself (and see Janssens "Qur'ān" 183–184 for further details), but most significantly, whereas Avicenna makes the lamp (*miṣbāḥ*) correspond to the actual intellect (*bi-l-fi'l*) and the "light upon light" (*nūr 'alā nūr*) to the acquired, the *Iṯbāt an-nubuwwa* text makes the former correspond to what it calls "actual acquired intellect" (§ 21: *al-'aql al-mustafād bi-l-fi'l*)—a nonsensical construction that Avicenna would not have used—and the latter to the actual intellect (§ 20).

Numerous other aspects of the *Iṯbāt an-nubuwwa* text also point to its inauthenticity, including the complete absence of any mention of *ḥads* in the explanation of the Light Verse, a theory central to Avicenna's thought almost from the very beginning. The *Iṯbāt an-nubuwwa* is thus definitely not a work by Avicenna, certainly not from his middle and later years. It may be thought that it is a very early work by him, before his theory of *ḥads* had developed (see above, Chapter 3.2), but it is incompatible also with what he says in his earliest work, the *Compendium on the Soul* (W1), and in any case it exhibits a certain confusion of terminology and notions that one would be hard put to ascribe even to the youngest Avicenna. Besides, had it been an early work, it would have been addressed to the dedicatee *by name*, and not anonymously, as here, and in a more obsequious manner than in

[41] The conception of the animal soul evidenced in this text of the *Iṯbāt an-nubuwwa* is quite different from that briefly indicated in the treatise on Prayer, which I have discussed in "Intuition and Thinking" 10. Eichner "*Prayer*" 173n8 puts their deviation from standard Avicennan theory on the same level and thus excuses the *Iṯbāt an-nubuwwa* text as "a very early work by Ibn Sīnā."

the peremptory, almost, tone of this text; at the very least one would have expected it to have been mentioned either in the Auto-/Biography or at least in the SB, but it is not. As a pseudepigraph, and given its muddling account of the faculties of the soul and the absence of any mention of Guessing Correctly middle terms, it exudes the same atmosphere as the writings of Ġazālī and his followers.[42] Pseudepigraphy in the name of Avicenna and Ġazālī was well under way after the latter's death in 1111, which would put the date of composition of the *Iṯbāt an-nubuwwa* some time by the end of the twelfth or the beginning of the thirteenth century, so that it was in circulation by the time the earliest manuscript to contain it, Bursa Hüseyin Çelebi 1194, came to be copied in 675/1277.

MSS: **Beirut** 410_{19}; **Bursa**, Hüseyin Çelebi 1194_{30} ff. 159^{a}–161^{b}; **Gotha** 1158_{5}; **Hyderabad** III 728; **Istanbul**, Ahmet III 1584_{3}, Ayasofya 4849_{15}, 4853_{16}, Feyzullah 213, Köprülü 868_{6}, Nuruosmaniye 4894_{90}, Ragıp Paşa 1483_{5}, Üniversite 1458_{17}, 4754_{5} ff. 51^{a}–61^{a}; **Leiden** 1464_{7} (1020a Warn.); **London**, Brit. Lib. 1349_{10}; **Meshed**, Riżavī IV 1/590; **Rampur** I 301, 712, II 774; **Tehran**, Majlis I 3070 ff. 305–326, Malik 2007_{14}, Miškāt 1037, 1079, 1149 ff. 384^{b}–386^{b}, Sipahsālār 1217_{15}, 8371_{7}.

Published: Marmura *Nubuwwāt*.

Translation: English, Marmura in Lerner and Mahdi 112–121.

GM-Ps 3. *R. fī ṣ-Ṣalāt* (M85, A227)—*On Prayer*

Alternate titles: *Asrār aṣ-ṣalāt, Māhiyyat aṣ-ṣalāt.*

The title of this treatise does not appear in any of the early bibliographies, which means that the treatise itself came into circulation under the name of Avicenna after the middle of the thirteenth century. All known manuscripts attribute it to Avicenna—and it has to be determined whether any of them is dated to before the middle of the thirtenth century—though it appears in none of the known early manuscripts; accordingly its authenticity is suspect, as also suggested by Mahdavī (175). The contents of the treatise have been studied in some detail by Eichner *"Prayer,"* who ascribes its discrepancies from standard Avicennan theories to its allegedly early date; but some of these discrepancies are also found in the *Proof of Prophecy* (Eichner 173n8), which is almost certainly not by Avicenna, as I argued above (GM-Ps 2). This

42 For the interpretation of the Light Verse by Ġazālī and the changes he wrought to Avicenna's account see the analysis by Treiger *Inspired Knowledge* 74–78.

set of questions presents starkly the problem I referred to at the beginning of this section on Metaphysics of the Rational Soul, whether works that contain these discrepancies are early works or pseudepigraphs.

MSS: **Bankipore** XIX 1606; **Berlin** 3512; **Calcutta**, Bengal I 1722_{2}; **Escorial** 703_{7}; **Dublin**, Chester Beatty 3045_{6} (699H); **Gotha** 1158_{7}; **Istanbul**, Ahmet III 1584_{6}, 3447_{5}, Ayasofya 2144_{7}, 4829_{40}, 4851_{1}, Carullah 2078_{4}, Hamidiye 1452_{1}, Köprülü 1613_{3}, Nuruosmaniye 4894_{79}, Ragıp Paşa 1461_{21}, Şehit Ali Paşa 2725, Serez 4009_{6}, Üniversite 1458_{24}, 2874_{2}, Veliyüddin 3263_{16}, Yeni Cami 1181_{34}; **Leiden** 2141 ff. 29[a]–33[b]; **London**, Brit. Lib. 978_{43}, 1349_{16}; **Oxford**, Bodleian 980_{4}; **Tehran**, Majlis 598_{7}, 634_{28}, 1768_{13}, 1859_{8}; Malik 2007_{13}, 2012_{3}, 2017_{4}; Millī 872_{9}; Miškāt 1149 ff. 37[a]–39[a], Sipahsālār 1217_{13}, 2912_{75}; Tangābunī 79_{12}.

Published: Mehren *Traités* III,28–43; ʿĀṣī *Tafsīr* 203–222.

Translation: English, Arberry *Theology* 50–63 (except the introduction).

GM-Ps 4. *R. fī Sirr al-qadar* (M4ḥ, A181)—*On the Secret of Predestination*

Alternate title: *Maʿnā qawl aṣ-ṣūfiyya.*

Not mentioned in any of the bibliographies, this treatise was also incorporated into the pseudepigraphic Avicenna—Ibn-Abī-l-Ḫayr correspondence. If not deliberate, the misattribution to Avicenna may be due to confusion with the authentic treatise *al-Qaḍāʾ wa-l-qadar* (GM 4); cf. Reisman *Avicennan Tradition* 140n79.

MSS: **Hyderabad** III,728; **Iṣfahān**, University 1048; **Istanbul**, Revan 2042_{9}, Üniversite 1458_{38}; **London**, Brit. Lib. 978_{16} (= Or. Add. 16659), Or. 12804; **Meshed**, Riżavī IV 1/653, 654; **Rampur**, Ḥikma 82; **Tehran**, Majlis 630_{4}, 1061_{17}, Millī 992_{10}, Miškāt 339_{10}, 876, 1030, Sipahsālār 1216, 1217_{25}, 2912, Ṭabāṭabāʾī 1373_{2}, Tangābunī 317_{5}.

Published: Hourani.

Translations: English, Arberry *Theology* 38–41; Hourani.

GM-Ps 5 (= GS 12a, 4a). *Fī Sabab ijābat ad-duʿāʾ wa-kayfiyyat az-ziyāra* (M4d, A213)—*On the Cause of the Efficacy of Prayer and Visitation* [*of Tombs*]

Alternate titles: *Ijābat ad-daʿawāt, az-Ziyāra, Kayfiyyat az-ziyāra, Maʿnā z-ziyāra.*

This work is listed in none of the bibliographies and is preserved in what appears to be late manuscripts. It is present in the early Ṣiġnāḫī codex (Cairo MS Muṣṭafā Fāḍil 6 Ḥikma), but it is written in a different hand from that of Ṣiġnāḫī and appears to be a subsequent interpolation (cf. Gutas "Ṣiġnāḫī" 14a). In some manuscripts it also appears as part of the pseudepigraphic

Avicenna—Ibn-Abī-l-Ḫayr correspondence. Some of the text itself may be related to the *Taʿlīqāt* (cf. Reisman *Avicennan Tradition* 140n83).

MSS: **Ankara**, Ismail Saib (Dil ve Tarih-Coğrafya Fakültesi) 4605; **Berlin** 3568, 4083; **Cairo**, Muṣṭafā Fāḍil 6 Ḥikma ff. 218^{a}–219^{a}, Taymūr 200 Majāmīʿ; **Damascus**, Ẓāhiriyya 5433; **Escorial** 703_{5}; **Istanbul**, Ahmet III 1584_{9}, 3063_{5}, 3447_{17}, Ayasofya 4851_{4}, Esat Efendi 1143_{13}, 3787_{37}, Fatih 5380_{3}, Hamidiye 1447, 1448_{29}, 1452_{3}, Köprülü 1602_{5}, Nuruosmaniye $4894_{23,70}$, Ragıp Paşa 1461_{8}, Üniversite 2874_{3}, Veliyüddin $3263_{9,17}$, Yeni Cami 1181 (560H); **London**, Brit. Lib. 978_{42}; **Meshed**, Riżavī IV 1/1027; **Oxford**, Bodleian 980_{6}; **Rampur** I 708; **Tehran**, Majlis 1768_{7}; Malik 2003_{6}; Miškāt 339_{6}, 861_{2}, Ṭabāṭabāʾī 1373_{5}; **Tübingen** 89_{20}.

Published: Mehren *Traités* III,44–48; ʿĀṣī *Tafsīr* 281–288; Šamsaddīn 388–391.

GM-Ps 6. *Al-Muʿāwada fī amr an-nafs wa-l-fayḍ* (M4j, A106, 204, 269)—*On the Return of the Soul*

Alternate title: *Mumkin al-wujūd.*

A letter addressed in some manuscripts to Jūzjānī, but actually it appears to have been originally addressed to Bahmanyār. Later it was incorporated into the pseudepigraphic Avicenna—Ibn-Abī-l-Ḫayr correspondence. See Reisman *Avicennan Tradition* 144–147.

MSS: **Istanbul**, Ahmet III 3447_{12} ff. 60^{b}–61^{b}, Ayasofya 4851_{2}, Hamidiye 1448_{16}, 1452_{3}, Hazine 1730_{36}, Nuruosmaniye $4894_{68,97}$, Pertev 617, Üniversite 1458_{75}, 4724_{1}; **London**, Brit. Lib. 978_{21}; **Manchester** 384_{b}; **Tehran**, Majlis 625_{4}, Miškāt 339_{5} ff. 68^{a}–70^{a}, 1149 ff. 342^{a-b}.

GM-Ps 7. *Ḥuṣūl ʿilm wa-ḥikma* (M4w, A260, 266, 268)—*Acquiring Knowledge and Philosophy*

A letter addressed to Ibn-Zayla in response to his letter when Ibn-Zayla "had decided to go into seclusion (*ʿuzla*)." A slightly abridged version was later incorporated into the pseudepigraphic Avicenna—Ibn-Abī-l-Ḫayr correspondence. See Reisman *Avicennan Tradition* 141n83 and 198, and Reisman "New Standard" 569–575.

MSS: **Berlin** 2297; **Bursa**, Hüseyin Çelebi 1194 ff. 148^{a-b}, 151^{b}–152^{a}; **Istanbul**, Ahmet III 1584_{18}, $3447_{27,40}$, Ayasofya 4829_{12}, 4849_{5} ff. 29–31, Esat Efendi 3688, Hamidiye $1448_{22,46}$, Nuruosmaniye 2718_{4}, $4894_{42,56,59}$, Ragıp Paşa 1461_{12}, Üniversite 1458_{60}; **London**, Brit. Lib. Or. 6572; **Tehran**, Majlis 1768_{11}, Miškāt 861_{1}, 871, 1079, 1257, Ṭabāṭabāʾī 1373_{6}.—For further MSS see Reisman "New Standard" 571.

Published: in the introduction to *Najāt*, pp. 11–15 Kurdī.

Translation: French, partial, Michot *Abū Saʿd* 120*-129*.

GM-Ps 8. *Salāmān wa-Absāl* (M204, A235)—*Salāmān and Absāl*

This appears to be another phantom work by Avicenna.[43] In all his works, he mentions Salāmān and Absāl together only once, and Absāl by itself only once. The former is in the *Išārāt*, II.9.1, 198–199/355, where he says,

> If among the things that reach your ear and the tales you hear there is the story of Salāmān and Absāl, know that Salāmān is an image referring to yourself and that Absāl is an image referring to the stage you [have reached] in Knowledge, if you are worthy of it. Now analyze the allegory, if you can.[44]

The second is in the first part of Avicenna's *al-Qaḍā' wa-l-qadar*, where he says, "Not everyone is endowed ... with the chastity of Absāl when there loomed over him a big thick cloud that lit up with a long streak and revealed to him her face."[45] In neither of these passages does Avicenna imply that the story of Salāmān and Absāl is something that he himself had written, which is borne out by the complete absence of the title from the oldest bibliographies. The mention of a detail of the story in the second passage, namely Absāl's recognition of the adulterous wife in the flash of lightning, at most indicates that this was a story that Avienna's circle was expected to know. But the problem of the absence of the story—if it was a story—from any record until Ṭūsī, more than two centuries after Avicenna's death, raises serious doubts even about its very existence.[46] Nobody in the circles of Avicenna's disciples and propagators and students of his works had heard of a such a story, let alone a work by Avicenna with that title, and the two earliest commentators on the *Išārāt*, al-Āmidī and Faḫraddīn ar-Rāzī, say nothing on the subject in the relevant passage at the beginning of the ninth *Namaṭ*.

---

[43] Discussed at great length, but uncritically, by Corbin *Recital* 204–241.

[44] For an analysis of this passage see above, Chapter 8.2, L78, and further Gutas "Ibn Ṭufayl" 234.

[45] *Al-Qaḍā' wa-l-qadar*, Mehren *Traités* IV,5–6. In the story, as reported by Ṭūsī, the wife of Salāmān, who was secretly in love with his half-brother, Absāl, stole into his bed at night but "the sky became overcast with dark clouds in which there flashed a lightning, and Absāl recognized her face in its light and pushed her away" (Ṭūsī *Šarḥ al-Išārāt* 54 Dunyā).

[46] The story to which Avicenna refers in these two works should not be confused with another story about Salāmān and Absāl—this time a man and a woman—which was allegedly translated from the Greek by Ḥunayn b. Isḥāq and is extant in a few manuscripts. For the Greek, Indian, or "Hermetic" pedigree of this story see Shlomo Pines, "The Origin of the Tale of Salāmān and Absāl—A Possible Indian Influence," in *The Collected Works of Shlomo Pines, III, Studies in the History of Arabic Philosophy*, Sarah Stroumsa, ed., Jerusalem: Magnes Press, 1996, 343–353, and N. Peter Joosse, "An Example of Medieval Arabic Pseudo-Hermetism: The Tale of Salāmān and Absāl," *Journal of Semitic Studies* 38 (1993) 279–293.

The first who claimed to have seen such a story and ascribe it to Avicenna is Naṣīr-ad-Dīn aṭ-Ṭūsī, and his testimony complicates matters. In his commentary on the *Išārāt* he says, "I came across (*waqaʿat ilayya*) the story twenty years after completing the *Commentary*. It is ascribed to Avicenna, and it is as if (*ka-annahā*) it is this [story] to which he is referring [in the *Išārāt*], for Jūzjānī, in his Bibliography of Avicenna's works (*fihrist taṣānīf aš-Šayḫ*), mentions the story of *Salāmān and Absāl* by him" (*Šarḥ* IV,53–54 Dunyā). Ṭūsī's reference to Jūzjānī's bibliography is certainly to the SB, for it was this list that, already embedded in Jūzjānī's biography by the middle of the thirteenth century, as discussed in Part One of the Appendix above, was considered to be by Jūzjānī. Now none of the extant manuscripts of the SB and its derivative lists contains such a title. Either, therefore, Ṭūsī (or whoever wrote this statement) is lying, or, more likely, some copy of the SB that was available to Ṭūsī contained the title as an addition to the original list by someone who had made the same calculations of attribution as Ṭūsī himself. In any case, the attribution cannot be taken seriously as it manifestly stems not from any circle of those with knowledge about Avicenna's works.

But even more problematic is the report that Ṭūsī came across this story twenty years after the completion of his *Commentary*. At the very least this implies that Ṭūsī was revising his commentary and that there were at least two, if not multiple, "editions" of the work as new materials were added and corrections registered. A detailed study of the transmission of the manuscripts of the *Šarḥ* should provide a clearer picture precisely how we are to understand Ṭūsī's "editions" and their number and nature. But repeated editions also leave open the possibility of interpolations, and it is at least questionable whether the paragraphs on the Salāmān and Absāl story were indeed additions made by Ṭūsī himself. All these uncertainties leave little doubt about the spuriousness of the work, if indeed a "work" it was.

MSS. Mahdavī does not list any MSS for this entry, but Anawati *Muʾallafāt* 293 does, though it is not clear what these MSS contain.

For translations and discussion see Corbin *Récit* and *Recital*.

GM-Ps 9. *Īḍāḥ barāhīn mustanbaṭa fī masāʾil ʿawīṣa* (M38, A79), incorporating *R. al-ʿArūs* (M89, A184)—*Explanation of Demonstrations Devised for Abstruse Problems*, incorporating *The Groom* / EB 55

Alternate titles: *al-ʿUrūš, al-ʿArš, Silsilat al-falāsifa, al-Ḥayra, Iṯbāt wujūd, Iṯbāt al-ʿuqūl, Kayfiyyat al-mawjūdāt.*

A cluster of works, or rather of interpenetrating segments of texts, going under the different titles listed above and extant in various recensions in the manuscripts, treat of the familiar subjects of the Metaphysics of the Rational Soul: the Creator, the soul, and its survival or Destination. Mahdavī, who identified them, also noted (179) that some version of them is ascribed to Fārābī, and the rest to Avicenna. The "Fārābī" text, *Šarḥ R. Zīnūn al-kabīr al-yūnānī* (published in Hyderabad: al-Maʿārif al-ʿUṯmāniyya, 1349), was recognized as spurious already in 1937 by Franz Rosenthal, "Arabische Nachrichten über Zenon den Eleaten," *Orientalia* 6 (1937) 64 (repr. in his *Greek Philosophy in the Arab World*, Aldershot: Variorum, 1990, no. I). It was later studied by Josep Puig, "Un tratado de Zenón el Mayor. Un comentario atribuido a al-Farabi," *La Ciudad de Dios* 201 (1988) 287–321 (with a Spanish translation on pp. 314–321, not 214–221 as listed in Janssens *Bibliography* 64), who even suggests it may be by Avicenna. A comprehensive examination of this entire cluster of texts, which remains to be done, should prove significant for an understanding of the currents of pseudepigraphy within two centuries after Avicenna, given that one part of it, the *ʿArūs*, is listed in the EB.

MSS of the *Īḍāḥ*: **Isfahan**, Dāneškade-ye Adabiyyāt 1048_{5}; **Istanbul**, Ayasofya 4853_{2} ff. 5^{b}–7^{b}; **London**, Brit. Lib. 978_{48}, 980_{9}; **Princeton**, Yehuda 2994_{14} (677H); **Tehran**, Majlis 1061_{3}; Malik 2007_{17}; Sipahsālār 1217_{18}, 8371_{11}.

MSS of the *ʿArūs*: **Berlin** 2295; **Cairo**, Taymūr 145 Ḥikma, 200 Majāmīʿ; **Escorial** 703_{6}; **Istanbul**, Ahmet III 1584_{28}, 3447_{22}, Hamidiye 1448_{41}, Hazine 1730_{45}, Köprülü 1589_{38}, Nuruosmaniye 4894_{101}, 9894_{4}, Ragıp Paşa $1461_{17,27}$, Serez 3824, Üniversite 1458_{22}, 3328_{8}, 4724_{9}, Veliyüddin 2134_{17}, 3237_{9}, 3275_{14}; **London**, Brit. Lib. 1349_{17}; **Meshed**, Riżavī IV 1/590, 666, 667; **Tehran**, Khān 875, Majlis 611_{2}, $1768_{12,17}$, Malik 2001_{11}, 2003_{8}, $2007_{3,16}$, 2012_{5}, Miškāt 339_{19}, 861_{6}, 871_{20}, 1035, 1088_{7}, 1149 ff. 343^{b}–344^{a}, Sipahsālār $1217_{6,17}$, Ṭabāṭabāʾī 1373_{4}, Tangābunī 79_{11}, 205_{7}, 317_{7}.

GM-Ps 10. *R. an-Nīranjāt* (M126, 210, A76, 69)—*Magical Practices*

The *nīranj* "is a magical practice which includes the mixing and processing of ingredients, the recitation of magical words, the burning of incense, and the making of figurines, in order to manipulate spiritual forces."[47] This treatise, attributed to Avicenna, "is a non-theoretical work that simply lists the days, nights and hours of the planets, their suitability for the work of friendship (*ʿamal aṣ-ṣadāqa*) and enmity (*ʿadāwa*), the races and kinds of

[47] Charles Burnett, "*Nīranj*: A Category of Magic (Almost) Forgotten in the Latin West", in *Natura, scienze e società medievali. Studi in onore di Agostino Paravicini Bagliani*, Claudio Leonardi and Francesco Santi, eds., Florence: SISMEL—Galluzzo, 2008, 37–66, at 42.

people attributed to them, their incenses, their letters, the letters of the four elements, and the prayers and fumigations accompanying the combinations of these letters (the charm: *ruqya*)."[48] The treatise, which appears in none of the early bibliographies, is known so far to exist in the two late manuscripts in Istanbul. The attribution to Avicenna can hardly be entertained.
MSS: **Istanbul**, Nuruosmaniye 4894_{41} ff. 246^{b}–247^{b}, Pertev 617_{48}.

GM-Ps 11. *R. fī l-Arzāq* (M23, A248)—*On Wealth*

The treatise begins with a note by an editor or scribe who describes it as an exchange between Avicenna and a contemporary "disputant" or "dialectician" (*jadalī*) in the Ayasofya MS, according to Mahdavī 28, or between Avicenna and Abū-Saʿīd b. Abī-l-Ḫayr in the Ahmet III MS. The editor then adds that after the disputation Avicenna "thoroughly revised it" (*haḏḏabahā ġāyata t-tahḏīb*). The subject is divine providence: the disputant asks why, if a wise God created the world, it shows no traces of wisdom, in particular regarding the distribution of wealth among people. This manifestly spurious work appears nowhere in the bibliographies.
MSS: **Isfahan**, Dāneškade-ye Adabiyyāt 1048_{6}; **Istanbul**, Ahmet III 1584_{10}, Ayasofya 4853_{1} ff. 2^{b}–6^{a}, Nuruosmaniye 4894; **Meshed**, Riżavī IV 1/591; **Oxford**, Bodleian 980_{6}; **Princeton**, Yehuda 16_{13} (677H); **Tehran**, Dānešgāh 2441, Majlis 1061_{15}, Miškāt 1149 ff. 383^{a}–384^{a}.
Published: Ritter; Šamsaddīn 273–279, who apparently "copied Ritter's edition and added his own corrections" (Reisman *Avicenniana* 28).

GM-Ps 12. *R. fī l-Ḥaṯṯ ʿalā l-ištiġāl bi-ḏ-ḏikr* (M54, A216, 221)—*Protreptic to Recitation of God's Name*

Alternate title: *Fī l-Ḫalwa wa-ḏ-ḏikr wa-l-ḥaṯṯ ʿalā taṣfiyat al-bāṭin.*

A one page protreptic to employ "the weapon of the recitation of Allāh" (*silāḥ ḏikr Allāh*), not mentioned in any bibliography.
MSS: **Istanbul**, Ahmet III 1584_{14}, Hazine 1730_{41}; **Manchester** 384_{R}; **Oxford**, Bodleian 980_{11}; **Rampur** H 82; **Tehran**, Miškāt 1149 ff. 147^{b}–148^{a}, Sipahsālār 8371_{16}, Ṭabāṭabāʾī 1367_{8}.
Published: ʿĀṣī *Tafsīr* 310–313.

---

48 *Ibid.* 44n20.

GM-Ps 13. *Fuṣūl ilāhiyya fī iṯbāt al-awwal* (M-, A-)—*Sections Relating to the Godhead on the Proof of the First* / LB 88, EB 79

Alternate (?) title: *R. fī Iṯbāt al-mabdaʾ al-awwal.*

The LB 88 lists this title, which appears to be a descriptive title by a scribe or the compiler for a collection of paragraphs on this subject. The EB 79 would seem to make a *risāla* out of it, if it is the same work.

F. Practical Philosophy (GPP)

Avicenna had little interest in the traditional branches of practical philosophy—ethics, oeconomics (household management), politics—; his interest in these matters expresed itself primarily in a fourth branch which he originated, in conjunction with his main preoccupation with the Metaphysics of the Rational Soul, as mentioned in the introduction to the peceding section, and left little room for theoretical treatment of traditional practical philosophy. Accordingly, he wrote little on the subject. As a matter of fact, other than the lost *al-Birr wa-l-iṯm* which he wrote while still in Buḫārā, and about whose precise contents we have little information, there is little evidence that he composed any other independent treatises on the traditional branches of practical philosophy. His view of practical philosophy as a somewhat separate and secondary part of philosophy is already indicated by his mentioning *al-Birr wa-l-iṯm* in the Autobiography (T3, §13) *separately* from *al-Ḥāṣil wa-l-maḥṣūl*: he says that Abū-Bakr al-Baraqī asked him "to comment on the books [i.e., on philosophy] and so I composed *The Available and the Valid* ... and I also composed a book for him on Ethics which I called *Piety and Sin*." Here *al-Birr wa-l-iṯm* is mentioned as not being part of "the books" on philosophy. Similarly, his very first summa of philosophy, *al-Ḥikma al-ʿArūḍiyya*, also did not include practical philosophy—there is no evidence for it in the extant texts—indicating that Avicenna thought of it in these terms from the very beginning. Thus the last sections of the Metaphysics of the *Šifāʾ* constitute just about the best and most basic extant expression of his ideas on practical philosophy in all its branches, both the traditional three and the new fourth one on the "discipline of legislating" (*aṣ-ṣināʿa aš-šāriʿa*).

The few treatises listed below on these subjects, except for *al-Birr wa-l-iṯm*, are of doubtful authenticity at best. In addition, they, as well as *al-Birr*, seem to be for the most part transcripts and paraphrases of work by earlier philosophers, and one is hard pressed to discern what is Avicennan. *Al-Birr* copies Fārābī extensively, and what is transmitted in some manuscripts as his essay on sorrow is a paraphrase of Kindī's work on the subject; the treatise on household governance remains to be investigated. If these paraphrases were made in fact by Avicenna himself, as *al-Birr* doubtless was, the rationale behind the pastiche style of composition may have been what Franz Rosenthal suggested some time ago: these are notes and transcripts made by Avicenna for his own use, an otherwise common scholarly practice (*Orientalia* 9 (1940) 185). If this is true, then these notes would have been transmitted among Avicenna's books—both his own and those he owned—

and ended up with scholars who had inherited or purchased them, as is the case with Avicenna's library that ended up in the possession of Ṣiġnāḫī (see Gutas "Ṣiġnāḫī"), and only then began circulating under Avicenna's name, which would explain the absence of most of these titles from the earliest bibliographies of his works.

i. *Expository*

GPP 1. ***K. al-Birr wa-l-iṯm—Piety and Sin***

For description and analysis see above, W3. The transmission history of this work, which has not survived intact, is extremely complicated; no other lost work by Avicenna has been so fragmented, adapted, and recopied—balkanized, really—as this one. Its sources are equally complex. For parts of it Avicenna used heavily some of Fārābī's works, as shown by Karlığa "Traité d'éthique" and Janssens "*Birr*", but also other works, including spin-offs of the Aristotelian *Ethics*. As was his wont, Avicenna also used some parts of it in later works of his. The publication record of its parts has followed suit: see the descriptions by Karlığa, Šamsaddīn 218–221, and Lizzini "Vie active" 207n1. Intensive work on the manuscripts containing its bits and pieces, as well as on its sources, will be required before some clarity emerges. At this stage, the following five texts, going under separate titles, appear to contain parts of it in various configurations. The first three texts are interpenetrating, the fourth appears to be independent but of similar style and content, while the fifth is questionable. How these are related to each other and to the lost original remains to be investigated.

a. ***K. al-Birr wa-l-iṯm*** **(M40, A249)—*Piety and Sin* / Autobio 3, SB 3, LB 4, EB 82**

MSS: **Istanbul**, Ahmet 1584_{19} ff. 137^{a}–145^{a}, 3447_{28}, Ayasofya 4829_{27}, Hamidiye 1448_{50}, Köprülü 1589_{40}, Nuruosmaniye 4894_{95}, Üniversite 1458_{42}, 4711_{10} ff. 67^{a}–74^{a} (579H); **Leiden**, Warner Or. 864 ff. 123^{b}, 124, 120, 126–129; **Tehran**, Miškāt 1149 ff. 360^{a}–363^{b}.

Published: Šamsaddīn 353–368.

b. ***R. fī l-Aḫlāq*** **1 (M13, A246)—*On Ethics* 1 / LB 54, EB 52**

Alternate title: *ʿIlm al-aḫlāq*.

MSS: **Berlin** 5391; **Gotha** 1158_{9}; **Hyderabad** III 728; **Istanbul**, Ahmet III 3447_{10}, Ayasofya 4853_{3}, Hamidiye 1448_{13}, Köprülü 868_{9}, 1589_{39}, 1601_{6}, Nuruosmaniye 4894_{13}, Ragıp Paşa 1461_{5}, 1483_{8}, Revan 2042_{24}, Üniversite 1458_{41} ff. 109^{b}–110^{b}, 4711_{9} (579H), 4724_{3}, 4754_{2}, 4755_{20} ff. 278^{a}–283^{a}; **Leiden** 1464_{6}, 2143; **Lon-**

don, Brit. Lib. Or. 6572; **Tehran**, Majlis 1264_{5}, Malik 2001_{10}, Miškāt 1074_{16}, 1079, 1149 ff. 363^{b}–364^{b}.
Published: Šamsaddīn 369–377.

c. *Al-ʿAhd* (M92, 149, A82, 232)—*The Pledge* / SB (36), LB 62, EB 50
Alternate titles: *Muʿāhada, ʿAhd fī tazkiyat an-nafs, Tazkiyat an-nafs.*

The fragmentation of *al-Birr wa-l-iṯm*, from which *al-ʿAhd* derives, must have occurred early, but not that early. The title does not appear in the original SB, thus it had not yet been concocted by mid-twelfth century, but it was added toward the end of the SB in the copy available to Ibn-Abī-Uṣaybiʿa a century later.

The text of *al-ʿAhd* has been transmitted in various recensions of two versions: a brief one in which one person makes a vow to God, and a longer and more detailed one, apparently the original, in which two people enter into covenant with God. See Reisman "New Standard" 575–577.

MSS: **Bursa**, Hüseyin Çelebi 1194 ff. 146^{b}–147^{a}, 150^{b}–151^{b}; **Cairo**, Muṣṭafā Fāḍil 6 Ḥikma; **Hyderabad** III 731; **Istanbul**, Ahmet III 3447_{21}, Ali Emiri Efendi 4353_{6}, Ayasofya 4829_{29}, 4849_{27} ff. 136^{b}–137^{a}, Esat Efendi 3688_{11} (contains both versions), Fatih 3170_{5}, Hamidiye 1448_{40}, Köprülü 868_{8}, 1589_{33}, Nuruosmaniye 4894_{100}, Ragıp Paşa 1483_{7}, Üniversite 1458_{14}; **London**, Brit. Lib. Or. 6572; **Rampur** I 390, 712; **Tehran**, Malik 2008_{6}, Miškāt 1149, Tangābunī 79_{14}.
Published, original version: Badawī *Arisṭū* 247–249; for the rest see Reisman "New Standard" 575–577.
Translation, original version: French, Michot *Abû Saʿd* 116–126.

d. *R. fī l-Aḫlāq* 2 (M-, A-)—*On Ethics* 2
This is a second treatise under this name ascribed to Avicenna in one Istanbul MS, Üniversite 1458, f. 185^{a} (copied in 1821, or shortly thereafter; cf. Reisman "ARCE" 141–142), while a second, Pertev Paşa 617, f. 235^{b}, which also contains the same text, has it anonymously. Karlığa "Ahlâk risalesi" and "Traité d'éthique," who noted that this text is different from the preceding one and discovered it also in the Pertev Paşa MS, claims it is an independent work by Avicenna. He also noted that it is quoted (anonymously) by Ġazālī, which establishes at least an upper date for it. But the text has certain definite affinities with spin-off material from the *Nicomachean Ethics*, also as Karlığa discovered, something which, in addition to its attribution to Avicenna in only one late manuscript, raises serious doubts about its authenticity. And if it is by Avicenna, it consists of an enumeration of virtues and vices, very much along the lines of some of the other pieces of his *al-Birr wa-l-iṯm*. The question remains.

MSS: **Istanbul**, Pertev Paşa 617 ff. 235[b]–240[a], Üniversite 1458_{57} ff. 185[a]–186[b].
Published: Karlığa, "Ahlâk risalesi".
Translation: Turkish, Karlığa, "Ahlâk risalesi".

e. *Al-Afʿāl wa-l-infiʿālāt* (M97, A190)—*Actions and Affections* / EB 80
Alternate titles: *al-Birr wa-l-iṯm, al-Fayḍ al-ilāhī, al-Fiʿl wa-l-infiʿāl.*

This text on the mutual actions and affections of souls and bodies on each other is made up, in the words of the scribe of MS Leiden Warn. Or 864 (1485_2), 123b, of "portions [that were] found of his [Avicenna's] work known as *al-Birr wa-l-iṯm*" (Reisman *Avicennan Tradition* 147). According to Mahdavī 187, the same notation is found in the MSS Brit. Lib. 1349 and Sipahsālār 2912, as follows: "This [text] is from Avicenna's book known as *al-Birr wa-l-iṯm,* though I think it to be not from that work but from his *al-ʿAzāʾim wa-ṭ-ṭilasmāt*; but thus I found it entitled." As Reisman notes, the evidence of the Leiden MS is respectable, though at some point this text also formed part of the pseudepigraphic Avicenna—Abū Saʿīd Ibn-Abī-l-Ḫayr correspondence. This is another piece in the *al-Birr wa-l-iṯm* puzzle that needs to be resolved.

MSS: **Berlin** 4094; **Cairo**, Ṭalʿat 197 Mā baʿd aṭ-ṭabīʿa, Taymūr 37 Ḥikma, 200 Majāmīʿ; **Hyderabad** III 728; **Istanbul**, Ahmet III 3447_{58}, Ayasofya 2048_4, 4851_3, Hamidiye 1452_3, Köprülü 1602_1, Nuruosmaniye $4894_{69,105}$, Pertev 617_{33}, Ragıp Paşa 1461_{19}, Revan 2042_{20}, Üniversite 1458_{16}, Veliyüddin 3263_2; **Leiden** 1481, 1485_2; **London**, Brit. Lib. 978_{17}, 1349_9; **Meshed**, Riżavī I 3/105, IV 1/919; **Rampur** I 392, II 772, 782; **Tehran**, Khān 875, Majlis 1061_{11}, Malik 2004_{14}, Miškāt 367_4, 1089_7, Sipahsālār 1217_{10}, 2912_{74}, Tangābunī $317_{14,19}$.
Published: Mūsawī, no. 1.
Translation: For partial French translations by Michot see Janssens *Bibliography* 62.

ii. *Pseudepigraphs, to be authenticated*

GPP-Ps 1. *R. fī s-Siyāsa* (M82, A253)—*On Governance* / EB 24, EB 101 (?)

Alternate title (?): *Tadbīr al-manzil.*

A treatise on management of the household (oeconomics). The title *Siyāsa* appears only in the late EB which, however, also lists another title, *Tadbīr al-manzil* (EB 101). Given that the treatise is actually on oeconomics rather than on political governance, this may have been an alternate (and original?) title that eventually fell into disuse. Janssens *Bibliography Suppl. I* 36 refers to a Dutch translation and commentary by T. Hoff which "indicates elements which sound rather un-Avicennian."

MSS: **Istanbul**, Ahmet III 3447_{30}, Hamidiye 1448_{51}, Nuruosmaniye 2718_{7}, 4898_{14} ff. 71[a]–74[b]; **Leiden** 1464_{5}; **Princeton** (ELS) 308 ff. 147[b]–154[a]; **Tehran**, Dānešgāh 2441 pp. 77–86.
Published: L. Cheikho in *Maqālāt falsafiyya qadīma*, Beirut 1911, 2–17; Šamsaddīn 232–260.
Translation: English, McGinnis and Reisman 224–237.

GPP-Ps 2. *R. fī l-Ḥuzn wa-asbābihi* (M59, A217)—*On Sorrow and Its Causes* / LB 83, (101), EB 106

Alternate title: *Māhiyyat al-ḥuzn*.

This is a paraphrastic extract of the first two sections of Kindī's *Fī l-Ḥīla li-dafʿ al-aḥzān*, as originally noted by Hellmut Ritter and registered by him and Richard Walzer in their *Studi su al-Kindī* II, Rome 1938, 8, repeated by Franz Rosenthal in his review of Ritter and Walzer in *Orientalia* 9 (1940) 184–185, and summarized by Hans Daiber, "Political Philosophy," in *History of Islamic Philosophy*, S.H. Nasr and O. Leaman, eds., London: Routledge, 1996, 860n24; see also Gätje "Seelenarzt." Some of the manuscripts in Istanbul examined by Ritter ascribe the piece to Avicenna, others do not. Nevertheless, it is to be noted that the misattribution, if misattribution it was, was early, as the piece appears in the early manuscripts, including the Marāġa MS, under Avicenna's name.
MSS: **Cairo**, Dār al-Kutub 345 Ḥikma, Taymūr 200 Majāmīʿ; **Istanbul**, Ahmet III 3447_{70}, Ayasofya 4849_{36} f. 167[b], 4851_{6}, Fatih 5380_{2}, Hamidiye 1452_{12}, Köprülü 1589_{35}, 1602_{4}, Nuruosmaniye 4894_{52}, Üniversite 1458_{40}, 4711_{8} (579H), Vehbi 148_{3}, Veliyüddin 3263_{8}; **Marāġa** p. 350 Pourjavady; **Tehran**, Millī 9_{2}, Miškāt 1308 f. 144[a], 1149 f. 146[a].
Published: ʿĀṣī *Tafsīr* 314–317; Šamsaddīn 386–387.
Translation: German, Gätje "Seelenarzt" 226–227.

G. Personal Writings (GPW): Controversies, Letters, Homilies, Poetry

Avicenna lived his philosophy, as discussed above (Chapter 5), or rather, theoretical matters were in his society very much part of the everyday intellectual and ideological life. His personal circumstances, in addition, forced him into public life, as he was involved in constant search for patronage when it was lacking, and in efforts to maintain it when present (cf. Reisman "Patronage"). Communicating his ideas, both his theoretical philosophy but also more personal and private opinions, in ways that would be widely disseminated and result in his being better understood and vindicated was vital to him (cf. Coda above). These circumstances led to his producing various writings which could be called personal, to distinguish them from his technical philosophical treatises, even if they incorporated and discussed many theoretical subjects. These writings include (I) correspondence depicting the controversies in which he was involved and seeking arbitration, as well as other (II) private letters, (III) homiletic literature artistically expressing religious sentiment, and (IV) poetry.

The transmission history of these writings and their authentication vary. The easiest to resolve are the letters of controversy: they are listed in the early bibliographies and their contents are of such historical specificity as to remove all doubt about them. The private letters are listed only generically in the bibliographies, but their authenticity can be verified through the study of the addressees, if they can be identified and their circumstances historically contextualized. The homiletic writings and the poetry present the greatest challenge to research. In the case of the former, Avicenna himself says in his *R. al-Intifāʾ ʿammā nusiba ilayhi min muʿāraḍat al-Qurʾān* that he had composed certain homilies (*ḫuṭab*) on various religious subjects and that these were taken by his detractors as attempts to imitate the style of the Qurʾān because of the rhymed prose (*sajʿ*) in which they were composed (cf. Mahdavī 98 and Michot "Riz" 94–96). The subjects included God's oneness (*tawḥīd*), the praise of God (read *taḥmīd*, as in some mss, for *tamjīd* in the text), proof of prophecy, signs indicating the prophethood of Muḥammad, some Qurʾānic verses, cosmology, embryology, and refutation of Ṣābians, Zoroastrians, Christians, Jews, and deniers of God's *qadar* (Michot "Riz" lines 38–62 of text and translation). Most of these subjects are treated in the works that have come down to us in manuscript, though in some cases it is difficult to decide on their authorship as they are couched in generic pietistic language. As for the poetry, although it is clear that Avicenna did engage in versification beyond his didactic poems, it presents intractable problems that have not been treated in any significant way and constitute a separate area for future research. For all these reasons I do not list any of the works in this category as pseudepigraphs but comment on their authenticity whenever possible.

I. *Controversies*

GPW 1. *R. ilā ʿUlamāʾ Baġdād yasʾaluhum al-inṣāf baynahu wa-bayna rajul Hamaḏānī yaddaʿī l-ḥikma* (M78, A-)—*Letter to the Scholars of Baġdād requesting they judge fairly between him and a man from Hamaḏān claiming [to know] philosophy* / LB 80

Letter describing the philosophical controversy between Avicenna and al-Kirmānī which took place shortly after Avicenna's arrival in Hamaḏān in 1015. See Reisman *Avicennan Tradition* 174–175, Michot *Abū Saʿd* 10*ff.
MSS: **Tehran**, Malik 2007$_{21}$, Millī Malik 4694, Miškāt 367$_{3}$, Sipahsālār 1216 ff. 112^{a}–114^{b}, 1217$_{22}$, 2912$_{60}$ ff. 268^{a}–269^{a}.
Published: Yarshater *Panj Resāle* 73–90.
Translation: German, Arnzen *Platonische Ideen*, Appendix II, pp. 355–370.

GPW 2. *R. ilā Ṣadīq yasʾaluhu l-inṣāf baynahu wa-bayna l-Hamaḏānī allaḏī yaddaʿī l-ḥikma* (M-, A-)—*Letter to a Friend requesting he judge fairly between him and a man from Hamaḏān who claims [to know] philosophy* / LB 81

This is the letter to the Vizir Abū Saʿd describing the same philosophical controversy between Avicenna and al-Kirmānī as in the preceding entry, which took place shortly after Avicenna's arrival in Hamaḏān in 1015. See Michot *Abū Saʿd*, who discovered the unique manuscript containing it.
MS: **Bursa**, Hüseyin Çelebi 1194, ff. 131^{b}–140^{a}.
Published, with French translation: Michot *Abū Saʿd*.

GPW 3. *R. fī Intifāʾ ʿammā nusiba ilayhi min muʿāraḍat al-Qurʾān* (M34, A204, 257)—*Repudiating Charges of Imitating the Qurʾān* / LB 67, EB 72

Alternate titles: *al-Iʿtiḏār fī-mā nusiba ilayhi min al-ḫuṭab, R. ilā Ṣadīq fī ibṭāl mā nusiba ilayhi fī l-ḫuṭab.*

A letter addressed to an anonymous friend or disciple, who in some manuscripts is said to be Jūzjānī. Both Reisman *Avicennan Tradition* 178–180 and Michot "Riz" 85–88 reject this, and the latter suggests instead Bahmanyār. Reisman and Michot, on the other hand, disagree about the dating of the letter; Reisman argues for a date after 1030, Michot for one soon after Avicenna's move to Iṣfahān in 1024.

MSS: **Berlin** 2072; **Cairo**, Ṭalʿat 197 Maʿārif ʿāmma; **Istanbul**, Ahmet III 3447_{31}, Ayasofya 4829_{12}, 4849_{5} ff. 27^{a}–28^{b} (677H), Esat Efendi 3688, Hamidiye 1448, Nuruosmaniye 4894_{15}; **Tehran**, Tangābunī 79_{15}.
Published, with French translation: Michot "Riz".

GPW 3.1. ***Masāʾil jarat baynahu wa-bayna baʿḍ al-fuḍalāʾ*** **(M-, A-)—*Issues between Avicenna and Some of his Contemporary Notables* / SB 37, LB 92**

No text in the known manuscripts bears such a title. Its presence in both the SB and LB indicates that at some point texts relating to the controversies to which Avicenna alludes in the letters in this section carried this title or, rather, description—if indeed it was these and not other disputes to which the title refers. The questions remain open.

II. *Correspondence*

GPW 4. ***Letters*** **/ SB (42):** ***Rasāʾil lahu iḫwāniyya wa-sulṭāniyya*****; LB 71:** ***Rasāʾil bi-l-fārisiyya wa-l-ʿarabiyya wa-muḫāṭabāt wa-mukātabāt wa-hazliyyāt***

Letters to various individuals are preserved in some manuscript copies, and they started circulating by the end of the twelfth century when they began to be listed in the bibliographies in generic terms. The authenticity of the letters themselves and the identity of some of their addressees have yet to be studied.

a. ***Ilā baʿḍ aḥibbāʾihi*** **(M79a, A261)—*Letter to a friend***
MSS: **Istanbul**, Ayasofya 4829_{12}, 4849_{5} f. 31^{a}, Nuruosmaniye 4894_{47}.

b. ***Ilā Abī Jaʿfar al-Qāsānī*** **(M79b, A267, 270)—*Letter to Abū-Jaʿfar al-Qāsānī***
MSS: **Istanbul**, Ahmet III 3447_{45}, Hamidiye 1448_{17}, Nuruosmaniye 4894_{53} f. 254^{a}; **Tehran**, Miškāt 1035_{31} f. 262^{a}.

c. ***Ilā Abī Ṭāhir b. Ḥassūl*** **(M79c, A262, 270)—*Letter to Abū-Ṭāhir Ibn-Ḥassūl* / EB 113**
MSS: **Bursa**, Hüseyin Çelebi 1194 f. 147^{a}; **Istanbul**, Ahmet III $3447_{34,46}$, Hamidiye $1448_{18,53}$, Nuruosmaniye $4894_{22,134}$ f. 594^{a}.

d. ***Ilā ʿAlāʾ ad-Dawla b. Kākūya*** **(M79d, A265)—*Letter to ʿAlāʾ-ad-Dawla***
MSS: **Cairo**, Ṭalʿat 197 Mā baʿd aṭ-ṭabīʿa; **Istanbul**, Ayasofya 4829_{12}, 4849_{5} ff. 28^{b}–29^{a}, Hamidiye 1448_{52}, Nuruosmaniye 4894_{18}.
Published: Šamsaddīn 399–400.

e. ***Ilā š-šayḫ Abī l-Faḍl b. Maḥmūd*** **(M79e, A364)—*Letter to Abū-l-Faḍl Ibn-Maḥmūd*** **/ EB 64, EB 85 (?)**
The second EB listing gives the name of the addressee as Abū l-Qāsim al-Faḍl b. Maḥmūd, who may be the recipient of the present or following letter.
MSS: **Istanbul**, Ahmet III 3447_{35}, Nuruosmaniye $4894_{17,48}$.

f. ***Ilā š-šayḫ Abī l-Qāsim b. Abī l-Faḍl*** **(M79f, A263)—*Letter to Abū-l-Qāsim Ibn-Abī-l-Faḍl*** **/ EB 85 (?)**
See the preceding entry.
MSS: **Istanbul**, Ahmet III 3447_{37}, Nuruosmaniye $4894_{16,135}$ f. 594[a].

g. ***K. ilā Abī l-Faḍl Māfīd b. Īrāmard*** **(?) (M-, A-)—*Letter to Abū-l-Faḍl Māfīd Ibn-Īrāmard*** **(?) / EB 87**
Listed only in the EB, nothing is known about this letter or the addressee.

h. ***R. ilā Abī l-Qāsim al-Kirmānī*** **(M-, A-)—*Letter to Abū-l-Qāsim al-Kirmānī*** **/ EB 46**
This letter is listed only in the EB and does appear in any known manuscript. Normally it would not be part of the *Mubāḥaṯāt* discussions insofar as Kirmānī's "participation is mediated almost entirely through Bahmanyār" (Reisman *Avicennan Tradition* 180). Independently Avicenna may or may not have written to al-Kirmānī, given their mutually abusive relationship. The *kunya* Abū l-Qāsim was popular, and the second preceding letter was addressed to one. The possibility of a confusion cannot be excluded.

i. ***R. ilā Abī Ṭāhir al-mutaṭabbib fī maʿnā s-sirāj*** **(M-, A-)—*Letter to Abū-Ṭāhir the Physician on the Meaning of the Lamp*** **(?) / EB 114**
Listed only in the EB, nothing is known about this letter or the addressee. The word *sirāj*, lamp, if it is correct, is problematic. It can hardly refer to anything in the Qurʾān, where its use is straightforward. Three times it is used to refer to the sun (25:61, 71:16, and 78:13), and a fourth to the Prophet Muḥammad as a light to people (33:46), the meaning of which would hardly need any elucidation or philosophical comment. But since the addressee was a physician, the word that is written as *sirāj* in the manuscripts may be most likely a corruption of a medical term, possibly *mizāj*, temperament.

j. ***Correspondence with al-Wazīr al-ʿAlawī*** **(M-, A-)**
Fragments of a correspondence with al-Wazīr al-ʿAlawī are extant in MS **Baghdad**, Iraq Museum 594 (639H) pp. 87–88; see Daiber *Naturwissenschaft* 7. This person may be identical with the Abū-Ṭālib al-ʿAlawī, in whose home Avicenna stayed, mentioned by Reisman *Avicennan Tradition* 49n54 (Daiber *Collection IV* 7).

III. *Homilies*

GPW 5. *Tafsīr ba'ḍ suwar kalām Allāh* (M50)—*Exegesis of various Qur'ānic verses* / EB 83, 92, 93, 94

Avicenna used allegorical interpretation of some Qur'ānic verses, notably the Light Verse (Q 24:35), in several of his authentic works. The procedure is very much in keeping with Avicenna's understanding of the nature of revelation as an imaginative "translation" of demonstrative truths in figurative language accessible to the masses. Accordingly he may have engaged in such allegorical exegeses independently of his treatises, and some such interpretations are transmitted in the manuscripts and listed in the bibliographies. Mahdavī lists the titles that are given below, and al-Ḫaṭīb (2001) 396 refers additionally to manuscripts containing interpretations of the opening sūra, the *Fātiḥa* (Q 1), and of the "usury" verse in the second (Q 2:275). The EB, which appears to refer collectively to such compositions in a generic entry (83), as given above, nevertheless lists three further titles by name (EB 92–94): one interpreting the "splitting of the moon" (Q 54:1), and the other two interpreting the story of the Seven Sleepers (Q 18:8–26) and verse 45 (Q 18:45) of the sūra of *The Cave*; none of these has been so far identified in the manuscripts. Doubtless there are others that future research will uncover. Other than a preliminary review of the published exegeses by Janssens "Qur'ān," in which he arrived at mixed results—some may be authentic others not—they have not been studied critically in any significant way. Their authenticity has yet to be established.

a. *Sūrat al-Iḫlāṣ* (M50a, A208)—*Sincere Religion* (Q 112)
Alternate titles: *at-Tawḥīd, aṣ-Ṣamadiyya.*

Al-Ḫaṭīb (2001) 403 defends its authenticity on the basis of its agreement with "all the philosophical views" of Avicenna. He also gives a list (396–402) of all the commentaries that were written on Avicenna's piece.

MSS: **Bankipore** 1646; **Berlin** 972; **Cairo**, Taymūr 200 Majāmī'; **Dublin**, Chester Beatty 3045_{10}; **Gotha** 543_{1}; **Hyderabad** I 534; **Istanbul**, Ahmet III 3447_{1}, Carullah 184, 2114_{2}, Esat Efendi 3688, Hamidiye 1448_{54}, Hazine 1723_{8}, Nuruosmaniye 4894_{1}, Ragıp Paşa 1461_{22}, 1469_{6}, Şehit Ali Paşa 321, Üniversite 1458_{1}, 1568_{5}, 2268, 2602_{2}, 3328_{10}, Vehbi 148, Veliyüddin 2134_{14}, 3228_{4}; **London**, Brit. Lib. 978_{38}; **Meshed**, Riżavī I 3/104, IV 5/283, 284; **Oxford**, Bodleian 980_{5}; **Princeton** (ELS) 308 ff. 123^{b}–128^{a}; **Tehran**, Majlis 625_{1}, 866_{1}, 1061_{4}, 1768_{2}, Malik 2003_{15}, 2017_{1}, Miškāt 1035, 1037, 1046_{9}, 1149 ff. 39^{b}–40^{b}, 1164 ff. 76^{a}–79^{a}, Sipahsālār 4474_{4}, 8371_{15}, Tangābunī 317_{2}.—See also al-Ḫaṭīb (2001).

Published: 'Āṣī *Tafsīr* 104–113; al-Ḫaṭīb (2002).

b. ***al-Muʿawwiḏatāni*****: i.** ***Sūrat al-Falaq*** **(M50b, A210)—*****Daybreak*** **(Q 113); ii.** ***Sūrat an-Nās*** **(M50b, A211)—*****Men*** **(Q 114)**

MSS: **Bankipore** 1646; **Berlin** 977_{1+2}; **Cairo**, Taymūr 200 Majāmīʿ; **Dublin**, Chester Beatty 3045_{11}; **Gotha** 543_{1}, 1158_{3+4}; **Hyderabad** I 344; **Istanbul**, Ahmet III 3447_{2+3}, Carullah 2114_{2}, Hamidiye 1441, 1448_{55}, Hazine 1723_{7+10}, Nuruosmaniye 4894_{2+3}, Ragıp Paşa 1461_{23}, 1469_{5+8}, Üniversite 1458_{2+3}, 1568_{5}, 2602_{2}, 3328_{16}, Vehbi 148, Veliyüddin 2134_{14}, 3228_{4}; **London**, Brit. Lib. 978_{39+40}, India Off. 1079; **Manchester** 384_{j}; **Meshed**, Riżavī I 3/104, 5/290, 299, 300; **Mosul** VII 73_{7}; **Oxford**, Bodleian 980_{5}; **Princeton** (ELS) 308 ff. 123^{b}–128^{a}; **Tehran**, Majlis 625_{1}, 866_{2}, 1061_{5+7}, 1768_{3}, Malik 2003_{16}, 2017_{2}, Miškāt 1035, 1037, 1046_{10+11}, 1149 ff. 41^{a}–42^{a}, 1164 ff. 69^{b}–76^{a}, 79^{b}–81^{a}, Sipahsālār 4474_{5+6}, 8371_{15}, Tangābunī 317_{3+4}.

Published: ʿĀṣī *Tafsīr* 114–125.

Translation: English, Kenny "Sūras."

c. ***Sūrat al-Aʿlā*** **(M50c, A209)—*****The Most High*** **(Q 87)**

MSS: **Istanbul**, Üniversite 1458_{5}; **Meshed**, Riżavī I 4/62; **Tehran**, Majlis 1061_{26}, Miškāt 1164 ff. 63^{a}–69^{b}.

Published: ʿĀṣī *Tafsīr* 94–103.

Translation: English, ʿAbdul Ḥaq.

d. ***Tafsīr qawlihi taʿālā: Ṯumma stawā ilā s-samāʾi wa-hiya duḫān*** **(M50d, A208)—*****Exegesis of the Verse, "Then He lifted Himself to heaven when it was smoke"*** **(Q 41:11)**

MSS: **Hyderabad** III 730; **Istanbul**, Ahmet III 1584_{29}, 3447_{7}, Fatih 5380_{5}, Hamidiye 1448_{56}, Hazine 1723_{2}, Nuruosmaniye 4894_{78}, Ragıp Paşa 1461_{54}, 1469_{1}; **Rampur** I 32; **Tehran**, Majlis 1768_{4}, Malik 2003_{17}, Miškāt 871 ff. 144^{a}–145^{a}.

Published: Michot "Puis Il se tourna"; ʿĀṣī *Tafsīr* 89–93.

Translation: French, Michot "Puis Il se tourna".

e. ***Tafsīr āyat an-nūr*** **(M50e, A-)—*****Exegesis of the Light Verse*** **(Q 24:35)**

MS: **Istanbul**, Üniversite 1458_{4}.

Published: ʿĀṣī *Tafsīr* 84–88.

f. ***Tafsīr sūrat al-Fātiḥa*** **(M-, A-)—*****Exegesis of the Opening Sūra*** **(Q 1)**

Reference to a Jordanian MS in al-Ḫaṭīb (2001) 396.

g. ***Tafsīr āyat ar-ribā*** **(M-, A-)—*****Exegesis of the Usury Verse*** **(Q 2:275)**

Reference to a Rampur MS in al-Ḫaṭīb (2001) 396.

h. ***R. fī Kayfiyyat Aṣḥāb al-kahf*** **(M-, A-)—*****On How [to understand] the "Seven Sleepers"*** **(Q 18:8–26) / EB 94**

Listed only in the EB, no manuscripts of it are known.

i. *R. fī Maʿnā ḥaqīqat Wa-ḍrib lahum maṯala l-ḥayāti d-dunyā ka-māʾin* (M-, A-)—*The True Meaning of, "And strike for them the similitude of the present life: it is as water"* (Q 18:45) / EB 92
Listed only in the EB, no manuscripts of it are known.

j. *R. fī Kayfiyyat inšiqāq al-qamar* (M-, A-)—*On How [to understand] the "Splitting of the Moon"* (Q 54:1) / EB 93
Listed only in the EB, no manuscripts of it are known.

k. *R. an-Nayrūziyya fī maʿānī al-ḥurūf al-hijāʾiyya* (M127, A49)—*The Nayrūziyya: On the Signification of the Qurʾānic Letters* / EB 37
Alternate titles: *Fawātiḥ as-suwar, Asrār al-ḥurūf.*

A commentary on some of the "mystical" letters with which some Qurʾānic chapters begin. In the introduction the author says that he wrote it as a new year's (Nayrūz) present for aš-Šayḫ al-Amīr Abū Bakr Muḥammad b. ʿAbdallāh (or ʿAbdarraḥīm in some MSS). Mahdavī 251 identifies him with the person for whom Avicenna also wrote the *Aḍḥawiyya* (above, GM 2), though this has to be verified just as much as the authenticity of the treatise.

MSS: **Cairo**, Dār al-Kutub 935 Falsafa ff. 1–5, Taymūr 121 Ḥikma, 200 Majāmīʿ ff. 193–195; **Gotha** 1158_{6}; **Hyderabad** II 1720; **Istanbul**, Ahmet III 3447_{49}, Ayasofya 2048_{3}, 4851_{10}, 4853_{11}, Carullah 2117_{8}, Hamidiye 1448_{57}, Hazine 1723_{11}, Köprülü 868_{7}, 1613_{2}, Nuruosmaniye 4894_{8}, Ragıp Paşa 1461_{7}, 1469_{9}, 1483_{6}, Üniversite 1458_{15}, 3328_{9}, 4724_{16}, 4754_{6}, Veliyüddin 2134_{16}; **London**, Brit. Lib. 978_{27}; **Manchester** 384_{A}; **Tehran**, Majlis 610_{3}, 1768_{6}, Malik 2003_{5}, 2007_{10}, 2008_{8}, Millī A 872_{7}, Miškāt 871_{13}, 1149 ff. 381[b]–383[a], Sipahsālār 1217_{24}, 2912_{9}.

Published: ʿAbdassalām Hārūn, *Nawādir al-maḫṭūṭāt*, Cairo: Maṭbaʿat Muṣṭafā al-Bābī al-Ḥalabī, [2]1393/1973, Vol. II, pp. 27–44.

GPW 6. Ḫuṭab wa-taḥmīdāt wa-asjāʿ—Homilies, Pieces in praise of God, Pieces in rhymed prose / LB 66

The letter in which Avicenna refers to his homilies, *R. al-Intifāʾ ʿammā nusiba ilayhi min muʿāraḍat al-Qurʾān*, cited above, is most likely dated to his Hamaḏān period, 1015–1024 (cf. Mahdavī 98, Michot "Riz" 94–96). Avicenna may well have continued composing such homiletic pieces in rhymed prose beyond that period. The LB lists them under the generic and descriptive heading given above. There are other such pieces in the manuscripts yet to be unearthed. M.T. Dānešpajūh lists two of them in the Tehran MS Miškāt 861, f. 4[a] (*Fehrest-e Ketābḫāne-ye ehdāʾī-ye Āqā-ye Sayyed Moḥammad Meškāt be Ketābḫāne-ye Dānešgāh-e Tehrān*, Tehran: Dānešgāh

1330/1951, 3:1, 512–513). Another can be found in MS Princeton (ELS) 308 ff. 1^{a}–2^{b}.

a. *Al-Ḫuṭba at-tawḥīdiyya* (M70, A177, 194)—*Homily on the Oneness of God* / LB 33

Alternate titles: *at-Tasbīḥiyya, at-Tamjīd, al-Ḫuṭba al-ġarrāʾ, Ḫuṭba fī l-ilāhiyyāt, al-ʿAṭiyya al-ilāhiyya, al-Kalima al-ilāhiyya.*

A eulogy of the prime mover and his attributes in rhyming prose (*sajʿ*). The Istanbul MS Üniversite 4755, f. 205^{a}, gives the title as *al-Kalima al-ilāhiyya llatī tuʿrafu bi-t-Tasbīḥiyya*, and the scribe writes in the margin next to the title, *ḏakarahā Abū ʿUbayd fī l-Fihrist al-Ḫuṭba at-tawḥīdiyya fī l-ilāhiyyāt.* If by Abū ʿUbayd is meant Jūzjānī, this is inaccurate; the bibliography that lists the title precisely in this fashion is the LB (33), not the SB, which is attributed in the tradition to Jūzjānī as embedded in his Biography. It can neither be held that the LB was thought to have been compiled by Jūzjānī; this is nowhere else attested. Most likely this is an oversight by the scribe. Mahdavī 99 mentions that Faḫr-ad-Din ar-Rāzī refers to this *ḫuṭba* in his *al-Mabāḥiṯ al-mašriqiyya* (II, 501, Hyderabad ed.) and that ʿUmar Ḫayyām translated it into Persian.

MSS: **Berlin** 2298; **Bursa**, Hüseyin Çelebi 1194 ff. 149^{b}–150^{b}; **Cairo**, Taymūr 482 Adab; **Gotha** 1158_{17}; **Hyderabad** III 730; **Istanbul**, Ahmet III 3447_{43}, Esat Efendi 3688, Hamidiye 1448_{32}, Köprülü 1602_{7}, Nuruosmaniye 4894_{62}, Revan 2042_{14}, Üniversite 4755_{11} ff. 204^{a}–206^{b} (588H), Veliyüddin 3263_{11}; **Leiden** 1464_{1}, 2139; **London**, Brit. Lib. 978_{46}; **Oxford**, Bodleian Persian 1422_{10}; **Rampur** I 341, 585, 712; **Tehran**, Malik 2005_{9}, 2017_{3}, 2019_{6}, Miškāt 1046_{22}, 1149 ff. 48^{b}–49^{a}, Tangābunī 79_{2}.

Published, with English translation: Akhtar.

b. *Ḫuṭba* (M69, A220)—*Homily*

A homily on the creator and creation in rhyming prose.

MSS: **Cairo**, Ṭalʿat 197 Mā baʿd aṭ-ṭabīʿa; **Istanbul**, Ayasofya 4849_{29} f. 142^{b}.

c. *Ḫuṭba fī l-ḫamr* (M71, A129)—*Homily on Wine*

Alternate title: *Ḫuṭba min maqālāt aš-Šayḫ ar-Raʾīs.*

This brief homily on wine interdiction (*taḥrīm hāḏihi l-ḫamra*) is unrelated to the medical treatise on the benefits and harms of wine, below, GMed 17.

MSS: **Gotha** 1158_{13}; **Istanbul**, Esat Efendi 3688 ff. 138^{b}–139^{a}, Hamidiye 1448_{26}; **Tehran**, Miškāt 861_{7}, Sipahsālār 1217_{2}.

d. *Fī d-Duʿāʾ* (M74, A222)—*Prayer*

Philosophical prayer to God in rhyming prose. One passage says, "Make me

one of the brethren of purity" (*wa-j'alnī min iḫwān aṣ-ṣafā' wa-aṣḥāb al-wafā' wa-sukkān as-samā'*, p. 394.2–3 Šamsaddīn).
MSS: **Istanbul**, Ahmet III 1584_{13} (partial), Nuruosmaniye 4894_{87}.
Published: 'Āṣī *Tafsīr* 295–299; Šamsaddīn 392–395.
Translation: English, Kenny "Prayer."

e. *Kalām aš-Šayḫ fī l-mawā'iẓ* (M102, A240, 243)—*Exhortations*
Alternate titles: *an-Naṣīḥa li-ba'ḍ al-iḫwān, al-Mawā'iẓ.*

Exhortations in rhyming prose to cultivate one's soul for happiness in this world and the next.
MSS: **Istanbul**, Ahmet III 1584, Ragıp Paşa 1461_{18}; **Tehran**, Majlis 1768_{16}.
Published: 'Āṣī *Tafsīr* 306–309; Šamsaddīn 396–397.

f. *Fī l-Ḥadīṯ* (M58, A214)—*On the Report*
Alternate title: *al-Aḥādīṯ al-marwiyya.*

An allegorical *ḥadīṯ* report on God and creation. It begins, without prologue, right after the *basmala*: *Ḥaddaṯanī nūr al-ḥayāt wa-nūr as-sam' wa-l-baṣar, qālā: ḥaddaṯanā l-aḥadiyya* (? undotted in the two MSS) *ta'ālā qāla: ḥaddaṯanī l-qidam, qāla: ḥaddaṯanī l-ġayb 'an al-ism al-mubīn 'an allāh jalla jalāluhu, qāla …*
MSS: **Istanbul**, Ayasofya 4829_{22} ff. 100[b]–101[a], Nuruosmaniye 4894_{135}.

g. *R. fī l-Malā'ika* (M113, A203)—*On Angels*
Homily in rhyming prose on the celestial host, called *karūb* in the text.
MSS: **Istanbul**, Ahmet III 3447_{13} ff. 62[b]–64[a], Hamidiye 1448_{19}, Köprülü 1589_{18}, Nuruosmaniye 4894_{98}, Üniversite 1458_{25}, 4724_{10}; **Tehran**, Miškāt 1079_{9}, 1149 ff. 353[b]–354[b].
Published: 'Āṣī *Tafsīr* 289–294.

h. *Al-Wird al-a'ẓam* (M128, A244)—*The Supreme Recitation*
An invocation to God in rhyming prose.
MS: **Istanbul**, Hamidiye 1448_{8}.
Published: 'Āṣī *Tafsīr* 318–320.

i. Min Kalimāt aš-Šayḫ ar-Ra'īs (M103, A5)—From Avicenna's Sayings
Alternate titles: *Aqwāl aš-Šayḫ, Fawā'id ḥikmiyya.*

Homiletic text in rhyming prose extolling philosophy which leads to knowledge of God and to things which "speech does not make [one] understand them, interpretation does not explain them, and statements do not disclose them, except the [faculty of] imagery" (*umūr lā yufhimuhā l-ḥadīṯ wa-lā tašraḥuhā l-'ibāra wa-lā yakšifu l-maqāl minhā ġayr al-ḫayāl; hāḏā wa-innī wa-in lam akun min al-ḥukamā' wa-lā min ḥizb al-'ulamā' wa-l-aṣfiyā'*

…, f. 75ᵇ in the Nuruosmaniye MS and MS A in Michot's text in "Sagesse;" Michot corrects himself in "Parfum" 58). The quotation is from the *Išārāt* II.9.20, 205/364,[49] while the following claim that he is no philosopher is beyond exaggeration. If authentic, this piece must have been composed during the last three or four years of Avicenna's life, after the composition of the *Išārāt*; but at that stage, but also for many years previously, he would not claim that he is not a philosopher, even for rhetorical effect. The piece must accordingly be thought pseudepigraphic, but its very air of authenticity and knowledge of Avicenna's works that it displays show the sophistication of the circles that are responsible for the forgeries and constitute an object lesson for the study of Avicennan pseudepigraphy.

MSS: **Cairo**, Ṭalʿat 197 Maʿārif ʿāmma f. 64^{a-b}; **Istanbul**, Ahmet III 3447_{33}, Nuruosmaniye 4894_{21}, Üniversite 1458_{33}.

Published, with French translation: Michot "Sagesse"

IV. *Poetry*

GPW 7. Ašʿār wa-qaṣāʾid (M29, A50)—Poetry / SB (26), LB 70, EB 88

Avicenna was certainly a versifier, using the *rajaz* meter to compose didactic poems presenting his views, in particular on logic and medicine, as registered in this inventory in the respective categories. In this regard he was following a practice already established not only in Arabic but also in Persian: an otherwise unknown Samanid physician named Maysarī composed a poem on medicine in 298 verses in the meter *hazaj* between the years 978 and 980, when Avicenna was a young boy. Significantly entitled also *Dānešnāme*, Maysarī's poem was dedicated to the Samanid vassal Abū-l-Ḥasan ibn-Sīmjūr;[50] Avicenna had thus respectable precedents to follow in this regard. But whether he was also a poet, composing or reciting poetry in the traditional Arabic meters in both Arabic and Persian, has yet to be investigated. The bibliographies refer to his poems in generic terms–*qaṣāʾid*, odes, poems composed in the traditional meters—while numerous such lines are credited to him in the manuscripts. No properly critical study has been conducted on them so far, and they cannot be listed individually here. See the references in Mahdavī and Anawati for the manuscripts, Lazard 63n2 for the basic references to earlier literature, and the entries in the bibliographies of Janssens.

49 For an interpretation of this passage and its place in Avicenna's epistemology see Gutas "Absence of Mysticism" 363–365.

50 Gilbert Lazard, *Les premiers poètes persans*, Paris: Adrien-Maisonneuve, 1964, 36–40.

H. Medicine (GMed)

Avicenna's medical works, both their contents and their transmission, have been studied very little, and at the present state of our knowledge it is impossible to make serious judgments about their authenticity. The manuscripts contain a large number of medical treatises and pieces or fragments of medical texts attributed to Avicenna, and much work is required before there is an accurate listing and subsequent examination of them all in order to determine whether they are by Avicenna, derive from the *Qānūn* or other authentic works by him, are paraphrases and extracts from his works, or simply misattributions and forgeries. Equally unsettled as a result is also the question of the titles of the medical works; many of those figuring in the list below are clearly scribes' and bibliographers' descriptions of the contents of the piece they were copying or cataloguing, not of the title of the piece, assuming even that it had one. I accordingly discuss the medical works in what follows all together without separating them into authentic and pseudepigraphic, and list them in decreasing order of attestation in the oldest bibliographies. I list only those titles included in Mahdavī and Ullmann *Medizin*; additional titles, even more questionable, are listed by Anawati, mainly followed by Scrimieri *Studi* 309–312.

i. *Expository*

GMed 1. ***K. al-Qānūn fī ṭ-ṭibb*** **(M98, 138, A140)—*The Canon of Medicine* / Bio 4, SB 5, LB 7, EB 6**

Jūzjānī reports (Gohlman 44.7, 74.2) that Avicenna began writing the *Qānūn* in Jurjān (ca. 403/1013). He went on writing it throughout his career until he finished it some time during his last stay in Iṣfahān, so that it was completed after 1024, perhaps significantly later than that.

In the following list of MSS given by Mahdavī, partial copies are indicated by the book number in Roman numerals in parentheses. For further manuscripts and the numerous commentaries, marginal notes and additions, summaries, versifications, and translations see Mahdavī, Anawati, *GAL* and *GALS*, Ullmann *Medizin* 152–154, and Janssens *Bibliography* and *Suppl. I*.

MSS: **Algiers** 1747 (II; 539H), 1748 (II), 1749 (IV), 1750 (IV), 1751 (IV); **Aligarh** 610/8, 18, 22, 616/8, 10; **Bankipore** IV 19–21, 22 (III–IV), 23, 24 (I), 25 (I); **Berlin** 6269 (I), 6270 (II), 6271 (III; 538H); **Cairo**, Dār al-Kutub Ṭibb 80, 83 (III), 494 (I), 508 (III), 797 (III), 1133 (III), 1564 (III), Ṭalʿat Ṭibb 590 (I), 604 (III), Taymūr Ṭibb 367 (I–II); **Escorial** 822–827 (I–IV), 862 (IV);

Gotha 1911; **Istanbul**, Ahmet III 1932, 1933, 1934 (I), 1935, 1936, Atıf Efendi 1965+1966, Ayasofya 3599 (I), 3638, 3684 (I), 3685 (I), 3686, 3687 (I), Beşir Ağa 513, Beyazıt (Umumi) 4126 (I), Carullah 1522+1523, 1524 (I–II), 1525 (I–II), Damat İbrahim Paşa 936, 938, 939 (I), Fatih 3594 (I), 3595 (I), 3596 (I), 3597 (I) 3598, 3599 (IV), 3600 (III), 3601 (II), 3602 (I), Feyzullah 1324, Halet Efendi 750 (I), Hazine 543, 573 (V), Köprülü 976, 977, Nuruosmaniye 3569, 3570, 3571, 3572 (III), Yeni Cami 923 (I–II); **Leiden** 1317 (I), 1318 (II), 1319 (III); **London**, Brit. Lib. 448, 449_1 (I), 450 (II), 1359, 1652 (III), Or. 4946, Or. 5033, Or. 5594 (I, III), Or. 5858_3 (II), Or. 6536_1 (III), Or. 6537 (III; 664H); **Manchester** 323–326; **Meshed**, Riżavī III 9/86 (I), 87 (I), 88, 89 (II), 90 (III); **Munich** 812 (I), 813 (I), 814 (I), 815 (I), 816 (III), 817 (IV); **Oxford**, Bodleian 532 (III), 534 (III), 556 (I–II), 575 (V), 591 (I), 613 (II), 621 (II); **Paris** 2885–2891 (593H), 2892–2916, 6265 (II), 6454, 6690 (II; 581H); **Rampur** I 490–491; **St. Petersburg**, Rosen 166; **Tehran**, Khān 654, Majlis 516 (I), 517 (IV), 518 (IV), 2343 (III–V; 586H), Malik 4235 (III), 4292 (I), 4403 (I), 4475 (I), 4494 (I), 4496 (I–II), 4499 (I), 4500 (IV; 591H), 4544, 4550 (IV), 4562, Sipahsālār 808, 809, 810 (III), 811 (III), Ṭabāṭabā'ī 650 (I), 1017 (I), 1117 (III).

Published: The Arabic text was published for the first time in Rome in 1593, together with the *Najāt*, in two parts; part one comprised Books 1–3 and part two Books 4–5. The print in use is that of Cairo, Būlāq 1294/1877, in three volumes, reprinted and reset by al-Qašš and Zayʿūr, in four volumes, with the Būlāq volume and page numbers given in the margins. For a new edition coming out in New Delhi see Janssens *Bibliography* 26, *Suppl. I* 16.

Translations: See Janssens *Bibliography* 30–35, *Suppl. I* 17–18.

Related to the *Qānūn* material are the following entries in the bibliographies:

a. *Muʿālajāt (ṭibbiyya li-l-Qānūn)* (M-, A-)—(*Medical*) *Treatments* (*in the Canon*) / Bio 16, LB 73

Alternate title (?): *Qawānīn wa-muʿālajāt ṭibbiyya.*

In the Biography Jūzjānī mentions (Gohlman 72.9–74.1) that Avicenna intended to include in the *Qānūn* the experience which he had gained in his medical practice (*muʿālajāt*), of which he gives two examples, but that these notes were lost before the book was completed. The compiler of the LB echoes Jūzjānī's description by registering it as a work, *Qawānīn wa-muʿālajāt ṭibbiyya*, the *Qawānīn* part presumably being added as reflecting the title of the book to which these treatments belonged, the *Qānūn*. It does not appear that he had a manuscript before him with a treatise bearing this title. No such treatise is known to be extant in manuscript. Gohlman 150n20 identifies this with *Dustūr ṭibbī*, (c) below.

b. ***K. al-Ḥawāšī ʿalā l-Qānūn*** **(M-, A-)—*Glosses on the Canon* / SB (44)**
The SB alone has this title, though not the original SB, but the version that came into the hands of Ibn-Abī-Uṣaybiʿa and was circulating in the middle of the thirteenth century. The title is thus an addition to the original SB, and thus of equal value as the later EB rather than the earlier SB. Again, it is not clear whether the person responsible for the addition found a manuscript text with this title or simply interpreted Jūzjānī's statement cited in the preceding entry (a) as constituting "glosses" on the *Qānūn*. No such treatise is known to be extant in manuscript.

c. ***Dustūr ṭibbī*** **(M 73, A128)—*Medical Code* / EB 104**
This title appears only in the EB, and thus came into circulation by mid-thirteenth century. Extant in manuscript, it is attributed to Avicenna and begins by stating that the first thing a physician should know is the genus and species of the disease. Such rules for therapy explain the title of the piece (*dustūr*), which itself may be a variant of the *qawānīn* in the second preceding title, (a) above, if Gohlman's suggestion that the two works are identical is right. Furthermore, Mahdavī 280 indicates that this treatise may be identical with the *Šaṭr al-ġibb* (*Intermittent Fever*), GMed 19 below.

MSS: **Gotha** 1930$_{3}$; **Istanbul**, Ahmet III 3447$_{42}$, Ayasofya 4849$_{28}$ ff. 139[b]–141[b], 4853$_{10}$, Hamidiye 1448$_{24}$, Hazine 1730$_{39}$, Nuruosmaniye 4894$_{61}$; **Rampur** I 475$_{47}$; **Tehran**, Malik 2005$_{3}$, 2012$_{7}$, Millī 9$_{6}$, Miškāt 1074$_{9}$, 1149 ff. 239[a–b].

GMed 2. ***M. al-Adwiya al-qalbiyya*** **(M14, A111)—*Cardiac Remedies* / Bio 11, SB 14, LB 20, EB 39**

Alternate title: *Aḥkām al-adwiya al-qalbiyya.*

Jūzjānī reports (Bio 11) that Avicenna composed this treatise on psychiatry soon after his arrival in Hamaḏān, i.e., about 405/1015. In the introduction Avicenna states that he wrote it for an ʿAlid dignitary (*aš-šarīf*), one as-Saʿīd Abū-l-Ḥusayn ʿAlī b. al-Ḥusayn b. al-Ḥasanī, who, as Mahdavī 24 suggests, may be the same person at whose home he stayed after his release from the fortress of Fardajān (Gohlman 60.6 and 61n82). Jūzjānī, who added some passages from this treatise at the end of Book Four, Section Four of the De anima of the *Šifāʾ* (*Nafs* 201 Rahman)—manifestly because in the last lines of that section Avicenna says that he treated extensively that subject in his medical books (*fī kutubinā ṭ-ṭibbiyya*)—adds that Avicenna composed this treatise for a friend of his who was a beginner (*baʿḍ al-mubtadiʾīn min aṣdiqāʾihi*; Mahdavī 24).—See further Ullmann *Medizin* 155–156.

MSS: **Berlin** 6359; **Dublin**, Chester Beatty 3676_{1}; **Gotha** 1995; **Istanbul**, Ahmet III 2119_{1}, 3447_{39}, Ayasofya 3699_{3}, Damat İbrahim Paşa 822, Esat Efendi 3790, Fatih 3627_{1}, 5316_{4}, Hamidiye 1448_{21}, Köprülü 869_{7} ff. 206^{b}–219^{b}, Lâleli 1647_{2}, Nuruosmaniye 3456_{1}, 3590_{1}, 4894_{58}, Şehit Ali Paşa 2031_{1}, 2092, Üniversite 6172, Vehbi Efendi 1477; **Leiden** 1330, 1331; **London**, Brit. Lib. Or. 5280, 5719_{2}, Wellcome Catal. p. 74, no. 73; **Meshed**, Riżavī III 9/14; **Mosul** 14_{2}; **St. Petersburg** 171 Rosen; **Tehran**, Malik 2005_{1}, Millī 9_{1+3}, Miškāt 861_{11}, 1074_{12}, 1149 ff. 51^{a}–61^{a}, Tangābunī 324_{3}.

Published: al-Bābā 221–294.

Translations: English, Hameed.

GMed 3. *K. al-Qawlanj* (M101, A142)—*Colic* / Bio 10, SB (13), LB 17, EB 75

Jūzjānī reports that Avicenna wrote the *K. al-Qawlanj* while imprisoned in the castle of Fardajān, i.e., around 414/1023.

MSS: **Hyderabad** III 736; **Istanbul**, Vehbi 1488_{13}; **Meshed**, Riżavī III 9/57; **Rampur** I 480, 712; **Tehran**, Malik 4573_{4}, Miškāt 861_{12}.—Ullmann *Medizin* 156.

Published: see Janssens *Bibliography* 57.

GMed 4. *R. fī l-Hindibāʾ* (M131, A150, 272)—*On Endive* / SB 36, LB 36, EB 42

Alternate titles: *Hindibāʾ ġayr maġsūla, ʿIllat al-amr bi-stiʿmāl al-hindibāʾ ġayr maġsūla.*

MSS: **Gotha** 1158_{26}, 1930_{5}; **Istanbul**, Ahmet III 2119_{2}, 3447_{48}, Ayasofya 3683_{2}, Hamidiye 1448_{35}, Kaptan Paşa 1262, Köprülü 869_{10}, Lâleli 1647_{1}, Nuruosmaniye 3590_{2}, 4894_{64}, Revan 2042, Şehit Ali Paşa 2034_{2}, Üniversite 1458_{37}, 4711_{6}, 4755_{25}, Vehbi 1488_{16}; **Lisbon**, Academia das Ciencias, Arab. V.293 ff. 70^{b}–74^{a}; **Meshed**, Riżavī III 9/58; **Tehran**, Malik 4573_{6}, Millī 9_{4}, Miškāt 861_{14}, 1046_{35}, 1074_{10}, Sipahsālār 4475, Ṭabāṭabāʾī 352_{6}.—See also Ullmann *Medizin* 201

Published: in the edition by Kilisli Rıfat Bilge in A. Süheyl Ünver, *İbni Sina: hayatı ve eserleri hakkında çalışmalar*, Istanbul: Burhaneddin Erenler Matbaası, 1955, 10–23.

GMed 5. *Resāle-ye Nabḍ* (M117, A149)—*On the Pulse* / SB 30, LB 21, EB 81

Alternate titles: *Nabḍiyya, Dāneš-e rag.*

Written in Persian; see Lazard 66. It is not clear whether the *R. Maʿrifat at-tanaffus wa-n-nabḍ* (*Diagnosis through breathing and pulse*) mentioned by Ullmann *Medizin* 156 is related to this work or not.

MSS: **Hyderabad** III 730, 732; **Meshed**, Rižavī III 9/65; **Rampur** I 481, 712; **Tehran**, Malik 2021_{1}, Miškāt 1074_{4}, Ṭabāṭabāʾī 352_{4}, 1373_{7}.
Published: Meškāt *Rag.*
Translation: Italian, Scrimieri *Studi* 212–232.

GMed 6. ***R. fī s-Sikanjubīn*** **(M81, A253)—*On Oxymel* / LB 39, EB 110**

Alternate title: *Manāfiʿ aš-šarāb al-musammā sikanjubīn.*
MSS: **Cairo** Dār al-Kutub 593 Ṭibb; **Istanbul**, Ahmet III 2119_{3}, Beyazıt (Umumi) 50_{3}, Lâleli 1647_{3}, Nuruosmaniye 3590_{3}, Vehbi 1488; **Tehran**, Malik 4753_{27}, Miškāt 1046_{34}, 1079 pp. 172–176, Ṭabāṭabāʾī 352_{14}.—See also Ullmann *Medizin* 200–201.
Published, with English translation: Marín and Waines.

GMed 7. ***M. fī Dafʿ al-maḍārr al-kulliyya ʿan al-abdān al-insāniyya bi-tadāruk anwāʿ ḫaṭaʾ at-tadbīr*** **(M75, A130)—*Averting General Harm to Human Bodies by Preventing Various Mistakes in Treatment* / LB 52, EB 52**

Alternate title: *Tadāruk al-ḫaṭaʾ al-wāqiʿ fī t-tadbīr aṭ-ṭibbī.*

Avicenna wrote this treatise for Abū l-Ḥasan Aḥmad b. Muḥammad as-Sahlī in Gurgānj some time between 389/999–402/1012, though in some manuscripts it is attributed to as-Sahlī himself; see *GAS* III, 334 and Daiber "Khwārazm" 285.
MSS: **Cairo**, Dār al-Kutub 19 Ṭibb Majāmīʿ, Taymūr 325 Ṭibb; **Istanbul**, Ahmet III 3447_{79}, Ayasofya 3698_{1}, 3699_{1}, Carullah 1528, Fatih 3627_{2}, Hamidiye 1448_{47}, Hazine 1730_{37}, Köprülü 869_{6}, 1589_{47}, Nuruosmaniye 3471, 4894_{57}, Şehit Ali Paşa 2034_{1}, Üniversite F 737_{2}, A 4201, 4711_{5} (579H); **London**, Brit. Lib. Or. 5820_{2}; **New Haven**, Yale Landberg 473 (Nemoy Cat. 1505);[51] **Paris** 5966_{1}; **Tehran**, Miškāt 1074_{13}, 1149 ff. 119^{b}–128^{b}, Sipahsālār 2034_{1}.—See also Ullmann *Medizin* 191.
Published: al-Bābā 11–73.

GMed 8. ***Masāʾil Ḥunayn*** **(M110, A144)—*On Ḥunayn's* Questions / LB 72, EB 108**

Alternate titles: *Taʿālīq Masāʾil Ḥunayn, Šarḥ Masāʾil Ḥunayn b. Isḥāq.*

---

51 The author in the Leon Nemoy catalogue (*Arabic Manucripts in the Yale University Library*, New Haven: Yale University Press, 1956, 159b) is listed as Aḥmad b. Muḥammad al-Ġāfiqī.

Notes and comments on Ḥunayn's *Questions*. Although it appears in the LB, which means that it was in circulation under Avicenna's name before the end of the twelfth century, it is preserved in only relatively late manuscripts.
MSS: **Istanbul**, Ahmet III 3447_{18} ff. 126^{b}–138^{a}, Hamidiye 1448_{30}, Köprülü 1589_{48}, Nuruosmaniye 4894_{24}; **Tehran**, Miškāt 1149 ff. 204^{a}–209^{a}.

GMed 9. Fuṣūl ṭibbiyya mustafāda min majlis an-naẓar li-š-Šayḫ Abī ʿAlī b. Sīnā (M96, A137, 138)—Medical Notes from Avicenna's Sessions / LB 93, EB 76

Alternate titles: *Taʿlīqāt istafādahā Abū l-Faraj al-Hamaḏānī aṭ-ṭabīb min majlisihi wa-jawābāt lahu, Fuṣūl aṭ-ṭibbiyyāt, Fī Fann aṭ-ṭibb, Fī r-Rūḥ.*
Mahdavī 187 reports that the last section of this treatise is taken from the *R. al-Ḥudūd*. This may be a compilation from some of Avicenna's works.
MSS: **London**, Brit. Lib. 1349_{12}; **Bankipore** IV 108_{23}; **Rampur** I 490, 712; **Istanbul**, Ahmet III 1548_{22}, 3447_{16} ff. 106^{b}–122^{b}, Ayasofya 3683_{1}, Hamidiye 1448_{28}, Köprülü 1589_{49}, Nuruosmaniye 4894_{92}, Üniversite 4711_{14}; **Tehran**, Malik 4573_{12}, Miškāt 1149 ff. 290^{b}–303^{b}.

GMed 10. *Ar-Radd ʿalā maqālat aš-Šayḫ Abī l-Faraj b. Abī Saʿīd al-Yamāmī* (M77, A145)—*Refutation of Statements by al-Yamāmī* / LB 24, EB 77

Alternate title: *Risāla katabahā š-Šayḫ ar-Raʾīs Abū ʿAlī Ibn Sīnā ilā š-Šayḫ Abī l-Faraj b. Abī Saʿīd al-Yamāmī fī masʾala ṭibbiyya dārat baynahumā, M. fī l-Quwā ṭ-ṭabīʿiyya ilā Abī Saʿīd al-Yamāmī.*
Avicenna refutes al-Yamāmī's misunderstanding of what Avicenna had said on issues relating to humoral temperament.
MSS: **Bursa**, Hüseyin Çelebi 1194 ff. 140^{a}–143^{a}; **Gotha** 1930_{6}; **Istanbul**, Hazine 1730_{37}, Nuruosmaniye 4894_{88}, Şehit Ali Paşa 2034_{4}, Üniversite 4711_{15} (579H), Vehbi 1488_{17}; **Tehran**, Malik 2005_{14}, 4753_{7}, Millī 9_{5} ff. 111^{a}–126^{a}.

GMed 11. *Fī Naqḍ Risālat Ibn aṭ-Ṭayyib fī l-quwā ṭ-ṭabīʿiyya* (M76, A141)—*Refutation of Ibn-aṭ-Ṭayyib's Treatise on the Natural Faculties* / LB 27

Alternate titles: *R. fī r-Radd ʿalā kitāb Abī l-Faraj Ibn aṭ-Ṭayyib, ar-Radd ʿalā r-risāla al-mutaqaddima.*
This brief treatise is a refutation of Abū-l-Faraj Ibn-aṭ-Ṭayyib's (d. 1043) essay on *al-Quwā l-arbaʿa* or *al-Quwā ṭ-ṭabīʿiyya*, the bodily functions of attraction, retention, digestion, and excretion. The LB lists it with this title. Cf. Ullmann *Medizin* 156. In the introduction Avicenna refers to his *Šifāʾ*

in which the question is discussed. The treatise was accordingly composed during Avicenna's final Iṣfahān period.

MSS: **Istanbul**, Ahmet III 3447_{69}, Ayasofya 4829_{37}, Hazine 1730_{35}, Nuruosmaniye 4894_{130}, Pertev Paşa 617_{21}, Şehit Ali Paşa 2034_{3}, Üniversite 4711_{12} (579H), 4724_{13}, Vehbi 1488_{19}; **Tehran**, Malik 4753_{14}, Miškāt 1074_{8} ff. 134^{a}–138^{a}, 1149 ff. 240^{a}–242^{a}.

GMed. 12. *Tadbīr manzil al-ʿaskar* (M46, A252)—*Regimen of Military Camps* / LB 64

Alternate titles: *Manzil al-ʿaskar, K. Tadbīr al-jund wa-l-mamālīk wa-l-ʿasākir wa-arzāqihim wa-ḫarāj al-jund wa-l-mamālik* (LB).

MSS: **Istanbul**, Ayasofya 4849_{20} f. 108^{b}, Carullah 1441_{1}, Nuruosmaniye 4894_{114}.

Published: Šamsaddīn 280.

GMed 13. *R. fī Tadbīr al-musāfirīn* (M45, A251)—*Viaticum* (*Regimen for Travelers*) / EB 102

Medical advice for travellers. Mahdavī 56 notes that some passages at the end of the treatise are expressly attributed to Rhazes, which makes the attribution to Avicenna doubtful, especially since it is listed only in the late EB.

MSS: **Istanbul**, Ahmet III 3447_{73}, Ayasofya 4849_{32} ff. 153^{a}–175^{b}, Nuruosmaniye 4894_{122}; **London**, Brit. Lib. 1349_{11}; **Tehran**, Miškāt 1149 ff. 272^{b}–274^{a}, Tangābunī 317_{18}.

Published: Šamsaddīn 285–294.

GMed 14. *R. fī l-Bāh* (M39, A143)—*On Coitus* / EB 109

Alternate title: *Masʾala ṭibbiyya*.

This treatise was composed in response to a question on the subject by "an eminent personality" (*baʿḍ al-akābir*). In the course of the exposition there occurs the name of aš-Šayḫ al-ʿAmīd Abū Sahl al-Ḥamdūnī (f. 591^{b} in the Nuruosmaniye MS), the governor of Rayy in the service of the Ghaznavid Maḥmūd whose Kurdish troops, according to Bayhaqī (*Tatimma* 55–56/67), rifled the bags of Avicenna causing the loss of some of his books in January 1030 (see above, W10, Test. 8). The treatise is accordingly to be dated to Avicenna's Iṣfahān period

MSS: **Istanbul**, Ahmet III. 3447_{71}, Ayasofya 4849_{33} ff. 158^{a}–163^{a}, Nuruosmaniye 4894_{131}; **London**, Brit. Lib. 1349_{13}; **Tehran**, Miškāt 1149 ff. 309^{a}–311^{b}, Tangābunī 317_{16}.—Ullmann *Medizin* 195.

GMed 15. *R. fī l-Faṣd* (M95, A136)—*On Phlebotomy* / EB 111

Alternate title: *Fī l-ʿUrūq al-mafṣūda*.

MSS: **Istanbul**, Ahmet III 3447_{72}, Ayasofya 4829_{3}, 4849_{30} ff. 143ᵃ–145ᵇ, Nuruosmaniye 2748_{2}, 4894_{137}.—Ullmann *Medizin* 156.

GMed 16. *R. fī Ḥifẓ aṣ-ṣiḥḥa* (M60, A126)—*On Hygiene* / EB 115

MSS: **Bankipore** IV 108_{12}; **Cairo**, Taymūr 378 Ṭibb; **Hyderabad** III 730; **Istanbul**, Ayasofya 4849_{31} ff. 146ᵃ–152ᵃ, Nuruosmaniye 4894_{121}, Revan 2042_{6}, Şehit Ali Paşa 2031_{2}; **London**, Brit. Lib. 981_{12}, 1349_{4}; **Rampur** I 479, 712; **Tehran**, Majlis 1061_{18}, Malik 2010_{1}, Miškāt 1149 ff. 270ᵃ–272ᵇ, Sipahsālār 2031_{2}.

GMed 17. *K. Siyāsat al-badan wa-faḍāʾil aš-šarāb wa-manāfiʿihi wa-maḍārrihi* (M83, A133)—*Benefits and Harms of Wine for Physical Regime* / EB 65, 66

Alternate title: *Ḫamriyya, maʿrūfa bi-l-mujadwal; R. fī š-Šarāb, mujadwal wa-ġayr mujadwal*.

This medical treatise is unrelated to the Homily on wine in GPW 6c above. The dual entry in EB listed in the alternate titles above indicates that the treatise at one point circulated in both expository and tabular (*mujadwal*) form in columns.

MSS: **Istanbul**, Ayasofya 4849_{34} ff. 163ᵇ–165ᵃ, Nuruosmaniye $4894_{45,123}$, Şehit Ali Paşa 2031_{3}; **Tehran**, Malik 2007_{33}.

Published: Šamsaddīn 281–284.

GMed 18. *R. fī l-Farq bayn al-ḥarāra al-ġarīziyya wa-l-ġarība* (M94, A66)—*On the Difference between Vital and External Heat*

MSS: **Bankipore** IV 108_{14}; **Hyderabad** III 728_{41}, 730; **London**, Brit. Lib. 978_{29}; **Rampur** I 480, 713; **Tehran**, Malik 2005_{5}, 2012.

GMed 19. *Šaṭr al-ġibb* (M179, A134)—*Intermittent Fever*

Alternate title: *ʿIlāj al-ḥummā*.

Mahdavī 280 notes that this treatise may be identified with the *Dustūr ṭibbī* (above, GMed 1c).

MSS: **Bankipore** IV 108; **Hyderabad** III 730; **Rampur** I 479, 712.—Ullmann *Medizin* 156.

GMed 20. *R. fī l-Bawl* (M140, A122)—*On Urine*

There is a Greek translation of an Arabic work on urine attributed to Avicenna (Ἄλλη Ἔμπνι τοῦ Σινᾶ), but Ullmann *Medizin* 156 reports that it is not the same as the Arabic text surviving in the Glasgow MS. There has been some work on the Greek text, though the attribution to Avicenna remains to be established (cf. D. Gutas, "Arabic into Byzantine Greek," in *Knotenpunkt Byzanz. Wissensformen und kulturelle Wechselbeziehungen*, Andreas Speer and Philipp Steinkrüger, eds., Berlin: De Gruyter, 2012, 246–262, at 253).
MS: Glasgow 121_3.

GMed 21. *Al-Aġḏiya wa-l-adwiya* (M31, A121)—*Nourishment and Medication*

MS: **Istanbul**, Ayasofya 4849_{24} ff. 131[b]–132[b].

GMed 22. *Tadbīr sayalān al-manīy* (M44, A124)—*Therapy of Gonorrhea*

MS: **Istanbul**, Üniversite 4711_{13} (10 lines).

GMed 23. *R. fī Ḏikr ʿadad al-amʿāʾ* (M-, A-)—*On the Number of Intestines*

MS: **Dublin**, Chester Beatty 3676_3.—Ullmann *Medizin* 156.

GMed 24. *R. fī ṭ-Ṭīb* (M87, A135)—*On Perfume*

MS: **Leiden** 2140 f. 255[a].
Published, with French translation: Michot "Parfum".

GMed 25. *Maqādīr aš-šurubāt min al-adwiya al-mufrada* [*wa-maḍārru-hā*] (M112, A147)—*Measures of Potions in Simple Medicaments*

MS: **Berlin** 6412 ff. 54[a]–60[a].

GMed 26. Masāʾil ʿidda ṭibbiyya (M225, A146)—Numerous medical questions / LB 75

These would appear to be extracts from some medical work, attributed to Avicenna, which the scribes and bibliographers had no recourse but to give such generic title. The title in the MSS listed by Mahdavī, *al-Masāʾil al-maʿdūda fī ṭ-ṭibb*, would appear to be a slight variant of the one in the LB.
MSS: **Hyderabad** 3/736; **Rampur** 1/481.

ii. *Versified*

GMed 27. *Urjūza fī ṭ-Ṭibb* (M15, A114)—*Medicine, in verse*

The *Qānūn* versified in 1326 lines. See Ullmann *Medizin* 154–155.

MSS: **Algiers** 1752, 1753; **Bankipore** IV 108_3; **Beirut**, St. Joseph 289; **Berlin** 6268; **Cairo** VI,2,3; **Cambridge** Suppl. 42_a; **Escorial** 788_{12}, 853_2; **Gotha** 2032_3; **Istanbul**, Ayasofya 3706_2, Ali Emiri Efendi 2849, Fatih 3526, Nuruosmaniye 3458_1, 4894_{39}; **Leiden** 1325; **London**, Brit. Lib. 893_3, Suppl. 801_1; **Manchester**, Mingana IV 826; **Mosul** I 152; **Oxford**, Bodleian 527_2, 645_1, 1264_1; **Paris** 2943_2, 3038_3; **Rampur** I 467_2; **Tehran**, Malik 4573_{15}, Miškāt 1149 ff. 61^b–69^b and 235^a–237^b.

Published: Jahier and Noureddine; al-Bābā 89–194.

Translation: French, Jahier and Noureddine.

GMed 28. *Urjūza fī Ḥifẓ aṣ-ṣiḥḥa* (M16, A117, 153)—*Hygiene, in verse*

Alternate title: *Urjūza fī ṭ-Ṭibb.*

Number of verses: 15; Anawati says 151 verses, though the Ayasofya MS has 15 and the Berlin MS 13.

MSS: **Berlin** 6396; **Escorial** 889_4; **Istanbul**, Ayasofya 4849_{28} f. 142^a; **Leiden** 526_{12}.

GMed 29. *Urjūzat Tadbīr al-fuḥūl fī l-fuṣūl* (M17, A115, 118)—*Seasonal Dietetics, in verse*

Alternate titles: *Fī l-Fuṣūl al-arbaʿa*; *Urjūza fī ṭ-Ṭibb*; *Urjūza fī Tadbīr aṣ-ṣiḥḥa fī l-fuṣūl al-arbaʿa.*

Dietetic advice according to the season. According to Mahdavī 26, the beginning varies in the manuscripts. Mahdavī registers the number of verses as 121, though the al-Bābā edition has 147 with an additional seven. See further Ullmann *Medizin* 201.

MSS: **Berlin** 6397, 6398, 6399; **Istanbul**, Atıf Efendi 2837, Damat İbrahim Paşa 839, Esat Efendi 3785, Lâleli 1643, Vehbi 1407_3; **Paris** 2562_{15}, 2942_1, 2992_3, 3039_9.

Published: al-Bābā 195–206.

GMed 30a. *Urjūza fī t-Tašrīḥ* (M18, A112)—*Anatomy, in verse*

Anawati 171 reports that the Vatican MS contains two poems on anatomy attributed to Avicenna, one after the other. The first, in 89 verses, on ff. 51–53 of the MS, is the only one registered by Mahdavī. Scrimieri *Testimonianze*

117, who does not discuss it, merely states that it is a "poetic summary" of the poem that follows ("88 versi introduttivi ... che in effetti si riducono ad un riassunto poetico della poesia seguente"), i.e., the one he publishes in 156 verses. All this material needs to be examined on the basis of the manuscripts.
MS: **Vatican**, Borgia 87_{9}.

GMed 30b. *Urjūza fī t-Tašrīḥ* (M-, A112)—*Anatomy, in verse*

In 156 verses. See the preceding entry.
MSS: **Cairo**, Dār al-Kutub 2 Ṭibb; **Gotha** 13; **Vatican**, Borgia 87_{10}.
Published, with Italian translation: Scrimieri *Testimonianze* 118–156.

GMed 31. *Urjūza fī l-Bāh* (M-, A116)—*On Coitus, in verse*

MS: **Istanbul**, Vehbi 1407. See further Anawati p. 176, no. 116.

GMed 32. *Urjūza fī Waṣāyā Abuqrāṭ* (M19, A120)—*Hippocratic Determinations ["Ivory Box"], in verse*

Versification of the Arabic translation of the late antique ps-Hippocratic work on signs prognosticating death (*Capsula eburnea*), in 95 verses in the edition of Kuhne Brabant. See Ullmann *Medizin* 33–34 and 155, and Strohmaier "Écrits pseudépigraphiques" 42–43.
MSS: **Berlin** 6229; **London**, Brit. Lib. 893_{6}.—Further MSS in the edition of Kuhne Brabant.
Published, with Spanish translation: Kuhne Brabant.

GMed 33. *Urjūza fī l-Mujarrabāt* (M20, A113)—*Tested Prescriptions, in verse*

Number of verses: 120. On the *mujarrabāt* see Ullmann *Medizin* 312.
MSS: **Escorial** 863_{2}; **Istanbul**, Ayasofya 4829_{30}, Nuruosmaniye 3458_{2}, 4894_{136}, Ragıp Paşa 1481_{1}; **London**, Brit. Lib. 893_{5}; **Paris** 2661_{4}, 2942_{2}; **Tehran**, Miškāt 1149 ff. 314^{a}–315^{a}; **Vienna** 1457_{2}.

GMed 34. *Urjūza fī l-Waṣāyā* (M21, A119)—[*Medical*] *Recommendations, in verse*

Alternate title: *Naṣāʾiḥ ṭibbiyya manẓūma*.
Number of verses: 72.
MSS: **Berlin** 6395; **Gotha** 2027_{4}, 2034_{2}; **Istanbul**, Ahmet III 3447_{76}, Nuruosmaniye 4894_{49}; **Tehran**, Miškāt 1149 ff. 315^{a-b}.

J. Spurious or Misattributed Works (listed alphabetically by title)

Asbāb ar-raʿd wa-l-barq, R. fī Ḏikr* (M26, A55)—*On the Causes of Thunder and Lightning

This is a portion of the meteorology by Theophrastus, wrongly attributed to Avicenna; see *GAS* VII,223, Janssens *Bibliography* 52, Reisman "ARCE" 144 and "Pseudo-Avicennan Corpus I" 10, and Daiber "Khwārazm."
MSS: **Cairo**[2] I 29; **Hyderabad** III 728; **London**, Brit. Lib. 978_{15} ff. 368–369; **Meshed**, Riżavī IV 1/605; **Rampur** I 389, 712, II 724; **Tehran**, Miškāt 1089_{6}.
Published: Mūsawī no. 2.

R. fī Dafʿ al-ġamm min al-mawt* (M168, A224)—*Dispelling Distress over Death

An extract from Miskawayh's *Tahḏīb al-aḫlāq*.
Published: Mehren *Traités* III.49–57; ʿĀṣī *Tafsīr* 270–280.

Dānešnāme-ye ʿAlāʾī* (M164, A13, 11)—*"Philosophy for ʿAlāʾ al-Dawla"

This is a Persian work on logic which is distinct from the *Dānešnāme*, and which Mahdavī 274 identifies from internal evidence as one of the works by Sāwī.
MSS: **Istanbul**, Ahmet III 3447_{81}, Ayasofya 2530, 2531, 4829_{17}, Hamidiye 1448_{4}, Nuruosmaniye 2748_{1}; **Tehran**, Majlis 108.

***Fuṣūṣ al-ḥikam* (M192, 206, A233, 95)—*Philosophical Bezels/Clauses* / LB (100), EB 34, 107**

Alternate titles: *al-Firdaws; al-Quwā l-insāniyya wa-idrākātuhā.*
An Avicennizing treatise attributed to Fārābī, Avicenna, and others in the manuscripts. See the discussion by Pines "*Fuṣūṣ.*"
Published: Dieterici *Abhandlungen* (text) 66–83; ʿĀṣī *Tafsīr* 126–147.
Translations: German, Dieterici *Abhandlungen* (translation) 108–138; Spanish, Manuel Alonso Alonso, "El "Kitāb Fusūs al-Ḥikam de al-Fārābī"," *Al-Andalus* 25 (1960) 1–40.

M. fī Ḥiṣb al-badan* (M66, A127)—*On Physical Well-being

Mahdavī 97 records that at the beginning of the treatise it is written, "This is the treatise by Galen *Fī Ḥiṣb al-badan*, as translated by Avicenna." This is in all probability a version of the Galenic treatise Περὶ εὐεξίας, possibly as reworked by Ibn Abī l-Ašʿaṯ; cf. Ullmann *Medizin* 40 and 138.

MS: **Istanbul**, Ayasofya 3572₃.—According to Mahdavī 97, Ergin and Anawati also list MS Ayasofya 4836 but the present treatise does not appear there.

Liber celi et mundi (M-, A-)—*On the Heavens and the World*

A paraphrase of books one and two of Aristotle's *De caelo*, surviving in Latin translation and falsely attributed to Avicenna. See Oliver Gutman, "On the Fringes of the *Corpus Aristotelicum*: the Pseudo-Avicenna *Liber celi et mundi*," *Early Science and Medicine* 2 (1997) 109–128, and his edition and translation of the Latin text in *Pseudo-Avicenna, Liber celi et mundi*, Leiden: Brill, 2003.

It has no resemblance to any surviving works by Avicenna on the subject and it cannot be identified as the Latin translation of his *Tafsīr as-Samāʾ wa-l-ʿālam* (GS 10b under Physics).

R. al-Mabdaʾ wa-l-maʿād (M106 p. 216, A196)—*"Epistle on the Provenance and Destination"*

A brief epistle under this title, providing answers to four questions (where we come from, why we have come, whither we go, what our state at the *Barzaḫ* will be) is attributed to Avicenna in some manuscripts. It is not attested in any of the medieval bibliographies and it has been conclusively shown to be inauthentic by Michot *"Épître sur la genèse,"* who also provides a French translation. The MSS are listed in Mahdavī, Anawati, and Michot, and the text is printed in al-Kurdī *Majmuʿāt ar-rasāʾil* 249–256.

R. fī Maʿrifat an-nafs an-nāṭiqa wa-aḥwālihā (M238, A103)—*On the Knowledge of the Rational Soul and its States*

Alternate titles: *R. fī ʿIlm an-nafs, R. fī n-Nafs an-nāṭiqa wa-kayfiyyat aḥwālihā, Ḥaqīqat annafs.*

As Mahdavī 302 reports, this treatise is anonymous in some manuscripts while in others it is attributed to any number of other authors. It is not listed in any bibliography of Avicenna's works, and its authenticity was questioned by both Mahdavī and Michot "Connaissance de l'âme," who thought that this treatise was written about 100 to 150 years after Avicenna's death, but that it is nevertheless imbued completely with Avicenna's thought. Michot also provided a critical translation. Marmura "Kalām" 203 defended its authenticity on the sole basis that "it is an expression of Avicenna's personal philosophy."

MSS: **Cairo**, Dār al-Kutub 343 Majāmīʿ ff. 127^b–130^a, Ṭalʿat 209 Majāmīʿ; **Cambridge** 1066; **Gotha** 52_6; **Istanbul**, Ahmet III 1302 ff. 91^b–99^a (605H), 3447_{80}, Ayasofya 2414_1, 4829_{39}, Carullah 2098_{13}, 2117, Esat Efendi 3688, Nuruosmaniye 4894_{77}, Üniversite 1458_{11}, Veliyüddin 3228_5, 3237_7, 3275_{24}, 3282_2; **Leiden** 1466; **Oxford**, Bodleian 1012_2 (696H); **Tehran**, Sipahsālār 4474.
Published: Ahwānī *Aḥwāl* 181–192.
Translation: French, Michot "Connaissance de l'âme."

Al-Muḫtaṣar fī ʿilm al-hayʾa (M197, 220, A166)—*Compendium of Astronomy*

Alternate titles: *al-Falak wa-l-manāzil*, *Risāla fī l-Hayʾa*.

As properly identified by Mahdavī and then by Ragep and Ragep 8, this is part from the *Rasāʾil Iḫwān aṣ-ṣafāʾ*. It seems to exist in relatively late manuscripts. Scrimieri *Testimonianze*, who provides an Italian translation to the first 14 sections (of the 25) on the basis of the Cairo MS Hayʾa 10, does not at all discuss how and where this treatise is ascribed to Avicenna. A brief review of the contents, on the basis of the London and Algiers MSS is offered by Ibn Ḥammūda aš-Šaršālī al-Jazāʾirī, "Muḫtaṣar ʿilm al-hayʾa li-š-Šayḫ ar-Raʾīs Abī ʿAlī b. Sīnā," *Le livre du millenaire d'Avicenne*, vol. III, Tehran 1956, 1–10.
MSS: **Algiers**, Nat. Libr. 1452 (1183H); **Cairo**, Dār al-Kutub 10 Hayʾa ff. 25^a–40^a, Hayʾa 43 (1337H);[52] **Istanbul**, Hüsrev Paşa 251; **London**, Brit. Lib. 977_{27} ff. 227–239.
Published: *Risāla fī l-hayʾa taʾlīf Abī ʿAlī ... Ibn Sīnā*, ed. Mahā Maẓlūm Ḫiḍr, Cairo: Maṭbaʿat Dār al-Kutub, 1427/2006.
Translation: Italian, Scrimieri *Testimonianze* 171–189.

R. fī n-Nafs (M124, A96)—*On the Soul*

This is the shorter version of a brief treatise on the soul by Gregory Thaumaturgos in seven sections, also as noted by Reisman "Pseudo-Avicennan Corpus I" 10 and note 16. For manuscripts, an edition, and translation of the text, together with a discussion of its transmission and of a scholium allegedly by Avicenna at the end of the treatise in the Leiden MS (the only one listed by Mahdavī), see Gätje *Psychologie* 114–129.

52 See David A. King, *A Survey of the Scientific Manuscripts in the Egyptian National Library* [ARCE / Catalogs 5], Indiana: Eisenbrauns, 1986, 49, no. B81.

Naṣāʾiḥ al-ḥukamāʾ li-l-Iskandar* (M119, A255)—*Philosophers' Advice to Alexander

Non-medical precepts by a Western (*maġrib*) sage to Alexander for staying healthy and avoiding aches and pains throughout the body.
MS: **Istanbul**, Nuruosmaniye 4894_{46} f. 252[a].
Published: Šamsaddīn 295–297.

An-Nukat wa-l-fawāʾid* (M-, A-)—*Useful Tidbits

For a description and study of this "stubbornly anonymous pseudo-Avicennian work," preserved only in the Istanbul MS Feyzullah 1217, see Michot "*Nukat*" (at 112).

***R. fī ṣ-Ṣanʿa ilā imām Abī ʿAbd Allāh al-Baraqī* (M86, A158)—*On Alchemy, to Abū-ʿAbdallāh al-Baraqī* / EB 69**

Alternate titles: *al-Iksīr al-aḥmar, Ḥaqīqat al-iksīr al-aḥmar, aṣ-Ṣanʿa al-ʿāliya.*

A spurious alchemical treatise; see above under Physics V.

MSS: **Istanbul**, Ayasofya 4849_{27} ff. 137[b]–139[a], Nuruosmaniye 4894_{14}, Üniversite 4724_{17} (700H); **Rampur** I 686; **Tehran**, Miškāt 1149 ff. 368[a–b].

***Taʿbīr ar-ruʾyā* (M47, A101, 156)—*Interpretation of Dreams* / LB (97), EB 74**

Alternate titles: *Taʾwīl ar-ruʾyā, Fī r-Ruʾyā, Manāmiyya.*

This treatise is by Abū-Sahl al-Masīḥī, as listed by Bayhaqī *Tatimma* 88/95 and Ibn-Abī-Uṣaybiʿa I,328.25 Müller; see Gutas "Agenda" 51 and Daiber "Khwārazm." Mahdavī 59 notes that there exists another treatise entitled *Taʿbīr ar-ruʾyā* or *Tafsīr ar-ruʾyā* having eleven chapters and attributed to Avicenna in the Tehran MSS Majlis 870_{7} ff. 243–249 and Miškāt 1045_{10}, which is not to be identified with the present one.

MSS: **Calcutta** (Bengal) II 787; **Hyderabad** III 728_{41}; **Istanbul**, Esat Efendi 3774_{6}; Vehbi 1488_{12}; **London**, Brit. Lib. 978_{44}; **Meshed**, Riżavī I 1/60; **Rampur** I 389_{76}, 692_{56}; **Tehran**, Majlis 756, 1859_{10}, Malik 2020_{1}, Miškāt 1040.
Published, with English translation, by Khan "Dreams" and "Ruya."

R. fī ṭ-Ṭibb* (M123, A107)—*On Medicine

Alternate titles: *Faṣl min kalām aš-Šayḫ ar-Raʾīs fī n-nafs; Fī n-Nafs.*

Dānešpažūh discovered (as cited by Michot *Destinée* p. xxix) that these four *fuṣūl* are from Abū-l-Ḥasan aṭ-Ṭabarī's (d. ca. 985) *al-Muʿālajāt al-Buqrāṭiyya*. They correspond to sections 13–14 and 24–25 of Book One, pp. 11–13 and 25–26 in the facsimile edition by Fuat Sezgin and others, *The Hippocratic Treatments*, Frankfurt: Institute for the History of Arabic-Islamic Science, 1990.

MSS: **Istanbul**, Ahmet III 3447_{62} ff. 475^b–477^b, Nuruosmaniye 4894_{82}, Pertev 617 ff. 19^b–21^b; **Leiden** 1469_{26} (= Warn. 958 ff. 80^b–81^b); **Tehran**, Miškāt 1149 ff. 244^b–245^b.

***Fī z-Zuhd, R. ilā Abī Saʿīd b. Abī l-Ḫayr* (M4z, A225, 256) —*On Asceticism, Letter to Ibn-Abī-l-Ḫayr* / LB 90, EB 60**

Alternate title: *al-Iršād.*

This is a passage from ʿAyn al-Quḍāt's *at-Tamhīdāt*, re-worked to form the pseudepigraphic Avicenna—Ibn-Abī-l-Ḫayr correspondence. The listing of the title in the LB (and then EB) indicates that the forgery was already in place before 1192, which was "after the composition of ʿAyn al-Quḍāt's *at-Tamhīdāt*. After ʿAyn al-Quḍāt the project was taken up by anonymous scholars who added yet other specimens of the correspondence, culled from both authentic and spurious texts, and at one point ordered sequentially through the introduction of epistolary elements attributed to Ibn Sīnā and Abū Saʿīd" (Reisman *Avicennan Tradition* 140). The sequence of letters was formed over a long period of time, and there was no canonical collection that would represent even a forged work. Mahdavī 3–11 lists ten such pieces as forming the correspondence under a title of his own, *ajwibat aš-Šayḫ ar-Raʾīs Abī ʿAlī Ibn Sīnā ilā Abī Saʿīd Ibn Abī l-Ḫayr*, which gives the false impression that this is actually a real work. As he says, he follows the collection of five of these pieces in the Istanbul MS Hamidiye 1452 (under the title *Ḫams asʾila li-Abī Saʿīd b. Abī l-Ḫayr maʿa ajwibat aš-Šayḫ ar-Raʾīs Abī ʿAlī Ibn Sīnā*), to which he added another five. I list in the inventory each individual piece under its category, as indicated.

MSS: **Cairo**, Dār al-Kutub 125 Majāmīʿ, 191 Majāmīʿ; **Istanbul**, Ahmet III 3447_{32}, Nuruosmaniye $4894_{20,43}$, Pertev 617_{45}; **Tehran**, Miškāt 339_{16}, 1030.

K. Unknown Works

Of all the works included in the bibliographies only the following four, listed only in the EB, are completely unknown and unaccounted for.

17. *Al-Istibṣār*
32. *K. Zubdat al-quwā l-ḥayawāniyya*
67. *R. fī t-Tuffāḥ*
90. *K. Yūṣaf ẓafar al-Amīr ʿAḍud ad-Dawla*

PART THREE

CONSPECTUS OF AVICENNA'S AUTHENTIC WORKS

A. SUMMAE (GS): WORKS COMPRISING ALL PHILOSOPHY

(i) Classificatory

GS 1. *M. fī Aqsām al-ḥikma—The Divisions of Philosophy*

(ii) Expository Summae

GS 2. *K. al-Majmūʿ/ al-Ḥikma al-ʿArūḍiyya—The Compilation / Philosophy for ʿArūḍī*
GS 3. *ʿUyūn al-ḥikma—Elements of Philosophy*
GS 4. *Al-Hidāya—The Guidance*
GS 5. *Aš-Šifāʾ—The Cure*
GS 6. *An-Najāt—The Salvation*
GS 7. *Dānešnāme-ye ʿAlāʾī—Philosophy for ʿAlāʾ-ad-Dawla*
GS 8. *Al-Mašriqiyyūn; al-Ḥikma al-mašriqiyya—The Easterners; Eastern Philosophy*
GS 9. *Al-Išārāt wa-t-tanbīhāt—Pointers and Reminders*

(iii) Commentaries and Notes

GS 10. *Al-Ḥāṣil wa-l-maḥṣūl—The Available and the Valid* [*of Philosophy*]
GS 11. *Al-Inṣāf—Fair Judgment*
(a) *Šarḥ K. al-Lām—Commentary on* [*Metaphysics*] *Lambda*
(b) *Tafsīr/Šarḥ K. Uṯūlūjiyā—Commentary on the Theologia Aristotelis*
(c) *At-Taʿlīqāt ʿalā ḥawāšī K. an-Nafs li-Arisṭūṭālīs—Marginal Glosses on Aristotle's De anima*
GS 12a. *At-Taʿlīqāt—Notes*
GS 12b. *Lawāḥiq—Appendices*
GS 13. Masāʾil tudʿā *l-Buḏūr*—Topics called *Seeds*

(iv) Responsa

GS 14. *K. al-Mubāḥaṯāt—Discussions*
(a) *Fī Masʾalat K. an-Nafs—Question on De anima*

(b) *Li-kull ḥayawān wa-nabāt ṯabāt—Every Animal and Plant has Permanence*
(c) *Al-Ajwiba ʿan al-masāʾil al-ʿašr II—Answers to Ten Questions II*
(d) *R. fī Ḏamm māḍiġ al-ḫarāʾ—Reproach of the Shit-eater*
(e) *Varia*

(v) Pseudepigraphs, to be authenticated

GS-Ps 1. *ʿUyūn al-masāʾil—Elements of [Philosophical] Topics*
GS-Ps 2. *Jawāb masāʾil kaṯīra—Answers to Many Questions*
(a) *Al-Ajwiba ʿan al-masāʾil al-ḥikmiyya—Answers to Philosophical Questions*
(b) *Al-Ajwiba ʿan al-masāʾil—Answers to Questions*
GS-Ps 3. *Al-Majālis as-sabʿa bayn aš-Šayḫ wa-l-ʿĀmirī—Seven Sessions between the Šayḫ and al-ʿĀmirī*
GS-Ps 4. Masāʾil tarjamahā bi-*t-Taḏkīr*—Questions which he entitled *Reminder*

B. LOGIC AND LANGUAGE (GL)

I. Logic

(i) General expository

GL 1. *Al-Muḫtaṣar al-awsaṭ fī l-manṭiq—Middle Summary on Logic*
GS 6a. *Al-Muḫtaṣar al-aṣġar fī l-manṭiq—Shorter Summary on Logic*
GL 2. *Ar-Risāla al-Mūjaza fī uṣūl al-manṭiq—Epitome of the Principles of Logic*
GL 3. *Al-Manṭiq al-mūjaz—Logic Epitomized*
GS 3a. *Al-Mūjaz aṣ-ṣaġīr fī l-manṭiq—Shorter Epitome on Logic*

(ii) General versified

GL 4. *Urjūza fī ʿilm al-manṭiq—The Science of Logic, in verse*

(iii) Particular Expository

GL 5. *M. fī l-Išāra ilā ʿilm al-manṭiq—Pointer to the Science of Logic*
GL 6. *K. al-Ḥudūd—Definitions*
(a) *Al-ʿUqūl—Intellects*
(b) *Jumal al-ḥudūd—Main Points of Definitions*
GL 7. *M. fi Ġaraḍ Qāṭīġūriyās—On the Purpose of the* Categories

GL 8. *R. fī Ḫaṭa' man qāla inna l-kammiyya jawhar—On the Error of Those Who Hold that Quantity Is Substance*
GL 9. *R. fī Ḫaṭa' man qāla inna š-šay' jawhar wa-ʿaraḍ—On the Error of Those Who Hold that Something Can Be Substance and Accident Simultaneously*
GL 10. *Bayān ḏawāt al-jiha—Explanation of the Modal Propositions*
GL 11. *An-Nukat fī l-manṭiq—Subtle Points in Logic*
GL 12. *Fī Uṣūl ʿilm al-burhān / Kitāb al-Mūjaz fī l-manṭiq—On the Principles of Demonstration / Epitome of Logic*
GL 13. *M. fī Taʿaqqub al-mawḍiʿ al-jadalī—Tracing the Dialectical Commonplace*
GL 14. *Fī anna ʿilm Zayd ġayr ʿilm ʿAmr—That the Knowledge of Zayd Is Other than the Knowledge of ʿAmr*

(iv) Responsa

GL 15. *Al-Ajwiba ʿan al-masā'il al-ʿišrīniyya—Answers to Twenty Questions* [*on Logic*]

(v) Pseudepigraphs, to be authenticated

GL-Ps 1. *Mafātīḥ al-ḫazā'in fī l-manṭiq—Keys to the Treasures in Logic*
GL-Ps 2. *Al-Bahja fī l-manṭiq / K. al-Muhja* (?)*—Splendor, on Logic / Book of the Lifeblood* (?)
GL-Ps 3. *Al-Qiyās—Syllogism*
GL-Ps 4. *Fī Ḍabṭ anwāʿ al-qaḍāyā—The Species of Propositions*
GL-Ps 5. *Talḫīṣ al-Manṭiq—Precise Exposition of Logic*
(a) *Al-Maʿānī fī l-manṭiq; al-Imlā' fī l-manṭiq—Subjects in Logic; Logic by Dictation*

II. Language

(i) Expository

GL 16. *Asbāb ḥudūṯ al-ḥurūf—On the Causes of the Articulation of the Letters*
GL 17. *K. Lisān al-ʿarab—The Language of the Arabs*
(a) *Qaḍā' Allāh taʿālā—The Decree of God*

(ii) Pseudepigraphs, to be authenticated

GL-Ps 6. *Muʿtaṣim aš-šuʿarā' fī l-ʿarūḍ—Poetic Guard (?), on Prosody*
GL-Ps 7. *K. al-Mulaḥ fī n-naḥw—Grammatical Witticisms*

C. PHYSICS (NATURAL SCIENCE) (GP)

I. Physics and On the Heavens

(i) Expository

GP1. *Kalām fī Ḥadd al-jism—On the Definition of Body*
GP2. *Fī anna Ab'ād al-ǧism ġayr ḏātiyya lahu—That the Dimensions of a Body Are not of Its Essence*
GP3. *Al-Ḥukūma fī ḥujaj al-muṯbitīn li-l-māḍī mabda'an zamāniy-yan—Judgment of the Arguments of Those Who Maintain that the Past Has a Temporal Beginning*
GP4. *R. fī l-Wus'a—On Space*
GP 5. *Jawhariyyat an-nār—That Fire Is a Substance*
GP 6. *Fī l-Ajrām al-'ulwiyya—On the Supernal Bodies*
GP 7. *R. fī 'Illat qiyām al-arḍ fī ḥayyizihā—On the Cause of the Earth's Remaining in Its Position*

(ii) Commentaries

GS 10a. *Tafsīr K. as-Samā' aṭ-ṭabī'ī—Commentary on [Aristotle's] Physics*
GS 10b. *Tafsīr as-Samā' wa-l-'ālam—Commentary on De caelo*

(iii) Responsa

GP 8. *Al-Ajwiba 'an masā'il Abī Rayḥān al-Bīrūnī—Answers to Questions Posed by Bīrūnī*
GP 9. *Al-Ajwiba 'an al-masā'il al-'ašr I—Answers to Ten Questions I*

(iv) Pseudepigraphs, to be authenticated

GP-Ps 1. *R. fī l-Ḥadaṯ—On Origination*
GP-Ps 2. *Mas'alatān—Two Questions*

II. Meteorology

(i) Pseudepigraph, to be authenticated

GP-Ps 3. *Al-Āṯār al-'ulwiyya—Meteorology*

III. On the Soul

(i) Expository

GP 10. *K. fī n-Nafs 'alā sunnat al-iḫtiṣār—Compendium on the Soul*
GP 11. *R. fī l-Kalām 'alā n-nafs an-nāṭiqa—On the Rational Soul*

GP 12. *Al-Jumal min al-adilla al-muḥaqqaqa li-baqāʾ an-nafs an-nāṭiqa—The Main Points of Verified Proofs on the Survival of the Rational Soul*

GP13. *Iḫtilāf an-nās fī amr an-nafs wa-amr al-ʿaql* (*R. ilā l-Kiyā*)—*Dispute on the Subject of Soul and Intellect* (*Letter to Kiyā*)

(ii) Commentary

GS 10c. *Šarḥ K. Arisṭūṭālīs fī n-Nafs—Commentary on Aristotle's De anima*

(iii) Pseudepigraphs, to be authenticated

GP-Ps 4. *Al-Qaṣīda al-ʿayniyya—Poem Rhyming in ʿayn*

GP-Ps 5. *R. fī Infisāḫ aṣ-ṣuwar al-mawjūda fī n-nafs—On the Disappearance of the Vain Intelligibles*

GP-Ps 6. *Taʿalluq an-nafs bi-l-badan—Association of the Soul with the Body*

GP-Ps 7. *Munāẓarāt jarat lahu fī n-nafs maʿa Abī ʿAlī an-Nīsābūrī—Disputations on the Soul with Abū-ʿAlī an-Nīsābūrī*

GP-Ps 8. *Fuṣūl fī n-nafs wa-ṭ-ṭabīʿiyyāt; R. fī n-Nafs—Sections on the Soul and Natural Science; On the Soul* (thrice)

IV. Astrology

GP 14. *Al-Išāra ilā ʿilm fasād aḥkām an-nujūm—The Pointer to Knowing the Fallacy of Astrology*

VI. Alchemy

(i) Pseudepigraph, to be authenticated

GP-Ps 9. *R. fī Amr mastūr, ilā s-Sahlī—On the Occult, to as-Sahlī*

D. MATHEMATICS (GMath)

I. Geometry—Geodesy

(i) Expository

GS 6b. *Muḫtaṣar Awqlīdis* (*Uṣūl al-handasa*)—*Compendium of Euclid* (*The Principles of Geometry*)

GMath 1. *R. fī z-Zāwiya—On the Angle*

GMath 2. *Muḫtaṣar fī anna z-zāwiya allatī min al-muḥīṭ wa-l-mumāss lā kammiyya lahā—Compendium on That the Angle which Is Formed by the Circumference and the Tangent Has no Magnitude*

(ii) Pseudepigraphs, to be authenticated

GMath-Ps 1. *Fī Ṭūl Jurjān—On the Longitude of Jurjān*
GMath-Ps 2. *M. fī l-Masālik wa-biqāʿ al-arḍ—On Roads and Provinces*

II. Astronomy

GS 6d. *Al-Arṣād al-kulliyya* (= *Muḫtaṣar al-Majisṭī*)*—Comprehensive Observations* (= *Compendium of the Almagest*)
GMath 3. *M. fī Kayfiyyat ar-raṣad wa-taṭābuqihi maʿa l-ʿilm aṭ-ṭabīʿī—On the Nature of* [*Astronomical*] *Observations and their Conformity with the Science of Physics*
GMath 4. *Al-Ālāt ar-raṣadiyya—Instruments of Astronomical Observation*
GMath 5. *M. fī Ḫawāṣṣ ḫaṭṭ al-istiwāʾ—On the Characteristics of the Equator*

III. Arithmetic

GS 6c. *M. fī l-Ariṯmāṭīqī—On Arithmetic*

IV. Music

(i) Expository

GS 6e. *R. fī l-Mūsīqā—Treatise on Music*

(ii) Pseudepigraph, to be authenticated

GMath-Ps 3. *Al-Madḫal ilā ṣināʿat al-mūsīqā—Introduction to the Science of Music*

E. METAPHYSICS OF THE RATIONAL SOUL (GM)

(i) Expository

GM 1. *K. al-Mabdaʾ wa-l-maʿād—The Provenance and Destination*
GM 2. *Al-Aḍḥawiyya fī l-maʿād—The Immolation Destination*
GM 3. *Al-Maʿād* [*al-aṣġar*] (*Ḥāl an-nafs al-insāniyya*)*—The* [*"Lesser"*] *Destination* (*State of the Human Soul*)
GM 4. *Fī l-Qaḍāʾ wa-l-qadar—On the* [*Divine*] *Decree and Predestination*
GM 5. *R. fī l-ʿIšq—On Love*
GM 6. *R. at-Tuḥfa—The Present*

(ii) Commentary

GS 10d. *Tafsīr Mā ba'd aṭ-ṭabī'a—Commentary on the Metaphysics*

(iii) Allegories

GM 7. *R. Ḥayy b. Yaqẓān—Ḥayy Ibn-Yaqẓān*
GM 8. *R. aṭ-Ṭayr—The Bird*

(iv) Versified

GM 9. *Al-Jumāna al-ilāhiyya fī t-tawḥīd—The Divine Pearl: On Professing the Unity of God*

(v) Pseudepigraps, to be authenticated

GM-Ps 1. *Ḥaqā'iq 'ilm at-tawḥīd* (*al-'Aršiyya?*)—*The Real Meaning of Theological Truths* (*Throne Philosophy?*)
GM-Ps 2. *R. fī Iṯbāt an-nubuwwa—Proof of Prophecy*
GM-Ps 3. *R. fī ṣ-Ṣalāt—On Prayer*
GM-Ps 4. *R. fī Sirr al-qadar—On the Secret of Predestination*
GM-Ps 5. *Fī Sabab ijābat ad-du'ā' wa-kayfiyyat az-ziyāra—On the Cause of the Efficacy of Prayer and Visitation* [*of Tombs*]
GM-Ps 6. *Al-Mu'āwada fī amr an-nafs wa-l-fayḍ—On the Return of the Soul*
GM-Ps 7. *Ḥuṣūl 'ilm wa-ḥikma—Acquiring Knowledge and Philosophy*
GM-Ps 8. *Salāmān wa-Absāl—Salāmān and Absāl*
GM-Ps 9. *Īḍāḥ barāhīn mustanbaṭa fī masā'il 'awīṣa*, incorporating *R. al-'Arūs—Explanation of Demonstrations Devised for Abstruse Problems*, incorporating *The Groom*
GM-Ps 10. *R. an-Nīranjāt—Magical Practices*
GM-Ps 11. *R. fī l-Arzāq—On Wealth*
GM-Ps 12. *R. fī l-Ḥaṯṯ 'alā l-ištiġāl bi-ḏ-ḏikr—Protreptic to Recitation of God's Name*
GM-Ps 13. *Fuṣūl ilāhiyya fī iṯbāt al-awwal—Selections Relating to the Godhead on the Proof of the First*

F. PRACTICAL PHILOSOPHY (GPP)

(i) Expository

GPP 1. *K. al-Birr wa-l-iṯm—Piety and Sin*
(a) *K. al-Birr wa-l-iṯm—Piety and Sin*

(b) *R. fī l-Aḫlāq* 1—*On Ethics* 1
(c) *Al-ʿAhd—The Pledge*
(d) *R. fī l-Aḫlāq* 2—*On Ethics* 2
(e) *Al-Afʿāl wa-l-infiʿālāt—Actions and Affections*

(ii) Pseudepigraphs, to be authenticated

GPP-Ps 1. *R. fī s-Siyāsa—On Governance*
GPP-Ps 2. *R. fī l-Ḥuzn wa-asbābihi—On Sorrow and Its Causes*

G. PERSONAL WRITINGS (GPW): Controversies, Letters, Homilies, Poetry

I. Controversies

GPW 1. *R. ilā ʿUlamāʾ Baġdād yasʾaluhum al-inṣāf baynahu wa-bayna rajul Hamaḏānī yaddaʿī l-ḥikma—Letter to the Scholars of Baġdād*
GPW 2. *R. ilā Ṣadīq yasʾaluhu l-inṣāf baynahu wa-bayna l-Hamaḏānī allaḏī yaddaʿī l-ḥikma—Letter to a Friend*
GPW 3. *R. fī Intifāʾ ʿammā nusiba ilayhi min muʿāraḍat al-Qurʾān—Repudiating Charges of Imitating the Qurʾān*
GPW 3.1. *Masāʾil jarat baynahu wa-bayna baʿḍ al-fuḍalāʾ—Issues between Avicenna and Some of his Contemporary Notables*

II. Correspondence

GPW 4.*Rasāʾil*—Letters
(a) *Ilā baʿḍ aḥibbāʾihi—Letter to a Friend*
(b) *Ilā Abī Jaʿfar al-Qāsānī—Letter to Abū-Jaʿfar al-Qāsānī*
(c) *Ilā Abī Ṭāhir b. Ḥassūl—Letter to Abū-Ṭāhir Ibn-Ḥassūl*
(d) *Ilā ʿAlāʾ ad-Dawla b. Kākūya—Letter to ʿAlāʾ-ad-Dawla*
(e) *Ilā š-šayḫ Abī l-Faḍl b. Maḥmūd—Letter to Abū-l-Faḍl Ibn-Maḥmūd*
(f) *Ilā š-šayḫ Abī l-Qāsim b. Abī l-Faḍl—Letter to Abū-l-Qāsim Ibn-Abī-l-Faḍl*
(g) *K. ilā Abī l-Faḍl Māfīd b. Īrāmard* (?) - *Letter to Abū-l-Faḍl Māfīd Ibn-Īrāmard* (?)
(h) *R. ilā Abī l-Qāsim al-Kirmānī—Letter to Abū-l-Qāsim al-Kirmānī*
(i) *R. ilā Abī Ṭāhir al-mutaṭabbib fī maʿnā s-sirāj—Letter to Abū-Ṭāhir the Physician on the Meaning of the Lamp* (?)
(j) *Correspondence with al-Wazīr al-ʿAlawī*

III. Homilies

GPW 5. *Tafsīr baʿḍ suwar kalām Allāh*—Exegesis of various Qurʾānic verses

(a) *Sūrat al-Iḫlāṣ—Sincere Religion* (Q 112)
(b) *Al-Muʿawwiḏatāni: Sūrat al-Falaq* and *Sūrat an-Nās—Daybreak* (Q 113) and *Men* (Q 114)
(c) *Sūrat al-Aʿlā—The Most High* (Q 87)
(d) *Tafsīr qawlihi taʿālā: Ṯumma stawā ilā s-samāʾi wa-hiya duḫān—Exegesis of the verse, "Then He lifted Himself to heaven when it was smoke"* (Q 41:11)
(e) *Tafsīr āyat an-nūr—Exegesis of the Light Verse* (Q 24:35)
(f) *Tafsīr sūrat al-Fātiḥa—Exegesis of the Opening Sūra* (Q 1)
(g) *Tafsīr āyat ar-Ribā—Exegesis of the Usury Verse* (Q 2:275)
(h) *R. fī Kayfiyyat Aṣḥāb al-kahf—On How [to understand] the "Seven Sleepers"* (Q 18:8–26)
(i) *R. fī Maʿnā ḥaqīqat Wa-ḍrib lahum maṯala l-ḥayāti d-dunyā ka-māʾin—The True Meaning of, "And strike for them the similitude of the present life: it is as water"* (Q 18:45)
(j) *R. fī Kayfiyyat inšiqāq al-qamar—On How [to understand] the "Splitting of the Moon"* (Q 54:1)
(k) *R. an-Nayrūziyya fī maʿānī al-ḥurūf al-hijāʾiyya—The Nayrūziyya: On the Signification of the Qurʾānic Letters*

GPW 6. Ḫuṭab wa-taḥmīdāt wa-asjāʿ—Homilies, Pieces in praise of God, Pieces in rhymed prose

(a) *Al-Ḫuṭba at-tawḥīdiyya—Homily on the Oneness of God*
(b) *Ḫuṭba—Homily*
(c) *Ḫuṭba fī l-ḫamr—Homily on Wine*
(d) *Fī d-Duʿāʾ—Prayer*
(e) *Kalām aš-Šayḫ fī l-mawāʿiẓ—Exhortations*
(f) *Fī l-Ḥadīṯ—On the Report*
(g) *R. fī l-Malāʾika—On Angels*
(h) *Al-Wird al-aʿẓam—The Supreme Recitation*
(i) Min Kalimāt aš-Šayḫ ar-Raʾīs—From Avicenna's sayings

IV. Poetry

GPW 7. Ašʿār wa-qaṣāʾid—Poetry

H. MEDICINE (GMed)

(i) Expository

GMed 1. *K. al-Qānūn fī ṭ-ṭibb—The Canon of Medicine*
(a) *Muʿālajāt (ṭibbiyya li-l-Qānūn)—(Medical) Treatments (in the Canon)*
(b) *K. al-Ḥawāšī ʿalā l-Qānūn—Glosses on the Canon*
(c) *Dustūr ṭibbī—Medical Code*
GMed 2. *M. al-Adwiya al-qalbiyya—Cardiac Remedies*
GMed 3. *K. al-Qawlanj—Colic*
GMed 4. *R. fī l-Hindibāʾ—On Endive*
GMed 5. *Resāle-ye Nabḍ—On the Pulse*
GMed 6. *R. fī s-Sikanjubīn—On Oxymel*
GMed 7. *M. fī Dafʿ al-maḍārr al-kulliyya ʿan al-abdān al-insāniyya bi-tadāruk anwāʿ ḫaṭaʾ at-tadbīr—Averting General Harm to Human Bodies*
GMed 8. *Masāʾil Ḥunayn—On Ḥunayn's* Questions
GMed 9. Fuṣūl ṭibbiyya mustafāda min majlis an-naẓar li-š-Šayḫ Abī ʿAlī b. Sīnā—Medical Notes from Avicenna's Sessions
GMed 10. *Ar-Radd ʿalā maqālat aš-Šayḫ Abī l-Faraj b. Abī Saʿīd al-Yamāmī—Refutation of Statements by al-Yamāmī*
GMed 11. *Fī Naqḍ Risālat Ibn aṭ-Ṭayyib fī l-quwā ṭ-ṭabīʿiyya—Refutation of Ibn-aṭ-Ṭayyib's Treatise on the Natural Faculties*
GMed 12. *Tadbīr manzil al-ʿaskar—Regimen of Military Camps*
GMed 13. *R. fī Tadbīr al-musāfirīn—Viaticum (Regimen for Travelers)*
GMed 14. *R. fī l-Bāh—On Coitus*
GMed 15. *R. fī l-Faṣd—On Phlebotomy*
GMed 16. *R. fī Ḥifẓ aṣ-ṣiḥḥa—On Hygiene*
GMed 17. *K. Siyāsat al-badan wa-faḍāʾil aš-šarāb wa-manāfiʿihi wa-maḍārrihi—Benefits and Harms of Wine for Physical Regime*
GMed 18. *R. fī l-Farq bayn al-ḥarāra al-ġarīziyya wa-l-ġarība—On the Difference between Vital and External Heat*
GMed 19. *Šaṭr al-ġibb—Intermittent Fever*
GMed 20. *R. fī l-Bawl—On Urine*
GMed 21. *Al-Aġḏiya wa-l-adwiya—Nourishment and Medication*
GMed 22. *Tadbīr sayalān al-manīy—Therapy of Gonorrhea*
GMed 23. *R. fī Ḏikr ʿadad al-amʿāʾ—On the Number of Intestines*
GMed 24. *R. fī ṭ-Ṭīb—On Perfume*

GMed 25. *Maqādīr aš-šurubāt min al-adwiya al-mufrada—Measures of Potions in Simple Medicaments*
GMed 26. Masāʾil ʿidda ṭibbiyya—Numerous medical questions

(ii) Versified

GMed 27. *Urjūza fī ṭ-Ṭibb—Medicine, in verse*
GMed 28. *Urjūza fī Ḥifẓ aṣ-ṣiḥḥa—Hygiene, in verse*
GMed 29. *Urjūzat Tadbīr al-fuḥūl fī l-fuṣūl—Seasonal Dietetics, in verse*
GMed 30a. *Urjūza fī t-Tašrīḥ—Anatomy, in verse*
GMed 30b. *Urjūza fī t-Tašrīḥ—Anatomy, in verse*
GMed 31. *Urjūza fī l-Bāh—On Coitus, in verse*
GMed 32. *Urjūza fī Waṣāyā Abuqrāṭ—Hippocratic Determinations ["Ivory Box"], in verse*
GMed 33. *Urjūza fī l-Mujarrabāt—Tested Prescriptions, in verse*
GMed 34. *Urjūza fī l-Waṣāyā—[Medical] Recommendations, in verse*

J. SPURIOUS or MISATTRIBUTED WORKS (listed alphabetically by title)

Asbāb ar-raʿd wa-l-barq, R. fī Ḏikr—On the Causes of Thunder and Lightning
R. fī Dafʿ al-ġamm min al-mawt—Dispelling Distress over Death
"Dānešnāme-ye ʿAlāʾī"—"Philosophy for ʿAlāʾ-ad-Dawla"
Fuṣūṣ al-ḥikam—Philosophical Bezels/Clauses
M. fī Ḫiṣb al-badan—On Physical Well-being
Liber celi et mundi—On the Heavens and the World
"R. al-Mabdaʾ wa-l-maʿād"—"Epistle on the Provenance and Destination"
R. fī Maʿrifat an-nafs an-nāṭiqa wa-aḥwālihā—On the Knowledge of the Rational Soul and Its States
Al-Muḫtaṣar fī ʿilm al-hayʾa—Compendium of Astronomy
R. fī n-Nafs—On the Soul
Naṣāʾiḥ al-ḥukamāʾ li-l-Iskandar—Philosophers' Advice to Alexander
An-Nukat wa-l-fawāʾid—Useful Tidbits
R. fī ṣ-Ṣanʿa ilā imām Abī ʿAbd Allāh al-Baraqī—On Alchemy, to Abū-ʿAbdallāh al-Baraqī
Taʿbīr ar-ruʾyā—Interpretation of Dreams
R. fī ṭ-Ṭibb—On Medicine
Fī z-Zuhd, R. ilā Abī Saʿīd b. Abī l-Ḫayr—On Asceticism, Letter to Ibn-Abī-l-Ḫayr

K. UNKNOWN WORKS

Al-Istibṣār
K. Zubdat al-quwā l-ḥayawāniyya
R. fī t-Tuffāḥ
K. Yūṣaf ẓafar al-Amīr ʿAḍud ad-Dawla

INDEX OF THE TITLES OF AVICENNA'S WORKS I: ARABIC & PERSIAN

To facilitate identification of individual works by Avicenna, most of which go under a variety of titles in Arabic and Persian, the index lists all known such, including the alternate titles given under each work in the Inventory, followed by their serial G-number there. The G-numbers of titles deemed authentic or most probably authentic and used throughout this study are printed in bold.

The order follows the Roman alphabet, but letters with diacritics are listed consecutively, as follows: D, Ḍ, D̠; H, Ḥ, H̱; S, Ṣ, Š; T, Ṭ, T̠; Z, Ẓ. The article, prepositions, conjunctions, and the words K(itāb), R(isāla), and M(aqāla), are disregarded in the alphabetization. Private letters by Avicenna are all entered under the rubric *Rasāʾil* and listed alphabetically by name of addressee; commentaries on the Qurʾān are listed in the order of the sūras under the rubric *Tafsīr baʿḍ suwar kalām Allāh.*

INDEX OF THE TITLES OF AVICENNA'S WORKS II: ENGLISH

Initial articles and prepositions in the titles are disregarded in the alphabetization.

Passages cited from these works in the body of the text are listed, under these titles, in the Index of Authors Cited, Names, and Places.

CORRESPONDENCE OF THE SERIAL NUMBERS OF THE WORKS IN MAHDAVĪ WITH THOSE IN ANAWATI AND GUTAS

The Mahdavī numbers missing in the following table after no. 131 are those of works manifestly spurious which have not been taken into consideration in the inventory in the Appendix (cf. p. 412 above). The correspondence of the Gutas numbers with those in Mahdavī and Anawatī can be seen in the inventory right after the title of each work.

Mahdavī	Anawati	Gutas (G+)	Mahdavī	Anawati	Gutas (G+)
1	164	Math 4	22	25, 33	L 4
2	52	P 14	23	248	M-Ps 11
3	245	M-Ps 2	24	51	P-Ps 3
4a	35	L-Ps 3	25	47	L 16
4b	83	P-Ps 6	26	55	Spur
4d	213	M-Ps 5	27	3, 239	S 9
4h	88	S 14a	28	37	L 5
4ḥ	181	M-Ps 4	29	50	PW 7
4j	106, 204, 269	M-Ps 6	30	200	M 2
4ṭ	192	L 17a	31	121	Med 21
4w	260, 266, 268	M-Ps 7	32	4	S 1
4y	S 14b		33	154	P-Ps 9
4z	225, 256	Spur	34	204, 257	PW 3
5	54	P 8	35	6	S 11
6	2, 38_2	P 9	36	81	P-Ps 5
7	38_1	S 14c	37	34	L-Ps 4
8	39	L 15	38	79	M-Ps 9
9	21	S-Ps 2b	39	143	Med 14
10	22	S-Ps 2a	40	249	PP 1a
11	63	P 5	41	42	L-Ps 2
12	78, 108, 259	P 13	42	42	L 10
13	246	PP 1b	43	84	M 6
14	111	Med 2	44	124	Med 22
15	114	Med 27	45	251	Med 13
16	117, 153	Med 28	46	252	Med 12
17	115,118	Med 29	47	101, 156	Spur
18	112	Med 30a	48	26	L 13
19	120	Med 32	49	8, 89, 271	S 12a
20	113	Med 33	50	PW 5	
21	119	Med 34	50a	208	PW 5a

Mahdavī	Anawati	Gutas (G+)	Mahdavī	Anawati	Gutas (G+)
50b	210, 211	PW 5b	84	14	S 5
50c	209	PW 5c	85	227	M-Ps 3
50d	208	PW 5d	86	158	Spur
50e		PW 5e	87	135	Med 24
51	178	M 9	88	229	M 8
52	80	P 12	89	184	M-Ps 9
53	53	P 6	90	230	M 5
54	216, 221	M-Ps 12	91	168	P 7
55	61	P-Ps 1	92	82, 232	PP 1c
56	56, 60, 64, 72	P 2	93	15	S 3
56b		P 1	94	66	Med 18
57	9, 90	L 6	95	136	Med 15
58	214	PW 6f	96	137, 138	Med 9
59	217	PP-Ps 2	97	190	PP 1e
60	126	Med 16	98	140	Med 1
61	179, 183	M-Ps 1	99	93	P-Ps 4
62	10, 28, 29, 32, 65, 247	S 2	100	193	M 4
			101	142	Med 3
63	12	S8	102	240, 243	PW 6e
64	75	P 3	103	5	PW 6i
65	219, 227	M 7	104		L 17
66	127	Spur	105	19, 257	S14
67	68	L 8	106	195	M 1
68	59	L 9	106, p. 216	196	Spur
69	220	PW 6b	107	20	S-Ps 3
70	177, 194	PW 6a	108	45	L 1
71	129	PW 6c	109	71	P-Ps 2
72	11, 13	S 7	110	144	Med 8
73	128	Med 1c	111		L-Ps 1
74	222	PW 6d	112	147	Med 25
75	130	Med 7	113	203	PW 6g
76	141	Med 11	114	44	L 3
77	145	Med 10	115	43	S 3a
78		PW 1	116	31, 44	L 2
79a	261	PW 4a	117	149	Med 5
79b	267, 270	PW 4b	118	23	S 6
79c	262, 270	PW 4c	119	255	Spur
79d	265	PW 4d	120	102	P 10
79e	364	PW 4e	121	74, 77, 109, 199, 201	M 3
79f	263	PW 4f			
80	160	Math 1	122	p. 165	P 11
81	253	Med 6	123	107	Spur
82	253	PP-Ps 1	124	96	Spur
83	133	Med 17	125	46	L 11

Mahdavī	Anawati	Gutas (G+)	Mahdavī	Anawati	Gutas (G+)
126	69, 76	M-Ps 10	186	90 [?], 186	L 6a
127	49	PW 5k	189	16	S-Ps 1
128	244	PW 6h	192	95, 233	Spur
129	68	P 4	193	8, 89, 271	S 12a (4b)
130	24	S 4	194		S 14e
131	150, 272	Med 4	196		S 12a (4b)
133		S 14e	197	166	Spur
134		S 14e	200		S 14e
137	10, 28, 29, 32,	S 2	202		S 14e
	65, 247		204	235	M-Ps 8
138	140	Med 1	206	95, 233	Spur
140	122	Med 20	207	74, 77, 109, 199,	M 3
142	171	S 6d		201	
149	82, 232	PP 1c	210	69, 76	M-Ps 10
152	27	L-Ps 5	211		S 12a (4b)
160	12	S 8	220	166	Spur
163	8, 89, 271	S 12a (4b)	224		S 14e
164	11, 13	Spur	225	146	Med 26
168	224	Spur	232	165	Math-Ps 3
179	134	Med 19	238	103	Spur
182	219, 227	M 7	242	173	Math 3

BIBLIOGRAPHY

The Bibliography includes all the works referred to in this study by author and short title if more than two publications by the same author have been consulted, and by author alone if not. The short titles used for this purpose are added in brackets after the citation. Incidental single references to works not directly relevant to the study of Avicenna have been provided with full bibliographical details in the appropriate notes and have not been repeated here.

All primary sources, including all the works of Avicenna, are listed not under the name of the authors but of their editors, to whom consistent reference has been made in all citations. Only references to web sites are under the name of the ancient or medieval author. In the very few cases where no name of editor is provided for the publication, it is listed alphabetically by title. In the case of Avicenna, the publication record of each of his works can be readily consulted in the Inventory in the Appendix. For conventions of reference to individual works see the section on the Layout of this study at the beginning of the book.

In the alphabetization, articles and prepositions of any language have not been taken into account. German umlaut (ä, ö, ü) is entered as ae, oe, ue, and the diacritics as well as the signs for *hamza* and *ʿayn* in the transliteration of Arabic and Persian have been disregarded.

ʿAbbās, Iḥsān, ed., *At-Taqrīb li-ḥadd al-manṭiq wa-l-madḫal ilayhi bi-l-alfāẓ al-ʿāmmiyya wa-l-amṯila al-fiqhiyya, taʾlīf Ibn Ḥazm al-Andalusī*, Beirut: Dār maktabat al-ḥayāt, n.y. [1959].

ʿAbduh, Muḥammad, ed., *Kitāb al-Hidāya ... li-š-Šayḫ ar-Raʾīs*, Cairo: Maktabat al-Qāhira al-ḥadīṯa, 1974.

ʿAbdul Ḥaq, Muḥammad, "Ibn Sīnā's Interpretation of the Qurān," *The Islamic Quarterly* 32 (1988) 46–56.

Abū-Rīda, Muḥammad ʿAbdalhādī, ed., *Rasāʾil al-Kindī al-falsafiyya*, 2 vols., Cairo: Maṭbaʿat al-iʿtimād, 1369/1950.

Achena, Mohammad and Henri Massé, *Le Livre de science*, Paris: Les Belles Lettres, [1]1955–1958; Paris: Les Belles Lettres / UNESCO, [2]1986 [references are to the second edition].

Adamson, Peter, "Non-Discursive Thought in Avicenna's Commentary on the *Theology of Aristotle*," in McGinnis with Reisman (2004) 87–111. ["Non-Discursive Thought"]

———, ed., *Interpreting Avicenna*, Cambridge: Cambridge University Press, 2013. [*Interpreting Avicenna*]

Adamson, Peter, and Peter E. Pormann, *The Philosophical Works of al-Kindī*, Karachi: Oxford University Press, 2012.

ʿAfīfī, Abū-l-ʿAlā, ed., *Ibn Sīnā. Aš-Šifāʾ, al-Manṭiq, al-Burhān*, Cairo: al-Maṭbaʿa al-amīriyya, 1375/1956.

Afifi al-Akiti, Muhammad, "The Three Properties of Prophethood in Certain Works of Avicenna and al-Ġazālī," in McGinnis with Reisman (2004) 189–212.

Afnan, Soheil M., *Avicenna. His Life and Works*, London: George Allen & Unwin, 1958.

Ahmed, Asad Q., *Avicenna's Deliverance: Logic*, Karachi: Oxford University Press, 2011.

al-Ahwānī, Aḥmad Fuʾād (El Ahwany), "La théorie de la connaissance et la psychologie d'Avicenne," *La Revue du Caire*, Vol. 27, No. 141 (June 1951) 23–43. ["Théorie de la connaissance"]

———, ed., *Aḥwāl an-nafs*, Cairo: Dār iḥyāʾ al-kutub al-ʿarabiyya, 1371/1952. [*Aḥwāl*]

———, ed., *Nukat fī aḥwāl aš-Šayḫ ar-Raʾīs Ibn Sīnā* [*Ḏikrā Ibn Sīnā III*], Cairo: Institut Français d'Archéologie Orientale, 1952. [*Nukat*]

———, ed., *Ibn Sīnā. Aš-Šifāʾ, al-Manṭiq, as-Safsaṭa*, Cairo: al-Maṭbaʿa al-amīriyya, 1958. [*Safsaṭa*]

———, ed., *Ibn Sīnā. Aš-Šifāʾ, al-Manṭiq, al-Jadal*, Cairo: al-Hayʾa al-ʿāmma li-šuʾūn al-maṭābiʿ al-amīriyya, 1385/1965. [*Jadal*]

Akasoy, Anna Ayşe, *Philosophie und Mystik in der späten Almohadenzeit. Die* Sizilianischen Fragen *des Ibn Sabʿīn*, Leiden: Brill, 2006.

Akhtar, Kazi Ahmad Mian, "A Tract of Avicenna (Translated by Umar Khayyam)," *Islamic Culture* 9 (1935) 218–233.

Alpago, Andrea, *Avicennae philosophi praeclarissimi ac medicorum principis Compendium de Anima, De Mahad*, etc., Venice: Junta, 1546; repr. Farnborough: Gregg International Publishers Limited, 1969.

d'Alverny, Marie-Thérèse, "Notes sur les traductions médiévales d'Avicenne," *Archives d'Histoire Doctrinale et Littéraire du Moyen Âge* 27 (1952). ["Notes"]

———, "Avendauth?," *Homenaje a Millás-Vallicrosa*, Vol. I, Barcelona: Consejo Superior de Investigaciones Científicas, 1954, 19–43. ["Avendauth?"]

———, "Avicenna Latinus [I–XI]," *Archives d'Histoire Doctrinale et Littéraire du Moyen Âge*, 1961–1972; repr. in d'Alverny *Codices*. ["Avicenna Latinus"]

———, *Avicenna Latinus. Codices*, descripsit Marie-Thérèse d'Alverny. Addenda collegerunt Simone Van Riet et Pierre Jordogne, Louvain-la-Neuve: E. Peeters and Leiden: E.J. Brill, 1994. [*Codices*]

Amīn, Aḥmad, ed., *Ḥayy b. Yaqẓān li-Ibn Sīnā wa-Ibn Ṭufayl wa-s-Suhrawardī*, Cairo: Muʾassasat al-Ḫānǧī, 1958.

Amīn, Aḥmad and Aḥmad az-Zayn, eds., *At-Tawḥīdī, al-Imtāʿ wa-l-muʾānasa*, Cairo: Lajnat at-taʾlīf wa-t-tarjama wa-n-našr, 1939–1944.

Anawati, Georges C., *Muʾallafāt Ibn Sīnā*, Cairo: Dār al-maʿārif, 1950. [*Muʾallafāt*]

———, "La tradition manuscrite orientale de l'œuvre d'Avicenne," *Revue Thomiste* 51 (1951) 407–440; repr. in his *Études* (1974) 229–262. ["Tradition manuscrite"]

———, "Le Manuscrit Nour Osmaniyye 4894," *MIDEO* 3 (1956) 381–386. ["Nour Osmaniyye"]

———, "La *Ḥikma ʿarūḍiyya* d'Ibn Sīnā," in *Proceedings of the Twenty-second Congress of Orientalists*, Zeki Velidi Togan, ed., Leiden: E.J. Brill, 1957, II,171–176. ["*Ḥikma ʿarūḍiyya*"]

———, "Études Avicenniennes," *Revue Thomiste* 61 (1961) 109–135. ["Études"]
———, "Avicenne et l'alchimie," in *Convegno Internazionale 9–15 Aprile 1969. Oriente e Occidente nel Medioevo: Filosofia e Scienze*, Rome: Accademia Nazionale dei Lincei, 1971. ["Alchimie"]
———, *Études de philosophie musulmane* [Études Musulmanes XV], Paris: Vrin, 1974. [*Études*]
———, "Les Divisions des sciences intellectuelles d'Avicenne (traduction)," *MIDEO* 13 (1977) 323–335. ["Divisions"]
Anawati, Georges C., Maḥmūd al-Ḫuḍayrī, Fu'ād al-Ahwānī, eds., *Ibn Sīnā. Aš-Šifā', al-Manṭiq, al-Madḫal*, Cairo: al-Maṭba'a al-amīriyya, 1371/1952. [*Madḫal*]
Anawati, Georges C., Maḥmūd al-Ḫudayrī, Aḥmad Fu'ād al-Ahwānī, Sa'īd Zāyid, eds., *Ibn Sīnā. Aš-Šifā', al-Manṭiq, al-Maqūlāt*, Cairo: al-Hay'a al-'āmma li-šu'ūn al-maṭābi' al-amīriyya, 1378/1959. [*Maqūlāt*]
Anawati, Georges C. and Sa'īd Zāyid, eds., *Ibn Sīnā. Aš-Šifā', al-Ilāhiyyāt (1)*, Cairo: al-Hay'a al-'āmma li-šu'ūn al-maṭābi' al-amīriyya, 1380/1960. [*Ilāhiyyāt*]
———, eds., *Ibn Sīnā. Aš-Šifā', aṭ-Ṭabī'iyyāt, an-Nafs*, Cairo: al-Hay'a al-miṣriyya al-'āmma li-l-kitāb, 1395/1975. [*Nafs*]
Anwar, Etin, "Ibn Sīnā's Philosophical Theology of Love: a Study of the *Risālah fī al-'Ishq*," *Islamic Studies* 42 (2003) 331–345.
Arberry, Arthur J., *The Spiritual Physick of Rhazes*, London: John Murray, 1950. [*Physick*]
———, *Avicenna on Theology*, London: John Murray, 1951. [*Theology*]
———, "Avicenna: His Life and Times," in Wickens *Avicenna* (1952) 9–28. ["Avicenna"]
Ardeshir, Mohammad, "Ibn Sīnā's Philosophy of Mathematics," in Shahid Rahman et al. (2008) 43–61.
Aristotle, Arabic Organon MS Paris. Arab. 2346, http://gallica.bnf.fr/Search?ArianeWireIndex=index&p=1&lang=FR&q=arabe+2346
Arnzen, Rüdiger, *Aristoteles'* De anima. *Eine verlorene spätantike Paraphrase in arabischer und persischer Überlieferung* [Aristoteles Semitico-Latinus 9], Leiden: Brill, 1998. [*Paraphrase*]
———, *Platonische Ideen in der arabischen Philosophie* [Scientia Graeco-Arabica 6], Berlin: De Gruyter, 2011. [*Platonische Ideen*]
'Āṣī, Ḥasan, ed., *at-Tafsīr al-Qur'ānī wa-l-luġa aṣ-ṣūfiyya fī falsafat Ibn Sīnā*, Beirut: al-Mu'assasa al-jāmi'iyya, 1402/1983. [*Tafsīr*]
———, ed., *al-Aḍḥawiyya fī l-ma'ād li-Ibn Sīnā*, Beirut: al-Mu'assasa al-jāmi'iyya, [2]1407/1987. [*Aḍḥawiyya*]
Ateş, Ahmed, "İbn Sīnā. Risālat al-iksīr," *Türkiyat Mecmuası* 10 (1951/1953) 27–54.
al-Bābā, Muḥammad Zuhayr, *Min mu'allafāt Ibn Sīnā aṭ-ṭibbiyya*, Aleppo: Ma'had at-turāṯ al-'ilmī al-'arabī, 1404/1984.
Badawī, 'Abdurraḥmān, ed., *Arisṭū 'inda l-'Arab*, Cairo: Maktabat an-nahḍa al-miṣriyya, 1947. [*Arisṭū*]
———, ed., *Manṭiq Arisṭū*, 3 vols., Cairo: Maṭba'at Dār al-kutub al-miṣriyya 1948–1952. [*Manṭiq*]
———, ed., *Avicennae Fontes Sapientiae* [Mémorial Avicenne—V], Cairo: Institut Français D'Archéologie Orientale, 1954. [*'Uyūn*]

——, ed., *Al-Mubaššir ibn-Fātik, Muḫtār al-ḥikam wa-maḥāsin al-kalim*, Madrid: Instituto Egipcio de Estudios Islámicos, 1958. [*Muḫtār*]

——, *At-Turāṯ al-yūnānī fī l-ḥaḍāra al-islāmiyya*, Cairo: Dār an-nahḍa al-ʿarabiyya, ³1965. [*Turāṯ*]

——, ed., *Ibn Sīnā. Aš-Šifāʾ, al-Manṭiq, aš-Šiʿr*, Cairo: ad-Dār al-miṣriyya li-t-taʾlīf wa-t-tarjama, 1386/1966. [*Šiʿr*]

——, *Histoire de la Philosophie en Islam*, Paris: Vrin, 1972. [*Histoire*]

——, ed., *Ibn Sīnā, at-Taʿlīqāt*, Cairo: al-Hayʾa al-miṣriyya al-ʿāmma li-l-kitāb, 1973. [*Taʿlīqāt*]

——, ed., *Ṣiwān al-ḥikma wa-ṯalāṯ rasāʾil, taʾlīf Abū* [*sic*] *Sulaymān al-Manṭiqī as-Sijistānī*, Tehran: Entešārāt-e Farhang-e Īrān, 1974. [*Ṣiwān*]

——, ed., *Ḥunayn ibn Isḥāq, Ādāb al-falāsifa*, Kuwayt: Maʿhad al-maḫṭūṭāt al-ʿarabiyya, 1406/1985. [*Ādāb*]

Bäck, Allan, "Avicenna the Commentator," in *Medieval Commentaries on Aristotle's* Categories, Lloyd A. Newton, ed., Leiden: Brill, 2008, 31–71.

——, *Avicenna's Commentary on Aristotle's De Interpretatione*, Munich: Philosophia Verlag, 2013.

Baffioni, Carmela, *La tradizione araba del IV Libro dei 'Meteorologica' di Aristotele*, Istituto Orientale di Napoli, *Annali* 40 (1980), fasc. 2, suppl. no. 23.

Barnes, Jonathan, *Aristotle. Posterior Analytics*, Oxford: Clarendon Press, ²1994.

Bell, Joseph Norment, "Avicenna's *Treatise on Love* and the Nonphilosophical Muslim Tradition," *Der Islam* 63 (1986) 73–89.

van den Bergh, Simon, *Averroes' Tahafut al-Tahafut*, Oxford: Oxford University Press, 1954.

Berjak, Rafiq and Muzaffar Iqbal, "Ibn Sīnā—al-Bīrūnī Correspondence," *Islam & Science* 1 (2003) 91–98, 253–260; 2 (2004) 57–62, 181–187; 3 (2005) 57–62, 166–170.

Bertolacci, Amos, "From al-Kindī to al-Fārābī: Avicenna's Progressive Knowledge of Aristotle's *Metaphysics* according to his Autobiography," *ASP* 11 (2001) 257–295 ["Autobiography"]; revised version in Bertolacci *Reception*, Chapter Two, 37–64.

——, "Ammonius and al-Fārābī: The Sources of Avicenna's Concept of Metaphysics," *Quaestio* 5 (2005) 287–305 ["Ammonius"]; revised and enlarged version in Bertolacci *Reception*, Chapter Three, 65–103.

——, *The Reception of Aristotle's* Metaphysics *in Avicenna's* Kitāb al-Šifāʾ, Leiden: Brill, 2006. [*Reception*]

——, "Avicenna and Averroes on the Proof of God's Existence and the Subject-Matter of Metaphysics," *Medioevo* 32 (2007) 61–97. ["Proof"]

——, *Libro della Guarigione. Le cose divine di Avicenna*, Torino: Unione Tipografico-Editrice Torinese, 2007. [*Guarigione*]

——, "The Distinction of Essence and Existence in Avicenna's Metaphysics: The Text and Its Context," in Opwis and Reisman (2012), 257–288. ["Distinction"]

Bīdārfar, Moḥsen, ed., *Al-Mubāḥaṯāt. Abū ʿAlī Ḥusayn b. ʿAbdallāh Ibn Sīnā*, Qum: Entešārāt-e Bīdār, 1371Š/1992.

Biesterfeldt, Hans Hinrich, *Galens Traktat 'Dass die Kräfte der Seele den Mischungen des Körpers folgen' in arabischer Übersetzung* [Abhandlungen für die Kunde des Morgenlandes XL, 4], Wiesbaden: Franz Steiner, 1973.

Bilge, Kilisli R., and İbnülemin M.K. İnal, eds., *Bağdatlı Ismail Paşa, Hadiyyat al-ʿārifīn*, 2 vols., Istanbul: Milli Eğitim Basımevi, 1951.

Birkenmajer, Aleksander, "Avicennas Vorrede zum 'Liber Sufficientiae' und Roger Bacon," *Revue Néo-scolastique de Philosophie* 36 (1934) 308–320; repr. in his *Études d'histoire des sciences et de la philosophie du Moyen Âge* [Studia Copernicana I], Wroclaw: Zakład Narodowy im. Ossolińskich, 1970, 89–101.

Blachère, Régis, *Kitāb Ṭabaḳāt al-umam (Livre des catégories des nations) [par] Ṣāʿid al-Andalusī*, Paris: Larose, 1935; repr. Frankfurt: Institute for the History of Arabic-Islamic Science, 1999.

Black, Deborah L., "Avicenna and the Ontological and Epistemic Status of Fictional Beings," *Documenti e Studi sulla Tradizione Filosofica Medievale*, 8 (1997) 425–453. ["Fictional Beings"]

———, "Avicenna on Self-Awareness and Knowing that One Knows," in Shahid Rahman et al. (2008) 63–87. ["Self-Awareness"]

Booth, Edward, *Aristotelian Aporetic Ontology in Islamic and Christian Thinkers*, Cambridge: Cambridge University Press, 1983.

Bosworth, Clifford E., "On the Chronology of the Ziyārids in Gurgān and Ṭabaristān," *Der Islam* 40 (1964) 25–34. ["Ziyārids"]

———, "Dailamīs in Central Iran: the Kākūyids of Jibāl and Yazd," *Iran* 8 (1970) 73–95 ["Kākūyids"]

Bouyges, Maurice, ed., *Averroès. Tafsir ma baʿd at-tabiʿat* [Bibliotheca Arabica Scholasticorum V–VII], Beirut: Dar el-Machreq, 4 vols., 1938–1952.

Brentjes, Burchard, and Sonja Brentjes, *Ibn Sina (Avicenna), der fürstliche Meister aus Buchara*, Leipzig: Teubner, 1979.

Brown, H.V.B., "Avicenna and the Christian Philosophers in Baghdad," in *Islamic Philosophy and the Classical Tradition. Essays Presented … to Richard Walzer*, S.M. Stern, A. Hourani, and V. Brown, eds., Oxford / Columbia, S.C.: Bruno Cassirer / University of S.C. Press, 1972 / 1973, 35–48.

Brunschvig, Robert, "Logic and Law in Classical Islam," in *Logic in Classical Islamic Culture* [First Giorgio Levi Della Vida Conference], G.E. von Grunebaum, ed., Wiesbaden: Harrassowitz, 1970, 9–20; French version repr. in his *Études d'Islamologie*, Abdel Magid Turki, ed., Paris: Maisonneuve et Larose, 1976, II,347–361.

Cheikho, Louis, ed., *Kitāb Ṭabaqāt al-umam li-Abī l-Qāsim Ṣāʿid ibn Aḥmad ibn Ṣāʿid al-Andalusī*, Beirut: al-Maṭbaʿa al-Kāṯūlīkiyya, 1912; repr. Frankfurt: Institute for the History of Arabic-Islamic Science, 1999.

Cheikho, Louis, L. Malouf, and C. Edde, eds., *Traités inédits d'anciens philosophes arabes*, Beirut: Imprimerie Catholique, 1911.

Corbin, Henry, ed., *Şihābaddīn Yaḥyā as-Suhrawardī. Opera Metaphysica et Mystica I* [Bibliotheca Islamica 16a], Leipzig/Istanbul: Brockhaus/Maarif Matbaası, 1945. [*Opera I*]

———, ed., *Œuvres philosophiques et mystiques de … Sohrawardi. (Opera Metaphysica et Mystica II)*, Tehran/Paris: Institut Franco-Iranien/Adrien-Maisonneuve, 1952. [*Opera II*]

———, *Avicenna and the Visionary Recital*, translated by Willard R. Trask, London: Routledge & Kegan Paul, 1960 [1961]. [*Recital*]

———, *Avicenne et le récit visionnaire*, Paris: Berg International, ²1979. [*Récit*]

Crawford, F. Stuart, ed., *Averrois Cordubensis Commentarium Magnum in Aristotelis De Anima libros*, Cambridge, Mass.: The Mediaeval Academy of America, 1953.

Cruz Hernández, Miguel, *La vida de Avicena como introducción a su pensamiento*, Salamanca: Anthema Ediciones, 1997.

Cureton, William, ed., *Aš-Šahrastānī, Kitāb al-Milal wa-n-niḥal*, London: The Society for the Publication of Oriental Texts, 1842–1846.

al-Daffa, Ali A. and John J. Stroyls, "Ibn Sīnā as a Mathematician," in their *Studies in the Exact Sciences in Medieval Islam*, Dhahran, Saudi Arabia: University of Petroleum and Minerals, and Chichester etc.: John Wiley & Sons, 1984, 60–118.

Dahiyat, Ismail M., *Avicenna's Commentary on the Poetics of Aristotle*, Leiden: Brill, 1974.

Daiber, Hans, *Naturwissenschaft bei den Arabern im 10. Jahrhundert n. Chr: Briefe des Abū l-Faḍl ibn al-ʿAmīd (gest. 360/970) an ʿAḍudaddaula*, Leiden: Brill, 1993. [*Naturwissenschaft*]

——, "Limitations of Knowledge according to Ibn Sīnā: Epistemological and Theological Aspects and the Consequences," in *Erkenntnis und Wissenschaft: Probleme der Epistemologie in der Philosophie des Mittelalters*, M. Lutz-Bachmann, A. Fidora, und P. Antolic, eds., Berlin: Akademie-Verlag, 2004, 25–34. ["Limitations"]

——, "Science Connecting Scholars and Cultures in Khwārazm," in *Knowledge, Language, Thought and the Civilization of Islam. Essays in Honor of Syed Muhammad Naquib al-Attas*, Wan Mohd Nor Wan Daud, Muhammad Zainiy Uthman, eds., Kuala Lumpur 2010, 283–294. ["Khwārazm"]

——, *Microfilms and Offprints from Arabic Manuscripts in Manuscript Libraries, including Some Persian and Syriac Texts and Two Latin Manuscripts*, unpublished typescript (PDF) privately given to me by the author. [*Collection IV*]

Dānešpažūh, Moḥammad Taqī, ed., *an-Najāt*, Tehran: Entešārāt-e Dānešgāh, 1364Š/ [1985].

Davidson, Herbert A., *Alfarabi, Avicenna, and Averroes, on Intellect*, Oxford / New York: Oxford University Press, 1992.

De Smet, Daniel, "Avicenne et l'Ismaélisme post-fatimide, selon la *Risāla al-mufīda fī īḍāḥ mulġaz al-qaṣīda* de ʿAlī b. Muḥammad b. al-Walīd," in Janssens and De Smet (2002) 1–20.

Dhanani, Alnoor, "Rocks in the Heavens?! The Encounter between ʿAbd al-Ǧabbār and Ibn Sīnā," in Reisman with Al-Rahim (2003), 127–144.

Dieterici, Friedrich, *Alfārābī's philosophische Abhandlungen*, Leiden: Brill, 1890. [*Abhandlungen* (text)].

——, *Alfārābī's philosophische Abhandlungen*, Leiden: Brill, 1892. [*Abhandlungen* (translation)]

Djebbar, Ahmed, "Les mathématiques dans l'oeuvre d'Ibn Sīnā (370/980–428/ 1037)," in *Journées d'études. Avicenne. Marrakech 25–26 Septembre 1998*, Marrakech: Publication du Groupe d'Étude Ibn Sīnā, 1999, 51–70.

Dodge, Bayard, *The Fihrist of al-Nadim*, New York: Columbia University Press, 1970.

Düring, Ingemar, *Aristotle in the Ancient Biographical Tradition* [Studia Graeca et Latina Gothoburgensia V], Göteborg: Institute of Classical Studies, 1957.

Dunlop, Douglas M., "Al-Fārābī's Introductory *Risālah* on Logic," *Islamic Quarterly* 3 (1956–1957) 224–235. ["Introductory *Risālah*"]

——, ed., *The Muntakhab Ṣiwān al-ḥikma of Abū Sulaimān as-Sijistānī*, The Hague: Mouton Publishers, 1979. [*Ṣiwān*]

Dunyā, Sulaymān, ed., *Manṭiq Tahāfut al-falāsifa al-musammā Miʿyār al-ʿilm li-l-Imām al-Ġazālī*, Cairo: Dār al-maʿārif, 1961. [*Miʿyār*]

——, ed., *Al-Išārāt wa-t-tanbīhāt li-Abī ʿAlī ibn Sīnā, maʿa Šarḥ Naṣīr ad-Dīn aṭ-Ṭūsī*, 4 vols., Cairo: Dār al-maʿārif, 1971ff. [*Šarḥ*]

Durusoy, Ali, "İbn Sīnā'nın *el-Mûcezil' sağīr fi'l-mantık* Adlı Risâlesi," *Marmara Üniversitesi İlahiyat Fakültesi Dergisi*, 13/5 (1995) 143–166.

van Dyck, Edward Abbot, *Hadiyyat ar-Raʾīs ... wa-hiya Mabḥaṯ ʿan al-quwā n-nafsāniyya aw Kitāb fī n-nafs ʿalā sunnat al-iḫtiṣār*, Cairo: Maṭbaʿat al-maʿārif, 1325. [*Hadiyya*]

——, *Avicena's Offering to the Prince. A Compendium on the Soul*, Verona: Stamperia di Nicola Paderno, 1906. [*Offering*]

Eichner, Heidrun, "Dissolving the Unity of Metaphysics: From Fakhr al-Dīn al-Rāzī to Mullā Ṣadrā al-Shīrāzī," *Medioevo* 32 (2007) 139–197. ["Dissolving"]

——, "Ibn Sīnā's *Epistle on Prayer* (*Risala fi al-salat*)," in *Uluslararası İbn Sînâ Sempozyumu* (2008) II,171–182. ["*Prayer*"]

——, *The Post-Avicennian Philosophical Tradition and Islamic Orthodoxy: Philosophical and Theological Summae in Context*, unpublished professorial dissertation (Habilitationsschrift), Halle 2009. [*Summae*]

——, "Al-Fārābī and Ibn Sīnā on 'Universal Science' and the System of Sciences: Evidence of the Arabic Tradition of the *Posterior Analytics*," *Documenti e Studi* 21 (2010) 71–95. ["Universal Science"]

——, "Essence and Existence. Thirteeth-Century Perspectives in Arabic-Islamic Philosophy and Theology," in Hasse and Bertolacci *Reception* (2012), 123–151. ["Essence"]

——, "The *Categories* in Avicenna: Material for Developing a Developmental Account?," in *Aristotle's* Categories *in the Byzantine, Arabic and Latin Traditions*, Sten Ebbesen, John Marenbon, and Paul Thom, eds., Copenhagen: The Royal Danish Academy of Sciences and Letters, 2013, 59–86. ["Categories"]

Endress, Gerhard, "Alexander Arabus on the First Cause. Aristotle's First Mover in an Arabic Treatise Attributed to Alexander of Aphrodisias," in *Aristotele e Alessandro di Afrodisia nella tradizione araba* (Subsidia Mediaevalia Patavina 3), C. D'Ancona and G. Serra, eds., Padova: Il Poligrafo, 2002, 19–74.

Ergin, Osman, "İbni Sina Bibliyografyası," in *Büyük Türk Filozof ve Tıb Üstadı İbni Sina. Şasiyeti* [*sic*] *ve eserleri hakkında tetkikler* [Türk Tarih Kurumu Yayınları, VII. 1], Istanbul: Muallim Ahmet Halit Kitap Evi, 1937, last fascicle in the volume.

——, *İbni Sina Bibliografyası* [İstanbul Üniversitesi Tıp Tarihi Enstitüsü, N. 51], Istanbul: Osman Yalçın Matbaası, ^{2}1956. References are to this second edition.

d'Erlanger, Baron Rodolphe, *La musique arabe*, Paris: P. Geuthner, 1930–1959.

van Ess, Josef, *Die Erkenntnislehre des ʿAḍudaddīn al-Īcī*, Wiesbaden: Steiner, 1966.

Fackenheim, Emil L., "A Treatise on Love by Ibn Sina," *Mediaeval Studies* 7 (1945) 208–228.

Fakhry, Majid, *A History of Islamic Philosophy*, New York: Columbia University Press, ^{1}1970, ^{2}1983, ^{3}2004. References are to the third edition unless otherwise indicated.

Finianos, Ghassan, *Les grandes divisions de l'être "mawjūd" selon Ibn Sīnā*, Fribourg: Éditions Universitaires, 1976.

Finnegan, James, "Avicenna's Refutation of Porphyrius," *Avicenna Commemoration Volume*, Calcutta: Iran Society, 1956, 187–203. ["Porphyrius"]

———, "Al-Fārābī et le ΠΕΡΙ ΝΟΥ d'Alexandre d'Aphrodise," *Mélanges Louis Massignon*, Damascus: Institut français de Damas, 1957, II, 133–152. ["Alexandre"]

Fiori, E., "L'épitomé syriaque du *Traité sur les causes du tout* d'Alexandre d'Aphrodise attribué à Serge de Rešʿaynā," *Le Muséon* 123 (2010) 127–158.

Flügel, Gustav, Johannes Roediger, and August Müller, eds., *Ibn-an-Nadîm, Kitāb al-Fihrist*, 2 vols., Leipzig: F.C.W. Vogel, 1871–1872.

Forget, Jacques, ed., *Ibn Sīnā. Le livre des théorèmes et des avertissements*, Leiden: E.J. Brill, 1892. [*Théorèmes*]

———, "Un chapître inédit de la philosophie d'Avicenne," *Revue Néo-scolastique* 1 (1894) 19–38. ["Chapître inédit"]

Frank, Richard M., "Some Fragments of Isḥāq's Translation of the *De Anima*," *Les Cahiers de Byrsa* 8 (1958–1959) 231–251; repr. in his *Texts and Studies I* (2005), no. II. ["*De Anima*"]

———, *Beings and Their Attributes*, Albany: State University of New York Press, 1978. [*Beings*]

———, *Philosophy, Theology and Mysticism in Medieval Islam. Texts and Studies on the Development and History of Kalām I*, Dimitri Gutas, ed., Aldershot: Ashgate / Variorum, 2005. [*Texts and Studies I*]

———, *Classical Islamic Theology: The Ashʿarites. Texts and Studies on the Development and History of Kalām III*, Dimitri Gutas, ed., Aldershot: Ashgate / Variorum, 2008. [*Texts and Studies III*]

Freudenthal, Gad, and Mauro Zonta, "Avicenna among Medieval Jews. The Reception of Avicenna's Philosophical, Scientific and Medical Writings in Jewish Cultures, East and West," *ASP* 22 (2012) 217–287.

Gacek, Adam, *The Arabic Manuscript Tradition. A Glossary of Technical Terms & Bibliography*, Leiden: Brill, 2001; *Supplement*, Leiden: Brill, 2008.

Gardet, Louis, *La pensée religieuse d'Avicenne*, Paris: Vrin, 1951.

Gätje, Helmut, "Avicenna als Seelenarzt," in *Avicenna Commemoration Volume*, Calcutta: Iran Society, 1956, 225–228. ["Seelenarzt"]

———, "Philosophische Traumlehren im Islam," *ZDMG* 109 (1959) 258–285. ["Traumlehren"]

———, *Studien zur Überlieferung der aristotelischen Psychologie im Islam*, Heidelberg: Carl Winter, 1971. [*Psychologie*]

Gauthier, Léon, *Hayy ben Yaqdhân. Roman philosophique d'Ibn Thofaïl*, Beirut: Imprimerie Catholique, [2]1936.

van Gelder, Geert Jan, and Marlé Hammond, eds. and transls., *Takhyīl. The Imaginary in Classical Arabic Poetics*, Exeter: Gibb Memorial Trust, 2008.

Genequand, Charles, *Alexander of Aphrodisias on the Cosmos*, Leiden: Brill, 2001.

Germann, Nadja, "Logik zwischen 'Kunst' und 'Wissenschaft': Avicenna zum Status der Logik in seiner *Isagoge*," *Recherches de Théologie et Philosophie Médiévales* 75 (2008) 1–32.

Gohlman, William E., *The Life of Ibn Sina*, Albany, N.Y.: State University of New York Press, 1974.

Goichon, Amélie-Marie, *La distinction de l'essence et de l'existence d'après Ibn Sīnā*, Paris: Desclée de Brouwer, 1937; repr. Frankfurt: Institute for the History of Arabic-Islamic Science, 1999. [*Distinction*]

——, *Lexique de la langue philosophique d'Ibn Sīnā*, Paris: Desclée de Brouwer, 1938. [*Lexique*]

——, *Vocabulaires comparés d'Aristote et d'Ibn Sīnā*, Paris: Desclée de Brouwer, 1939. [*Vocabulaires*]

——, "L'évolution philosophique d'Avicenne," *Revue Philosophique de la France et de l'Étranger* 138 (1948) 318–329. ["Évolution"]

——, *Ibn Sīnā, Livre des Directives et Remarques*, Beirut/Paris: J. Vrin, 1951. [*Directives*]

——, "La personnalité d'Avicenne," *Institut des Belles Lettres Arabes* (Tunis) 15 (1952) 265–282. ["Personnalité"]

——, "L'unité de la pensée avicennienne," *Archives Internationales d'Histoire des Sciences* 5 (1952) 290–308. ["Unité"]

——, "La nouveauté de la logique d'Ibn Sina," *Millénaire d'Avicenne, Congrès de Bagdad*, 20–28 Mars 1952, Cairo 1952, 41–58. ["Nouveauté"]

——, "Philosophie et histoire des sciences," *Les Cahiers de Tunisie* 3 (1955) 17–40. ["Philosophie"]

——, *Le Récit de Ḥayy Ibn Yaqẓān commenté par des textes d'Avicenne*, Paris: Desclée De Brouwer, 1959. [*Ḥayy*]

——, *Avicenne. Livre des Définitions* [Mémorial Avicenne—VI] Cairo: Institut Français d'Archéologie Orientale, 1963. [*Définitions*]

——, "Le Sirr 'l'intime du cœur' dans la doctrine avicennienne de la connaissance," *Studia Semitica Ioanni Bakoš Dicata*, Bratislava 1965, 119–126. ["Sirr"]

——, review of Gohlman in *Arabica* 24 (1977) 98. [Gohlman review]

González Palencia, Angel, ed., *Al-Farabi. Catálogo de las ciencias*, Madrid: Imp. de Estanislao Maestre, 1932.

Goodman, Lenn E., *Avicenna*, Ithaca / London: Cornell University Press, [2]2006.

Griffel, Frank, "Al-Ghazālī's Use of 'Original Human Disposition' (*Fiṭra*) and Its Background in the Teachings of al-Fārābī and Avicenna," *The Muslim World* 102 (2012) 1–32.

Gruner, Oskar Cameron, *A Treatise on the Canon of Medicine of Avicenna*, London: Luzac & Co., 1930.

Guidi, Michelangelo, and Richard Walzer, "Studi su al-Kindi I: Uno scritto introduttivo allo studio di Aristotele," *Memorie della R. Accademia Nazionale dei Lincei*, Classe di Sc. Mor. Stor. e Fil., Ser. VI, Vol. VI, Fasc. V, Rome 1940.

Gutas, Dimitri, *Greek Wisdom Literature in Arabic Translation*, New Haven: American Oriental Society, 1975. [*Wisdom Literature*]

——, "Paul the Persian on the Classification of the Parts of Aristotle's Philosophy: A Milestone between Alexandria and Baġdād," *Der Islam* 60 (1983) 231–267; repr. in his *Greek Philosophers* (2000), no. IX. ["Paul the Persian"]

——, "The Starting Point of Philosophical Studies in Alexandrian and Arabic Aristotelianism," *Rutgers University Studies in Classical Humanities* 2 (1985) 115–123; repr. in his *Greek Philosophers* (2000), no. X. ["Starting Point"]

——, "The Spurious and the Authentic in the Arabic Lives of Aristotle," in *Pseudo-Aristotle in the Middle Ages*, J. Kraye, W.F. Ryan, and C.B. Schmitt, eds., London: The Warburg Institute, 1986, 15–36; repr. in his *Greek Philosophers* (2000), no. VI. ["Lives"]

——, "Philoponos and Avicenna on the Separability of the Intellect," *The Greek*

Orthodox Theological Review 31 (1986) 121–129; repr. in his *Greek Philosophers* (2000), no. XI. ["Separability"]

———, "Notes and Texts from Cairo MSS, II: Texts from Avicenna's Library in a Copy by ʿAbd-ar-Razzāq aṣ-Ṣiġnāḫī," *Manuscripts of the Middle East* 2 (1987) 18–26. ["Ṣiġnāḫī"]

———, "Avicenna ii, Biography," *Encyclopaedia Iranica* III.67–70 (1987). ["Biography"]

———, "Avicenna's *Maḏhab*, With an Appendix on the Question of His Date of Birth," *Quaderni di Studi Arabi* [Atti del XIII Congresso dell'Union Européenne d'Arabisants et d'Islamisants. Venezia, 29 settembre–4 ottobre 1986] 5–6 (1987–1988) 323–336. [*"Maḏhab"*]

———, "Aspects of Literary Form and Genre in Arabic Logical Works," in *Glosses and Commentaries on Aristotelian Logical Texts* [Warburg Institute, Surveys and Texts XXIII], Charles Burnett, ed., London: The Warburg Institute, 1993, 29–76. ["Logical Works"]

———, "Ibn Ṭufayl on Ibn Sīnā's Eastern Philosophy," *Oriens* 34 (1994) 222–241. ["Ibn Ṭufayl"]

———, "Pre-Plotinian Philosophy in Arabic (Other than Platonism and Aristotelianism). A Review of the Sources," in *Aufstieg und Niedergang der Römischen Welt*, W. Haase, ed., Part II, Vol. 36.7, Berlin/New York: De Gruyter, 1994, 4939–4973; repr. in his *Greek Philosophers* (2000), no. I. ["Pre-Plotinian Philosophy"]

———, "Avicenna: *De anima* (*V 6*). Über die Seele, über Intuition and Prophetie," in *Interpretationen. Hauptwerke der Philosophie. Mittelalter*, Kurt Flasch, ed., Stuttgart: Philipp Reclam, 1998, 90–107. ["Über die Seele"]

———, *Greek Thought, Arabic Culture. The Graeco-Arabic Translation Movement in Baghdad and Early ʿAbbāsid Society (2nd–4th/8th–10th c.)*, London: Routledge, 1998. [*Translation Movement*]

———, "The 'Alexandria to Baghdad' Complex of Narratives. A Contribution to the Study of Philosophical and Medical Historiography among the Arabs," *Documenti e Studi sulla Tradizione Filosofica Medievale* 10 (1999) 155–193. ["Alexandria to Baghdad"]

———, "Avicenna's Eastern ("Oriental") Philosophy: Nature, Contents, Transmission," in *ASP* 10 (2000) 159–180. ["Eastern Philosophy"]

———, *Greek Philosophers in the Arabic Tradition* [Variorum Collected Studies Series: CS 6981], Ashgate: Aldershot, 2000. [*Greek Philosophers*]

———, "Intuition and Thinking: The Evolving Structure of Avicenna's Epistemology," *Princeton Papers. Interdisciplinary Journal of Middle Eastern Studies* 9 (2001) 1–38; repr. in Wisnovsky *Aspects* (2001) 1–38. ["Intuition and Thinking"]

———, "The Study of Arabic Philosophy in the Twentieth Century. An Essay on the Historiography of Arabic Philosophy." *British Journal of Middle Eastern Studies* 29 (2002) 5–25. ["Historiography"]

———, "The Heritage of Avicenna: The Golden Age of Arabic Philosophy, 1000–ca. 1350," in Janssens and De Smet (2002) 81–97. ["Heritage"]

———, "Avicenna's Marginal Glosses on *De anima* and the Greek Commentatorial Tradition," in *Philosophy, Science & Exegesis in Greek, Arabic & Latin Commentaries* (Essays in Honour of Richard Sorabji), P. Adamson, H. Baltussen, and M.W.F. Stone, eds., London (Bulletin of the Institute of Classical Studies Supplement 83.2), London 2004, vol. II,77–88. ["Glosses"]

———, "Geometry and the Rebirth of Philosophy in Arabic with al-Kindī," in *Words, Texts and Concepts Cruising the Mediterranean Sea, Studies ... Dedicated to Gerhard Endress on his Sixty-fifth Birthday* [Orientalia Lovaniensia Analecta 139], R. Arnzen and J. Thielmann, eds., Leuven: Peeters, 2004, 195–209. ["Geometry"]

———, "Intellect Without Limits: The Absence of Mysticism in Avicenna," in *Intellect et imagination dans la Philosophie Médiévale (Actes du XIe Congrès International de Philosophie Médiévale de la S.I.E.P.M.*, Porto, du 26 au 31 août 2002), M.C. Pacheco and J.F. Meirinhos, eds., Turnhout: Brepols, 2006, 351–372. ["Absence of Mysticism"]

———, "Imagination and Transcendental Knowledge in Avicenna," in Montgomery (2006) 337–354. ["Imagination"]

———, "The Study of Avicenna. Status quaestionis atque agenda," *Documenti e Studi sulla Tradizione Filosofica Medievale* 21 (2010) 45–69. ["Agenda"]

———, "Origins in Baghdad," in *The Cambridge History of Medieval Philosophy*, Robert Pasnau, ed., Cambridge: Cambridge University Press, 2010, 11–25. ["Origins"]

———, "The Empiricism of Avicenna," *Oriens* 40 (2012) 391–436. ["Empiricism"]

———, "Avicenna: The Metaphysics of the Rational Soul," *The Muslim World* 102 (2012) 417–425. ["Rational Soul"]

———, "From Greek to Arabic Philosophy: Curricula, Texts, Translations," in *The Blackwell History of Philosophy*, Taneli Kukkonen et al., eds., forthcoming. ["Greek to Arabic"]

Hameed, Hakeem Abdul, *Avicenna's Tract on Cardiac Drugs*, Karachi: Hamdard Foundation Press, 1983, 11–75.

Ḫānlarī, Parvīz Nātil, ed., *Ibn Sīnā. Risāla fī Maḫārij al-ḥurūf*, Tehran: Entešārāt-e Dānešgāh, 1333.

Hansberger, Rotraud, "*Kitāb al-Ḥiss wa-l-maḥsūs*: Aristotle's *Parva Naturalia* in Arabic Guise," in *Les* Parva naturalia *d'Aristote: Fortune antique et médiévale*, C. Grellard and P.-M. Morel, eds., Paris: Publications de la Sorbonne, 2010, 143–162.

Hasnaoui, Ahmad, "Avicenne et le livre IV des *Météorologiques* d'Aristote," in *Aristoteles Chemicus. Il IV libro dei 'Meteorologica' nella tradizione antica e medievale*, Cristina Viano, ed., [International Aristotle Studies, vol. 1], Sankt Augustin: Academia Verlag, 2002, 133–143.

Harvey, Steven, ed., *Anthology of the Writings of Avicenna*. Tel Aviv: The Haim Rubin Tel Aviv University Press, 2009 [in Hebrew].

Hasse, Dag N., "Das Lehrstück von den vier Intellekten in der Scholastik: von den arabischen Quellen bis zu Albertus Magnus." *Recherches de Théologie et Philosophie Médiévales* 66 (1999) 21–77.

Hasse, Dag N., and Amos Bertolacci, eds., *The Arabic, Hebrew and Latin Reception of Avicenna's Metaphysics* [Scientia Graeco-Arabica 7], Berlin: De Gruyter, 2012.

al-Ḫaṭīb, ʿAbdallāh ʿAbdurraḥmān, "Tafsīr Sūrat al-Iḫlâṣ li-š-Šayḫ ar-Raʾīs Abī ʿAlī al-Ḥusayn b. ʿAbdallāh Ibn Sīnā," *al-Machriq* 75 (2001) 383–433, 76 (2002) 121–200.

Heath, Peter, "Disorientation and Reorientation in Ibn Sina's *Epistle of the Bird*: A Reading," in *Intellectual Studies on Islam. Essays written in honor of Martin B. Dickson*, Michel M. Mazzaoui and Vera B. Moreen, eds., Salt Lake City, Utah: University of Utah Press, 1990, 163–183.

El Hefny, Mahmoud, *Ibn Sina's Musiklehre hauptsächlich an seinem "Nağāt" erläutert. Nebst Übersetzung und Herausgabe des Musikabschnittes des "Nağāt"*, Berlin-Wilmersdorf: O. Hellwig, 1931.

Hein, Christel, *Definition und Einteilung der Philosophie. Von der spätantiken Einleitungsliteratur zur arabischen Enzyklopädie* [Europäische Hochschulschriften XX/177], Frankfurt / Bern / New York: Peter Lang, 1985.

Hilāl, Ibrāhīm Ibrāhīm, *Ar-Risāla al-ʿAršiyya fī ḥaqāʾiq at-tawḥīd wa-iṯbāt an-nubuwwa*, Cairo: al-Azhar, 1400/1980.

Hourani, George F., "Ibn Sīnā's 'Essay on the Secret of Destiny'," *BSOAS* 29 (1966) 25–48.

Inati, Shams C., *Ibn Sīnā, Remarks and Admonitions. Part One: Logic*, Toronto: Pontifical Institute of Mediaeval Studies, 1984. [*Logic*]

———, *Ibn Sīnā and Mysticism. Remarks and Admonitions: Part Four*, London and New York: Kegan Paul International, 1996. [*Mysticism*]

Ivry, Alfred L., *Al-Kindi's Metaphysics*, Albany: State University of New York Press, 1974.

Jabre, Farid (Farīd Jabr), *Essai sur le lexique de Ghazālī*, Beirut: Université Libanaise, 1970. [*Lexique*]

———, (Farīd Jabr), ed., *an-Naṣṣ al-kāmil li-Manṭiq Arisṭū*, 2 vols., Beirut: Dār al-fikr al-lubnānī, 1999. [*Manṭiq*]

Jahier, Henri, and Abdelkader Noureddine, eds., *Avicenne, Poème de la médecine*, Paris: Les Belles Lettres, 1956.

Janos, Damien, *Method, Structure, and Development in al-Fārābī's Cosmology*, Leiden: Brill, 2012.

Janssens, Jules L., "Le Dānesh-Nāmeh d'Ibn Sīnā: un texte à revoir?" *Bulletin de philosophie médiévale* 28 (1986) 163–177; repr. in his *Ibn Sīnā and His Influence* (2006), no. VII. ["Dānesh-Nāmeh"]

———, *An Annotated Bibliography on Ibn Sînâ (1970–1989)*, Leuven: Leuven University Press, 1991. [*Bibliography*]

———, "Le *maʿārij al-quds fī madārij maʿrifat al-nafs*: un élément-clé pour le dossier Ghazzālī-Ibn Sīnā," *Archives d'Histoire Doctrinale et Littéraire du Moyen Âge* 60 (1993) 27–55; repr. in his *Ibn Sīnā and His Influence* (2006), no. VIII. ["*Maʿārij al-quds*"]

———, "Les Taʿlīqāt d'Ibn Sīnā. Essai de structuration et de datation", in de Libera et al. (1997) 109–122; repr. in his *Ibn Sīnā and His Influence* (2006), no. VI. ["Structuration"]

———, *An Annotated Bibliography on Ibn Sīnā: First Supplement (1990–1994)*, Louvain-la-Neuve: Fédération Internationale des Instituts d'Études Médiévales, 1999. [*Bibliography Suppl. I*]

———, "Bahmanyār ibn Marzubān: A Faithful Disciple of Ibn Sīnā?" in Reisman with Al-Rahim (2003), 177–197; repr. in his *Ibn Sīnā and His Influence* (2006), no. XII. ["Bahmanyār"]

———, "Avicenne et sa "paraphrase-commentaire" du livre Lambda (*Kitāb al-inṣāf*)," *Recherches de Théologie et Philosophie Médiévales* 70 (2003) 401–416. ["Lambda"]

———, "Avicenna and the Qurʾān. A Survey of His Qurʾānic Commentaries," *MIDEO*, 25–26 (2004) 177–192. ["Qurʾān"]

——, *Ibn Sīnā and His Influence on the Arabic and Latin World* [Variorum Collected Studies 843], Aldershot, Hampshire: Ashgate, 2006. [*Ibn Sīnā and His Influence*]

——, "Bahmanyâr, and his Revision of Ibn Sīnā's Metaphysical Project," *Medioevo* 32 (2007) 99–117. ["Revision"]

——, "Ibn Sînâ (Avicenna), The Latin Translations of," in *Encyclopedia of Medieval Philosophy. Philosophy between 500 and 1500*, Henrik Lagerlund, ed., Springer, 2011, Part 9, pp. 522–527. ["Latin Translations"]

——, "Al-Lawkarī's Reception of Ibn Sīnā's Ilāhiyyāt," in Hasse and Bertolacci (2012), 7–26. ["Lawkarī"]

——, "Ibn Sīnā's *Taʿlīqāt*: The Presence of Paraphrases of and Super-Commentaries on the *Ilāhīyāt* of the *Šifāʾ*," in Opwis and Reisman (2012), 201–222. ["*Taʿlīqāt*"]

——, "*Al-Birr wa-l-ithm, Piety and Sin*: Possible Farabian Influences on the Young Ibn Sīnā," *Ishraq. Islamic Philosophy Yearbook* 3 (2012) 412–422. ["*Birr*"]

Janssens, Jules, and Daniel De Smet, *Avicenna and His Heritage*, Leuven: Leuven University Press, 2002.

Jolivet, Jean et Roshdi Rashed, *Études sur Avicenne*, Paris: Les Belles Lettres, 1984.

Jonaydī, Farīdūn, *Kārnāme-ye Ebn-e Sīnā*, Tehran: Entešārāt-e Balḫ, 1360/1981.

Kalbarczyk, Alexander, "The *Kitāb al-Maqūlāt* of the *Muḫtaṣar al-awsaṭ fī l-manṭiq*: A Hitherto Unknown Source for Studying Ibn Sīnā's Reception of Aristotle's *Categories*," *Oriens* 40 (2012) 305–354.

Karlığa, Bekir, "Un nouveau traité d'éthique d'Ibn Sīnā inconnu jusqu'à nos jours," in Janssens and De Smet (2002), 21–35. ["Traité d'éthique"]

——, "İbn Sina'nın şimdiye kadar bilinmeyen yeni bir ahlâk risalesi," draft copy prepared for publication in the Turkish journal *Erdem*. ["Ahlâk risalesi"]

——, "Mustafa Behçet Efendi ve İbn Sina'nın Yeni Bir Ahlâk Risalesi," *Tıp Tarihi Araştırmaları* 6 (1997) 121–142. ["Mustafa Behçet"]

Kaya, M. Cüneyt, ed. and transl., *Dimitri Gutas. İbn Sînâ'nın Mirası*, Istanbul: Klâsik Yayınları, ^{2}2010. [*Miras*]

——, "Şukûk alâ *'Uyûn*: *'Uyûnü'l-mesâ'il*'in Fârâbî'ye Âidiyeti Üzerine," *İslâm Araştırmaları Dergisi* 27 (2012) 29–67. ["Şukûk"]

——, "Prophetic Legislation: Avicenna's View of Practical Philosophy Revisited," in *Philosophy and the Abrahamic Religions: Scriptural Hermeneutics and Epistemology*, Torrance Kirby, Rahim Acar, and Bilal Baş, eds., Newcastle upon Tyne: Cambridge Scholars Publishing, 2013, 205–223. ["Prophetic Legislation"]

Kenny, Joseph, "Sûras 113 & 114: Commented by Ibn-Sīnā," *Orita* 35 (2003) 1–16. ["Sûras"]

——, "A Philosophical Prayer, *Risâla fî d-duʿāʾ*," *Orita* 37 (2005) 1–10. ["Prayer"].

Khan, M. ʿAbdul Muʿid, "A Unique Treatise on the Interpretation of Dreams by Ibn Sina, Edited with an Introduction," *Avicenna Commemoration Volume*, Calcutta: Iran Society, 1956, 257–307. ["Dreams"]

——, "Kitabu Taʿbir-ir-Ruya of Abu ʿAli b. Sina," *Indo-Iranica* 9 (1956) 15–57. ["Ruya"]

El-Khodeiri, Maḥmoud, "Silsila muttaṣila min talāmīḏ Ibn Sīnā fi mi'atay ʿām (Une série continue de disciples d'Avicenne pendant deux siècles)," *Millénaire d'Avicenne* [Congrès de Bagdad, 20–28 Mars 1952], Cairo 1952, 53–59. ["Silsila"]

——, "Autour de deux opuscules d'Avicenne traduits en Latin," *MIDEO* 2 (1955) 341–350. ["Opuscules"]

——, ed., *Ibn Sīnā. Aš-Šifāʾ, al-Manṭiq, al-ʿIbāra*, Cairo: al-Hayʾa al-miṣriyya al-ʿāmma li-t-taʾlīf wa-n-našr, 1390/1970.

Kraemer, Joel L., *Philosophy in the Renaissance of Islam*, Leiden: Brill, 1986.

Kraus, Paul, "Eine arabische Biographie Avicennas," *Klinische Wochenschrift* 11 (1932) 1880a–1884b. ["Biographie"]

——, "Raziana I," *Orientalia* 4 (1935) 300–334.

——, "Raziana II," *Orientalia* 5 (1936) 35–56.

——, "Plotin chez les Arabes," *Bulletin de l'Institut d'Égypte* 23 (1940–1941) 263–295. ["Plotin"]

Kuhne Brabant, R. "La *Urŷūza laṭīfa fī qaḍāyā Ibuqrāṭ al-jams wa-l-ʿišrīn* de Avicena," in *Homenaje al Prof. Darío Cabanelas Rodriguez, O.F.M.*, Granada: Universidad de Granada 1987, II,343–366.

Kurd ʿAlī, Muḥammad, ed., *Taʾrīḫ ḥukamāʾ al-Islām, Taʾlīf Ẓahīr ad-Dīn al-Bayhaqī*, Damascus: Maṭbaʿat at-taraqqī, 1365/1946.

al-Kurdī, Muḥyīddīn Ṣabrī, ed./publisher, *Majmūʿat ar-rasāʾil*, Cairo: Maṭbaʿat Kurdistān al-ʿilmiyya, 1328/[1910]. [*Majmūʿat ar-rasāʾil*]

——, ed./publisher, *Kitāb an-Najāt*, Cairo: Maṭbaʿat as-saʿāda, 1331/[1913]. [*Najāt*]

——, ed./publisher, *Jāmiʿ al-badāʾiʿ*, Cairo; Maṭbaʿat as-saʿāda, 1335/1917. [*Jāmiʿ*]

Kutsch, Wilhelm, "Muḥaṣṣal—Ġayr Muḥaṣṣal," *Mélanges de l'Université Saint Joseph* 27 (1947–1948) 169–176.

Lagerlund, Henrik, "Avicenna and Tusi on Modal Logic," *History and Philosophy of Logic* 30 (2009) 227–239.

Lameer, Joep, *Conception and Belief in Ṣadr al-Dīn Shīrāzī. Al-Risāla fī l-taṣawwur wa-l-taṣdīq*, Tehran: Iranian Institute of Philosophy, 2006. [*Conception*]

——, "Avicenna's Concupiscence," *ASP* 23 (2013) 277–289. ["Concupiscence"]

——, "Towards a New Edition of Avicenna's *Kitāb al-Ishārat wa-l-tanbīhāt*," *Journal of Islamic Manuscripts* 4 (2013) 199–248. [*"Ishārāt"*]

Landauer, Samuel, "Die Psychologie des Ibn Sīnā," *ZDMG* 29 (1875) 335–418.

Langermann, Tzvi, *Avicenna and His Legacy. A Golden Age of Science and Philosophy*, Turnhout: Brepols, 2009.

Langhade, Jacques and Mario Grignaschi, *Al-Fārābī, Deux ouvrages inédits sur la Réthorique* [*sic*], Beirut: Dar el-Machreq, 1971.

Lazard, Gilbert, *La langue des plus anciens monuments de la prose persane* [Études Linguistiques 2], Paris: Klincksieck, 1963.

Lerner, Ralph, and Muhsin Mahdi, *Medieval Political Philosophy: A Sourcebook*, New York: The Free Press, 1963.

Libera, Alain de, Abdelali Elamrani-Jamal, Alain Galonnier, eds., *Langages et philosophie. Hommage à Jean Jolivet*, Paris: Vrin, 1997.

Lippert, Julius, ed., *Ibn al-Qifṭī's Taʾrīḫ al-ḥukamāʾ*, Leipzig: Dieterich'sche Verlagsbuchhandlung, 1903.

Lizzini, Olga, "La Metafisica del *Libro della Guida*. Presentazione e traduzione della terza parte (*bâb*) del *Kitâb al-Hidâya* di Avicenna," *Le Muséon* 108 (1995) 367–424. [*Guida*]

——, *Avicenna. Metafisica*, Milano: Bompiani, [2]2006. [*Metafisica*]

——, "L'*Epistola sulle divisioni delle scienze intellettuali* di Avicenna," in *"Ad ingenii acuitionem". Studies in Honour of Alfonso Maierù*, Stefano Caroti, Ruedi Imbach,

Zénon Kaluza, Giorgio Stabile & Loris Sturlese, eds. [Textes et Études du Moyen Âge 38], Louvain-la-Neuve: Collège Cardinal Mercier, 2006, pp. 221–248. ["Divisioni"]

——, "Vie active, vie contemplative et philosophie chez Avicenne," in *Vie active et vie contemplative au Moyen Âge et au seuil de la Renaissance*, Christian Trottmann, ed., Rome: École Française de Rome, 2009, 207–239. ["Vie contemplative"]

Lucchetta, Francesca, *Avicenna. Epistola sulla vita futura*, Padova: Antenore, 1969. [*Epistola*]

——, "Le dieci questioni di Avicenna," *Quaderni di Studi Arabi* 19 (2001) 101–134. ["Dieci questioni"]

Lüling, Günther, "Ein anderer Avicenna. Kritik seiner Autobiographie und ihrer bisherigen Behandlung," *ZDMG* Suppl. III.1 (1977) 496–513.

Luther, Irina, "The Conception of the Angle in the Works of Ibn Sīnā and aš-Šīrāzī," in McGinnis with Reisman (2004) 112–125.

Madelung, Wilferd, "An Ismaili Interpretation of Ibn Sīnā's *Qaṣīdat al-Nafs*," in *Reason and Inspiration in Islam: Theology, Philosophy and Mysticism in Muslim Thought. Essays in Honour of Hermann Landolt*, Todd Lawson, ed., London/New York: I.B. Tauris, 2005, 157–168.

Madkour, Ibrahim, *L'Organon d'Aristote dans le monde arabe*, Paris: Vrin, [1]1934, [2]1969.

Madwar, Muḥammad Riḍā, and Imām Ibrāhīm Aḥmad, eds., *Ibn Sīnā. Aš-Šifāʾ, ar-Riyāḍiyyāt, ʿIlm al-Hayʾa*, Cairo: al-Hayʾa al-miṣriyya al-ʿāmma li-l-kitāb, 1980.

Mahdavī, Yaḥyā, *Fehrest-e nosḫahā-ye moṣannafāt-e Ebn-e Sīnā*, Tehran: Dānešgāh-e Tehrān, 1333Š/1954.

Manṭiq al-mašriqiyyīn wa-l-Qaṣīda al-muzdawija, taṣnīf ar-Raʾīs Abī ʿAlī Ibn Sīnā, Cairo: al-Maktaba as-salafiyya, 1910. [*Manṭiq al-mašriqiyyīn*]

Marín, Manuela, and David Waines, "Ibn Sīnā on *Sakanjabīn*," *Bulletin des Études Orientales* 47 (1995) 81–97.

Marmura, Michael E., ed., *Ibn Sīnā. Fī Ithbāt al-nubuwwāt*, Beirut: Dār an-nahār, 1968. [*Nubuwwāt*]

——, "Ghazali's Attitude to the Secular Sciences and Logic," in George F. Hourani, ed., *Essays on Islamic Philosophy and Science*, Albany, N.Y.: SUNY Press, 1975, 100–111. ["Ghazali's Attitude"]

——, "Avicenna's Proof from Contingency for God's Existence in the *Metaphysics* of the *Shifā*," *Medieval Studies* 42 (1980) 337–352; repr. in his *Probing* (2005) 131–148. ["Proof from Contingency"]

——, "Plotting the Course of Avicenna's Thought," *JAOS* 111 (1991) 333–342. ["Avicenna's Thought"]

——, "Avicenna and the Kalām," *ZGAIW* 7 (1991–1992) 172–206; repr. in his *Probing* (2005) 97–130. ["Kalām"]

——, *Avicenna. The Metaphysics of* The Healing, Provo: Brigham Young University Press, 2005. [*Metaphysics*]

——, *Probing in Islamic Philosophy: Studies in the Philosophies of Ibn Sīnā, al-Ghazālī and Other Major Muslim Thinkers*, State University of N.Y at Binghamton: Global Academic Publishing, 2005. [*Probing*]

——, "Avicenna's Critique of Platonists in Book VII, Chapter 2 of the *Metaphysics* of His *Healing*," in Montgomery (2006) 355–369. ["Critique of Platonists"]

——, "Some Questions Regarding Avicenna's Theory of the Temporal Origination of the Human Rational Soul," *ASP* 18 (2008) 121–138. ["Rational Soul"]

Martini Bonadeo, Cecilia, *Al-Fārābī. L'armonia delle opinioni dei due sapienti, il divino Platone e Aristotele*, Pisa: Edizioni Plus, Pisa University Press, 2008.

Mawāldī, Muṣṭafā, "Risāla fī z-zāwiya li-Ibn Sīnā," *Majallat Maʿhad al-Maḫṭūṭāt al-ʿArabiyya* 42 (1998) 33–93.

Maẓhar, ʿAbdalḥamīd Luṭfī, ed., *Ibn Sīnā. Aš-Šifāʾ, ar-Riyāḍiyyāt, al-Ḥisāb*, Cairo: al-Hayʾa al-miṣriyyah al-ʿāmma li-l-kitāb, 1975.

McGinnis, Jon, *Avicenna. The Physics of* The Healing, Provo: Brigham Young University Press, 2009. [*Physics*]

——, *Avicenna*, Oxford: Oxford University Press, 2010. [*Avicenna*]

McGinnis, Jon, and David C. Reisman, *Classical Arabic Philosophy*, Indianapolis: Hackett, 2007.

McGinnis, Jon, with the assistance of David C. Reisman, *Interpreting Avicenna: Science and Philosophy in Medieval Islam* [Proceedings of the Second Conference of the Avicenna Study Group], Leiden: Brill, 2004.

Mehren, Michael August Ferdinand, ed., *Traités mystiques d'Abou Alî al-Hosain b. Abdallah b. Sînâ ou d'Avicenne*, 4 fascicles, Leiden: E.J. Brill, 1889–1899; repr. Frankfurt: Institute for the History of Arabic-Islamic Science, 1999.

Merkle, Karl, *Die Sittensprüche der Philosophen*, Leipzig: G. Kreysing, 1921.

Meškāt, Moḥammad, ed., *Ragšenāsī yā Resāle dar Nabḍ*, Tehran: Entešārāt-e Anjoman-e Āṯār-e Mellī, 1330Š/1951. [*Rag*]

——, ed., *Manṭiq. Dānešnāme-ye ʿAlāʾī*, Tehran: Anjoman-e Āṯār-e Mellī, 1331Š/[1952]. [*Manṭiq*]

——, ed., *Ṭabīʿiyyāt. Dānešnāme-ye ʿAlāʾī*, Tehran: Anjoman-e Āṯār-e Mellī, 1331Š/[1952]. [*Ṭabīʿiyyāt*]

Meyer, Egbert, "Philosophischer Gottesglaube: Ibn Sīnās Thronschrift," *ZDMG* 130 (1980) 226–278.

Meyerhof, Max, "ʿAlī al-Bayhaqī's Tatimmat Ṣiwān al-Ḥikma," *Osiris* 8 (1948) 122–216.

Michot, Jean R. (Yahya), "Paroles d'Avicenne sur la sagesse," *Bulletin de Philosophie Médiévale* 19 (1977) 45–49. ["Sagesse"]

——, "L'Épître d'Avicenne sur le parfum," *Bulletin de Philosophie Médiévale* 20 (1978) 53–58. ["Parfum"]

——, "Le commentaire avicennien du verset: 'Puis Il se tourna vers le ciel …'. Édition, traduction, notes," *MIDEO* 14 (1980) 317–328. ["Puis Il se tourna"]

——, "Tables de correspondance des 'Taʿlīqāt' d'al-Fārābī, des 'Taʿlīqāt' d'Avicenne et du 'Liber Aphorismorum' d'Andrea Alpago," *MIDEO* 15 (1982) 231–250. ["Taʿlīqāt"]

——, "Les questions sur les états de l'esprit. Problèmes d'attribution et essai de traduction critique," *Bulletin de Philosophie Médiévale* 24 (1982) 44–53. ["États de l'esprit"]

——, "De la joie et du bonheur. Essai de traduction critique de la section II, 8 des "Ishârât" d'Avicenne," *Bulletin de Philosophie Médiévale* 25 (1983) 49–60. ["Joie"]

——, ""L'épître sur la connaissance de l'âme rationnelle et de ses états" attribuée à Avicenne. Présentation et essai de traduction," *Revue Philosophique de Louvain* 82 (1984) 479–499. ["Connaissance de l'âme"]

——, "L'*Épître sur la genèse et le retour* attribuée à Avicenne. Présentation et essai de traduction critique," *Bulletin de Philosophie Médiévale* 26 (1984) 104–118. [*"Épître sur la genèse"*]

——, "Prophétie et divination selon Avicenne. Présentation, essai de traduction critique et index de l'"Épître de l'âme de la sphère"," *Revue Philosophique de Louvain* 83 (1985) 507–535. ["Prophétie"]

——, "Avicenna's 'Letter on the Disappearance of the Vain Intelligible Forms after Death.' Presentation and translation," *Bulletin de Philosophie Médiévale*, 27 (1985) 94–103. ["Disappearance"]

——, *La destinée de l'homme selon Avicenne. Le retour à Dieu (ma'ād) et l'imagination*, Leuven: Peeters, 1986. [*Destinée*]

——, ""L'épître sur la disparition des formes intelligibles après la mort" d'Avicenne. Édition critique, traduction et index," *Bulletin de Philosophie Médiévale* 29 (1987) 152–170. ["Disparition"]

——, "L'eschatologie dans le "Livre de la Guidance" d'Avicenne. Présentation, traduction et index de la dernière section du *Kitâb al-Hidâya*," *Bulletin de Philosophie Médiévale* 30 (1988) 138–152. ["Eschatologie"]

——, "Un important recueil avicennien du VIIe/XIIIe s.: la *majmû'a* Hüseyin Çelebi 1194 de Brousse," *Bulletin de Philosophie Médiévale* 33 (1991) 121–129. ["Recueil avicennien"]

——, "Avicenne, *La définition de l'âme*. Section I de l'*Épître des états de l'âme*. Traduction critique et lexique," in de Libera et al. (1997), 239–256. [*"Définition"*]

——, "La réponse d'Avicenne à Bahmanyār et al-Kirmānī. Présentation, traduction critique et lexique arabe-français de la *Mubāḥatha III*," *Le Muséon* 110 (1997) 143–221. ["Réponse"]

Michot, Yahya (Jean R.), *Ibn Sînâ. Lettre au vizir Abû Sa'd*. Editio princeps d'après le manuscrit de Bursa, traduction de l'arabe, introduction, notes et lexique [Sagesses musulmanes 4], Beirut/Paris: Al-Bouraq, 2000. Reviewed by Reisman "A New Standard," and by Gutas in *JIS* 14 (2003) 379–381. [*Abû Sa'd*]

——, *Avicenne, Livre de la genèse et du retour*, "Version exploratoire," Oxford 2002, on-line PDF version available at http://www.muslimphilosophy.com/sina/works/AN195.pdf. [*Livre de la genèse*]

——, *Avicenne. Réfutation de l'astrologie*. Édition et traduction du texte arabe, introduction, notes et lexique [Sagesses Musulmanes, 5], Beirut/Paris: Albouraq, 1427/2006. [*Astrologie*]

——, "*Al-Nukat wa-l-fawâ'id*: An Important *Summa* of Avicennian *Falsafa*," in *Classical Arabic Philosophy: Sources and Reception*, Peter Adasmson, ed., London: The Warburg Institute—Turin: Nino Aragno Editore, 2007, 90–124. [*"Nukat"*]

——, "Le Riz trop cuit du Kirmânî. Présentation, édition, traduction et lexique de l'*Épître d'Avicenne contestant l'accusation d'avoir pastiché le Coran*," in *Mélanges offerts à Hossam Elkhadem par ses amis et élèves*, Frank Daelemans, Jean-Marie Duvosquel, Robert Halleux, and David Juste, eds., *Archives et Bibliothèques de Belgique*, Numéro Spécial 83, Brussels: Bibliothèque Royale de Belgique, 2007, 81–129. ["Riz"]

Mimoune, Rabia, "Épître sur les parties des sciences intellectuelles d'Abū 'Alī al-Ḥusayn ibn Sīnā," in Jolivet and Rashed (1984) 143–151.

Minorsky, Vladimir, "Avicenne l'homme," *Le livre du millénaire d'Avicenne*, vol. IV, Tehran: Dānešgāh-e Tehran, 1956, 3–12.

Mīnovī, Mojtabā, ed., *Riyāḍiyyāt. Dānešnāme-ye ʿAlāʾī*, Tehran: Anjoman-e Āṯār-e Mellī, 1331/[1952].

Mohaghegh, Mehdi, ed., *Ḥudūṯ al-ʿālam, Afḍal-ad-Dīn ... Ibn Ġaylān; al-Ḥukūma ..., Ibn Sīnā*, Tehran: Dānešgāh-e Tehrān, 1377/1998.

Mohaghegh, Mehdi, and Toshihiko Izutsu, eds., *Collected Texts and Papers on Logic and Language* [Wisdom of Persia VIII], Tehran: Tehran University Press, 1974.

Moʿīn, Moḥammad, ed., *Ilāhiyyāt. Dānešnāme-ye ʿAlāʾī*, Tehran: Anjoman-e Āṯār-e Mellī, 1331/[1952].

Montgomery, James E., ed., *Arabic Theology, Arabic Philosophy. From the Many to the One: Essays in Celebration of Richard M. Frank*, Leuven: Peeters, 2006.

Morewedge, Parviz, *The* Metaphysica *of Avicenna* (*ibn Sīnā*) [Pesian Heritage Series No. 13], London: Routledge & Kegan Paul, 1973.

Moṭahharī, Mortaḍā, ed., *Bahmanyār b. al-Marzubān, at-Taḥṣīl*, Tehran: Dānešgāh-e Tehrān, 1375Š/1996.

Mousavian, Seyyed Hossein, ed., *Ibn Sīnā. At-Taʿlīqāt*, Tehran: Iranian Institute of Philosophy, 2013.

Müller, August, ed., *Ibn Abī Uṣaybiʿa, ʿUyūn al-anbāʾ fī ṭabaqāt al-aṭibbāʾ*, Königsberg / Cairo: al-Maṭbaʿa al-wahbiyya, 1882–1884.

Muntaṣir, ʿAbdalḥalīm, Saʿīd Zāyid, and ʿAbdallāh Ismāʿīl, eds., *Ibn Sīnā. Aš-Šifāʾ, aṭ-Ṭabīʿiyyāt, an-Nabāt*, Cairo: al-Hayʾa al-ʿāmma li-šuʾūn al-maṭābiʿ al-amīriyya, 1384/1965.

———, eds., *Ibn Sīnā. Aš-Šifāʾ, aṭ-Ṭabīʿiyyāt, al-Maʿādin wa-l-āṯār al-ʿulwiyya*, Cairo: al-Hayʾa al-ʿāmma li-šuʾūn al-maṭābiʿ al-amīriyya, 1385/1965.

———, eds., *Ibn Sīnā. Aš-Šifāʾ, aṭ-Ṭabīʿiyyāt, al-Ḥayawān*, Cairo: al-Hayʾa al-miṣriyya al-ʿāmma li-t-taʾlīf wa-n-našr, 1970.

Mūsā, Muḥammad Yūsuf, Sulaymān Dunyā, and Saʿīd Zāyid, eds., *Ibn Sīnā. Aš-Šifāʾ, al-Ilāhiyyāt* (2), Cairo: al-Hayʾa al-ʿāmma li-šuʾūn al-maṭābiʿ al-amīriyya, 1380/1960.

al-Mūsawī, Zayn-al-ʿĀbidīn, ed., *Majmūʿ rasāʾil aš-Šayḫ ar-Raʾīs Abī ʿAlī al-Ḥusayn b. ʿAbdallāh Ibn Sīnā al-Buḫārī*, Hyderabad: Dāʾirat al-maʿārif al-ʿuṯmāniyya, 1353–1354/[1934–1935].

Nafīsī, Saʿīd, *Zendegī va kār va andīše va rūzgār-e Pūr-e Sīnā*, Tehran 1333/1954.

Nallino, Carlo Alfonso, "Filosofia "Orientale" od "Illuminativa" d'Avicenna?," *Rivista degli Studi Orientali* 10 (1923–1925) 433–467.

Nasr, Seyyed Hossein, *An Introduction to Islamic Cosmological Doctrines*, Cambridge, Mass.: Belknap Press, Harvard, [1]1964; London: Thames and Hudson, [2]1978. [*Cosmological Doctrines*]

———, "Ibn Sīnā's 'Oriental Philosophy'," in *History of Islamic Philosophy* [Routledge History of World Philosophies, Volume I], Seyyed Hossein Nasr and Oliver Leaman, eds., London: Routledge, 1994, 247–251. ["Oriental Philosophy"]

Nasr, Seyyed Hossein, and Mehdi Aminrazavi, *An Anthology of Philosophy in Persia*, Volume I, New York and Oxford: Oxford University Press, 1999.

Nasr, Seyyed Hossein, and Mehdi Mohaghegh, *Abū Reyḥān Bērūnī va Ebn-e Sīnā, Al-Asʾila wa-l-ajwiba*, Tehran: Dānešgāh-e Tehrān, 1352/1974.

Nūraddīn, Muḥammad, ed., *Ṣadr-ad-Dīn al-Ḥusaynī, Zubdat at-tawārīḫ, Aḫbār al-umarāʾ wa-l-mulūk as-Saljūqiyya*, Beirut: Dār Iqraʾ, 1405/1985.

Nūrānī, ʿAbdallāh, *al-Mabdaʾ wa-l-maʿād li-š-Šayḫ ar-Raʾīs* [Wisdom of Persia XXXVI], Tehran: The Institute of Islamic Studies, 1984.

Opwis, Felicitas, and David C. Reisman, eds., *Islamic Philosophy, Science, Culture, and Religion. Studies in Honor of Dimitri Gutas* [Islamic Philosophy, Theology and Science 83], Leiden: Brill, 2012.

Peters, Francis E., *Aristotle and the Arabs*, New York: New York University Press, 1968.

Pines, Shlomo, "Ibn Sīnā et l'auteur de la *Risālat al-Fuṣūṣ fī'l-ḥikma*: Quelques données du problème," *Revue des Études Islamiques* 19 (1951) 121–124; repr. in *Collected Works of Shlomo Pines, III. Studies in the History of Arabic Philosophy*, Sarah Stroumsa, ed., Jerusalem: The Magnes Press, 1996, 297–300. ["*Fuṣūṣ*"]

———, "La 'Philosophie Orientale' d'Avicenne et sa polémique contre les Bagdadiens," *Archives d'Histoire Doctrinale et Littéraire du Moyen Âge* 27 (1952) 5–37; repr. in *Collected Works of Shlomo Pines, III. Studies in the History of Arabic Philosophy*, Sarah Stroumsa, ed., Jerusalem: The Magnes Press, 1996, 301–333. ["Philosophie Orientale"]

Pourjavady, Nasrollah, ed., *Majmūʿah-ye Falsafī-e Marāghah. A Philosophical Anthology from Maraghah*, Tehran: Iran University Press, 2002.

Qāsim, Maḥmūd, *Ibn Sīnā. Aš-Šifāʾ, aṭ-Ṭabīʿiyyāt: as-Samāʾ wa-l-ʿālam, al-Kawn wa-l-fasād, al-Afʿāl wa-l-infiʿālāt*, Cairo: Dār al-kitāb al-ʿarabī li-ṭ-ṭibāʿa wa-n-našr, 1969.

al-Qašš, Edouard (Idwār), and ʿAlī Zayʿūr, eds., *Al-Qānūn fī ṭ-ṭibb*, 4 vols., Beirut: Muʾassasat ʿIzzaddīn, 1413/1993.

Ragep, F. Jamil and Sally P. Ragep, "The Astronomical and Cosmological Works of Ibn Sīnā: Some Preliminary Remarks," in *Sciences, techniques et instruments dans le monde iranien (Xe–XIXe siècle)*, ed. by N. Pourjavady & Ž. Vesel, Tehran: Presses Universitaires d'Iran & Institut Français de Recherche en Iran, 2004, 3–15.

al-Rahim, Ahmed H., "Avicenna's Immediate Disciples: Their Lives and Works," in Langermann (2009) 1–25.

Rahman, Fazlur, *Avicenna's Psychology. An English Translation of* Kitāb al-Najāt, *Book II, Chapter VI*, London: Oxford University Press, 1952. [*Psychology*]

———, *Prophecy in Islam*, London: George Allen & Unwin, 1958; repr. Chicago: The University of Chicago Press, 2011. [*Prophecy*]

———, ed., *Avicenna's De anima*, London: Oxford University Press, 1959. [*Nafs*]

Rahman, Shahid, Tony Street, and Hassan Tahiri, eds., *The Unity of Science in the Arabic Tradition*, n.p.: Springer, 2008.

Ramón Guerrero, Rafael, *La recepción arabe del* De anima *de Aristoteles: Al-Kindi y al-Farabi*, Madrid: Consejo Superior de Investigaciones Científicas, 1992.

Rashed, Roshdi, "Mathématiques et philosophie chez Avicenne," in Jolivet and Rashed (1984) 29–39.

Rashed, Roshdi et Jean Jolivet, *Œuvres philosophiques et scientifiques d'al-Kindī. Volume II. Métaphysique et cosmologie*, Leiden: Brill, 1998.

Reisman, David C., "Avicenna at the ARCE," in Wisnovsky *Aspects* (2001) 131–182. ["ARCE"]

———, *The Making of the Avicennan Tradition: The Transmission, Contents, and Structure of Ibn Sīnā's* al-Mubāḥaṯāt (*The Discussions*), Leiden: Brill, 2002. [*Avicennan Tradition*]

———, "A New Standard for Avicenna Studies," *JAOS* 122 (2002) 562–577. ["New Standard"]

——, "Stealing Avicenna's Books: A Study of the Historical Sources for the Life and Times of Avicenna," in Reisman with Al-Rahim (2003) 91–126. ["Stealing"]
——, "The Pseudo-Avicennan Corpus, I: Methodological Considerations," in McGinnis with Reisman (2004) 3–21. ["Pseudo-Avicennan Corpus, I"]
——, *Avicenniana. A Guide to the Manuscripts of Avicenna, Being a Revision of the Bibliographies of Anawati and Mahdavī*, First Incomplete Draft 2007; unpublished computer print-out privately given to me by the author. [*Avicenniana*]
——, "The Ps.-Avicenna Corpus II: The Ṣūfistic Turn," *Documenti e Studi sulla Tradizione Filosofica Medievale* 21 (2010) 243–258. ["Ps.-Avicenna Corpus II"]
——, "The Life and Times of Avicenna: Patronage and Learning in Medieval Islam," in Adamson *Interpreting Avicenna* (2013) 7–27. ["Patronage"]
Reisman, David C., with the assistance of Ahmed H. Al-Rahim, eds., *Before and after Avicenna. Proceedings of the First Conference of the Avicenna Study Group*, Leiden: Brill, 2003.
Remondon, Denise, "*Al-aḫlāq wa-l-infiʿālāt an-nafsāniyya*," in *Miscellanea* [Mémorial Avicenne IV], Cairo: Institut Français d'Archéologie Orientale, 1954, 19–29.
Ritter, Hellmut, "Risālat Ibn Sīnā fī l-Arzāq," *Majallat al-Majmaʿ al-ʿIlmī al-ʿArabī bi-Dimašq* 25 (1950) 199–209.
Rosenthal, Franz, "Die arabische Autobiographie," *Studia Arabica I* [Analecta Orientalia 14], Rome: Pontificium Institutum Biblicum, 1937, 1–40. ["Autobiographie"]
——, *The Technique and Approach of Muslim Scholarship*, Rome: Pontificium Institutum Biblicum, 1947. [*Muslim Scholarship*]
——, *Knowledge Triumphant*, Leiden: Brill, 1970, ^{2}2007. [*Knowledge*]
——, *The Classical Heritage in Islam*, translated by E. and J. Marmorstein, Berkeley and Los Angeles: University of California Press, 1975. [*Classical Heritage*]
Rowson, Everett K., *A Muslim Philosopher on the Soul and Its Fate: Al-ʿĀmirī's* Kitāb al-Amad ʿalā l-abad, New Haven: American Oriental Society, 1988.
Rudolph, Ulrich, unter Mitarbeit von Renate Würsch, *Philosophie in der islamischen Welt. Band 1: 8.-10. Jahrhundert* [Grundriss der Geschichte der Philosophie, begründet von Friedrich Ueberweg], Basel: Schwabe Verlag, 2012.
Rundgren, Frithiof, "Avicenna on Love. Studies in the 'Risāla fī māhīyat alʿišq' I," *Orientalia Suecana* 27–28 (1978–1979) 42–62.
Ruska, Julius, "Die Alchemie des Avicenna," *Isis* 21 (1934) 14–51.
Sabra, Abdelhamid I., "Avicenna on the Subject Matter of Logic," *The Journal of Philosophy* 77 (1980) 746–764.
Ṣabra, ʿAbdelḥamīd and ʿAbdelḥamīd Luṭfī Maẓhar, eds., *Ibn Sīnā. Aš-Šifāʾ, ar-Riyāḍiyyāt, Uṣūl al-handasa*, Cairo: al-Hayʾa al-miṣriyya al-ʿāmma li-l-kitāb, 1977.
Sabri, Tahani, "Traité d'Avicenne sur le destin (*Al-Qadar*). Traduction et commentaire," *Revue des Études Islamiques* 55–57 (1987–1989 [1992]) 181–204.
Sagadeev, Artur Vladimirovich, *Ibn-Sina*, Moscow: Mysl', ^{1}1980, ^{2}1985.
Sālem, Muḥammad Silīm, *Ibn Sīnā, Kitāb al-majmūʿ aw al-ḥikma al-ʿarūḍiyya fī maʿānī Kitāb Rīṭūrīqā*, Cairo: Maktabat an-nahḍa al-miṣriyya, 1950. [*Rīṭūrīqā*]
——, *Ibn Sīnā. Aš-Šifāʾ, al-Manṭiq, al-Ḫiṭāba*, Cairo: al-Maṭbaʿa al-amīriyya, 1373/1954. [*Ḫiṭāba*]
——, *Ibn Sīnā, Kitāb al-majmūʿ aw al-ḥikma al-ʿarūḍiyya fī maʿānī Kitāb aš-Šiʿr*, Cairo: Maktabat Dār al-Kutub, 1969. [*Šiʿr*]

Saliba, George, "Ibn Sīnā and Abū ʿUbayd al-Jūzjānī: The Problem of the Ptolemaic Equant," *Journal for the History of Arabic Science* 4 (1980) 377–403, repr. in his *A History of Arabic Astronomy*, New York: New York University Press, 1994, 85–112.

Ṣāliḥ, Muḥsin, *Kitāb al-Majmūʿ aw al-Ḥikma al-ʿArūḍiyya*, Beirut: Dār al-Hādī, 1428/2007.

Šamsaddīn, ʿAbdalamīr Z., ed., *Al-Maḏhab at-tarbawī ʿinda Ibn Sīnā*, Beirut: aš-Širka al-ʿālamiyya li-l-kitāb, 1988.

as-Saqā, Aḥmad Ḥijāzī Aḥmad, ed., *Faḫr-ad-Dīn ar-Rāzī, Šarḥ ʿUyūn al-ḥikma*, Tehran: Muʾassasat aṣ-ṣādiq li-ṭ-ṭibāʿa wa-n-našr, 1415H/1373Š.

Sara, Solomon I., *A Treatise on Arabic Phonetics* [LINCOM Studies in Phonetics 04], München: LINCOM GmbH, 2009.

Schacht, Joseph, and Max Meyerhof, *The Medico-Philosophical Controversy between Ibn Butlan of Baghdad and Ibn Ridwan of Cairo*, Cairo: Egyptian University, Faculty of Arts, 1937.

Schmoelders, Augustus, *Documenta philosophiae Arabum*, Bonn: Eduard Weber, 1836.

Scrimieri, Giorgio, *Testimonianze medievali e pensiero moderno—Carme sull' anatomia, Epistola sull' astronomia, Inediti di Ibn Sina*, Bari: Edizioni Levante, 1970. [*Testimonianze*]

———, *Degli Studi su Ibn Sīnā I. Teoresi Fisica*, Bari: Edizioni Levante, 1973. [*Studi*]

Sebti, Meryem, "Une épître inédite d'Avicenne, *Taʿalluq al-nafs bi-l-badan* (De l'attachement de l'âme et du corps): édition critique, traduction et annotation," *Documenti e Studi sulla Tradizione Filosofica Medievale* 15 (2004) 141–200. ["*Taʿalluq*"]

———, "La question de l'authenticité de l'*Épître des états de l'âme* (*Risāla fī aḥwāl al-nafs*) d'Avicenne," *Studia Graeco-Arabica* 2 (2012) 331–354. ["Authenticité"]

Sellheim, Rudolf, review of Ergin, *İbni Sina Bibliyografyası*, 2nd ed., in *Oriens* 11 (1958) 231–239.

Semaan, Khalil I., *Arabic Phonetics. Ibn Sīnā's Risālah on the Points of Articulation of the Speech-sounds*, Lahore: Sh. Muhammad Ashraf, 1963.

Sezgin, Fuat, "Qaḍiyyat iktišāf al-āla ar-raṣadiyya ʿaṣā Yaʿqūb," *ZGAIW* 2 (1985) 7–73.

Shafīʿ, Moḥammad, ed., *Tatimmat Ṣiwān al-ḥikma of ʿAlī b. Zaid al-Baihaḳī* [Panjab University Oriental Publications Series No. 20], Lahore: L. Ishwar Das, University of the Panjab, 1935.

Shehaby, Nabil, *The Propositional Logic of Avicenna*, Dordrecht/Boston: Springer Netherlands 1973.

Soreth, Marion, "Text- und quellenkritische Bemerkungen zu Ibn Sīnā's Risāla fī l-ʿIšq," *Oriens* 17 (1964) 118–131.

Stapleton, H.E., R.F. Azo, M. Hidāyat Ḥusain, and G.L. Lewis, "Two Alchemical Treatises Attributed to Avicenna," *Ambix* 10 (1962) 41–82.

Stern, Samuel Miklos, "Ibn al-Samḥ," *Journal of the Royal Asiatic Society* (1956) 31–44.

Street, Tony, "Medieval and Modern Interpretations of Avicenna's Modal Syllogistic," in Opwis and Reisman (2012), 233–255.

Strohmaier, Gotthard, *Al-Bīrūnī. In den Gärten der Wissenschaft*, Leipzig: Reclam-Verlag, 1991. [*Al-Bīrūnī*]

———, "Avicenna und al-Bīrūnī im Dialog über aristotelische Naturphilosophie," in *Antike Naturwissenschaft und ihre Rezeption*, K. Döring und G. Wöhrle, eds., Bamberg: Colibri Verlag, 1992, 115–130; repr. in his *Von Demokrit bis Dante*, Hildesheim: Georg Olms Verlag, 1996, 342–357. ["Dialog"]

———, "Avicenne et le phénomène des écrits pseudépigraphiques," in Janssens and De Smet (2002) 37–46. ["Écrits pseudépigraphiques"]

Szpiech, Ryan, "In Search of Ibn Sīnā's 'Oriental Philosophy' in Medieval Castile," *ASP* 20 (2010) 185–207.

aṭ-Ṭayyān, Muḥammad Ḥassān and Yaḥyā Mīr 'Alam, eds., *Risālat Asbāb ḥudūṯ al-ḥurūf li-š-Šayḫ ... Ibn Sīnā*, Damascus: Majma' al-luġa al-'arabiyya, 1983.

Taghi, Shokoufeh, *The Two Wings of Wisdom. Mysticism and Philosophy in the* Risālat uṭ-ṭair *of Ibn Sina*, Uppsala: Acta Universitatis Upsaliensis, 2000. Reviewed by David C. Reisman in *JNES* 65 (2006) 59–62.

Takahashi, Hidemi, "The Reception of Ibn Sīnā in Syriac. The Case of Gregory Barhebraeus," in Reisman with al-Rahim (2003) 249–281.

Thom, Paul, *Medieval Modal Systems*, Aldershot: Ashgate, 2003.

Tis' Rasā'il fī l-ḥikma wa-ṭ-ṭabī'iyyāt, Cairo: Maṭba'a hindiyya, 1326/1908.

Tornberg, Carolus Johannes, ed., *Ibn-el-Athiri chronicon*, Leiden: E.J. Brill, 1851–1876.

Treiger, Alexander, *Inspired Knowledge in Islamic Thought. Al-Ghazâlî's Theory of Mystical Cognition and Its Avicennian Foundation*, London: Routledge, 2012. [*Inspired Knowledge*]

———, "Avicenna's Notion of Transcendental Modulation of Existence (*taškīk al-wujūd, analogia entis*) and Its Greek and Arabic Sources," in Opwis and Reisman (2012), 327–363. ["Modulation"]

Türker Küyel, Mubahat, ed., "İbn Sīnā'nın *On sorunun* karşılıkları," in *Beyruni'ye Armağan*, Ankara: Türk Tarih Kurumu Basımevi, 1974, 103–112.

al-'Ubaydī, Ḥasan Majīd, ed., *Ibn Sīnā. Kitāb at-Ta'līqāt*, Damascus: at-Takwīn, ²2008 (Baghdad: Bayt al-Ḥikma, ¹2002).

Ülken, Hilmi Ziya, *İbn Sina Risâleleri*, 2 vols., Istanbul: İbrahim Horoz Basımevi, 1953.

Ullmann, Manfred, *Die Medizin im Islam*, Leiden: E.J. Brill, 1970. [*Medizin*]

———, *Die Natur- und Geheimwissenschaften im Islam*, Leiden: E.J. Brill, 1972. [*Geheimwissenschaften*]

———, "Neues zu den diätetischen Schriften des Rufus von Ephesos," *Medizinhistorisches Journal* 9 (1974) 23–40. ["Rufus"]

———, review of Gohlman, *Der Islam* 52 (1975) 148–151. [Gohlman review]

———, *Islamic Medicine* [Islamic Surveys 11], Edinburgh: University Press, 1978, ²1997. [*Medicine*]

———, *Untersuchungen zur arabischen Überlieferung der* Materia medica *des Dioskurides*. Mit Beiträgen von Rainer Degen, Wiesbaden: Harrassowitz, 2009. [*Dioskurides*]

Uluslararası İbn Sînâ Sempozyumu. Bildiriler. 22–24 Mayıs 2008, İstanbul (*International Ibn Sina Symposium. Papers*), 2 vols., Istanbul: İstanbul Büyükşehir Belediyesi Kültür Yayınları, 2008.

Vajda, Georges, "Les notes d'Avicenne sur la "Théologie d'Aristote"," *Revue Thomiste* 51 (1951) 346–406. ["Théologie"]

———, "Deux manuscrits des *Muḥākamāt* de Quṭb ad-Dīn at-Taḥtānī," in *Miscellanea* [Mémorial Avicenne IV], Cairo: Institut Français d'Archéologie Orientale, 1954, 31–32. [*Muḥākamāt*]

Van Riet, Simone, "Données biographiques pour l'histoire du *Shifā'* d'Avicenne," *Bulletin de la Classe des Lettres et des Sciences Morales et Politiques*, Académie Royale de Belgique, Bruxelles, 66 (1980) 314–329.
Versteegh, *Greek Elements in Arabic Linguistic Thinking*, Leiden: Brill, 1977.
van Vloten, Gerlof, ed., *Al-Ḫwārizmī, Mafātīḥ al-ʿulūm*, Leiden: Brill, 1895.
Weisweiler, Max, "Avicenna und die iranischen Fürstenbibliotheken seiner Zeit," *Avicenna Commemoration Volume*, Calcutta: Iran Society, 1956, 47–63.
Wickens, G.M., ed., *Avicenna: Scientist & Philosopher. A Millenary Symposium*, London: Luzac & Company, Ltd., 1952. [*Avicenna*]
———, "Some Aspects of Avicenna's Work," in his *Avicenna* (1952) 49–65. ["Aspects"]
Wiedemann, E., "Avicennas Schrift über ein von ihm ersonnenes Beobachtungsinstrument," *Acta Orientalia* 11 (1926) 81–167; repr. in his *Gesammelte Schriften zur arabisch-islamischen Wissenschaftsgeschichte*, D. Girke and D. Bischoff, eds. [Institut für Geschichte der Arabisch-Islamischen Wissenschaften, B/1,2], Frankfurt 1984, II.1117–1203.
Wisnovsky, Robert, ed., *Aspects of Avicenna*, Princeton: Markus Wiener, 2001 [= *Princeton Papers: Interdisciplinary Journal of Middle Eastern Studies*, vol. IX]. [*Aspects*]
———, *Avicenna's Metaphysics in Context*, Ithaca, N.Y.: Cornell University Press, 2003. [*Metaphysics*]
———, "The Nature and Scope of Arabic Philosophical Commentary in Post-classical (ca. 1100–1900 AD) Islamic Intellectual History: Some Preliminary Observations," in *Philosophy, Science & Exegesis in Greek, Arabic and Latin Commentaries II*, P. Adamson, H. Baltussen and M.W.F. Stone, eds., *Supplement to the Bulletin of the Institute Of Classical Studies* 83/1–2, London: Institute of Classical Studies, 2004, 149–191. ["Philosophical Commentary"]
———, "Towards a History of Avicenna's Distinction between Immanent and Transcendent Causes," in Reisman with Al-Rahim (2003) 49–68. ["Causes"]
———, "Jowzjāni," in *EIr* XV,82–84, 2007.
———, "Avicenna's Islamic Reception," in Adamson *Interpreting Avicenna* (2013) 190–213. ["Islamic Reception"]
Würsch, Renate, *Avicenna's Bearbeitungen der aristotelischen Rhetorik*, Berlin: Schwarz, 1991.
al-Yāfī, ʿAbdalkarīm, ed., *Ḥiwār al-Bīrūnī wa-Ibn Sīnā*, Damascus: Dār al-fikr, 2002.
Yaltkaya, Şerefettin, and Kilisli Rifat Bilge, eds., *Keşf-el-Zunun. Kâtib Çelebi*, Istanbul: Maarif Matbaası, 1941.
Yarshater, Ehsan, ed., *Panj Resāle*, Tehran: Ānjomān-e Āṯār-e Mellī, 1332Š/1953.
Yūsuf, Zakariyā, ed., *Ibn Sīnā. Aš-Šifāʾ, ar-Riyāḍiyyāt, Jawāmiʿ ʿilm al-mūsīqā*, Cairo: al-Hayʾa al-miṣriyya al-ʿāmma li-l-kitāb, 1956.
Zāreʿī, Mojtabā, ed., *Al-Išārāt wa-t-tanbīhāt li-š-Šayḫ ar-Raʾīs Ibn Sīnā*, Qum: Būstān-e Ketāb-e Qom, 1381Š/2002.
Zāyid, Saʿīd, ed., *Ibn Sīnā. Aš-Šifāʾ, al-Manṭiq, al-Qiyās*, Cairo: al-Hayʾa al-ʿāmma li-šuʾūn al-maṭābiʿ al-amīriyya, 1373/1964. [*Qiyās*]
———, ed., *Ibn Sīnā. Aš-Šifāʾ, aṭ-Ṭabīʿiyyāt, as-Samāʿ aṭ-ṭabīʿī*, Cairo: al-Hayʾa al-miṣriyya al-ʿāmma li-l-kitāb, 1983 [*Samāʿ*]
Zonta, Mauro, "Possible Hebrew Quotations of the Metaphysical Section of Avicenna's *Oriental Philosophy* and Their Historical Meaning," in Hasse and Bertolacci (2012), 177–195.

INDEX OF SUBJECTS

INDEX OF AUTHORS CITED, NAMES, AND PLACES

Initial articles and prepositions in any language have been disregarded in the alphabetical order, except for initial prepositions in European names which form part of the surname and are capitalized, and the preposition *De* in Latin titles. Compound Arabic proper names connected with a hyphen (-) that form a unit of nomenclature (see p. XXVIII) are treated as a single name and listed in strict alphabetical order, counting any articles. The diacritics of transliterated Arabic letters, as well as the German umlauts, have been disregarded in the alphabetical order.

References to authors, names, and places in footnotes are given with the page number followed by the letter "n." When a name or place occurs in both the body of the text and in a footnote, only the reference to the former is given.

This Index includes the works of Avicenna actually referred to in the body of the text, listed alphabetically under his name with their English titles and their corresponding G-number, through which their original language titles can be located in the Conspectus in Part Three of the Appendix. The works listed in the Appendix are not included in this Index.

INDEX OF LEMMATA (L PASSAGES)

INDEX OF QUR'ĀNIC PASSAGES

INDEX OF MANUSCRIPTS

The Index lists manuscripts mentioned or discussed in the body of the text only, not in the Appendix.

INDEX OF GREEK WORDS

INDEX OF ARABIC WORDS

The index follows the order of the Arabic alphabet. For the English equivalents of the technical terms listed below see the Index of Technical Terms.

INDEX OF TECHNICAL TERMS

NOTE. Ethics, Logic, Mathematics, Metaphysics, and Physics, as well as the titles of Aristotle's books that begin with a capital letter but are not italicized, refer to the field of study covered by these subjects or books, as classified in the Aristotelian tradition. This is intended to distinguish them both from the titles Aristotle's books and from the corresponding general concepts such as, e.g., logic or categories.

Unless preceded by the initials for T(exts), W(orks), and L(emmata), the numbers below refer to chapters and sections.

See also the Index of Arabic Words.

Acumen, *ḏakāʾ*; L8, L9
Adherence, Partisan Adherence, *taʿaṣṣub*; 3.3E.ii
Ascertain, Ascertainment, *taḥaqquq*; 3.3E.i
Authority, Following Authority, *taqlīd*; 3.3E.ii

Comprehension, *fahm*; L9
Corollary Principle, *farʿ*, *furūʿ*; Derive, Work out C.P., *tafrīʿ*; 5.1
Custom, Customary Practice, *ʿāda*; 5.2

Derive Corollary Principles → Corollary Principle
Destination, *maʿād*; T4, preface
Determine Validity → Validity
Discover, Discovery, *istinbāṭ*; 3.3E.i; 3.2, note 33

Fair Judgment, *inṣāf*; 3.3E.iii
Following Authority → Authority
Fundamental Principle, *aṣl*, *uṣūl* (as opposed to *mabdaʾ*, first principle) 5.1

Guessing Correctly, *ḥads*; 3.2

Judgment → Fair judgment

Knowledge, Philosophy, Philosophical Sciences, *al-ʿilm*; 3.1 end; 3.2 end, §ii

Mind, *ḏihn*; L9

Partisan Adherence → Adherence
Philosophy, Philosophical Sciences → Knowledge
Pointer, *išāra*; 8.3, W11
Principle → Corollary Principle, Fundamental Principle
Provenance, *mabdaʾ*; T4, preface

Theology, *al-ʿilm al-ilāhī*, *ilahiyyāt* (the part of Metaphysics not dealing with "being as such") cf. 6.1

Thinking, *fikr*; L13
Thought, *fikra*; L9

Validate, Determine Validity, *ḥaṣṣala*;
Validating, *muḥaṣṣil*; 3.3E.i
Valid, *maḥṣūl*; W3

Verify, Verification, *ḥaqqaqa, taḥqīq*; 3.3E.i

Withhold, *ḍanna bi-*; 5.3
Work out Corollary Principles → Corollary Principle